IVOR HORTON'S
BEGINNING VISUAL C++® 2013

IVOR HORTON'S
BEGINNING
Visual C++® 2013

IVOR HORTON'S
BEGINNING

Visual C++® 2013

Ivor Horton

Ivor Horton's Beginning Visual C++® 2013

Published by
John Wiley & Sons, Inc.
10475 Crosspoint Boulevard
Indianapolis, IN 46256
www.wiley.com

Copyright © 2014 by Ivor Horton

Published by John Wiley & Sons, Inc., Indianapolis, Indiana

Published simultaneously in Canada

ISBN: 978-1-118-84571-4
ISBN: 978-1-118-84568-4 (ebk)
ISBN: 978-1-118-84577-6 (ebk)

Manufactured in the United States of America

10 9 8 7 6 5 4 3 2 1

This book is for my dear wife, Eve.

ABOUT THE AUTHOR

IVOR HORTON graduated as a mathematician and was lured into information technology by promises of great rewards for very little work. In spite of the reality usually being a great deal of work for relatively modest rewards, he has continued to work with computers to the present day. He has been engaged at various times in programming, systems design, consultancy, and the management and implementation of projects of considerable complexity.

Horton has many years of experience in the design and implementation of computer systems applied to engineering design and manufacturing operations in a variety of industries. He has considerable experience in developing occasionally useful applications in a wide variety of programming languages, and in teaching primarily scientists and engineers to do likewise. He has been writing books on programming for several years, and his currently published works include tutorials on C, C++, and Java. At the present time, when he is not writing programming books or providing advice to others, he spends his time fishing, traveling, and enjoying life in general.

ABOUT THE TECHNICAL EDITORS

GIOVANNI DICANIO is a Microsoft Visual C++ MVP, computer programmer, and Pluralsight author. His computer programming experience dates back to the glorious Commodore 64 and Commodore Amiga 500 golden days. He started with C=64 BASIC, then moved to assembly, Pascal, C, C++, Java, and C#. Giovanni wrote computer programming articles on C++, MFC, OpenGL, and other programming subjects in Italian computer magazines. He contributed code to some open-source projects as well, including a mathematical expression parser written in C++ for one of the first versions of QCAD. Giovanni's programming experience includes Windows programming using C++, Win32, COM, and ATL. His favorite programming languages are C and C++.

He has recently started cultivating an interest for mobile platforms and embedded systems.

He can be contacted via e-mail at `giovanni.dicanio@gmail.com`.

MARC GREGOIRE is a software engineer from Belgium. He graduated from the University of Leuven, Belgium, with a degree in "Burgerlijk ingenieur in de computer wetenschappen" (equivalent to Master of Science in engineering in computer science). The year after, he received the cum laude degree of master in artificial intelligence at the same university. After his studies, Marc started working for a software consultancy company called Ordina Belgium. As a consultant, he worked for Siemens and Nokia Siemens Networks on critical 2G and 3G software running on Solaris for telecom operators. This required working in international teams stretching from South America and the United States to EMEA and Asia. Now, Marc is working for Nikon Metrology on 3D laser scanning software.

His main expertise is C/C++, and specifically Microsoft VC++ and the MFC framework. He has experience in developing C++ programs running 24x7 on Windows and Linux platforms; for example, KNX/EIB home automation software. Next to C/C++, Marc also likes C# and uses PHP for creating web pages.

Since April 2007, he received the yearly Microsoft MVP (Most Valuable Professional) award for his Visual C++ expertise.

Marc is the founder of the Belgian C++ Users Group (www.becpp.org), author of *Professional C++*, Wrox, 2011 (ISBN 978-047-0-93244-9) and a member on the CodeGuru forum (as Marc G). He maintains a blog on www.nuonsoft.com/blog/.

CREDITS

Executive Editor
Robert Elliott

Project Editors
Sydney Jones Argenta
Edward Connor

Technical Editors
Giovani Dicanio
Marc Gregoire

Production Editor
Christine Mugnolo

Copy Editor
Charlotte Kughen

Manager of Content Development and Assembly
Mary Beth Wakefield

Director of Community Marketing
David Mayhew

Marketing Manager
Ashley Zurcher

Business Manager
Amy Knies

Vice President and Executive Group Publisher
Richard Swadley

Associate Publisher
Jim Minatel

Project Coordinator, Cover
Todd Klemme

Proofreader
Sarah Kaikini, Word One New York

Indexer
Johnna VanHoose Dinse

Cover Designer
Wiley

Cover Image
©iStockphoto.com/xyno

ACKNOWLEDGMENTS

THE AUTHOR is only one member of the large team of people necessary to get a book into print. I'd like to thank the John Wiley & Sons and Wrox Press editorial and production teams for their help and support throughout.

I would particularly like to thank my technical editors, Marc Gregoire and Giovanni Dicanio, for doing such a fantastic job of reviewing the text and checking out all the code fragments and examples. Their many constructive comments and suggestions have undoubtedly made the book a much better tutorial.

CONTENTS

INTRODUCTION

WELCOME TO *Ivor Horton's Beginning Visual C++ 2013*. With this book, you can become an effective C++ programmer using Microsoft's latest application-development system, Visual Studio Professional 2013. I aim to teach you the C++ programming language, and then how to apply C++ in the development of your own Windows applications. Along the way, you will also learn about many of the exciting new capabilities introduced by this latest version of Visual C++.

Visual C++ 2013 comes with the Microsoft development environment Visual Studio Professional 2013. When I refer to Visual C++ in the rest of the book, I mean the Visual C++ 2013 capability that comes as part of Visual Studio Professional 2013. Note that the Visual Studio Express 2013 Edition *does not* provide sufficient facilities for this book. None of the examples in Chapters 11 through 18 can be created with Visual Studio Express 2013.

WHO THIS BOOK IS FOR

This book is for anyone who wants to learn how to write C++ applications for Microsoft Windows using Visual C++. I make no assumptions about prior knowledge of any programming language, so there are no prerequisites other than some aptitude for programming and sufficient enthusiasm and commitment for learning C++. This tutorial is for you if:

➤   You are a newcomer to programming and sufficiently keen to jump into the deep end with C++. To be successful, you need to have at least a rough idea of how your computer works.

➤   You have a little experience of programming in some other language, such as BASIC, and you want to learn C++ and develop practical Microsoft Windows programming skills.

➤   You have some experience in C or C++, but not in a Microsoft Windows context and want to extend your skills to program for the Windows environment using the latest tools and technologies.

WHAT THIS BOOK COVERS

The first part of the book teaches you the essentials of C++ programming using Visual Studio Professional 2013 through a detailed, step-by-step tutorial. You'll learn the syntax and use of the C++ language and gain experience and confidence in applying it in a practical context through working examples. You'll find complete code for the examples that demonstrate virtually all aspects of C++. There are also exercises that you can use to test your knowledge, with solutions available for download if you get stuck.

The language tutorial also introduces and demonstrates the use of the C++ standard library facilities you are most likely to need. You'll add to your knowledge of the standard libraries incrementally as you progress through the C++ language. You'll also learn about the powerful tools provided by the Standard Template Library (STL).

When you are confident in applying C++, you move on to Windows programming. You will learn how to develop Windows desktop applications using the Microsoft Foundation Classes (MFC) by creating a substantial working application of more than 2,000 lines of code. You develop the application over several chapters, utilizing a broad range of user interface capabilities provided by the MFC. You also learn the essentials of programming applications targeting tablets running Windows 8. You learn about creating an application with the Windows 8 Modern interface by incrementally developing a working example of a game.

HOW THIS BOOK IS STRUCTURED

The book is structured so that as far as possible, each chapter builds on what you have learned in previous chapters:

- ➤ Chapter 1 introduces you to the basic concepts you need to understand for programming in C++ and the main ideas embodied in the Visual C++ development environment. It describes how you use Visual C++ to create the various kinds of applications you'll learn about in the rest of the book.

- ➤ Chapters 2 through 9 teach you the C++ language. You start with simple procedural program examples and progress to learning about classes and object-oriented programming.

- ➤ Chapter 10 teaches you how you use the Standard Template Library (STL). The STL is a powerful and extensive set of tools for organizing and manipulating data in your C++ programs. The STL is application-neutral, so you can apply it in a wide range of contexts.

- ➤ Chapter 11 discusses how Microsoft Windows desktop applications are structured and describes and demonstrates the essential elements that are present in every desktop application written for the Windows operating system. The chapter explains through elementary examples how Windows applications work, and you'll create programs that use C++ with the Windows API and with the MFC.

- ➤ Chapters 12 through 17 teach you Windows desktop application programming. You learn to write Windows applications using the MFC for building a GUI. You'll be creating and using common controls to build the graphical user interface for your application, and you'll learn how to handle the events that result from user interactions with your program. In addition to the techniques you learn for building a GUI, the application you develop will show you how to handle printing and how your application can work with files.

- ➤ Chapter 18 introduces the fundamental ideas involved in writing applications for Windows 8. You'll develop a fully working application that uses the Windows 8 Modern user interface.

All chapters include working examples that demonstrate the programming techniques discussed. Every chapter concludes with a summary of the key points that were covered, and most chapters include a set of exercises at the end that you can attempt, to apply what you have learned. Solutions to all the exercises, and all the code from the examples in the book are available for download from the publisher's website.

WHAT YOU NEED TO USE THIS BOOK

There are several versions of Visual Studio 2013, and they each have a different range of capabilities. This book assumes you have the Visual Studio Professional 2013 Edition (or a superior edition) installed. To put it another way, any of the paid versions of Visual Studio 2013 are okay. There are lower cost student versions of these available if you are in full-time education. None of the free Express editions will suffice.

All the examples in Chapters 1 through 17 will work if you have Visual Studio installed with Windows 7 or Windows 8. To work with Chapter 18, your version of Visual Studio must be installed in a Windows 8 environment.

The examples in Chapters 2 through 10 can be created and executed with the Visual Studio Express 2013 for Windows Desktop, but none of the examples in Chapters 11 through 18 can.

CONVENTIONS

To help you get the most from the text and keep track of what's happening, we've used a number of conventions throughout the book.

TRY IT OUT

The *Try It Out* is an exercise you should work through, following the text in the book.

1. They usually consist of a set of steps.
2. Each step has a number.
3. Follow the steps through with your copy of the program.

How It Works

After each *Try It Out*, the code you've typed will be explained in detail.

> **WARNING** *Boxes like this one hold important, not-to-be-forgotten information that is directly relevant to the surrounding text.*

> **NOTE** *Notes, tips, hints, tricks, and asides to the current discussion are offset and placed in italics like this.*

As for styles in the text:

➤ We *highlight* new terms and important words when we introduce them.

➤ We show keyboard strokes like this: Ctrl+A.

➤ We show filenames, URLs, and code within the text like so: `persistence.properties`.

➤ We present code in two different ways:

```
We use a monofont type with no highlighting for most code examples.
```

We use bold highlighting to emphasize code that is of particular importance in the present context.

SOURCE CODE

You should type in the code for all the examples yourself; this greatly helps memory and the learning process. However, you can download all the source code files for examples in the book, so if you can't work out why your code doesn't work, you'll have some available that does. The code downloads for the examples are located at `www.wrox.com/go/beginningvisualc` on the Download Code tab.

> **NOTE** *Because many books have similar titles, you may find it easiest to search by ISBN; this book's ISBN is 978-1-118-84571-4.*

Once you download the code, just decompress it with your favorite compression tool. Alternately, you can go to the main Wrox code download page at `www.wrox.com/dynamic/books/download .aspx` to see the code available for this book and all other Wrox books.

EXERCISES

Many of the chapters have a set of exercises for you to test your knowledge. I encourage you to try all of these. If you get stuck you can download solutions to all of these exercises from `www.wrox .com/go/beginningvisualc`.

ERRATA

We make every effort to ensure that there are no errors in the text or in the code. However, no one is perfect, and mistakes do occur. If you find an error in one of our books, like a spelling mistake or faulty piece of code, we would be very grateful for your feedback. By sending in errata, you may save another reader hours of frustration, and at the same time, you will be helping us provide even higher quality information.

To find the errata page for this book, go to `http://www.wrox.com` and locate the title using the Search box or one of the title lists. Then, on the book's detail page, click the Book Errata link. On this page, you can view all errata that has been submitted for this book and posted by Wrox editors. A complete book list, including links to each book's errata, is also available at `www.wrox.com/misc-pages/booklist.shtml`.

If you don't spot "your" error on the Book Errata page, go to `www.wrox.com/contact/techsupport.shtml` and complete the form there to send us the error you have found. We'll check the information and, if appropriate, post a message to the book's errata page and fix the problem in subsequent editions of the book.

P2P.WROX.COM

For author and peer discussion, join the P2P forums at `p2p.wrox.com`. The forums are a web-based system for you to post messages relating to Wrox books and related technologies and interact with other readers and technology users. The forums offer a subscription feature to e-mail you topics of interest of your choosing when new posts are made to the forums. Wrox authors, editors, other industry experts, and your fellow readers are present on these forums.

At `http://p2p.wrox.com`, you will find a number of different forums that will help you, not only as you read this book, but also as you develop your own applications. To join the forums, just follow these steps:

1. Go to `p2p.wrox.com` and click the Register link.

2. Read the terms of use and click Agree.

3. Complete the required information to join, as well as any optional information you wish to provide, and click Submit.

4. You will receive an e-mail with information describing how to verify your account and complete the joining process.

> **NOTE** *You can read messages in the forums without joining P2P, but in order to post your own messages, you must join.*

Once you join, you can post new messages and respond to messages other users post. You can read messages at any time on the web. If you would like to have new messages from a particular forum e-mailed to you, click the Subscribe to this Forum icon by the forum name in the forum listing.

For more information about how to use the Wrox P2P, be sure to read the P2P FAQs for answers to questions about how the forum software works, as well as many common questions specific to P2P and Wrox books. To read the FAQs, click the FAQ link on any P2P page.

1

Programming with Visual C++

WHAT YOU WILL LEARN IN THIS CHAPTER:

➤   What the principal components of Visual C++ are

➤   What solutions and projects are and how you create them

➤   About console programs

➤   How to create and edit a program

➤   How to compile, link, and execute C++ console programs

➤   How to create and execute basic Windows programs

WROX.COM CODE DOWNLOADS FOR THIS CHAPTER

You can find the wrox.com code downloads for this chapter on the Download Code tab at www.wrox.com/go/beginningvisualc. The code is in the Chapter 1 download and individually named according to the names throughout the chapter.

LEARNING WITH VISUAL C++

Windows programming isn't difficult. Microsoft Visual C++ makes it remarkably easy, as you'll see throughout the course of this book. There's just one obstacle in your path: Before you get to the specifics of Windows programming, you have to be thoroughly familiar with the capabilities of the C++ programming language, particularly the object-oriented capabilities. Object-oriented techniques are central to the effectiveness of all the tools provided by Visual C++ for Windows programming, so it's essential that you gain a good understanding of them. That's exactly what this book provides.

This chapter gives you an overview of the essential concepts involved in programming applications in C++. You'll take a rapid tour of the integrated development environment (IDE) that comes with Visual C++. The IDE is straightforward and generally intuitive in its operation, so you'll be able to pick up most of it as you go along. The best way to get familiar with it is to work through the process of creating, compiling, and executing a simple program. So power up your PC, start Windows, load the mighty Visual C++, and begin your journey.

WRITING C++ APPLICATIONS

You have tremendous flexibility in the types of applications and program components that you can develop with Visual C++. Applications that you can develop fall into two broad categories: *desktop applications* and *Windows Store apps*. Desktop applications are the applications that you know and love; they have an application window that typically has a menu bar and a toolbar and frequently a status bar at the bottom of the application window. This book focuses primarily on desktop applications.

Windows Store apps only run under Windows 8 or later versions and have a user interface that is completely different from desktop applications. The focus is on the content where the user interacts directly with the data, rather than interacting with controls such as menu items and toolbar buttons.

Once you have learned C++, this book concentrates on using the Microsoft Foundation Classes (MFC) with C++ for building desktop applications. The application programming interface (API) for Windows desktop applications is referred to as *Win32*. Win32 has a long history and was developed long before the object-oriented programming paradigm emerged, so it has none of the object-oriented characteristics that would be expected if it were written today. The MFC consists of a set of C++ classes that encapsulate the Win32 API for user interface creation and control and greatly eases the process of program development. You are not obliged to use the MFC, though. If you want the ultimate in performance you can write your C++ code to access the Windows API directly, but it certainly won't be as easy.

Figure 1-1 shows the basic options you have for developing C++ applications.

Figure 1-1 is a simplified representation of what is involved. Desktop applications can target Windows 7, Windows 8, or Windows Vista. Windows Store apps execute only with Windows 8 and its successors and you must have Visual Studio 2013 installed under Windows 8 or later to develop them. Windows Store apps communicate with the operating system through the Windows Runtime, WinRT. I'll introduce you to programming Windows 8 applications in Chapter 18.

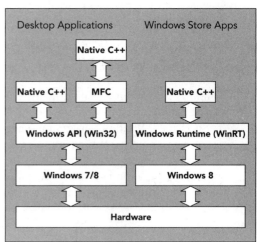

FIGURE 1-1

LEARNING DESKTOP APPLICATIONS PROGRAMMING

There are always two basic aspects to interactive desktop applications executing under Windows: You need code to create the *graphical user interface* (GUI) with which the user interacts, and you need code to process these interactions to provide the functionality of the application. Visual C++ provides you with a great deal of assistance in both aspects. As you'll see later in this chapter, you can create a working Windows program with a GUI without writing any code at all. All the basic code to create the GUI can be generated automatically by Visual C++. Of course, it's essential to understand how this automatically generated code works because you need to extend and modify it to make the application do what you want. To do that, you need a comprehensive understanding of C++.

For this reason you'll first learn C++ without getting involved in Windows programming considerations. After you're comfortable with C++ you'll learn how to develop fully fledged Windows applications. This means that while you are learning C++, you'll be working with programs that involve only command line input and output. By sticking to this rather limited input and output capability, you'll be able to concentrate on the specifics of how the C++ language works and avoid the inevitable complications involved in GUI building and control. Once you are comfortable with C++ you'll find that it's an easy and natural progression to applying C++ to the development of Windows applications.

> **NOTE** As I'll explain in Chapter 18, Windows Store apps are different. You specify the GUI in XAML, and the XAML is processed to generate the C++ code for GUI elements.

Learning C++

Visual C++ supports the C++ language defined by the most recent ISO/IEC C++ standard that was published in 2011. The standard is defined in the document ISO/IEC 14882:2011 and commonly referred to as *C++ 11*. The Visual C++ compiler supports most of the language features introduced by this latest standard, and it includes some features from the draft for the next standard, C++ 14. Programs that you write in standard C++ can be ported from one system environment to another reasonably easily; although, the library functions that a program uses — particularly those related to building a graphical user interface — are a major determinant of how easy or difficult it will be. C++ is the first choice of a great many professional program developers because it is so widely supported, and because it is one of the most powerful programming languages available today.

Chapters 2 through 9 of this book teach you the C++ language and introduce some of the most commonly used C++ standard library facilities along the way. Chapter 10 explains how you can use the Standard Template Library (STL) for C++ for managing collections of data.

C++ Concepts

As with virtually all programming languages, there's a chicken and egg problem in explaining C++. Inevitably there are occasions when I need to reference or make use of a language feature before I have discussed it in detail. This section is intended to help with this conundrum by outlining the principle C++ language elements. Of course, everything I mention here will be explained fully later in the book.

Functions

Every C++ program consists of at least one, and usually many, *functions*. A function is a named block of executable code that you invoke or *call* using its name. There must always be one function with the name `main`, and execution always starts with the `main()` function. The parentheses following the function name can specify what information is passed to a function when you call it. I'll always put parentheses after a function name in the text to distinguish it from other things. All the executable code in a program is contained in functions. The simplest C++ program consists of just the `main()` function.

Data and Variables

You store an item of data in a *variable*. A variable is a named memory area that can store a data item of a particular type. There are several standard *fundamental data types* that store integers, non-integral numerical values, and character data. You can also define your own data types, which makes writing a program that deals with real-world objects much easier. Variables of types that you define store *objects*. Because each variable can only store data of a given type, C++ is said to be a *type-safe* language.

Classes and Objects

A *class* is a block of code that defines a data type. A class has a name that is the name for your data type. An item of data of a class type is referred to as an *object*. You use the class type name when you create variables that can store objects of your data type.

Templates

Circumstances often arise when you need several different classes or functions in a program where the code for these only differs in the kind of data they work with. Templates save a lot of coding effort in such situations.

A *template* is a recipe or specification that you create that can be used by the compiler to generate code automatically in a program when requested. You can define *class templates* that the compiler can use to generate one or more of a family of classes. You can also define *function templates* that the compiler can use to generate functions. Each template has a name that you use when you want the compiler to create an instance of it.

The code for the class or function that the compiler generates from a template depends on one or more *template arguments*. The arguments are usually types, but not always. Typically you specify the template arguments explicitly when you use a class template. The compiler can usually deduce the arguments for a function template from the context.

Program Files

C++ program code is stored in two kinds of files. *Source files* contain executable code and have the extension `.cpp`. *Header files* contain definitions for things, such as classes and templates, that are used by the executable code. Header files have the extension `.h`.

Console Applications

Visual C++ *console applications* enable you to write, compile, and test C++ programs that have none of the baggage required by Windows desktop applications. These programs are called console applications because you communicate with them through the keyboard and the screen in character mode, so they are essentially character-based, command-line programs.

In Chapters 2 through 10 you'll only be working with console applications. Writing console applications might seem to be side-tracking you from the main objective of programming Windows applications with a GUI. However, when it comes to learning C++, it's by far the best way to proceed in my view. There's a *lot* of code in even a simple Windows program, and it's very important not to be distracted by the complexities of Windows when learning the ins and outs of C++. In the early chapters of the book you'll be learning C++ with a few lightweight console applications, before you get to work with the heavyweight sacks of code that are implicit in the world of Windows.

Windows Programming Concepts

The project creation facilities in Visual C++ can generate skeleton code automatically for a variety of applications. A Windows program has a completely different structure from that of the typical console program, and it's much more complicated. In a console program, you can get user input from the keyboard and write output back to the command line directly, and that is essentially it. A Windows application can access the input and output facilities of the computer only by way of functions supplied by the host environment; no direct access to the hardware resources is permitted. Several programs can be executing concurrently under Windows, so the operating system has to determine which application should receive a given raw input, such as a mouse click or the pressing of a key on the keyboard, and signal the program accordingly. Thus, the Windows operating system always manages all communications with the user.

The nature of the interface between a user and a Windows desktop application is such that a wide range of different inputs is usually possible at any given time. A user may select any of a number of menu options, click any of several toolbar buttons, or click the mouse somewhere in the application window. A well-designed Windows application has to be prepared to deal with any of these possible types of input at any time because there is no way of knowing in advance which type of input is going to occur. These user actions are received by the operating system in the first instance, and are all regarded by Windows as *events*. An event that originates with the user interface for your application will typically result in a particular piece of your program code being executed. How execution proceeds is therefore determined by the sequence of user actions. Programs that operate in this way are referred to as *event-driven programs*, and are different from traditional procedural programs that have a single order of execution. Input to a procedural program is controlled by the program code and can occur only when the program permits it. A Windows program consists primarily of pieces of code that respond to events caused by the action of the user, or by Windows itself. This sort of program structure is illustrated in Figure 1-2.

Each block within the Desktop Application block in Figure 1-2 represents a piece of code that deals with a particular kind of event. The program may appear to be somewhat fragmented because of the disjointed blocks of code, but the primary factor welding the program into a whole is the Windows operating system itself. You can think of your program as customizing Windows to provide a particular set of capabilities.

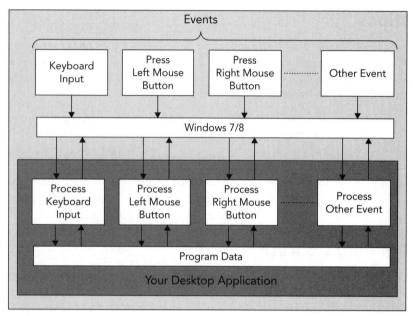

FIGURE 1-2

Of course, modules servicing external events, such as the selection of a menu or a mouse click, will typically need access to a common set of application-specific data. This data contains information that relates to what the program is about — for example, blocks of text recording scoring records for a player in a program aimed at tracking how your baseball team is doing — as well as information about some of the events that have occurred during execution of the program. This shared data allows various parts of the program that look independent to communicate and operate in a coordinated and integrated fashion. I will go into this in much more detail later in the book.

Even an elementary Windows program involves several lines of code, and with Windows programs generated by the application wizards that come with Visual C++, "several" turns out to be "very many". To simplify the process of understanding how C++ works, you need a context that is as uncomplicated as possible and at the same time has the tools to make it easy to create and navigate around sacks of code. Fortunately, Visual C++ comes with an environment that is designed specifically for the purpose.

THE INTEGRATED DEVELOPMENT ENVIRONMENT

The *integrated development environment* (IDE) is a self-contained environment in Visual C++ for creating, compiling, linking, testing, and debugging C++ programs of any kind. It also happens to be a great environment in which to learn the language (particularly when combined with a great book). The IDE incorporates a range of fully integrated tools that make the whole process of writing programs easy. You will see something of these in this chapter, but rather than grind through a boring litany of features and options in the abstract, I'll introduce you to the basics to get a view of how the IDE works and then you'll be able to pick up the rest in context as you go along.

The fundamental elements you'll be working with through the IDE are the editor, the C++ compiler, the linker, and the libraries. These are the basic tools that are essential to writing and executing a C++ program.

The Editor

The *editor* is an interactive environment in which you create and edit C++ source code. As well as the usual facilities such as cut and paste that you are certainly already familiar with, the editor offers a wide range of capabilities to help you get things right. For example:

➤ Code is automatically laid out with standard indentation and spacing. There's a default arrangement for code, but you can customize how your code is arranged in the dialog that displays when you select Tools ⇨ Options from the menu.

➤ Fundamental words in C++ are recognized automatically and colored according to what they are. This makes your code more readable and easier to follow.

➤ *IntelliSense* analyzes code as you enter it. Anything that is incorrect or any words IntelliSense doesn't recognize are underlined with a red squiggle. It also provides prompts when it can determine the options for what you need to enter next. This saves typing because you can just select from a list.

> **NOTE** *IntelliSense doesn't just work with C++. It works with XAML too.*

The Compiler

You execute the *compiler* when you have entered the C++ code for your program. The compiler converts your source code into *object code*, and detects and reports errors in the compilation process. The compiler detects a wide range of errors caused by invalid or unrecognized program code, as well as structural errors, such as parts of a program that can never be executed. The object code generated by the compiler is stored in *object files* that have the extension `.obj`.

The Linker

The *linker* combines the modules generated by the compiler from source code files, adds required code modules from the standard libraries that are supplied as part of C++, and welds everything into an executable whole, usually in the form of an `.exe` file. The linker can also detect and report errors — for example, if part of your program is missing, or a non-existent library component is referenced.

The Libraries

A *library* is a collection of prewritten routines that support and extend the C++ language by providing standard professionally produced code units for common operations that you can incorporate into your programs. The operations implemented by the libraries greatly enhance productivity by saving you the effort of writing and testing the code for such operations yourself.

The Standard C++ Library

The *Standard C++ Library* defines a set of facilities that are common to all ISO/IEC standard-conforming C++ compilers. It contains a vast range of commonly used routines, including numerical functions, such as calculating square roots and evaluating trigonometrical functions; character- and string-processing functions, such as the classification of characters and the comparison of character strings; and many others. It also defines data types and standard templates for generating customized data types and functions. You'll learn about many of these as you develop your knowledge of C++.

Microsoft Libraries

Windows desktop applications are supported by a library called the *Microsoft Foundation Classes* (MFC). The MFC greatly reduces the effort needed to build the GUI for an application. (You'll see a lot more of the MFC when you finish exploring the nuances of the C++ language.) There are other Microsoft libraries for desktop applications, but you won't be exploring them in this book.

USING THE IDE

All program development and execution in this book is performed from within the IDE. When you start Visual C++ you'll see an application window similar to that shown in Figure 1-3.

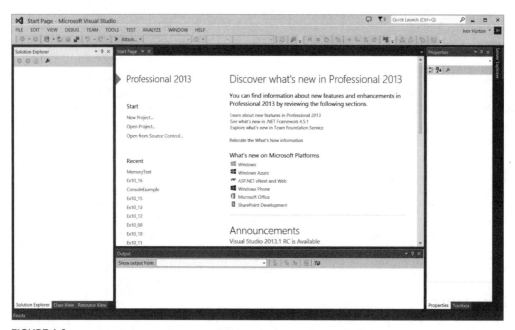

FIGURE 1-3

The pane to the left in Figure 1-3 is the *Solution Explorer window*, the middle pane presently showing the Start page is the *Editor window*, and the tab visible in the pane at the bottom is the *Output window*. The Properties pane on the right displays properties for a variety of entities in your program. The Solution Explorer pane enables you to navigate through your program files and display their contents in the Editor window, and to add new files to your program. You can dock several windows where the Solution Explorer pane is located. Three are shown in Figure 1-3 and you can select other windows to be displayed here from the View menu. You can rearrange the windows by dragging their labels. The Editor window is where you enter and modify source code and other components of your application. The Output window displays the output from build operations during which a project is compiled and linked. You can choose to display other windows by selecting from the View menu.

Note that a window can be undocked from its position in the Visual Studio application window. Just right-click the title bar of the window you want to undock and select Float from the pop-up menu. In general, I will show windows in their undocked state in the book. You can restore a window to its docked state by right-clicking its title bar and selecting Dock from the pop-up or by dragging it with the left mouse button down to the position that you want in the application window.

Toolbar Options

You can choose which toolbars are displayed by right-clicking in the toolbar area. The range of toolbars in the list depends on which edition of Visual Studio 2013 you have installed. A pop-up menu with a list of toolbars (Figure 1-4) appears, and the toolbars that are currently displayed have checkmarks alongside them.

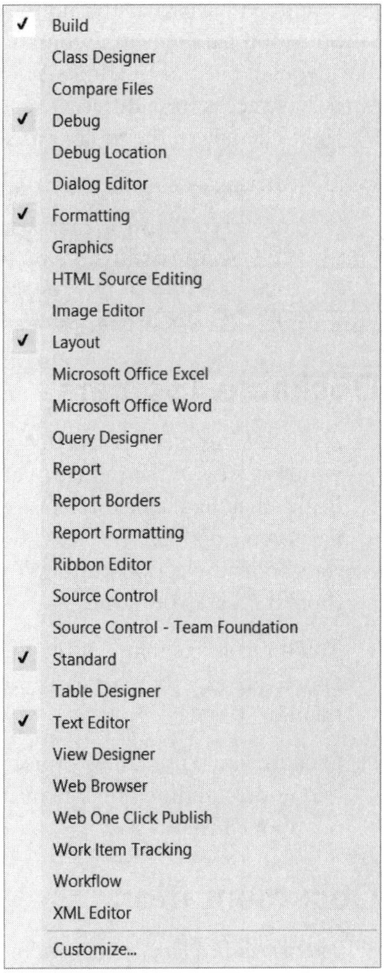

This is where you decide which toolbars are visible at any one time. To start with, make sure the Build, Debug, Formatting, Layout, Standard, and Text Editor menu items are selected. Clicking a toolbar in the list checks it if it is deselected, and results in it being displayed; clicking a toolbar that is selected deselects it and hides the toolbar.

✓	Build
	Class Designer
	Compare Files
✓	Debug
	Debug Location
	Dialog Editor
✓	Formatting
	Graphics
	HTML Source Editing
	Image Editor
✓	Layout
	Microsoft Office Excel
	Microsoft Office Word
	Query Designer
	Report
	Report Borders
	Report Formatting
	Ribbon Editor
	Source Control
	Source Control - Team Foundation
✓	Standard
	Table Designer
✓	Text Editor
	View Designer
	Web Browser
	Web One Click Publish
	Work Item Tracking
	Workflow
	XML Editor
	Customize...

FIGURE 1-4

> **NOTE** A toolbar won't necessarily display all of its buttons. You can add or remove buttons for a toolbar by clicking the down arrow that appears at the right of the button set. The buttons in the Text Editor toolbar that indent and unindent a set of highlighted statements are particularly useful, as are the buttons that comment out or uncomment a selected set of statements, so make sure these are displayed.

You don't have to clutter up the application window with all the toolbars you think you might need. Some toolbars appear automatically when required, and you'll find that the default set of toolbars is adequate most of the time. As you develop your application, it may sometimes be more convenient to have access to a different set of toolbars. You can change the set of visible toolbars at any time by right-clicking in the toolbar area and choosing from the context menu.

> **NOTE** As in many other Windows applications, the toolbars come complete with tooltips. If you let the mouse pointer linger over a toolbar button for a second or two, a label will display the function of that button.

Dockable Toolbars

A *dockable toolbar* is one that you can move around to position it at a convenient place in the window. Any of the toolbars can be docked at any of the four sides of the application window. Right-clicking in the toolbar area and selecting Customize from the pop-up will display the Customize dialog. You can choose where a particular toolbar is docked by selecting it and clicking the Modify Selection button. You can then choose from the drop-down list that appears to dock the toolbar where you want.

You'll recognize many of the toolbar icons from other Windows applications, but you may not appreciate exactly what these icons do in the context of Visual C++, so I'll describe them as we use them.

Because you'll use a new project for every program you develop, looking at what exactly a project is and understanding how the mechanism for defining a project works is a good place to start finding out about Visual C++.

Documentation

There will be plenty of occasions when you'll want to find out more information about Visual C++ and its features and options. Pressing Ctrl+F1 will display the online product documentation in your browser. Pressing F1 with the cursor on a C++ language element in your code or a standard library item will open a browser window showing documentation for the element. The Help menu also provides various routes into the documentation, as well as access to program samples and technical support.

Projects and Solutions

A *project* is a container for all the things that make up a program of some kind — it might be a console program, a window-based program, or some other kind of program. A project usually consists of several source files containing your code, plus possibly other files containing auxiliary data. All the files for a project are stored in the *project folder* and detailed information about the project is stored in an XML file with the extension .vcxproj, which is also in the project folder. The project folder contains other folders that are used to store the output from compiling and linking your project.

A *solution* is a mechanism for bringing together one or more programs and other resources that represent a solution to a particular data-processing problem. For example, a distributed order-entry system for a business operation might be composed of several different programs, each of which is a project within a single solution. Therefore a solution is a folder in which all the information relating to one or more projects is stored, and there will be one or more project folders as subfolders of the solution folder. Information about the projects in a solution is stored in a file with the extension .sln. When you create a project, a new solution is created automatically, unless you elect to add the project to an existing solution. The .suo file is not that important. You can even delete the .suo file and Visual C++ will re-create it when opening the solution.

When you create a project along with a solution, you can add projects to the same solution. You can add any kind of project to an existing solution, but you will usually add only projects that are related in some way to the existing project or projects in the solution. Generally, unless you have a good reason to do otherwise, each of your projects should have its own solution. Each example you create with this book will be a single project within its own solution.

Defining a Project

The first step in writing a Visual C++ program is to create a project for it using the File ➪ New ➪ Project menu option from the main menu or by pressing Ctrl+Shift+N. You can also simply click New Project on the Start page. As well as containing files that define the code and any other data that makes up your program, the project XML file in the project folder also records the options you've set for the project. That's enough introductory stuff for the moment. It's time to get your hands dirty.

TRY IT OUT   Creating a Project for a Win32 Console Application

First, select File ➪ New ➪ Project, or use one of the other possibilities I mentioned earlier to bring up the New Project dialog. The left pane in the dialog displays the types of projects you can create; in this case, click Win32. This selection identifies an application wizard that creates the initial contents for the project. The right pane displays a list of templates for the project type you have chosen in the left pane. The template you select is used to create the files that make up the project. In the next dialog you can customize the files that are created when you click the OK button in this dialog. For most type/template combinations a basic set of source files is created automatically. Choose Win32 Console Application in this instance.

Enter a suitable name for your project by typing into the Name: text box — for example, you could call it Ex1_01, or you can choose your own project name. Visual C++ supports long filenames, so you have a lot of flexibility. The name of the solution folder appears in the bottom text box and by default it is the same as the project name. You can change this if you prefer. The dialog also enables you to modify the location for the solution that contains your project — this appears in the Location: text box. If you simply enter a name for your project, the solution folder is automatically set to a folder with that name, with the path shown in the Location: text box. By default the solution folder is created for you if it doesn't already exist. To specify a different path for the solution folder, just enter it in the Location: text box. Alternatively, you can use the Browse button to select a path for your solution. Clicking OK displays the Win32 Application Wizard dialog.

This dialog explains the settings currently in effect. You can click Application Settings on the left to display the Application Settings page of the wizard, shown in Figure 1-5.

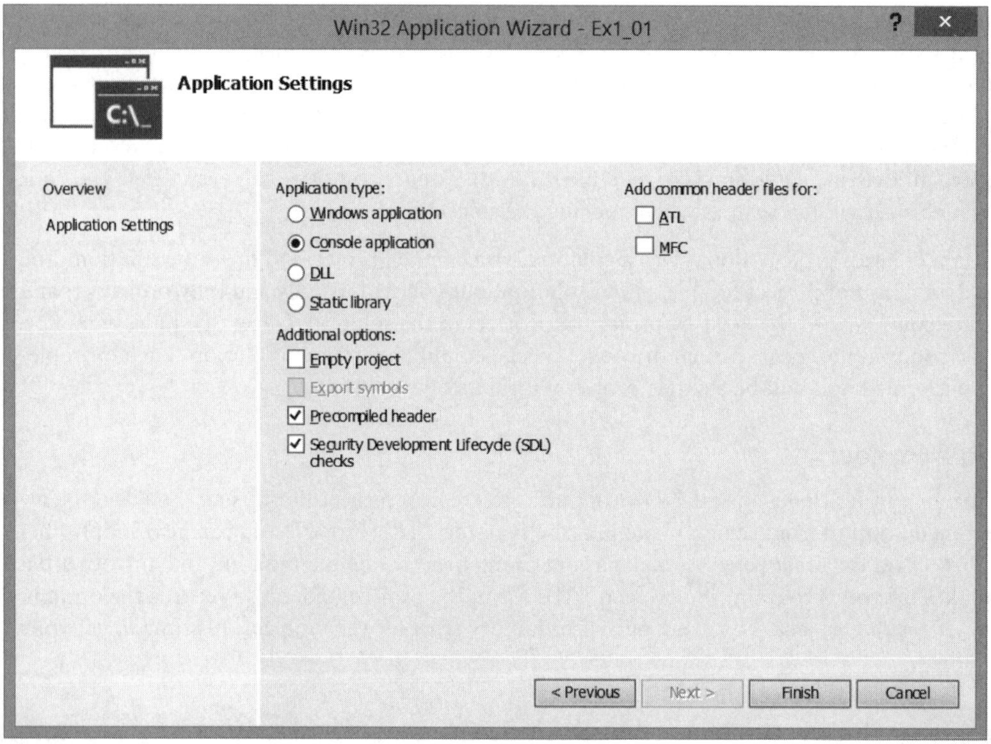

FIGURE 1-5

The Application Settings page enables you to choose options that apply to the project. You can see that you are creating a console application and not a Windows application. The Precompiled header option is a facility for compiling header files such as those from the standard library that do not change frequently. When you compile your program after making changes or additions to your code, the pre-compiled code that has not been changed will be reused as is. This makes compiling your program faster. You can uncheck the Security Development Lifecycle Checks checkbox option; this feature adds functionality for managing large-scale professional projects and we won't be using these. On the right of the dialog there are options for using MFC, which I have mentioned, and ATL, which is outside the scope of this book. For this project you can leave the rest of the options as they are and click Finish. The application wizard will create the project with default files.

The project folder will have the name that you supplied as the project name and will hold the files making up the project definition. If you didn't change it, the solution folder has the same name as the project folder and contains the project folder plus the files defining the contents of the solution. If you use Windows Explorer to inspect the contents of the solution folder, you'll see that it contains four files:

➤ A file with the extension `.sln` that records information about the projects in the solution.

➤ A file with the extension `.suo` in which user options that apply to the solution will be recorded.

➤ A file with the extension `.sdf` that records data about IntelliSense for the solution. IntelliSense is the facility that I mentioned earlier that provides auto-completion and prompts you for code in the Editor window as you enter it.

➤ A file with the extension `.opensdf` that records information about the state of the project. This file exists only while the project is open.

If you use Windows Explorer to look in the `Ex1_01` project folder, you will see that there are seven files initially, including a file with the name `ReadMe.txt` that contains a summary of the contents of the files that have been created. The project will automatically open with the Solution Explorer pane, as in Figure 1-6.

The Solution Explorer tab presents a view of all the projects in the current solution and the files they contain — here, of course, there is just one project. You can display the contents of any file as an additional tab in the Editor pane by double-clicking the name in the Solution Explorer tab. In the Editor pane, you can switch instantly to any of the files that have been displayed by clicking the appropriate tab.

The Class View tab displays the classes in your project and shows the contents of each class. You don't have any classes in this application, so the view is empty. When I discuss classes you will see that you can use the Class View tab to move quickly and easily around the code relating to your application classes.

You can display the Property Manager tab by selecting it from the View menu. It shows the properties that have been set for the Debug and Release versions of your project. I'll explain these a little later in this chapter. You can change any of the properties for a version by right-clicking it and selecting Properties from the context menu; this displays a dialog where you can set the project properties. You can also press Alt+F7 to display the Property Pages dialog at any time. I'll discuss this in more detail when I go into the Debug and Release versions of a program.

If it's not already visible, you can display the Resource View tab by selecting from the View menu or by pressing Ctrl+Shift+E. Resource View shows the dialog boxes, icons, menus, toolbars, and other resources used by the project. Because this is a console program, no resources are used; when you start writing Windows applications, you'll see a lot of things here. Through this tab you can edit or add to the resources available to the project.

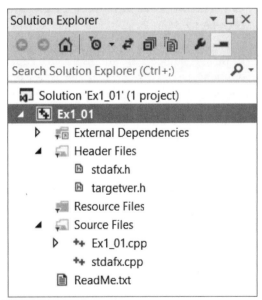

FIGURE 1-6

As with most elements of the IDE, the Solution Explorer and other tabs provide context-sensitive pop-up menus when you right-click items displayed in the tab, and in some cases when you right-click in the empty space in the tab. If you find that the Solution Explorer pane is in the way when you're writing code, you can hide it by clicking the Auto Hide icon. To redisplay it, click the Name tab on the left of the IDE window.

Modifying the Source Code

The application wizard generates a complete Win32 console program that you can compile and execute. The program doesn't do anything as it stands so to make it a little more interesting you need to change it. If it is not already visible in the Editor pane, double-click Ex1_01.cpp in the Solution Explorer pane. This is the main source file for the program and is shown in Figure 1-7.

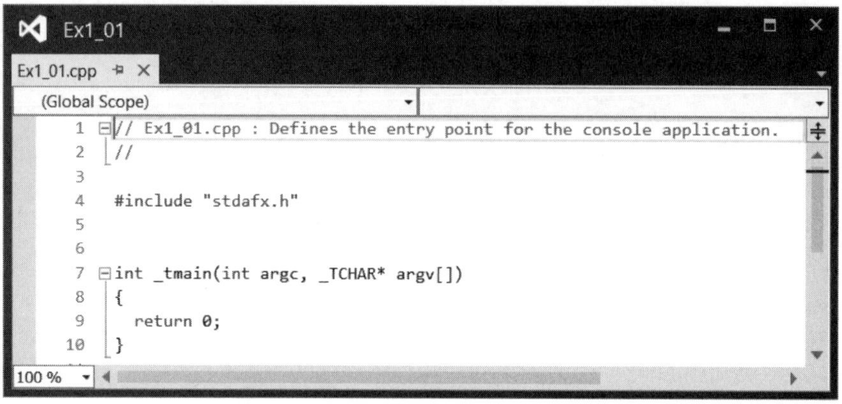

FIGURE 1-7

If the line numbers are not displayed, select Tools ➪ Options from the main menu to display the Options dialog. If you extend the C/C++ option in the Text Editor subtree in the left pane and select General from the extended tree, you can check the Line numbers option in the right pane of the dialog. I'll give you a rough guide to what this code in Figure 1-7 does, and you'll see more on all of this later.

The first two lines are just comments. Anything following // in a line is ignored by the compiler. When you want to add descriptive comments in a line, precede your text with //.

Line 4 is an #include directive that adds the contents of the file stdafx.h to this file, and the contents are inserted in place of the #include directive. This is the standard way to add the contents of .h header files to a .cpp source file in a C++ program.

Line 7 is the first line of the executable code in this file and the beginning of the function called _tmain(). A function is simply a named unit of executable code in a C++ program; every C++ program consists of at least one — and usually many more — functions.

Lines 8 and 10 contain left and right braces, respectively, that enclose all the executable code in the _tmain() function. The executable code is just the single line 9, and this ends the program.

Now you can add the following two lines of code in the Editor window:

```
// Ex1_01.cpp : Defines the entry point for the console application.
//

#include "stdafx.h"
#include <iostream>
```

```
int _tmain(int argc, _TCHAR* argv[])
{
    std::cout << "Hello world!\n";
    return 0;
}
```

The new lines you should add are shown in bold; the others are generated for you. To introduce each new line, place the cursor at the end of the text on the preceding line and press Enter to create an empty line in which you can type the new code. Make sure it is exactly as shown in the preceding example; otherwise the program may not compile.

The first new line is an #include directive that adds the contents of one of the standard library files to the Ex1_01.cpp source file. The iostream library defines facilities for basic I/O operations, and the one you are using in the second line that you added writes output to the command line. std::cout is the name of the standard output stream, and you write the string "Hello world!\n" to std::cout in the second addition statement. Whatever appears between the pair of double-quote characters is written to the command line.

Building the Solution

To build the solution, press F7 or select the Build ⇨ Build Solution menu item. Alternatively, you can click the toolbar button corresponding to this menu item. The toolbar buttons for the Build menu may not be displayed, but you can fix this by right-clicking in the toolbar area and selecting the Build toolbar from those in the list. The program should compile successfully. If there are errors, it may be that you created them while entering the new code, so check the two new lines very carefully.

Files Created by Building a Console Application

After the example has been built without error, take a look in the project folder by using Windows Explorer. You'll see a new subfolder to the solution folder Ex1_01 called Debug. This is the folder Ex1_01\Debug, not the folder Ex1_01\Ex1_01\Debug. This folder contains the output of the build you just performed. Notice that this folder contains three files.

The .exe file is your program in executable form. You don't need to know much about what's in the other files. In case you're curious, the .ilk file is used by the linker when you build your project. It enables the linker to incrementally link object files produced from modified source code into the existing .exe file. This avoids the need to relink everything each time you change the program. The .pdb file contains debugging information that is used when you execute the program in debug mode. In this mode, you can dynamically inspect information generated during program execution.

There's a Debug subdirectory in the Ex1_01 project folder too. This contains a large number of files that were created during the build process, and you can see what kind of information they contain from the Type description in Windows Explorer.

Debug and Release Versions of Your Program

You can set options for a project through the Project ⇨ Ex1_01 Properties menu item. These options determine how your source code is processed during the compile and link stages. The set of options that produces a particular executable version of your program is called a *configuration*. When you create a new project workspace, Visual C++ automatically creates configurations for producing two versions of your application. The Debug version includes additional information that helps you debug the program. With the Debug version of a program, you can step through the code when things go wrong, checking on the data values in the program as you go. The Release version has no debug information included and has the code-optimization options for the compiler turned on to provide the most efficient executable module. These two configurations are sufficient for your needs throughout this book, but when you need to add other configurations for an application you can do so through the Build ⇨ Configuration Manager menu. (Note that this menu item won't appear if you haven't got a project loaded. This is obviously not a problem, but might be confusing if you're just browsing through the menus to see what's there.)

You can choose which configuration of your program to work with by selecting from the drop-down list in the toolbar. Selecting Configuration Manager from the drop-down list will display the Configuration Manager dialog. You use this dialog when your solution contains multiple projects. Here you can choose configurations for each of the projects and choose which ones you want to build.

After your application has been tested using the debug configuration and appears to be working correctly, you typically rebuild the program as a release version; this produces optimized code without the debug and trace capability, so the program runs faster and occupies less memory.

Executing the Program

After you have successfully compiled the solution, you can execute the program by pressing Ctrl+F5. You should see the window shown in Figure 1-8.

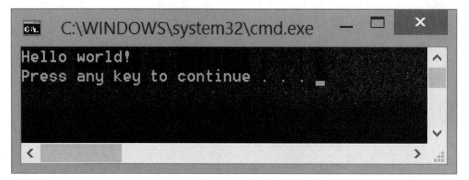

FIGURE 1-8

As you see, you get the text between the double quotes written to the command line. The "\n" that was at the end of the text string is a special sequence called an *escape sequence* that denotes a new-line character. Escape sequences are used to represent characters in a text string that you cannot enter directly from the keyboard. The last line prompting how you continue always appears with console program output. Pressing Enter will close the window. I won't show this last line when I show output from a program in the book.

TRY IT OUT   Creating an Empty Console Project

The previous project contained a certain amount of excess baggage that you don't need when working with simple examples. The precompiled headers option chosen by default resulted in the stdafx.h file being created in the project. This is a mechanism for making the compilation process more efficient when there are a lot of files in a program, but it won't be necessary for most of our examples. In these instances, you start with an empty project to which you can add your own source files. You can see how this works by creating a new project in a new solution for a Win32 console program with the name **Ex1_02**. After you have entered the project name and clicked OK, click Application Settings on the left side of the dialog box that follows. You can then select Empty project from the additional options and uncheck SDL. When you click Finish, the project is created as before, but this time without any source files.

Next, you can add a new source file to the project. Right-click the Solution Explorer pane and then select Add ➪ New Item from the context menu. A dialog displays: click Code in the left pane and C++ File(.cpp) in the right pane. Enter the filename as **Ex1_02**.

When you click Add in the dialog, the new file is added to the project and is displayed in the Editor window. The file is empty, of course, so nothing will be displayed. Enter the following code in the Editor window:

```
// Ex1_02.cpp A simple console program
#include <iostream>                      // Basic input and output library

int main()
{
  std::cout << "This is a simple program that outputs some text." << std::endl;
  std::cout << "You can output more lines of text" << std::endl;
  std::cout << "just by repeating the output statement like this." << std::endl;
  return 0;                              // Return to the operating system
}
```

Note the automatic indenting that occurs as you type the code. C++ uses indenting to make programs more readable, and the editor automatically indents each line of code that you enter based on what was in the previous line. You can change the indenting by selecting the Tools ➪ Options... menu item to display the Options dialog. Selecting Text Editor ➪ C/C++ ➪ Tabs in the left pane of the dialog displays the indenting options in the right pane. The editor inserts tabs by default, but you can change it to insert spaces if you prefer.

You'll see the syntax color highlighting in action as you type. Some elements of the program are shown in different colors, as the editor automatically assigns colors to language elements depending on what they are.

The preceding code is the complete program. You probably noticed a couple of differences compared to the code generated by the application wizard in the previous example. There's no #include directive for the stdafx.h file. You don't have this file as part of the project because you are not using the precompiled headers facility. The name of the function here is main; before it was _tmain. In fact all ISO/IEC standard C++ programs start execution in a function called main(). Microsoft uses wmain for this function when Unicode characters are used, and the name _tmain is defined to be either main or wmain (in the tchar.h header file), depending on whether or not the program is going to use Unicode characters. In the previous example the name _tmain is defined behind the scenes to be wmain because the project settings were set to Unicode. I'll use the standard name `main` in all the examples. The output statements are a little different. The first statement in `main()` is:

```
std::cout << "This is a simple program that outputs some text." << std::endl;
```

You have two occurrences of the `<<` operator, and each one sends whatever follows to `std::cout`, the standard output stream. First, the string between double quotes is sent to the stream, and then `std::endl`, where `std::endl` is defined in the standard library as a newline character. Earlier, you used the escape sequence `\n` for a newline character within a string between double quotes. You could have written the preceding statement as follows:

```
std::cout << "This is a simple program that outputs some text.\n";
```

This is not identical to using `std::endl` though. Using `std::endl` writes a newline and then flushes the output buffer. Using just `\n`, the buffer is not flushed immediately.

The last statement is the `return` statement that ends `main()` and thus the program. This is not strictly necessary here and you could leave it out. If execution reaches the end of `main()` without encountering a return statement, it is equivalent to executing `return 0`.

You can build this project in the same way as the previous example. Note that any open source files in the Editor pane are saved automatically if you have not already saved them when you build the project. When you have compiled the program successfully, press Ctrl+F5 to execute it. If everything works as it should, the output will be as follows:

```
This is a simple program that outputs some text.
You can output more lines of text
just by repeating the output statement like this.
```

Note that pressing Ctrl+F5 will build the project before executing it if it is not up to date.

Dealing with Errors

Of course, if you didn't type the program correctly, you get errors reported. To see how this works you could deliberately introduce an error into the program. If you already have errors of your own, you can use those to perform this exercise. Go back to the Editor pane and delete the semicolon at the end of the second-to-last line between the braces (line 8); then rebuild the source file. The Output pane at the bottom of the application window will include the following error message:

```
C2143: syntax error : missing ';' before 'return'
```

Every error message during compilation has an error number that you can look up in the documentation. Here the problem is obvious, but in more obscure cases the documentation may help you figure out what is causing the error. To get the documentation on an error, click the line in the Output pane that contains the error number and then press F1. A new window displays containing further information about the error. You can try it with this simple error, if you like.

When you have corrected the error, you can rebuild the project. The build operation works efficiently because the project definition keeps track of the status of the files making up the project. During a normal build, Visual C++ recompiles only the files that have changed since the program was last compiled or built. This means that if your project has several source files, and you've edited only one of them since the project was last built, only that file is recompiled before linking to create a new `.exe` file. If you modify a header file, all files that include that header will be recompiled.

Setting Options in Visual C++

Two sets of options are available. You can set options that apply to the tools provided by Visual C++, which apply in every project context. You also can set options that are specific to a project that determine how the project code is to be processed when it is compiled and linked. Options that apply to every project are set through the Options dialog that's displayed when you select Tools ➪ Options from the main menu. You used this dialog earlier to change the code indenting used by the editor. The Options dialog box is shown in Figure 1-9.

Clicking the arrow symbol to the left of any of the items in the left pane displays a list of subtopics. Figure 1-9 shows the options for the General subtopic under Projects and Solutions. The right pane displays the options you can set for the topic you have selected in the left pane. You should concern yourself with only a few of these at this time, but you'll find it useful to spend a little time browsing the range of options available to you. Clicking the Help button (the one with the question mark) at the top right of the dialog box displays an explanation of the current options.

You probably want to choose a path to use as a default when you create a new project, and you can do this through the first option shown in Figure 1-9. Just set the path to the location where you want your projects and solutions stored.

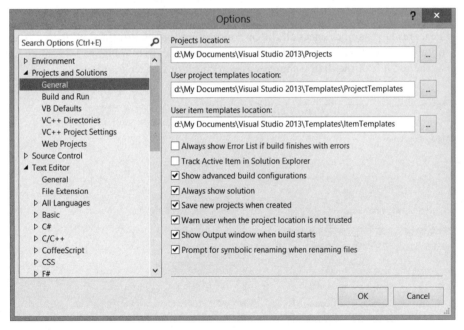

FIGURE 1-9

You can set options that apply to every project by selecting the Projects and Solutions ➪ VC++ Project Settings topic in the left pane of the Options dialog. You set options specific to the current project through the dialog that displays when you select the Project ➪ Ex1_02 Properties menu item in the main menu, or by pressing Alt+F7. The label for this menu item is tailored to reflect the name of the current project.

Creating and Executing Windows Applications

Just to show how easy it's going to be, you can now create a working Windows application. I'll defer discussion of the program until I've covered the necessary ground for you to understand it in detail. You will see, though, that the processes are straightforward.

Creating an MFC Application

To start with, if an existing project is active — as indicated by the project name appearing in the title bar of the Visual C++ main window — you can select Close Solution from the File menu. Alternatively, you can create a new project and have the current solution closed automatically. Create directory for solution is selected by default in the New Project dialog.

To create the Windows program, select New ➪ Project from the File menu or press Ctrl+Shift+N; then set the project type as MFC in the left pane, and select MFC Application as the project template. Enter the project name as **Ex1_03**. When you click OK, the MFC Application Wizard dialog is displayed. The dialog has options for the features you can include in your application. These are identified by the items in the list on the left of the dialog.

Click Application Type to display these options. Click the Tabbed documents option to deselect it and select Windows Native/Default from the drop-down list to the right. The dialog should then look as shown in Figure 1-10.

Click Advanced Features next, and deselect all the options except for the Printing and Print Preview and Common Control Manifest options so that the dialog looks as shown in Figure 1-11. Note how the small image at the top left of the dialog changes as you check or uncheck options.

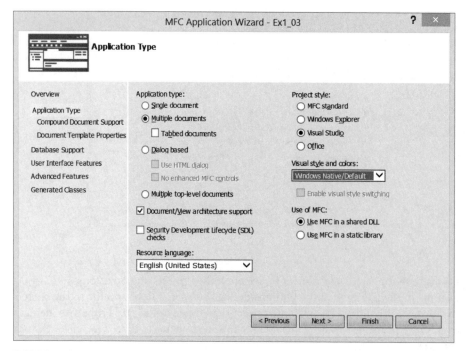

FIGURE 1-10

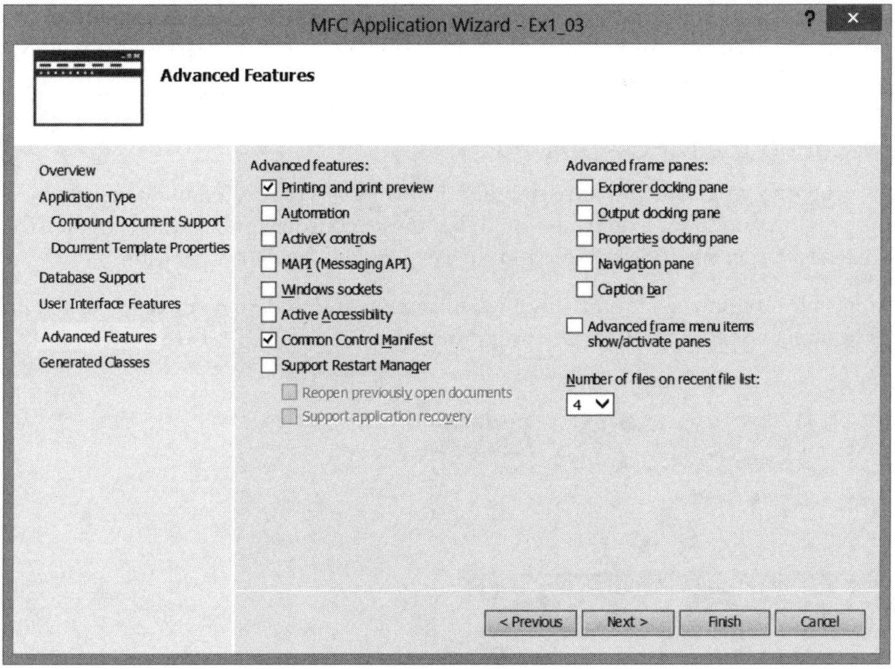

FIGURE 1-11

Finally, click Finish to create the project. The undocked Solution Explorer pane in the IDE window will look like Figure 1-12. The list shows the large number of source files that have been created, and several resource files. The files with the extension .cpp contain executable C++ source code, and the .h files, called header files, contain C++ code for definitions such as classes that are used by the executable code. The .ico files contain icons. The files are grouped into subfolders in the Solution Explorer pane for ease of access. These aren't real folders though, so they won't appear in the project folder on your disk.

If you look at the contents of the Ex1_03 solution folder and subfolders using Windows Explorer, you'll notice that you have generated a large number of files. Four of these are in the solution folder that includes the transient .opensdf file, there are many more in the project folder, and the rest are in the res subfolder of the project folder. The files in the res subfolder contain the resources used by the program, such as the toolbars and icons. You get all this as a result of just entering the name for the project. You can see why, with so many files and filenames being created automatically, a separate folder for each project becomes more than just a good idea.

FIGURE 1-12

One of the files in the `Ex1_03` project directory is `ReadMe.txt`, and it provides an explanation of the files that the MFC Application Wizard has generated. You can view this file in the Editor window by double-clicking it in the Solution Explorer pane.

Building and Executing the MFC Application

Before you can execute the program, you have to build the project — that is, compile the source code and link the program modules, exactly as you did with the console application example. To save time, press Ctrl+F5 to get the project built and then executed in a single operation.

After the project has been built, the Output window indicates that there are no errors, and the program executes. The application window for the program is shown in Figure 1-13.

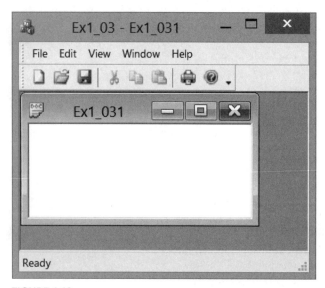

FIGURE 1-13

As you see, the window is complete with menus and a toolbar. Although there is no specific functionality in the program — you must add code for that to make it *your* program — all the menus work. You can try them out. You can even create further windows by selecting New from the File menu.

I think you'll agree that creating a Windows program with the MFC Application Wizard hasn't stressed too many brain cells. You'll need to get a few more ticking away when it comes to developing the basic program you have here into a program that does something more interesting, but it won't be that hard. Certainly, for many people, writing a serious Windows program the old-fashioned way, without the aid of Visual C++, required at least a couple of months on a brain-enhancing fish diet before making the attempt. That's why so many programmers used to eat sushi. That's all gone now with Visual C++. However, you never know what's around the corner in programming technology. If you like sushi, it's best to continue eating it — just to be on the safe side.

SUMMARY

In this chapter you have run through the basic mechanics of using Visual C++ to create applications. You created and executed console programs, and with the help of the application wizard you created an MFC-based Windows program. You should be reasonably comfortable with creating and executing projects.

Starting with the next chapter, all the examples illustrating how C++ language elements are used are executed using Win32 console applications. You will return to the application wizard for MFC-based programs as soon as you have finished learning the basics of C++.

➤ WHAT YOU LEARNED IN THIS CHAPTER

TOPIC	CONCEPT
C++	Visual C++ supports C++ that conforms to the C++ 11 language standard that is defined in the document ISO/IEC 14882:2011. Visual C++ implements most of the language features defined by this standard and some features from the draft of the next standard, C++ 14.
Solutions	A solution is a container for one or more projects that form a solution to an information-processing problem of some kind.
Projects	A project is a container for the code and resource elements that make up a functional unit in a program.
Project View Panes	The Solution Explorer pane displays one or more tabs and shows the project files. The Class View pane shows classes in the project. The Resource View pane shows project resources.
Project Options	You can display and modify the options that apply to all C++ projects through the dialog that is displayed when you select Options from the Tools menu.
Project Properties	You can set values for properties for the current project through the dialog that is displayed when you select Properties from the Project menu.
Console Applications	A console application is a basic C++ application with no GUI. Typically, input is from the keyboard and output is to the command line.
The `main()` function	The starting point for a standard C++ program is the `main()` function. The New Project dialog generates a console application that starts with the `_tmain()` function.
Unicode	If you want to use the standard `main()` function in a console program, you can generate an empty Win32 project and add the source file for `main()`.
Windows Store Apps	Windows Store apps target tablet computers and desktop PCs running the Windows 8 operating system.
Windows Runtime	The Windows Runtime, WinRT, provides the interface to the Windows 8 and later operating systems for Windows Store apps.
Windows Desktop Applications	Windows desktop applications have an application window and a GUI incorporating controls such as menus, toolbars, and dialogs. Desktop applications interface to the operating system through the Win32 set of functions. Desktop applications execute under Windows 7 and Windows 8 and it successors.
The Microsoft Foundation Classes	The MFC is a set of C++ classes that encapsulate the functions provided by Win32. MFC makes it easier to develop Windows desktop applications.
MFC Projects	You create an MFC project by selecting MFC then MFC Application in the New Project dialog.

2

Data, Variables, and Calculations

WHAT YOU WILL LEARN IN THIS CHAPTER:

- ➤ C++ program structure
- ➤ Namespaces
- ➤ Variables in C++
- ➤ Defining variables and constants
- ➤ Basic input from the keyboard and output to the screen
- ➤ Performing arithmetic calculations
- ➤ Casting operands
- ➤ Variable scope
- ➤ What the auto keyword does
- ➤ How to discover the type of an expression

WROX.COM CODE DOWNLOADS FOR THIS CHAPTER

You can find the wrox.com code downloads for this chapter on the Download Code tab at `www.wrox.com/go/beginningvisualc` . The code is in the Chapter 2 download and files are individually named according to the names throughout the chapter.

THE STRUCTURE OF A C++ PROGRAM

Console applications are programs that read data from the command line and output results to the command line. All the examples that you'll write to understand how the C++ language works will be console programs. This avoids having to dig into the complexities of creating and managing Windows applications before you have enough knowledge of how they work. You will be able to focus entirely on C++. After you have mastered that, you'll be ready to deal with creating and managing Windows applications and the sacks of code that it involves. I'll start by explaining how console programs are structured.

A C++ program consists of one or more functions. A function is a self-contained block of code with a unique name that you use to identify the function when you want to execute it. Chapter 1 includes an example of a Win32 console program consisting of just the main() function, where main is the name of the function. Every C++ program contains the main() function, and that is where execution always starts. Programs of any size consist of several functions — the main() function, plus a number of others.

You saw in Chapter 1 that a console program generated by the Application Wizard has a main function with the name _tmain. This is a Microsoft-specific programming construct to allow the function name to be wmain or main, depending on whether or not the program is using Unicode characters. The names wmain and _tmain are also Microsoft-specific and therefore not standard C++. The name for the main function in standard C++ is main. I'll use the name main for all our console examples because this is the most portable option. If you intend to compile your code only with Visual C++, and you want to use the Microsoft-specific name for main, you can use the default console application the Application Wizard generates. In this case, just copy the code that is shown in the body of main() in the console program examples to _tmain().

Figure 2-1 shows how a typical console program might be structured. Execution starts at the beginning of main(). From main() execution transfers to an input_names() function, which returns execution to the position immediately following where it was called in main(). The sort_names() function is called next from main() and when control returns to main(), the output_names() function is called. When output_names() finishes, execution returns again to main() and the program ends.

Of course, different programs may have radically different functional structures, but they all start execution at the beginning of main(). Defining a program as a number of functions allows you to write and test each function separately. Segmenting your programs in this way offers other advantages. A function you write to perform a general task can often be reused in other programs. The libraries that come with C++ provide a large number of standard functions that you can use to save yourself a great deal of work.

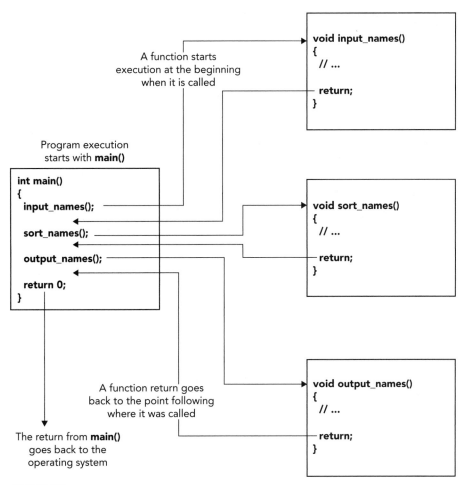

FIGURE 2-1

> **NOTE** *You'll see more about creating and using functions in Chapter 5.*

TRY IT OUT A Simple Program Using main()

This example demonstrates what you need to do to use main() in a Visual C++ console program. Start by creating a new project — you can use the Ctrl+Shift+N key combination as a shortcut for this. When the dialog appears, select Win32 as the project type and Win32 Console Application as the template. You can name the project **Ex2_01**.

When you click the OK button, you'll see the dialog in Figure 2-2 that shows an overview of what the Application Wizard will generate.

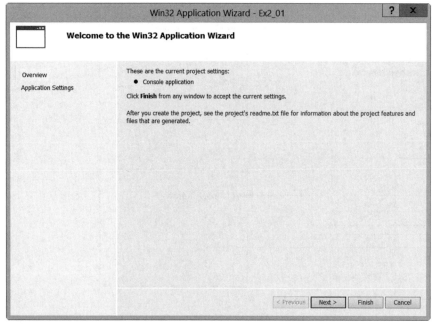

FIGURE 2-2

If you now click Application Settings on the left of this dialog, you'll see further options for a Win32 application displayed, as shown in Figure 2-3.

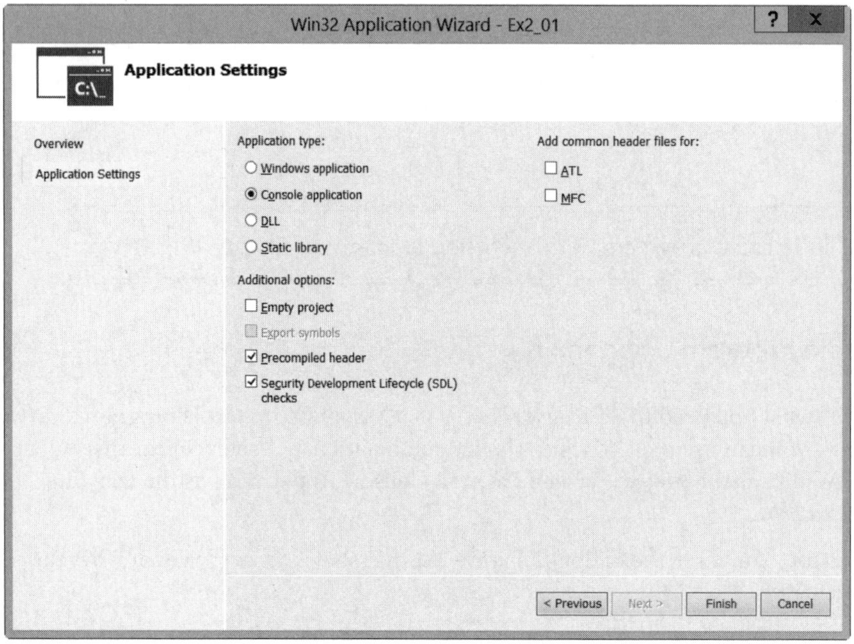

FIGURE 2-3

The default setting is a Console application that includes a file containing a default version of `main()` with the name `_tmain()`. You start from the most basic project structure that contains no source files, so choose Empty project and uncheck SDL checks from the set of options and click the Finish button.

You can see what the project contains from the Solution Explorer pane on the left of the main window, as shown in Figure 2-4.

You start by adding a new source file to the project. Right-click Source Files in the Solution Explorer pane and select the Add ⇨ New Item menu option. The Add New Item dialog displays, showing the options available.

Select Code in the left pane, select the C++ File (.cpp) template in the middle pane, and enter the filename as **Ex2_01**. The file is automatically given the extension

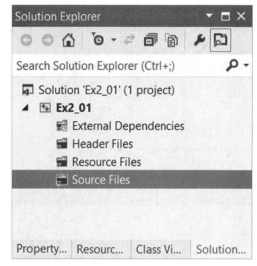

FIGURE 2-4

.cpp, so you don't have to enter this. There is no problem making the name of the file the same as the name of the project. The project file will have the extension `.vcxproj`, so that will differentiate it from the source file.

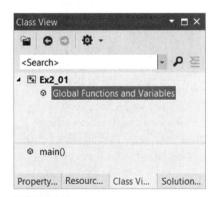

FIGURE 2-5

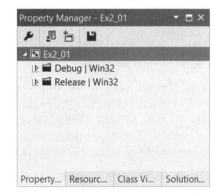

FIGURE 2-6

Click the Add button to create the file. You can then type the following code in the Editor pane of the IDE window:

```cpp
// Ex2_01.cpp
// A Simple Example of a Program
#include <iostream>

using std::cout;
using std::endl;

int main()
{
```

```
    int apples, oranges;                // Define two integer variables
    int fruit;                          // ...then another one

    apples = 5; oranges = 6;            // Set initial values
    fruit = apples + oranges;           // Get the total fruit

    cout << endl;                       // Start output on a new line
    cout << "Oranges are not the only fruit... " << endl
         << "- and we have " << fruit << " fruits in all.";
    cout << endl;                       // Output a new line character

    return 0;                           // Exit the program
  }
```

This illustrates some of the ways in which you can write statements and is not a model of good programming style. The editor checks the code as you type. Anything it thinks is not correct is underlined with a red squiggle, so look out for these. If you see one, it usually means that you have mistyped something. When you hover the mouse cursor over a red squiggle, a message displays to indicate what is wrong.

The source file is identified by its extension as a file containing C++ code so language elements of various kinds that the editor recognizes will be colored to highlight them. I say more about color highlighting later in this chapter.

If you look at the Solution Explorer pane (press Ctrl+Alt+L to display it); you'll see the new source file name. Solution Explorer always shows all the files in a project. You can display the Class View pane by selecting from the View menu or by pressing Ctrl+Shift+C. This consists of two panes. The upper pane shows global functions and macros within the project (and classes when you get to create a project involving classes), and the lower pane is presently empty. The main() function will appear in the lower pane if you select Global Functions and Variables in the upper pane; this is shown in Figure 2-5. I explain what this means in more detail later, but essentially, *globals* are functions and/or variables that are accessible from anywhere in a program.

You can display the Property Manager pane by selecting from the View menu. If you expand the items in the tree that is displayed by clicking the unfilled arrow symbols, it will look like Figure 2-6. This shows the two possible versions you can build, the Debug version for testing and the Release version when your program has been tested. The properties for each version are shown, and double-clicking any of them displays a dialog showing the Property Pages where you can change properties, if necessary.

You have three ways to compile and link the program; you can select the Build Ex2_01 menu item from the Build menu, you can press the F7 function key, or you can select the appropriate toolbar button. To identify what a toolbar button does just hover the mouse cursor over it. If there is no toolbar button that shows the tooltip Build Ex2_01, then the Build toolbar is not currently displayed. You can remedy this by right-clicking an empty part of the toolbar and selecting Build from the list. It's a very long list and you will probably want to choose to display different sets of toolbars, depending on what you are doing.

If the build operation is successful, you can execute the program by pressing Ctrl+F5 or by selecting Start Without Debugging from the Debug menu. You should get the following output in a command-line window:

```
    Oranges are not the only fruit...
    - and we have 11 fruits in all.
    Press any key to continue ...
```

The first two lines were produced by the program, and the last line indicates how you can end the execution and close the command-line window. I won't show this last line of output from other console examples but it's always there.

Program Comments

The first two lines in the program are *comments*. Comments are an important part of any program, but they're not executable code — they are there to help the human reader. The compiler ignores all comments. On any line of code, two successive slashes (//) that are not contained within a text string (you'll see what text strings are later) indicate that the rest of the line is a comment. You can see that several lines contain comments.

There's another form of comment bounded by /* and */. For example, the first line of the program could have been written:

```
/*   Ex2_01.cpp   */
```

A comment using // covers only the portion of the line following the two successive slashes, whereas the /*...*/ form defines whatever is enclosed between the /* and the */ as a comment, and this can span several lines. For example, you could write:

```
/*
   Ex2_01.cpp
   A Simple Program Example
*/
```

All four lines are comments and are ignored by the compiler. If you want to highlight some particular comment lines, you can embellish them:

```
/*****************************
 *   Ex2_01.cpp              *
 *   A Simple Program Example *
 *****************************/
```

As a rule, you should always comment your programs comprehensively. The comments should be sufficient for another programmer, or you at a later date, to understand the purpose of the code and how it works. I will often use more detailed comments in examples than you would in a production program.

The #include Directive — Header Files

Following the comments, you have an #include directive:

```
#include <iostream>
```

This is called a *directive* because it directs the compiler to do something — in this case, to insert the contents of the file, iostream, that is identified between the angled brackets, <>, into the program source file before compilation. The iostream file is called a *header file* because it's invariably inserted in another source file. iostream is part of the standard C++ library and contains the definitions necessary to allow you to use input and output statements. If you didn't include iostream into the program, it wouldn't compile, because you use output statements in the program that depend on definitions in this file. There are many different standard header files that cover a wide range of capabilities. You'll see more of them as you progress through the language facilities.

The name of the file to be inserted by an `#include` directive does not have to be written between angled brackets. It can be between double quotes, thus:

```
#include "iostream"
```

The difference between this and the preceding version is the places where the compiler will look for the file. If you write the header filename between double quotes, the compiler first searches the directory that contains the source file in which the directive appears. If the header file is not there, the compiler searches the directories containing the standard header files.

When the filename is enclosed between angled brackets, the compiler only searches the directories containing the standard header files. Thus, when you want to include a standard header in a source file, placing the name between angled brackets ensures it will be found more quickly. When you are including other header files, typically ones that you create yourself, place the name between double quotes; otherwise, the files will not be found at all.

An `#include` directive is one of several *preprocessor directives*, and I'll be introducing more of these as you need them. The editor highlights preprocessor directives in blue in the edit window. Preprocessor directives are commands executed by the preprocessor phase of compilation that executes before your code is compiled into object code, and they generally act on your source code in some way. They all start with the # character.

Namespaces and the Using Declaration

As you saw in Chapter 1, the *standard library* is an extensive set of routines that carry out many common tasks, such as dealing with input and output and performing basic mathematical calculations. There are a large number of these routines as well as other kinds of things that have names in the standard library so it is possible that you might accidentally use a name for your own purposes that is already used in the library. A *namespace* is a mechanism for minimizing the risk of inadvertently using duplicate names. It does this by associating a given set of names, such as those from the standard library, with a sort of family name, which is the *namespace name*.

Every name that is defined in code within a namespace has the namespace name associated with it. The standard library facilities are defined within a namespace with the name `std`, so every item from the standard library has its own name, plus the namespace name, `std`, as a qualifier. The full names for `cout` and `endl` from the standard library are `std::cout` and `std::endl`; you saw these in action in Chapter 1. The two colons that separate the namespace name from the entity name form an operator called the *scope resolution operator*. I'll discuss other uses for this operator later in the book. Using full names in a program can make the code look a bit cluttered, so it would be nice to have the option to use simple names, unqualified by the namespace name, `std`. The two lines in our program following the `#include` directive for `iostream` make this possible:

```
using std::cout;
using std::endl;
```

These are *using declarations*. They tell the compiler that you intend to use the names `cout` and `endl` from the namespace `std` without specifying the namespace name. The compiler assumes that wherever you use `cout` subsequent to the first `using` declaration, you mean `std::cout`. The name `cout` represents the standard output stream that corresponds to the command line and the name `endl` represents the newline character and flushes the output buffer. You learn more about namespaces a little later in this chapter, including how you define your own namespaces.

> **WARNING** Be careful with using declarations in header files, especially when the header files are included into several other source files. In header files you should avoid placing using declarations at global scope because they will apply within any source file that includes the header file.

The main() Function

The `main()` function in the example consists of the function header defining it as `main()` plus everything from the first opening brace, {, to the corresponding closing brace, }. The braces enclose the executable statements in the function, which are referred to collectively as the *body* of the function.

As you'll see, all functions consist of a header that defines (among other things) the function name, followed by the function body that consists of a number of program statements enclosed between braces. The body of a function may contain no statements at all, in which case, it doesn't do anything.

A function that doesn't do anything may seem somewhat superfluous, but when you're writing a large program, you may map out the complete program structure in functions initially, but omit the code for many of the functions, leaving them with empty or minimal bodies. Doing this means that you can compile and execute the whole program with all its functions at any time and add detailed coding for the functions incrementally.

Program Statements

Each program statement in the body of `main()` is terminated with a semicolon. It's the semicolon that marks the end of a statement, not the end of a line. Consequently, you can spread a statement over several lines when this makes the code easier to follow, and several statements can appear in a single line. The program statement is the basic unit for defining what a program does. This is a bit like a sentence in a paragraph of text, where each sentence stands by itself in expressing an action or an idea, but relates to and combines with the other sentences in the paragraph in expressing a more general concept. A statement is a self-contained definition of an action that the computer is to carry out, but that can be combined with other statements to define a more complex action or calculation.

The action of a function is always expressed by a number of statements, each ending with a semicolon. Take a look at the statements in the example just written, just to get a feel for how it works. I will discuss each type of statement later in this chapter.

The first statement in the body of `main()` is:

```
int apples, oranges;          // Declare two integer variables
```

This defines two variables, `apples` and `oranges`. A *variable* is a named bit of computer memory that you use to store data, and a statement that introduces the names of one or more variables is called a *variable declaration*. The `int` keyword indicates that the variables with the names `apples` and `oranges` are to store values that are whole numbers, or integers. Whenever you introduce the name of a variable into a program, you always specify what kind of data it will store, and this is called the `type` of the variable.

The next statement defines another integer variable, `fruit`:

```
int fruit;                              // ...then another one
```

While you can define several variables in the same statement, as in the preceding statement for `apples` and `oranges`, it's generally a good idea to define each variable in a separate statement on its own line. This enables you to comment them individually to explain how you will use them.

The next line in the example is:

```
apples = 5; oranges = 6;        // Set initial values
```

This line contains two statements, each terminated by a semicolon. I put this here to demonstrate that you can put more than one statement in a line. Although it isn't obligatory, it's generally good programming practice to write only one statement on a line because it makes the code easier to understand. Good programming practice is about adopting approaches that make your code easy to follow and that minimize the likelihood of errors.

The two statements store the values 5 and 6 in the variables `apples` and `oranges`, respectively. These statements are called *assignment statements*, because they assign new values to variables; the = is the assignment operator.

The next statement is:

```
fruit = apples + oranges;       // Get the total fruit
```

This is also an assignment statement, but is a little different. You have an *arithmetic expression* to the right of the assignment operator. This statement sums the values stored in `apples` and `oranges` and stores the result in `fruit`.

The next three statements are:

```
cout << endl;                   // Start output on a new line
cout << "Oranges are not the only fruit... " << endl
     << "- and we have " << fruit << " fruits in all.";
cout << endl;                   // Output a new line character
```

These are all *output statements*. The first sends a newline character, denoted by the word `endl`, to the command line on the screen. A source of input or a destination for output in C++ is referred to as a *stream*. The name `cout` specifies the "standard" output stream, and the operator `<<` indicates that what appears to the right of the operator is to be sent to `cout`. The `<<` operator "points" in the direction that the data flows — from the variable, string, or expression that appears on the right of the operator to the output destination that is on the left. Thus in the first statement, the value represented by the name `endl` — a newline character — is sent to the stream identified by the name `cout` — and data transferred to `cout` is written to the command line. Sending `endl` to the stream also causes the stream buffer to be flushed so all output is sent to the command line at that point.

The meaning of the name `cout` and the `<<` operator are defined in the `iostream` header file that you added to the program code by means of the `#include` directive. `cout` is a name in the standard library so it is within the `std` namespace. Without the `using` directive, it would not be recognized unless you used its fully qualified name, `std::cout`. `cout` has been defined to represent the standard output stream so you shouldn't use `cout` for other purposes. Using the same name for different things is likely to cause confusion.

The second output statement of the three is spread over two lines:

```
cout << "Oranges are not the only fruit... " << endl
        << "- and we have " << fruit << " fruits in all.";
```

As I said earlier, you can spread each statement over as many lines as you wish. The end of a statement is always signalled by a semicolon, not the end of a line. Successive lines are read and combined into a single statement by the compiler until it finds the semicolon that defines the end of the statement. Of course, this means that if you forget to put a semicolon at the end of a statement, the compiler will assume the next line is part of the same statement and join them together. This usually results in something the compiler cannot understand, so you'll get an error message.

The statement sends the text string `"Oranges are not the only fruit..."` to the command line, followed by another newline character (`endl`), then another text string, `"- and we have "`, followed by the value stored in the variable `fruit`, then, finally, another text string, `" fruits in all."`. There is no problem stringing together a sequence of things that you want to output in this way. The statement executes from left to right, with each item being sent to `cout` in turn. Note that each item to be sent to `cout` is preceded by its own `<<` operator.

The third and last output statement sends another newline character to the screen, and the three statements produce the output that you see. The last statement is:

```
return 0;                       // Exit the program
```

This terminates execution of `main()`, which ends the program. Control returns to the operating system, and the `0` is a return code that tells the operating system that the application terminated successfully. You can omit the return statement from `main()` and it will still compile and run. I'll discuss all these statements in more detail later.

Program statements execute in the sequence in which they are written, unless a statement specifically causes the natural sequence to be altered. In Chapter 3, you'll look at statements that alter the sequence of execution.

Whitespace

Whitespace is any sequence of blanks, tabs, newline characters, form feed characters, and comments. Whitespace serves to separate one part of a statement from another and enables the compiler to identify where one element in a statement, such as `int`, ends and the next element begins. Otherwise, whitespace is ignored and has no effect.

For example, consider the following statement:

```
int fruit;                      // ...then another one
```

There must be at least one whitespace character between `int` and `fruit` for the compiler to be able to distinguish them, but if you add more whitespace characters, they will be ignored. The content of the line following the semicolon is all whitespace and is therefore ignored.

On the other hand, look at this statement:

```
fruit = apples + oranges;       // Get the total fruit
```

No whitespace characters are necessary between `fruit` and `=`, or between `=` and `apples`, although you are free to include some if you wish. This is because the `=` is not alphabetic or numeric, so the compiler can separate it from its surroundings. Similarly, no whitespace characters are necessary on either side of the + sign, but you can include some if you want.

Apart from its use as a separator between elements, the compiler ignores whitespace (except, of course, in a string of characters between double quotes). You can include as much whitespace as you like to make your program more readable. Remember that the end of a statement is wherever the semicolon occurs.

Statement Blocks

You can enclose several statements between a pair of braces, in which case, they become a *block*, or a *compound statement*. The body of a function is an example of a block. Such a compound statement can be thought of as a single statement (as you'll see when you look at the decision-making possibilities in Chapter 3). Wherever you can put a single statement, you could equally well put a block of statements between braces. As a consequence, blocks can be placed inside other blocks. In fact, blocks can be nested, one within another, to any depth.

> **NOTE** A statement block has important effects on variables, but I will defer discussion of this until the "Understanding Storage Duration and Scope" section later in this chapter.

Automatically Generated Console Programs

In the last example, you opted to produce the project as an empty project with no source files, and you added the source file subsequently. If you allow the Application Wizard to generate the project as you did in Chapter 1, the project will contain several files, so let's look at their contents in a little more depth. Create a new Win32 console project with the name **Ex2_01A**, and this time allow the Application Wizard to finish without setting any options in the Application Settings dialog. The project will have four files containing code: the `Ex2_01A.cpp` and `stdafx.cpp` source files, the `stdafx.h` header file, and the `targetver.h` file that specifies the earliest version of Windows that is capable of running your application. They represent a working program that does nothing. You can close an open project by selecting File ➪ Close Solution on the main menu. You can create a new project with an existing project open, in which case, the old project will be closed automatically unless you elect to add it to the same solution.

`Ex2_01A.cpp` contains the following:

```
// Ex2_01A.cpp : Defines the entry point for the console application.
//

#include "stdafx.h"

int _tmain(int argc, _TCHAR* argv[])
{
  return 0;
}
```

This is decidedly different from the previous example. There is an `#include` directive for the `stdafx.h` header file and the function where execution starts is called `_tmain()`, not `main()`. Chapter 5 explains the things between the parentheses in the function header.

Precompiled Header Files

The Application Wizard generated the `stdafx.h` header file as part of the project, and if you look at the code in there, you'll see three further `#include` directives for the `targetver.h` header that I mentioned earlier, plus the standard library header files `stdio.h` and `tchar.h`. The old-style header `stdio.h` is for standard I/O and was used before the current C++ standard; this covers ground similar to the `iostream` header but does not define the same names. Our console examples will use `iostream` so you will need to include it. `tchar.h` is a Microsoft-specific header file defining text functions.

The idea of `stdafx.h` is that it will be compiled only when its contents change and not recompiled every time you compile the program. Compiling `stdafx.h` results in a `.pch` file (precompiled header file). The compiler only recompiles `stdafx.h` if there is no corresponding `.pch` file, or if the time-stamp for the `.pch` file is earlier than the timestamp for the `stdafx.h` file. Some standard library header files are very large, so this feature can significantly reduce the time it takes to compile a project. If you only put an `#include` directive for `iostream` in `Ex2_01A.cpp`, the header is recompiled each time you compile the program. If you put it in `stdafx.h`, `iostream` will only be compiled once. Thus `stdafx.h` should contain `#include` directives for all header files that are not going to be changed very often, if at all. These will be standard header files for your project plus any of your own project header files that are rarely changed. While you are learning C++, you won't be using either of the headers that appear in `stdafx.h`.

Main Function Names

As I explained, Visual C++ supports `wmain()` as an alternative to `main()` when you are writing a program that's using Unicode characters — `wmain()` being a Microsoft-specific definition for `main()` that is not part of standard C++. The `tchar.h` header defines the name `_tmain` such that it will normally be replaced by `main`, but will be replaced by `wmain` if the symbol `_UNICODE` is defined. To identify a program as using Unicode, you could add the following statements to the beginning of the `stdafx.h` header file:

```
#define _UNICODE
#define  UNICODE
```

So why do you need two statements? Defining the `_UNICODE` symbol causes the Windows header files to assume Unicode characters are the default. Defining `_UNICODE` does the same for the C runtime header files that come with the C++ standard library. You don't need to do this with the `Ex2_01A` project because the `Character Set` project property will have been set to use the Unicode character set by default. Now that I've explained all that, I'll stick to plain old `main()` for our C++ console examples because this option is standard C++ and therefore the most portable coding approach.

> **NOTE** *You can use the default console project for the console examples in the book if you wish. In this case just put the code from the body of* `main()` *in an example as the body of* `_tmain()`. *You can put any* `#include` *directives for standard library headers in* `stdafx.h`.

DEFINING VARIABLES

A fundamental objective in all computer programs is to manipulate data and get some answers. An essential element in this process is having a piece of memory that you can call your own, that you can refer to using a meaningful name, and where you can store an item of data. Each piece of memory specified is called a *variable*.

As you know, each variable will store a particular kind of data, and the type of data that can be stored is fixed when you define the variable. One variable might store whole numbers (that is, integers), in which case you can't use it to store fractional values. The value that a variable contains at any point is determined by the statements in your program and will usually change many times as the program progresses.

Naming Variables

Names of variables, or indeed names of anything in C++, can be any sequence of letters and digits, where the underscore, _, counts as a letter in this context. No other characters are allowed. If you use some other character in a name, you will get an error message when you compile the program. Names must begin with either a letter or an underscore and are usually chosen to indicate the kind of information stored. Names are also referred to as *identifiers*.

Names can be up to 2,048 characters in Visual C++ so you have a more than reasonable amount of flexibility. Using long names can make your programs difficult to read, and unless you have amazing keyboard skills, they are the very devil to type in. A more serious consideration is that not all compilers support very long names. Realistically, you rarely need to use names of more than 10 or 15 characters.

Names that begin with an underscore and include uppercase letters (for example, _Upper and _Lower) are best avoided because of potential clashes with standard library names that have this form. You should also avoid using names that include a double underscore for the same reason.

Here are some examples of valid variable names:

```
price  discount  pShape  value_  COUNT

five NaCl sodiumChloride tax_rate
```

Meaningful names involving two or more words can be constructed in various ways — capitalizing the first letter of the second and subsequent words or inserting underscores between words, for instance. There are examples in the preceding list. I'll use various styles for names in code in the book, but it's a good idea to stick to one style, at least within a single program.

8_Ball, 7Up, and 6_pack are not legal names. Neither is Hash! nor Mary-Ann. This last example is a common mistake, although Mary_Ann with an underscore is okay. Of course, Mary Ann is not, because variable names cannot contain whitespace. The names republican and Republican are different because names are case-sensitive. A common convention is to reserve names beginning with a capital letter for classes and to use names beginning with a lowercase letter for variables. I'll discuss classes in Chapter 8.

Keywords

Keywords are reserved words in C++ that have special significance within the language. You must not use keywords as names in your code. Keywords are highlighted with a particular color by the editor and the default is blue. If a keyword does not appear highlighted, then you have entered it incorrectly. If you don't like the default highlighting colors used by the editor to identify various language elements, you can change them. First select Options from the Tools menu, then make whatever changes you want after selecting Environment/Fonts and Colors in the left dialog pane.

Remember that keywords, like names, are case-sensitive. For example, the program you entered earlier in the chapter contained the keywords `int` and `return`; if you write `Int` or `Return`, these are not keywords and therefore will not be recognized and won't be highlighted in blue. You will see many more keywords as you progress through the book.

Declaring Variables

As you know, a variable *declaration* is a statement that specifies the name of a variable and its type. For example:

```
int value;
```

This declares a variable with the name `value` that can store integers. The type of data that can be stored in `value` is specified by the keyword `int`, so you can only use `value` to store data of type `int`.

A single declaration can specify the names of several variables:

```
int cost, discount_percent, net_price;
```

This is not recommended. It is generally better to declare variables in individual statements, one per line. I'll deviate from this from time to time in this book, usually in the interests of not spreading code over too many pages.

To store an item of data you need to have a memory location associated with the variable name. This process is called variable *definition*. Except in a few special cases that you will meet in the book, a variable declaration is also a definition so it introduces the variable name and ties it to an appropriately sized piece of memory.

Consider the statement:

```
int value;
```

This is a declaration and a definition. You use the variable *name*, `value`, that you have declared, to access the *memory* associated with it, and that can store a single value of type `int`. The reason for this apparently pedantic differentiation between a declaration and a definition is that you will meet statements that are declarations but not definitions. To avoid error messages from the compiler, you must declare a variable before the variable is used for the first time. It is good practice to declare variables close to their first point of use.

Initial Values for Variables

You can assign an initial value to a variable when you declare it. A declaration that assigns an initial value to a variable is called an *initialization*. There are three forms of syntax available to do this, and I show you the recommended approach last. The following statements give each of the variables an initial value:

```
int value = 0;
int count = 10;
int number = 5;
```

value will have the value 0, count will have the value 10, and number will have the value 5.

A second way to initialize a variable uses *functional notation*. Instead of an equal sign and the value, you write the value in parentheses following the variable name. You could rewrite the previous statements like this:

```
int value(0);
int count(10);
int number(5);
```

The third possibility and the recommended approach is to use an *initializer list*. The previous three statements can be written:

```
int value{};
int count{10};
int number{5};
```

The initial value appears between braces, following the variable name. If the braces are empty, as in the definition for value, 0 is assumed so value will be 0. This notation was introduced by the C++ 11 standard, and although the previous two methods are still valid, this is now the preferred approach. The reason is that the same notation can be used in almost every context, thus making initialization uniform. I use it throughout the rest of the book and indicate the few circumstances where it cannot be used.

If you don't supply an initial value, a variable will usually contain garbage left in the memory it occupies by a previous program (there is an exception to this that you will meet later in this chapter). Wherever possible, you should initialize variables when you define them. If your variables start out with known values, it is easier to work out what is happening when things go wrong. And you can be sure that things *will* go wrong.

FUNDAMENTAL DATA TYPES

The sort of information that a variable can hold is determined by its *data type*. All data and variables in your program must be of some defined type. C++ provides a range of *fundamental data types*, specified by particular keywords. Fundamental data types are so-called because they store values that represent fundamental data in your computer, essentially numerical values. Characters are numeric because a character is represented by a numeric character code. You have already seen type int for integer variables.

The fundamental types fall into three categories:

➤ Types that store integers

➤ Types that store non-integral values, called *floating-point* types

➤ The void type that specifies an empty set of values or no type

Integer Variables

Integer variables can only store whole numbers. The number of players in a football team is an integer, at least at the beginning of the game. You already know that you can declare integer variables using the keyword int. Variables of type int occupy 4 bytes in memory and can store both positive and negative integers. The upper and lower limits for values of type int correspond to the maximum and minimum signed binary numbers that can be represented by 32 bits. The upper limit is $2^{31} - 1$, which is 2,147,483,647, and the lower limit is $-(2^{31})$, which is -2,147,483,648. Here's an example of defining a variable of type int:

```
int toeCount {10};
```

The short keyword defines an integer variable occupying 2 bytes. The keyword short is equivalent to short int, so you could define two variables of type short with the following statements:

```
short feetPerPerson {2};
short int feetPerYard {3};
```

Both variables are of the same type because short means exactly the same as short int. I used both forms of the type name to show them in use, but it is best to stick to one representation, and short is used most often.

The integer type, long, occupies 4 bytes in Visual C++ and therefore can store the same range of values as type int. You'll find type long occupies 8 bytes with some other C++ compilers. The type can also be written as long int. Here's how you can declare variables of type long:

```
long bigNumber {1000000L};
long int largeValue {};
```

These statements declare the variables bigNumber and largeValue with initial values 1000000 and 0, respectively. The letter L appended to the literals specifies that they are of type long. You can use a small letter l but it has the disadvantage that it is easily confused with the digit 1. Integer literals without an L appended are of type int.

> **NOTE** You must not include commas when writing numeric values in your code. In text you can write the number 12,345, but in code you must write it as 12345.

You can use variables of type long long to store integers of an even greater magnitude:

```
long long huge {100000000LL};
```

Variables of type long long occupy 8 bytes and store values from -9,223,372,036,854,775,808 to 9,223,372,036,854,775,807. The suffix to identify an integer as type long long is LL or ll. The latter is best avoided because it looks like eleven.

Character Data Types

The char data type serves a dual purpose. It specifies a one-byte variable that can store integers within a given range, or it can store the code for a single *ASCII* character (the *American Standard Code for Information Interchange*). You can declare a char variable with this statement:

```
char letter {'A'};
```

This declares the variable letter and initializes it with the constant 'A'. You specify a value that is a single character between single quotes. Because 'A' is represented in ASCII by the decimal value 65, you could have written the statement as:

```
char letter {65};          // Equivalent to A
```

This produces the same result as the previous statement. The range of integers that can be stored in a variable of type char is from -128 to 127.

> **NOTE** The C++ standard does not require that type char should represent signed 1-byte integers. It is the compiler implementer's choice as to whether type char stores signed integers in the range -128 to +127 or unsigned integers in the range 0 to 255. You need to keep this in mind if you are porting your code to a different environment.

The type wchar_t is so-called because it is a *wide character type*. Variables of this type in Visual C++ store 2-byte character codes with values in the range from 0 to 65,535. Here's an example of defining a variable of type wchar_t:

```
wchar_t letter {L'Z'};     // A variable storing a 16-bit character code
```

This defines letter and initializes it with the 16-bit code for the letter Z. The L preceding the character constant, 'Z', tells the compiler that this is a 16-bit character code value.

You can also use hexadecimal constants to initialize integer variables, including those of type char. A hexadecimal number is written using the standard representation for hexadecimal digits: 0 to 9, and A to F (or a to f) for digits with values from 10 to 15. It's also prefixed by 0x (or 0X) to distinguish it from a decimal value. Thus, to get exactly the same result again, you could rewrite the last statement as follows:

```
wchar_t letter{0x5A};      // A variable storing a 16-bit character code
```

> **WARNING** Don't write decimal integer values with a leading zero. The compiler will interpret such values as octal (base 8), so a value written as 065 will be equivalent to 53 in decimal notation.

Microsoft Windows provides a Character Map utility that enables you to locate characters from any of the fonts available. It will show the character code in hexadecimal and tell you the keystroke to use for entering the character.

Integer Type Modifiers

Variables of the types `char`, `int`, `short`, `long`, or `long long` store `signed` integer values so you can use these types to store either positive or negative values. This is because these types are assumed to have the default *type modifier* `signed`. So, wherever you wrote `int` or `long`, you could have written `signed int` or `signed long`, respectively.

You can also use the `signed` keyword by itself to specify the type of a variable, in which case, it means `signed int`. For example:

```
signed value {-5};          // Equivalent to signed int
```

This usage is not common. I prefer to use `int` because it is more obvious what is meant.

The range of values you can store as type `char`, -128 to 127, is the same as the range of values you can store in a variable of type `signed char`. In spite of this, `char` and `signed char` are different types so you should not make the mistake of assuming they are the same. Whether type `char` is signed or unsigned is implementation defined in general. Visual C++ defines it as `signed char` but it may be different with other compilers.

If you are sure that you don't need to store negative values (for example, if you were recording the number of miles you drive in a week), you can specify a variable as `unsigned`:

```
unsigned long mileage {0UL};
```

The minimum value that can be stored in `mileage` is zero and the maximum is 4,294,967,295 (that's 2^{32} - 1). Compare this to the range for a `signed long`, -2,147,483,648 to 2,147,483,647 (that's -2^{31} to 2^{31} - 1). The bit that is used in a `signed` variable as the sign is part of the numeric value in an `unsigned` variable. Consequently, an `unsigned` variable can store larger positive values, but it can't represent a negative value. Note how a `U` (or `u`) is appended to `unsigned` constants. In the preceding example, I also appended `L` to indicate that the constant is `long`. You can use either upper- or lowercase for `U` and `L`, and the sequence is unimportant. However, it's a good idea to adopt a consistent approach.

You can also use `unsigned` by itself as the type specification for a variable, in which case, you are specifying the type as `unsigned int`.

> **NOTE** Remember, both `signed` *and* `unsigned` *are keywords, so you can't use them as variable names.*

The Boolean Type

Boolean variables can store one of two values: a value called `true` and a value called `false`. Boolean variables are also referred to as *logical variables*. The type for a logical variable is `bool`, named after George Boole, who developed Boolean algebra, and it is regarded as an integer type. Variables of type `bool` are used to store the results of tests that can be either `true` or `false`, such as whether two values are equal.

You could declare a variable of type `bool` with the statement:

```
bool testResult;
```

Of course, you can also initialize `bool` variables when you declare them:

```
bool colorIsRed {true};
```

> **NOTE** The values TRUE and FALSE are used quite extensively with variables of numeric types, and particularly of type `int`. This is a hangover from the time before type `bool` was implemented in C++ when variables of type `int` were typically used to represent logical values. In this case a zero-value is treated as false and a non-zero value as true. The symbols TRUE and FALSE are still used within the MFC where they represent a non-zero integer value and 0, respectively. Note that TRUE and FALSE — written with capital letters — are not keywords; they are just symbols defined in the Win32 SDK. TRUE and FALSE are not legal `bool` values, so don't confuse `true` with TRUE.

Floating-point Types

Values that aren't integral are stored as *floating-point* numbers. A floating-point number can be expressed as a decimal value such as 112.5, or with an exponent such as 1.125E2 where the decimal part is multiplied by the power of 10 specified after the E (for Exponent). Thus 1.125E2 is 1.125×10^2, which is 112.5.

> **NOTE** A floating-point constant must contain a decimal point, or an exponent, or both. If you write a numerical value with neither, you have an integer.

You can specify a floating-point variable using the keyword `double`, as in this statement:

```
double in_to_mm {25.4};
```

A variable of type `double` occupies 8 bytes and stores values accurate to approximately 15 decimal digits. The range of values stored is much wider than the 15 digits' accuracy indicates, being from 1.7×10^{-308} to 1.7×10^{308}, positive and negative. If you don't need 15 digits' precision, and you don't need the massive range of values provided by `double` variables, you can use the keyword `float` to declare floating-point variables that occupy 4 bytes. For example:

```
float pi {3.14159f};
```

This defines `pi` with the initial value 3.14159. The `f` at the end of the constant specifies that it is of type `float`. Without the `f`, the constant would be type `double`. Variables of type `float` have approximately 7 decimal digits of precision and can have values from 3.4×10^{-38} to 3.4×10^{38}, positive and negative.

The C++ standard also defines the `long double` floating-point type, which is implemented with the same range and precision as type `double` in Visual C++. With some compilers, `long double` corresponds to a 16-byte floating-point value with a much greater range and precision than type `double`.

Fundamental Types in C++

The following table summarizes all the fundamental types and the range of values that are supported for these in Visual C++:

TYPE	SIZE IN BYTES	RANGE OF VALUES
bool	1	true or false
char	1	By default, the same as type signed char: -128 to 127; optionally, you can make char the same range as type unsigned char
signed char	1	-128 to 127
unsigned char	1	0 to 255
wchar_t	2	0 to 65,535
short	2	-32,768 to 32,767
unsigned short	2	0 to 65,535
int	4	-2,147,483,648 to 2,147,483,647
unsigned int	4	0 to 4,294,967,295
long	4	-2,147,483,648 to 2,147,483,647
unsigned long	4	0 to 4,294,967,295
long long	8	-9,223,372,036,854,775,808 to 9,223,372,036,854,775,807
unsigned long long	8	0 to 18,446,744,073,709,551,615
float	4	$\pm 3.4 \times 10^{\pm 38}$ with approximately 7-digit accuracy
double	8	$\pm 1.7 \times 10^{\pm 308}$ with approximately 15-digit accuracy
long double	8	$\pm 1.7 \times 10^{\pm 308}$ with approximately 15-digit accuracy

Literals

I have already used a lot of explicit constants to initialize variables. Constant values of any kind are referred to as *literals*. A literal is a value of a specific type, and values such as 23, 3.14159, 9.5f, and true are examples of literals of types int, double, float, and bool, respectively. "Samuel Beckett" is an example of a literal that is a string, but I'll defer discussion of exactly what type this is until Chapter 4. Here's a summary of how you write literals of the types you have met:

TYPE	EXAMPLES OF LITERALS
char, signed char, or unsigned char	'A', 'Z', '8', '*'
wchar_t	L'A', L'Z', L'8', L'*'
int	-77, 65, 12345, 0x9FE
unsigned int	10U, 64000u
long	-77L, 65L, 123451
unsigned long	5UL, 999999UL, 25ul, 35Ul
long long	-777LL, 66LL, 123456711
unsigned long long	55ULL, 999999999ULL, 885ull, 445Ull
float	3.14f, 34.506F
double	1.414, 2.71828
long double	1.414L, 2.718281
bool	true, false

You can't specify literals of type short or unsigned short, but the compiler will accept initial values of type int for variables of these types, provided the value is within the range of the type.

You will often need to use literals in calculations, for example, conversion values such as 12 for feet to inches or 25.4 for inches to millimeters. However, you should avoid using numeric literals explicitly where their significance is not obvious. It is not necessarily apparent to everyone that 2.54 is the number of centimeters in an inch. It is better to declare a variable with a fixed value — you might name a variable with the value 2.54 as inchesToCentimeters, for example. Then wherever you use inchesToCentimeters in your code, it will be quite obvious what it is. You will see how to fix the value of a variable a little later in this chapter.

Defining Type Aliases

The typedef keyword enables you to define your own name for an existing type. For example, you could define the name BigOnes as equivalent to the standard long int type with this declaration:

```
typedef long int BigOnes;      // Defining BigOnes as a type name
```

This defines BigOnes as an alias for long int, so you could declare a variable mynum as type long int with the declaration:

```
BigOnes mynum {};              // Define a long int variable
```

There's no difference between this and the declaration using the built-in type name. You could equally well use:

```
long int mynum {};             // Define a long int variable
```

When you define a type alias such as `BigOnes`, you can use both type specifiers within the same program for variables and the variables will have the same type.

The C++ 11 standard introduced an alternative syntax for defining a type alias that uses the `using` keyword. You could write the definition of the `BigOnes` alias as:

```
using BigOnes = long int;
```

You write the type alias on the left of the = and the original type on the right. The effect of this statement is identical to using `typedef`. I use this form in subsequent examples but `typedef` is just as good.

A type alias is only a synonym for an existing type so it may appear to be a bit superficial, but it isn't. You'll see later that it fulfills a very useful role in simplifying complex declarations by defining a simple name for a more convoluted type specification. This can make your code more readable.

BASIC INPUT/OUTPUT OPERATIONS

Here, you will only look at enough of input and output to get you through learning about C++. It's not that it's difficult — quite the opposite, in fact — but for Windows programming, you won't need it at all. C++ input/output incorporates the notion of a *data stream*. You can insert data into an output stream or extract data from an input stream. You have already seen that the standard output stream to the command line is referred to as `cout`. The complementary input stream from the keyboard is `cin`. Of course, both names are defined in the `std` namespace.

Input from the Keyboard

You obtain input from the keyboard through the standard input stream, `cin`, using the extraction operator for a stream, `>>`. To read integer values from the keyboard into integer variables `num1` and `num2`, you can write this statement:

```
std::cin >> num1 >> num2;
```

The *extraction operator*, `>>`, "points" in the direction that data flows — in this case, from `cin` to each of the two variables in turn. The types of the variables storing the input determines the type of data that is expected. Any leading whitespace in the input is skipped, and the first integer value you enter is read into `num1`. This is because the input statement executes from left to right. Any whitespace following `num1` is ignored, and the second integer value you enter is stored in `num2`. There has to be whitespace between successive values so that they can be differentiated. The stream input operation ends when you press the Enter key, and execution then continues with the next statement. Of course, errors can arise if you key in the wrong data, but I will assume that you always get it right!

Floating-point values are read in exactly the same way as integers, and of course, you can mix the two. The stream input and operations automatically deal with variables and data of any of the fundamental types. For example:

```
int num1 {}, num2 {};
double factor {};
std::cin >> num1 >> factor >> num2;
```

The last line reads an integer into num1, then a floating-point value into factor, and finally, an integer into num2.

Output to the Command Line

You have already seen output to the command line, but I'll revisit it anyway. Output operates in a complementary fashion to input. The standard output stream is std::cout, and you use the insertion operator, <<, to transfer data to it. This operator also "points" in the direction of data movement. You have already used this operator to output a text string. I can demonstrate outputting the value of a variable with a simple program.

TRY IT OUT   Output to the Command Line

I'll assume that you've got the hang of creating a new empty project by adding a new source file to the project and building it into an executable. Here's the code that you need to put in the source file once you have created the Ex2_02 project:

```
// Ex2_02.cpp
// Exercising output
#include <iostream>

using std::cout;
using std::endl;

int main()
{
    int num1 {1234}, num2 {5678};
    cout << endl;                       // Start on a new line
    cout << num1 << num2;               // Output two values
    cout << endl;                       // End on a new line
    return 0;                           // Exit program
}
```

How It Works

You have using declarations for std::cout and std::endl so you can use the unqualified names in the code. The first statement in main() declares and initializes two integer variables, num1 and num2. This is followed by three output statements, the first of which moves the screen cursor position to a new line. Because output statements execute from left to right, the second output statement displays the value of num1 followed by the value of num2.

When you compile and execute this, you will get the output:

```
12345678
```

The output is correct, but it's not exactly helpful. You really need the two output values to be separated by at least one space. The default for stream output is to just output the value, which doesn't provide for spacing successive values so they can be differentiated. As it is, you have no way to tell where the first number ends and the second number begins.

Formatting the Output

You can fix the problem quite easily by outputting a space between the two values. You can do this by replacing the following line in your original program:

```
cout << num1 << num2;                      // Output two values
```

Just substitute the statement:

```
cout << num1 << ' ' << num2;               // Output two values
```

If you had several rows of output that you wanted to align in columns, you would need some extra capability because you do not know how many digits there will be in each value. You can take care of this by using a *manipulator*, which modifies the way in which output to (or input from) a stream is handled.

Manipulators are defined in the header file iomanip, so you need an #include directive for it. The manipulator that you'll use is std::setw(n), which sets the output field width as n characters for the next output value, and the output will be right-justified. Thus std::setw(6) causes the next output value to be presented in a field with a width of six spaces. Let's see it working.

TRY IT OUT   Using Manipulators

To get something more like the output you want, you can change the program to the following:

```
// Ex2_03.cpp
// Exercising output
#include <iostream>
#include <iomanip>

using std::cout;
using std::endl;
using std::setw;

int main()
{
   int num1 {1234}, num2 {5678};
   cout << endl;                            // Start on a new line
   cout << setw(6) << num1 << setw(6) << num2;  // Output two values
   cout << endl;                            // Start on a new line
   return 0;                                // Exit program
}
```

How It Works

The changes from Ex2_02.cpp are the addition of the #include directive for the iomanip header, the addition of a using declaration for the setw name in the std namespace, and the insertion of the setw() manipulator in the output stream preceding each value. Now you get nice, neat output:

```
  1234  5678
```

Note that the `setw()` manipulator applies only for the next single output value after its insertion into the stream. Subsequent values will be output in the default manner. You must insert the manipulator into the stream immediately preceding each value that you want to output within a given field width.

Another useful manipulator in the `iomanip` header is `std::setiosflags`. One thing it does is to enable you to have the output left-aligned in a given field width instead of right-aligned by default. Here's how you can do that:

```
cout << std::setiosflags(std::ios::left);
```

`std::ios::left` is the flag that is set by the manipulator, which causes output to be left-aligned in a field. You can use `std::setiosflags` to control the appearance of numerical output in other ways by setting other flags, so it is worth exploring.

Escape Sequences

When you specify a single character or a character string between double quotes, you specify some characters by special character sequences called *escape sequences*. They are called escape sequences because they allow characters to be specified that otherwise could not be represented, and they do this by escaping from the default interpretation of the characters. An obvious example of a character you can't include in a string between double quotes or specify as a single character literal is a new-line. Pressing Enter for a newline just moves the cursor to the next line — the character itself won't be entered in the code.

An escape sequence starts with a backslash character, \, and the backslash cues the compiler to interpret the character that follows in a special way. For example, a tab character is written as \t, so the t is understood by the compiler to represent a tab, and not the letter t. Look at these two statements:

```
cout << endl << "This is output.";
cout << endl << "\tThis is output after a tab.";
```

They will produce these output lines:

```
This is output.
    This is output after a tab.
```

The \t in the second statement causes the output to be indented to the first tab position. Instead of using `endl`, you could use the escape sequence for the newline character, \n, in each string, so you could rewrite the statements as:

```
cout << "\nThis is output.";
cout << "\n\tThis is output after a tab.";
```

The output is the same, but note that \n is not quite the same as `endl`. `endl` will output a newline and flush the stream, while \n will output the newline without flushing the stream. Flushing an output stream causes all data in the stream buffer in memory to be written to the device.

Here are some escape sequences that may be particularly useful:

ESCAPE SEQUENCE	WHAT IT DOES	ESCAPE SEQUENCE	WHAT IT DOES
\a	Sounds a beep	\b	Backspace
\n	Newline	\t	Tab
\'	Single quote	\"	Double quote
\\	Backslash	\?	Question mark

Obviously, if you want to be able to include a backslash or a double quote as a character in a string, you must use the appropriate escape sequences to represent them. Otherwise, the backslash would be interpreted as the start of another escape sequence, and the double quote would indicate the end of the character string. Similarly, to define a single quote character literal you must use '\''.

Of course, you can use escape sequences in the initialization of variables of type char. For example:

```
char Tab {'\t'};                    // Initialize with tab character
```

> **NOTE** You can put a question mark in a string or a character literal. The \? escape sequence is there to avoid conflicts with trigraphs, which are a C language construct consisting of three characters that begin with ??. Trigraphs are for defining characters in environments that have a limited character set where the characters otherwise could not be specified. Trigraphs are rarely used today, but they are still part of the language standard.

TRY IT OUT Using Escape Sequences

Here's a program that uses some of the escape sequences from the table in the previous section:

```cpp
// Ex2_04.cpp
// Using escape sequences
#include <iostream>

using std::cout;

int main()
{
   char newline {'\n'};                    // Newline escape sequence
   cout << newline;                        // Start on a new line
   cout << "\"We\'ll make our escapes in sequence\", he said.";
   cout << "\n\tThe program\'s over, it\'s time to make a beep beep.\a\a";
   cout << newline;                        // Start on a new line
   return 0;                               // Exit program
}
```

If you compile and execute this example, it will produce the following output:

```
"We'll make our escapes in sequence", he said.
        The program's over, it's time to make a beep beep.
```

How It Works

The first line in `main()` defines `newline` as type `char` and initializes it with the escape sequence for a newline. You can then use `newline` instead of `endl` from the standard library.

After writing `newline` to `cout`, you output a string that uses the escape sequences for a double quote (`\"`) and a single quote (`\'`). You don't have to use the escape sequence for a single quote here because the string is delimited by double quotes, and the compiler will recognize a single quote character as just that, and not a delimiter. You must use the escape sequence for the double quote in a string though. The second string starts with a newline then a tab, so the output is indented by the tab distance. The string ends with two instances of the escape sequence for a beep, so you should hear a beep from the PC.

CALCULATING IN C++

This is where you start doing something with the data that you enter. You know how to carry out simple input and output; now, you'll be coding the bit in the middle, the "processing" part of a program. Almost all of the computational aspects of C++ are intuitive, so you should slice through this like a hot knife through butter.

The Assignment Statement

You have already seen examples of the assignment statement. A typical assignment statement looks like this:

```
whole = part1 + part2 + part3;
```

The assignment statement calculates the value of the expression that appears on the right of the assignment operator, = — in this case the sum of `part1`, `part2`, and `part3` — and stores the result in the variable specified on the left, the variable with the name `whole`. In this statement, the `whole` is exactly the sum of its parts, and no more.

You can also write repeated assignments, such as:

```
a = b = 2;
```

This is equivalent to assigning the value 2 to `b` and then assigning the value of `b` to `a`, so both variables end up with the value 2.

Arithmetic Operations

The basic arithmetic operators are addition, subtraction, multiplication, and division, represented by the operators `+`, `-`, `*`, and `/`, respectively. Generally, these work as you would expect, with the exception of division, which has a slight aberration when applied to integers, as you'll see. Look at this:

```
netPay = hours * rate - deductions;
```

Here, the product of `hours` and `rate` will be calculated and then `deductions` subtracted from the value produced. Multiply and divide operations are executed before addition and subtraction, as you would expect. I discuss the order of execution of operators in expressions later in this chapter. The overall result of evaluating the expression `hours * rate - deductions` will be stored in the variable `netPay`.

The minus sign used in the last statement has two operands — it subtracts the value of its right operand from the value of its left operand. This is called a *binary operation* because two values are involved. The minus sign can also be used with one operand to change the sign of a value to which it is applied, in which case it is called a *unary minus*. You could write this:

```
int a {};
int b {-5};
a = -b;                       // Changes the sign of the operand so a is 5
```

Here, `a` will be assigned the value +5 because the unary minus in the expression on the right changes the sign of the value of the operand `b`.

An assignment is not the equivalent of the equations you saw in high-school algebra. It specifies an action to be carried out rather than a statement of fact. The expression to the right of the assignment operator is evaluated and the result is stored in the location specified on the left.

Look at this statement:

```
number = number + 1;
```

This means "add 1 to the current value stored in `number` and then store the result back in `number`." As a normal algebraic statement, it wouldn't make sense, but as a programming action, it obviously does.

> **NOTE** Typically, the expression on the left of an assignment is a single variable name but it doesn't have to be. It can be an expression of some kind but if it is an expression then the result of evaluating it must be an lvalue. An lvalue, as you will see later, is a persistent location in memory where the result of the expression to the right of the assignment operator can be stored.

TRY IT OUT   Exercising Basic Arithmetic

You can exercise basic arithmetic by calculating how many standard rolls of wallpaper are needed to paper a room. The following example does this:

```
// Ex2_05.cpp
// Calculating how many rolls of wallpaper are required for a room
#include <iostream>

using std::cout;
using std::cin;
using std::endl;

int main()
{
    double height {}, width {}, length {};       // Room dimensions
    double perimeter {};                         // Room perimeter
```

```
    const double rollWidth {21.0};            // Standard roll width
    const double rollLength {12.0*33.0};      // Standard roll length(33ft.)

    int strips_per_roll {};                   // Number of strips in a roll
    int strips_reqd {};                       // Number of strips needed
    int nrolls {};                            // Total number of rolls

    cout << endl                              // Start a new line
        << "Enter the height of the room in inches: ";
    cin >> height;

    cout  << endl                             // Start a new line
        << "Now enter the length and width in inches: ";
    cin >> length >> width;

    strips_per_roll = rollLength / height;    // Get number of strips per roll
    perimeter = 2.0*(length + width);         // Calculate room perimeter
    strips_reqd = perimeter / rollWidth;      // Get total strips required
    nrolls = strips_reqd / strips_per_roll;   // Calculate number of rolls

    cout << endl
        << "For your room you need " << nrolls << " rolls of wallpaper."
        << endl;

    return 0;
}
```

Unless you are more adept than I am at typing, chances are there will be a few errors when you compile this for the first time. Once you have fixed the typos, it will compile and run just fine. You'll get a couple of warning messages from the compiler. Don't worry about them — the compiler is just making sure you understand what's going on. I'll explain the reason for the warnings.

How It Works

One thing needs to be clear at the outset — I assume no responsibility if you run out of wallpaper as a result of using this program! As you'll see, all errors in the estimate of the number of rolls required are due to the way C++ works and to the wastage that inevitably occurs when you hang your own wallpaper — usually 50 percent plus!

I'll work through the statements in sequence, picking out the interesting, novel, or even exciting features. The statements down to the start of the body of main() are familiar territory by now, so I will take those for granted.

A couple of general points about the layout of the code are worth noting. First, the statements in main() are indented to make the extent of the body easier to see, and second, sets of statements are separated by a blank line to indicate that they are functional groups. Indenting statements is a fundamental technique in laying out C++ code. You will see that this is applied universally to provide visual cues to the logical blocks in a program.

The const Modifier

You have a block of declarations for the variables used in the program at the beginning of `main()`. These are familiar, but two contain new features:

```
const double rollWidth {21.0};           // Standard roll width
const double rollLength {12.0*33.0};      // Standard roll length(33ft.)
```

They both start out with a new keyword: `const`. This is a *type modifier* that indicates that the variables are not just of type `double`, but are also constants. Because you tell the compiler that these are constants, the compiler will check for any statements that attempt to change the values of these variables, and if it finds any, it will generate an error message. You could check this out by adding this statement anywhere after the declaration of `rollWidth`:

```
rollWidth = 0;
```

Now the program no longer compiles, and you'll see the message:

```
'error C3892: 'rollWidth' : you cannot assign to a variable that is const'.
```

It is very useful to define constants as `const` variables, particularly when you use the same constant several times in a program. For one thing, it is much better than sprinkling literals throughout your program that may not have blindingly obvious meanings; the value 42 could be referring to the meaning of life, the universe, and everything, but if you use a `const` variable with the name `myAge` that has a value of 42, it becomes obvious that you are not. For another thing, if you change the initial value of a `const` variable, the change will take effect everywhere in a source file. If you use explicit literals, you have to change all occurrences individually.

Constant Expressions

The `const` variable `rollLength` is initialized with an arithmetic expression (`12.0*33.0`). Being able to use constant expressions to initialize variables saves having to work out the value yourself. It can also be more meaningful, as in this case, because 33 feet times 12 inches is a much clearer expression of what the value represents than simply writing 396. The compiler will evaluate constant expressions accurately, whereas if you do it, depending on the complexity of the expression and your ability to number-crunch, there is a finite probability that it may be wrong.

You can use any expression that can be evaluated as a constant at compile time, including `const` variables that you have already defined. So, for instance, if it were useful in the program to do so, you could declare the area of a standard roll of wallpaper as:

```
const double rollArea {rollWidth*rollLength};
```

This statement would need to be placed after the declarations for the two `const` variables used in the initialization of `rollArea`, because all the variables that appear in a constant expression must be known to the compiler at the point where the constant expression appears.

Program Input

After declaring some integer variables, the next four statements in the program handle input from the keyboard:

```
cout << endl                                    // Start a new line
     << "Enter the height of the room in inches: ";
cin >> height;

cout << endl                                    // Start a new line
     << "Now enter the length and width in inches: ";
cin >> length >> width;
```

You write text to `cout` to prompt for the input required, and then read the input from the keyboard using `cin`, the standard input stream. You first obtain the value for `height` and then read `length` and `width`, successively. In a practical program, you would need to check for errors and possibly make sure that the input values are sensible, but you don't have enough knowledge to do that yet!

Calculating the Result

You have four statements involved in calculating the number of standard rolls of wallpaper required for the size of the room:

```
strips_per_roll = rollLength / height;    // Get number of strips in a roll
perimeter = 2.0*(length + width);         // Calculate room perimeter
strips_reqd = perimeter / rollWidth;      // Get total strips required
nrolls = strips_reqd / strips_per_roll;   // Calculate number of rolls
```

The first statement calculates the number of strips of paper with a length corresponding to the height of the room that you can get from a standard roll, by dividing one into the other. So, if the room is 8 feet high, you divide 96 into 396, which would produce the floating-point result 4.125. There is a subtlety here. The variable where you store the result, `strips_per_roll`, is type `int`, so it can store only integers. Any floating-point value that is to be stored as an integer is rounded down to the nearest integer, 4 in this case, and this value is stored. This is actually the result you want here because, although they may fit under a window or over a door, fractions of a strip are best ignored when estimating.

The conversion of a value from one type to another is called *type conversion*. This particular example is an *implicit type conversion*, because the code doesn't explicitly state that a conversion is needed, and the compiler has to supply it. The two warnings you got during compilation were because information could be lost as a result of the implicit conversions that were inserted to change values from one type to another.

You should beware when your code necessitates implicit conversions. Compilers do not always supply a warning that an implicit conversion is being made, and if you are assigning a value of one type to a variable of a type with a lesser range of values, there is a danger that you will lose information. If there are implicit conversions in your program that you have included accidentally, they may represent bugs that may be difficult to locate.

Where a conversion that may result in the loss of information is unavoidable, you should specify the conversion explicitly to demonstrate that it is no accident. You do this by making an *explicit type conversion* or *cast* of the value on the right of the assignment to `int`, so the statement would become:

```
strips_per_roll = static_cast<int>(rollLength / height);    // Get number
                                                            // of strips in
                                                            // a roll
```

The addition of `static_cast<int>` with the parentheses around the expression on the right tells the compiler that you want to convert the value of the expression between the parentheses to the type between the angled brackets, `int`. Although you still lose the fractional part of the value, the compiler assumes that you know what you are doing and will not issue a warning. You'll see more about `static_cast<>()` and other type conversions later in this chapter.

Note how you calculate the perimeter of the room in the next statement. To multiply the sum of the `length` and the `width` by 2.0, you enclose the expression summing the two variables between parentheses. The parentheses ensure that the addition is performed first and the result is multiplied by 2.0 to produce the value for the perimeter. You can use parentheses to make sure that a calculation is carried out in the order you require because expressions in parentheses are always evaluated first. Where there are nested parentheses, the expressions within the parentheses are evaluated in sequence, from the innermost to the outermost.

The third statement that calculates how many strips of paper are required to cover the room uses the same effect that you saw in the first statement: the result is rounded down to the nearest integer because it is stored in the integer variable, `strips_reqd`. This is not what you need in practice. It would be best to round up for estimating, but you don't have enough knowledge to do this yet. Once you have read the next chapter, you can come back and fix it!

The last arithmetic statement calculates the number of rolls needed by dividing the number of strips required (an integer) by the number of strips in a roll (also an integer). Because you are dividing one integer by another, the result has to be an integer, and any remainder is ignored. This would still be the case if the `nrolls` was floating-point; the integer value resulting from the expression would be converted to floating-point form before it was stored in `nrolls`. The result that you obtain is essentially the same as if you had produced a floating-point result and rounded down to the nearest integer. Again, this is not what you want, so if you want to use this, you will need to fix it.

Displaying the Result

The following statement displays the result of the calculation:

```
cout << endl
     << "For your room you need " << nrolls << " rolls of wallpaper."
     << endl;
```

This is a single output statement spread over three lines. It first outputs a newline character and then the text string `"For your room you need"`. This is followed by the value of the variable `nrolls` and, finally, the text string `" rolls of wallpaper."`. As you see, output statements are very easy. You could have written the statement using escape characters for the newlines:

```
cout << "\nFor your room you need " << nrolls << " rolls of wallpaper.\n";
```

Finally, the program ends when this statement is executed:

```
return 0;
```

The value zero here is a return value that will be returned to the operating system. You will learn more about return values in Chapter 5.

Calculating a Remainder

You saw that dividing one integer value by another produces an integer result that ignores any remainder, so 11 divided by 4 gives the result 2. Because the remainder after division can be of great interest, particularly when you are dividing cookies amongst children for example, C++ provides a special operator, %, for this. The following statements handle the cookie-sharing problem:

```
int residue {}, cookies {19}, children {5};
residue = cookies % children;
```

`residue` will end up with the value 4, which is the number left after dividing 19 by 5. To calculate how many cookies each child receives, you just use division, as in the statement:

```
each = cookies / children;
```

Modifying a Variable

It's often necessary to modify the current value of a variable by incrementing it or doubling it. You could increment count using the statement:

```
count = count + 5;
```

This adds 5 to the current value of count and stores the result back in count, so if count started out as 10, it would end up as 15.

You have an alternative, shorthand way of writing the same thing:

```
count += 5;
```

This says, "Take the value in count, add 5 to it, and store the result back in count." You can use other operators with this notation:

```
count *= 5;
```

This multiplies the current value of count by 5 and stores the result back in count. In general, you can write statements of the form:

```
lhs op=  rhs;
```

lhs stands for any legal expression for the left-hand side of the statement and is usually (but not necessarily) a variable name.

rhs stands for any legal expression on the right-hand side of the statement.

op is any of the following operators:

+	-	
*	/	%
<<	>>	
&	^	|

You have already met the first five of these operators, and you'll see the others, which are the shift and logical operators, later in this chapter.

The general form of the statement is equivalent to this:

```
lhs = lhs op (rhs);
```

The parentheses around `rhs` imply that this expression is always evaluated first, and the result becomes the right operand for `op`.

This means that you can write statements such as:

```
a /= b + c;
```

This will be identical in effect to this statement:

```
a = a/(b + c);
```

The value of `a` is divided by the sum of `b` and `c`, and the result is stored back in `a`, overwriting the original value.

The Increment and Decrement Operators

I'll now introduce some unusual arithmetic operators called the *increment* and *decrement operators*. You will find them to be quite an asset once you get further into applying C++. These are unary operators that you use to increment or decrement a value stored in a variable by 1. For example, assuming `count` is of type `int`, the following three statements all have exactly the same effect:

```
count = count + 1;      count += 1;       ++count;
```

They each increment `count` by 1. The last statement uses the increment operator and is clearly the most concise.

The increment operator not only changes the value of the variable to which you apply it, but also results in a value. Thus, using the increment operator to increase the value of a variable by 1 can also appear as part of a more complex expression. The expression `++count` increments the value of the variable and the value that results is the value of the expression. For example, suppose `count` has the value 5, and you have defined `total` as type `int`. Suppose you write the following statement:

```
total = ++count + 10;
```

This increments `count` to 6. The expression `++count` has the resultant value of `count`, 6, which is added to 10 so `total` is assigned the value 16.

So far you have written the increment operator, `++`, in front of the variable to which it applies. This is called the *prefix* form of the operator. The operator also has a *postfix* form, where you write the operator *after* the variable to which it applies and the effect is slightly different. The variable is incremented only *after* its value has been used in context. For example:

```
total = count++ + 10;
```

If `count` has the value 5, `total` is assigned the value 15, because the initial value of `count` is used to evaluate the expression before the increment is applied. The preceding statement is equivalent to the two statements:

```
total = count + 10;
++count;
```

The clustering of + signs in the preceding example of the postfix form is likely to lead to confusion. Generally, it isn't a good idea to write the increment operator in the way that I have written it here. It would be clearer to write:

```
total = 6 + count++;
```

Alternatively you could put parentheses around count++. Where you have an expression such as a++ + b, or even a+++b, it becomes less obvious what is meant or what the compiler will do. They are actually the same, but in the second case, you might really have meant a + ++b, which is different. It evaluates to one more than the other two expressions.

The rules I have discussed in relation to the increment operator also apply to the decrement operator, --. For example, if count has the initial value 5, then the statement,

```
total = --count + 10;
```

results in total having the value 14 assigned, whereas,

```
total = 10 + count--;
```

sets the value of total to 15. Both operators are usually applied to integers, particularly in the context of loops, as you will see in Chapter 3, but you can also use them with floating-point variables. You will see in later chapters that they can also be applied to other data types, notably variables that store addresses.

TRY IT OUT   The Comma Operator

The comma operator allows you to specify several expressions where normally only one might occur. This is best understood by looking at an example that demonstrates how it works:

```
// Ex2_06.cpp
// Exercising the comma operator
#include <iostream>

using std::cout;
using std::endl;

int main()
{
    long num1 {}, num2 {}, num3 {}, num4 {};

    num4 = (num1 = 10L, num2 = 20L, num3 = 30L);
    cout << endl
            << "The value of a series of expressions "
            << "is the value of the rightmost: "
            << num4;
    cout << endl;

    return 0;
}
```

How It Works

If you compile and run this program you will get this output:

```
The value of a series of expressions is the value of the rightmost: 30
```

This is fairly self-explanatory. The first statement in `main()` creates four variables, `num1` through `num4`, and initializes them to zero. The variable `num4` receives the value of the last of the series of three assignments, the value of an assignment operation being the value assigned to the left-hand side. The parentheses in the assignment for `num4` are essential. You could try executing this without them to see the effect. Without the parentheses, the first expression in the series of expressions separated by commas in the series will become:

```
num4 = num1 = 10L
```

So, `num4` will have the value `10L`.

Of course, expressions separated by the comma operator don't have to be assignments. You could equally well write the following:

```
long num1 {1L}, num2 {10L}, num3 {100L}, num4 {};
num4 = (++num1, ++num2, ++num3);
```

The effect of the assignment statement will be to increment the variables `num1`, `num2`, and `num3` by 1, and to set `num4` to the value of the last expression, which will be 101L. This example is aimed at illustrating the effect of the comma operator and is not an example of how to write good code.

The Sequence of Calculation

So far, I haven't talked about how you arrive at the sequence of calculations involved in evaluating an expression. It corresponds to what you have learned at school when dealing with basic arithmetic operators, but there are many other operators in C++. To understand what happens with these, you need to look at the mechanism used in C++ to determine this sequence. It's referred to as *operator precedence*.

Operator Precedence

Operator precedence orders the operators in a priority sequence. In any expression, operators with the highest precedence are executed first, followed by operators with the next highest precedence, and so on, down to those with the lowest precedence. The precedence of the operators is as follows:

PRECEDENCE	OPERATORS	ASSOCIATIVITY
1	`::`	None

2	`()` `[]` `->` `.`
	postfix `++` postfix `--`
	`typeid`
	`const_cast` `dynamic_cast` `static_cast` `reinterpret_cast`
		Left

continues

(continued)

PRECEDENCE	OPERATORS	ASSOCIATIVITY

3	logical not `!` one's complement `~`
	unary `+` unary `-`
	prefix `++` prefix `--`
	address-of `&` indirection `*`
	type cast `(type)`
	`sizeof` `decltype`
	`new` `new[]` `delete` `delete[]`
		Right

4	`.*` `->*`	Left
5	`*` `/` `%`	Left
6	`+` `-`	Left
7	`<<` `>>`	Left
8	`==` `!=`	Left
9	`&`	Left
10	`^`	Left
11	`|`	Left
12	`&&`	Left
13	`||`	Left
14	`?:` (conditional operator)	Right
15	`=` `*=` `/=` `%=` `+=` `-=` `&=` `^=` `|=` `<<=` `>>=`	Right
16	`throw`	Right
17	`,`	Left

There are also `const_cast`, `static_cast`, `dynamic_cast`, `reinterpret_cast`, and `typeid` that are not included in the table because they are never ambiguous. There are a lot of operators here that you haven't seen yet, but you will know them all by the end of the book. I have introduced all the operators here so that you can refer to the table if you are uncertain about the precedence of one operator relative to another.

Operators with the highest precedence appear at the top of the table. All the operators in the same row have equal precedence. If there are no parentheses in an expression, operators with equal precedence are executed in a sequence determined by their *associativity*. If the associativity is "left," the left-most operator in an expression executes first, progressing through the expression to the right-most. This means that an expression such as `a+b+c+d` is executed as though it was written `(((a+b)+c)+d)` because binary `+` is left-associative.

Note that where an operator has a unary (working with one operand) and a binary (working with two operands) form, the unary form is always of higher precedence and is therefore executed first.

> **NOTE** You can always override the precedence of operators by using parentheses. Because there are so many operators, it's sometimes hard to be sure what takes precedence over what. It's a good idea to insert parentheses to make sure. A further plus is that parentheses often make the code much easier to read.

TYPE CONVERSION AND CASTING

Calculations can be carried out only between values of the same type. When you write an expression involving variables or constants of different types, for each binary operation, the compiler has to arrange to convert the type of one operand to match that of the other. This process is called *implicit type conversion*. For example, if you add a `double` value to a value of an integer type, the integer value is converted to `double` before the addition is carried out. Of course, the variable that contains the value to be converted is, itself, not changed. The compiler stores the converted value in a temporary location and discards it when the calculation is finished.

There are rules that govern the selection of the operand to be converted in any operation. Any expression breaks down into a series of operations between two operands. For example, the expression `2*3-4+5` amounts to the series `2*3` resulting in `6`, `6-4` resulting in `2`, and finally `2+5` resulting in `7`. Thus, the rules for converting the type of operands where necessary need to be defined only in terms of decisions about pairs of operands. For any pair of operands of different types, the compiler decides which operand to convert to the other considering types to be in the following rank from high to low:

1. `long double`	2. `double`	3. `float`
4. `unsigned long long`	5. `long long`	
6. `unsigned long`	7. `long`	
8. `unsigned int`	9. `int`	

Thus, in an operation where the operands are of type `long long` and type `unsigned int`, the latter will be converted to type `long long`. Any operand of type `char`, `signed char`, `unsigned char`, `short`, or `unsigned short` is at least converted to type `int` before an operation.

Implicit type conversions can produce unexpected results. For example, consider these statements:

```
unsigned int a {10u};
signed int b {20};
std::cout << a - b << std::endl;
```

You might expect this code to output -10, but it doesn't. It outputs 4294967286. This is because the value of b is converted to `unsigned int` to match the type of a, and the subtraction results in an unsigned integer value. This implies that when you write integer operations with operands of different types, you should not rely on implicit type conversion to produce the result you want unless you are quite certain it will do so.

Type Conversion in Assignments

You saw in example `Ex2_05.cpp` that an implicit type conversion is inserted when the expression on the right of an assignment results in a value of a different type from the variable on the left. This can cause information to be lost. For instance, if you assign an expression that results in a `float` or `double` value to a variable of type `int` or `long`, the fractional part of the `float` or `double` result will be lost and just the integer part will be stored. (You may lose even more information if the result exceeds the range for the integer type.)

For example, consider the following code:

```
int number {};
float decimal {2.5f};
number = decimal;
```

The value of `number` will be 2. The `f` at the end of `2.5f` indicates to the compiler that it is single-precision floating-point. Without the `f`, it would have been type `double`. Any constant containing a decimal point is floating-point. If you don't want it to be double-precision, you need to append the `f`. A capital `F` would do the job just as well.

Explicit Type Conversion

With mixed expressions involving the basic types, your compiler automatically arranges type conversions where necessary, but you can force a conversion from one type to another by using an *explicit type conversion*, which is also referred to as a *cast*. To cast the value of an expression to a given type, you write the cast in the form:

```
static_cast<the_type_to_convert_to>(expression)
```

The `static_cast` keyword reflects the fact that the cast is checked statically — that is, when your program is compiled. No checks are made to see if this cast is safe to apply when you execute the program. Later, when you get to deal with classes, you will meet `dynamic_cast`, where the conversion is checked dynamically — that is, when the program is executing. There are two other kinds of cast — `const_cast` for removing the const-ness of an expression, and `reinterpret_cast`, which is an unconditional cast — but I'll say no more about these here.

The effect of the `static_cast` operation is to convert the value that results from evaluating expression to the type between the angled brackets. `expression` can be anything from a single variable to a complex expression involving lots of nested parentheses.

Here's an example of the use of `static_cast<>()`:

```
double value1 {10.5};
double value2 {15.5};
int whole_number {};
whole_number = static_cast<int>(value1) + static_cast<int>(value2);
```

The value assigned to `whole_number` is the sum of the integral parts of `value1` and `value2`, so they are each explicitly cast to type `int`. `whole_number` will therefore have the value 25. The casts do *not* affect the values stored in value1 and value2, which will remain as 10.5 and 15.5, respectively. The values produced by the casts are stored temporarily for use in the calculation and then discarded. Although both casts cause a loss of information, the compiler assumes that you know what you are doing with an explicit cast.

You can apply an explicit cast to any numeric type, but you should be conscious of the possibility of losing information. If you cast a value of type float or double to an integer type, you will lose the fractional part of the value, so if the value started out as less than 1.0, the result will be 0. If you cast a value of type double to type float, you will lose accuracy because a float variable has only 7-digit precision, whereas double variables maintain 15. Even casting between integer types provides the potential for losing data, depending on the values involved. For example, the value of an integer of type long long can exceed the maximum that you can store in a variable of type int, so casting from a long long value to type int may lose information.

In general, you should avoid casting as far as possible. If you find that you need a lot of explicit casts in your program, you should look at the structure of the program and the ways in which you have chosen data types to see whether you can eliminate, or at least reduce, the number of casts.

Old-style Casts

Prior to the introduction of static_cast<>() (and the other casts: const_cast<>(), dynamic_cast<>(), and reinterpret_cast<>(), which I'll discuss later in the book) into C++, an explicit cast was written as:

```
(the_type_to_convert_to)expression
```

The result of expression is cast to the type between parentheses. For example, the statement to calculate strips_per_roll could be written:

```
strips_per_roll = (int)(rollLength / height);    //Get number of strips in a roll
```

There are four different kinds of casts and the old-style casting syntax covers them all. Because of this, code using the old-style casts is more error-prone — it is not always clear what you intended, and you may not get the result you expected. Although you will still see the old style of casting used extensively (it's still part of the language and you will see it in MFC code for historical reasons), I strongly recommend that you stick to using only the new casts.

THE auto KEYWORD

You can use the auto keyword as the type of a variable in a definition statement and have its type deduced from the initial value you supply. Here are some examples:

```
auto n = 16;                // Type is int
auto pi = 3.14159;          // Type is double
auto x = 3.5f;              // Type is float
auto found = false;         // Type is bool
```

In each of these cases, the type assigned to the variable you are defining is the same as that of the literal used as the initializer. Of course, when you use the auto keyword in this way, you must supply an initial value for the variable.

Note that you should *not* use the initializer list form with `auto` because an initializer list has a type. The compiler will not deduce the type from the items in the list, but from the list itself. Suppose you write:

```
auto n {16};
```

The type assigned to n will not be `int`, but will be `std::initializer_list<int>`, which is the type of this particular initializer list. You learn more about the `std::initializer_list<>` type later in the book.

You can use the functional form of initialization with `auto`:

```
auto n(16);
```

The variable n will be type `int`. Variables defined using the `auto` keyword can be specified as constants:

```
const auto e = 2.71828L;          // Type is const long double
```

Of course, you can also use functional notation:

```
const auto dozen(12);             // Type is const int
```

The initial value can also be an expression:

```
auto factor(n*pi*pi);             // Type is double
```

In this case, the definitions for n and pi must precede this statement.

When you use `auto`, you are telling the compiler to figure out the type of the variable. The `auto` keyword may seem at this point to be a somewhat trivial feature of C++, but you'll see later in the book, especially in Chapter 10, that it can save a lot of effort in determining complicated variable types and make your code more elegant. I recommend that you limit the use of `auto` to situations where it has advantages; don't use it for defining variables of fundamental types.

DISCOVERING TYPES

The `typeid` operator enables you to discover the type of an expression. To obtain the type of an expression, you simply write `typeid(expression)`. This results in an object of type `type_info` that encapsulates the type of the expression. Let's look at an example.

Suppose variables x and y are of type `int` and type `double`, respectively. The expression `typeid(x*y)` results in a `type_info` object representing the type of x*y, which by now you know to be `double`. Because the result of the `typeid` operator is an object, you can't write it to the standard output stream just as it is. However, you can output the type of the expression x*y like this:

```
cout << "The type of x*y is " << typeid(x*y).name() << endl;
```

This will result in the output:

```
The type of x*y is double
```

You will understand better how this works when you have learned more about classes and functions in Chapter 7. You won't need to use the `typeid` operator very often but when you do, it is invaluable.

THE BITWISE OPERATORS

Bitwise operators treat their operands as a series of bits rather than as a numerical value. They work only with integer variables or constants so only types short, int, long, long long, signed char, and char and the unsigned variants of these can be used. The bitwise operators are useful in programming hardware devices, where the status of a device is often represented as a series of individual flags (that is, each bit of a byte signifies the status of some aspect of the device). They also help in situations where you want to pack a set of on-off flags into a single variable. You will see them in action when you look at input/ output in detail, where single bits are used to control options for how data is handled.

There are six bitwise operators:

& bitwise AND	| bitwise OR	^ bitwise exclusive OR
~ bitwise NOT	>> shift right	<< shift left

The following sections explain how each of these works.

The Bitwise AND

The bitwise AND, &, is a binary operator that combines corresponding bits in its operands such that if both corresponding bits are 1, the result is a 1-bit, and if either or both bits are 0, the result is a 0-bit.

The effect of a particular binary operator can be shown in a *truth table* that shows the results for various combinations of operands. The truth table for & is:

Bitwise AND	0	1
0	0	0
1	0	1

For each row and column combination, the result of the operation is the entry at the intersection of the row and column. You can see this in an example:

```
char letter1 {'A'}, letter2 {'Z'}, result {};
result = letter1 & letter2;
```

You need to look at the bit patterns to see what happens. The letters 'A' and 'Z' correspond to hexadecimal values 0x41 and 0x5A, respectively. The way in which the bitwise AND operates on these values is shown in Figure 2-7. You can confirm this by looking at how corresponding bits combine in the truth table. After the assignment, result will be 0x40 — the code for the '@' character.

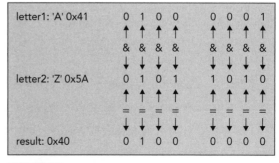

FIGURE 2-7

Because & produces zero if *either* bit is zero, you can use this operator to set specific bits in a variable to 0. You achieve this by creating what is called a *mask* and combining it with the original variable using &. The value of the mask will have a 1 where you want to keep a bit, and 0 where you want to set a bit to zero. The result of AND-ing the mask with a variable will be 0 bits where the mask bit is 0, and the original bit value where the mask bit is 1. Suppose letter is of type char and you want to zero the high-order 4 bits but keep the low-order 4 bits. This is easily done by combining 0x0F with letter like this,

```
letter = letter & 0x0F;
```

or, more concisely:

```
letter &= 0x0F;
```

If letter started out as 0x41, it would end up as 0x01 as a result of either of these statements. This operation is shown in Figure 2-8. 0-bits in the mask cause corresponding bits in letter to be set to 0; 1-bits in the mask cause corresponding bits in letter to be kept as they are.

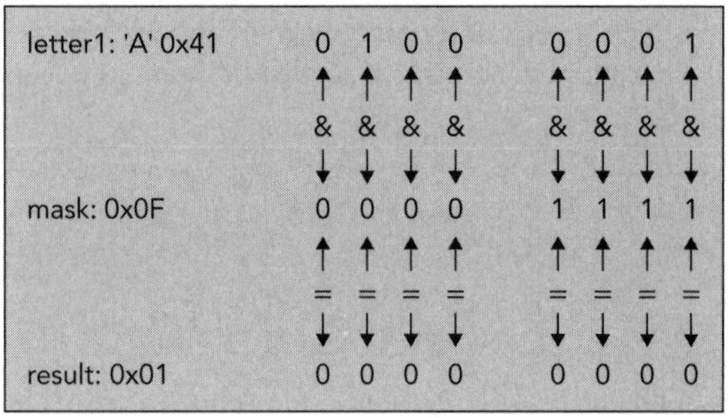

FIGURE 2-8

Similarly, you can use a mask of 0xF0 to keep the 4 high-order bits and zero the 4 low-order bits. This statement does it:

```
letter &= 0xF0;
```

The value of letter will be changed from 0x41 to 0x40.

The Bitwise OR

The bitwise OR, |, sometimes called the *inclusive OR*, combines corresponding bits such that the result is a 1 if either bit is 1, and 0 if both bits are 0. The truth table for the bitwise OR is:

Bitwise OR	0	1
0	0	1
1	1	1

You can exercise this with an example of how you could set individual flags packed into a variable of type int. Suppose style is of type short and contains 16 individual 1-bit flags. Suppose further that you want to set some of the flags to 1. You could define a mask to set the rightmost bit like this:

```
short vredraw {0x01};
```

To set the second-to-rightmost bit, you could define hredraw as:

```
short hredraw {0x02};
```

This statement will set the rightmost two bits in style to 1:

```
style = hredraw | vredraw;
```

This is illustrated in Figure 2-9. Of course, to set the third bit of style to 1, you would use 0x04.

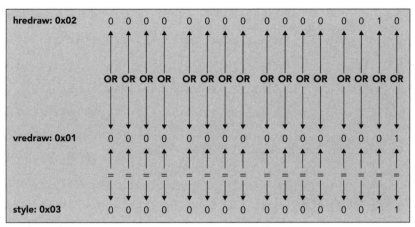

FIGURE 2-9

Setting particular bits in a word to 1 is a common requirement. You can do this quite easily with a statement such as:

```
style |= hredraw | vredraw;
```

This statement sets the two rightmost bits of `style` to 1 and leaves the other bits in their original state.

The Bitwise Exclusive OR

The *exclusive OR*, ^, is so-called because it operates similarly to the inclusive OR but produces 0 when both operand bits are 1. Its truth table is:

Bitwise XOR	0	1
0	0	1
1	1	0

Assuming the same variable values that I used with &, consider this:

```
result = letter1 ^ letter2;
```

This operation is XOR-ing these binary values:

```
letter1  0100 0001
letter2  0101 1010
```

This produces:

```
result  0001 1011
```

The variable `result` is set to 0x1B, or 27 in decimal notation.

The ^ operator has a rather surprising property. Suppose that you have char variables, `first` and `last`, with values `'A'` and `'Z'`. Look at these statements:

```
first ^= last;          // Result first is 0001 1011
last ^= first;          // Result last is 0100 0001
first ^= last;          // Result first is 0101 1010
```

The result of executing these is that `first` and `last` exchange values without using any intermediate memory location. This works with any integer values.

The Bitwise NOT

The bitwise NOT, ~, takes a single operand, for which it inverts the bits: 1 becomes 0, and 0 becomes 1. Here's an example:

```
result = ~letter1;
```

If `letter1` is 0100 0001, `result` will have the value 1011 1110, which is 0xBE, or 190 as a decimal value.

The Bitwise Shift Operators

These operators shift the value of an integer variable a specified number of bits left or right. The `>>` operator shifts to the right, while `<<` shifts to the left. Bits that "fall off" either end of a variable are lost. Figure 2-10 shows the effect of shifting a 2-byte variable left and right, with the initial value shown.

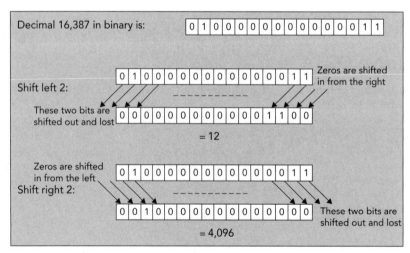

FIGURE 2-10

You declare and initialize `number` with the statement:

```
unsigned short number {16387U};
```

As you know, you write unsigned integer literals with `U` or `u` appended. You can shift the contents of `number` left with the statement:

```
number <<= 2;                // Shift left two bit positions
```

The left operand of the shift operator is the value to be shifted, and the right operand is the number of bit positions that the value is to be shifted. Figure 2-10 shows the effect. Shifting 16,387 two positions left produces 12. The rather drastic change is the result of losing the high-order 1-bit.

You can also shift a value right. Let's reset the value of number to its initial value of 16,387. Then you can write:

```
number >>= 2;              // Shift right two bit positions
```

This shifts 16,387 two bits right, storing 4,096. Shifting right 2 bits is effectively dividing the value by 4 (discarding the remainder). This is also shown in the illustration.

As long as bits are not lost, shifting n bits to the left is equivalent to multiplying the value by 2, n times. In other words, it is equivalent to multiplying by 2^n. Similarly, shifting right n bits is equivalent to dividing by 2^n. But beware: as you saw with the left shift of number, if significant bits are lost, the result is nothing like what you would expect. However, this is no different from the multiply operation. If you multiplied number by 4, you would get the same result, so shifting left and multiply are equivalent. The problem of accuracy arises because the result of the multiplication is outside the range of a 2-byte integer.

You might imagine that confusion could arise between the operators for input and output and the shift operators. As far as the compiler is concerned, the meaning will always be clear from the context. If it isn't, the compiler will generate an error message, but you need to be careful. For example, suppose you want to output the result of shifting number left by 2 bits:

```
cout << (number << 2);
```

The parentheses are essential here. Without them, the shift operator will be interpreted as a stream operator, so you won't get the result that you intended; the output would be the value of number followed by the value 2.

The right-shift operation is similar to the left-shift. For example, suppose number has the value 24, and you execute the statement:

```
number >>= 2;
```

This results in number having the value 6, effectively dividing the original value by 4. However, right shift operates in a special way with signed integer types that are negative, where the sign bit, which is the leftmost bit, is 1. In this case, the sign bit is propagated to the right. For example, declare and initialize a variable number of type char with the value -104 in decimal:

```
char number {-104};        // Binary representation is 1001 1000
```

Now you can shift it right 2 bits with the operation:

```
number >>= 2;              // Result 1110 0110
```

The value of the result is -26, because the sign bit is repeated. With this operation on unsigned integer types, there is no sign bit and zeros appear.

> **NOTE** You may be wondering how the shift operators, << and >>, can be the same as the operators used with the standard streams. cin and cout are stream objects, and because they are objects it is possible to redefine the meaning of operators in their context by a process called operator overloading. The >> operator has been redefined for input stream objects such as cin so you can use it in the way you have seen. The << operator has also been redefined for use with output stream objects such as cout. You'll learn about operator overloading in Chapter 8.

INTRODUCING LVALUES AND RVALUES

Every expression results in either an *lvalue* or an *rvalue* (sometimes written *l-value* and *r-value* and pronounced like that). An lvalue refers to an address in memory in which something can be stored on an ongoing basis. An rvalue, on the other hand, is the result of an expression that is stored transiently. An lvalue is so called because any expression that results in an lvalue can appear on the left of the equals sign in an assignment statement. If the result of an expression is not an lvalue, it is an rvalue.

Consider the following statements:

```
int a {}, b {1}, c {2};
a = b + c;
b = ++a;
c = a++;
```

The first statement declares a, b, and c to be of type int and initializes them to 0, 1, and 2, respectively. In the second statement, the expression b+c is evaluated and the result is stored in a. The result of evaluating b+c is stored temporarily and the value is copied to a. Once execution of the statement is complete, the memory holding the result of b+c is discarded. Thus, the result of evaluating b+c is an rvalue.

In the third statement, the expression ++a is an lvalue because its result is a after its value is incremented. The expression a++ in the fourth statement is an rvalue because it stores the value of a temporarily as the result of the expression and then increments a.

An expression that consists of a single named variable is always an lvalue.

> **NOTE** *This is by no means all there is to know about lvalues and rvalues. Most of the time, you don't need to worry very much about whether an expression is an lvalue or an rvalue but sometimes you do. Lvalues and rvalues will pop up at various times throughout the book so keep the idea in mind.*

UNDERSTANDING STORAGE DURATION AND SCOPE

All variables have a finite lifetime. They come into existence at the point at which you declare them and then, at some point, they disappear — at the latest, when your program terminates. How long a particular variable lasts is determined by a property called its *storage duration*. There are three different kinds of storage duration that a variable can have:

➤ Automatic storage duration

➤ Static storage duration

➤ Dynamic storage duration

Which of these a variable will have depends on how you create it. I will defer discussion of variables with dynamic storage duration until Chapter 4, but you will be exploring the characteristics of the other two in this chapter.

Another property that variables have is *scope*. The scope of a variable is that part of your program over which the variable name is valid. Within a variable's scope, you can legally refer to it, either to set its value or to use it in an expression. Outside of the scope of a variable, you cannot refer to its name — any attempt to do so will cause a compiler error. Note that a variable may still *exist* outside of its scope, even though you cannot refer to it. You will see examples of this a little later in this discussion.

All the variables that you have declared up to now have had *automatic storage duration*, and are therefore called *automatic variables*. Let's take a closer look at these first.

Automatic Variables

The variables that you have declared so far have been declared within a block — that is, within the extent of a pair of braces. These are *automatic* variables and have *local scope* or *block scope*. An automatic variable is "in scope" from the point at which it is declared until the end of the block containing its declaration. The space that an automatic variable occupies is allocated in a memory area called the *stack* that is set aside specifically for this purpose. The default size for the stack is 1 MB, which is adequate for most purposes. If this is insufficient, you can increase the stack by adding a / STACK or /F compiler command-line option for the project to a value of your choosing. You can also set the stack size as a linker property.

An automatic variable is created when it is defined and space for it is allocated on the stack; it automatically ceases to exist at the end of the block containing its definition. This will be at the closing brace matching the first opening brace that precedes the declaration of the variable. Every time a block of statements containing a declaration for an automatic variable is executed, the variable is re-created, and if you specified an initial value for it, it will be reinitialized each time. When an automatic variable dies, its memory on the stack is freed for use by other automatic variables. Let's look at an example demonstrating some of what I've discussed so far about scope.

TRY IT OUT   Automatic Variables

The following example shows the effect of scope on automatic variables:

```cpp
// Ex2_07.cpp
// Demonstrating variable scope
#include <iostream>

using std::cout;
using std::endl;

int main()
{                                       // Function scope starts here
    int count1 {10};
    int count3 {50};
    cout << endl
        << "Value of outer count1 = " << count1
        << endl;

    {                                   // New scope starts here...
        int count1 {20};                // This hides the outer count1
```

```
        int count2 {30};
        cout << "Value of inner count1 = " << count1
            << endl;
        count1 += 3;                // This affects the inner count1
        count3 += count2;
    }                               // ...and ends here

    cout << "Value of outer count1 = " << count1
        << endl
        << "Value of outer count3 = " << count3
        << endl;

//  cout << count2 << endl;        // uncomment to get an error

    return 0;
}                                   // Function scope ends here
```

The output from this example will be:

```
Value of outer count1 = 10
Value of inner count1 = 20
Value of outer count1 = 10
Value of outer count3 = 80
```

How It Works

The first two statements declare and define count1 and count3, with initial values of 10 and 50, respectively. Both exist from this point to the closing brace at the end of the program. The scope of these variables also extends to the closing brace at the end of main().

Remember that lifetime and scope are two different things. It's important not to get these two ideas confused. The lifetime is the period from when a variable is first created to when it is destroyed and the memory it occupies is freed. Scope is the region of program code over which a variable may be accessed.

Following the variable definitions, the value of count1 is written to cout to produce the first output line. There's then a second brace, which starts a new block. Two variables, count1 and count2, are defined within this block, with values 20 and 30, respectively. The count1 here is *different* from the first count1. The first count1 still exists, but its name is masked by the second count1. Any use of the name count1 following the declaration within the inner block refers to the count1 declared within that block.

I used a duplicate of the variable name count1 here to illustrate what happens. Although this code is legal, it's a bad approach to programming. In a real-world environment, it would be confusing, and using duplicate names makes it very easy to hide variables defined in an outer scope accidentally.

The value shown in the second output line shows that within the inner block, you are using the count1 in the inner scope — that is, inside the innermost braces:

```
cout << "Value of inner count1 = " << count1
    << endl;
```

Had you still been using the outer count1, then this would output 10. count1 is then incremented by this statement:

```
count1 += 3;                // This affects the inner count1
```

The increment applies to the variable in the inner scope because the outer one is still hidden. However, count3 that was defined in the outer scope is incremented in the next statement without any problem:

```
count3 += count2;
```

This shows that the variables that were declared at the beginning of the outer scope are accessible from within the inner scope. If count3 had been declared *after* the second of the inner pair of braces, then it would still be within the outer scope but it would not exist in the inner scope.

After the brace ending the inner scope, count2 and the inner count1 cease to exist. count1 and count3 are still there in the outer scope, and the values displayed show that count3 was indeed incremented in the inner scope.

If you uncomment the line,

```
// cout << count2 << endl;        // uncomment to get an error
```

the program will no longer compile because this attempts to output a non-existent variable. You will get an error message something like:

```
c:\microsoft visual studio\myprojects\Ex2_07\Ex2_07.cpp(29) : error
    C2065: 'count2' : undeclared identifier
```

This is because count2 is out of scope at this point.

Positioning Variable Declarations

You have great flexibility as to where you can place variable definitions. The most important aspect to consider is what scope the variables need to have. Beyond that, you should place a definition close to where the variable is to be first used. You should write your programs with the intention of making them as easy as possible for another programmer to understand, and declaring a variable at its first point of use is helpful in achieving that.

It is possible to place definitions for variables outside of all of the functions that make up a program. The next section looks at what effect that has.

Global Variables

Variables declared outside of all blocks and classes (I will discuss classes later in the book) are called *globals* and have *global scope* , which is also called *global namespace scope* or *file scope*. This means that they are accessible throughout all the functions in the file following the point at which they are declared. If you declare a variable at the beginning of a source file, it will be accessible from anywhere in the file.

Globals have *static storage duration* by default. Static storage duration means they exist from the start of execution of a program until the program ends. If you do not specify an initial value for a global variable, it will be initialized with 0 by default. Global variables are created and initialized before the execution of main() begins, so they are always accessible by any code within the variable's scope.

Figure 2-11 shows the contents of a source file, Example.cpp, and the arrows indicate the scopes of the variables.

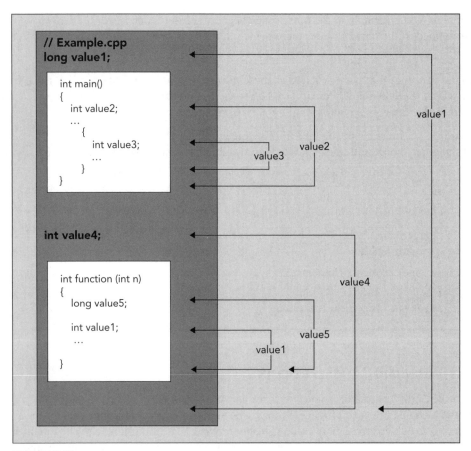

FIGURE 2-11

`value1` appears at the beginning of the file so it is declared at global scope, as is `value4`, which appears after the function `main()`. The scope of each global variable extends from the point at which it is defined to the end of the file. Even though `value4` exists when execution starts, it cannot be referred to in `main()` because `main()` is not within the variable's scope. For `main()` to use `value4`, its definition must precede `main()`.`value1` and `value4` will be initialized with 0 by default, which is not the case for the automatic variables. The local variable, `value1`, in `function()` hides the global `value1`.

Global variables continue to exist for as long as a program is running, which raises the question "Why not make all variables global and avoid this messing about with local variables that disappear?" This sounds attractive but as with the Sirens of mythology, there are serious side effects that completely outweigh any advantages. Real programs are generally composed of a large number of statements, a significant number of functions, and a great many variables. Declaring all variables at global scope greatly magnifies the possibility of accidental erroneous modification of a variable, as well as making the job of naming them sensibly quite intractable. They will also occupy memory for the duration of program execution. By keeping variables local to a function or a block, you can be sure they have almost complete protection from external effects, they will only exist and occupy memory from the point at which they are defined to the end of the enclosing block, and the whole development process becomes much easier to manage. That's not to say you should never define variables at global scope. Sometimes it can be very convenient.

If you look at the Class View pane for any of the examples that you have created so far and extend the class tree for the project by clicking on the unfilled arrow, you will see an entry called Global Functions and Variables. Clicking this will display a list of everything that has global scope. This will include all the global functions, as well as any global variables.

TRY IT OUT   The Scope Resolution Operator

As you have seen, a global variable can be hidden by a local variable with the same name. However, it's still possible to get at the global variable by using the *scope resolution operator* (::), which you saw in Chapter 1 when I was discussing namespaces. I can demonstrate this with a revised version of Ex2_07.cpp:

```
// Ex2_08.cpp
// Demonstrating variable scope
#include <iostream>

using std::cout;
using std::endl;

int count1 {100};                         // Global version of count1

int main()
{                                         // Function scope starts here
   int count1 {10};
   int count3 {50};
   cout << endl
        << "Value of outer count1 = " << count1
        << endl;
   cout << "Value of global count1 = " << ::count1        // From outer block
        << endl;

  {                                 // New scope starts here...
      int count1 {20};              // This hides the outer count1
      int count2 {30};
      cout << "Value of inner count1 = " << count1
           << endl;
      cout << "Value of global count1 = " << ::count1        // From inner block
           << endl;

      count1 += 3;                  // This affects the inner count1
      count3 += count2;
   }                                // ...and ends here.

   cout << "Value of outer count1 = " << count1
        << endl
        << "Value of outer count3 = " << count3
```

```
                    << endl;

        //cout << count2 << endl;          // uncomment to get an error
        return 0;
    }                                      // Function scope ends here
```

This produces the following output:

```
    Value of outer count1 = 10
    Value of global count1 = 100
    Value of inner count1 = 20
    Value of global count1 = 100
    Value of outer count1 = 10
    Value of outer count3 = 80
```

How It Works

The shaded code marks the changes I have made to the previous example; I'll just discuss the effects of those. The definition of count1 prior to the definition of main() is global, so in principle, it is available anywhere through main(). This global variable is initialized with the value of 100:

```
    int count1 {100};                      // Global version of count1
```

However, you have two other variables called count1 defined within main() so throughout the program the global count1 is hidden by the local count1 variables. The first new output statement is:

```
    cout << "Value of global count1 = " << ::count1          // From outer block
        << endl;
```

This uses the scope resolution operator (::) to reference the global count1, *not* the local one. You can see that this works from the value in the output.

In the inner block, the global count1 is hidden by *two* variables called count1: the inner count1 and the outer count1. The global scope resolution operator gets over this within the inner block, as you can see from the output generated by the statement we have added there:

```
    cout << "Value of global count1 = " << ::count1          // From inner block
        << endl;
```

This outputs the value 100, as before — the long arm of the scope resolution operator used in this fashion always reaches a global variable.

You have seen earlier that you can refer to a name in the std namespace by qualifying the name with the namespace name, such as with std::cout or std::endl. The compiler searches the namespace that has the name specified by the left operand of the scope resolution operator for the name that you specify as the right operand. In the preceding example, you are using the scope resolution operator to search the global namespace for the variable count1. By not specifying a namespace name in front of the operator, you are telling the compiler to search the global namespace for the name that follows it. You'll see a lot more of this operator when you get to explore object-oriented programming in Chapter 9, where it is used extensively.

Static Variables

It's conceivable that you might want a variable that's defined and accessible locally, but which also continues to exist after exiting the block in which it is declared. In other words, you need to declare a variable with block scope, but to give it *static storage duration*. The `static` specifier enables you to do this, and the need for this will become more apparent when we come to deal with functions in Chapter 5.

A static variable continues to exist for the life of a program even though it is declared within a block and available only from within that block (or its sub-blocks). It still has block scope, but it has static storage duration. To declare a static integer variable called `count`, you would write:

```
static int count;
```

If you don't provide an initial value for a static variable, it will be initialized with 0 converted to the type applicable to the variable. Remember that this is *not* the case with automatic variables.

VARIABLES WITH SPECIFIC SETS OF VALUES

You will sometimes need variables that have a limited set of possible values that can be usefully referred to by labels — the days of the week, for example, or months of the year, or the suits in a card deck. An *enumeration* provides this capability. There are two kinds of enumerations: those defined using syntax introduced in the C++ 11 standard, and those defined using older syntax. I'll describe both because the old syntax is used widely, but the new syntax has several real advantages so you should only use that.

Old Enumerations

Take one of the examples I mentioned — a variable that can assume values corresponding to days of the week. Here's how you can define this:

```
enum Weekdays{Mon, Tues, Wed, Thurs, Fri, Sat, Sun} today;
```

This declares an enumeration type with the name `Weekdays` and a variable `today`, which is an instance of that type. A variable of type `Weekdays` can assume only the constant values specified between the braces. If you try to set `today` to anything other than one of the set of values specified, it will cause an error. The names between the braces are called *enumerators*. Each enumerator will be automatically defined as a fixed integer value that will be type `int` by default. The first name in the list, `Mon`, will have the value 0, `Tues` will be 1, and so on.

You could assign one of the enumeration constants as the value of `today` like this:

```
today = Thurs;
```

The value of `today` will be 3 because the enumerators are assigned values in sequence, starting with 0 by default. Each successive enumerator is one larger than the previous one. If you would prefer the implicit numbering to start at a different value, you can change it. For example:

```
enum Weekdays {Mon = 1, Tues, Wed, Thurs, Fri, Sat, Sun} today;
```

Now the enumeration constants will be 1 through 7. Enumerators don't even need to have unique values. You could define `Mon` and `Tues` as both having the value 1, for example, with the statement:

```
enum Weekdays {Mon = 1, Tues = 1, Wed, Thurs, Fri, Sat, Sun} thisWeek;
```

Because the enumerators for `Weekdays` are of type `int`, `today` stores a value of type `int` and it will occupy 4 bytes, as will all variables of type `Weekdays`. Enumerators and variables of an enumeration type will be implicitly converted to type `int` when required. For example, you can assign an enumerator as a value for an integer variable:

```
int value {};
value = Wed;
```

If you wish, you can assign specific values to all the enumerators. For example, you could define this enumeration:

```
enum Punctuation {Comma = ',', Exclamation = '!', Question = '?'} things;
```

You have defined the possible values for `things` as the code values of the corresponding characters. The enumerators are 44, 33, and 63, respectively, in decimal. As you can see, the enumerator values don't have to be in ascending order. Any enumerator for which you don't specify a value will be assigned a value 1 greater than the preceding enumerator value.

You can write enumerator values to the standard output stream:

```
cout << today << endl;
```

The compiler inserts a conversion to type `int` for the value of `today`. In general, if you use an enumerator or a variable of an enumeration type, the compiler will insert a conversion of the value to the required numeric type for the expression. This is an undesirable feature because it allows the accidental use of a variable of an enumeration type as though it was a numeric type.

Having defined an enumeration type, you can define another variable:

```
enum Weekdays tomorrow;
```

This defines `tomorrow` as type `Weekdays`. You can omit the `enum` keyword so you could write:

```
Weekdays tomorrow;
```

You can declare and initialize a variable of an enumeration type like any other variable. For example:

```
Weekdays myBirthday {Tues};
Weekdays yourBirthday {Thurs};
```

You don't need to qualify an enumeration constant with the name of the enumeration, although you can if you wish:

```
Weekdays myBirthday {Weekdays::Tues};
```

The `enum` type name is separated from the enumerator name by the scope resolution operator.

You can omit the enumeration type name from the definition if you don't need to define other variables of this type. For example:

```
enum {Mon, Tues, Wed, Thurs, Fri, Sat, Sun} today, tomorrow, yesterday;
```

You have three variables declared that can assume any of the values from `Mon` to `Sun`. Because the enumeration type is not specified, you cannot refer to it. This implies that you cannot define other variables for this enumeration type because you would not be permitted to repeat the definition. Doing so would imply that you were redefining values for `Mon` to `Sun`, and this isn't allowed.

You don't have to accept the default type for the enumerators. You can explicitly specify the enumerator type as any integer type except `wchar_t`. Here's an example that shows how you do that:

```
enum Workdays : unsigned long {Mon, Tues, Wed, Thurs, Fri} tomorrow;
```

The enumerators for `Workdays` will be of type `unsigned long`.

The enumerator names are exported into the enclosing scope by default. This is why there is no need to qualify their names. This can create a problem. Look at these two enumerations:

```
enum Suit {Clubs, Diamonds, Hearts, Spades};
enum Jewels {Diamonds, Emeralds, Opals, Rubies, Sapphires};
```

If you put these definitions in `main()` they won't compile. Both sets of enumerator names are in the enclosing scope, that is, throughout the body of `main()`. The `Jewels` enumeration is seen to redefine `Diamonds`, which is not allowed.

Type-safe Enumerations

C++ 11 introduced a new form of enumeration. These enumerations are said to be *type-safe* because implicit conversion of enumerator values to another type will not occur. You use the `class` keyword following `enum` to specify the new enumeration type. Here's an example:

```
enum class Suit {Clubs, Diamonds, Hearts, Spades};
```

The enumerator names are not exported into the enclosing scope. You must always qualify them using the type name, like this:

```
Suit suit {Suit::Diamonds};
```

You can rewrite the two enumerations from the previous section that did not compile as type-safe enumerations:

```
enum class Suit {Clubs, Diamonds, Hearts, Spades};
enum class Jewels {Diamonds, Emeralds, Opals, Rubies, Sapphires};
```

These statements will compile. There are no name conflicts because the enumerator names are not exported into the enclosing scope. You must always qualify the enumerator names with the type name so `Suit::Diamonds` is always distinct from `Jewels::Diamonds`.

If you want to convert an enumerator value to another type, you can use an explicit cast. For example:

```
Suit suit{Suit::Diamonds};               // Create and initialize suit
int suitValue {static_cast<int>(suit)};  // Convert suit to int
```

This will not compile without the explicit conversion of `suit` to type `int`.

The enumerator values are type `int` by default, but you can change this:

```
enum class Jewels : char {Diamonds, Emeralds, Opals, Rubies, Sapphires};
```

Here, enumerator values will be of type `char`. The next example demonstrates aspects of both kinds of enumerations.

TRY IT OUT   Using Enumerations

This example demonstrates both types of enumerations:

```cpp
// Ex2_09.cpp
// Demonstrating type-safe and non-type-safe enumerations
#include <iostream>

using std::cout;
using std::endl;

// You can define enumerations at global scope
//enum Jewels {Diamonds, Emeralds, Rubies};  // Uncomment this for an error
enum Suit : long {Clubs, Diamonds, Hearts, Spades};

int main()
{
  // Using the old enumeration type...
    Suit suit {Clubs};                      // You can use old enumerator names directly
    Suit another {Suit::Diamonds};          // or you can qualify them

  // Automatic conversion from enumeration type to integer
    cout << "suit value: " << suit << endl;
    cout << "Add 10 to another: " << another + 10 << endl;

  // Using type-safe enumerations...
    enum class Color : char {Red, Orange, Yellow, Green, Blue, Indigo, Violet};
    Color skyColor{Color::Blue};            // You must qualify enumerator names
  // Color grassColor{Green};                // Uncomment for an error

  // No auto conversion to numeric type
    cout << endl
         << "Sky color value: "
         << static_cast<long>(skyColor) << endl;

  //cout << skyColor + 10L << endl;          // Uncomment for an error
    cout << "Incremented sky color: "
         << static_cast<long>(skyColor) + 10L // OK with explicit cast
         << endl;
    return 0;
}
```

If you compile and run this example, you'll get the following output:

```
suit value: 0
Add 10 to another: 11
Sky color value: 4
Incremented sky color: 14
```

How It Works

You can see that you can define enumerations at global scope, in which case they are accessible throughout the source file. Enumerations defined locally within a block are available from where they are defined to the end of the block. You could put the definition of the enumeration type into a `.h` file that you create; you could then `#include` the header into any source file that is to use the enumeration.

Uncommenting the definition for the `Jewels` enumeration will result in a compiler error because of the duplication of `Diamonds`. If the `Suit` and `Jewels` types were defined as type-safe enums, no name collision would occur.

The `main()` function exercises the old-style enumerations first by showing that type qualification of enumerator names is optional. These statements show automatic conversions in operation:

```
cout << "suit value: " << suit << endl;
cout << "Add 10 to another: " << another + 10 << endl;
```

The compiler will happily allow you to output `suit` as though it is an integer, even though it is of type `Suit`. You can also use it in an arithmetic expression.

The `Color` enumeration is type-safe:

```
enum class Color : char {Red, Orange, Yellow, Green, Blue, Indigo, Violet};
```

If you attempt to use the enumerator names without qualification, you will get an error message from the compiler. The compiler will insist that if you want to convert a `Color` value to another type, you must insert an explicit cast.

> **NOTE** *Always use type-safe enumerations. This will make your code less error-prone.*

NAMESPACES

I have mentioned namespaces several times, so it's time you got a better idea of what they are about. They are not used in the libraries supporting MFC, but the standard library uses namespaces throughout.

You know already that the names in the standard library are defined in a namespace with the name `std`. This means that the names have an additional qualifying name, `std`; for example, `cout` is really `std::cout`. You have already seen how a `using` declaration imports a name from the `std` namespace into your source file. For example:

```
using std::cout;
```

This allows you to use `cout` and have it interpreted as `std::cout`.

Namespaces provide a way to separate names used in one part of a program from those used in another. This is invaluable with large projects involving several teams of programmers working on different parts of a program. Each team can have its own namespace name, and worries about two teams accidentally using the same name for different functions disappear.

Look at this line of code:

```
using namespace std;
```

This is a *using directive* and is different from a `using` declaration. The effect of this is to import *all* the names from the `std` namespace into the source file so you can refer to anything that is defined in this namespace without qualifying the name. Thus, you can write `cout` instead of `std::cout` and `endl` instead of `std::endl`. This sounds like a big advantage, but the downside of this blanket `using` directive is that it effectively negates the primary reason for using a namespace — that is, preventing accidental name clashes. There are two ways to access names from a namespace without negating its intended effect. One way is to qualify each name explicitly with the namespace name; however, this can make the code very verbose and reduce its readability. The other possibility is to introduce just the names that you use in your code with `using` declarations as you have seen in earlier examples, like this for example:

```
using std::cout;            // Allows cout usage without qualification
using std::endl;            // Allows endl usage without qualification
```

Each `using` declaration introduces a single name from the specified namespace and allows it to be used unqualified within the program code that follows. This can be a better way of importing names from a namespace, as you only import the names you actually use. However, you may find the number of using declarations becomes excessive. Of course, you can define your own namespace that has a name that you choose. The following section shows how.

> **WARNING** You should not use `using` directives in a headers file because they will apply in all source files that include the header file. You should avoid `using` declarations at global scope in a header file.

Declaring a Namespace

You use the `namespace` keyword to declare a namespace — like this:

```
namespace myStuff
{
   // Code that I want to have in the namespace myStuff...
}
```

This defines a namespace with the name `myStuff`. All name declarations in the code between the braces will be defined within the `myStuff` namespace. To access any name in this namespace from outside it requires that the name is qualified by the namespace name. Inside the `myStuff` namespace you just use the unqualified names.

You can't declare a namespace inside a function. It's intended to be used the other way around; you use a namespace to contain functions, global variables, and other named entities such as classes. You must not put the definition of `main()` in a namespace though. `main()` is where execution starts and it must always be at global scope; otherwise the compiler won't recognize it.

You could define a variable `value` in a namespace and use it in an example:

```
// Ex2_10.cpp
// Declaring a namespace
#include <iostream>

namespace myStuff
{
  int value {};
}

int main()
{
  std::cout << "enter an integer: ";
  std::cin  >> myStuff::value;
  std::cout << "\nYou entered " << myStuff::value
          << std::endl;
  return 0;
}
```

The `myStuff` namespace defines a scope, and every name defined within that scope is qualified by the namespace name. To refer to a name declared within a namespace from outside, you must qualify it with the namespace name. Inside the namespace scope, any of the names within it can be referred to without qualification — they are all part of the same family. You must qualify the name `value` with `myStuff`, the name of the namespace. If not, the program will not compile. `main()` refers to names in two different namespaces and in general you can have as many namespaces in your program as you need. You could remove the need to qualify `value` by adding a `using` directive:

```
// Ex2_11.cpp
// Using a using directive
#include <iostream>

namespace myStuff
{
  int value {};
}

using namespace myStuff;              // Make all the names in myStuff available

int main()
{
  std::cout << "enter an integer: ";
  std::cin  >> value;
  std::cout << "\nYou entered " << value
          << std::endl;
  return 0;
}
```

You could also have a `using` directive for `std`. Generally if you use namespaces, you should not add `using` directives for them throughout your code; otherwise, you might as well not bother with namespaces in the first place. I'll add a `using` directive for `std` in some of the examples to keep the code less cluttered and easier to read. When you are starting out with a new programming language, you can do without clutter, no matter how useful it is in practice.

Multiple Namespaces

A real-world program is likely to involve multiple namespaces. You can have multiple declarations of a namespace with a given name, and the contents of all namespace blocks with the same name are within the same namespace. For example, you might have a program file with two namespaces:

```
namespace sortStuff
{
    // Everything in here is within sortStuff namespace
}

namespace calculateStuff
{
  // Everything in here is within calculateStuff namespace
  // To refer to names from sortStuff they must be qualified
}

namespace sortStuff
{
  // This is a continuation of the namespace sortStuff
  // so from here you can refer to names in the first sortStuff namespace
  // without qualifying them
}
```

A second declaration of a namespace with a given name is a continuation of the first, so you can reference names in the first namespace block from the second without qualifying them. They are all in the same namespace. Of course, you would not organize a source file in this way deliberately, but it can arise quite naturally with header files. For example, you might have something like this:

```
#include <iostream>     // Contents are in namespace std
#include "myheader.h"   // Contents are in namespace myStuff
#include <string>       // Contents are in namespace std

// and so on...
```

Here, `iostream` and `string` are standard library headers, and `myheader.h` represents a header file that contains our program code. You have a situation with the namespaces that is an exact parallel of the previous illustration.

This has given you a basic idea of how namespaces work. There is a lot more to namespaces than I have discussed here, but if you grasp this bit, you should be able to find out more about it when you need to without difficulty.

SUMMARY

This chapter covered the basics of computation. You have learned about all the fundamental types of data provided for in the language, and all the operators that manipulate these types directly.

Although I have discussed all the fundamental types, don't be misled into thinking that's all there is. There are more complex types based on the basic set, as you'll see, and eventually you will be creating original types of your own.

EXERCISES

1. Write a program that asks the user to enter a number and then prints it out, using an integer as a local variable.

2. Write a program that reads an integer value from the keyboard into a variable of type `int`, and uses one of the bitwise operators (i.e., not the `%` operator!) to determine the positive remainder when divided by 8. For example, 29 = (3 x 8) + 5 and -14 = (-2 x 8) + 2 have positive remainder 5 and 2, respectively, when divided by 8.

3. Fully parenthesize the following expressions, in order to show the precedence and associativity:

   ```
   1 + 2 + 3 + 4

   16 * 4 / 2 * 3

   a > b? a: c > d? e: f

   a & b && c & d
   ```

4. Create a program that will calculate the aspect ratio of your computer screen, given the width and height in pixels, using the following statements:

   ```
   int width {1280};
   int height {1024};

   double aspect {width / height};
   ```

   When you output the result, what answer will you get? Is it satisfactory — and if not, how could you modify the code, without adding more variables?

5. (Advanced) Without running it, can you work out what value the following code is going to output, and why?

   ```
   unsigned s {555};

   int i {static_cast<int>((s >> 4) & ~(~0 << 3))};
   cout << i;
   ```

➤ WHAT YOU LEARNED IN THIS CHAPTER

TOPIC	CONCEPT
The `main()` function	A C++ program consists of one or more functions and must include a global function called `main()`, which is where execution starts.
The function body	The executable part of a function is made up of statements contained between braces.
Statements	A statement is terminated by a semicolon and can be spread over several lines.
Names	Named objects, such as variables or functions, can have names that consist of a sequence of letters, underscores, and digits, the first of which is a letter or an underscore. Uppercase and lowercase letters are distinguished.
Reserved words	Reserved words in C++ are called keywords. You must not use keywords as names for things in your code.
Fundamental types	All constants and variables in C++ are of a given type. The fundamental types are `char`, `signed char`, `unsigned char`, `wchar_t`, `short`, `unsigned short`, `int`, `unsigned int`, `long`, `unsigned long`, `long long`, `unsigned long long`, `bool`, `float`, `double`, and `long double`.
Declarations	You define the name and type of a variable in a definition statement that ends with a semicolon. You can also specify initial values for variables in a definition.
The `const` modifier	You can protect the value of a variable by using the `const` modifier. This prevents direct modification of the variable within the program. Any attempt to modify a `const` variable will result in a compiler error message.
Automatic variables	By default, a variable is automatic, which means that it exists only from the point at which it is declared to the end of the scope in which it is defined, indicated by the first closing brace after its definition.
`static` variables	A variable may be declared as `static`, in which case, it continues to exist for the life of the program. It can be accessed only within the scope in which it was defined.
Global variables	Variables can be declared outside of all blocks within a program, in which case, they have global namespace scope. Variables with global namespace scope are accessible throughout a program, except where a local variable exists with the same name as the global variable. Even then, they can still be reached by using the scope resolution operator.
Enumerations	An enumeration is a type that you define with a fixed set of values. You should use type-safe enumerations that you define using the keywords `enum class`.
Namespaces	A namespace defines a scope where each of the names declared within it is qualified by the namespace name. Referring to names from outside a namespace requires the names to be qualified. You can access individual objects in a namespace from outside the namespace by using the namespace name to qualify the object name. Alternatively, you can supply a `using` declaration for each name from the namespace that you want to reference.

TOPIC	CONCEPT
The Stanrd Library	The Stanrd Library defines a vast range of functions, operators, and constants that you can use in your programs. Everything in the Stanrd Library is defined in the `std` namespace.
Lvalues and rvalues	Every expression in C++ results in either an lvalue or an rvalue. An lvalue is a persistent address and can appear on the left side of an assignment. Non-`const` variables are examples of lvalues. Any result that is not an lvalue is an rvalue. This implies that an rvalue cannot be used on the left side of an assignment.

3

Decisions and Loops

WHAT YOU WILL LEARN IN THIS CHAPTER:

- ➤ How to compare data values
- ➤ How to alter the sequence of program execution based on the result
- ➤ How to apply logical operators and expressions
- ➤ How to deal with multiple choice situations
- ➤ How to write and use loops in your programs

WROX.COM CODE DOWNLOADS FOR THIS CHAPTER

You can find the wrox.com code downloads for this chapter on the Download Code tab at www.wrox.com/go/beginningvisualc. The code is in the Chapter 3 download and individually named according to the names throughout the chapter.

COMPARING VALUES

Unless you want to make decisions on a whim, you need a mechanism for comparing things. This involves some new operators called relational operators. Because all information in your computer is ultimately represented by numerical values (in the last chapter you saw how character information is represented by numeric codes), comparing numerical values is the essence of all decision making. You have six operators for comparing two values:

<	less than	<=	less than or equal to
>	greater than	>=	greater than or equal to
==	equal to	!=	not equal to

> **NOTE** The "equal to" comparison operator has two successive = signs. This is not the same as the assignment operator, which consists only of a single = sign. It's a common mistake to inadvertently use the assignment operator instead of the comparison operator, so watch out for this.

Each operator compares the values of two operands and returns one of the two possible values of type `bool`: `true` if the comparison is true, or `false` if it is not. You can see how this works by having a look at a few simple examples. The operands can be variables, literals, or expressions. Suppose you have created integer variables `i` and `j` with the values 10 and −5, respectively. The expressions,

```
i > j      i != j      j > -8      i <= j + 15
```

all return the value `true`.

Assume that you have defined the following variables:

```
char first {'A'}, last {'Z'};
```

Here are some examples of comparisons using these:

```
first == 65      first < last      'E' <= first      first != last
```

All four expressions compare ASCII code values. The first expression returns `true` because `first` was initialized with `'A'`, which is the equivalent of decimal 65. The second expression checks whether the value of `first`, which is `'A'`, is less than the value `last`, which is `'Z'`. The ASCII codes for the capital letters are represented by an ascending sequence of numerical values from 65 to 90, 65 representing `'A'` and 90 representing `'Z'`, so this comparison also returns the value `true`. The third expression returns the value `false` because `'E'` is greater than the value of `first`. The last expression returns `true` because `'A'` is definitely not equal to `'Z'`.

Let's consider some slightly more complicated comparisons with variables defined by the statements:

```
int i {-10}, j {20};
double x {1.5}, y {-0.25E-10};
```

Take a look at the following expressions:

```
-1 < y      j < (10 - i)      2.0*x >= (3 + y)
```

Here you use expressions that result in numerical values as operands. The precedence table for operators that you saw in Chapter 2 shows that none of the parentheses are strictly necessary, but they do help to make the expressions clearer. The first comparison is true, and so returns the `bool` value `true`. The variable y has a very small negative value, -0.000000000025, and so is greater than -1. The second comparison returns the value `false`. The expression `10 - i` has the value 20, which is the same as `j`. The third expression returns `true` because the expression `3 + y` is slightly less than 3.

You can use relational operators to compare values of any of the fundamental types or of the enumeration types, so all you need now is a way of using the results of a comparison to modify the behavior of a program.

The if Statement

The basic `if` statement allows your program to execute a single statement — or a block of statements enclosed within braces — if a given conditional expression evaluates to `true`, or to skip the statement or block of statements if the condition evaluates to `false`. This is illustrated in Figure 3-1.

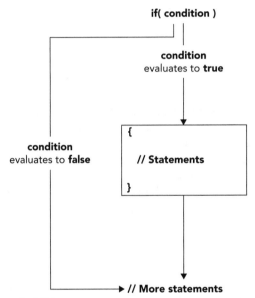

if(condition)

condition
evaluates to **true**

condition
evaluates to **false**

{

// **Statements**

}

// **More statements**

FIGURE 3-1

A simple example of an `if` statement is:

```
if('A' == letter)
    cout << "The first capital, alphabetically speaking.";
```

The condition to be tested appears in parentheses immediately following the keyword, `if`, and this is followed by the statement to be executed when the condition is `true`. Note the position of the semicolon. It goes after the statement *following* the `if` and the condition between parentheses; there shouldn't be a semicolon after the condition in parentheses because the two lines essentially make up a single statement. You also can see how the line following the `if` is indented to indicate that it is only executed when the `if` condition returns the value `true`. The indentation is not essential, but it helps you to recognize the relationship between the `if` condition and the statement that depends on it. The output statement in the code fragment is executed only if the variable `letter` has the value 'A'.

> **NOTE** *When you are comparing a variable to a constant of some kind using the == operator, it is a good idea to write the constant on the left of the == operator, as in* 'A' == letter. *That way, if you accidentally write* 'A' = letter, *you will get an error message from the compiler. If you write* letter = 'A', *this is perfectly legal, though not what you intended, and no error message will be produced.*

You could extend this example to change the value of letter if it contains the value 'A':

```
if('A' == letter)
{
  cout << "The first capital, alphabetically speaking.";
  letter = 'a';
}
```

The block of statements that is controlled by the if statement is delimited by the curly braces. You execute the statements in the block only if the condition ('A' == letter) evaluates to true. Without the braces, only the first statement would be the subject of the if, and the statement assigning the value 'a' to letter would always be executed. Note that there is a semicolon after each of the statements in the block, but not after the closing brace at the end of the block. There can be as many statements as you like within a block. Now, as a result of letter having the value 'A', you change its value to 'a' after outputting the same message as before. If the condition returns false, neither of these statements is executed.

Nested if Statements

The statement to be executed when the condition in an if statement is true can also be an if. This arrangement is called a *nested* if. The condition for the inner if is only tested if the condition for the outer if is true. An if that is nested inside another can also contain a nested if. You can generally continue nesting ifs one inside the other like this for as long as you still know what you are doing.

TRY IT OUT   Using Nested ifs

The following is a working example of the nested if:

```
// Ex3_01.cpp
// A nested if demonstration
#include <iostream>

using std::cin;
using std::cout;
using std::endl;

int main{}
{
  char letter {};                       // Store input in here
```

```
    cout << endl
        << "Enter a letter: ";          // Prompt for the input
    cin >> letter;                      // then read a character

    if(letter >= 'A')                   // Test for 'A' or larger
    {
        if(letter <= 'Z')               // Test for 'Z' or smaller
        {
            cout << endl
                << "You entered a capital letter."
                << endl;
            return 0;
        }
    }

    if(letter >= 'a')                   // Test for 'a' or larger
    {
        if(letter <= 'z')               // Test for 'z' or smaller
        {
            cout << endl
                << "You entered a lowercase letter."
                << endl;
            return 0;
        }
    }

    cout << endl << "You did not enter a letter." << endl;
    return 0;
}
```

How It Works

This program starts with the usual comment lines, then the `#include` statement for the header file supporting input/output, followed by the `using` declarations for `cin`, `cout`, and `endl` that are in the `std` namespace. The first action in the body of `main()` is to prompt for a letter to be entered. This is stored in the `char` variable with the name `letter`.

The `if` statement that follows the input checks whether the character entered is `'A'` or larger. The ASCII codes for lowercase letters (97 to 122) are greater than those for uppercase letters (65 to 90). Entering a lowercase letter causes the program to execute the first `if` block, because `(letter >= 'A')` returns `true` for all lowercase letters. In this case, the nested `if`, which checks for an input of `'Z'` or less, is executed. If `letter` is `'Z'` or less, you know that you have a capital letter, so the appropriate message is displayed, and because there is nothing more to do, you execute a `return` statement to end the program. Both statements are between braces, so they are both executed when the nested `if` condition returns `true`.

The next `if` checks whether the character entered is lowercase using essentially the same mechanism as the first `if`, then displays a message and returns.

If the character entered is not a letter, the output statement following the last `if` block is executed. This displays a message to the effect that the character entered was not a letter. The `return` is then executed.

You can see that the relationship between the nested `if`s and the output statement is much easier to follow because of the indentation applied to each.

A typical output from this example is:

```
Enter a letter: T
You entered a capital letter.
```

You could easily arrange to change uppercase to lowercase by adding just one extra statement to the `if`, checking for uppercase:

```
if(letter >= 'A')                    // Test for 'A' or larger
  if(letter <= 'Z')                  // Test for 'Z' or smaller
  {
    cout << endl
         << "You entered a capital letter."
         << endl;
    letter += 'a' - 'A';             // Convert to lowercase
    return 0;
  }
```

The statement for converting from uppercase to lowercase increments the `letter` variable by the value 'a' - 'A'. It works because the ASCII codes for 'A' to 'Z' and 'a' to 'z' are two groups of consecutive numerical codes, decimal 65 to 90 and 97 to 122, respectively, so the expression 'a' - 'A' represents the value to be added to an uppercase letter to get the equivalent lowercase letter and corresponds to 97–65, which is 32. Thus, if you add 32 to the code value for 'K', which is 75, you get 107, which is the code value for 'k'.

You could equally use the equivalent ASCII values for the letters here, but by using the letters you've ensured that this code would work on computers where the characters were not ASCII, as long as both the upper- and lowercase sets are represented by a contiguous sequence of numeric values.

There is a standard library function to convert letters to uppercase, so you don't normally need to program this yourself. It has the name `toupper()` and appears in the `ctype` standard header file. You will see more about standard library facilities when you get to look at how functions are written.

The Extended if Statement

The `if` statement that you have been using so far executes a statement if the condition specified returns `true`. Program execution then continues with the next statement in sequence. You also have a version of the `if` that allows one statement to be executed if the condition returns `true`, and a different statement to be executed if the condition returns `false`. Execution then continues with the next statement in sequence. As you saw in Chapter 2, a block of statements can always replace a single statement, so this also applies to these `if`s.

TRY IT OUT   Extending the if

Here's an extended `if` example:

```
// Ex3_02.cpp
// Using the extended if
#include <iostream>

using std::cin;
using std::cout;
using std::endl;

int main()
{
  long number {};              // Store input here
  cout << endl
       << "Enter an integer number less than 2 billion: ";
  cin >> number;

  if(number % 2L)              // Test remainder after division by 2
     cout << endl              // Here if remainder 1
          << "Your number is odd." << endl;
  else
     cout << endl              // Here if remainder 0
          << "Your number is even." << endl;

  return 0;
}
```

Typical output from this program is:

```
Enter an integer less than 2 billion: 123456
Your number is even.
```

How It Works

After reading the input value into `number`, the value is tested by taking the remainder after division by two (using the remainder operator `%` that you saw in the previous chapter) and using that as the condition for the `if`. In this case, the condition of the `if` statement returns an integer, not a boolean. The `if` statement interprets a non-zero value returned by the condition as `true`, and interprets zero as `false`. In other words, the condition expression for the `if` statement

```
(number % 2L)
```

is equivalent to

```
(number % 2L != 0)
```

If the remainder is 1, the condition is `true`, and the statement immediately following the `if` is executed. If the remainder is 0, the condition is `false`, and the statement following the `else` keyword is executed. It's obvious here what the `if` expression is doing, but with more complicated expressions it's better to add the extra few characters needed for the comparison with zero to ensure that the code is easily understood.

> **NOTE** The condition in an `if` statement can be an expression that results in a value of any of the fundamental data types that you saw in Chapter 2. When the conditional expression evaluates to a numerical value, the compiler inserts an automatic conversion of the value to type `bool`. Casting a non-zero value to type `bool` results in `true`, and casting a zero value results in `false`.
>
> The remainder from the division of an integer by two can only be one or zero. After either outcome, the return statement is executed to end the program.

> **NOTE** The `else` keyword is written without a semicolon, similar to the `if` part of the statement. Again, indentation is used as a visible indicator of the relationship between various statements. You can clearly see which statement is executed for a `true` or non-zero result, and which for a `false` or zero result. You should always indent the statements in your programs to show their logical structure.

The `if-else` combination provides a choice between two options. The general logic of the `if-else` is shown in Figure 3-2.

The arrows in the diagram indicate the sequence in which statements are executed, depending on whether the `if` condition returns `true` or `false`.

Nested if-else Statements

As you have seen, you can nest `if` statements within `if` statements. You can also nest `if-else` statements within `ifs`, `ifs` within `if-else` statements, and `if-else` statements within `if-else` statements. This provides considerable room for confusion, so let's take a look at a few examples. The following is an example of an `if-else` nested within an `if`:

```
if('y' == coffee)
  if('y' == donuts)
    cout << "We have coffee and donuts.";
  else
    cout << "We have coffee, but not donuts";
```

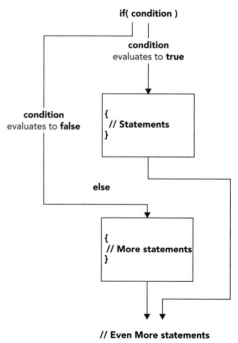

FIGURE 3-2

The test for `donuts` is executed only if the result of the test for `coffee` returns `true`, so the messages reflect the correct situation in each case; however, it is easy to get this confused. If you write much the same thing with incorrect indentation, you can be trapped into the wrong conclusion:

```
if('y' == coffee)
  if('y' == donuts)
    cout << "We have coffee and donuts.";
else                                    // This else is indented incorrectly
  cout << "We have no coffee...";      // Wrong!
```

The mistake is easy to see here, but with more complicated `if` structures you need to keep in mind the rule about which `if` owns which `else`.

> **NOTE** An `else` *always belongs to the nearest preceding* `if` *that is not already spoken for by another* `else`.

Whenever things look a bit complicated, you can apply this rule to sort things out. When you are writing your own programs you can always use braces to make the situation clearer. It isn't essential but it's a good idea to write the last example as follows:

```
if('y' == coffee)
{
  if('y' == donuts)
    cout << "We have coffee and donuts.";
  else
    cout << "We have coffee, but not donuts";
}
```

and it should be absolutely clear. Now that you know the rules, understanding the case of an `if` nested within an `if-else` becomes easy:

```
if('y' == coffee)
{
  if('y' == donuts)
    cout << "We have coffee and donuts.";
}
else
  if('y' == tea)
    cout << "We have tea, but not coffee";
```

Here, the braces are essential. If you leave them out, the `else` would belong to the second `if`, which is looking out for `donuts`. In this kind of situation, it is easy to forget to include the braces and create an error that may be hard to find. A program with this kind of error compiles fine and even produces the right results some of the time.

If you removed the braces in this example, you get the correct results only as long as `coffee` and `donuts` are both equal to `'y'` so that the `if('y' == tea)` check wouldn't be executed.

`if-else` statements nested in `if-else` statements can get very messy, even with just one level of nesting:

```
if('y' == coffee)
  if('y' == donuts)
    cout << "We have coffee and donuts.";
```

```
    else
      cout << "We have coffee, but not donuts";
  else
    if('y' == tea)
      cout << "We have no coffee, but we have tea, and maybe donuts...";
    else
      cout << "No tea or coffee, but maybe donuts...";
```

The logic here doesn't look quite so obvious, even with the correct indentation. No braces are necessary. The rule you saw earlier verifies that each `else` belongs to the correct `if`, but it would be a lot clearer if you included them:

```
if('y' == coffee)
{
  if('y' == donuts)
    cout << "We have coffee and donuts.";
  else
    cout << "We have coffee, but not donuts";
}
else
{
  if('y' == tea)
    cout << "We have no coffee, but we have tea, and maybe donuts...";
  else
    cout << "No tea or coffee, but maybe donuts...";
}
```

There are much better ways of dealing with this kind of logic in a program. If you put enough nested `if`s together, you can almost guarantee a mistake somewhere. The next section will help to simplify things.

Logical Operators and Expressions

As you have just seen, using `if`s where you have two or more related conditions can be a bit cumbersome. We have tried our iffy talents on looking for coffee and donuts, but in practice you may want to test much more complex conditions.

Logical operators provide a neat and simple solution. Using logical operators, you can combine a series of comparisons into a single logical expression, so you end up needing just one `if`, virtually regardless of the complexity of the set of conditions, as long as the decision ultimately boils down to a choice between two possibilities — true or false.

You have just three logical operators:

&&	Logical AND
||	Logical OR
!	Logical negation (NOT)

Logical AND

You would use the AND operator, &&, where you have two conditions that must both be true for a true result. You want to be rich *and* healthy. Thus the && operator produces the result true when both operands have the value true, and false otherwise.

You could use the && operator when you are testing a character to determine whether it's an uppercase letter; the value being tested must be both greater than or equal to 'A' and less than or equal to 'Z'. Both conditions must return true for the value to be a capital letter.

> **NOTE** As before, the conditions you combine using logical operators may return numerical values. Remember that a non-zero value converts to the value true; zero converts to false.

Taking the example of a value stored in a char variable letter, you could replace the test that uses two ifs with one that uses only a single if and the && operator:

```
if((letter >= 'A') && (letter <= 'Z'))
   cout << "This is a capital letter.";
```

The parentheses inside the expression that is the if condition ensure that there is no doubt that the comparison operations are executed first, which makes the statement clearer. Here, the output statement is executed only if *both* of the conditions that are combined by the && operator are true.

> **NOTE** If the left operand for the && operator is false, the right operand will not be evaluated. This becomes significant if the right operand is an expression that can change something, such as an expression involving the ++ or -- operator. For example, in the expression x>=5 && ++n<10, n will not be incremented if x is less than 5.

Logical OR

The OR operator, ||, applies when you have two conditions where you want a true result if either or both of them are true. For example, you might be considered credit worthy for a loan from the bank if your income was at least $100,000 a year, or if you had $1,000,000 in cash. This could be tested using the following if:

```
if((income >= 100000.00) || (capital >= 1000000.00))
   cout << "How much would you like to borrow, Sir (grovel, grovel)?";
```

The ingratiating response emerges when either or both of the conditions are true. (A better response might be, "Why do you want to borrow?" It's strange how banks lend you money only if you don't need it.)

You only get a false result with the || operator when both operands are false.

> **NOTE** If the left operand for the || operator is `true`, the right operand will not be evaluated. For example, in the expression `x>=5 || ++n<10`, the variable n will not be incremented if `x` is greater than or equal to 5.

Logical NOT

The third logical operator, `!`, takes one operand of type `bool` and inverts its value. So, if the value of a variable `test` is `true`, `!test` is `false`; and if `test` is `false`, `!test` is `true`. To take the example of a simple expression, if `x` has the value 10, the expression `!(x > 5)` evaluates to `false`, because `x > 5` is true.

You could also apply the `!` operator in an expression that was a favorite of Charles Dickens':

```
!(income > expenditure)
```

If this expression is `true`, the result is misery, at least as soon as the bank starts bouncing your checks.

Finally, you can apply the `!` operator to other basic data types. Suppose you have a variable, `rate`, that is of type `float` and has the value 3.2. For some reason, you might want to verify that the value of `rate` is non-zero, in which case you could use the expression:

```
!(rate)
```

The value 3.2 is non-zero and thus converts to the `bool` value `true`, so the result of this expression is `false`.

TRY IT OUT Combining Logical Operators

You can combine conditional expressions and logical operators to any degree that you feel comfortable with. For example, using just a single `if`, you could construct a test for whether a variable contained a letter. Let's write it as a working example:

```cpp
// Ex3_03.cpp
// Testing for a letter using logical operators
#include <iostream>

using std::cin;
using std::cout;
using std::endl;

int main()
{
  char letter {};                              // Store input in here

  cout << endl
       << "Enter a character: ";
  cin >> letter;

  if(((letter >= 'A') && (letter <= 'Z')) ||
      ((letter >= 'a') && (letter <= 'z')))    // Test for alphabetic
    cout << endl
         << "You entered a letter." << endl;
  else
```

```
    cout << endl
        << "You didn't enter a letter." << endl;

  return 0;
}
```

How It Works

This starts out in the same way as `Ex3_01.cpp`, by reading a character after a prompt for input. The interesting part of the program is in the `if` statement condition. This consists of two logical expressions combined with the `||` (OR) operator, so that if either is `true`, the condition returns `true` and the following message is displayed:

```
You entered a letter.
```

If both logical expressions are `false`, the `else` statement is executed, which displays this message:

```
You didn't enter a letter.
```

Each logical expression combines a pair of comparisons with the operator `&&` (AND), so both comparisons must return `true` if the expression is to be `true`. The first logical expression returns `true` if the input is an uppercase letter, and the second returns `true` if the input is a lowercase letter.

The Conditional Operator

The conditional operator is sometimes called the ternary operator because it involves three operands. It is best understood by looking at an example. Suppose you have two variables, a and b, and you want to assign the maximum of a and b to a third variable, c. You can do this with the following statement:

```
c = a > b ? a : b;          // Set c to the maximum of a or b
```

The first operand for the conditional operator must be an expression that results in a `bool` value, `true` or `false`, and in this case it is a `>` b. If this expression returns `true`, the second operand — in this case a — is selected as the value resulting from the operation. If the first argument returns `false`, the third operand — in this case b — is selected as the value that results from the operation. Thus, the result of a `>` b `?` a `:` b is a, if a is greater than b, and b otherwise. This value is stored in c by the assignment operation. The use of the conditional operator in this assignment statement is equivalent to the `if` statement:

```
if(a > b)
  c = a;
else
  c = b;
```

The conditional operator can be written generally as:

```
condition ? expression1 : expression2
```

If *condition* evaluates to `true`, the result is the value of *expression1*, and if it evaluates to `false`, the result is the value of *expression2*.

A common use of the conditional operator is to control output based on the result of an expression or the value of a variable. You can vary a message by selecting one text string or another, depending on the condition specified:

```cpp
// Ex3_04.cpp
// The conditional operator selecting output
#include <iostream>

using std::cout;
using std::endl;

int main()
{
  int nCakes {1};            // Count of number of cakes

  cout << endl
       << "We have " << nCakes << " cake" << ((nCakes > 1) ? "s." : ".")
       << endl;

  ++nCakes;

  cout << endl
       << "We have " << nCakes << " cake" << ((nCakes > 1) ? "s." : ".")
       << endl;
  return 0;
}
```

The output from this program is:

```
We have 1 cake.
We have 2 cakes.
```

How It Works

You first create the `nCakes` variable with the initial value 1; then you have an output statement that shows the number of cakes. The part that uses the conditional operator simply tests the variable to determine whether you have a singular cake or several cakes:

```cpp
((nCakes > 1) ? "s." : ".")
```

This expression evaluates to `"s."` if `nCakes` is greater than 1, or `"."` otherwise. This enables you to use the same output statement for any number of cakes and get grammatically correct output. You make use of this in the example by incrementing the `nCakes` variable and repeating the output statement.

There are many other situations where you can apply this sort of mechanism; selecting between `"is"` and `"are"`, for example.

The switch Statement

The `switch` statement enables you to select from multiple choices based on a set of fixed values for a given expression. It operates like a physical rotary switch in that you can select one of a number of choices. Some washing machines provide a means of choosing an operation for processing your laundry in this way. There are a number of possible positions for the switch, such as cotton, wool, synthetic fiber, and so on, and you can select one of them by turning the knob to point to the option you want.

In the `switch` statement, the selection is determined by the value of an expression that you specify. You define the possible `switch` positions by one or more *case values*, a particular one being selected if the value of the `switch` expression is the same as the particular case value. There is one case value for each possible choice in the `switch`, and all the case values must be distinct.

The general form of the `switch` statement is:

```
switch(expression)
{
case c1:
  // One or more statements for c1...
  break;
case c2:
  // One or more statements for c2...
  break;
// More case statements...
default:
  // Statements for default case...
  break;
}
```

Both `switch` and `case` are keywords. `c1`, `c2`, and so on are integer constants, or expressions that the compiler can evaluate to produce an integer constant; that is, not an expression that has to be executed at run time. The cases can be in any sequence and each case value must be unique to allow the compiler to differentiate between them. When `expression` evaluates to one of the case values, the statements following that case statement are executed.

If the value of the `switch` expression does not match any of the case values, the `switch` automatically selects the `default` case. You can omit the `default` case, in which case the default is to do nothing.

The `break` statement at the end of each case statement causes execution to transfer to the statement following the `switch` block after a case statement executes. If you leave it out, statements for the next case will execute. The `break` at the end of the `default` case is not necessary, but including it is a good idea to provide for the possibility that you add a `case` statement after the `default` case later. Let's see it working.

TRY IT OUT   The switch Statement

You can examine how the `switch` statement works with the following example:

```cpp
// Ex3_05.cpp
// Using the switch statement
#include <iostream>

using std::cin;
```

```cpp
using std::cout;
using std::endl;

int main()
{
  int choice {};                     // Store selection value here

  cout << endl
      << "Your electronic recipe book is at your service." << endl
      << "You can choose from the following delicious dishes: "
      << endl
      << endl << "1 Boiled eggs"
      << endl << "2 Fried eggs"
      << endl << "3 Scrambled eggs"
      << endl << "4 Coddled eggs"
      << endl << endl << "Enter your selection number: ";
  cin >> choice;

  switch(choice)
  {
  case 1: cout << endl << "Boil some eggs." << endl;
          break;
  case 2: cout << endl << "Fry some eggs." << endl;
          break;
  case 3: cout << endl << "Scramble some eggs." << endl;
           break;
  case 4: cout << endl << "Coddle some eggs." << endl;
          break;
  default: cout << endl <<"You entered a wrong number, try raw eggs."
                  << endl;
           break;
  }

  return 0;
}
```

How It Works

The stream output statement displays the input options, and then a selection number is read into the variable choice. The switch statement has the condition specified as simply choice, in parentheses, immediately following the keyword switch. The possible options in the switch are enclosed between braces and are each identified by a *case label*. A case label is the keyword case, followed by the value of choice that corresponds to this option, and terminated by a colon.

As you can see, the statements to be executed for a particular case follow the colon at the end of the case label, and are terminated by a break statement. The break transfers execution to the statement after the switch. The break isn't mandatory, but if you don't include it, execution continues with the statements for the case that follows, which isn't usually what you want. You can demonstrate this by removing the break statements from this example and seeing what happens.

You can put the statements to be executed for a particular case between braces and sometimes this is necessary. For example, if you create a variable within a case statement, you must include braces. The following statement will result in an error message:

```
switch(choice)
{
case 1:
  int count {2};
  cout << "Boil " << count
       << " eggs." << endl;
  // Code to do something with count...
  break;

default:
  cout << endl <<"You entered a wrong number, try raw eggs." << endl;
  break;
}
```

Because it is possible that `count` may not get initialized within the block for the `switch`, you get the following error message:

```
error C2360: initialization of 'count' is skipped by 'default' label
```

You can fix this by writing it as:

```
switch(choice)
{
case 1:
  {
    int count {2};
    cout << "Boil " << count
         << " eggs." << endl;
    // Code to do something with count...
    break;
  }

default:
  cout << endl <<"You entered a wrong number, try raw eggs." << endl;
  break;
}
```

If the value of `choice` doesn't correspond with any of the case values, the statements following the `default` label are executed. A `default` case isn't essential. In its absence, if the value of the test expression doesn't correspond to any of the cases, the `switch` is exited, and the program continues with the next statement after the `switch`.

TRY IT OUT   Sharing a Case

Each of the case expressions in a `switch` statement must be constant expressions that can be evaluated at compile time and must evaluate to a unique integer value. The reason that no two case values can be the same is that the compiler would have no way of knowing which case statement should be executed for that particular value; however, different cases don't need to have a unique action. Several cases can share the same action, as shown here:

```
// Ex3_06.cpp
// Multiple case actions
```

```
#include <iostream>

using std::cin;
using std::cout;
using std::endl;

int main()
{
  char letter {};
  cout << endl
       << "Enter a small letter: ";
  cin >> letter;

  switch(letter*(letter >= 'a' && letter <= 'z'))
  {
   case 'a':  case 'e': case 'i': case 'o': case 'u':
     cout << endl << "You entered a vowel.";
     break;

   case 0:
     cout << endl << "That is not a small letter.";
     break;

   default: cout << endl << "You entered a consonant.";
  }

  cout << endl;
  return 0;
}
```

How It Works

In this example, you have a more complex expression in the switch. If the character entered isn't a lowercase letter, the expression

```
(letter >= 'a' && letter <= 'z')
```

results in the value false; otherwise it evaluates to true. Because letter is multiplied by this expression, the value of the logical expression is converted to an integer — 0 if the logical expression is false and 1 if it is true. Thus, the switch expression evaluates to 0 if a lowercase letter was not entered, and to the value of letter if it was. The statements following the case label case 0 are executed whenever the character code stored in letter does not represent a lowercase letter.

If a lowercase letter was entered, the switch expression evaluates to the same value as letter; so, for all values corresponding to vowels, the output statement following the sequence of case labels that have vowels as values is executed. The same statement executes for any vowel because when any of these case labels is chosen, the following statements are executed until the break statement is reached. You can see that a single action can be taken for a number of different cases by writing the case labels, one after the other, before the statements to be executed. If a lowercase letter that is a consonant is entered, the default case is executed.

Unconditional Branching

The `if` statement provides you with the flexibility to choose to execute one set of statements or another, depending on a specified condition, so the statement execution sequence is varied, depending on the values of the data in the program. The `goto` statement, in contrast, is a blunt instrument. It enables you to branch to a specified program statement unconditionally. The statement to be branched to must be identified by a statement label, which is an identifier defined according to the same rules as a variable name. This is followed by a colon and placed before the statement requiring labeling. Here is an example of a labeled statement:

```
myLabel: cout << "myLabel branch has been activated" << endl;
```

This statement has the label `myLabel`, and an unconditional branch to this statement would be written as follows:

```
goto myLabel;
```

Whenever possible, you should avoid using `goto`s in your program. They tend to encourage convoluted code that can be extremely difficult to follow.

> **NOTE** Because the `goto` is theoretically unnecessary in a program — there's always an alternative approach to using `goto` — a significant cadre of programmers say you should never use it. I don't subscribe to such an extreme view. It is a legal statement, after all, and there are occasions when it can be convenient, such as when you must exit from a deeply nested set of loops (you learn about loops in the next section). I do, however, recommend that you only use it where you can see an obvious advantage over other options that are available; otherwise, you may end up with convoluted, error-prone code that is hard to understand and even harder to maintain.

REPEATING A BLOCK OF STATEMENTS

The capability to repeat a group of statements is fundamental to most applications. Without this, an organization would need to modify the payroll program every time an extra employee was hired, and you would need to reload your favorite game every time you wanted to play. So, let's first understand how a loop works.

What Is a Loop?

A loop executes a sequence of statements subject to a given condition. You can write a loop with the statements that you have met so far. You just need an `if` and the dreaded `goto`. Look at the following example:

```cpp
// Ex3_07.cpp
// Creating a loop with an if and a goto
#include <iostream>

using std::cout;
using std::endl;

int main()
{
  int i {1}, sum {};
  const int max {10};

loop:
  sum += i;              // Add current value of i to sum
  if(++i <= max)
    goto loop;           // Go back to loop until i = 11

  cout << endl
       << "sum = " << sum << endl
       << "i = "   << i   << endl;
  return 0;
}
```

This example accumulates the sum of integers from 1 to 10. The first time through the sequence of statements, i has the initial value 1 and is added to sum, which starts out as zero. In the `if`, i is incremented to 2 and, as long as it is less than or equal to max, the unconditional branch to `loop` occurs, and the value of i, now 2, is added to sum. This continues with i being incremented and added to sum each time, until finally, when i is incremented to 11 in the `if`, the branch back is not executed. If you run this example, you get the following output:

```
sum = 55
i = 11
```

This shows quite clearly how the loop works; however, it uses a `goto` and introduces a label into the program, both of which you should avoid, if possible. You can achieve the same thing, and more, with the `for` statement, which is specifically for writing a loop.

TRY IT OUT   Using the for Loop

You can rewrite the last example using what is known as a `for` loop:

```cpp
// Ex3_08.cpp
// Summing integers with a for loop
#include <iostream>

using std::cout;
```

```
using std::endl;

int main()
{
  int i {1}, sum {};
  const int max {10};

  for(i = 1; i <= max; i++)        // Loop specification
      sum += i;                    // Loop statement

  cout << endl
       << "sum = " << sum << endl
       << "i = "   << i   << endl;
  return 0;
}
```

How It Works

If you compile and run this, you get exactly the same output as the previous example, but the code is much simpler here. The conditions determining the operation of the loop appear in parentheses after the keyword for. There are three expressions that appear within the parentheses, separated by semicolons:

➤ The first expression executes once at the outset and sets the initial conditions for the loop. In this case, it sets i to 1.

➤ The second expression is a logical expression that determines whether the loop statement (or block of statements) should continue to be executed. If the second expression is true, the loop continues to execute; when it is false, the loop ends, and execution continues with the statement that follows the loop. In this case, the loop statement on the following line is executed as long as i is less than or equal to max.

➤ The third expression is evaluated after the loop statement (or block of statements) executes, and in this case increments i at each iteration. After this expression has been evaluated, the second expression is evaluated once more to see whether the loop should continue.

This loop is not exactly the same as the version in Ex3_07.cpp. You can demonstrate this if you set the value of max to 0 in both programs and run them again; then, you will find that the value of sum is 1 in Ex3_07.cpp and 0 in Ex3_08.cpp, and the value of i differs too. The reason for this is that the if version of the program always executes the loop at least once, because you don't check the condition until the end. The for loop doesn't do this, because the condition is checked at the beginning.

The general form of the for loop is:

```
for (initializing_expression ; test_expression ; increment_expression)
     loop_statement;
```

Of course, loop_statement can be a single statement, or a block of statements between braces. The sequence of events in executing the for loop is shown in Figure 3-3.

for loop logic

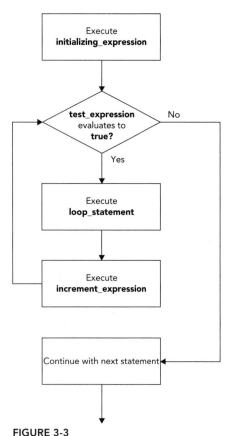

FIGURE 3-3

The expressions controlling the `for` loop are very flexible. You can even write two or more expressions, separated by the comma operator, for each control expression. This gives you a lot of scope in what you can do with a `for` loop.

> **NOTE** The more mathematically minded will know that you can sum the first n integers without using a loop. The sum of the integers from 1 to n is given by the expression ½n(n+1). Using this wouldn't teach you much about loops though.

Variations on the for Loop

Most of the time, the expressions in a `for` loop are used in a fairly standard way: the first to initialize one or more loop counters, the second to test if the loop should continue, and the third to increment or decrement one or more loop counters. You are not obliged to use these expressions in this way, however, and quite a few variations are possible.

The initialization expression can also include a definition for a loop variable. In the previous example, you could have written the loop to include the definition for the loop counter i in the first control expression.

```
for(int i {1}; i <= max; i++)        // Loop specification
    sum += i;                        // Loop statement
```

Naturally, the original definition for i would need to be omitted. If you make this change to the last example, you will find that it does not compile because the loop variable, i, ceases to exist after the loop, so you cannot refer to it in the output statement. A loop has a scope which extends from the for expression to the end of the body of the loop, which of course can be a block of code between braces, as well as just a single statement. The counter i is now defined within the loop scope, so you cannot refer to it in the output statement, which is outside the scope of the loop. If you need to use the value in the counter after the loop has executed, you must define the counter variable *outside the scope of the loop.*

You can omit the initialization expression altogether from the loop. Because i has the initial value 1, you can write the loop as:

```
for(; i <= max; i++)                 // Loop specification
    sum += i;                        // Loop statement
```

You still need the semicolon that separates the initialization expression from the test condition. In fact, both semicolons must always be present, regardless of whether any or all of the control expressions are omitted. If you omit the first semicolon, the compiler is unable to decide which expression has been omitted, or even which semicolon is missing.

The loop statement can be empty. For example, you could place the loop statement in the for loop from the previous example inside the increment expression; in this case the loop becomes:

```
for(; i <= max; sum += i++);         // The whole loop
```

You still need the semicolon after the closing parentheses, to indicate that the loop statement is now empty. If you omit this, the statement immediately following this line is interpreted as the loop statement. Sometimes you'll see the empty loop statement written on a separate line, like the following:

```
for(; i <= max; sum += i++)          // The whole loop
    ;
```

TRY IT OUT   Using Multiple Counters

You can use the comma operator to include multiple counters in a for loop. You can see this in operation in the following program:

```
// Ex3_09.cpp
// Using multiple counters to show powers of 2
#include <iostream>
#include <iomanip>

using std::cout;
```

```
using std::endl;
using std::setw;

int main()
{
  const long max {10L};

  for(long i {}, power {1L}; i <= max; i++, power += power)
     cout << endl
            << setw(10) << i << setw(10) << power;      // Loop statement

  cout << endl;
  return 0;
}
```

How It Works

You create and initialize two variables in the initialization section of the for loop and increment each of them in the increment section. You can create as many variables as you want here, as long as they are of the same type.

You can also specify multiple conditions, separated by commas, in the second expression that represents the test part of the for loop that determines whether it should continue, but this is not generally useful because only the right-most condition affects when the loop ends.

For each increment of i, the value of the variable power is doubled by adding it to itself. This produces the powers of two that we are looking for, and so the program produces the following output:

```
 0           1
 1           2
 2           4
 3           8
 4          16
 5          32
 6          64
 7         128
 8         256
 9         512
10        1024
```

You use the setw() manipulator that you saw in the previous chapter to align the output nicely. You have included the iomanip header file and added a using declaration for the name in the std namespace, so you can use setw() without qualifying the name.

TRY IT OUT   The Indefinite for Loop

If you omit the second control expression that specifies the test condition for a for loop, the value is assumed to be true, so the loop continues indefinitely unless you provide some other means of exiting from it. In fact, you can omit all the expressions in the parentheses after for. This may not seem to be useful, but the reverse is true. You will often come across situations where you want to execute a loop a number of times, but you do not know in advance how many iterations you will need. Have a look at the following:

```
// Ex3_10.cpp
// Using an indefinite for loop to compute an average
#include <iostream>

using std::cin;
using std::cout;
using std::endl;

int main()
{
  double value {};               // Value entered stored here
  double sum {};                 // Total of values accumulated here
  int i {};                      // Count of number of values
  char indicator {'n'};          // Continue or not?

  for(;;)                        // Indefinite loop
{
    cout << endl
         << "Enter a value: ";
    cin >> value;                // Read a value
    ++i;                         // Increment count
    sum += value;                // Add current input to total

    cout << endl
         << "Do you want to enter another value (enter y or n)? ";
    cin >> indicator;            // Read indicator
    if (('n' == indicator) || ('N' == indicator))
      break;                     // Exit from loop
  }

  cout << endl
       << "The average of the " << i
       << " values you entered is " << sum/i << "."
       << endl;
  return 0;
}
```

How It Works

This program computes the average of an arbitrary number of values. After each value is entered, you must indicate whether you want to enter another value, by entering a single character, y or n. Typical output from executing this example is:

```
Enter a value: 10

Do you want to enter another value (enter y or n)? y

Enter a value: 20

Do you want to enter another value (enter y or n)? y

Enter a value: 30

Do you want to enter another value (enter y or n)? n
```

```
The average of the 3 values you entered is 20.
```

After defining and initializing the variables that you're going to use, you start a `for` loop with no expressions specified, so there is no provision for ending it here. The block immediately following is the subject of the loop that is to be repeated.

The loop block performs three basic actions:

➤ It reads a value.

➤ It adds the value read from `cin` to `sum`.

➤ It checks whether you want to continue to enter values.

The first action within the block is to prompt you for input and then read a value into the variable `value`. The value that you enter is added to `sum`, and the count of the number of values, `i`, is incremented. After accumulating the value in `sum`, you are asked if you want to enter another value, and prompted to enter 'y' or 'n' if you have finished. The character that you enter is stored in `indicator`, for testing against 'n' or 'N' in the `if` statement. If neither is found, the loop continues; otherwise, a `break` is executed. The effect of `break` in a loop is similar to its effect in the context of the `switch` statement. It exits the loop immediately by transferring control to the statement following the closing brace of the loop block.

Finally, you output the count of the number of values entered and their average, which is calculated by dividing `sum` by `i`. Of course, `i` is promoted to type `double` before the calculation, as you remember from the casting discussion in Chapter 2.

Using the continue Statement

You write the `continue` statement simply as:

```
continue;
```

Executing `continue` within a loop starts the next loop iteration immediately, skipping over any statements remaining in the body of the loop. I can show how this works with the following code:

```cpp
#include <iostream>

using std::cin;
using std::cout;
using std::endl;

int main()
{
  int value {}, product {1};

  for(int i {1}; i <= 10; i++)
  {
    cout << "Enter an integer: ";
```

```
        cin >> value;

        if(0 == value)              // If value is zero
            continue;               // skip to next iteration

        product *= value;
    }

    cout << "Product (ignoring zeros): " << product
        << endl;

    return 0;
}
```

This loop reads 10 values with the intention of producing the product of the values entered. The `if` checks each value, and if it is zero, the `continue` statement skips to the next iteration. This is so that you don't end up with a zero product if one of the values is zero. Obviously, if a zero value occurred on the last iteration, the loop would end. There are other ways of achieving the same result, but `continue` provides a very useful capability, particularly with complex loops where you may need to skip to the end of the current iteration from various points in the loop.

The effect of the `break` and `continue` statements on the logic of a `for` loop is illustrated in Figure 3-4.

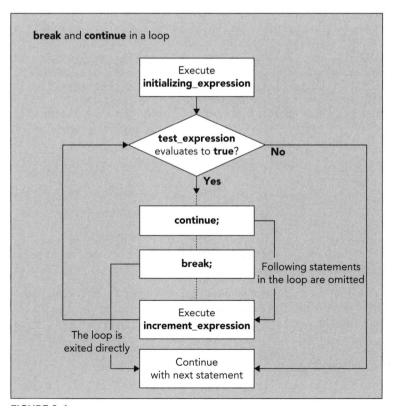

FIGURE 3-4

Obviously, in a real situation, you would use the `break` and `continue` statements with some condition-testing logic to determine when the loop should be exited, or when an iteration of the loop should be skipped. You can also use the `break` and `continue` statements with the other kinds of loop, which I'll discuss later on in this chapter, where they work in exactly the same way.

TRY IT OUT   Using Other Types in Loops

So far, you have only used integers to count loop iterations. You are in no way restricted as to what type of variable you use to count iterations. Look at the following example:

```cpp
// Ex3_11.cpp
// Display ASCII codes for alphabetic characters
#include <iostream>
#include <iomanip>

using std::cout;
using std::endl;
using std::hex;
using std::dec;
using std::setw;

int main()
{
  for(char capital {'A'}, small {'a'}; capital <= 'Z'; capital++, small++)
  {
    cout << endl
         << "\t" << capital                             // Output capital as a character
         << hex << setw(10) << static_cast<int>(capital)   // and as hexadecimal
         << dec << setw(10) << static_cast<int>(capital)   // and as decimal
         << " " << small                         // Output small as a character
         << hex << setw(10) << static_cast<int>(small)   // and as hexadecimal
         << dec << setw(10) << static_cast<int>(small);  // and as decimal
  }

  cout << endl;
  return 0;
}
```

How It Works

Here we have `using` declarations for the names of some new manipulators that are used in the program to affect how the output is presented.

The loop in this example is controlled by the `char` variable `capital`, which you declare along with the variable `small` in the initializing expression. You increment both variables in the third control expression for the loop, so that the value of `capital` varies from 'A' to 'Z', and the value of `small` correspondingly varies from 'a' to 'z'.

The loop contains just one output statement spread over seven lines. The first line is:

```cpp
cout << endl
```

This starts a new line on the screen.

The next three lines are:

```
<< "\t" << capital                                 // Output capital as a character
<< hex << setw(10) << static_cast<int>(capital)    // and as hexadecimal
<< dec << setw(10) << static_cast<int>(capital)    // and as decimal
```

After outputting a tab character on each iteration, the value of capital is displayed three times: as a character, as a hexadecimal value, and as a decimal value.

Inserting the hex manipulator into the cout stream causes subsequent integer data values to be displayed as hexadecimal values, rather than the default decimal representation, so the second output of capital is as a hexadecimal representation of the character code.

You then insert the dec manipulator into the stream to cause succeeding values to be output as decimals once more. By default, a variable of type char is interpreted by the stream as a character, not a numerical value. You get the char variable capital to output as a numerical value by casting its value to type int, using the static_cast<>() operator that you saw in the previous chapter.

The value of small is output in a similar way by the next three lines of the output statement:

```
<< " " << small                                    // Output small as a character
<< hex << setw(10) << static_cast<int>(small)      // and as hexadecimal
<< dec << setw(10) << static_cast<int>(small);     // and as decimal
```

As a result, the program generates the following output:

A	41	65	a	61	97
B	42	66	b	62	98
C	43	67	c	63	99
D	44	68	d	64	100
E	45	69	e	65	101
F	46	70	f	66	102
G	47	71	g	67	103
H	48	72	h	68	104
I	49	73	i	69	105
J	4a	74	j	6a	106
K	4b	75	k	6b	107
L	4c	76	l	6c	108
M	4d	77	m	6d	109
N	4e	78	n	6e	110
O	4f	79	o	6f	111
P	50	80	p	70	112
Q	51	81	q	71	113
R	52	82	r	72	114
S	53	83	s	73	115
T	54	84	t	74	116
U	55	85	u	75	117
V	56	86	v	76	118
W	57	87	w	77	119
X	58	88	x	78	120
Y	59	89	y	79	121
Z	5a	90	z	7a	122

Floating-Point Loop Counters

You can use a floating-point value as a loop counter. Here's an example of a for loop with this kind of counter:

```
double a {0.3}, b {2.5};
for(double x {}; x <= 2.0; x += 0.25)
  cout << "\n\tx = " << x
          << "\ta*x + b = " << a*x + b;
```

This code fragment calculates the value of a*x + b for values of x from 0.0 to 2.0, in steps of 0.25; however, you need to take care when using a floating-point counter in a loop. Many decimal values cannot be represented exactly in binary floating-point form, so discrepancies can build up with cumulative values. This means that you should not code a for loop such that ending the loop depends on a floating-point loop counter reaching a precise value. For example, the following poorly-designed loop never ends:

```
for(double x {}; x != 1.0; x += 0.1)
  cout << x << endl;
```

The intention with this loop is to output the value of x as it varies from 0.0 to 1.0; however, 0.1 has no exact representation as a binary floating-point value, so the value of x is never exactly 1. Thus, the second loop control expression is always false, and the loop continues indefinitely.

> **NOTE** It's easy to see why some decimal fractional values cannot be represented exactly as binary values. In a binary fraction, the digits to the right of the binary point are equivalent to the decimal fractions 1/2, 1/4, 1/8, 1/16, and so on. Thus any binary fraction as a decimal value is the sum of one or more of these decimal fractions. Decimal fractions such as 1/3 or 1/10 that have a denominator that is odd or has an odd factor can never by represented exactly by a sum of fractions that all have an even denominator.

The while Loop

A second kind of loop in C++ is the while loop. Where the for loop is primarily used to repeat a statement or a block for a prescribed number of iterations, the while loop is used to execute a statement or block of statements as long as a specified condition is true. The general form is:

```
while(condition)
  loop_statement;
```

Here loop_statement is executed repeatedly, as long as the condition expression has the value true. After the condition becomes false, the program continues with the statement following the loop. As always, a block of statements between braces could replace loop_statement.

The logic of the while loop is shown in Figure 3-5.

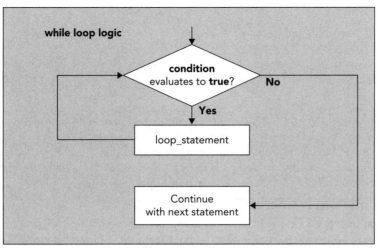

FIGURE 3-5

TRY IT OUT Using the while Loop

You could rewrite the earlier example that computes averages (Ex3_10.cpp) to use the while loop.

```cpp
// Ex3_12.cpp
// Using a while loop to compute an average
#include <iostream>

using std::cin;
using std::cout;
using std::endl;

int main()
{
  double value {};              // Value entered stored here
  double sum {};                // Total of values accumulated here
  int i {};                     // Count of number of values
  char indicator {'y'};         // Continue or not?

  while('y' == indicator )      // Loop as long as y is entered
  {
    cout << endl
         << "Enter a value: ";
    cin >> value;               // Read a value
    ++i;                        // Increment count
    sum += value;               // Add current input to total

    cout << endl
         << "Do you want to enter another value (enter y or n)? ";
    cin >> indicator;           // Read indicator
  }

  cout << endl
```

```
                << "The average of the " << i
                << " values you entered is " << sum/i << "."
                << endl;
      return 0;
    }
```

How It Works

For the same input, this version of the program produces the same output as before. One statement has been updated, and another has been added — they are highlighted in the code. The `for` loop statement has been replaced by the `while` statement, and the test for `indicator` in the `if` has been deleted, as this function is performed by the `while` condition. You have to initialize `indicator` with 'y', in place of the 'n' which appeared previously — otherwise the `while` loop terminates immediately. As long as the condition in the `while` returns `true`, the loop continues.

You can use any expression resulting in `true` or `false` as a `while` loop condition. The example would be better if the loop condition was extended to allow 'Y' to be entered to continue the loop, as well as 'y'. You could modify the `while` as follows to do the trick:

```
    while(('y' == indicator) || ('Y' == indicator))
```

You can also create a `while` loop that potentially executes indefinitely, by using a condition that is always `true`. This can be written as follows:

```
    while(true)
    {
    ...
    }
```

You could also write the loop control expression as the integer value 1, which would be converted to the `bool` value `true`. Naturally, the same requirement applies here as in the case of the indefinite `for` loop: namely, you must provide some way of exiting the loop within the loop block. You'll see other ways to use the `while` loop in Chapter 4.

The do-while Loop

The `do-while` loop is similar to the `while` loop in that the loop continues as long as the specified loop condition remains `true`. The main difference is that the condition is checked at the end of the loop — which contrasts with the `while` loop and the `for` loop, where the condition is checked at the beginning. Consequently, the `do-while` loop statement is always executed at least once. The general form of the `do-while` loop is:

```
    do
    {
       loop_statements;
    }while(condition);
```

The logic of this form of loop is shown in Figure 3-6.

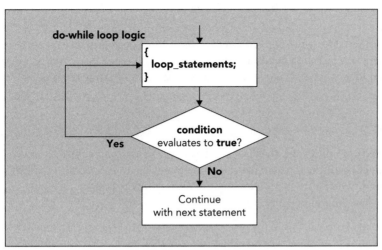

FIGURE 3-6

You could replace the `while` loop in the last version of the program to calculate an average with a do-while loop:

```
do
{
  cout << endl
       << "Enter a value: ";
  cin >> value;                    // Read a value
  ++i;                             // Increment count
  sum += value;                    // Add current input to total

  cout << "Do you want to enter another value (enter y or n)?";
  cin >> indicator;                // Read indicator
} while(('y' == indicator) || ('Y' == indicator));
```

There's little difference between the two versions of the loop, except that this version doesn't depend on the initial value set in `indicator` for correct operation. As long as you want to enter at least one value, which is not unreasonable for the calculation in question, this version is preferable.

The Range-Based for Loop

I am introducing this loop here so all the loops that you have available appear together. The range-based `for` loop enables you to iterate over each of the items in a collection of items in a very simple way. You have not met any collections to which you can apply this loop so far, but you will meet arrays in the next chapter where you can use this loop. I'll discuss how the range-based `for` loop works in more detail then, and you will learn about other kinds of collections that you can apply the range-based `for` loop to in Chapter 10.

Nested Loops

You can nest one loop inside another. The usual application for this will become apparent in Chapter 4 — it's typically applied to repeating actions at different levels of classification. An example might be calculating the total marks for each student in a class, and then repeating the process for each class in a school.

Nested Loops

You can see the effects of nesting one loop inside another by calculating the values of a simple formula. A factorial of an integer is the product of all the integers from 1 to the integer in question; the factorial of 3, for example, is 1 times 2 times 3, which is 6. The following program computes the factorial of integers that you enter (until you've had enough):

```
// Ex3_13.cpp
// Demonstrating nested loops to compute factorials
#include <iostream>

using std::cin;
using std::cout;
using std::endl;

int main()
{
  char indicator {'n'};
  long value {}, factorial {};

  do
  {
     cout << endl << "Enter an integer value: ";
     cin >> value;

     factorial = 1L;
     for(long i {2L}; i <= value; i++)
        factorial *= i;

     cout << "Factorial " << value << " is " << factorial;
     cout << endl << "Do you want to enter another value (y or n)? ";
     cin >> indicator;
  } while(('y' == indicator) || ('Y' == indicator));

  return 0;
}
```

If you compile and execute this example, the typical output produced is:

```
Enter an integer value: 5
Factorial 5 is 120
Do you want to enter another value (y or n)? y

Enter an integer value: 10
Factorial 10 is 3628800
```

```
Do you want to enter another value (y or n)? y

Enter an integer value: 13
Factorial 13 is 1932053504
Do you want to enter another value (y or n)? y

Enter an integer value: 22
Factorial 22 is -522715136
Do you want to enter another value (y or n)? n
```

How It Works

Factorial values grow very fast. In fact, 12 is the largest input value for which this example produces a correct result. The factorial of 13 is actually 6,227,020,800, not 1,932,053,504 as the program tells you. If you run it with even larger input values, leading digits are lost in the result stored in the variable `factorial`, and you may well get negative values for the factorial, as you do when you ask for the factorial of 22.

This situation doesn't cause any error messages, so it is of paramount importance that you are sure that the values you're dealing with in a program can be contained in the permitted range of the type of variable you're using. You also need to consider the effects of incorrect input values. Errors of this kind, which occur silently, can be very hard to find.

The outer of the two nested loops is the `do-while` loop, which controls when the program ends. As long as you keep entering y or Y at the prompt, the program continues to calculate factorial values. The factorial for the integer entered is calculated in the inner `for` loop. This is executed `value-1` times, to multiply the variable `factorial` (with an initial value of 1) with successive integers from 2 to `value`.

TRY IT OUT   Another Nested Loop

Nested loops can be a little confusing, so let's try another example. This program generates a multiplication table of a given size:

```cpp
// Ex3_14.cpp
// Using nested loops to generate a multiplication table
#include <iostream>
#include <iomanip>

using std::cout;
using std::endl;
using std::setw;

int main()
{
  const int size {12};                 // Size of table
  int i {}, j {};                      // Loop counters

  cout << endl                         // Output table title
       << size << " by " << size << " Multiplication Table" << endl << endl;
```

```
    cout << endl << "     |";

    for(i = 1; i <= size; i++)            // Loop to output column headings
        cout << setw(3) << i << " ";

    cout << endl;                         // Newline for underlines

    for(i = 0; i <= size; i++)
        cout << "_____";                  // Underline each heading

    for(i = 1; i <= size; i++)            // Outer loop for rows
    {
        cout << endl
            << setw(3) << i << " |";       // Output row label
        for(j = 1; j <= size; j++)        // Inner loop for the rest of the row
            cout << setw(3) << i*j << " "; // End of inner loop
    }                                     // End of outer loop
    cout << endl;

    return 0;
}
```

The output from this example is:

```
12 by 12 Multiplication Table

     |  1   2   3   4   5   6   7   8   9  10  11  12

  1  |  1   2   3   4   5   6   7   8   9  10  11  12
  2  |  2   4   6   8  10  12  14  16  18  20  22  24
  3  |  3   6   9  12  15  18  21  24  27  30  33  36
  4  |  4   8  12  16  20  24  28  32  36  40  44  48
  5  |  5  10  15  20  25  30  35  40  45  50  55  60
  6  |  6  12  18  24  30  36  42  48  54  60  66  72
  7  |  7  14  21  28  35  42  49  56  63  70  77  84
  8  |  8  16  24  32  40  48  56  64  72  80  88  96
  9  |  9  18  27  36  45  54  63  72  81  90  99 108
 10  | 10  20  30  40  50  60  70  80  90 100 110 120
 11  | 11  22  33  44  55  66  77  88  99 110 121 132
 12  | 12  24  36  48  60  72  84  96 108 120 132 144
```

How It Works

The table title is produced by the first output statement. The next output statement, combined with the loop following it, generates the column headings. Each column is five characters wide, so the heading value is displayed in a field width of three, specified by the setw(3) manipulator, followed by two spaces. The output statement preceding the loop outputs four spaces and a vertical bar above the first column, which contains the row headings. A series of underline characters is then displayed beneath the column headings.

The nested loop generates the main table contents. The outer loop repeats once for each row, so i is the row number. The output statement

```
cout << endl
     << setw(3) << i << " |";        // Output row label
```

goes to a new line for the start of a row, and then outputs the row heading given by the value of i in a field width of three, followed by a space and a vertical bar.

A row of values is generated by the inner loop:

```
for(j = 1; j <= size; j++)          // Inner loop for the rest of the row
   cout << setw(3) << i*j << " ";    // End of inner loop
```

This loop outputs values i*j, corresponding to the product of the current row value i, and each of the column values in turn by varying j from 1 to size. So, for each iteration of the outer loop, the inner loop executes size iterations. The values are positioned in the same way as the column headings. When the outer loop ends, a new line is printed and the return is executed to end the program.

SUMMARY

In this chapter, you learned all the essential mechanisms for making decisions in C++ programs. The ability to compare values and change the course of program execution is what differentiates a computer from a simple calculator. You need to be comfortable with all of the decision-making statements I have discussed because they are all used very frequently. You have also gone through all the facilities for repeating a group of statements. Loops are a fundamental programming technique that you will need to use in every program of consequence that you write. You will find you use the for loop most often, closely followed by the while loop.

EXERCISES

1. Write a program that reads numbers from cin and then sums them, stopping when 0 has been entered. Construct three versions of this program, using the while, do-while, and for loops.

2. Write a program to read characters from the keyboard and count the vowels. Stop counting when a Q (or a q) is encountered. Use a combination of an indefinite loop to get the characters, and a switch statement to count them.

3. Write a program to print out the multiplication tables from 2 to 12, in columns.

4. Imagine that in a program you want to set a 'file open mode' variable based on two attributes: the file type, which can be text or binary, and the way in which you want to open the file to read or write it, or append data to it. Using the bitwise operators (& and |) and a set of flags, devise a method to allow a single integer variable to be set to any combination of the two attributes. Write a program that sets such a variable and then decodes it, printing out its setting, for all possible combinations of the attributes.

➤ WHAT YOU LEARNED IN THIS CHAPTER

TOPIC	CONCEPT
Relational operators	The relational operators allow you to combine logical values or expressions that result in a logical value. They yield a `bool` value — `true` or `false` — as the result that you can use in an `if` statement.
Decisions based on numerical values	You can make decisions based on conditions that return non-`bool` values. Any non-zero value is cast to `true` when a condition is tested; zero casts to `false`.
Statements for decision-making	The `if` statement provides the primary decision-making capability in C++. Further flexibility is provided by the `switch` statement and the conditional operator.
Loop statements	There are four basic methods for repeating a block of statements: the `for` loop, the `while` loop, the `do-while` loop, and the range-based `for` loop. The `for` loop allows the loop to repeat a given number of times. The `while` loop allows a loop to continue as long as a specified condition returns `true`. The `do-while` executes the loop at least once and allows continuation of the loop as long as a specified condition returns `true`. The range-based `for` loop iterates over the items in a collection.
Nested loops	Any kind of loop may be nested within any other kind of loop.
The `continue` keyword	The keyword `continue` allows you to skip the remainder of the current iteration in a loop and go straight to the next iteration.
The `break` keyword	The keyword `break` provides an immediate exit from a loop. It also provides an exit from a `switch` at the end of statements in a `case`.

Arrays, Strings, and Pointers

WHAT YOU WILL LEARN IN THIS CHAPTER:

- ➤ How to use arrays
- ➤ How to define and initialize arrays of different types
- ➤ How to use the range-based `for` loop with an array
- ➤ How to define and use multidimensional arrays
- ➤ How to use pointers
- ➤ How to define and initialize pointers of different types
- ➤ The relationship between arrays and pointers
- ➤ How to define references and some initial ideas on their uses

WROX.COM CODE DOWNLOADS FOR THIS CHAPTER

You can find the wrox.com code downloads for this chapter on the Download Code tab at www.wrox.com/go/beginningvisualc. The code is in the Chapter 4 download and individually named according to the names throughout the chapter.

HANDLING MULTIPLE DATA VALUES OF THE SAME TYPE

You already know how to define and initialize variables of various types that each holds a single item of information; I'll refer to single items of data as *data elements*. The most obvious extension to the idea of a variable is to be able to reference several data elements of a particular type with a single variable name. This would enable you to handle applications of a much broader scope.

Let's consider an example. Suppose that you needed to write a payroll program. Using a separate variable for each individual's pay, tax liability, and so on, would be an uphill task to say the least. A more convenient way to handle such a problem would be to reference an employee by some kind of generic name — employeeName to take an imaginative example — and to have other generic names for the kinds of data related to each employee, such as pay and tax. Of course, you would need some means of picking out a particular employee from the whole bunch, together with the data from the generic variables associated with them. This kind of requirement arises with any collection of like entities that you want to handle, whether they're baseball players or battleships. Naturally, C++ provides you with a way to deal with this.

Arrays

One way to solve these problems is to use an *array*. An array is a number of memory locations called *array elements* or simply *elements*, each of which stores an item of data of the same given data type, and which are all referenced through the same variable name. The employee names in a payroll program could be stored in one array, the pay for each employee in another, and the tax due for each employee could be stored in a third array.

You select an element in an array using an *index* value. An index is an integer representing the sequence number of the element in the array. The first element has the index 0, the second 1, and so on. You can also envisage the index for an array element as being the offset from the first element. The first element has an offset of 0 and therefore an index of 0, and an index value of 3 will refer to the fourth element of an array.

The basic structure of an array is illustrated in Figure 4-1.

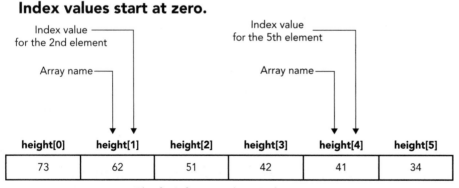

The **height** array has 6 elements.

FIGURE 4-1

Figure 4-1 shows an array with the name height that has six elements. These might be the heights of the members of a family, for instance, recorded to the nearest inch. Because there are six elements, the index values run from 0 through 5. You refer to a particular element by writing the array name followed by the index value of the element between square brackets. The third element is height [2], for example. If you think of the index as the offset from the first element, it's easy to see that the index for the fourth element will be 3.

The memory required to store each element is determined by its type, and all the elements of an array are stored in a contiguous block of memory.

Declaring Arrays

You define an array in essentially the same way as you defined the variables that you have seen up to now. The only difference is that you specify the number of array elements between square brackets following the array name. For example, you could define the integer array height, shown in the previous figure, with the following statement:

```
long height[6];
```

A long value occupies 4 bytes, so the whole array requires 24 bytes. Arrays can be of any size, subject to the constraints imposed by the amount of memory in the computer on which your program is running.

Arrays can be of any type. For example, to define arrays to store the capacity and power output of a series of engines, you could write:

```
double engine_size[10];      // Engine size in cubic inches
double horsepower[10];       // Engine power output
```

If auto mechanics is your thing, this would enable you to store the cubic capacity and power output of up to 10 engines, referenced by index values from 0 to 9. As you have seen with other variables, you can define several arrays of a given type in a single statement, but in practice it is almost always better to define them in separate statements.

TRY IT OUT   Using Arrays

Imagine that you have recorded the amount of gasoline you have bought for the car and the odometer reading each time. You can write a program to analyze this data to see how the gas consumption looks on each occasion you bought gas:

```cpp
// Ex4_01.cpp
// Calculating gas mileage
#include <iostream>
#include <iomanip>

using std::cin;
using std::cout;
using std::endl;
using std::setw;

int main()
{
   const int MAX {20};                  // Maximum number of values
   double gas[ MAX ];                    // Gas quantity in gallons
   long miles[ MAX ];                    // Odometer readings
   int count {};                         // Loop counter
   char indicator {'y'};                 // Input indicator

   while( ('y' == indicator || 'Y' == indicator) && count < MAX )
   {
```

```
      cout << endl << "Enter gas quantity: ";
      cin >> gas[count];                     // Read gas quantity
      cout << "Enter odometer reading: ";
      cin >> miles[count];                   // Read odometer value

      ++count;
      cout << "Do you want to enter another(y or n)? ";
      cin >> indicator;
    }

    if(count <= 1)                           // count = 1 after 1 entry completed
    {                                        // ... we need at least 2
      cout << endl << "Sorry - at least two readings are necessary.";
      return 0;
    }

    // Output results from 2nd entry to last entry
    for(int i {1}; i < count; i++)
    {
      cout << endl
           << setw(2) << i << "."            // Output sequence number
           << "Gas purchased = " << gas[i] << " gallons" // Output gas
           << " resulted in "                // Output miles per gallon
           << (miles[i] - miles[i - 1])/gas[i] << " miles per gallon.";
    }
    cout << endl;
    return 0;
}
```

The program assumes that you fill the tank each time, so the gas bought was the amount used by driving the distance recorded. Here's an example of the output:

```
Enter gas quantity: 12.8
Enter odometer reading: 25832
Do you want to enter another(y or n)? y

Enter gas quantity: 14.9
Enter odometer reading: 26337
Do you want to enter another(y or n)? y

Enter gas quantity: 11.8
Enter odometer reading: 26598
Do you want to enter another(y or n)? n

 1.Gas purchased = 14.9 gallons resulted in 33.8926 miles per gallon.
 2.Gas purchased = 11.8 gallons resulted in 22.1186 miles per gallon.
```

How It Works

Because you need to take the difference between two odometer readings to calculate the miles covered for the gas used, you use only the odometer reading from the first pair of input values — you ignore the gas bought in the first instance as that would have been used earlier. During the second period in the output, the traffic must have been really bad — or maybe the parking brake was left on.

The dimensions of the arrays gas and miles that store the input data are determined by the value of the constant, MAX. By changing the value of MAX, you can change the program to accommodate a different maximum number of input values. This technique makes a program flexible in the amount of information that it can handle. Of course, all the program code must be written taking account of the array dimensions, or of any other parameters specified by `const` variables. This presents little difficulty in practice, so there's no reason not to adopt this approach. You'll see later how to allocate memory as the program executes, so that you don't need to fix the memory for data storage in advance.

Entering the Data

The data values are read in the `while` loop. Because the loop variable `count` can run from 0 to `MAX - 1`, the user cannot enter more values than the array can handle. You initialize `count` and `indicator` to 0 and `'y'` respectively, so the `while` loop is entered at least once. There's a prompt for each input value and the value is read into the appropriate array element. The element used to store a particular value is determined by `count`, which is 0 for the first input. The array element is specified in the `cin` statement by using `count` as an index, and `count` is then incremented, ready for the next value.

After you enter each value, the program prompts for confirmation that another value is to be entered. The character entered is read into `indicator` and tested in the loop condition. The loop will terminate unless `'y'` or `'Y'` is entered and `count` is less than the specified maximum value, `MAX`.

After the input loop ends (by whatever means), `count` contains one more than the index of the last element entered in each array. (Remember, you increment it after you enter each value). This is checked to verify that at least two pairs of values were entered. If this wasn't the case, the program ends with a suitable message because two odometer values are needed to calculate a mileage value.

Producing the Results

The output is generated in the `for` loop. The control variable `i` runs from 1 to `count-1`, allowing mileage to be calculated as the difference between the current element, `miles[i]`, and the previous element, `miles[i - 1]`. An index value can be any expression evaluating to an integer that represents a legal index for the array in question, which is a value from 0 to one less than the number of elements in the array.

If the value of an index is outside the range of the array elements, you will reference a spurious location that may contain other data, garbage, or even program code. If the reference to such an element is in an expression, you will use some arbitrary value in the calculation, which certainly produces a result that you did not intend. If you are storing a result in an array element using an illegal index, you will overwrite whatever happens to be in that location. When this is part of your program code, the results are catastrophic. If you use illegal index values, there are no warnings produced, either by the compiler or at run time. The only way to guard against this is to code your program to prevent it from happening.

NOTE *Visual C++ has a code analysis feature that you can access via the ANALYZE menu. This will scan your code for issues and can sometimes detect and warn against problems such as accessing array elements out of bounds.*

The output is generated by a single statement in the last loop for all values entered after the first. A line number is generated for each line of output using the loop control variable `i`. Miles per gallon is calculated directly in the output statement. You can use array elements in the same way as any other variables in an expression.

Initializing Arrays

To initialize an array in its definition, you put the initializing values in an initializer list. Here's an example:

```
int engine_size[5] { 200, 250, 300, 350, 400 };
```

The array has the name `engine_size` and has five elements that each store a value of type `int`. The values in the initializing list correspond to successive index values, so in this case `engine_size[0]` has the value 200, `engine_size[1]` the value 250, `engine_size[2]` the value 300, and so on.

You must not specify more initializing values than there are elements in the array, but you can include fewer. If there *are* fewer, the values are assigned to successive elements, starting with the first — which is the one corresponding to index 0. Array elements for which you don't provide a value are initialized with zero. This isn't the same as supplying no initializing list. Without an initializing list, the array elements contain junk values. You can initialize all array elements to zero with an empty initializer list. For example:

```
long data[100] {};          // Initialize all elements to zero
```

You can also omit the dimension of an array, provided you supply initializing values. The number of array elements will be the number of initializing values. For example:

```
int value[] { 2, 3, 4 };
```

This defines an array with three elements that have initial values 2, 3, and 4.

> **NOTE** *The older syntax for initializing arrays has* = *preceding the initializer list, thus:*
>
> ```
> int value[] = { 2, 3, 4 };
> ```
>
> *This syntax is still valid so you will come across it from time to time.*

TRY IT OUT Initializing an Array

This example demonstrates that you'll have junk values in arrays that you don't initialize:

```cpp
// Ex4_02.cpp
// Demonstrating array initialization
#include <iostream>
#include <iomanip>

using std::cout;
using std::endl;
using std::setw;

int main()
{
    int value[5] { 1, 2, 3 };
    int junk [5];

    cout << endl;
    for(int i {}; i < 5; i++)
```

```
            cout << setw(12) << value[i];

        cout << endl;
        for(int i {}; i < 5; i++)
            cout << setw(12) << junk[i];

        cout << endl;
        return 0;
    }
```

You define two arrays, `value` and `junk`. You initialize `value` in part, and you don't initialize `junk` at all. The program generates two lines of output, which on my computer look like this:

```
            1            2            3            0            0
    -858993460   -858993460   -858993460   -858993460   -858993460
```

The second line (corresponding to values of `junk[0]` to `junk[4]`) may be different on your PC.

How It Works

The first three values of the `value` array are the initializing values, and the last two have the default value of `0`. In the case of `junk`, all the values are meaningless in the context of your program because you didn't provide any initial values.

> **NOTE** *In debug mode bytes in uninitialized variables will be set to 0xcc so the values will not be arbitrary. You can see in the previous output that the uninitialized variable values are all identical because this was compiled in debug mode.*

Using the Range-based for Loop

You have seen that you can use a `for` loop to iterate over all the elements in an array. The range-based `for` loop makes this even easier. The loop is easy to understand through an example:

```
double temperatures[] {65.5, 68.0, 75.0, 77.5, 76.4, 73.8,80.1};
double sum {};
int count {};
for(double t : temperatures)
{
  sum += t;
  ++count;
}
double average = sum/count;
```

This calculates the average of the values in the `temperatures` array. The parentheses following `for` contain two things separated by a colon; the first specifies the variable that will access each of the values from the collection specified by the second. The `t` variable will be assigned the value of each element in the `temperatures` array in turn before executing the loop body. This accumulates the sum of the array elements . The loop also accumulates the total number of elements in `count` so the average can be calculated after the loop.

You could also write the loop using the `auto` keyword:

```
for(auto temperature : temperatures)
{
  sum += temperature;
  ++count;
}
```

The `auto` keyword tells the compiler to determine the type for the local variable that holds the current value from the array type. The compiler knows that the array elements are of type `double`, so t will be of type `double`.

You cannot modify the values of the array elements in the range-based `for` loop as it is written here. You can only access the element values for use elsewhere. With the loop written as it is, element values are copied to the loop variable. You could access the array elements directly specifying the loop variable as a *reference*. You learn about references later in this chapter.

> **NOTE** *The C++ library provides the* `_countof()` *function that returns the number of elements in an array. You just put the array name between the parentheses. The* `cstdlib` *header needs to be included to use this function. Many other standard library headers such as* `iostream` *include* `cstdlib`*. You could calculate the average temperature like this:*
>
> ```
> for(auto temperature : temperatures)
> {
>   sum += temperature;
> }
> sum /= _countof(temperatures);
> ```
>
> `_countof()` *is a Microsoft extension and not standard C++.*

Multidimensional Arrays

Arrays with one index are referred to as *one-dimensional arrays*. You can define an array with more than one index, in which case it is a *multidimensional* array. Suppose you have a field in which you are growing bean plants in rows of 10, and the field contains 12 rows so there are 120 plants in all. You could define an array to record the weight of beans produced by each plant using the statement:

```
double beans[12][10];
```

This defines the two-dimensional array `beans`, the first index being the row number, and the second index the plant number within the row. To refer to an element requires two index values. For example, you could set the value of the element reflecting the fifth plant in the third row with the statement:

```
beans[2][4] = 10.7;
```

Remember that index values start from zero, so the row index is 2 and the index for the fifth plant within the row is 4.

Being a successful bean farmer, you might have several identical fields planted with beans in the same pattern. Assuming that you have eight fields, you could use a three-dimensional array to record data about these, defined thus:

```
double beans[8][12][10];
```

This records production for the 10 plants in each of the 12 rows in a field and the leftmost index references one of the 8 fields. If you ever get to bean farming on an international scale, you can use a four-dimensional array, with the extra dimension designating the country. Assuming that you're as good a salesman as you are a farmer, growing this quantity of beans is likely to affect the ozone layer.

Arrays are stored in memory such that the rightmost index varies most rapidly. Thus, the array `data[3][4]` is three one-dimensional arrays of four elements each. The arrangement of this array is illustrated in Figure 4-2.

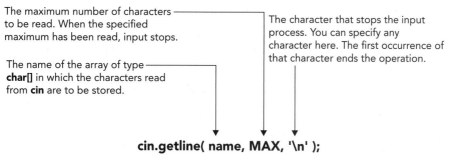

FIGURE 4-2

The elements of the array are stored in a contiguous block of memory, as indicated by the arrows in Figure 4-2. The first index selects a particular row within the array, and the second index selects an element within a row.

A two-dimensional array is really a one-dimensional array of one-dimensional arrays. An array with three dimensions is actually a one-dimensional array of elements where each element is a one-dimensional array of one-dimensional arrays. This is not something you need to worry about most of the time. However, it implies that for the array in Figure 4-2, the expressions `data[0]`, `data[1]`, and `data[2]` reference one-dimensional arrays.

Initializing Multidimensional Arrays

To initialize a multidimensional array, you use an extension of the method used for a one-dimensional array. For example, you can define and initialize a two-dimensional array, `data`, with the statement:

```
long data[2][4] {
                  { 1,  2,  3,  5 },
                  { 7, 11, 13, 17 }
                };
```

The initial values for each row are within their own pair of braces. Because there are four elements in each row, there are four initial values in each group, and because there are two rows, there are two groups between braces, each group of initial values being separated from the next by a comma.

You can omit initial values in any row, in which case the remaining elements in the row are zero. For example:

```
long data[2][4] {
                    { 1,  2,  3      },
                    { 7, 11          }
                };
```

I have spaced out the initial values to show where values have been omitted. The elements `data[0]` `[3]`, `data[1][2]`, and `data[1][3]` have no initializing values and are therefore zero.

To initialize the entire array with zeros you can write:

```
long data[2][4] {};
```

If you are initializing arrays with even more dimensions, remember that you need as many nested braces for groups of initial values as there are dimensions in the array — unless you're initializing the array with zeros.

You can let the compiler work out the first dimension in an array, but only the first, regardless of the number of dimensions.

TRY IT OUT Using a Multidimensional Array

You can use a multidimensional array to figure out the average bean plant production in each of a number of rows in a field:

```
// Ex4_03.cpp
// Storing bean plant production in an array
#include <iostream>              // For stream I/O
#include <iomanip>               // For stream manipulators
using namespace std;            // Any name in std namespace

int main()
{
  const int plant_row_count{ 6 };       // Count of plants in a row
  double beans[][plant_row_count] {     // Production for each plant
    { 12, 15 },
    { 0, 10, 13, 0, 11, 2 },
    { 8, 7, 10, 10, 13      },
    { 9, 8, 11, 13, 16      }
  };

  double averages[_countof(beans)] {};    // Stores average plant production
  for (int row{}; row < _countof(beans); ++row)
  {
    for (int plant{}; plant < plant_row_count; ++plant)
    {
      averages[row] += beans[row][plant];
    }
```

```
        averages[row] /= plant_row_count;
    }

    cout << "Average production per row is :"
            << setiosflags(ios::fixed)              // Fixed point output
            << setprecision(2)                      // 2 decimal places
            << endl;

    int n{};                                        // Row number
    for (double ave : averages)
        cout << "Row " << ++n << setw(10) << ave << endl;

    return 0;
}
```

How It Works

There's a `using` directive so all names in the `std` namespace can be used without qualification. The first statement in `main()` defines `plant_row_count` as a `const` variable, and this stores the number of plants in a row. The next statement defines and initializes the two-dimensional `beans` array. The first dimension is deduced by the compiler from the initializer list and the second dimension is specified by `plant_row_count`. This would result in an error message if `plant_row_count` was not `const`. The initial values for elements in each row are between braces, and the number of pairs of inner braces determines the first row dimension. The number of elements in a row is defined explicitly, so if you inadvertently specify more initial values than there are elements in a row, you will get an error message. Where you specify fewer than `plant_row_count` values for a row, the remaining elements in the row will be 0.

The next statement defines and initializes an array to hold the average plant production for each row:

```
        double averages[_countof(beans)] {};    // Stores average plant production
```

The `_countof()` macro determines the number of rows in `beans`. Specifying just the array name references the array of rows. The array name with a single index would reference a particular row, so `_countof(beans[0])` would return the number of elements in the first row. There are no values in the initializer list so all elements in `averages` will be initialized to 0.

The averages for the rows are calculated in nested loops:

```
        for (int row{}; row < _countof(beans); ++row)
        {
          for (int plant{}; plant < plant_row_count; ++plant)
          {
            averages[row] += beans[row][plant];
          }
          averages[row] /= plant_row_count;
        }
```

The outer `for` loop iterates over the rows. The inner loop iterates over the plants in a row, adding each production value to the `averages` element for the row. The average is calculated by dividing the sum accumulated in `averages[row]` by the number of plants in a row.

When the nested loops end, this statement executes:

```
cout << "Average production per row is :"
     << setiosflags(ios::fixed)              // Fixed point output
     << setprecision(2)                      // 2 decimal places
     << endl;
```

This outputs a message to precede the output of the averages and writes two manipulators to the stream. The `std::setiosflags()` manipulator is used to set flags that affect how output is presented. In this case `ios::fixed` appears between the parentheses, which ensures a floating-point value is displayed with fixed-point notation and not in scientific notation. Sending `std::setprecision()` to the stream causes subsequent floating-point output to include the number of decimal places specified between the parentheses.

The averages are output using a range-based `for` loop:

```
int n{};                                     // Row number
for (double ave : averages)
   cout << "Row " << ++n << setw(10) << ave << endl;
```

The loop variable `ave` will be assigned each of the values in the `averages` array in turn. You could use `auto` instead of type `double`.

WORKING WITH C-STYLE STRINGS

An array of `char` elements is called a *character array* and is generally used to store a C-style string. A character string is a sequence of characters with a special character appended to indicate the end of the string. This character is defined by the escape sequence `\0`. It's referred to as the *null or NUL character* because it's a byte with all bits zero. A string terminated by null is referred to as a *C-style string* because it originated in the C language.

This is not the only representation of a string. You'll meet much safer representations in Chapter 8. You should avoid using C-style strings in new code, but they often occur in existing programs so you need to know about them.

Each character in a non-Unicode string occupies one byte, so with the terminating null, the number of bytes a string occupies is one more than the number of characters in the string. You can define a character array and initialize it with a string literal like this:

```
char movie_star[15] {"Marilyn Monroe"};    // 14 characters plus null
```

The terminating `'\0'` is supplied automatically. If you include one explicitly in the string literal, you'll end up with two. You must allow for the terminating null when you specify the array dimension.

You can omit the dimension and let the compiler work it out:

```
char president[] {"Ulysses Grant"};
```

The compiler allocates enough elements to hold the characters in the string plus the terminating null, so this array will have 14 elements. Of course, if you use the array later to store a different string, the new string must not exceed 14 bytes including its terminating null character. In general, it is your responsibility to ensure that an array is large enough for any string you store in it.

You can create strings of Unicode characters, the characters in the string being of type `wchar_t`:

```
wchar_t president[] {L"Ulysses Grant"};
```

The `L` prefix indicates that the literal is a wide character string, so each character, including the terminating null, will occupy two bytes. Of course, indexing the string references characters, not bytes, so `president[2]` corresponds to the character `L'y'`.

The Unicode encoding for type `wchar_t` is UTF-16. There are other encodings such as UTF-8 and UTF-32. Whenever I refer to just Unicode in the book I mean UTF-16.

> **NOTE** You can also initialize a character array with = preceding the initializer list, but the syntax without = is preferred.

String Input

The `iostream` header contains definitions of functions for reading characters from the keyboard. The one that you'll look at here is the `getline()` function that reads a sequence of characters from the keyboard and stores it in an array as a string terminated by `'\0'`. You typically use `getline()` like this:

```
const int MAX {80};               // Maximum string length including \0
char name[MAX];                   // Array to store a string
cin.getline(name, MAX, '\n');     // Read input line as a string
```

These statements define the `char` array `name` with `MAX` elements and then read characters from `cin` using `getline()`. The source of the data, `cin`, is written as shown, with a period separating it from the function name. The period indicates that the `getline()` function is the one belonging to the `cin` object. You will learn more about this syntax when you learn about classes. Meanwhile, just take it for granted. The significance of each argument to the `getline()` function is shown in Figure 4-3.

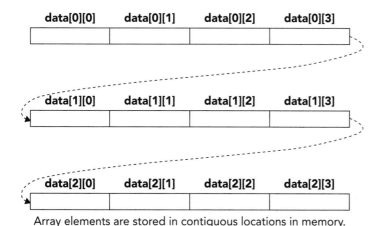

Array elements are stored in contiguous locations in memory.

FIGURE 4-3

Because the last argument is '\n' (newline or end line character) and the second argument is MAX, characters are read from cin until the '\n' character is read, or when MAX-1 characters have been read, whichever occurs first. The maximum number of characters read is MAX-1 rather than MAX to allow for the '\0' character to be appended to the characters stored in the array. The '\n' character is generated when you press the *Return* key and is therefore usually the most convenient character to end input. You can specify something else by changing the last argument. The '\n' isn't stored in the array name, but as I said, '\0' is stored at the end of the input string in the array.

TRY IT OUT Programming with Strings

This program reads a string from the keyboard and counts its characters.

```cpp
// Ex4_04.cpp
// Counting string characters
#include <iostream>
using std::cin;
using std::cout;
using std::endl;

int main()
{
    const int MAX {80};              // Maximum array dimension
    char buffer[MAX];                // Input buffer
    int count {};                    // Character count

    cout << "Enter a string of less than "
         << MAX << " characters:\n";
    cin.getline(buffer, MAX, '\n');  // Read a string until \n

    while(buffer[count] != '\0')     // Increment count as long as
        count++;                     // the current character is not null

    cout << endl
         << "The string \"" << buffer
         << "\" has " << count << " characters.";
    cout << endl;
    return 0;
}
```

Typical output from this program is as follows:

```
Enter a string of less than 80 characters:
Radiation fades your genes
The string "Radiation fades your genes" has 26 characters.
```

How It Works

This program defines a character array buffer and reads a string into it from the keyboard after prompting for the input. Input ends when the user presses Enter, or when MAX-1 characters have been read.

A `while` loop counts the number of characters in `buffer`. The loop continues as long as the character in `buffer[count]` is not `'\0'`. This sort of checking on the current element while stepping through an array is a common technique. The only action in the loop is to increment `count` for each non-null character. There is a library function that will do what this loop does; you learn about it later in this chapter.

Finally, the string and the character count are displayed by a single output statement. Note the use of the escape sequence `'\"'` to output a double quote.

String Literals

You have seen that you can write a string literal between double quotes and you can add `L` as a prefix to specify a Unicode string. You can split a long string over more than one line with each segment between double quotes. For example:

```
"This is a very long string that "

"has been spread over two lines."
```

C++ supports the use of *regular expressions* through the `regex` header. I don't have the space to cover these in this book, but regular expressions typically involve strings with lots of backslash characters. Having to use the escape sequence for each backslash character makes regular expressions hard to enter correctly and even harder to read. The *raw string literal* gets over the problem. A raw string literal can contain any character, without necessitating the use of escape sequences. Here's an example:

```
R"(The "\t" escape sequence is a tab character.)"
```

As a normal string literal, this would be:

```
"The \"\\t\" escape sequence is a tab character."
```

The `R` indicates the start of a raw string literal and the string is delimited by `"(` and `)"`. All characters between the delimiters are "as is" — escape sequences are not recognized as such. This immediately raises the question of how you include `)"` as part of a raw string literal. This is not a problem. The delimiters for a raw string literal in general can be `"char_sequence(` at the beginning and `)char_sequence"` at the end. `char_sequence` is a sequence of characters that must be the same at both ends and can be up to 16 characters; it must not contain parentheses, spaces, control characters, or backslashes. Here's an example:

```
R"*("a = b*(c-d)")*"
```
is equivalent to `"\"a = b*(c-d)\""`

The raw string contains the characters between `"*(` and `)*"`. You can define a raw string of wide characters by prefixing R with L.

Using the Range-based for Loop with Strings

You can use a range-based `for` loop to access the characters in a string:

```cpp
char text[] {"Exit signs are on the way out."};
int count {};
cout << "The string contains the following characters:" << endl;
for (auto ch : text)
{
  ++count;
  cout << ch << " ";
}
cout << endl << "The string contains "
<< (count-1) << " characters." << endl;
```

The loop outputs each string character, including the null at the end, and accumulates a count of the total number of characters. The count includes the null that terminates the string so its value is reduced by 1 before output.

TRY IT OUT Storing Multiple Strings

You can use a two-dimensional array to store several C-style strings. You can see how this works with an example:

```cpp
// Ex4_05.cpp
// Storing strings in an array
#include <iostream>
using std::cout;
using std::cin;
using std::endl;

int main()
{
    char stars[6][80] { "Robert Redford",
                        "Hopalong Cassidy",
                        "Lassie",
                        "Slim Pickens",
                        "Boris Karloff",
                        "Oliver Hardy"
                      };
    int dice {};

    cout << endl
         << "Pick a lucky star!"
         << "Enter a number between 1 and 6: ";
    cin >> dice;

    if(dice >= 1 && dice <= 6)          // Check input validity
       cout << endl                     // Output star name
            << "Your lucky star is " << stars[dice - 1];
    else
       cout << endl                     // Invalid input
            << "Sorry, you haven't got a lucky star.";
```

```
        cout << endl;
        return 0;
    }
```

How It Works

Apart from its incredible inherent entertainment value, the main point of interest in this example is the definition of the `stars` array. It is a two-dimensional array of elements of type `char` that can hold up to six strings, each of which can be up to 80 characters, including the terminating null. The initializing strings for the array are enclosed between braces and separated by commas.

A disadvantage of using arrays in this way is the memory that is almost invariably left unused. All of the strings are fewer than 80 characters, and the surplus elements in each row of the array are wasted. You'll see later in this chapter how you could avoid this.

You can let the compiler work out how many strings you have by omitting the first array dimension:

```
char stars[][80] { "Robert Redford",
                   "Hopalong Cassidy",
                   "Lassie",
                   "Slim Pickens",
                   "Boris Karloff",
                   "Oliver Hardy"
                 };
```

This causes the compiler to define the first dimension to accommodate the initializing strings. Because you have six, the result is exactly the same, but it avoids the possibility of an error. You can't omit both array dimensions. You can only omit the first dimension in an array.

Of course, if you do omit the first array dimension, you would need to update the rest of the code to figure out the dimension instead of hard-coding 6. The `_countof()` function helps. The statement affected would then look like this:

```
cout << endl
    << "Pick a lucky star!"
    << "Enter a number between 1 and " << _countof(stars) << ": ";
cin >> dice;

if (dice >= 1 && dice <= _countof(stars))      // Check input validity
    cout << endl                               // Output star name
    << "Your lucky star is " << stars[dice - 1];
else
    cout << endl                               // Invalid input
    << "Sorry, you haven't got a lucky star.";
```

Where you reference a string for output in `Ex4_05.cpp`, you only specify the first index value:

```
cout << endl                               // Output star name
    << "Your lucky star is " << stars[dice - 1];
```

A single index selects a particular 80-element subarray, and the output operation displays the contents up to the terminating null. The index is `dice-1` because `dice` varies from 1 to 6 and the index values need to be from 0 to 5.

INDIRECT DATA ACCESS

Variables you have dealt with so far provided you with the ability to name a memory location in which you can store data of a particular type. The contents of a variable are either entered from an external source, such as the keyboard, or calculated from other values. There is another kind of variable that does not store data that you normally enter or calculate, but greatly extends the power and flexibility of your programs. This kind of variable is called a *pointer.*

What Is a Pointer?

Each memory location in your PC has an address. The address provides the means for the hardware to reference that location. A *pointer* is a variable that stores the address of another variable of a given type. A pointer has a variable name just like any other variable and also has a type that designates what kind of variables its contents refer to. Note that the type of a pointer variable includes the fact that it's a pointer. A variable that is a pointer, that can hold an address of a location containing a value of type int, is of type 'pointer to int'.

Declaring Pointers

A definition for a pointer is similar to that of an ordinary variable, except that the pointer name has an asterisk in front of it to indicate that it's a pointer. For example, to define a pointer pnumber of type pointer to long, you could use the following statement:

```
long* pnumber;
```

This definition has been written with the asterisk close to the type name. If you want, you can also write it as:

```
long *pnumber;
```

The compiler won't mind; however, the type of pnumber is 'pointer to long', which is often indicated by placing the asterisk close to the type name. Whichever way you choose to write a pointer type, be consistent.

You can mix definitions of ordinary variables and pointers in the same statement. For example:

```
long* pnumber, number {99};
```

This defines pnumber of type 'pointer to long' as before, and also defines the variable number, of type long. On balance, it's probably better to define pointers separately from other variables; otherwise, the statement can appear misleading as to the type of variables defined, particularly if you prefer to place the * adjacent to the type name. The following statements certainly look clearer, and putting definitions on separate lines enables you to add comments for them individually, making for a program that is easier to read:

```
long number {99};      // Declaration and initialization of long variable
long* pnumber;         // Declaration of variable of type pointer to long
```

It's a common convention to use variable names beginning with p to denote pointers. This makes it easier to see which variables are pointers, which in turn can make a program easier to follow.

Let's take an example to see how this works, without worrying about what it's for. I will get to how you use pointers very shortly. Suppose you have the long variable number containing the value 99 because you defined it in the preceding code. You could use the pointer pnumber of type pointer to long to store the address of number. But how do you obtain the address of a variable?

The Address-of Operator

What you need is the *address-of operator*, &. This is a unary operator that obtains the address of a variable. It's also called the reference operator, for reasons I discuss later in this chapter. To set up the pointer, you could write this assignment statement:

```
pnumber = &number;            // Store address of number in pnumber
```

The result of this operation is illustrated in Figure 4-4.

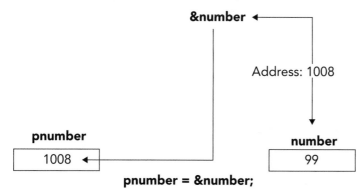

FIGURE 4-4

The & operator obtains the address of any variable, but you need a pointer of the appropriate type to store it. To store the address of a double variable for example, the pointer must be of type double*, which is 'pointer to double'.

Using Pointers

Taking the address of a variable and storing it in a pointer is all very well, but the really interesting aspect is how you can use it. Fundamental to using a pointer is accessing the data in the variable to which it points. You do this using the indirection operator, *.

The Indirection Operator

You use the *indirection operator*, *, to access the contents of the variable to which a pointer points. The name "indirection operator" stems from the fact that the data is accessed indirectly. It is also called the *dereference operator*, and the process of accessing the data in the variable pointed to by a pointer is termed *de-referencing the pointer*.

One aspect of this operator that can seem confusing is the fact that you now have several different uses for the same symbol, *. It is the multiply operator, it is the indirection operator, and it is used in the definition of a pointer. Each time you use *, the compiler can distinguish its meaning by the context. When you multiply two variables, A*B for instance, there's no meaningful interpretation of this expression for anything other than a multiply operation.

Why Use Pointers?

A question that usually springs to mind at this point is, "Why use pointers at all?" After all, taking the address of a variable you already know and sticking it in a pointer so that you can dereference it seems like overhead you can do without. There are several reasons why pointers are important.

As you will see, you can use pointer notation to operate on data stored in an array. Also, when you get to define your own functions, you will see that pointers are used extensively for enabling access within a function to large blocks of data, such as arrays, that are defined outside the function. Most importantly, you will see that you can allocate space for variables dynamically — that is, during program execution. This capability allows your program to adjust its use of memory depending on the input. Because you don't know in advance how many variables you are going to create dynamically, the way for doing this is using pointers — so make sure you get the hang of this bit.

Initializing Pointers

Using pointers that aren't initialized is extremely hazardous. You can easily overwrite random areas of memory through an uninitialized pointer. The resulting damage depends on how unlucky you are, so it's more than just a good idea to initialize your pointers. It's very easy to initialize a pointer to the address of a variable that has already been defined. Here you can see that I have initialized the pointer pnumber with the address of the variable number just by using the operator & with the variable name:

```
int number {};                    // Initialized integer variable
int* pnumber {&number};           // Initialized pointer
```

When initializing a pointer with the address of another variable, remember that the variable must already have been defined prior to the pointer definition.

Of course, you may not want to initialize a pointer with the address of a specific variable when you define it. In this case, you can initialize it with the pointer equivalent of zero, nullptr, which is a pointer that doesn't point to anything. You can define and initialize a pointer using the following statement:

```
int* pnumber {nullptr};           // Pointer not pointing to anything
```

Because nullptr is the equivalent of zero for pointers, an empty initializer list would work just as well. Setting a pointer to nullptr ensures that it doesn't contain an address that will be accepted as valid, and provides the pointer with a value that you can check in an if statement, such as:

```
if(pnumber == nullptr)
    cout << endl << "pnumber does not point to anything.";
```

Before nullptr was added to C++, 0 or NULL (which is a macro for which the compiler will substitute 0) was used to initialize a pointer, and of course, these still work. However, it is much better to use nullptr.

> **NOTE** `nullptr` *was introduced into C++ to remove potential confusion between the literal 0 as an integral value and 0 as a pointer. Having a dual meaning for 0 caused problems in some circumstances.* `nullptr` *is of type* `std::nullptr_t` *and cannot be confused with a value of any other type.* `nullptr` *can be implicitly converted to any pointer type but cannot be implicitly converted to any integral type except type* `bool`*.*

Because the literal `nullptr` can be implicitly converted to type `bool`, you can check the status of the pointer pnumber like this:

```
if(!pnumber)
    cout << endl << "pnumber does not point to anything.";
```

`nullptr` converts the `bool` value to `false`, and any other pointer value converts to `true`. Thus, if pnumber contains `nullptr`, the `if` expression will be `true` and will cause the message to be written to the output stream.

TRY IT OUT Using Pointers

You can try out various aspects of pointer operations with an example:

```cpp
// Ex4_06.cpp
// Exercising pointers
#include <iostream>
using std::cout;
using std::endl;
using std::hex;
using std::dec;

int main()
{
   long* pnumber {};             // Pointer definition & initialization
   long number1 {55}, number2 {99};

   pnumber = &number1;           // Store address in pointer
   *pnumber += 11;               // Increment number1 by 11
   cout << endl
        << "number1 = " << number1
        << "    &number1 = " << hex << pnumber;

   pnumber = &number2;           // Change pointer to address of number2
   number1 = *pnumber*10;        // 10 times number2

   cout << endl
        << "number1 = " << dec << number1
        << "    pnumber = " << hex << pnumber
        << "    *pnumber = " << dec << *pnumber;

   cout << endl;
   return 0;
}
```

You should compile and execute the release version of this example. The debug version will add extra bytes that are used for debugging purposes; these will cause the variables to be separated by 12 bytes instead of 4. On my computer, this example generates the following output:

```
number1 = 66    &number1 = 003CF7F0
number1 = 990   pnumber = 003CF7F4   *pnumber = 99
```

How It Works

There is no input. All operations are carried out with the initial values for the variables. After storing the address of number1 in the pointer pnumber, the value of number1 is incremented indirectly through the pointer in this statement:

```
*pnumber += 11;                  // Increment number1 by 11
```

The indirection operator determines that you are adding 11 to the contents of the variable pointed to by pnumber, which is number1. If you forgot the * in this statement, you would be attempting to add 11 to the address in the pointer.

The values of number1, and the address of number1 that is stored in pnumber, are displayed. You use the hex manipulator to generate the address output in hexadecimal notation. You can output the values of ordinary integer variables as hexadecimal using the hex manipulator. You send it to the output stream in the same way as endl, with the effect that all following output is in hexadecimal notation. To restore decimal output, you use the dec manipulator in the next output statement, which switches output back to decimal mode.

After the first line of output, pnumber is set to the address of number2. number1 is then changed to the value of 10 times number2:

```
number1 = *pnumber*10;           // 10 times number2
```

This is calculated by accessing the contents of number2 indirectly through the pointer. The second line of output shows the results.

The address values you see in your output may well be different from those shown here because they reflect where the program is loaded in memory, which depends on the state of your operating system environment.

Note that the addresses &number1 and &number2 differ by four bytes. This shows that number1 and number2 occupy adjacent memory locations, because each long variable occupies four bytes. The output demonstrates that everything is working as you would expect.

Pointers to char

A pointer of type const char* has the interesting property that it can be initialized with a string literal. For example, you can define and initialize such a pointer with the statement:

```
const char* proverb {"A miss is as good as a mile."};
```

This looks similar to initializing a char array, but it's quite different. This creates a string literal (actually an array of type const char[]) with the character string appearing between the quotes and terminating with '\0', and stores the address of the literal in the pointer proverb. The address of the literal will be the address of its first character. This is shown in Figure 4-5.

char* proverb {"A miss is as good as a mile."};

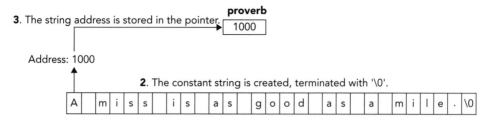

1. The pointer **proverb** is created.

3. The string address is stored in the pointer.

proverb
1000

Address: 1000

2. The constant string is created, terminated with '\0'.

| A | | m | i | s | s | | i | s | | a | s | | g | o | o | d | | a | s | | a | | m | i | l | e | . | \0 |

FIGURE 4-5

NOTE You can store the address of a string literal in a pointer that is not const. This was removed from C++ by the C++ 11 standard but is still allowed by the Visual C++ compiler so as not to break existing code. Storing the address of a string literal in a non-const pointer is dangerous; you should not do it. Setting the /Zc:strictStrings compiler option causes the compiler to enforce the standard.

TRY IT OUT   Lucky Stars with Pointers

You could rewrite the lucky stars example using pointers instead of an array:

```
// Ex4_07.cpp
// Initializing pointers with strings
#include <iostream>
using std::cin;
using std::cout;
using std::endl;

int main()
{
    const char* pstr1 {"Robert Redford"};
    const char* pstr2 {"Hopalong Cassidy"};
    const char* pstr3 {"Lassie"};
    const char* pstr4 {"Slim Pickens"};
    const char* pstr5 {"Boris Karloff"};
    const char* pstr6 {"Oliver Hardy"};
    const char* pstr {"Your lucky star is "};

    int dice {};

    cout << endl
         << "Pick a lucky star!"
         << "Enter a number between 1 and 6: ";
    cin >> dice;

    cout << endl;
```

```
    switch(dice)
    {
        case 1: cout << pstr << pstr1;
                break;
        case 2: cout << pstr << pstr2;
                break;
        case 3: cout << pstr << pstr3;
                break;
        case 4: cout << pstr << pstr4;
                break;
        case 5: cout << pstr << pstr5;
                break;
        case 6: cout << pstr << pstr6;
                break;

        default: cout << "Sorry, you haven't got a lucky star.";
    }

    cout << endl;
    return 0;
}
```

How It Works

The array in Ex4_05.cpp has been replaced by the six pointers, pstr1 to pstr6, each initialized with the name of a star. You have also defined pstr, initialized with the phrase that you'll use at the start of a normal output line. Because you have discrete pointers, it is easier to use a switch statement to select the appropriate output message rather than an if, as you did in the original version. Incorrect values entered are taken care of by the default option of the switch.

Outputting the string pointed to couldn't be easier. As you can see, you simply write the pointer name. It may cross your mind at this point that in Ex4_06.cpp you wrote a pointer name in the output statement, and the address that it contained was displayed. Why is it different here? The answer is in the way the stream output operation views a pointer of type 'pointer to char.' It treats a pointer of this type in a special way, in that it regards it as a string (which is an array of char), and so outputs the string, rather than its address.

Using pointers has eliminated the waste of memory that occurred with the array version of this program, but the program seems a little long-winded now. There must be a better way. Indeed there is — using an array of pointers.

TRY IT OUT   Arrays of Pointers

With an array of pointers of type char, each element can point to an independent string, and the lengths of each of the strings can be different. You can define an array of pointers in the same way that you define a normal array. Let's go straight to rewriting the previous example using a pointer array:

```
// Ex4_08.cpp
// Initializing pointers with strings
#include <iostream>
```

```
using std::cin;
using std::cout;
using std::endl;

int main()
{
    const char* pstr[] { "Robert Redford",   // Initializing a pointer array
                         "Hopalong Cassidy",
                         "Lassie",
                         "Slim Pickens",
                         "Boris Karloff",
                         "Oliver Hardy"
                       };
    const char* pstart {"Your lucky star is "};

    int dice {};

    cout << endl
         << "Pick a lucky star!"
         << "Enter a number between 1 and "<< _countof(pstr) << ": ";
    cin >> dice;

    cout << endl;
    if(dice >= 1 && dice <= _countof(pstr))    // Check input validity
        cout << pstart << pstr[dice - 1];      // Output star name

    else
        cout << "Sorry, you haven't got a lucky star."; // Invalid input

    cout << endl;
    return 0;
}
```

How It Works

In this case, you are nearly getting the best of all possible worlds. You have a one-dimensional array of pointers to type char defined, such that the compiler works out what the dimension should be from the number of initializing strings. The memory usage that results from this is illustrated in Figure 4-6.

Compared to using a "normal" array, a pointer array generally carries less overhead in terms of space. With an array, you would need to make each row the length of the longest string, and six rows of seventeen bytes each is 102 bytes, so by using a pointer array you have saved a whole -1 bytes! What's gone wrong? The simple truth is that for this small number of relatively short strings, the size of the extra array of pointers is significant. You would make savings if you were dealing with more strings that were longer and more variable in length.

Space saving isn't the only advantage of using pointers. In many circumstances you save time, too. Think of what happens if you want to move "Oliver Hardy" to the first position and "Robert Redford" to the end. With the pointer array in Ex4_08.cpp, you just swap the pointers — the strings themselves stay where they are. If you had stored these simply as strings, a great deal of copying would be necessary — you'd need to copy the string "Robert Redford" to a temporary location while you copied "Oliver Hardy" in its place. Then you'd need to copy "Robert Redford" to the end position. This requires significantly more computer time.

Because you use `pstr` as the array name, the variable holding the start of the output message needs to be different; it is called `pstart`. You select the string to output by means of an `if` statement, similar to that in the original version of the example. You either display a star selection, or a suitable message if the user enters an invalid value.

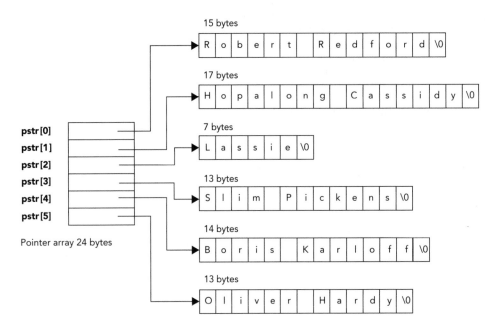

Total memory is 103 bytes

FIGURE 4-6

The sizeof Operator

The `sizeof` operator produces an integer value of type `size_t` that gives the number of bytes occupied by its operand, where `size_t` is a type defined by the standard library. Many standard library functions return a value of type `size_t`, and `size_t` is defined using a `typedef` statement to be equivalent to one of the fundamental types, usually `unsigned int`. The reason for using `size_t` rather than a fundamental type directly is that it allows flexibility in what the actual type is in different C++ implementations. The C++ standard permits the range of values accommodated by a fundamental type to vary, to make the best of a given hardware architecture, and `size_t` can be defined to be the equivalent of the most suitable fundamental type in the current machine environment.

Look at this statement that refers to `dice` in the previous example:

```
cout << sizeof dice;
```

The value of the expression `sizeof dice` is 4 because `dice` is type `int` and therefore occupies 4 bytes. Thus, this statement outputs the value 4.

The `sizeof` operator can be applied to an element in an array or to the whole array. When you apply the operator to an array name by itself, it produces the number of bytes occupied by the whole array, whereas when you apply it to a single element, it results in the number of bytes occupied by that element. In the last example, you could output the number of elements in `pstr` with the expression:

```
cout << (sizeof pstr)/(sizeof pstr[0]);
```

The expression `(sizeof pstr)/(sizeof pstr[0])` divides the number of bytes occupied by the whole array, by the number of bytes occupied by the first element. Because each array element occupies the same amount of memory, the result is the number of elements in the array. The code fragment you saw earlier that computed the average for an array of temperatures could be written like this:

```
double temperatures[] {65.5, 68.0, 75.0, 77.5, 76.4, 73.8, 80.1};
double sum {};
for(auto t : temperatures)
  sum += t;
double average = sum/((sizeof temperatures)/(sizeof temperatures[0]));
```

Of course, as I noted earlier, you can use `_countof()` to obtain the number of array elements and this is much clearer and will result in a compile-time error message if you pass a pointer to it instead of an array name.

You can apply the `sizeof` operator to a type name, in which case the result is the number of bytes occupied by a variable of that type. In this case, the type name should be enclosed in parentheses. For example:

```
size_t long_size {sizeof(long)};
```

The variable `long_size` will be initialized with the value 4. The variable `long_size` is of type `size_t` to match the type of value produced by the `sizeof` operator. Using a different integer type for `long_size` may result in a warning message from the compiler.

Constant Pointers and Pointers to Constants

You defined `pstr` in `Ex4_08.cpp` like this:

```
const char* pstr[]   { "Robert Redford",  // Initializing a pointer array
                       "Hopalong Cassidy",
                       "Lassie",
                       "Slim Pickens",
                       "Boris Karloff",
                       "Oliver Hardy"
                     };
```

Each pointer in the array is initialized with the address of a string literal, `"Robert Redford"`, `"Hopalong Cassidy"`, and so on. The type of a string literal is 'array of `const char`,' so you are storing the address of a `const` array in a `const` pointer. This prevents modification of the literal used as the initializer, which is quite a good idea. There is no ambiguity about the `const`-ness of the strings pointed to by the elements of the `pstr` pointer array. If you now attempt to change these strings, the compiler flags this as an error at compile time.

However, you could still legally write this:

```
pstr[0] = pstr[1];
```

Those lucky individuals due to be awarded Mr. Redford would get Mr. Cassidy instead since both pointers now point to the same name. Note that this isn't changing the strings pointed to — it is changing the address stored in pstr[0]. You probably want to inhibit this kind of change as well; some people may reckon that good old Hoppy may not have the same sex appeal as Robert. You can do this with the following statement:

```
// Array of constant pointers to constants
const char* const pstr[] = { "Robert Redford",
                             "Hopalong Cassidy",
                             "Lassie",
                             "Slim Pickens",
                             "Boris Karloff",
                             "Oliver Hardy"
                           };
```

Now the characters in the strings cannot be modified and neither can any of the addresses in the array.

You can distinguish three situations relating to const, pointers, and the objects to which they point:

➤ A pointer to a constant object

➤ A constant pointer to an object

➤ A constant pointer to a constant object

In the first situation, the object pointed to cannot be modified, but you can set the pointer to point to something else:

```
int value {5};
const int* pvalue {&value};
*pvalue = 6;                    // Will not compile!
pvalue = nullptr;              // OK
```

In the second situation, the address stored in the pointer can't be changed, but the object pointed to can be:

```
int value {5};
int* const pvalue {&value};
*pvalue = 6;                    // OK
pvalue = nullptr;              // Will not compile!
```

Finally, in the third situation, both the pointer and the object pointed to have been defined as constant and, therefore, neither can be changed:

```
int value {5};
const int* const pvalue {&value};
*pvalue = 6;                    // Will not compile!
pvalue = nullptr;              // Will not compile!
```

> **NOTE** *Of course, all this applies to pointers that point to any type. A pointer to type* int *is used here purely for illustrative purposes. In general, to interpret more complex pointer types correctly, you just read them from right to left. The type* const char* *is a pointer (***) to characters (*char*) that are* const *and the type* char* const *is a const pointer to characters.*

Pointers and Arrays

Array names can behave like pointers under some circumstances. In most situations, if you use the name of a one-dimensional array by itself, it is automatically interpreted as a pointer to the first array element . Note that this is not the case when the array name is used as the operand of the sizeof operator.

If you have these definitions,

```
double* pdata {};
double data[5];
```

you can write this assignment:

```
pdata = data;        // Initialize pointer with the array address
```

This assigns the address of the first element of the data to the pointer pdata. Using the array name by itself refers to the address of the array. If you use the array name data with an index value, it refers to the contents of the element corresponding to that index value. So, to store the address of an element in the pointer you use the address-of operator like this:

```
pdata = &data[1];
```

Here, pdata contains the address of the second array element.

Pointer Arithmetic

You can perform arithmetic operations with pointers. You are limited to addition and subtraction, but you can also compare pointer values to produce a logical result. Arithmetic with a pointer implicitly assumes that the pointer points to an array, and that the arithmetic operation is on the address contained in the pointer. For the pointer pdata, for example, you could assign the address of the third element of the data array to it with this statement:

```
pdata = &data[2];
```

In this case, the expression pdata+1 would refer to the address of data[3], the fourth element of the data array, so you could make pdata point to this element by writing this statement:

```
pdata += 1;          // Increment pdata to the next element
```

This increments the address in pdata by the number of bytes occupied by one element of the data array. In general, pdata+n, where n can be any expression resulting in an integer, adds n*sizeof(double) to the address in pdata, because it is of type pointer to double. This is illustrated in Figure 4-7.

In other words, incrementing or decrementing a pointer works in terms of the type of the object pointed to. Increasing a pointer to long by one changes its contents to the next long address, and so increments the address by four. Similarly, incrementing a pointer to

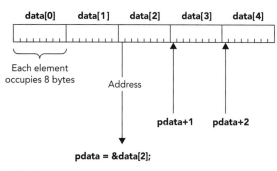

FIGURE 4-7

`short` by one increments the address by two. The more common notation for incrementing a pointer by one is using the increment operator. For example:

```
pdata++;              // Increment pdata to the next element
```

This is equivalent to (and more common than) the `+=` operator. However, I used `+=` earlier to make it clear that although the increment value is specified as one, the effect is always an address increment greater than one except for the case of a pointer to type `char`.

> **NOTE** *A valid address resulting from an arithmetic operation on a pointer can be a value ranging from the address of the first element of the array to the address that is one beyond the last element, although there's nothing to prevent you from writing expressions that result in values outside this range. Accessing an address that does not refer to an element within the array results in undefined behavior; this includes one beyond the last element of course.*

You can, of course, dereference a pointer on which you have performed arithmetic (there wouldn't be much point to it otherwise). For example, if `pdata` is still pointing to `data[2]`, this statement,

```
*(pdata + 1) = *(pdata + 2);
```

is equivalent to this:

```
data[3] = data[4];
```

The parentheses are necessary when you want to dereference a pointer after incrementing the address it contains because the precedence of the indirection operator is higher than that of the arithmetic operators, `+` and `-`. If you write `*pdata+1`, instead of `*(pdata+1)`, this adds one to the value stored at the address in `pdata`, which is equivalent to executing `data[2]+1`. Because this isn't an lvalue, its use in the previous assignment statement would cause the compiler to generate an error message.

You can use an array name as though it were a pointer for addressing elements of an array. Suppose you have the array defined as:

```
long data[5];
```

Using pointer notation, you can refer to the element `data[3]`, for example, as `*(data+3)`. This kind of notation can be applied generally so that, corresponding to the elements `data[0]`, `data[1]`, `data[2]`, you can write `*data`, `*(data+1)`, `*(data+2)`, and so on.

TRY IT OUT   Array Names as Pointers

You can practice this aspect of array addressing with a program to calculate prime numbers (a prime number is divisible only by itself and one):

```
// Ex4_09.cpp
// Calculating primes
#include <iostream>
#include <iomanip>
using std::cout;
```

```
using std::endl;
using std::setw;

int main()
{
   const int MAX {100};              // Number of primes required
   long primes[MAX] { 2,3,5 };       // First three primes defined
   long trial {5};                   // Candidate prime
   int count {3};                    // Count of primes found
   bool found {false};               // Indicates when a prime is found

   do
   {
      trial += 2;                    // Next value for checking
      found = false;                 // Set found indicator

      for(int i {}; i < count; i++)  // Try division by existing primes
      {
         found = (trial % *(primes + i)) == 0;// True for exact division
           if(found)                            // If division is exact
              break;                             // it's not a prime
      }

      if (!found)                    // We got one...
         *(primes + count++) = trial;  // ...so save it in primes array
   }while(count < MAX);

   // Output primes 5 to a line
   for(int i {}; i < MAX; i++)
   {
      if(i % 5 == 0)                 // New line on 1st, and every 5th line
         cout << endl;
      cout << setw(10) << *(primes + i);
   }
   cout << endl;

   return 0;
}
```

If you compile and execute this example, you should get the following output:

```
         2         3         5         7        11
        13        17        19        23        29
        31        37        41        43        47
        53        59        61        67        71
        73        79        83        89        97
       101       103       107       109       113
       127       131       137       139       149
       151       157       163       167       173
       179       181       191       193       197
       199       211       223       227       229
       233       239       241       251       257
       263       269       271       277       281
       283       293       307       311       313
       317       331       337       347       349
```

353	359	367	373	379
383	389	397	401	409
419	421	431	433	439
443	449	457	461	463
467	479	487	491	499
503	509	521	523	541

How It Works

You have the usual #include statements for the iostream header for input and output, and for iomanip, because you use a stream manipulator to set the field width for output.

You use the constant MAX to define the number of primes that you want the program to produce. The primes array, which stores the results, is initialized with the first three primes to start the process off. All the work is done in two loops. The outer do-while loop picks the next value to be checked and adds the value to the primes array if it is prime, and the inner for loop that checks the value to see whether it's prime or not.

The algorithm in the for loop is very simple and is based on the fact that if a number is not a prime, it must be divisible by one of the primes found so far — all of which are less than the number in question because all numbers are either prime or a product of primes. In fact, it is only necessary to divide by primes less than or equal to the square root of the number in question, so this example isn't as efficient as it might be:

```
found = (trial % *(primes + i)) == 0;  // True for exact division
```

This statement sets found to true if there's no remainder from dividing trial by the current prime *(primes + i) (remember that this is equivalent to primes[i]), and to false otherwise. The if statement causes the for loop to be terminated if found is true because the candidate in trial can't be a prime in that case.

After the for loop ends (for whatever reason), it's necessary to decide whether or not the value in trial was prime. This is indicated by the value in found:

```
*(primes + count++) = trial;   // ...so save it in primes array
```

If trial does contain a prime, this statement stores the value in primes[count] and then increments count through the postfix increment operator.

After MAX primes have been found, they are output with a field width of 10 characters, 5 to a line, as a result of this statement:

```
if(i % 5 == 0)               // New line on 1st, and every 5th line
    cout << endl;
```

This starts a new line when i has the values 0, 5, 10, and so on.

TRY IT OUT Counting Characters Revisited

To see how to handle strings in pointer notation, you could produce a version of the program you looked at earlier for counting the characters in a string:

```cpp
// Ex4_10.cpp
// Counting string characters using a pointer
#include <iostream>
using std::cin;
using std::cout;
using std::endl;

int main()
{
   const int MAX {80};                  // Maximum array dimension
   char buffer[MAX];                    // Input buffer
   char* pbuffer {buffer};              // Pointer to array buffer

   cout << endl                         // Prompt for input
        << "Enter a string of less than "
        << MAX << " characters:"
        << endl;

   cin.getline(pbuffer, MAX, '\n');     // Read a string until \n

   while(*pbuffer)                      // Continue until \0
      pbuffer++;

   cout << endl
        << "The string \"" << buffer
        << "\" has " << pbuffer - buffer << " characters.";
   cout << endl;

   return 0;
}
```

Here's an example of output from this example:

```
Enter a string of less than 80 characters:
The tigers of wrath are wiser than the horses of instruction.
The string "The tigers of wrath are wiser than the horses of
instruction." has 61 characters.
```

How It Works

The program uses the pointer pbuffer rather than the array name buffer. You don't need the count variable because the pointer is incremented in the while loop until '\0' is found. When '\0' is found, pbuffer will contain the address of that position in the string. The count of the number of characters in the string is therefore the difference between the address in pbuffer, and the address of the beginning of the array denoted by buffer.

You could have incremented the pointer in the loop by writing the loop like this:

```cpp
while(*pbuffer++);                      // Continue until \0
```

Now the loop contains no statements, only the test condition. This would work adequately, except that the pointer would be incremented after '\0' was encountered, so the address would be one more than the last position in the string. You would therefore need to express the count of the number of characters in the string as pbuffer-buffer-1.

Note that you can't use the array name here in the same way that you have used the pointer. The expression `buffer++` is strictly illegal because you can't modify the address value that an array name represents. Even though you can use an array name in an expression as though it is a pointer, it isn't a pointer, because the address value that it represents is fixed.

Using Pointers with Multidimensional Arrays

Using a pointer to store the address of a one-dimensional array is relatively straightforward, but with multidimensional arrays, things can get a little complicated. If you don't intend to use pointers with multidimensional arrays, you can skip this section, as it's a little obscure; however, if you have previous experience with C++, this section is worth a glance.

If you have to use a pointer with multidimensional arrays, you need to keep clear in your mind what is happening. By way of illustration, you can use an array `beans`, defined as follows:

```
double beans[3][4];
```

You can define and assign a value to the pointer `pbeans`, as follows:

```
double* pbeans;
pbeans = &beans[0][0];
```

Here, you are setting the pointer to the address of the first element of the array, which is of type `double`. You could also set the pointer to the address of the first row in the array with the statement:

```
pbeans = beans[0];
```

This is equivalent to using the name of a one-dimensional array, which is replaced by its address. You used this in the earlier discussion; however, because `beans` is a two-dimensional array, you cannot set an address in the pointer with the following statement:

```
pbeans = beans;          // Will cause an error!!
```

The problem is one of type. The type of the pointer is `double*`, but the array is of type `double[3][4]`. A pointer to store the address of this array must be of type `double*[4]`. C++ associates the dimensions of the array with its type, and the preceding statement is only legal if the pointer has been defined with the dimension required. This can be done with a slightly more complicated notation than you have seen so far:

```
double (*pbeans)[4];
```

The parentheses here are essential; otherwise, you would be declaring an array of pointers. Now the previous statement is legal, but this pointer can only be used to store addresses of an array with the dimensions shown. The `auto` keyword can help out here. You can write the statement as:

```
auto pbeans = beans;
```

Now the compiler will deduce the correct type for you.

Pointer Notation with Multidimensional Arrays

You can use pointer notation with an array name to reference elements of the array. You can reference each element of the array `beans` that you defined earlier, which had three rows of four elements, in two ways:

➤ Using the array name with two index values

➤ Using the array name in pointer notation

Therefore, the following two expressions are equivalent:

```
beans[i][j]
*(*(beans + i) + j)
```

Let's look at how these work. The first expression uses normal array indexing to refer to the element with offset `j` in row `i` of the array.

You can determine the meaning of the second expression by working from the inside outwards. `beans` refers to the address of the first row of the array, so `beans+i` refers to row `i`. The expression `*(beans+i)` is the address of the first element of row `i`, so `*(beans+i)+j` is the address of the element in row `i` with offset `j`. The whole expression therefore refers to the value of that element.

If you really want to be obscure — and it isn't recommended that you should be — the following two statements, where you have mixed array and pointer notation, are also legal references to the same element of the array:

```
*(beans[i] + j)
(*(beans + i))[j]
```

There is yet another aspect to using pointers that is the most important of all: the ability to allocate memory dynamically. You'll look into that next.

DYNAMIC MEMORY ALLOCATION

Working with a fixed set of variables in a program can be very restrictive. You'll often want to allocate space for variables at execution time, depending on the input data. Any program that processes a number of data items that is not known in advance can take advantage of the ability to allocate memory at run time. For example, in a program that stores information about the students in a class, the number of students is not fixed and their names will vary in length, so to deal with the data most efficiently, you'll want to allocate space at execution time.

Obviously, because dynamically allocated variables can't have been defined at compile time, they can't be named in your code. When they are created, they are identified by their address, which you store in a pointer. With the power of pointers, and the dynamic memory management tools in Visual C++, writing your programs to have this kind of flexibility is quick and easy.

The Free Store, Alias the Heap

In most instances, when your program is executed, there is unused memory in your computer. This unused memory is called the *heap*, or the *free store*. You can allocate space within the free store for a new variable of a given type using a special operator that returns the address of the space allocated. This operator is `new`, and it's complemented by the operator `delete`, which releases memory previously allocated by `new`.

You can allocate space in the free store for variables in one part of a program, and then release the space and return it to the free store after you have finished with it. This makes the memory available for reuse by other dynamically allocated variables. This is a powerful technique; it enables you to use memory very efficiently and in many cases results in programs that can handle much larger problems, involving considerably more data than otherwise might be possible.

The new and delete Operators

Suppose that you need space for a `double` variable. You can define a pointer to type `double` and then request that the memory be allocated at execution time. You can do this using the `new` operator:

```
double* pvalue {};
pvalue = new double;        // Request memory for a double variable
```

This is a good moment to recall that *all pointers should be initialized.* Using memory dynamically typically involves a number of pointers floating around, so it's important that they should not contain spurious values. You always set a pointer that doesn't contain a legal address value to `nullptr`.

The `new` operator in the second line of code should return the address of the memory in the free store allocated to a `double` variable, and this address is stored in the pointer `pvalue`. You can then use this pointer to reference the variable using the indirection operator, as you have seen. For example:

```
*pvalue = 9999.0;
```

Of course, the memory may not have been allocated because the free store had been used up, or because the free store is fragmented by previous usage — meaning that there aren't sufficient contiguous bytes to accommodate the variable for which you want to obtain space. You don't have to worry too much about this. The `new` operator will throw an *exception* if the memory cannot be allocated for any reason, which terminates your program. Exceptions are a mechanism for signaling errors in C++; you learn about these in Chapter 6.

You can initialize a variable created by `new`. Taking the example of the `double` variable that was allocated by `new` and the address stored in `pvalue`, you could have set the value to 999.0, as it was created with this statement:

```
pvalue = new double {999.0};    // Allocate a double and initialize it
```

Of course, you could create the pointer and initialize it in a single statement, like this:

```
double* pvalue { new double{999.0} };
```

When you no longer need a variable that has been dynamically allocated, you can free the memory that it occupies with the `delete` operator:

```
delete pvalue;                  // Release memory pointed to by pvalue
```

This ensures that the memory can be used for something else. If you don't use `delete`, and you store a different address in `pvalue`, it will be impossible to free the memory or to use the data that it contains, because access to the address is lost. In this situation, you have what is referred to as a *memory leak*, especially when it recurs in your program.

You should set a pointer to `nullptr` when you release the memory to which it points. If you don't, you have what is called a *dangling pointer*, through which you might attempt to access memory that has been freed.

> **NOTE** *In Chapter 10 I'll explain smart pointers, which is an alternative to the pointers I have discussed in this chapter. When you are allocating memory dynamically, especially for arrays or more complex objects, it is often better to use a smart pointer. A smart pointer takes care of deleting the memory automatically when it is no longer required so you no longer have to worry about it. I'll defer discussion of smart pointers until Chapter 10 because there are several things you need to learn about before you can understand smart pointers.*

Allocating Memory Dynamically for Arrays

Allocating memory for an array dynamically is very straightforward. To allocate an array of type `char`, you could write this statement:

```
char* pstr {new char[20]};      // Allocate a string of twenty characters
```

This allocates space for a `char` array of 20 characters and stores its address in `pstr`. To remove the array that you have just created, you use the `delete` operator. The statement would look like this:

```
delete [] pstr;                 // Delete array pointed to by pstr
```

Note the use of square brackets to indicate that you are deleting an array. When removing arrays from the free store, you should always include the square brackets, or the results will be unpredictable. Note that you do not specify any dimensions here, simply use `[]`.

Of course, `pstr` now contains the address of memory that may already have been allocated for some other purpose, so it certainly should not be used. When you use `delete` to discard memory you previously allocated, you should always reset the pointer, like this:

```
pstr = nullptr;
```

This ensures that you cannot access the memory that has been released.

You can initialize an array allocated in the free store:

```
int *data {new int[10] {2,3,4}};
```

This statement creates an array of 10 integer elements and initializes the first three with 2, 3, and 4. The remaining elements will be initialized to 0.

> **NOTE** *In Chapter 10 I'll also explain containers, which you can use to store collections of items in a much more flexible way than standard arrays.*

TRY IT OUT   **Using Free Store**

You can see how dynamic memory allocation works by rewriting the program that calculates an arbitrary number of primes, this time using memory in the free store to store the primes:

```
// Ex4_11.cpp
// Calculating primes using dynamic memory allocation
#include <iostream>
```

```cpp
#include <iomanip>
using std::cin;
using std::cout;
using std::endl;
using std::setw;

int main()
{
   int max {};                            // Number of primes required
   cout << endl
        << "Enter the number of primes you would like (at least 4): ";
   cin >> max;

   if(max < 4)                            // Test the user input, if less than 4
      max = 4;                            // ensure it is at least 4

   // Allocate prime array and initialize with seed primes
   long* pprime {new long[max] {2L, 3L, 5L} };

   long trial {5L};                       // Candidate prime
   int count {3};                         // Count of primes found
   bool found {false};                    // Indicates when a prime is found



   do
   {
      trial += 2L;                        // Next value for checking
      found = false;                      // Set found indicator

      for(int i {}; i < count; i++)       // Division by existing primes
      {
         found =(trial % *(pprime + i)) == 0;// True for exact division
         if(found)                        // If division is exact
            break;                        // it's not a prime
      }

      if (!found)                         // We got one...
         *(pprime + count++) = trial;     // ...so save it in primes array
   } while(count < max);

   // Output primes 5 to a line
   for(int i {}; i < max; i++)
   {
      if(i % 5 == 0)                      // New line on 1st, and every 5th line
         cout << endl;
      cout << setw(10) << *(pprime + i);
   }

   delete [] pprime;                      // Free up memory...
   pprime = nullptr;                      // ...and reset the pointer
   cout << endl;
   return 0;
}
```

Here's an example of the output from this program:

```
Enter the number of primes you would like (at least 4): 20
        2        3        5        7       11
       13       17       19       23       29
       31       37       41       43       47
       53       59       61       67       71
```

How It Works

After receiving the number of primes required in the `int` variable `max`, you make sure that `max` can be no less than 4. This is because the program requires space to be allocated for at least the three seed primes, plus one new one. You specify the size of the array by putting the variable `max` between the square brackets following the array type specification:

```
long* pprime {new long[max] {2L, 3L, 5L} };
```

The program would terminate at this point if the memory could not be allocated for `pprime`. The statement also initializes the first three elements of the array to the first three prime values. The remaining elements will be 0.

The calculation of the primes is exactly as before; the only change is that the name of the pointer, `pprime`, replaces the array name, `primes`, that you used in the previous version. Equally, the output process is the same. Acquiring space dynamically is really not a problem. After it has been allocated, it in no way affects how the computation is written.

After you finish with the array, you remove it from the free store using `delete`, remembering to include the square brackets to indicate that it is an array:

```
delete [] pprime;             // Free up memory
```

Although it's not essential here, you also reset the pointer:

```
pprime = nullptr;             // and reset the pointer
```

All memory allocated in the free store is released when your program ends, but it is good to get into the habit of resetting pointers to `nullptr` when they no longer point to valid memory areas.

Dynamic Allocation of Multidimensional Arrays

Allocating memory in the free store for a multidimensional array involves using the `new` operator in a slightly more complicated form than is used for a one-dimensional array. Suppose that you define the pointer `pbeans` like this:

```
double (*pbeans)[4] {};
```

To obtain the space for the array `beans[3][4]` that you used earlier in this chapter, you could write this:

```
pbeans = new double [3][4];             // Allocate memory for a 3x4 array
```

You just specify both array dimensions between square brackets after the type name for the elements. Of course, you could do it all in one go:

```
double (*pbeans)[4] {new double [3][4]};
```

Allocating space for a three-dimensional array simply requires that you specify the extra dimension, as in this example:

```
auto pBigArray (new double [5][10][10]); // Allocate memory for a 5x10x10 array
```

This uses auto to have the pointer type determined automatically. Don't forget — you can't use an initializer list with auto. You could write it as:

```
auto pBigArray = new double [5][10][10]; // Allocate memory for a 5x10x10 array
```

However many dimensions there are in the array that has been created, to destroy it and release the memory back to the free store, you write the following:

```
delete [] pBigArray;                    // Release memory for array
pBigArray = nullptr;
```

You always use just one pair of square brackets following the delete operator, regardless of the dimensionality of the array.

You have already seen that you can use a variable as the specification of the dimension of a one-dimensional array to be allocated by new. This extends to two or more dimensions, but with the restriction that only the leftmost dimension may be specified by a variable. All the other dimensions must be constants or constant expressions. So, you could write this,

```
pBigArray = new double[max][10][10];
```

where max is a variable; however, specifying a variable for any dimension other than the leftmost causes an error message to be generated by the compiler.

USING REFERENCES

A *reference* appears to be similar to a pointer in many respects, which is why I'm introducing it here, but it really isn't. The importance of references becomes apparent only when you get to explore their use with functions, particularly in the context of object-oriented programming. Don't be misled by their simplicity and what might seem to be a trivial concept here. As you'll see later, references provide some extraordinarily powerful facilities, and in some contexts enable you to achieve results that would be impossible without them.

What Is a Reference?

Essentially, a reference is a name that can be used as an alias for something else. There are two kinds of references: *lvalue references* and *rvalue references*.

An lvalue reference is an alias for another variable; it is called an *lvalue* reference because it refers to a persistent storage location that can appear on the left of an assignment operation. Because an lvalue reference is an alias, the variable for which it is an alias has to exist when the reference is defined. Unlike a pointer, a reference cannot be altered to represent something else.

An *rvalue* reference can be used as an alias for a variable, just like an lvalue reference, but it differs from an lvalue reference in that it can also reference an rvalue, which is a temporary value that is essentially transient.

Declaring and Initializing Lvalue References

Suppose that you have defined a variable as:

```
long number {};
```

You can define an lvalue reference for this variable using this statement:

```
long& rnumber {number};        // Declare a reference to variable number
```

The ampersand following the type name `long` and preceding the variable name `rnumber`, indicates that an lvalue reference is being defined, and that the variable name it represents, `number`, is specified as the initializing value between the parentheses; therefore `rnumber` is of type 'reference to long'. You can use the reference in place of the original variable name. For example:

```
rnumber += 10L;
```

This will increment `number` by 10.

Note that you cannot write:

```
int& rfive {5};                // Will not compile!
```

The literal 5 is constant and cannot be changed. To protect the integrity of constant values, you must use a `const` reference:

```
const int& rfive {5};          // OK
```

Now you can access the literal 5 through the `rfive` reference. Because you define `rfive` as `const`, it cannot be used to change the value it references.

Let's contrast the lvalue reference `rnumber` in the previous code with the pointer `pnumber`, defined in this statement:

```
long* pnumber {&number};       // Initialize a pointer with an address
```

This defines the pointer `pnumber`, and initializes it with the address of `number`. This allows `number` to be incremented with a statement such as:

```
*pnumber += 10L;               // Increment number through a pointer
```

There is a significant distinction between using a pointer and using a reference. You must dereference the pointer to access the variable to which it points in the expression. With a reference, there is no need for dereferencing. In some ways, a reference is like a pointer that has already been dereferenced, although it can't be changed to reference something else. An lvalue reference is the complete equivalent of the variable for which it is a reference.

Using References in a Range-based for Loop

Earlier in this chapter you saw a code snippet using a range-based `for` loop to iterate over an array of temperatures:

```
for(auto t : temperatures)
{
  sum += t;
  ++count;
}
```

The t variable does not reference an array element, only its value, so you cannot use it to modify the element. However, you can by using a reference:

```
const double FtoC {5.0/9.0};          // Convert Fahrenheit to Centigrade
for(auto& t : temperatures)
   t = (t - 32)*FtoC;
for(auto& t : temperatures)
   cout << "  " << t;
cout << endl;
```

The variable t will now be of type double& and will reference each array element directly. This loop changes the values in the array from Fahrenheit to Centigrade.

Using a reference in a range-based for loop is particularly valuable when you are working with collections of objects. Copying objects can be expensive on time, so avoiding copying by using a reference type makes your code more efficient. You will learn about collections of objects in Chapter 10 when the range-based for loop comes into its own.

If you want to use references with the range-based for loop for performance reasons, but you don't want to be able to modify the values, you can use const auto&, as in:

```
for (const auto& t : temperatures)
   cout << "  " << t;
```

Creating Rvalue References

I am explaining rvalue references here because the concept is related to that of lvalue references, but I cannot go into the significance of rvalue references at this point. Rvalue references are particularly important in the context of functions, which you'll learn about in Chapter 5. You'll also learn more about rvalue references in subsequent chapters.

As you know, every expression is either an rvalue or an lvalue. A variable is an lvalue because it represents a location in memory. An rvalue is different. It represents the result of evaluating an expression. Thus, an lvalue reference is a reference to a variable that has a name, and allows the contents of the memory that the variable represents to be accessed through the lvalue reference. An rvalue reference is a reference to memory containing the result of evaluating an expression.

You specify an rvalue reference type using two ampersands following the type name. Here's an example:

```
int x {5};
int&& rExpr {2*x + 3};                // rvalue reference
cout << rExpr << endl;
int& rx {x};                          // lvalue reference
cout << rx << endl;
```

Here, the rvalue reference is initialized to reference the result of evaluating the expression 2*x+3, which is a temporary value — an rvalue. The output will be 13. You cannot do this with an lvalue reference. Is this useful? In this case, no, indeed it is not recommended at all; but in a different context, it is very useful.

> **WARNING** *The preceding code fragment will compile and execute, but it is definitely NOT the way to use an rvalue reference. This is just to illustrate what an rvalue reference is.*

LIBRARY FUNCTIONS FOR STRINGS

The `cstring` standard header defines functions that operate on null-terminated strings. These are functions that are specified in the C++ standard and are defined in the `std` namespace. There are alternatives to some of these that are not standard and therefore not in the `std` namespace, but which provide a more secure implementation of the function than the original versions. In general, the secure functions have names ending with _s and I'll use the more secure versions in examples. Let's explore some of the most useful functions provided by the `cstring` header.

> **NOTE** *The `string` standard header defines the `string` and `wstring` classes that represent character strings. The `string` class represents strings of characters of type `char` and the `wstring` class represents strings of characters of type `wchar_t`. Both are defined in the `string` header as template classes that are instances of the `basic_string<T>` class template. I won't be discussing templates and the `string` and `wstring` classes until Chapter 8, but I am mentioning them here because they are much better and safer to use.*

Finding the Length of a Null-terminated String

The `strlen()` function returns the length of the argument string of type `char*` as a value of type `size_t`. The `wcslen()` function does the same thing for strings of type `wchar_t*`.

Here's how you use the `strlen()` function:

```
const char* str {"A miss is as good as a mile."};
std::cout << "The string contains " <<  std::strlen(str) << " characters.";
```

The output produced when this fragment executes is:

```
The string contains 28 characters.
```

As you can see from the output, the length that is returned does not include the terminating null. It is important to keep this in mind, especially when you are using the length of one string to create another.

Both `strlen()` and `wcslen()` find the length by looking for the null at the end. If there isn't one, the functions will happily continue beyond the end of the string, checking throughout memory in the hope of finding a null. For this reason, these functions represent a security risk when you are working with data from an untrusted external source. It is generally better to use the `strnlen()`

and `wcsnlen()` functions, both of which require a second argument that specifies the length of the buffer in which the string specified by the first argument is stored. For example:

```
char str[30] {"A miss is as good as a mile."};
std::cout << "The string contains " << strnlen(str, _countof(str))
        << " characters.";
```

The second argument to `strnlen()` is provided by the `_countof()` macro.

> **NOTE** In this example I switched to using `char str[30]` *while in the previous example it was* `const char*`. *This is because* `_countof()` *doesn't work with type* `const char*`.

Joining Null-terminated Strings

The `strcat()` function that concatenates two null-terminated strings is deprecated because it is unsafe. The `strcat_s()` function is the safe alternative. The string specified by the second argument to `strcat_s()` is appended to the string specified by the first argument. Here's an example of how you might use it:

```
const size_t count {30};
char str1[count] {"Many hands"};
const char* str2 {" make light work."};

errno_t error {strcat_s(str1, str2)};

if(error == 0)
    std::cout << "Strings joined successfully.\n"
            << str1 << std::endl;

else if(error == EINVAL)
    std::cout <<"Error! Source or destination string address is a null pointer."
            << std::endl;

else if(error == ERANGE)
    std::cout << "Error! Destination string too small." << std::endl;
```

For convenience, I defined the array size as the constant `count`. The first argument to `strcat_s()` is the destination string to which the source string specified by the second argument is to be appended. The function returns an integer value of type `errno_t` to indicate how things went. The return value will be zero if the operation is successful, `EINVAL` if the source or destination is `nullptr`, or `ERANGE` if the destination length is too small. In the event of an error, the destination will be left unchanged. The error code values `EINVAL` and `ERANGE` are defined in the `cerrno` header, which is included indirectly in the `iostream` header. Of course, you are not obliged to test for the error codes that the function might return but it is good practice.

As Figure 4-8 shows, the first character of the string specified by the second argument overwrites the terminating null of the first argument, and all the remaining characters of the second string are copied across, including the terminating null. Thus, the output from the fragment will be:

```
Strings joined successfully.
Many hands make light work.
```

The `wcscat_s()` function is the safe alternative to `wcscat()` that concatenates wide-character strings, and works in the same way as the `strcat_s()` function.

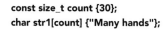

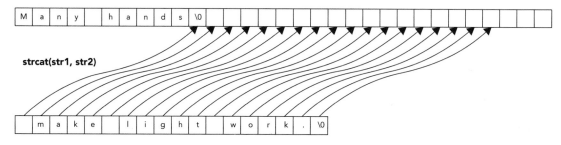

FIGURE 4-8

With the `strncat_s()` function you can append part of one null-terminated string to another. The first two arguments are the destination and source strings respectively, and the third argument is a count of the number of characters from the source string that are to be appended. With the strings as defined in Figure 4-8, here's an example of using `strncat_s()`:

```
errno_t error{ strncat_s(str1, str2, 11) };
```

After executing this statement, `str1` contains the string `"Many hands make light"`. The operation appends 11 characters from `str2` to `str1`, overwriting the terminating `'\0'` in `str1`, and then appends a final `'\0'` character. The `wcsncat_s()` provides the same capability as `strncat_s()` but for wide-character strings.

Copying Null-terminated Strings

The standard library function `strcpy()` copies a string from a source location to a destination. The `strcpy_s()` function is a more secure version of `strcpy()`. The first argument is a pointer to the destination, and the second is a pointer to the source string; the first argument is of type `char*` and the second is type `const char*`. `strcpy_s()` verifies that the source and destination are not `nullptr` and that the destination has sufficient space to accommodate the source string. If either argument is `nullptr` or the destination is too small, the program will crash and offer you the option to close the program or start debugging it, thus preventing an uncontrolled copy operation. `wcscpy_s()` provides analogous wide-character versions of this copy function.

Comparing Null-terminated Strings

The `strcmp()` function compares two null-terminated strings that you specify by arguments of type `const char*`. The function returns a value of type `int` that is less than zero, zero, or greater than zero, depending on whether the string pointed to by the first argument is less than, equal to, or greater than the string pointed to by the second argument. Here's an example:

```
const char* str1 {"Jill"};
const char* str2 {"Jacko"};
int result {std::strcmp(str1, str2)};
if(result < 0)
   std::cout << str1 << " is less than " << str2 << '.' << std::endl;
else if(0 == result)
   std::cout << str1 << " is equal to " << str2 << '.' << std::endl;
else
   std::cout << str1 << " is greater than " << str2 << '.' << std::endl;
```

This fragment compares the strings str1 and str2, and uses the value returned by strcmp() to execute one of three possible output statements.

Comparing strings works by comparing the character codes of successive pairs of corresponding characters. The first pair of characters that are different determines whether the first string is less than or greater than the second string. Two strings are equal if they contain the same number of characters, and the corresponding characters are identical. Of course, the output is:

```
Jill is greater than Jacko.
```

The wcscmp() function is the wide-character string equivalent of strcmp().

Searching Null-terminated Strings

The strspn() function searches a string for the first character that is not in a given set and returns the index of the character found. The first argument is a pointer to the string to be searched, and the second is a pointer to a string containing the set of characters. You could search for the first character that is not a vowel like this:

```
char str[] {"I agree with everything."};
const char* vowels {"aeiouAEIOU "};
size_t index {std::strspn(str, vowels)};
std::cout << "The first character that is not a vowel is '" << str[index]
          << "' at position " << index << std::endl;
```

This searches str for the first character that is not contained in vowels. Note that I included a space in the vowels set, so a space will be ignored so far as the search is concerned. The output from this fragment is:

```
The first character that is not a vowel is 'g' at position 3
```

Another way of looking at the return value from strspn() is that it represents the length of the substring, starting from the first character in the first argument string that consists entirely of characters in the second argument string. In the example it is the first three characters "I a". The wcsspn() function is the wide-character string equivalent of strspn().

The strstr() function returns a pointer to the position in the first argument of a substring specified by the second argument. Here's a fragment that shows this in action:

```
char str[] {"I agree with everything."};
const char* substring {"ever"};
```

```
char* psubstr {std::strstr(str, substring)};

if(!psubstr)
  std::cout << "\"" << substring << "\" not found in \"" << str << "\"" <<
std::endl;
else
  std::cout << "The first occurrence of \"" << substring
            << "\" in \"" << str << "\" is at position "
            << psubstr-str << std::endl;
```

The third statement calls `strstr()` to search `str` for the first occurrence of `substring`. The function returns a pointer to the position of the substring if it is found, or `nullptr` when it is not found. The `if` statement outputs a message, depending on whether or not `substring` was found in `str`. The expression `psubstr-str` gives the index position of the first character in the substring. The output produced by this fragment is:

```
The first occurrence of "ever" in "I agree with everything." is at position 13
```

TRY IT OUT   **Searching Null-terminated Strings**

This example searches a given string to determine the number of occurrences of a given substring:

```cpp
// Ex4_12.cpp
// Searching a string
#include <iostream>
#include <cstring>
using std::cout;
using std::endl;

int main()
{
  char str[] { "Smith, where Jones had had \"had had\" had had \"had\"."
    "\n\"Had had\" had had the examiners' approval." };
  const char* word { "had" };
  cout << "The string to be searched is: " << endl << str << endl;

  int count {};                            // Number of occurrences of word in str
  char* pstr { str };                      // Pointer to search start position
  char* found {};                          // Pointer to occurrence of word in str
  const size_t wordLength { std::strlen(word) };
  while (true)
  {
    found = std::strstr(pstr, word);
    if (!found)
      break;
    ++count;
    pstr = found + wordLength;
// Set next search start as 1 past the word found
  }
  cout << "\"" << word << "\" was found "
       << count << " times in the string." << endl;
  return 0;
}
```

The output from this example is:

```
The string to be searched is: Smith, where Jones had had "had had" had had "had".
"Had had" had had the examiners' approval.
"had" was found 10 times in the string.
```

How It Works

All the action takes place in the indefinite `while` loop:

```
while(true)
{
  found = std::strstr(pstr, word);
  if (!found)
    break;
  ++count;
  pstr = found + wordLength;
// Set next search start as 1 past the word found
}
```

You first search the string for `word` starting at position `pstr`, which initially is the beginning of the string. You store the address `strstr()` returns in `found`, which will be `nullptr` if `word` was not found so the `if` statement ends the loop in that case.

If `found` is not `nullptr`, you increment the number of occurrences of `word`, and update `pstr` so that it points to one character past the `word` instance that was found. This will be the starting point for the search on the next loop iteration. From the output, you can see that `word` was found ten times in `str`. Of course, `"Had"` doesn't count because it starts with an uppercase letter.

SUMMARY

You are now familiar with all of the basic types of values in C++, how to create and use arrays of those types, and how to create and use pointers. You have also been introduced to the idea of a reference. However, we have not exhausted all of these topics. I'll come back to arrays, pointers, and references later in the book.

The pointer mechanism is sometimes a bit confusing because it can operate at different levels within the same program. Sometimes it is operating as an address, and at other times it can be operating with the value stored at an address. It's very important that you feel at ease with the way pointers are used, so if you find that they are in any way unclear, try them out with a few examples of your own until you feel confident about applying them.

EXERCISES

1. Write a program that allows an unlimited number of values to be entered and stored in an array allocated in the free store. The program should then output the values, five to a line, followed by the average of the values entered. The initial array size should be five elements. The program should create a new array with five additional elements, when necessary, and copy values from the old array to the new.

2. Repeat the previous exercise but use pointer notation throughout instead of arrays.

3. Declare a character array, and initialize it to a suitable string. Use a loop to change every other character to uppercase.

Hint: In the ASCII character set, values for uppercase characters are 32 less than their lowercase counterparts.

4. Define an array of elements of type `double` that contains twelve arbitrary values that represent monthly average temperatures in Fahrenheit. Use a range-based `for` loop to convert the values to Centigrade and find and output the maximum, minimum, and average Centigrade temperatures.

➤ WHAT YOU LEARNED IN THIS CHAPTER

TOPIC	CONCEPT
Arrays	An array allows you to manage a number of variables of the same type using a single name. Each dimension of an array is defined between square brackets, following the array name in the definition of the array.
Array dimensions	Each dimension of an array is indexed starting from zero. Thus, the fifth element of a one-dimensional array has the index value 4.
Initializing arrays	Arrays can be initialized by placing the initializing values between curly braces in the definition — in other words, in an initializer list.
Range `for` loop	You can use the range-based `for` loop to iterate over each of the elements in an array.
Pointers	A pointer is a variable that contains the address of another variable. A pointer is defined as a 'pointer to type' and may only be assigned addresses of variables of the given type.
Pointers to `const` and `const` pointers	A pointer can point to a constant object. Such a pointer can be reassigned to another object. A pointer may also be defined as `const`, in which case it can't be reassigned.
References	A reference is an alias for something else. An lvalue reference can be used in place of the variable it references. An rvalue reference can refer to a value stored in a temporary location. A reference must be initialized when it is defined. A reference can't be reassigned to another variable.
The `sizeof` operator	The `sizeof` operator returns the number of bytes occupied by the object specified as its argument. Its argument may be a variable, or a type name between parentheses.
The `new` operator	The `new` operator allocates memory in the free store. When memory has been assigned, it returns a pointer to the beginning of the memory area. If memory cannot be allocated for any reason, an exception is thrown that by default causes the program to terminate.
The `delete` operator	You use the `delete` operator to release memory that you previously allocated using the `new` operator.

5

Introducing Structure into Your Programs

WHAT YOU WILL LEARN IN THIS CHAPTER:

- ➤ How to declare and write your own C++ functions
- ➤ How function arguments are defined and used
- ➤ How to pass arrays to and from a function
- ➤ What pass-by-value means
- ➤ How to pass pointers to functions
- ➤ How to use references as function arguments, and what pass-by-reference means
- ➤ How the `const` modifier affects function arguments
- ➤ How to return values from a function
- ➤ How to use recursion

WROX.COM CODE DOWNLOADS FOR THIS CHAPTER

You can find the wrox.com code downloads for this chapter on the Download Code tab at `www.wrox.com/go/beginningvisualc`. The code is in the Chapter 5 download and individually named according to the names throughout the chapter.

UNDERSTANDING FUNCTIONS

Up to now, you haven't really been able to structure your program code in a modular fashion, because you only know how to construct a program as a single function, `main()`; but you *have* been using library functions of various kinds as well as functions belonging to objects.

Whenever you write a C++ program, you should have a modular structure in mind from the outset, and as you'll see, a good understanding of how to implement functions is essential to object-oriented programming.

There's quite a lot to structuring your C++ programs, so to avoid indigestion, you won't try to swallow the whole thing in one gulp. After you have chewed over and gotten the full flavor of these morsels, you move on to the next chapter, where you get further into the meat of the topic.

First, I'll explain the broad principles of how a function works. A function is a self-contained block of code with a specific purpose. A function has a name that both identifies it and is used to call it for execution in a program. The name of a function is global if it is not defined within a namespace, otherwise the name is qualified by the namespace name. The name of a function is not necessarily unique, as you'll see in the next chapter; however, functions that perform different actions should generally have different names.

The name of a function is governed by the same rules as those for a variable. A function name is, therefore, a sequence of letters and digits, the first of which is a letter, where an underscore (_) counts as a letter. The name of a function should generally reflect what it does, so, for example, you might call a function that counts beans count_beans().

You pass information to a function by means of *arguments* specified when you invoke it. These arguments must correspond with *parameters* that appear in the definition of the function. The arguments that you specify replace the parameters used in the definition of the function when the function executes. The code in the function then executes as though it were written using your argument values. Figure 5-1 illustrates the relationship between arguments in the function call and the parameters you specify in the definition of the function.

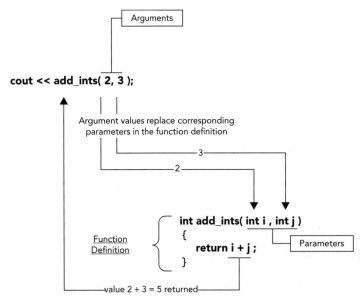

FIGURE 5-1

In Figure 5-1, the `add_ints()` function returns the sum of the two arguments passed to it. In general, a function returns either a single value to the point in the program where it was called, or nothing at all, depending on how you define the function. You might think that returning a single value from a function is a constraint, but the single value returned can be a pointer that could contain the address of an array, for example. You will learn more about how data is returned from a function a little later in this chapter.

Why Do You Need Functions?

One major advantage that a function offers is that it can be executed as many times as necessary from different points in a program. Without the ability to package a block of code into a function, programs would end up being much larger, because you would typically need to replicate the same code at various points in them. You also use functions to break up a program into easily manageable chunks for development and testing; a program of significant size and complexity that consists of several small blocks of code is much easier to understand and test than if it were written as one large chunk.

Imagine a really big program — let's say a million lines of code. A program of this size would be virtually impossible to write and debug without functions. Functions enable you to segment the program so that you can write the code piecemeal. You can test each piece independently before bringing it together with the other pieces. This approach also allows the development work to be divided among members of a programming team, with each team member taking responsibility for a tightly specified piece of the program that has a well-defined, functional interface to the rest of the code.

Structure of a Function

As you have seen when writing the function `main()`, a function consists of a *function header* that identifies the function, followed by the *body* of the function between braces that makes up the executable code for the function. Let's look at an example. You could write a function to raise a value to a given power; that is, to compute the result of multiplying the value x by itself n times, which is x^n:

```
// Function to calculate x to the power n, with n greater than or
// equal to 0
double power(double x, int n)          // Function header
{                                      // Function body starts here...
  double result {1.0};                 // Result stored here
  for(int i {1}; i <= n; i++)
    result *= x;

  return result;
}                                      // ...and ends here
```

The Function Header

Let's first examine the function header in this example. The following is the first line of the function:

```
double power(double x, int n)          // Function header
```

It consists of three parts:

➤ The type of the *return value* (`double`, in this case)

➤ The name of the function (`power`, in this case)

➤ The parameters of the function enclosed between parentheses (x and n, in this case, of types `double` and `int`, respectively)

The return value is returned to the calling function when the function is executed, so when the function is called, it results in a value of type `double` in the expression in which it appears.

Our function has two parameters: x, the value to be raised to a given power, which is of type `double`, and the value of the power, n, which is of type `int`. The computation that the function performs is written using these parameter variables together with another variable, `result`, declared in the body of the function. The parameter names and any variables defined in the body of the function are local to the function.

> **NOTE** *No semicolon is required at the end of the function header or after the closing brace for the function body.*

The General Form of a Function Header

The general form of a function header can be written as follows:

```
return_type function_name(parameter_list)
```

The `return_type` can be any legal type. If the function does not return a value, the return type is specified by the keyword `void`. The keyword `void` is also used to indicate the absence of parameters, so a function that has no parameters and doesn't return a value would have the following function header.

```
void my_function(void)
```

An empty parameter list also indicates that a function takes no arguments, so you could omit the keyword `void` between the parentheses like:

```
void my_function()
```

> **NOTE** *A function with a return type specified as* void *should not be used in an expression in the calling program. Because it doesn't return a value, it can't sensibly be part of an expression, so using it in this way causes the compiler to generate an error message.*

The Function Body

The desired computation in a function is performed by the statements in the function body that follow the function header. The first of these in our power() example declares a variable result that is initialized with the value 1.0. The variable result is local to the function, as are all automatic variables that you declare within the function body. This means that the variable result ceases to exist after the function has completed execution. What might immediately strike you is that if result ceases to exist on completing execution of the function, how is it returned? The answer is that a copy of the value to be returned is made automatically, and this copy is made available to the return point in the program.

The calculation in power() is performed in the for loop. A loop control variable i is declared in the for loop, which assumes successive values from 1 to n. The variable result is multiplied by x once for each loop iteration, so this occurs n times to generate the required value. If n is 0, the statement in the loop won't be executed at all because the loop continuation condition immediately fails, and so result is left as 1.0.

As I've said, the parameters and all the variables declared within the body of a function are local to the function. There is nothing to prevent you from using the same names for variables in other functions for quite different purposes. Indeed, it's just as well this is so because it would be extremely difficult to ensure variables' names were always unique within a program containing a large number of functions, particularly if the functions were not all written by the same person.

The scope of variables declared within a function is determined in the same way that I have already discussed. A variable is created at the point at which it is defined and ceases to exist at the end of the block containing it. There is one type of variable that is an exception to this — variables declared as static. I'll discuss static variables a little later in this chapter.

> **NOTE** *Take care not to mask global variables with local variables of the same name. You first met this situation back in Chapter 2, where you saw how you could use the scope resolution operator* :: *to access global variables.*

The return Statement

The return statement returns the value of result to the point where the function was called. The general form of the return statement is

```
return expression;
```

where *expression* must evaluate to a value of the type specified in the function header for the return value. The expression can be any expression you want, as long as you end up with a value of the required type. It can include function calls — even a call of the same function in which it appears, as you'll see later in this chapter.

If the type of return value has been specified as `void`, there must be no expression appearing in the `return` statement. It must be written simply as:

```
return;
```

You can also omit the `return` statement when it is the last statement in the function body and there is no return value.

Alternative Function Syntax

There is an alternative syntax for writing the function header. Here's an example of the `power()` function that you saw earlier defined using it:

```
auto power(double x, int n)-> double     // Function header
{                                        // Function body starts here...
  double result {1.0};                   // Result stored here
  for(int i {1}; i <= n; i++)
    result *= x;

  return result;
}                                        // ...and ends here
```

This will work in exactly the same way as the previous version of the function. The return type of the function appears following the `->` in the header. This is referred to as a `trailing return type`. The `auto` keyword at the beginning indicates to the compiler that the return type is determined later.

So why was it necessary to introduce the alternative syntax? Isn't the old syntax good enough? The answer is no. In the next chapter you'll learn about *function templates*, where situations can arise when you need to allow for the return type from a function to vary depending on the result of executing the body of the function. You can't specify that with the old syntax. The alternative function syntax does allow you to do that, as you'll see in Chapter 6.

Using a Function

At the point at which you use a function in a program, the compiler must know something about it to compile the function call. It needs enough information to be able to identify the function, and to verify that you are using it correctly. If the definition of the function that you intend to use does not appear earlier in the same source file, you must declare the function using a statement called a *function prototype*.

Function Prototypes

The prototype of a function provides the basic information that the compiler needs to check that you are using the function correctly. It specifies the parameters to be passed to the function, the function name, and the type of the return value — basically, it contains the same information as appears in the function header, with the addition of a semicolon. Clearly, the number of parameters and their types must be the same in the function prototype as they are in the function header in the definition of the function.

A prototype or a definition for each function that you call from within another function must appear before the statements doing the calling. Prototypes are usually placed at the beginning of the program source file. The header files that you've been including for standard library functions contain the prototypes of the functions provided by the library, amongst other things.

For the `power()` function example, you could write the prototype as:

```
double power(double value, int index);
```

> **NOTE** Don't forget that a semicolon is required at the end of a function prototype. Without it, you get error messages from the compiler.

Note that I have specified names for the parameters in the function prototype that are different from those I used in the function header when I defined the function. This is just to indicate that it's possible. Most often, the same names are used in the prototype and in the function header in the definition of the function, but this doesn't *have* to be so. You can use longer, more expressive parameter names in the function prototype to aid understanding of the significance of the parameters, and then use shorter parameter names in the function definition where the longer names would make the code in the body of the function less readable.

If you like, you can even omit the names altogether in the prototype, and just write:

```
double power(double, int);
```

This provides enough information for the compiler to do its job; however, it's better practice to use some meaningful name in a prototype because it aids readability and, in some cases, makes all the difference between clear code and confusing code. If you have a function with two parameters of the same type (suppose our index was also of type `double` in the function `power()`, for example), the use of suitable names indicates clearly which parameter appears first and which second. Without parameter names it would be impossible to tell.

TRY IT OUT   Using a Function

You can see how all this goes together in an example that exercises the `power()` function:

```cpp
// Ex5_01.cpp
// Declaring, defining, and using a function
#include <iostream>
using std::cout;
using std::endl;

double power(double x, int n);    // Function prototype

int main()
{
```

```
    int index {3};                 // Raise to this power
    double x {1};                  // Different x from that in function power
    double y {};

    y = power(5.0, 3);             // Passing constants as arguments
    cout << endl << "5.0 cubed = " << y;

    cout << endl << "3.0 cubed = "
         << power(3.0, index);     // Outputting return value

    x = power(x, power(2.0, 2.0)); // Using a function as an argument
    cout << endl                   // with auto conversion of 2nd parameter
         << "x = " << x;

    cout << endl;
    return 0;
}

// Function to compute positive integral powers of a double value
// First argument is value, second argument is power index
double power(double x, int n)
{                                  // Function body starts here...
    double result {1.0};           // Result stored here
    for(int i {1}; i <= n; i++)
        result *= x;
    return result;
}                                  // ...and ends here
```

This program shows some of the ways in which you can use the function power(), specifying the arguments to the function in a variety of ways. If you run this example, you get the following output:

```
5.0 cubed = 125
3.0 cubed = 27
x = 81
```

How It Works

After the usual #include statement for input/output and the using declarations, you have the prototype for the function power(). If you were to delete this and try recompiling the program, the compiler wouldn't be able to process the calls to the function in main() and would instead generate a whole series of error messages:

```
error C3861: 'power': identifier not found
```

In a change from previous examples, I've used the keyword void in the function main() where the parameter list would usually appear to indicate that no parameters are to be supplied. Previously, I left the parentheses enclosing the parameter list empty, which is also interpreted in C++ as indicating that there are no parameters. Using void in this way is a remnant from the practice in C but you won't see it very often in C++. As you saw, the keyword void is used as the return type for a function to indicate that no value is returned. If you specify the return type of a function as void, you must not place a value in any return statement within the function; otherwise, you get an error message from the compiler.

You gathered from some of the previous examples that using a function is very simple. To use the function power() to calculate 5.0^3 and store the result in a variable y in our example, you have the following statement:

```
y = power(5.0, 3);
```

The values 5.0 and 3 here are the arguments to the function. They happen to be constants, but you can use any expression as an argument, as long as a value of the correct type is ultimately produced. The arguments to the power() function substitute for the parameters x and n, which were used in the definition of the function. The computation is performed using these values, and then, a copy of the result, 125, is returned to the calling function, main(), which is then stored in y. You can think of the function as having this value in the statement or expression in which it appears. You then output the value of y:

```
cout << endl << "5.0 cubed = " << y;
```

The next call of the function is used within the output statement:

```
cout << endl << "3.0 cubed = "
     << power(3.0, index);          // Outputting return value
```

Here, the value returned by the function is transferred directly to the output stream. Because you haven't stored the returned value anywhere, it is otherwise unavailable to you. The first argument in the call of the function here is a constant; the second argument is a variable.

The function power() is used next in this statement:

```
x = power(x, power(2.0, 2.0));      // Using a function as an argument
```

Here, the power() function is called twice. The first call to the function is the rightmost in the expression, and the result supplies the value for the second argument to the leftmost call. Although the arguments in the sub-expression power(2.0, 2.0) are both specified as the double literal 2.0, the function is actually called with the first argument as 2.0 and the second argument as the integer literal, 2. The compiler converts the double value specified for the second argument to type int, because it knows from the function prototype (shown again here) that the type of the second parameter has been specified as int.

```
double power(double x, int n);      // Function prototype
```

The double result 4.0 is returned by the first call to the power() function, and after conversion to type int, the value 4 is passed as the second argument in the next call of the function, with x as the first argument. Because x has the value 3.0, the value of 3.0^4 is computed and the result, 81.0, stored in x. This sequence of events is illustrated in Figure 5-2.

This statement involves two implicit conversions from type double to type int that were inserted by the compiler. There's a possible loss of data when converting from type double to type int, so the compiler issues warning messages when this occurs, even though the compiler itself has inserted the conversations. Generally, relying on automatic conversions where there is potential for data loss is a dangerous programming practice, and it is not at all obvious from the code that this conversion is intended. It is far better to be explicit in your code by using the `static_cast` operator when necessary. The statement in the example is much better written as:

```
x = power(x, static_cast<int>(power(2.0, 2)));
```

Coding the statement like this avoids both the compiler warning messages that the original version caused. Using a static cast does not remove the possibility of losing data in the conversion of data from one type to another. Because you specified it, though, it is clear that this is what you intended, recognizing that data loss might occur.

You could write the loop in the `power()` function like this:

```
for(auto i = 1; i <= n; i++)
    result *= x;
```

The compiler will deduce the appropriate type for i from the initial value. I prefer to explicitly specify the type as `int` in this instance because I think it makes the code more readily understood.

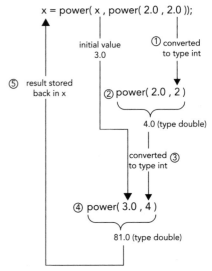

FIGURE 5-2

PASSING ARGUMENTS TO A FUNCTION

It's very important to understand how arguments are passed to a function, because it affects how you write functions and how they ultimately operate. There are also a number of pitfalls to be avoided, so we'll look at the mechanism for this quite closely.

The arguments you specify when a function is called should usually correspond in type and sequence to the parameters that appear in the definition of the function. As you saw in the last example, if the type of an argument you specify in a function call doesn't correspond with the type of the parameter in the function definition, the compiler arranges for the argument to be converted to the required type, obeying the same rules as those for converting operands that I discussed in Chapter 2. If the conversion is not possible, you get an error message from the compiler. However, even if the conversion is possible and the code compiles, it could result in the loss of data (for example, a conversion from type `long` to type `short`) and should therefore be avoided.

There are two mechanisms used to pass arguments to functions. The first mechanism applies when you specify the parameters in the function definition as ordinary variables (*not* references). This is called the *pass-by-value* method of transferring data to a function, so let's look into that first.

The Pass-by-Value Mechanism

With this mechanism, the variables, constants, or expression values that you specify as arguments are not passed to a function at all. Instead, copies of the argument values are created, and these copies are used as the values to be transferred to the function. Figure 5-3 shows this using the example of our power() function.

int index {2};
double value {10.0};
double result {power(value, index)} ;

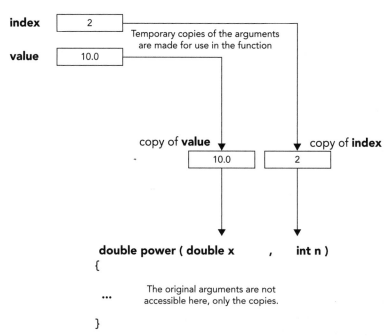

FIGURE 5-3

In Figure 5-3, the value returned by power() is used to initialize result. Each time you call the power() function, the compiler arranges for copies of the arguments to be stored in temporary location plural in memory. During execution of the function, all references to the function parameters are mapped to these temporary copies of the arguments.

TRY IT OUT   **Passing-by-Value**

One consequence of the pass-by-value mechanism is that a function can't directly modify the arguments passed to it. You can demonstrate this by deliberately trying to do so in an example:

```
// Ex5_02.cpp
// A futile attempt to modify caller arguments
#include <iostream>
using std::cout;
using std::endl;

int incr10(int num);              // Function prototype

int main()
{
  int num {3};

  cout << endl << "incr10(num) = " << incr10(num) << endl
       << "num = " << num << endl;
  return 0;
}

// Function to increment a variable by 10
int incr10(int num)               // Using the same name might help...
{
  num += 10;                      // Increment the caller argument - hopefully
  return num;                     // Return the incremented value
}
```

Of course, this program is doomed to failure. If you run it, you get this output:

```
incr10(num) = 13
num = 3
```

How It Works

The output confirms that the original value of num remains untouched. The copy of num that was generated and passed as the argument to the incr10() function was incremented and was eventually discarded on exiting from the function.

Clearly, the pass-by-value mechanism provides you with a high degree of protection from having your caller arguments mauled by a rogue function, but it is conceivable that you might actually want to modify caller arguments. Of course, there is a way to do this. Didn't you just know that pointers would turn out to be incredibly useful?

Pointers as Arguments to a Function

When you use a pointer as an argument, the pass-by-value mechanism still operates as before; however, a pointer is an address of another variable, and if you take a copy of this address, the copy still points to the same variable. This is how specifying a pointer as a parameter enables your function to get at a caller argument.

Pass-by-Pointer

You can change the last example to use a pointer to demonstrate the effect:

```cpp
// Ex5_03.cpp
// A successful attempt to modify caller arguments
#include <iostream>
using std::cout;
using std::endl;

int incr10(int* num);                   // Function prototype

int main()
{
  int num {3};

  int* pnum {&num};                      // Pointer to num

  cout << endl << "Address passed = " << pnum;

  int result {incr10(pnum)};
  cout << endl << "incr10(pnum) = " << result;

  cout << endl << "num = " << num << endl;
  return 0;
}

// Function to increment a variable by 10
int incr10(int* num)                     // Function with pointer argument
{
  cout << endl << "Address received = " << num;

  *num += 10;                            // Increment the caller argument
                                         //  - confidently
  return *num;                           // Return the incremented value
}
```

The output from this example is:

```
Address passed = 0012FF6C
Address received = 0012FF6C
incr10(pnum) = 13
num = 13
```

The address values produced by your computer may be different from those shown here, but the two values should be identical.

How It Works

In this example, the principal alterations from the previous version relate to passing a pointer, pnum, in place of the original variable, num. The prototype for the function now has the parameter type specified as a pointer to int, and the main() function has the pointer pnum declared and initialized with the address of num. The function main(), and the function incr10(), output the address sent and the address received, respectively, to verify that the same address is indeed being used in both places. Because the incr10() function is writing to cout, you now call it before the output statement and store the return value in result:

```
int result {incr10(pnum)};
cout << endl << "incr10(pnum) = " << result;
```

This ensures proper sequencing of the output. The output shows that this time, the variable num has been incremented and has a value that's now identical to that returned by the function.

In the rewritten version of incr10(), both the statement incrementing the value passed to the function and the return statement now de-reference the pointer to use the value stored.

Passing Arrays to a Function

You can pass an array to a function, but in this case, the array is not copied, even though a pass-by-value method of passing arguments still applies. The array name is converted to a pointer, and a copy of the pointer to the beginning of the array is passed by value to the function. This is quite advantageous because copying large arrays is very time-consuming. As you may have worked out, elements of the array may be changed within a function, and thus, an array is the only type that cannot be passed by value.

TRY IT OUT Passing Arrays

You can illustrate the ins and outs of this by writing a function to compute the average of a number of values passed to a function in an array:

```
// Ex5_04.cpp
// Passing an array to a function
#include <iostream>
using std::cout;
using std::endl;

double average(double array[], int count);        //Function prototype

int main()
{
  double values[] { 1.0, 2.0, 3.0, 4.0, 5.0, 6.0, 7.0, 8.0, 9.0, 10.0 };

  cout << endl << "Average = "
       << average(values, _countof(values)) << endl;
  return 0;
}

// Function to compute an average
double average(double array[], int count)
{
  double sum {};                       // Accumulate total in here
```

```
    for(int i {}; i < count; i++)
        sum += array[i];                // Sum array elements

    return sum/count;                   // Return average
}
```

The program produces the following output:

```
Average = 5.5
```

How It Works

The `average()` function is designed to work with an array of any length. As you can see from the prototype, it accepts two arguments: the array and a count of the number of elements. The function is called in `main()` in this statement:

```
cout << endl << "Average = "
    << average(values, _countof(values)) << endl;
```

The function is called with the first argument as the array name, `values`, and the second argument as an expression that evaluates to the number of elements in the array.

The number of elements is produced by the _countof() macro. Note that you cannot apply this macro to an array parameter in a function because only the address of the array is known.

Within the body of the function, the computation is expressed in the way you would expect. There's no significant difference between this and the way you would write the computation if you implemented it directly in `main()`.

The output confirms that everything works as we anticipated.

TRY IT OUT   **Using Pointer Notation When Passing Arrays**

You haven't exhausted all the possibilities here. As you determined at the outset, the array name is passed as a pointer — to be precise, as a copy of a pointer — so within the function, you are not obliged to work with the data as an array at all. You could modify the function in the example to work with pointer notation throughout, in spite of the fact that you are using an array.

```
// Ex5_05.cpp
// Handling an array in a function as a pointer
#include <iostream>
using std::cout;
using std::endl;

double average(double* array, int count);        //Function prototype

int main()
{
    double values[] { 1.0, 2.0, 3.0, 4.0, 5.0, 6.0, 7.0, 8.0, 9.0, 10.0 };

    cout << endl << "Average = "
```

```
            << average(values, _countof(values)) << endl;
   return 0;
}

// Function to compute an average
double average(double* array, int count)
{
   double sum {};                      // Accumulate total in here
   for(int i {}; i < count; i++)
      sum += *array++;                 // Sum array elements

   return sum/count;                   // Return average
}
```

The output is exactly the same as in the previous example.

How It Works

As you can see, the program needed very few changes to make it work with the array as a pointer. The prototype and the function header have been changed, although neither change is absolutely necessary. If you change both back to the original version, with the first parameter specified as a `double` array, and leave the function body written in terms of a pointer, it works just as well. The most interesting aspect of this version is the body of the `for` loop statement:

```
      sum += *array++;                 // Sum array elements
```

Here, you apparently break the rule about not being able to modify an address specified as an array name because you are incrementing the address stored in `array`. In fact, you aren't breaking the rule at all. Remember that the pass-by-value mechanism makes a copy of the original array address and passes that to the function, so you are just modifying the copy here — the original array address is quite unaffected. As a result, whenever you pass a one-dimensional array to a function, you are free to treat the value passed as a pointer in every sense, and change the address in any way that you want.

> **NOTE** An array records no information about its size, so you cannot use the range-based `for` loop with an array passed as an argument to a function.

Passing Multidimensional Arrays to a Function

Passing a multidimensional array to a function is quite straightforward. The following statement declares a two-dimensional array, `beans`:

```
double beans[2][4];
```

You could then write the prototype of a hypothetical function, `yield()`, like this:

```
double yield(double beans[2][4]);
```

> **NOTE** *You may be wondering how the compiler knows that this is defining an array of the dimensions shown as a parameter, and not a single array element. The answer is simple — you can't write a single array element as a parameter in a function definition or prototype, although you can pass one as an argument when you call a function. For a parameter accepting a single element of an array as an argument, the parameter would have just a variable name and its type. The array context doesn't apply.*

When you are defining a multidimensional array as a parameter, you can also omit the first dimension value. Of course, the function needs some way of knowing the extent of the first dimension. For example, you could write this:

```
double yield(double beans[][4], int index);
```

Here, the second parameter provides the necessary information about the first dimension. The function can operate with a two-dimensional array, with the value for the first dimension specified by the second argument and with the second dimension fixed at 4.

TRY IT OUT   Passing Multidimensional Arrays

You define such a function in the following example:

```cpp
// Ex5_06.cpp
// Passing a two-dimensional array to a function
#include <iostream>
using std::cout;
using std::endl;

double yield(double array[][4], int n);

int main()
{
  double beans[3][4]    {    { 1.0,  2.0,  3.0,  4.0 },
                             { 5.0,  6.0,  7.0,  8.0 },
                             { 9.0, 10.0, 11.0, 12.0 }   };

  cout << endl << "Yield = " << yield(beans, _countof(beans))
       << endl;
  return 0;
}

// Function to compute total yield
double yield(double beans[][4], int count)
{
  double sum {};
```

```
    for(int i {}; i < count; i++)      // Loop through number of rows
        for(int j {}; j < 4; j++)      // Loop through elements in a row
            sum += beans[i][j];
    return sum;
}
```

The output from this example is:

```
Yield = 78
```

How It Works

I have used different names for the parameters in the function header from those in the prototype, just to remind you that this is possible — but in this case, it doesn't really improve the program at all. The first parameter is defined as an array of an arbitrary number of rows, each row having four elements. You call the function using the array beans with three rows. The second argument is specified by dividing the total size of the array in bytes by the size of the first row. This evaluates to the number of rows in the array.

The computation in the function is a nested for loop with the inner loop summing elements of a single row and the outer loop repeating this for each row.

Using a pointer in a function rather than a multidimensional array as an argument doesn't really apply particularly well in this example. When the array is passed, it passes an address value that points to an array of four elements (a row). This doesn't lend itself to an easy pointer operation within the function. You would need to modify the statement in the nested for loop to the following:

```
    sum += *(*(beans + i) + j);
```

So the computation is probably clearer in array notation.

References as Arguments to a Function

We now come to the second of the two mechanisms for passing arguments to a function. Specifying a parameter to a function as a reference changes the method of passing data for that parameter. The method used is not pass-by-value, where an argument is copied before being transferred to the function, but *pass-by-reference*, where the parameter acts as an alias for the argument passed. This eliminates any copying of the argument supplied and allows the function to access the caller argument directly. It also means that the de-referencing, which is required when passing and using a pointer to a value, is also unnecessary.

Using reference parameters to a function has particular significance when you are working with objects of a class type. Objects can be large and complex, in which case, the copying process can be very time-consuming. Using reference parameters in these situations can make your code execute considerably faster.

TRY IT OUT   Pass-by-Reference

Let's go back to a revised version of a very simple example, Ex5_03.cpp, to see how it would work using reference parameters:

```cpp
// Ex5_07.cpp
// Using an lvalue reference to modify caller arguments
#include <iostream>
using std::cout;
using std::endl;

int incr10(int& num);                  // Function prototype

int main()
{
  int num {3};
  int value {6};

  int result {incr10(num)};
  cout << endl  << "incr10(num) = " << result
       << endl << "num = " << num;

  result = incr10(value);
  cout << endl << "incr10(value) = " << result
       << endl << "value = " << value << endl;
  return 0;
}

// Function to increment a variable by 10
int incr10(int& num)                    // Function with reference argument
{
  cout << endl << "Value received = " << num;
  num += 10;                            // Increment the caller argument
                                        //  - confidently
  return num;                           // Return the incremented value
}
```

This program produces the output:

```
Value received = 3
incr10(num) = 13
num = 13
Value received = 6
incr10(value) = 16
value = 16
```

How It Works

You should find the way this works quite remarkable. This is essentially the same as Ex5_03.cpp, except that the function uses an lvalue reference as a parameter. The prototype has been changed to reflect this. When the function is called, the argument is specified just as though it were a pass-by-value operation, so it's used in the same way as the earlier version. The argument value isn't passed to the function. The function parameter is *initialized* with the address of the argument, so whenever the parameter num is used in the function, it accesses the caller argument directly.

Just to reassure you that there's nothing fishy about the use of the identifier num in main() as well as in the function, the function is called a second time with the variable value as the argument. At first sight, this may give you the impression that it contradicts what I said was a basic property of a reference — that after being declared and initialized, it couldn't be reassigned to another variable. The reason it isn't contradictory is that a reference as a function parameter is created and initialized each time the function is called, and is destroyed when the function ends, so you get a completely new reference created each time you use the function.

Within the function, the value received from the calling program is displayed onscreen. Although the statement is essentially the same as the one used to output the address stored in a pointer, because num is now a reference you obtain the data value rather than the address.

This clearly demonstrates the difference between a reference and a pointer. A reference is an alias for another variable, and therefore can be used as an alternative way of referring to it. It is equivalent to using the original variable name. The output shows that the incr10() function is directly modifying the variable passed as a caller argument.

You will find that if you try to use a numeric value, such as 20, as an argument to incr10(), the compiler outputs an error message. This is because the compiler recognizes that a reference parameter can be modified within a function, and the last thing you want is to have your constants changing value now and again. This would introduce a kind of excitement into your programs that you could probably do without. You also cannot use an expression for an argument corresponding to an lvalue reference parameter unless the expression is an lvalue. Essentially, the argument for an lvalue reference parameter must result in a persistent memory location in which something can be stored.

> **NOTE** I'm sure that you remember that there is another type of reference called an rvalue reference that I mentioned in Chapter 4. A parameter of an rvalue reference type allows an expression that is an rvalue to be passed to a function. You'll learn more about this later in this chapter.

The security you get by using an lvalue reference parameter is all very well, but if the function didn't modify the value, you wouldn't want the compiler to create all these error messages every time you passed a reference argument that was a constant. Surely, there ought to be some way to accommodate this? As Ollie would have said, "There most certainly is, Stanley!"

Use of the const Modifier

You can apply the const modifier to a function parameter to tell the compiler that you don't intend to modify it in any way. This causes the compiler to check that your code indeed does not modify the argument, and there are no error messages when you use a constant argument.

TRY IT OUT   **Passing a const**

You can modify the previous program to show how the const modifier changes the situation:

```cpp
// Ex5_08.cpp
// Using a reference to modify caller arguments

#include <iostream>
using std::cout;
using std::endl;

int incr10(const int& num);                 // Function prototype

int main()
{
  const int num {3};        // Declared const to test for temporary creation
  int value {6};

  int result {incr10(num)}
  cout << endl << "incr10(num) = " << result
       << endl << "num = " << num;

  result = incr10(value);
  cout << endl << "incr10(value) = " << result;
  cout << endl << "value = " << value;

  cout << endl;
  return 0;
}

// Function to increment a variable by 10
int incr10(const int& num)        // Function with const reference argument
{
  cout << endl << "Value received = " << num;
//    num += 10;                  // this statement would now be illegal
  return num+10;                  // Return the incremented value
}
```

The output when you execute this is:

```
Value received = 3
incr10(num) = 13
num = 3
Value received = 6
incr10(value) = 16
value = 6
```

How It Works

You declare the variable num in main() as const to show that when the parameter to the function incr10() is declared as const, you no longer get a compiler message when passing a const object.

It has also been necessary to comment out the statement that increments num in the function incr10(). If you uncomment this line, you'll find the program no longer compiles, because the compiler won't allow num to appear on the left of an assignment. When you specified num as const in the function header and prototype, you promised not to modify it, so the compiler checks that you kept your word. Everything works as before, except that the variables in main() are no longer changed by the function.

By using lvalue reference parameters, you now have the best of both worlds. On one hand, you can write a function that can access caller arguments directly and avoid the copying that is implicit in the pass-by-value mechanism. On the other hand, where you don't intend to modify an argument, you can get all the protection against accidental modification you need by using a const modifier with an lvalue reference type.

Rvalue Reference Parameters

I'll now illustrate briefly how parameters that are rvalue reference types differ from parameters that are lvalue reference types. Keep in mind that this won't be how rvalue references are intended to be used. You'll learn about that later in the book. Let's look at an example that is similar to Ex5_07.cpp.

TRY IT OUT **Using rvalue Reference Parameters**

Here's the code for this example:

```
// Ex5_09.cpp
// Using an rvalue reference parameter

#include <iostream>
using std::cout;
using std::endl;

int incr10(int&& num);              // Function prototype

int main()
{
  int num {3};
  int value {6};
  int result {};
/*
  result = incr10(num);                         // Increment num
  cout << endl << "incr10(num) = " << result
       << endl << "num = " << num;

  result = incr10(value);                       // Increment value
  cout << endl << "incr10(value) = " << result
       << endl << "value = " << value;
*/
  result = incr10(value+num);                   // Increment an expression
  cout << endl << "incr10(value+num) = " << result
```

```
           << endl << "value = " << value;

    result = incr10(5);                              // Increment a literal
    cout << endl << "incr10(5) = " << result
         << endl << "5 = " << 5;

    cout << endl;
    return 0;
}

// Function to increment a variable by 10
int incr10(int&& num)          // Function with rvalue reference argument
{
    cout << endl << "Value received = " << num;
    num += 10;
    return num;               // Return the incremented value
}
```

Compiling and executing this produces the output:

```
Value received = 9
incr10(value+num) = 19
value = 6
Value received = 5
incr10(5) = 15
5 = 5
```

How It Works

The incr10() function now has an rvalue reference parameter type. In main(), you call the function with the expression value+num as the argument. The output shows that the function returns the value of the expression incremented by 10. Of course, you saw earlier that if you try to pass an expression as the argument for an lvalue reference parameter, the compiler will not allow it.

Next, you pass the literal, 5, as the argument, and again, the value returned shows the incrementing works. The output also shows that the literal 5 has not been changed, but why not? The argument in this case is an expression consisting of just the literal 5. The expression has the value 5 when it is evaluated, and this is stored in a temporary location that is referenced by the function parameter.

If you uncomment the statements at the beginning of main(), the code will not compile. A function that has an rvalue reference parameter can only be called with an argument that is an rvalue. Because num and value are lvalues, the compiler flags the statements that pass these as arguments to incr10() as errors.

While this example shows that you can pass an expression as the argument corresponding to an rvalue reference, and that within the function, the temporary location holding the value of the expression can be accessed and changed, this serves no purpose in this context. You will see when we get to look into defining classes that in some circumstances, rvalue reference parameters offer significant advantages.

> **NOTE** An important point to keep in mind is that even though an rvalue reference parameter may refer to an rvalue — the result of an expression that is temporary — the rvalue reference parameter itself is not an rvalue, it is an lvalue. There are circumstances where you will want to convert the rvalue reference parameter from an lvalue to an rvalue. You will see in Chapter 8 how this can arise and how you can use the `std::move()` library function to convert an lvalue to an rvalue.

Arguments to main()

You can define `main()` with no parameters or you can specify a parameter list that allows the `main()` function to obtain values from the command line from the execute command for the program. Values passed from the command line as arguments to `main()` are always interpreted as strings. If you want to get data into `main()` from the command line, you must define it like this:

```
int main(int argc, char* argv[])
{
   // Code for main()...
}
```

The first parameter is the count of the number of strings found on the command line, including the program name, and the second parameter is an array that contains pointers to these strings plus an additional element that is *null*. Thus, `argc` is always at least 1, because you at least must enter the name of the program. The number of arguments received depends on what you enter on the command line to execute the program. For example, suppose that you execute the `DoThat` program with the command:

```
DoThat.exe
```

There is just the name of the `.exe` file for the program, so `argc` is 1 and the `argv` array contains two elements — `argv[0]` pointing to the string `"DoThat.exe"`, and `argv[1]` that contains `nullptr`.

Suppose you enter this on the command line:

```
DoThat or else "my friend" 999.9
```

Now `argc` is 5 and `argv` contains six elements, the last element being `nullptr` and the first five pointing to the strings:

```
"DoThat" "or" "else" "my friend" "999.9"
```

You can see from this that if you want to have a string that includes spaces received as a single string, you must enclose it between double quotes. You can also see that numerical values are read as strings, so if you want conversion to the numerical value, that is up to you.

Let's see it working.

TRY IT OUT   **Receiving Command-Line Arguments**

This program just lists the arguments it receives from the command line:

```
// Ex5_10.cpp
// Reading command line arguments
#include <iostream>
using std::cout;
using std::endl;

int main(int argc, char* argv[])
{
  cout << endl << "argc = " << argc << endl;
  cout << "Command line arguments received are:" << endl;
  for(int i {}; i <argc; i++)
    cout << "argument " << (i+1) << ": " << argv[i] << endl;
  return 0;
}
```

You have two choices as to how you enter the command-line arguments. After you build the example, you can open a command window at the folder containing the .exe file, and then enter the program name followed by the command-line arguments. Alternatively, you can specify the command-line arguments in the IDE before you execute the program. Just open the project properties window by selecting Project ⇨ Properties from the main menu and then extend the Configuration Properties tree in the left pane by clicking the arrow. Click the Debugging folder and enter the items to be passed to the application as values for the Command Arguments property.

I enter the following in the command window with the current directory containing the .exe file for the program:

```
Ex5_10 trying multiple "argument values" 4.5 0.0
```

Here is the output resulting from my input:

```
argc = 6
Command line arguments received are:
argument 1: Ex5_10
argument 2: trying
argument 3: multiple
argument 4: argument values
argument 5: 4.5
argument 6: 0.0
```

How It Works

The program first outputs the value of `argc` and then the values of each argument from the `argv` array in the `for` loop. You can see from the output that the first argument value is the program name. `"argument values"` is treated as a single argument because of the enclosing double quotes.

You could make use of the fact that the last element in `argv` is `nullptr` and code the output of the command-line argument values like this:

```
int i{-1};
while(argv[++i]
    cout << "argument " << (i+1) << ": " << argv[i] << endl;
```

The `while` loop ends when `argv[argc]` is reached because that element contains `nullptr`.

Accepting a Variable Number of Function Arguments

You can define a function so that it allows any number of arguments to be passed to it. You indicate that a variable number of arguments can be supplied by placing an ellipsis (which is three periods, . . .) at the end of the parameter list in the function definition. For example:

```
int sumValues(int first,...)
{
  //Code for the function
}
```

There must be at least one ordinary parameter, but you can have more. The ellipsis must always be placed at the end of the parameter list.

Obviously, there is no information about the type or number of arguments in the variable list, so your code must figure out what is passed to the function when it is called. The C++ library defines `va_start`, `va_arg`, and `va_end` macros in the `cstdarg` header to help you do this. It's easiest to show how these are used with an example.

TRY IT OUT   **Receiving a Variable Number of Arguments**

This program uses a function that just sums the values of a variable number of arguments passed to it:

```
// Ex5_11.cpp
// Handling a variable number of arguments
#include <iostream>
#include <cstdarg>
using std::cout;
using std::endl;

int sum(int count, ...)
{
  if(count <= 0)
    return 0;

  va_list arg_ptr;                    // Declare argument list pointer
  va_start(arg_ptr, count);           // Set arg_ptr to 1st optional argument

  int sum {};
  for(int i {}; i<count; i++)
```

```
            sum += va_arg(arg_ptr, int);        // Add int value from arg_ptr and increment

        va_end(arg_ptr);                        // Reset the pointer to null
        return sum;
}

int main(int argc, char* argv[])
{
    cout << sum(6, 2, 4, 6, 8, 10, 12) << endl;
    cout << sum(9, 11, 22, 33, 44, 55, 66, 77, 66, 99) << endl;
    return 0;
}
```

This example produces the following output:

```
42
473
```

How It Works

The main() function calls the sum() function in the two output statements, in the first instance with seven arguments and in the second with ten arguments. The first argument in each case specifies the number of arguments that follow. It's important not to forget this, because if you omit the count argument, the result will be rubbish.

The sum() function has a single normal parameter of type int that represents the count of the number of arguments that follow. The ellipsis in the parameter list indicates that an arbitrary number of arguments can be passed. Basically, you have two ways of determining how many arguments there are when the function is called — you can require that the number of arguments is specified by a fixed parameter, as in the case of sum(), or you can require that the last argument has a special marker value that you can check for and recognize.

To start processing the variable argument list, you declare a pointer of type va_list:

```
        va_list arg_ptr;                        // Declare argument list pointer
```

The va_list type is defined in the cstdarg header file, and the pointer is used to point to each argument in turn.

The va_start macro is used to initialize arg_ptr so that it points to the first argument in the list:

```
        va_start(arg_ptr, count);               // Set arg_ptr to 1st optional argument
```

The second argument to the macro is the name of the fixed parameter that precedes the ellipsis in the parameter list, and this is used by the macro to determine where the first variable argument is.

You retrieve the values of the arguments in the list in the for loop:

```
        int sum {};
        for(int i {} ; i<count; i++)
            sum += va_arg(arg_ptr, int);        // Add int value from arg_ptr and increment
```

The `va_arg` macro returns the value of the argument at the location specified by `arg_ptr` and increments `arg_ptr` to point to the next argument value. The second argument to the `va_arg` macro is the argument type, and this determines the value that you get as well as how `arg_ptr` increments, so if this is not correct, you get chaos; the program probably executes, but the values you retrieve are rubbish, and `arg_ptr` is incremented incorrectly to access more rubbish.

When you are finished retrieving argument values, you reset `arg_ptr` with the statement:

```
va_end(arg_ptr);                    // Reset the pointer to null
```

The `va_end` macro resets the pointer of type `va_list` that you pass as the argument to it to null. It's a good idea to always do this because after processing the arguments, `arg_ptr` points to a location that does not contain valid data.

RETURNING VALUES FROM A FUNCTION

All the example functions that you have created have returned a single value. Is it possible to return anything other than a single value? Well, not directly, but as I said earlier, the single value returned need not be a numeric value; it could also be an address, which provides the key to returning any amount of data. You simply use a pointer. Unfortunately, this also is where the pitfalls start, so you need to keep your wits about you for the adventure ahead.

Returning a Pointer

Returning a pointer value is easy. A pointer value is just an address, so if you want to return the address of some variable `value`, you can just write the following:

```
return &value;                      // Returning an address
```

As long as the function header and function prototype indicate the return type appropriately, you have no problem — or at least, no apparent problem. Assuming that the variable `value` is of type `double`, the prototype of a function called `treble`, which might contain the preceding `return` statement, could be as follows:

```
double* treble(double data);
```

I have defined the parameter list arbitrarily here.

So let's look at a function that returns a pointer. It's only fair that I warn you in advance — this function doesn't work, but it is educational. Let's assume that you need a function that returns a pointer to a memory location containing three times its argument value. Our first attempt to implement such a function might look like this:

```
// Function to treble a value - mark 1
double* treble(double data)
{
```

```
      double result {};
      result = 3.0*data;
      return &result;
   }
```

TRY IT OUT   Returning a Bad Pointer

You could create a little test program to see what happens (remember that the `treble` function won't work as expected):

```
// Ex5_12.cpp
#include <iostream>
using std::cout;
using std::endl;

double* treble (double);                  // Function prototype

int main()
{
   double num {5.0};                      // Test value
   double* ptr {};                        // Pointer to returned value

   ptr = treble(num);

    out << endl << "Three times num = " << 3.0*num;

   cout << endl << "Result = " << *ptr;   // Display 3*num

   cout << endl;
   return 0;
}

// Function to treble a value - mark 1
double* treble(double data)
{
   double result {};
   result = 3.0*data;
   return &result;
}
```

There's a hint that everything is not as it should be, because compiling this program results in a warning from the compiler:

```
warning C4172: returning address of local variable or temporary
```

The output that I got from executing the program was:

```
Three times num = 15
Result = 4.10416e-230
```

How It Works (or Why It Doesn't)

The function `main()` calls `treble()` and stores the address returned in the pointer `ptr`, which should point to a value that is three times the argument, `num`. It then displays the result of computing three times `num`, followed by the value at the address returned from the function.

Clearly, the second line of output doesn't reflect the correct value of 15, but where's the error? Well, it's not exactly a secret because the compiler gives fair warning of the problem. The error arises because the variable `result` in the function `treble()` is created when the function begins execution, and is destroyed on exiting from the function — so the memory that the pointer is pointing to no longer contains the original variable value. The memory previously allocated to `result` becomes available for other purposes, and here, it has evidently been used for something else.

A Cast-Iron Rule for Returning Addresses

There is an absolutely cast-iron rule for returning addresses:

> *Never, ever, return the address of a local automatic variable from a function.*

You obviously can't use a function that doesn't work, so what can you do to rectify that? You could use a reference parameter and modify the original variable, but that's not what you set out to do. You are trying to return a pointer to some useful data so that, ultimately, you can return more than a single item of data. One answer lies in dynamic memory allocation (you saw this in action in the previous chapter). With the operator `new`, you can create a new variable in the free store that continues to exist until it is eventually destroyed by `delete` — or until the program ends. With this approach, the function looks like this:

```
// Function to treble a value - mark 2
double* treble(double data)
{
  double* result {new double{}};
  *result = 3.0*data;
  return result;
}
```

Rather than declaring `result` to be type `double`, you now declare it to be of type `double*` and store in it the address returned by the operator `new`. Because the result is a pointer, the rest of the function is changed to reflect this, and the address contained in the result is finally returned to the calling program. You could exercise this version by replacing the function in the last working example with this version.

You need to remember that with dynamic memory allocation from within a function such as this, more memory is allocated each time the function is called. The onus is on the calling program to delete the memory when it's no longer required. It's easy to forget to do this in practice, with the result that the free store is gradually eaten up until, at some point, it is exhausted and the program fails. As mentioned before, this sort of problem is referred to as a *memory leak*.

Here you can see how the function would be used. The only necessary change to the original code is to use delete to free the memory as soon as you have finished with the pointer returned by the treble() function.

```
#include <iostream>

using std::cout;
using std::endl;

double* treble(double);               // Function prototype

int main()
{
  double num {5.0};                   // Test value
  double* ptr {};                     // Pointer to returned value

  ptr = treble(num);

  cout << endl << "Three times num = " << 3.0*num;

  cout << endl << "Result = " << *ptr;   // Display 3*num
  delete ptr;                            // Don't forget to free the memory
  ptr = nullptr;
  cout << endl;
  return 0;
}

// Function to treble a value - mark 2
double* treble(double data)
{
  double* result {new double{}}
  *result = 3.0*data;
  return result;
}
```

> **NOTE** In Chapter 10 you'll learn about smart pointers that eliminate the need to use delete to free memory you have allocated with new. By using smart pointers you can remove the risk of memory leaks too.

Returning a Reference

You can also return an lvalue reference from a function. This is just as fraught with potential errors as returning a pointer, so you need to take care with this, too. Because an lvalue reference has no existence in its own right (it's always an alias for something else), you must be sure that the object that it refers to still exists after the function completes execution. It's very easy to forget this when you use references in a function because they appear to be just like ordinary variables.

References as return types are of primary significance in the context of object-oriented programming. As you will see later in the book, they enable you to do things that would be impossible without them. (This particularly applies to "operator overloading," which I'll come to in Chapter 8.) Returning an lvalue reference from a function means that you can use the result of the function on the left side of an assignment statement.

TRY IT OUT   Returning a Reference

Let's look at an example that illustrates the use of reference return types, and also demonstrates how a function can be used on the left of an assignment operation when it returns an lvalue. This example assumes that you have an array containing a mixed set of values. Whenever you want to insert a new value into the array, you want to replace the element with the lowest value.

```cpp
// Ex5_13.cpp
// Returning a reference
#include <iostream>
#include <iomanip>
using std::cout;
using std::endl;
using std::setw;

double& lowest(double values[], int length); // Function prototype

int main()
{

  double data[] { 3.0, 10.0, 1.5, 15.0, 2.7, 23.0,
                  4.5, 12.0, 6.8, 13.5, 2.1, 14.0 };
  int len {_countof(data)}                    // Number of elements
  for(auto value : data)
     cout << setw(6) << value;

  lowest(data, len) = 6.9;                    // Change lowest to 6.9
  lowest(data, len) = 7.9;                    // Change lowest to 7.9

  cout << endl;
  for (auto value : data)
     cout << setw(6) << value;

  cout << endl;
  return 0;
}

// Function returning a reference
double& lowest(double a[], int len)
{
  int j {};                                   // Index of lowest element
  for(int i {1}; i < len; i++)
     if(a[j] > a[i])                          // Test for a lower value...
         j = i;                               // ...if so update j
  return a[j];                                // Return reference to lowest element
}
```

The output from this example is:

```
3    10    1.5    15    2.7    23    4.5    12    6.8    13.5    2.1    14
3    10    6.9    15    2.7    23    4.5    12    6.8    13.5    7.9    14
```

How It Works

Let's first look at how the function is implemented. The prototype for the function `lowest()` uses `double&` as the specification of the return type, which is therefore of type "reference to `double`." You write a reference type return value in exactly the same way as you have seen for variable declarations, by appending `&` to the data type. The function has two parameters — a one-dimensional array of type `double` and a parameter of type `int` that specifies the length of the array.

The body of the function has a straightforward `for` loop to determine which element of the array passed contains the lowest value. The index, `j`, of the array element with the lowest value is arbitrarily set to 0 at the outset, and then modified within the loop if the current element, `a[i]`, is less than `a[j]`. Thus, on exit from the loop, `j` contains the index value corresponding to the array element with the lowest value. The `return` statement is:

```
    return a[j];                      // Return reference to lowest element
```

In spite of the fact that this looks identical to the statement that would return a value, because the return type was declared as a reference, this returns a reference to the array element `a[j]` rather than the value that the element contains. The address of `a[j]` is used to initialize the reference to be returned. This reference is created by the compiler because the return type was declared as a reference.

Don't confuse returning `&a[j]` with returning a reference. If you write `&a[j]` as the return value, you are specifying the address of `a[j]`, which is a *pointer*. If you do this after having specified the return type as a *reference*, you get an error message from the compiler. Specifically, you get this:

```
    error C2440: 'return' : cannot convert from 'double * ' to 'double &'
```

The function `main()`, which exercises the `lowest()` function, is very simple. An array of type `double` is declared and initialized with 12 arbitrary values, and an `int` variable `len` is initialized to the length of the array using the `_countof()` macro. The initial values in the array are output for comparison purposes.

Again, the program uses the stream manipulator `setw()` to space the values uniformly, requiring the `#include` directive for iomanip.

The function `main()` then calls the function `lowest()` on the left of an assignment to change the lowest value in the array. This is done twice to show that it does actually work and is not an accident. The contents of the array are then output to the display again, with the same field width as before, so corresponding values line up.

As you can see from the output with the first call to `lowest()`, the third element of the array, `data[2]`, contained the lowest value, so the function returned a reference to it and its value was changed to 6.9. Similarly, on the second call, `data[10]` was changed to 7.9. This demonstrates quite clearly that returning a reference allows the use of the function on the left of an assignment. The effect is as if the variable specified in the `return` statement appeared on the left of the assignment.

Of course, if you want to, you can also use it on the right of an assignment, or in any other suitable expression. If you had two arrays, x and y, with the number of array elements specified by lenx and leny, respectively, you could set the lowest element in the array x to twice the lowest element in the array y with this statement:

```
lowest(x, lenx) = 2.0*lowest(y, leny);
```

This statement would call lowest() twice — once with arguments y and leny in the expression on the right of the assignment, and once with arguments x and lenx to obtain the address where the result of the right-hand expression is to be stored.

A Cast-Iron Rule: Returning References

A similar rule to the one concerning the return of a pointer from a function also applies to returning references:

Never, ever, return a reference to a local variable from a function.

I'll leave the topic of returning a reference from a function for now, but I haven't finished with it yet. I will come back to it again in the context of user-defined types and object-oriented programming, when you will unearth a few more magical things that you can do with references.

Static Variables in a Function

There are some things you can't do with automatic variables within a function. You can't count how many times a function is called, for example, because you can't accumulate a value from one call to the next. There's more than one way to get around this. For instance, you could use a reference parameter to update a count in the calling program, but this wouldn't help if the function was called from lots of different places within a program. You could use a global variable that you incremented from within the function, but globals are risky things to use. Because globals can be accessed from anywhere in a program, it is very easy to change them accidentally.

Global variables are also risky in applications that have multiple threads of execution that access them, and you must take special care to manage how globals are accessed from different threads. The basic problem that has to be addressed when more than one thread can access a global variable is that one thread can change the value of a global variable while another thread is working with it. The best solution in such circumstances is to avoid the use of global variables altogether.

To create a variable whose value persists from one call of a function to the next, you can declare a variable within a function as static. You use exactly the same form of declaration for a static variable that you saw in Chapter 2. For example, to declare a variable count as static, you could use this statement:

```
static int count {};
```

This also initializes the variable to zero.

> **NOTE** *Initialization of a static variable within a function only occurs the first time that the function is called. On the first call of a function, the static variable is created and initialized. It then continues to exist for the duration of program execution, and whatever value it contains when the function is exited is available when the function is next called.*

TRY IT OUT **Using Static Variables in Functions**

You can demonstrate how a static variable behaves in a function with the following simple example:

```cpp
// Ex5_14.cpp
// Using a static variable within a function
#include <iostream>
using std::cout;
using std::endl;

void record();        // Function prototype, no arguments or return value

int main()
{
  record();

  for(int i {}; i <= 3; i++)
     record();

  cout << endl;
  return 0;
}

// A function that records how often it is called
void record()
{
  static int count {};
  cout << endl << "This is the " << ++count;
  if((count > 3) && (count < 21))          // All this....
     cout <<"th";
  else
     switch(count%10)                      // is just to get...
     {
     case 1: cout << "st";
             break;
     case 2: cout << "nd";
             break;
     case 3: cout << "rd";
             break;
     default: cout << "th";                // the right ending for...
     }                                     // 1st, 2nd, 3rd, 4th, etc.
  cout << " time I have been called";
  return;
}
```

Our function here serves only to record the fact that it was called. If you build and execute it, you get this output:

```
This is the 1st time I have been called
This is the 2nd time I have been called
This is the 3rd time I have been called
This is the 4th time I have been called
This is the 5th time I have been called
```

How It Works

You initialize the static variable `count` with 0 and increment it in the first output statement in the function. Because the increment operator is prefixed, the incremented value is displayed by the output statement. It will be 1 on the first call, 2 on the second, and so on. Because `count` is static, it continues to exist and retain its value from one call of the function to the next.

The remainder of the function is concerned with working out when `"st"`, `"nd"`, `"rd"`, or `"th"` should be appended to the value of `count` that is displayed. It's surprisingly irregular.

Note the `return` statement. Because the return type of the function is `void`, to include a value would cause a compiler error. You don't actually need to put a `return` statement in this particular case, because running off the closing brace for the body of the function is equivalent to executing a `return` statement without a value. The program would compile and run without error even if you didn't include the `return`.

RECURSIVE FUNCTION CALLS

When a function contains a call to itself, it's referred to as a *recursive function*. A recursive function call can also be indirect, where a function `fun1` calls a function `fun2`, which, in turn, calls `fun1`.

Recursion may seem to be a recipe for an indefinite loop, and if you aren't careful, it certainly can be. An indefinite loop will lock up your machine and require *Ctrl+Alt+Del* to end the program, which is always a nuisance. A prerequisite for avoiding an indefinite loop is that the function contains some means of stopping the process.

Unless you have come across the technique before, the sort of things to which recursion may be applied may not be obvious. In physics and mathematics, there are many things that can be thought of as involving recursion. A simple example is the factorial of an integer, which, for a given integer N, is the product $1 \times 2 \times 3 \ldots \times N$. This is very often the example given to show recursion in operation. Recursion can also be applied to the analysis of programs during the compilation process; however, you will look at something even simpler.

TRY IT OUT   A Recursive Function

At the start of this chapter (see `Ex5_01.cpp`), you produced a function to compute the integral power of a value; that is, to compute x^n. This is equivalent to x multiplied by itself n times. You can implement this as a recursive function as an elementary illustration of recursion in action. You can also improve the implementation of the function to deal with negative index values, where x^{-n} is equivalent to $1/x^n$.

```
// Ex5_15.cpp (based on Ex5_01.cpp)
// A recursive version of x to the power n
#include <iostream>
using std::cout;
using std::endl;

double power(double x, int n);      // Function prototype

int main()
{
  double x {2.0};                   // Different x from that in function power
  double result {};

  // Calculate x raised to powers -3 to +3 inclusive
  for(int index {-3}; index <= 3; index++)
    cout << x << " to the power " << index << " is " << power(x, index)<< endl;

  return 0;
}

// Recursive function to compute integral powers of a double value
// First argument is value, second argument is power index
double power(double x, int n)
{
  if(n < 0)
  {
    x = 1.0/x;
    n = -n;
  }
  if(n > 0)
    return x*power(x, n-1);
  else
    return 1.0;
}
```

The output from this program is:

```
2 to the power -3 is 0.125
2 to the power -2 is 0.25
2 to the power -1 is 0.5
2 to the power 0 is 1
2 to the power 1 is 2
2 to the power 2 is 4
2 to the power 3 is 8
```

How It Works

The function now supports positive and negative powers of x, so the first action is to check whether the value for the power that x is to be raised to, n, is negative:

```
if(n < 0)
{
  x = 1.0/x;
  n = -n;
}
```

Supporting negative powers is easy; the code just uses the fact that x^{-n} can be evaluated as $(1/x)^n$. Thus, if n is negative, you set x to be `1.0/x` and change the sign of n so it's positive.

The next `if` statement decides whether or not the `power()` function should call itself once more:

```
if(n > 0)
   return x*power(x, n-1);
else
   return 1.0;
```

The `if` statement provides for the value 1.0 being returned if n is zero, and in all other cases, it returns the result of the expression, `x*power(x, n-1)`. This causes a further call to the function `power()` with the index value reduced by 1. Thus, the `else` clause in the `if` statement provides the essential mechanism necessary to avoid an indefinite sequence of recursive function calls.

Clearly, if the value of n is other than zero within the function `power()`, a further call to `power()` occurs. In fact, for any given value of n other than 0, the function calls itself n times, ignoring the sign of n. Figure 5-4 shows the mechanism when the index argument is 3.

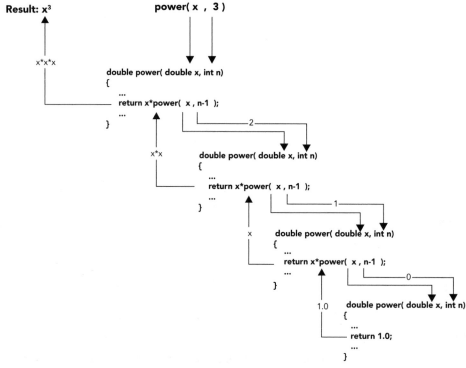

FIGURE 5-4

As you see, the `power()` function is called a total of four times to generate x^3, three of the calls being recursive where the function is calling itself.

Using Recursion

Unless you have a problem that particularly lends itself to using recursive functions, or if you have no obvious alternative, it's generally better to use a different approach, such as a loop, because it will be much more efficient than using recusion. Think about what happens with our last example to evaluate a simple product, x multiplied by itself n times. On each call, the compiler generates copies of the two arguments to the function, and also has to keep track of the location to return to when each `return` is executed. It's also necessary to arrange to save the contents of various registers in your computer so that they can be used within `power()`, and, of course, these need to be restored to their original state at each return from the function. With a quite modest depth of recursive call, the overhead will be considerably greater than if you use a loop.

This is not to say you should never use recursion. Where the problem suggests the use of recursive function calls as a solution, it can be an immensely powerful technique, greatly simplifying the code. You'll see an example where this is the case in the next chapter.

SUMMARY

In this chapter, you learned about the basics of program structure. You should have a good grasp of how functions are defined, how data can be passed to a function, and how results are returned to a calling program. Functions are fundamental to programming in C++, so everything you do from here on will involve using multiple functions in a program.

The use of references as arguments is a very important concept, so make sure you are confident about using them. You'll see a lot more about references as arguments to functions when you look into object-oriented programming.

EXERCISES

1. The *factorial* of 4 (written as 4!) is $4 \times 3 \times 2 \times 1 = 24$, and 3! is $3 \times 2 \times 1 = 6$, so it follows that 4! is $4 \times 3!$, or more generally:

    ```
    fact(n) = n*fact(n - 1)
    ```

    The limiting case is when n is 1, in which case, 1! = 1. Because of this, 0! is defined to be 1. Write a recursive function that calculates factorials, and test it.

2. Write a function that swaps two integers, using pointers as arguments. Write a program that uses this function and test that it works correctly.

3. The trigonometry functions (`sin()`, `cos()`, and `tan()`) in the standard `cmath` library take arguments in radians. Write three equivalent functions, called `sind()`, `cosd()`, and `tand()`, which take arguments in degrees. All arguments and return values should be type `double`.

4. Write a program that reads a number (an integer) and a name (less than 15 characters) from the keyboard. Design the program so that the data entry is done in one function, and the output in another. Store the data in the `main()` function. The program should end when zero is entered for the number. Think about how you are going to pass the data between functions — by value, by pointer, or by reference?

5. (Advanced) Write a function that, when passed a string consisting of words separated by single spaces, returns the first word; calling it again with an argument of `nullptr` returns the second word, and so on, until the string has been processed completely, when `nullptr` is returned. This is a simplified version of the way the C run-time library routine `strtok()` works. So, when passed the string `"one two three"`, the function returns `"one"` after the first call, then `"two"` after the second, and finally `"three"`. Passing it a new string results in the current string being discarded before the function starts on the new string.

➤ WHAT YOU LEARNED IN THIS CHAPTER

TOPIC	CONCEPT
Functions	Functions should be compact units of code with a well-defined purpose. A typical program will consist of a large number of small functions, rather than a small number of large functions.
Function prototypes	Always provide a function prototype for each function defined in your program, positioned before you call that function.
Reference parameters	Passing values to a function using a reference can avoid the copying implicit in the pass-by-value transfer of arguments. Parameters that are not modified in a function should be specified as const.
Returning references or pointers	When returning a reference or a pointer from a function, ensure that the object being returned has the correct scope. Never return a pointer or a reference to an object that is local to a function.
static variables in a function	A static variable that is defined within the body of a function retains its value from one function call to the next.

6

More about Program Structure

WHAT YOU WILL LEARN IN THIS CHAPTER:

- ➤ What a pointer to a function is
- ➤ How to define and use pointers to functions
- ➤ How to define and use arrays of pointers to functions
- ➤ What an exception is and how to write exception handlers that deal with them
- ➤ How to write multiple functions with a single name to handle different kinds of data automatically
- ➤ What function templates are and how to define and use them
- ➤ How to write a substantial program using several functions

WROX.COM CODE DOWNLOADS FOR THIS CHAPTER

You can find the wrox.com code downloads for this chapter on the Download Code tab at www.wrox.com/go/beginningvisualc. The code is in the Chapter 6 download and individually named according to the names throughout the chapter.

POINTERS TO FUNCTIONS

A pointer stores an address value that up to now has been the address of another variable. This has provided considerable flexibility in allowing you to use different variables at different times through a single pointer. A pointer can also store the address of a function. This enables you to call a function through a pointer, which will be the function at the address that was last assigned to the pointer.

Obviously, a pointer to a function must contain the address of the function that you want to call. To work properly, the pointer must also maintain information about the parameter list for the function it points to, as well as the return type. Therefore, the type for a pointer to a function must incorporate the parameter types and the return type of the functions to which it can point. Clearly, this is going to restrict what you can store in a particular pointer to a function.

If you have declared a pointer to functions that accept one argument of type int and return a value of type double, you can only store the address of a function that has exactly this form. If you want to store the address of a function that accepts two arguments of type int and returns type char, you must define another pointer with a type that includes these characteristics.

Declaring Pointers to Functions

You can declare a pointer pfun that you can use to point to functions that take two arguments, of type char* and int, and return a value of type double like this:

```
double (*pfun)(char*, int);              // Pointer to function declaration
```

At first, you may find that the parentheses make this look a little weird. This declares a pointer with the name pfun that can point to functions that accept two arguments, one of type pointer to char and another of type int, and return a value of type double. The parentheses around the pointer name, pfun, and the asterisk are essential; without them, the statement would be a function declaration rather than a pointer declaration. In this case, it would look like this:

```
double *pfun(char*, int);
```

This is a prototype for a function pfun() that has two parameters, and returns a pointer to a double value. The general form of a declaration of a pointer to a function looks like this:

```
return_type (*pointer_name)(list_of_parameter_types);
```

The declaration of a pointer to a function consists of three components:

➤ The return type of the functions that can be pointed to

➤ The pointer name preceded by an asterisk to indicate it is a pointer

➤ The parameter types of the functions that can be pointed to

> **NOTE** *The pointer can only point to functions with the same* return _ type *and* list _ of _ parameter _ types *specified in the declaration. If you attempt to assign a function to a pointer that does not conform to the types in the pointer declaration, the compiler generates an error message.*

You can initialize a pointer to a function with the name of a function within the declaration of the pointer. The following is an example of this:

```
long sum(long num1, long num2);        // Function prototype
long (*pfun)(long, long) {sum};        // Pointer to function points to sum()
```

In general, you can set the `pfun` pointer that you declared here to point to any function that accepts two arguments of type `long` and returns a value of type `long`. In the first instance, you initialized it with the address of the `sum()` function that has the prototype given by the first statement.

When you initialize a pointer to a function in the declaration, you can use the `auto` keyword for the type. You can write the previous declaration as:

```
auto pfun = sum;
```

As long as the prototype or definition for `sum()` precedes this statement in the source file, the compiler can work out the pointer type.

Of course, you can also initialize a pointer to a function by using an assignment statement. Assuming the pointer `pfun` has been declared as in the preceding code, you could set the value of the pointer to a different function with these statements:

```
long product(long, long);              // Function prototype
...
pfun = product;                        // Set pointer to function product()
```

As with pointers to variables, you must ensure that a pointer to a function is initialized before you use it. Without initialization, catastrophic failure of your program is guaranteed.

TRY IT OUT   Pointers to Functions

To get a proper feeling for these newfangled pointers and how they perform in action, try one out in a program:

```
// Ex6_01.cpp
// Exercising pointers to functions
#include <iostream>
using std::cout;
using std::endl;

long sum(long a, long b);              // Function prototype
long product(long a, long b);          // Function prototype

int main()
{
  long (*pdo_it)(long, long);          // Pointer to function declaration

  pdo_it = product;
  cout << endl
       << "3*5 = " << pdo_it(3, 5);    // Call product thru a pointer

  pdo_it = sum;                        // Reassign pointer to sum()
  cout << endl
```

```
                << "3*(4 + 5) + 6 = "
                << pdo_it(product(3, pdo_it(4, 5)), 6);    // Call thru a pointer,
                                                           // twice
     cout << endl;
     return 0;
}

// Function to multiply two values
long product(long a, long b)
{
   return a*b;
}

// Function to add two values
long sum(long a, long b)
{
   return a + b;
}
```

This example produces the output:

```
3*5 = 15
3*(4 + 5) + 6 = 33
```

How It Works

This is hardly a useful program, but it does show very simply how a pointer to a function is declared, assigned a value, and subsequently used to call a function.

After the usual preamble, you declare a pointer to a function, pdo_it, which can point to either of the other two functions that you have defined, sum() or product(). The pointer is given the address of the function product() in this assignment statement:

```
pdo_it = product;
```

You just supply the name of the function as the initial value for the pointer, and no parentheses or other adornments are required. The function name is automatically converted to an address, which is stored in the pointer. You could replace the first two statements in main() with this statement:

```
auto pdo_it = product;
```

This declares and initializes pdo_it with the address of the product() function.

The function product() is called indirectly through the pointer pdo_it in the output statement.

```
        cout << endl
             << "3*5 = " << pdo_it(3, 5);        // Call product thru a pointer
```

You use the name of the pointer just as if it was a function name, followed by the arguments between parentheses exactly as they would appear if you were using the original function name directly.

Just to show that you can, you change the pointer to point to sum():

```
    pdo_it = sum;                                // Reassign pointer to sum()
```

You then use it again in a ludicrously convoluted expression to do some simple arithmetic:

```
cout << endl
     << "3*(4 + 5) + 6 = "
     << pdo_it(product(3, pdo_it(4, 5)), 6);   // Call thru a pointer,
                                                 // twice
```

This shows that you can use a pointer to a function in exactly the same way as the function that it points to. The sequence of actions in the expression is shown in Figure 6-1.

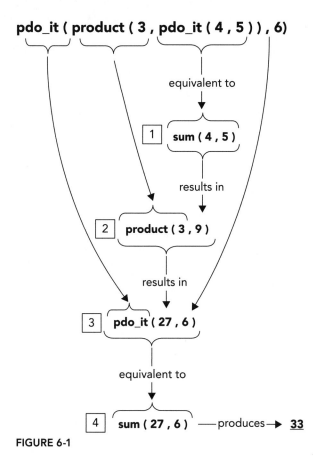

FIGURE 6-1

A Pointer to a Function as an Argument

Because "pointer to a function" is a perfectly reasonable type, a function can also have a parameter that is of a pointer to a function type. The function can then call the function pointed to by the argument. The pointer can point to different functions in different circumstances, which allows the particular function that is to be called from inside a function to be determined in the calling program. You can pass a function name explicitly as the argument for a parameter that is of a pointer to function type.

Passing a Function Pointer

Suppose you need a function that processes an array of values by producing the sum of the squares of each of the elements on some occasions, and the sum of the cubes on other occasions. One way of achieving this is by using a pointer to a function as a parameter.

```cpp
// Ex6_02.cpp
// A pointer to a function as an argument
#include <iostream>
using std::cout;
using std::endl;

// Function prototypes
double squared(double);
double cubed(double);
double sumarray(const double data[], size_t len, double (*pfun)(double));

int main()
{
  double data[] { 1.5, 2.5, 3.5, 4.5, 5.5, 6.5, 7.5 };
  size_t len {_countof(data)};

  cout << endl << "Sum of squares = " << sumarray(data, len, squared);
  cout << endl << "Sum of cubes = " << sumarray(data, len, cubed);
  cout << endl;
  return 0;
}

// Function for a square of a value
double squared(double x)
{
  return x*x;
}

// Function for a cube of a value
double cubed(double x)
{
  return x*x*x;
}

// Function to sum functions of array elements
double sumarray(const double data[], size_t len, double (*pfun)(double))
{
  double total {};                      // Accumulate total in here

  for(size_t i {}; i < len; i++)
    total += pfun(data[i]);

  return total;
}
```

If you compile and run this code, you should see the following output:

```
Sum of squares = 169.75
Sum of cubes = 1015.88
```

How It Works

The first statement of interest is the prototype for the function `sumarray()`. Its third parameter is a pointer to a function that has a parameter of type `double`, and returns a value of type `double`.

```
double sumarray(double array[], int len, double (*pfun)(double));
```

The function `sumarray()` processes each element of the array passed as its first argument with whatever function is pointed to by its third argument. The function then returns the sum of the processed array elements. The third argument must be a function that returns a `double` value and accepts an argument of type `double`.

You call `sumarray()` twice in `main()`, the first time with the function name `squared` as the third argument, and the second using `cubed`. In each case, the address corresponding to the function name that you use as the argument is substituted for the function pointer in the body of `sumarray()`, so the appropriate function is called within the `for` loop.

There are obviously easier ways of achieving what this example does, but using a pointer to a function provides you with a lot of generality. You could pass any function to `sumarray()` that you care to define as long as it takes one `double` argument and returns a value of type `double`.

Arrays of Pointers to Functions

In the same way as with regular pointers, you can declare an array of pointers to functions. You can also initialize them in the declaration. Here is an example:

```
double sum(const double, const double);          // Function prototype
double product(const double, const double);       // Function prototype
double difference(const double, const double);    // Function prototype
double (*pfun[])( const double, const double)
                { sum, product, difference };     // Array of function pointers
```

Each array element is initialized by the corresponding function address in the initializing list. The array length is determined by the number of values in the list. You cannot use `auto` to deduce an array type, so you must put the specific type here.

To call `product()` using the second element of the pointer array, you would write:

```
pfun[1](2.5, 3.5);
```

The square brackets that select the function pointer array element appear immediately after the array name and before the arguments to the function being called. Of course, you can place a function call through an element of a function pointer array in any appropriate expression that the original function might legitimately appear in, and the index value selecting the pointer can be any expression producing a valid index.

INITIALIZING FUNCTION PARAMETERS

With all the functions you have used up to now, you have had to take care to provide an argument corresponding to each parameter in a function call. It can be quite handy to be able to omit one or more arguments in a function call and have some default values supplied automatically for the arguments that you leave out. You can arrange this by providing initial values for the parameters to a function in its prototype.

Suppose that you write a function to display a message, where the message is passed as the argument. Here is the definition of such a function:

```
void showit(const char message[])
{
  cout << endl
       << message;
  return;
}
```

You can specify a default value for the parameter to this function by specifying the initializing string in the function prototype, as follows:

```
void showit(const char message[] = "Something is wrong.");
```

The default value for the message parameter is the string literal shown. If you omit the argument when you call the function, the default value is used.

TRY IT OUT   Omitting Function Arguments

Leaving out the function argument when you call the function executes it with the default value. If you supply the argument, it replaces the default value. You can use the showit() function to output a variety of messages.

```
// Ex6_03.cpp
// Omitting function arguments
#include <iostream>
using std::cout;
using std::endl;

void showit(const char message[] = "Something is wrong.");

int main()
{
  const char mymess[] {"The end of the world is nigh."};

  showit();                                // Display the basic message
  showit("Something is terribly wrong!");  // Display an alternative
```

```
      showit();                          // Display the default again
      showit(mymess);                    // Display a predefined message

      cout << endl;
      return 0;
   }
   void showit(const char message[])
   {
      cout << endl
           << message;
      return;
   }
```

If you execute this example, it produces the following apocalyptic output:

```
Something is wrong.
Something is terribly wrong!
Something is wrong.
The end of the world is nigh.
```

How It Works

As you see, you get the default message specified in the function prototype whenever the argument is left out; otherwise, the function behaves normally.

If you have a function with several arguments, you can provide initial values for as many of them as you like. If you want to omit more than one argument to take advantage of a default value, all arguments to the right of the leftmost argument that you omit must also be left out. For example, suppose you have this function:

```
   int do_it(long arg1 = 10, long arg2 = 20, long arg3 = 30, long arg4 = 40);
```

If you want to omit one argument in a call to it, you can omit only the last one, arg4. If you want to omit arg3, you must also omit arg4. If you omit arg2, arg3 and arg4 must also be omitted, and if you want to use the default value for arg1, you have to omit all of the arguments.

You can conclude from this that you need to put the parameters that have default values in the function prototype together in sequence at the end of the parameter list, with the parameter most likely to be omitted appearing last.

EXCEPTIONS

If you've had a go at the exercises that appear at the end of the previous chapters, you've more than likely come across compiler errors and warnings, as well as errors that occur while the program is running. *Exceptions* are a way of flagging errors or unexpected conditions that occur in your programs, and you already know that the new operator throws an exception if the memory you request cannot be allocated.

So far, you have typically handled error conditions by using an `if` statement to test some expression, and then executing some specific code to deal with the error. C++ provides another, more general mechanism for handling errors that allows you to separate the code that deals with these conditions from the code that executes when such conditions do not arise. It is important to realize that exceptions are not intended to be used as an alternative to the normal data checking and validating that you might do in a program. The code that is generated when you use exceptions carries quite a bit of overhead with it, so exceptions are really intended to be applied in the context of exceptional, near-catastrophic conditions that might arise, but are not expected to occur in the normal course of events. An error reading a disk might be something that you use exceptions for. An invalid data item being entered is not a good candidate for using exceptions.

The exception mechanism uses three new keywords:

➤ `try`—Identifies a code block in which an exception can occur. A `try` block must be immediately followed by at least one `catch` block.

➤ `throw`—Causes an exception condition to be originated and throws an exception of a particular type.

➤ `catch`—Identifies a block of code that handles the exception. A `catch` block is executed when an exception is thrown in the preceding `try` block that is of the type that is specified between parentheses following the `catch` keyword. A `try` block may be followed by several `catch` blocks, each catching a different type of exception.

In the following Try It Out, you can see how they work in practice.

TRY IT OUT Throwing and Catching Exceptions

You can easily see how exception handling operates by working through an example. Let's use a very simple context for this. Suppose that you are required to write a program that calculates the time it takes in minutes to make a part on a machine. The number of parts made in each hour is recorded, but you must keep in mind that the machine breaks down regularly and may not make any parts.

You could code this using exception handling as follows:

```
// Ex6_04.cpp  Using exception handling
#include <iostream>
using std::cout;
using std::endl;

int main()
{
  int counts[] {34, 54, 0, 27, 0, 10, 0};
  double time {60};                       // One hour in minutes
  int hour {};                            // Current hour

  for(auto count : counts)
  {
    try
    {
      cout << endl << "Hour " << ++hour;
```

```
      if(0 == count)
        throw "Zero count - calculation not possible.";

      cout << " minutes per item: " << time/count;
    }
    catch(const char aMessage[])
    {
      cout << endl << aMessage << endl;
    }
  }
  return 0;
}
```

If you run this example, the output is:

```
Hour 1 minutes per item: 1.76471
Hour 2 minutes per item: 1.11111
Hour 3
Zero count - calculation not possible.

Hour 4 minutes per item: 2.22222
Hour 5
Zero count - calculation not possible.

Hour 6 minutes per item: 6
Hour 7
Zero count - calculation not possible.
```

How It Works

The code in the `try` block is executed in the normal sequence. The `try` block serves to define where an exception can be raised. You can see from the output that when an exception is thrown, the sequence of execution continues with the `catch` block. The `catch` block will execute when an exception of type `const char[]` is thrown. After the code in the `catch` block has been executed, execution continues with the next loop iteration. Of course, when no exception is thrown, the `catch` block is not executed.

The division is carried out in the output statement that follows the `if` statement checking the divisor. When a `throw` statement is executed, control passes immediately to the first statement in the `catch` block, so the statement that performs the division is bypassed when an exception is thrown. After the statement in the `catch` block executes, the loop continues with the next iteration, if there is one.

Throwing Exceptions

You can throw an exception anywhere within a `try` block using a `throw` statement, and the `throw` statement operand determines the type of the exception. The exception thrown in the example is a string literal and, therefore, of type `const char[]`. The operand following the `throw` keyword can be any expression, and the type of the result of the expression determines the type of exception thrown. There must be a `catch` block to catch an exception of the type that may be thrown.

Exceptions can also be thrown in functions that are called from within a try block and can be caught by a catch block following the try block if they are not caught within the function. You could add a function to the previous example to demonstrate this, with the definition:

```
void testThrow()
{
  throw " Zero count - calculation not possible.";
}
```

You place a call to this function in the previous example in place of the throw statement:

```
if(0 == count)
  testThrow();                 // Call a function that throws an exception
```

The exception is thrown by the testThrow() function and caught by the catch block whenever the array element is zero, so the output is the same as before. Don't forget the function prototype if you add the definition of testThrow() to the end of the source code.

Catching Exceptions

The catch block following the try block in our example catches any exception of type const char[]. This is determined by the parameter specification that appears in parentheses following the keyword catch. You must supply at least one catch block for a try block, and the catch blocks must immediately follow the try block. A catch block catches all exceptions (of the specified type) that occur anywhere in the code in the immediately preceding try block, including those thrown and not caught in any functions called directly or indirectly within the try block.

If you want to specify that a catch block is to handle any exception thrown in a try block, you put an ellipsis (...) between the parentheses enclosing the exception declaration:

```
catch (...)
{
  // code to handle any exception
}
```

This catch block catches exceptions of any type. It must appear last if you have other catch blocks defined for the try block.

Here's how a try block followed by two catch blocks looks:

```
try
{
  ...
}
catch (const type1& ex)
{
  ...
}
catch (type2 ex)
{
  ...
}
```

When an exception is thrown in a try block with more than one catch block, the catch blocks are checked in sequence until a match for the exception type is found. The code in the first catch block that matches will be executed.

Nested try Blocks

You can nest try blocks one within another. With this situation, if an exception is thrown from within an inner try block that is not followed by a catch block corresponding to the type of exception thrown, the catch handlers for the outer try block are searched. You can demonstrate this with the following example:

```cpp
// Ex6_05.cpp
// Nested try blocks
#include <iostream>
using std::cin;
using std::cout;
using std::endl;

int main()
{
  int height {};
  const int minHeight {9};                 // Minimum height in inches
  const int maxHeight {100};               // Maximum height in inches
  const double inchesToMeters {0.0254};
  char ch {'y'};

  try                                      // Outer try block
  {
    while('y' == ch || 'Y' == ch)
    {
      cout << "Enter a height in inches: ";
      cin >> height;                       // Read the height to be
                                           // converted

      try                                  // Defines try block in which
      {                                    // exceptions may be thrown
        if(height > maxHeight)
          throw "Height exceeds maximum";  // Exception thrown
        if(height < minHeight)
          throw height;                    // Exception thrown

        cout << static_cast<double>(height)*inchesToMeters
             << " meters" << endl;
      }
      catch(const char aMessage[])         // start of catch block which
      {                                    // catches exceptions of type
        cout << aMessage << endl;          // const char[]
      }
      cout << "Do you want to continue(y or n)?";
      cin >> ch;
    }
  }
}
```

```
    catch(int badHeight)
    {
      cout << badHeight << " inches is below minimum" << endl;
    }
    return 0;
}
```

How It Works

There is a `try` block enclosing the `while` loop and an inner `try` block in which two different types of exception may be thrown. The exception of type `const char[]` is caught by the `catch` block for the inner `try` block, but the exception of type `int` has no catch handler associated with the inner `try` block; therefore, the `catch` handler in the outer try block is executed. In this case, the program ends immediately because the statement following the `catch` block is a `return`.

Rethrowing Exceptions

It may be that when you catch an exception, you want to pass it on the calling program for some additional action, rather that handling it entirely in the `catch` block. In this case you can rethrow the exception for onward processing. For example:

```
    try
    {
      ...
    }
    catch (const type1& ex)
    {
      ...
    }
    catch (type2 ex)
    {
      // Process the exception...
      throw;                   // Rethrow the exception for processing by the caller
    }
```

Using `throw` without an operand causes the exception that is being handled to be rethrown. You can only use `throw` without an operand within a `catch` block. Rethrowing an exception allows the exception to be caught by an enclosing `try/catch` block or by a caller of this function. The calling function must place its call to the function in a `try` block to catch the rethrown exception.

Exception Handling in the MFC

This is a good point to raise the question of MFC and exceptions because they are used to some extent. If you browse the documentation that came with Visual C++, you may come across TRY, THROW, and CATCH in the index. These are macros defined within the MFC that were created before exception handling was implemented in the C++ language. They mimic the operation of `try`, `throw`, and `catch` in C++, but the language facilities for exception handling really render these obsolete, so you should not use them. They are, however, still there for two reasons. There are large numbers of programs still around that use these macros, and it is important to ensure that, as far as possible, old code still compiles. Also, most of the MFC that throws exceptions was implemented in terms of these macros. In any event, any new programs should use the try, throw, and catch keywords because they work with the MFC.

There is one slight anomaly you need to keep in mind when you use MFC functions that throw exceptions. The MFC functions that throw exceptions generally throw exceptions of class types — you will find out about class types before you get to use the MFC. Even though the exception that an MFC function throws is of a given class type — CDBException, say — you need to catch the exception as a pointer, not as the type of the exception. So, with the exception thrown being of type CDBException, the type that appears as the catch block parameter is CBDException*. If you are not rethrowing the exception, you must also delete the exception object in the catch block by calling its Delete() function. For example:

```
try
{
    // Execute some code that might throw an MFC exception...
}
catch (CException* ex)
{
    // Handle the exception here...
    ex->Delete();                           // Delete the exception object
}
```

You should not use delete to delete the exception object because the object may not be allocated on the heap. CException is the base class for all MFC exceptions so the catch block here will catch MFC exceptions of any type.

HANDLING MEMORY ALLOCATION ERRORS

When you used the new operator to allocate memory (as you saw in Chapters 4 and 5), you ignored the possibility that the memory might not be allocated. If the memory isn't allocated, an exception is thrown that results in the termination of the program. Ignoring this exception is quite acceptable in most situations because having no memory left is usually a terminal condition for a program that you can usually do nothing about. However, there can be circumstances where you might be able to do something about it if you had the chance, or you might want to report the problem in your own way. In this situation, you can catch the exception that the new operator throws. Let's contrive an example to show this happening.

TRY IT OUT   Catching an Exception Thrown by the new Operator

The exception that the new operator throws when memory cannot be allocated is of type std::bad_alloc. bad_alloc is a class type defined in the new standard header file, so you'll need an #include directive for that. Here's the code:

```
// Ex6_06.cpp
// Catching an exception thrown by new
#include<new>                    // For bad_alloc type
```

```
#include<iostream>
using std::bad_alloc;
using std::cout;
using std::endl;

int main()
{
  char* pdata {};
  size_t count {~static_cast<size_t>(0)/2};
  try
  {
    pdata = new char[count];
    cout << "Memory allocated." << endl;
  }
  catch(bad_alloc& ex)
  {
    cout << "Memory allocation failed." << endl
         << "The information from the exception object is: "
         << ex.what() << endl;
  }
  delete[] pdata;
  return 0;
}
```

On my machine, this example produces the following output:

```
Memory allocation failed.
The information from the exception object is: bad allocation
```

How It Works

The example allocates memory dynamically for an array of type `char[]` where the length is specified by the `count` variable that you define as:

```
size_t count {~static_cast<size_t>(0)/2};
```

The size of an array is an integer of type `size_t`, so you declare `count` to be of this type. The value for `count` is generated by a somewhat complicated expression. The value 0 is type `int`, so the value produced by the expression `static_cast<size_t>(0)` is a zero of type `size_t`. Applying the `~` operator to this flips all the bits so you then have a `size_t` value with all the bits as 1, which corresponds to the maximum value you can represent as `size_t`, because `size_t` is an unsigned type. This value exceeds the maximum amount of memory that the `new` operator can allocate in one go, so you divide by 2 to bring it within the bounds of what is possible. This is still a very large value, so, unless your machine is exceptionally well endowed with memory, the allocation request will fail.

The allocation of the memory takes place in the `try` block. If the allocation succeeds, you'll see a message to that effect, but if, as you expect, it fails, an exception of type `bad_alloc` will be thrown by the `new` operator. This causes the code in the `catch` block to be executed. Calling the `what()` function for the `bad_alloc` object reference `ex` returns a string describing the problem that caused the exception, and you see the result of this call in the output. All standard exception classes implement the `what()` function to provide a string describing why the exception was thrown.

To handle out-of-memory situations with some positive effect, clearly, you must have some means of returning memory to the free store. In most practical cases, this involves some serious work on the program to manage memory, so it is not often undertaken.

FUNCTION OVERLOADING

Suppose you have written a function that determines the maximum value in an array of values of type `double`:

```
// Function to generate the maximum value in an array of type double
double maxdouble(const double data[], const size_t len)
{
    double maximum {data(0)};

    for(size_t i {1}; i < len; i++)
        if(maximum < data[i])
            maximum = data[i];

    return maximum;
}
```

You now want to create a function that produces the maximum value from an array of type `long`, so you write another function similar to the first, with this prototype:

```
long maxlong(const long data[], const size_t len);
```

You have chosen the function name to reflect the particular task in hand, which is OK for two functions, but you may also need the same function for several other types of argument. It seems a pity that you have to keep inventing names. Ideally, you would use the same function name `max()` regardless of the argument type, and have the appropriate version executed. It probably won't be any surprise to you that you can, indeed, do this, and the C++ mechanism that makes it possible is called *function overloading*.

What Is Function Overloading?

Function overloading allows you to use several functions with the same name as long as they each have different parameter lists. When one of the functions is called, the compiler chooses the correct version for the job based on the list of arguments. Obviously, the compiler must always be able to decide unequivocally which function should be selected in any particular instance of a function call, so the parameter list for each function in a set of overloaded functions must be unique. Following on from the `max()` function example, you could create overloaded functions with the following prototypes:

```
int max(const int data[], const size_t len);        // Prototypes for
long max(const long data[], const size_t len);      // a set of overloaded
double max(const double data[], const size_t len);  // functions
```

These functions share a common name, but have different parameter lists. Overloaded functions that have the same number of parameters must have at least one parameter with a unique type. An overloaded function can have a different number of parameters from the others in the set.

Note that a different return type does not distinguish a function adequately. You can't add the following function to the previous set:

```
double max(const long data[], const size_t len);              // Not valid overloading
```

The reason is that this function would be indistinguishable from the function that has this prototype:

```
long max(const long data[], const size_t len);
```

If you define functions like this, it causes the compiler to complain with the following error:

```
error C2556: 'double max(const long [],const size_t)' :
    overloaded function differs only by return type from 'long max(const long
[],const size_t)'
```

This may seem slightly unreasonable, until you remember that you can write statements such as these:

```
long numbers[] {1, 2, 3, 3, 6, 7, 11, 50, 40};
const size_t len {_countof(numbers)}
max(numbers, len);
```

The call for the `max()` function doesn't make much sense here because you discard the result, but this does not make it illegal. If the return type were permitted as a distinguishing feature, the compiler would be unable to decide whether to choose the version with a `long` or a `double` return type. For this reason, the return type is not considered to be a differentiating feature of overloaded functions.

Every function — not just overloaded functions — is said to have a *signature*, where the signature of a function is determined by its name and its parameter list. All functions in a program must have unique signatures, otherwise the program does not compile.

TRY IT OUT   Using Overloaded Functions

You can exercise the overloading capability with the function `max()` that you have already defined. Try an example that includes the three versions for `int`, `long`, and `double` arrays.

```
// Ex6_07.cpp
// Using overloaded functions
#include <iostream>
using std::cout;
using std::endl;

int max(const int data[],const size_t  len);              // Prototypes for
long max(const long data[],const size_t  len);            // a set of overloaded
double max(const double data[],const size_t  len);        // functions
```

```cpp
int main()
{
  int small[] {1, 24, 34, 22};
  long medium[] {23, 245, 123, 1, 234, 2345};
  double large[] {23.0, 1.4, 2.456, 345.5, 12.0, 21.0};

  const size_t lensmall {_countof(small)};
  const size_t lenmedium {_countof(medium)};
  const size_t lenlarge {_countof(large)};

  cout << endl << max(small, lensmall);
  cout << endl << max(medium, lenmedium);
  cout << endl << max(large, lenlarge);

  cout << endl;
  return 0;
}

// Maximum of ints
int max(const int x[],const size_t len)
{
  int maximum {x[0]};
  for(size_t i {1}; i < len; i++)
    if(maximum < x[i])
      maximum = x[i];
  return maximum;
}

// Maximum of longs
long max(const long x[],const size_t  len)
{
  long maximum {x[0]};
  for(size_t i {1}; i < len; i++)
    if(maximum < x[i])
      maximum = x[i];
  return maximum;
}

// Maximum of doubles
double max(const double x[],const size_t len)
{
  double maximum {x[0]};
  for(size_t i {1}; i < len; i++)
    if(maximum < x[i])
      maximum = x[i];
  return maximum;
}
```

The example works as you would expect and produces this output:

```
34
2345
345.5
```

How It Works

You have three prototypes for the three overloaded versions of the function max(). In each of the three output statements, the appropriate version of the function max() is selected by the compiler based on the argument list types. This works because each of the versions of max() has a unique signature, because each parameter list is different from that of the others.

Reference Types and Overload Selection

When you use reference types for parameters in overloaded functions, you must take care to ensure the compiler can select an appropriate overload. Suppose you define functions with the following prototypes:

```
void f(int n);
void f(int& rn);
```

These functions are differentiated by the type of the parameter, but code using these will not compile. When you call f() with an argument of type int, the compiler has no means of determining which function should be selected because either function is equally applicable. In general, you cannot overload on a given type, type, and an lvalue reference to that type, type&.

However, the compiler can distinguish the overloaded functions with the following prototypes:

```
void f(int& arg);      // Lvalue reference parameter
void f(int&& arg);     // Rvalue reference parameter
```

Even though for some argument types, either function could apply, the compiler adopts a preferred choice. The f(int&) function will always be selected when the argument is an lvalue. The f(int&&) version will be selected only when the argument is an rvalue. For example:

```
int num{5};
f(num);        // Calls f(int&)
f(2*num);      // Calls f(int&&)
f(25);         // Calls f(int&&)
f(num++);      // Calls f(int&&)
f(++num);      // Calls f(int&)
```

Only the first and last statements call the overload with the lvalue reference parameter, because the other statements call the function with arguments that are rvalues.

> **NOTE** The rvalue reference type parameter is intended primarily for addressing specific problems that you'll learn about when you look into defining classes.

When to Overload Functions

Function overloading provides you with the means of ensuring that a function name describes the function being performed and is not confused by extraneous information such as the type of data being processed. This is akin to what happens with basic operations in C++. To add two numbers, you use the same operator, regardless of the types of the operands. Our overloaded function max() has the same name, regardless of the type of data being processed. This helps to make the code more readable and makes these functions easier to use.

> **NOTE** *The intent of function overloading is clear: to enable the same operation to be performed with different operands using a single function name. So, whenever you have a series of functions that do essentially the same thing, but with different types of arguments, you should overload them and use a common function name, or write a function template, which is coming up next.*

FUNCTION TEMPLATES

The last example was somewhat tedious in that you had to repeat essentially the same code for each function, but with different variable and parameter types. However, there is a way of avoiding this. You have the possibility of creating a recipe that will enable the compiler to automatically generate functions with various parameter types. The code defining the recipe for generating a particular group of functions is called a *function template*.

A function template has one or more *type parameters*, and you generate a particular function by supplying a concrete type argument for each of the template's parameters. Thus, the functions generated by a function template all have the same basic code, but customized by the type arguments that you supply. You can see how this works in practice by defining a function template for the function max() in the previous example.

Using a Function Template

You can define a template for the function max() as follows:

```
template<class T> T max(const T x[], const size_t len)
{
  T maximum {x[0]};
  for(size_t i{1}; i < len; i++)
    if(maximum < x[i])
      maximum = x[i];
  return maximum;
}
```

The template keyword identifies this as a template definition. The angled brackets following the template keyword enclose the type parameters that are used to create a particular instance of the function separated by commas; in this instance, you have just one type parameter, T. The class keyword before the T indicates that the T is the type parameter for this template, class being the generic term for type. Later in the book, you will see that defining a class is essentially defining your own data type. Consequently, you have fundamental types in C++, such as type int and type char, and you also have the types that you define yourself. You can use the keyword typename instead of class to identify the parameters in a function template, in which case, the template definition would look like this:

```
template<typename T> T max(const T x[], const size_t len)
{
  T maximum {x[0]};
  for(size_t i {1}; i < len; i++)
    if(maximum < x[i])
      maximum = x[i];
  return maximum;
}
```

Some programmers prefer to use the typename keyword as the class keyword tends to connote a user-defined type, whereas typename is more neutral and, therefore, is more readily understood to imply fundamental types as well as user-defined types. In practice, you'll see both used widely.

Wherever T appears in the definition of a function template, it is replaced by the specific type argument, such as long, that you supply when you create an instance of the template. If you try this out manually by plugging in long in place of T in the template, you'll see that this generates a perfectly satisfactory function for calculating the maximum value from an array of type long:

```
long max(const long x[], const size_t len)
{
  long maximum {x[0]};
  for(size_t i {1}; i < len; i++)
    if(maximum < x[i])
      maximum = x[i];
  return maximum;
}
```

The creation of a particular function instance is referred to as *instantiation*. Each time you use max() in your program, the compiler checks to see if a function corresponding to the type of arguments that you have used in the function call already exists. If the function required does not exist, the compiler creates one by substituting the argument type that you have used in your function call in place of the parameter T throughout the template definition.

> **NOTE** *The compiler will only process a template definition if you use it in your code. This means that errors in the template will not be identified if you don't use it.*

You could exercise the template for the max() function with the same main() function that you used in the previous example.

TRY IT OUT Using a Function Template

Here's a version of the previous example modified to use a template for the max() function:

```cpp
// Ex6_08.cpp
// Using function templates

#include <iostream>
using std::cout;
using std::endl;

// Template for function to compute the maximum element of an array
template<typename T> T max(const T x[], const size_t len)
{
  T maximum {x[0]};
  for(size_t i {1}; i < len; i++)
    if(maximum < x[i])
      maximum = x[i];
  return maximum;
}

int main()
{
  int small[] { 1, 24, 34, 22};
  long medium[] { 23, 245, 123, 1, 234, 2345};
  double large[] { 23.0, 1.4, 2.456, 345.5, 12.0, 21.0};

  size_t lensmall {_countof(small)};
  size_t lenmedium {_countof(medium)};
  size_t lenlarge {_countof(large)};


  cout << endl << max(small, lensmall);
  cout << endl << max(medium, lenmedium);
  cout << endl << max(large, lenlarge);

  cout << endl;
  return 0;
}
```

This program produces exactly the same output as the previous example.

How It Works

For each of the statements outputting the maximum value in an array, a new version of max() is instantiated using the template. Of course, if you add another statement calling the function max() with one of the types used previously, no new version of the template code is generated.

Using a template doesn't reduce the size of your compiled program in any way. The compiler generates a version of the source code for each unique function that you require. In fact, using templates can *increase* the size of your program, because functions may be created even though an existing version might satisfactorily be used by casting because the argument. You can force the creation of particular instance of a template by explicitly including a declaration for it. For example, if you wanted to ensure that an instance of the template for the function max() was created corresponding to type float, you could place the following declaration after the definition of the template:

```
float max (const float[], const size_t);
```

This forces the creation of this version of the function template. It does not have much value in the case of our program example, but it can be useful when you know that several versions of a template function might be generated, but you want to force the generation of a subset that you plan to use, with arguments cast to the appropriate type where necessary.

USING THE DECLTYPE OPERATOR

You use the decltype operator to obtain the type of an expression, so decltype(exp) is the type of the value that results from evaluating the expression exp. For example, you could write the following statements:

```
double x {100.0};
int n {5};
decltype(x*n) result(x*n);
```

The last statement specifies the type of result to be the type of the expression x*n, which is type double. While this shows the mechanics of what the decltype operator does, the primary use for the decltype operator is in defining function templates. Occasionally, the return type of a template function with multiple type parameters may depend on the types used to instantiate the template. Suppose you want to write a template function to multiply corresponding elements of two arrays, possibly of different types, and return the sum of these products. Because the types of the two arrays may be different, the type of the result will depend on the actual types of the array arguments, so you cannot specify a particular return type. The function template might notionally look like this:

```
template<typename  T1, typename  T2>
return_type f(T1 v1[], T2 v2[], const size_t count)
{
  decltype(v1[0]*v2[0]) sum {};
  for(size_t i {}; i<count; i++) sum += v1[i]*v2[i];
  return sum;
}
```

return_type needs to be the type of the result of multiplying corresponding elements of the array arguments. The decltype operator can help, but unfortunately the following will not compile:

```
template<typename  T1, typename  T2>
decltype(v1[0]*v2[0]) f(T1 v1[], T2 v2[], const size_t count)    // Will not compile!
{
  decltype(v1[0]*v2[0]) sum {};
  for(size_t i {}; i<count; i++) sum += v1[i]*v2[i];
  return sum;
}
```

This specifies what you want, but the compiler cannot compile this because v1 and v2 are not defined at the point where the return type specification is processed.

It requires a different syntax to take care of it:

```
template<typename T1, typename T2>
auto f(T1 v1[], T2 v2[], const size_t count) -> decltype(v1[0]*v2[0])
{
  decltype(v1[0]*v2[0]) sum {};
  for(size_t i {}; i<count; i++) sum += v1[i]*v2[i];
  return sum;
}
```

As you saw in Chapter 5, this is referred to as a *trailing return type*. You specify the return type using the auto keyword. The actual return type can be determined by the compiler when an instance of the template is created because, at that point, the parameters v1 and v2 have been parsed. The decltype expression following the -> determines the return type for any instance of the template. Let's see if it works.

TRY IT OUT Using the decltype Operator

Here's a simple example to exercise the template you have just seen:

```
// Ex6_09.cpp Using the decltype operator
#include <iostream>
using std::cout;
using std::endl;

template<typename T1, typename T2>
auto product(T1 v1[], T2 v2[], const size_t count) -> decltype(v1[0]*v2[0])
{
  decltype(v1[0]*v2[0]) sum {};
  for(size_t i {}; i<count; i++) sum += v1[i]*v2[i];
  return sum;
}

int main()
{
  double x[] {100.5, 99.5, 88.7, 77.8};
  short y[] {3, 4, 5, 6};
  long z[] {11L, 12L, 13L, 14L};
  size_t n {_countof(x)};
  cout << "Result type is " << typeid(product(x, y, n)).name() << endl;
  cout << "Result is " << product(x, y, n) << endl;
  auto result = product(z, y, n);
  cout << "Result type is " << typeid(result).name() << endl;
  cout << "Result is " << result << endl;

  return 0;
}
```

This produces the following output:

```
Result type is double
Result is 1609.8
Result type is long
Result is 230
```

How It Works

The return types for functions generated from the `product()` function template are determined by the expression `decltype(v1[0]*v2[0])`. The first instantiations of the template in `main()` are due to the statements:

```
cout << "Result type is "<< typeid(product(x, y, n)).name() << endl;
cout << "Result is " << product(x, y, n) << endl;
```

You can see from the output that the type of the value returned by the `product()` function instance is type `double` when the first two arguments are arrays of type `double` and type `short`, respectively, which is as it should be. Executing the next three statements shows that the type for the value returned is type `long` when the arguments are arrays of type `short` and `long`. You obtain the type of `result` where the `auto` keyword determines the type of the variable to be that of the value returned by `product()`. Clearly, the `decltype` operator is working exactly as advertised.

The type of `result` will be the same as the type of value returned by `product()`, which is determined by the `auto` keyword.

```
template<typename T> auto max(const T x[], const size_t len) -> T
{
  T maximum {x[0]};
  for (size_t i {1}; i < len; i++)
    if (maximum < x[i])
      maximum = x[i];
  return maximum;
}
```

AN EXAMPLE USING FUNCTIONS

You have covered a lot of ground in C++ up to now and a lot on functions in this chapter alone. After wading through a varied menu of language capabilities, it's not always easy to see how they relate to one another. Now would be a good point to see how some of this goes together to produce something with more meat than a simple demonstration program.

Let's work through a more realistic example to see how a problem can be broken down into functions. The process involves defining the problem to be solved, analyzing the problem to see how it can be implemented in C++, and, finally, writing the code. The approach here is aimed at illustrating how various functions go together to make up the final result, rather than providing a tutorial on how to develop a program.

Implementing a Calculator

Suppose you need a program that acts as a calculator; not one of these fancy devices with lots of buttons and gizmos designed for those who are easily pleased, but one for people who know where they are going, arithmetically speaking. You can really go for it and enter a calculation from the keyboard as a single arithmetic expression, and have the answer displayed immediately. An example of the sort of thing that you might enter is:

```
2*3.14159*12.6*12.6 / 2 + 25.2*25.2
```

To avoid unnecessary complications for the moment, you won't allow parentheses in the expression and the whole computation must be entered in a single line; however, to allow the user to make the input look attractive, you *will* allow spaces to be placed anywhere. The expression may contain the operators multiply, divide, add, and subtract represented by *, /, +, and –, respectively, and it will be evaluated with normal arithmetic rules, so that multiplication and division take precedence over addition and subtraction.

The program should allow as many successive calculations to be performed as required, and should terminate if an empty line is entered. It should also have helpful and friendly error messages.

Analyzing the Problem

A good place to start is with the input. The program reads in an arithmetic expression of any length on a single line, which can be any construction within the terms given. Because nothing is fixed about the elements making up the expression, you have to read it as a string of characters and then work out within the program how it's made up. You can decide arbitrarily that you will handle a string of up to 80 characters, so you could store it in an array declared within these statements:

```
const size_t MAX {80};       // Maximum expression length including '\0'
char buffer[MAX];            // Input area for expression to be evaluated
```

To change the maximum length of the string processed by the program, you will only need to alter the initial value of MAX.

> **NOTE** In Chapter 8 you'll learn about the string class that enables you to handle strings of any length without having to decide the length in advance.

You'll need to analyze the basic structure of the information that appears in the input string, so let's break it down step by step.

You will want to make sure that the input is as uncluttered as possible when you are processing it, so before you start analyzing the input string, you will get rid of any spaces in it. You can call the function that will do this eatspaces(). This function can work by stepping through the input buffer — which is the array `buffer[]` — and shuffling characters up to overwrite any spaces. This process uses two indexes to the buffer array, `i` and `j`, which start out at the beginning of the buffer; in general, you'll store element `j` at position `i`. As you progress through the array elements, each time you find a space, you increment `j` but not `i`, so the space at position `i` gets overwritten by the next character you find at index position `j` that is not a space. Figure 6-2 illustrates the logic of this.

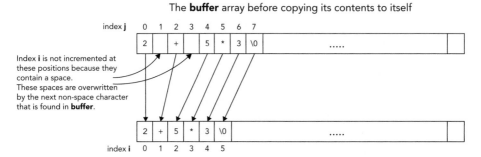

FIGURE 6-2

This process is one of copying the contents of the `buffer` array to itself, excluding any spaces. Figure 6-2 shows the `buffer` array before and after the copying process, and the arrows indicate which characters are copied and the position to which each character is copied.

When you have removed spaces from the input, you are ready to evaluate the expression. You define the `expr()` function that returns the value that results from evaluating the whole expression in the input buffer. To decide what goes on inside the `expr()` function, you need to look into the structure of the input in more detail. The add and subtract operators have the lowest precedence and so are evaluated last. You can think of the input string as comprising one or more *terms* connected by operators, which can be either the operator + or the operator -. You can refer to either operator as an addop. With this terminology, you can represent the general form of the input expression like this:

```
expression: term addop term ... addop term
```

The expression contains at least one `term` and can have an arbitrary number of following addop term combinations. In fact, assuming that you have removed all the blanks, there are only three legal possibilities for the character that follows each `term`:

➤ The next character is `'\0'`, so you are at the end of the string.

➤ The next character is `'-'`, in which case you should subtract the next `term` from the value accrued for the expression up to this point.

➤ The next character is `'+'`, in which case you should add the value of the next `term` to the value of the expression accumulated so far.

If anything else follows a `term`, the string is not what you expect, so you'll throw an exception. Figure 6-3 illustrates the structure of a sample expression.

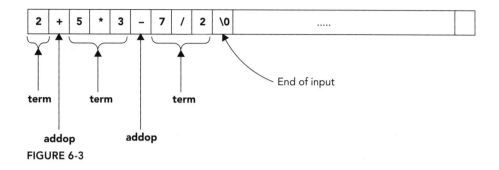

FIGURE 6-3

Next, you need a more detailed and precise definition of a `term`. A `term` is simply a series of numbers connected by either the operator `*` or the operator `/`. Therefore, a `term` (in general) looks like this:

```
term: number multop number ... multop number
```

`multop` represents either a multiply or a divide operator. You could define a `term()` function to return the value of a term. This needs to scan the string to a number first and then to look for a `multop` followed by another number. If a character is found that isn't a `multop`, the `term()` function assumes that it is an `addop` and returns the value that has been found up to that point.

The last thing you need to figure out before writing the program is how you recognize a number. To minimize the complexity of the code, you'll only recognize unsigned numbers; therefore, a number consists of a series of digits that optionally may be followed by a decimal point and some more digits. To determine the value of a number, you step through the buffer looking for digits. If you find anything that isn't a digit, you check whether it's a decimal point. If it's not a decimal point, it has nothing to do with a number, so you return what you have got. If you find a decimal point, you look for more digits. As soon as you find anything that's not a digit, you have the complete number and you return that. Imaginatively, you'll call the function to recognize a number and return its value `number()`. Figure 6-4 shows an example of how an expression breaks down into terms and numbers.

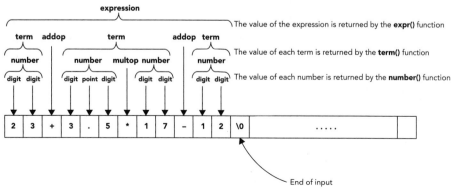

FIGURE 6-4

You now have enough understanding of the problem to write some code. You can work through the functions you need and then write a main() function to tie them all together. The first and, perhaps, easiest function to write is eatspaces(), which will eliminate spaces from the input string.

Eliminating Blanks from a String

You can write the prototype for the eatspaces() function as follows:

```
void eatspaces(char* str);            // Function to eliminate blanks
```

The function doesn't need to return any value because spaces can be eliminated from the string *in situ*, modifying the original string directly through the pointer that is passed as the argument. The process for eliminating spaces is very simple. You copy the string to itself, overwriting any spaces, as you saw earlier in this chapter.

You can define the function to do this as follows:

```
// Function to eliminate spaces from a string
void eatspaces(char* str)
{
  size_t i {};                            // 'Copy to' index to string
  size_t j {};                            // 'Copy from' index to string

  while((*(str + i) = *(str + j++)) != '\0')   // Loop while character is not \0
    if(*(str + i) != ' ')                  // Increment i as long as
      i++;                                 // character is not a space
  return;
}
```

How the Function Functions

All the action is in the while loop. The loop condition copies the string by moving the character at position j to the character at position i, and then increments j to the next character. If the character copied was '\0', you have reached the end of the string and you're done.

The only action in the loop statement is to increment i to the next character if the last character copied was not a blank. If it *is* a blank, i is not to be incremented and the blank can therefore be overwritten by the character copied on the next iteration.

That wasn't hard, was it? Next, you can try writing the function that returns the result of evaluating the expression.

Evaluating an Expression

The expr() function returns the value of the expression specified in a string that is supplied as an argument, so you can write its prototype as:

```
double expr(char* str);                // Function evaluating an expression
```

The function declared here accepts a string as an argument and returns the result as type `double`. Based on the structure for an expression that you worked out earlier, you can draw a logic diagram for the process of evaluating an expression, as shown in Figure 6-5.

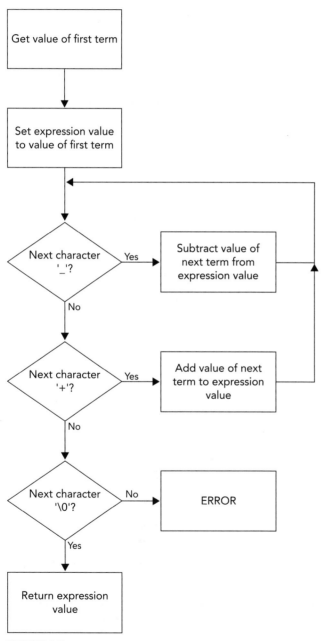

FIGURE 6-5

Using this basic definition of the logic, you can now write the function:

```
// Function to evaluate an arithmetic expression
double expr(const char* str)
{
  double value {};                      // Store result here
  int index {};                         // Keeps track of current character position

  value = term(str, index);             // Get first term

  for(;;)                               // Indefinite loop, all exits inside
  {
    switch(*(str + index++))            // Choose action based on current character
    {
      case '\0':                        // We're at the end of the string
        return value;                   // so return what we have got

      case '+':                         // + found so add in the
        value += term(str, index);      // next term
        break;

      case '-':                         // - found so subtract
        value -= term(str, index);      // the next term
        break;

      default:                          // If we reach here the string is junk
        char message[38] {"Expression evaluation error. Found: "}
        strncat_s(message, str + index - 1, 1);  // Append the character
        throw message;
        break;

    }
  }
}
```

How the Function Functions

Considering this function is analyzing any arithmetic expression that you care to throw at it (as long as it uses our operator subset), it's not a lot of code. You define a variable `index` of type `int`, which keeps track of the current position in the string where you are working, and you initialize it to 0, which corresponds to the index position of the first character in the string. You also define a variable `value` of type `double` in which you'll accumulate the value of the expression that is passed to the function in the char array `str`.

Because an expression must have at least one term, the first action in the function is to get the value of the first term by calling the function `term()`, which you have yet to write. This actually places three requirements on the function `term()`:

1. It should accept a `char*` and an `int` parameter, the second parameter being an index to the first character of the term in the string supplied through the first parameter.

2. It should update the index value passed so that it references the string character following the last character of the term found.

3. It should return the value of the term as type `double`.

The rest of the program is an indefinite `for` loop. Within the loop, the action is determined by a `switch` statement, which is controlled by the current character in the string. If it is a `'+'`, you call the `term()` function to get the value of the next term in the expression and add it to the variable `value`. If it is a `'-'`, you subtract the value returned by `term()` from `value`. If it is a `'\0'`, you are at the end of the string, so you return the current contents of `value` to the calling function. If it is any other character, it shouldn't be there, so throw an exception. The exception is a string that has the offending character appended.

As long as either a `'+'` or a `'-'` is found, the loop continues. Each call to `term()` moves the value of `index` to the character following the term that was evaluated, and this should be either another `'+'` or `'-'`, or the end-of-string character `'\0'`. Thus, the function either terminates normally when `'\0'` is reached, or abnormally by throwing an exception.

You could also analyze an arithmetic expression using a recursive function. If you think about the definition of an expression slightly differently, you could specify it as being either a term, or a term followed by an expression. The definition here is recursive (i.e., the definition involves the item being defined), and this approach is very common in defining programming language structures. This definition provides just as much flexibility as the first, but using it as the base concept, you could arrive at a recursive version of `expr()` instead of using a loop as you did in the implementation of `expr()`. You might want to try this alternative approach as an exercise after you have completed the first version.

Getting the Value of a Term

The `term()` function returns a value for a term as type `double` and receives two arguments: the string being analyzed and an index to the current position in the string. There are other ways of doing this, but this arrangement is quite straightforward. The prototype of the function `term()` is:

```
double term(const char* str, size_t& index);        // Function analyzing a term
```

The second parameter is a reference. This is because you want the function to be able to modify the value of the `index` variable in the calling program to position it at the character following the last character of the term found in the input string. You could return `index` as a value, but then you would need to return the value of the term in some other way, so this arrangement seems quite natural.

The logic for analyzing a term is going to be similar to that for an expression. A term is a number, potentially followed by one or more combinations of a multiply or a divide operator and another number. You can write the definition of the `term()` function as:

```
// Function to get the value of a term
double term(const char* str, size_t& index)
{
  double value {};                        // Somewhere to accumulate
                                          // the result

  value = number(str, index);             // Get the first number in the term

  // Loop as long as we have a good operator
  while(true)
```

```
  {
    if(*(str + index) == '*')          // If it's multiply,
      value *= number(str, ++index);   // multiply by next number

    else if(*(str + index) == '/')     // If it's divide,
      value /= number(str, ++index);   // divide by next number
    else
      break;
  }
  return value;                        // We've finished, so return what
                                       // we've got

}
```

How the Function Functions

You first declare a local `double` variable, `value`, in which you'll accumulate the value of the current term. Because a term must contain at least one number, the first action is to obtain the value of the first number by calling the `number()` function and storing the result in `value`. The code implicitly assumes that `number()` accepts the string and an index to a position in the string as arguments, and returns the value of the number found. Because the `number()` function must also update the index to the string to the position after a number is found, you'll specify the second parameter for the function as a reference.

The rest of the `term()` function is a `while` loop that continues as long as the next character is `'*'` or `'/'`. Within the loop, if the character found at the current position is `'*'`, you increment `index` to position it at the beginning of the next number, call the function `number()` to get the value of the next number, and then multiply the contents of `value` by the value returned. In a similar manner, if the current character is `'/'`, you increment `index` and divide the contents of `value` by the value returned from `number()`. Because `number()` automatically alters the value of `index` to the character following the number found, `index` is already set to select the next available character in the string on the next iteration. The loop terminates when a character other than a multiply or divide operator is found, whereupon the current value of the term accumulated in the variable `value` is returned to the calling function.

The last analytical function that you require is `number()`, which determines the numerical value of any number appearing in the string.

Analyzing a Number

Based on the way you have used `number()` within the `term()` function, you need to declare it with this prototype:

```
  double number(const char* str, size_t& index);   // Function to recognize a number
```

The specification of the second parameter as a reference allows the function to update the argument in the calling program directly, which is what you require.

You can make use of a function provided by the standard library here. The `cctype` header file provides definitions for a range of functions for testing single characters. These functions return values of type int where nonzero values correspond to true and zero corresponds to false. Four of these functions are shown in the following table:

FUNCTIONS	DESCRIPTION
int isalpha(int c)	Returns nonzero if the argument is alphabetic; otherwise, returns 0
int isupper(int c)	Returns nonzero if the argument is an uppercase letter; otherwise, returns 0.
int islower(int c)	Returns nonzero if the argument is a lowercase letter; otherwise, returns 0.
int isdigit(int c)	Returns nonzero if the argument is a digit; otherwise, returns 0.

> **NOTE** *A number of other functions are provided by the* cctype *header but I won't grind through all the details. If you're interested, you can look them up in the Visual C++ Help. A search on "is routines" should find them.*

You only need the last of the functions shown in the table in the program. Remember that isdigit() is testing a character, such as the character '9' (ASCII character 57 in decimal notation) for instance, not a numeric 9, because the input is a string. You can define the function number() as:

```
// Function to recognize a number in a string
double number(const char* str, size_t& index)
{
  double value {};                  // Store the resulting value

  // There must be at least one digit...
  if(!isdigit(*(str + index)))
  { // There's no digits so input is junk...
    char message[31] {"Invalid character in number: "}
    strncat_s(message, str+index, 1);  // Append the character
    throw message;

  }

  while(isdigit(*(str + index)))         // Loop accumulating leading digits
    value = 10*value + (*(str + index++) - '0');

                                    // Not a digit when we get to here
  if(*(str + index) != '.')          // so check for decimal point
```

```
    return value;                    // and if not, return value

  double factor {1.0};               // Factor for decimal places
  while(isdigit(*(str + (++index)))) // Loop as long as we have digits
  {
    factor *= 0.1;                   // Decrease factor by factor of 10
    value = value + (*(str + index) - '0')*factor;   // Add decimal place
  }

  return value;                      // On loop exit we are done
}
```

How the Function Functions

You declare the local variable `value` as type `double` that holds the value of the number that is found. You initialize it with 0.0 because you add in the digit values as you go along. There must always be at least one digit present for the number to be valid, so the first step is to verify that this is the case. If there is no initial digit, the input is badly formed, so you throw an exception that identifies the problem and the erroneous character.

A number in the string is a series of digits as ASCII characters so the function steps through the string accumulating the value of the number digit by digit. This occurs in two phases — the first phase accumulates digits before the decimal point; then, if you find a decimal point, the second phase accumulates the digits after it.

The first step is in the `while` loop that continues as long as the current character selected by the variable `index` is a digit. The value of the digit is extracted and added to the variable `value` in the loop statement:

```
value = 10*value + (*(str + index++) - '0');
```

The way this is constructed bears a closer examination. A digit character has an ASCII value between 48, corresponding to the digit 0, and 57, corresponding to the digit 9. Thus, if you subtract the ASCII code for `'0'` from the code for a digit, you convert it to its equivalent numeric digit value from 0 to 9. You have parentheses around the subexpression:

```
*(str + index++) - '0'
```

These are not essential, but they do make what's going on a little clearer. The contents of `value` are multiplied by 10 to shift the value one decimal place to the left before adding in the digit value, because you'll find digits from left to right — that is, the most significant digit first. This process is illustrated in Figure 6-6.

As soon as you come across something other than a digit, it is either a decimal point or something else. If it's not a decimal point, you've finished, so you return the current contents of `value` to the calling function. If it is a decimal point, you accumulate the digits corresponding to the fractional part of the number in the second loop. In this loop, you use the `factor` variable, which has the initial value 1.0, to set the decimal place for the current digit, and, consequently, `factor` is multiplied by 0.1 for each digit found. Thus, the first digit after the decimal point is multiplied by 0.1, the second by 0.01, the third by 0.001, and so on. This process is illustrated in Figure 6-7.

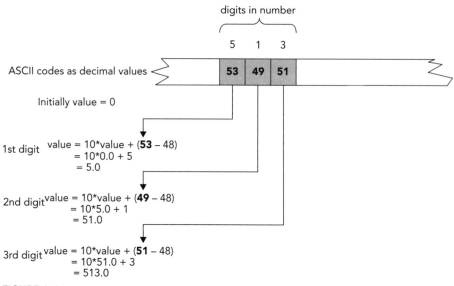

FIGURE 6-6

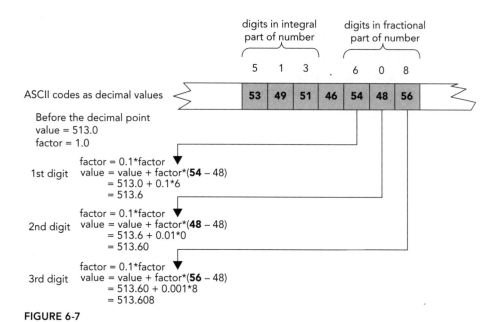

FIGURE 6-7

As soon as you find a non-digit character, you are done, so after the second loop you return `value`. You almost have the whole thing now. You just need a `main()` function to read the input and drive the process.

Putting the Program Together

You can collect the `#include` statements together and assemble the function prototypes at the beginning of the program for all the functions used in this program:

```
// Ex6_10.cpp
// A program to implement a calculator

#include <iostream>                               // For stream input/output
#include <cstdlib>                                // For the exit() function
#include <cctype>                                 // For the isdigit() function
using std::cin;
using std::cout;
using std::cerr;
using std::endl;

void eatspaces(char* str);                        // Function to eliminate blanks
double expr(char* str);                           // Function evaluating an expression
double term(const char* str, size_t& index);      // Function analyzing a term
double number(const char* str, size_t& index);    // Function to recognize a number

const size_t MAX {80};                            // Maximum expression length,
                                                  // including '\0'
```

You have also defined a global variable MAX, which is the maximum number of characters in the expression processed by the program (including the terminating `'\0'` character).

Now, you can add the definition of the `main()` function, and your program is complete. The `main()` function should read a string and exit if it is empty; otherwise, call `expr()` to evaluate the input and display the result. This process should repeat indefinitely. That doesn't sound too difficult, so let's give it a try.

```
int main()
{
  char buffer[MAX] {};      // Input area for expression to be evaluated

  cout << endl
       << "Welcome to your friendly calculator."
       << endl
       << "Enter an expression, or an empty line to quit."
       << endl;

  for(;;)

  {
    cin.getline(buffer, sizeof buffer);         // Read an input line
    eatspaces(buffer);                          // Remove blanks from input

    if(!buffer[0])                              // Empty line ends calculator
      return 0;

    try
    {
      cout << "\t= " << expr(buffer)            // Output value of expression
           << endl << endl;
    }
```

```
        catch( const char* pEx)
        {
          cerr << pEx << endl;
          cerr << "Ending program." << endl;
          return 1;
        }
    }
}
```

How the Function Functions

In `main()`, you set up the `char` array, `buffer`, to accept an expression up to 80 characters long (including the string termination character). The expression is read within the indefinite `for` loop using the `getline()` function. After obtaining the input, spaces are removed from the string by calling `eatspaces()`.

All the other things that `main()` provides for are also within the loop. It checks for an empty string, which consists of just the null character, `'\0'`, in which case the program ends. It also outputs the value returned by `expr()` function. The statement that does this is in a `try` block, because both `expr()` and the `number()` function that it calls indirectly can throw an exception when things go wrong. The exception thrown by both functions is of the same type. The `catch` block will catch exceptions of type `const char*` so it will catch an exception thrown by either function. When an exception is thrown, the `catch` block outputs the string that is the exception and ends the program.

After you add all the function definitions to the code and compile and run it, you should get output similar to the following:

```
2 * 35
          = 70
2/3 + 3/4 + 4/5 + 5/6 + 6/7
          = 3.90714
1 + 2.5 + 2.5*2.5 + 2.5*2.5*2.5
          = 25.375
```

You can enter as many calculations as you like, and when you are fed up with it, just press Enter to end the program. If you want to see the error handling in action, just enter an invalid expression.

Extending the Program

Now that you have got a working calculator, you can start to think about extending it. Wouldn't it be nice to be able to handle parentheses in an expression? It can't be that difficult, can it? Let's give it a try.

Think about the relationship between something in parentheses that might appear in an expression and the kind of expression analysis that you have made so far. Look at an example of the kind of expression you want to handle:

```
2*(3 + 4) / 6 - (5 + 6) / (7 + 8)
```

Notice that an expression between parentheses always forms part of a `term` in our original parlance. Whatever sort of computation you come up with, this is always true. In fact, if you could substitute the value of the expressions within parentheses back into the original string, you would have something that you can already deal with. This indicates a possible approach to handling parentheses. You might be able to treat an expression in parentheses as just another number, and modify the number() function to sort out the value of whatever appears between the parentheses.

That sounds like a good idea, but "sorting out" the expression in parentheses requires a bit of thought: the clue to success is in the terminology used here. An expression that appears within parentheses is a perfectly good example of a full-blown expression, and you already have the expr() function that will return the value of an expression. If you can get the number() function to work out what lies between the parentheses and extract those from the string, you could pass the substring to the expr() function, and recursion would really simplify the problem. What's more, you don't need to worry about nested parentheses. Any set of parentheses contains what you have defined as an expression, so nested parentheses are taken care of automatically. Recursion wins again.

Let's take a stab at rewriting number() to recognize an expression between parentheses:

```cpp
// Function to recognize an expression in parentheses
// or a number in a string
double number(const char* str, size_t& index)
{
  double value {};                      // Store the resulting value

  if(*(str + index) == '(')             // Start of parentheses
  {
    char* psubstr {};                   // Pointer for substring
    psubstr = extract(str, ++index);    // Extract substring in brackets
    value = expr(psubstr);              // Get the value of the substring
    delete[]psubstr;                    // Clean up the free store
    return value;                       // Return substring value
  }

  // There must be at least one digit...
  if(!isdigit(*(str + index)))
  { // There's no digits so input is junk...
    char message[31] {"Invalid character in number: "}
    strncat_s(message, str+index, 1);   // Append the character
    throw message;

  }

  while(isdigit(*(str + index)))        // Loop accumulating leading digits
    value = 10*value + (*(str + index++) - '0');
                                        // Not a digit when we get to here
  if(*(str + index) != '.')             // so check for decimal point
    return value;                       // and if not, return value

  double factor{1.0};                   // Factor for decimal places
  while(isdigit(*(str + (++index))))    // Loop as long as we have digits
  {
    factor *= 0.1;                      // Decrease factor by factor of 10
    value = value + (*(str + index) - '0')*factor;  // Add decimal place
  }
  return value;                         // On loop exit we are done
}
```

This is not yet complete, because you still need the extract() function, but you'll fix that in a moment.

How the Function Functions

Very little has been changed to support parentheses. I suppose it is a bit of a cheat, because you use the extract() function that you haven't written yet, but for one extra function, you get as many levels of nested parentheses as you want. This really is icing on the cake, and it's all down to the magic of recursion!

The first thing that number() does now is to test for a left parenthesis. If it finds one, it calls another function, extract() to extract the substring between the parentheses from the original string. The address of this new substring is stored in the pointer psubstr, so you then apply the expr() function to the substring by passing this pointer as an argument. The result is stored in value, and after releasing the memory allocated on the free store in the extract() function (as you will eventually implement it), you return the value obtained for the substring as though it were a regular number. Of course, if there is no left parenthesis to start with, the function number() continues exactly as before.

Extracting a Substring

You now need to write the extract() function. It's not difficult, but it's also not trivial. The main complication comes from the fact that the expression within parentheses may also contain other sets of parentheses, so you can't just go looking for the first right parenthesis after you find a left parenthesis. You must watch out for more left parentheses as well, and for every one that you find, ignore the corresponding right parenthesis. You can do this by maintaining a count of left parentheses as you go along, adding one to the count for each left parenthesis you find. If the left parenthesis count is not zero, you subtract one for each right parenthesis. Of course, if the left parenthesis count is zero and you find a right parenthesis, you're at the end of the substring. The mechanism for extracting a parenthesized substring is illustrated in Figure 6-8.

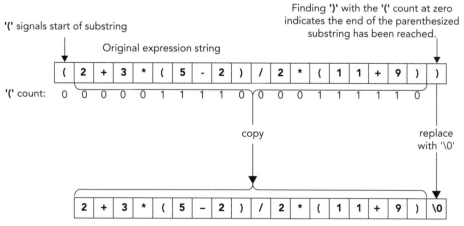

FIGURE 6-8

Because the string you extract here contains subexpressions between parentheses, eventually extract() is called again to deal with those.

The extract() function also needs to allocate memory for the substring and return a pointer to it. Of course, the index to the current position in the original string must end up selecting the character following the substring, so the parameter for that should be specified as a reference. Thus the prototype of extract() is:

```
char* extract(const char* str, size_t& index); //Function to extract a substring
```

You can now have a shot at the definition of the function:

```
// Function to extract a substring between parentheses
// (requires cstring header file)
char* extract(const char* str, size_t& index)
{
  char* pstr {};                        // Pointer to new string for return
  size_t numL {};                       // Count of left parentheses found
  size_t bufindex {index};              // Save starting value for index

  do
  {
    switch(*(str + index))
    {
      case ')':
        if(0 == numL)
        {
          ++index;
          pstr = new char[index - bufindex];
          if(!pstr)
          {
            throw "Memory allocation failed.";
          }
          // Copy substring to new memory
          strncpy_s(pstr, index-bufindex, str+bufindex, index-bufindex-1);

          return pstr;                   // Return substring in new memory
        }
        else
          numL--;                        // Reduce count of '(' to be matched
          break;

      case '(':
        numL++;                          // Increase count of '(' to be
                                         // matched

        break;
    }
  } while(*(str + index++) != '\0');     // Loop - don't overrun end of string

  throw "Ran off the end of the expression, must be bad input.";
}
```

How the Function Functions

You declare a pointer to a string, `pstr`, that will eventually point to the substring that you will return. You declare a counter `numL` to keep track of left parentheses in the substring. The initial value of `index` (when the function begins execution) is stored in the variable `bufindex`. You use this in combination with incremented values of `index` to determine the range of characters to be extracted from `str` and returned.

The executable part of the function is basically one big `do-while` loop that walks through `str` looking for parentheses. You check for left or right parentheses during each cycle. If a left parenthesis is found, `numL` is incremented, and if a right parenthesis is found and `numL` is non-zero, it is decremented. When you find a right parenthesis and `numL` is zero, you have found the end of the substring. Sufficient memory is obtained on the heap to hold the substring and the address is stored in `pstr`. The substring that you want from `str` is then copied to the memory that you obtained through the operator `new` by using the `strncpy_s()` function that is declared in the `cstring` header. This function copies the string specified by the third argument, `str+bufindex`, to the address specified by the first argument, `pstr`. `str+bufindex` is a pointer to the character in `str` where the substring starts. The second argument is the length of the destination string, `pstr` and the fourth argument is the number of characters to be copied from the source string.

If you fall through the bottom of the loop, it means that you hit the `'\0'` at the end of the expression in `str` without finding the complementary right parenthesis, so you throw an exception that will be caught in `main()`.

Running the Modified Program

After replacing the `number()` function in the old version of the program, adding the `#include` directive for `cstring`, and incorporating the prototype and the definition for the new `extract()` function you have just written, you're ready to roll with an all-singing, all-dancing calculator. If you have assembled all that without error, you can get output like this:

```
Welcome to your friendly calculator.
Enter an expression, or an empty line to quit.
1/(1+1/(1+1/(1+1)))
        = 0.6
(1/2-1/3)*(1/3-1/4)*(1/4-1/5)
        = 0.000694444
3.5*(1.25-3/(1.333-2.1*1.6))-1
        = 8.55507
2,4-3.4
Expression evaluation error. Found:, Ending program.
```

The friendly and informative error message in the last output line is due to the use of the comma instead of the decimal point in the expression above it, in what should be 2.4. As you can see, you get nested parentheses to any depth with a relatively simple extension of the program, all due to the amazing power of recursion.

SUMMARY

You now have a reasonably comprehensive knowledge of writing and using functions, and you have used overloading to implement a set of functions providing the same operation with different types of parameters. You have also seen how you can define function templates that you can use to generate different versions of essentially the same function. You'll see more about overloading functions in the following chapters.

You also got some experience of using several functions in a program by working through the calculator example. But remember that all the uses of functions up to now have been in the context of a traditional procedural approach to programming. When you come to look at object-oriented programming, you will still use functions extensively, but with a very different approach to program structure and to the design of the solution to a problem.

EXERCISES

1. Consider the following function:

```
int ascVal(size_t i, const char* p)
{
    // Return the ASCII value of the char
    if (!p || i > strlen(p))
        return -1;
    else
        return p[i];
}
```

Write a program that will call this function through a pointer and verify that it works. You'll need an #include directive for the cstring header in your program to use the strlen() function.

2. Write a family of overloaded functions called equal(), which take two arguments of the same type, returning 1 if the arguments are equal, and 0 otherwise. Provide versions having char, int, double, and char* arguments. (Use the strcmp() function from the runtime library to test for equality of strings. If you don't know how to use strcmp(), search for it in the online help. You'll need an #include directive for the cstring header file in your program.) Write test code to verify that the correct versions are called.

3. At present, when the calculator hits an invalid input character, it prints an error message, but doesn't show you where the error was in the line. Write an error routine that prints out the input string, putting a caret (^) below the offending character, like this:

```
12 + 4,2*3
      ^
```

4. Add an exponentiation operator, ^, to the calculator, fitting it in alongside * and /. What are the limitations of implementing it in this way, and how can you overcome them?

5. (Advanced) Extend the calculator so it can handle trig and other math functions, allowing you to input expressions such as:

```
2 * sin(0.6)
```

The math library functions all work in radians; provide versions of the trigonometric functions so that the user can use degrees, for example:

```
2 * sind(30)
```

➤ WHAT YOU LEARNED IN THIS CHAPTER

TOPIC	CONCEPT
Pointers to functions	A pointer to a function stores the address of a function, plus information about the number and types of parameters and return type for a function.
Exceptions	An exception is a way of signaling an error in a program so that the error handling code can be separated from the code for normal operations.
Throwing exceptions	You throw an exception with a statement that uses the keyword `throw`.
try blocks	Code that may throw exceptions should be placed in a `try` block, and the code to handle a particular type of exception is placed in a `catch` block immediately following the `try` block. There can be several `catch` blocks following a `try` block, each catching a different type of exception.
Overloaded functions	Overloaded functions are functions with the same name, but with different parameter lists.
Calling an overloaded function	When you call an overloaded function, the function to be called is selected by the compiler based on the number and types of the arguments that you specify.
Function templates	A function template is a recipe for generating overloaded functions automatically.
Function template parameters	A function template has one or more parameters that are type variables. An instance of the function template — that is, a function definition — is created by the compiler for each function call that corresponds to a unique set of type arguments for the template.
Function template instances	You can force the compiler to create a particular instance from a function template by specifying the function you want in a prototype declaration.
The `decltype` operator	You use the `decltype` operator to determine the type of the result of an expression.
Trailing return types	When a function template has a return type that depends on the arguments types, you can specify the return type using the `auto` keyword and define the return type using the `decltype` operator following `->` after the function header.

Defining Your Own Data Types

THE STRUCT IN C++

This chapter is about creating your own data types to suit your particular problem. It's also about creating objects, the building blocks of object-oriented programming. An object can seem a bit mysterious at first, but as you'll see in this chapter, an object can be just an instance of one of your own data types.

A structure is a user-defined type that you define using the struct keyword so it is often referred to as a *struct*. The struct originated back in C and C++ incorporates and expands on the C struct. A struct in C++ is functionally replaceable by a class insofar as anything you can do with a struct, you can also achieve by using a class. However, because Windows was written in C before C++ became widely used, the struct appears pervasively in Windows programming. It is also used today, so you really need to know something about structs. You'll first look at structs before exploring the more extensive capabilities offered by classes.

What Is a struct?

Almost all the variables that you have seen up to now have been able to store a single type of entity — a number of some kind, a character, or an array of elements of the same type. The real world is a bit more complicated than that, and just about any physical object you can think of needs several items of data to describe it even minimally. Think about the information that might be needed to describe something as simple as a book. You might consider title, author, publisher, date of publication, number of pages, price, topic or classification, and ISBN number, just for starters, and you can probably come up with a few more without too much difficulty. You could specify separate variables to contain each of the parameters that you need to describe a book, but ideally, you would have a single data type, Book, say, which embodied all of the things that you need to describe a book. I'm sure you won't be surprised to hear that this is exactly what a struct can do for you.

Defining a struct

Let's stick with the notion of a book, and suppose that you just want to include the title, author, publisher, and year of publication within your definition of a book. You could define a structure to accommodate this as follows:

```
struct Book
{
  char title[80];
  char author[80];
  char publisher[80];
  int year;
};
```

This doesn't define any variables, but it does define a new type, and the name of the type is Book. The struct keyword defines Book as a structure, and the elements making up an object of this type are defined within the braces. Note that each line defining an element in the struct is terminated by a semicolon, and that a semicolon also appears after the closing brace. The elements of a struct can be of any type, except the same type as the struct being defined. You couldn't have an element of type Book included in the structure definition for Book, for example. You may think this is a limitation, but note that you could include a pointer of type Book*, as you'll see a little later on.

The elements title, author, publisher, and year enclosed between the braces in the preceding definition are referred to as *members* or *fields* of the Book structure. A Book object is called an *instance* of the type. Every object of type Book contains its own set of the members title, author, publisher, and year. You can now create variables of type Book in exactly the same way as you create variables of any other type:

```
Book novel;                          // Declare variable novel of type Book
```

This defines a variable with the name novel that you can now use to store information about a book. All you need now is to understand how you get data into the members that make up a variable of type Book.

Initializing a struct

The first way to get data into members of a `struct` object is to define initial values for them in the definition of the object. Suppose you wanted to initialize novel to contain the data for one of your favorite books, *Paneless Programming*, published in 1981 by the Gutter Press. This is a story of a guy performing heroic code development while living in an igloo, and, as you probably know, inspired the famous Hollywood box office success, *Gone with the Window*. It was written by I.C. Fingers, who is also the author of that seminal three-volume work, *The Connoisseur's Guide to the Paper Clip*. With this wealth of information, you can write the definition for novel as:

```
Book novel
{
  "Paneless Programming",        // Initial value for title
  "I.C. Fingers",                // Initial value for author
  "Gutter Press",                // Initial value for publisher
   1981                          // Initial value for year
};
```

The initializing values appear in an initializer list in much the same way as for elements of an array. As with arrays, the sequence of initial values needs to be the same as the sequence of the members of the struct in its definition. Each member of the novel structure has the corresponding initial value assigned to it, as indicated in the comments.

Accessing the Members of a struct

To access individual members of a `struct`, you use the *member selection operator*, which is a period; this is sometimes referred to as the *member access operator*. To refer to a member, you write the struct variable name, followed by a period, followed by the name of the member. To change the year member of the novel structure, you could write:

```
novel.year = 1988;
```

This sets the value of the year member to 1988. You can use a member of a struct in exactly the same way as any other variable. To increment the member year by two, for example, you can write:

```
novel.year += 2;
```

This increments the value of the year member of novel.

TRY IT OUT **Using structs**

This example shows how referencing the members of a `struct` works. Suppose you want to write a program to deal with some of the things you might find in a yard, such as those illustrated in the professionally landscaped yard in Figure 7-1.

I have arbitrarily assigned the coordinates 0,0 to the top-left corner of the yard. The bottom-right corner has the coordinates 100,120. Thus, the first coordinate value is a measure of the horizontal position relative to the top-left corner, with values increasing from left to right, and the second coordinate is a measure of the vertical position from the same reference point, with values increasing from top to bottom. Figure 7-1 also shows the position of the pool and those of the two huts relative to the top-left corner of the yard. Because the yard, huts, and pool are all rectangular, you could define a struct type to represent any of these:

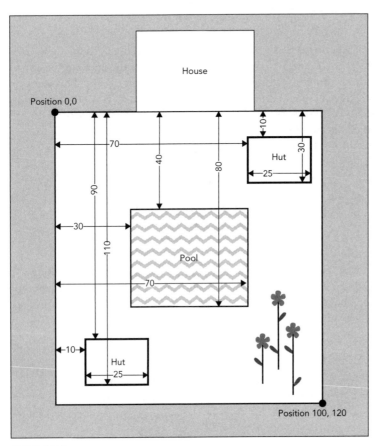

FIGURE 7-1

```
struct Rectangle
{
  int left;                          // Top-left point
  int top;                           // coordinate pair

  int right;                         // Bottom-right point
  int bottom;                        // coordinate pair
};
```

The first two members of the Rectangle structure type correspond to the coordinates of the top-left point of a rectangle, and the next two to the coordinates of the bottom-right point. You can use this in an elementary example representing rectangular objects in the yard:

```
// Ex7_01.cpp
// Exercising structures in the yard
#include <iostream>
using std::cout;
using std::endl;

// Definition of a struct to represent rectangles
struct Rectangle
{
  int left;                          // Top-left point
```

```
    int top;                            // coordinate pair

  int right;                            // Bottom-right point
  int bottom;                           // coordinate pair
};

// Prototype of function to calculate the area of a rectangle
long area(const Rectangle& aRect);

// Prototype of a function to move a rectangle
void moveRect(Rectangle& aRect, const int x, const int y);

int main()
{
  Rectangle yard { 0, 0, 100, 120 };
  Rectangle pool { 30, 40, 70, 80 };
  Rectangle hut1, hut2;


  hut1.left = 70;
  hut1.top = 10;
  hut1.right = hut1.left + 25;
  hut1.bottom = 30;

  hut2 = hut1;                          // Define hut2 the same as hut1
  moveRect(hut2, 10, 90);               // Now move it to the right position

  cout << "Coordinates of hut2 are "
       << hut2.left << "," << hut2.top << " and "
       << hut2.right << "," << hut2.bottom << endl;

  cout << "The area of the yard is " << area(yard) << endl;

  cout << "The area of the pool is " << area(pool) << endl;

  return 0;
}

// Function to calculate the area of a rectangle
long area(const Rectangle& aRect)
{
  return (aRect.right - aRect.left)*(aRect.bottom - aRect.top);
}

// Function to Move a Rectangle
void moveRect(Rectangle& aRect, const int x, const int y)
{
  const int length {aRect.right - aRect.left}; // Get length of rectangle
  const int width {aRect.bottom - aRect.top};  // Get width of rectangle

  aRect.left = x;                              // Set top-left point
  aRect.top = y;                              // to new position
  aRect.right = x + length;                    // Get bottom-right point as
  aRect.bottom = y + width;                    // increment from new position
  return;
}
```

The output from this example is:

```
Coordinates of hut2 are 10,90 and 35,110
The area of the yard is 12000
The area of the pool is 1600
```

How It Works

Note that the `struct` definition appears at global scope in this example. You'll be able to see it in the Class View tab for the project. Putting the definition of the `struct` at global scope allows you to define a variable of type `Rectangle` anywhere in the `.cpp` file. In a larger program, such definitions would be stored in an `.h` file that would be added to each `.cpp` file where necessary, using an `#include` directive.

You have defined two functions to process `Rectangle` objects. The `area()` function calculates the area of the `Rectangle` object that you pass as a reference argument as the product of the length and the width, where the length is the difference between the horizontal positions of the defining points, and the width is the difference between the vertical positions of the defining points. The parameter is `const` because the function does not change the argument that is passed to it. By passing a reference, the code runs a little faster because the argument is not copied. The `MoveRect()` function modifies the defining points of a `Rectangle` object to position it at the coordinates x, y, which are passed as arguments.

The position of a `Rectangle` object is assumed to be the position of the `left`, `top` point. Because the `Rectangle` object is passed as a reference, the function can modify the members of the `Rectangle` object directly. After calculating the length and width of the `Rectangle` object passed, the `left` and `top` members are set to x and y, respectively, and the new `right` and `bottom` members are calculated by incrementing x and y by the length and width of the original `Rectangle` object.

In the `main()` function, you initialize the yard and pool variables with their coordinate positions, as shown in Figure 7-1. The `hut1` variable represents the hut at the top-right in the illustration, and its members are set to the appropriate values using assignment statements. The `hut2` variable, corresponding to the hut at the bottom-left of the yard, is first set to be the same as `hut1` in the assignment statement:

```
hut2 = hut1;                          // Define Hut2 the same as Hut1
```

This copies the values of the members of `hut1` to the corresponding members of `hut2`. You can only assign a `struct` of a given type to another of the same type. You can't increment a `struct` directly or use a `struct` in an arithmetic expression.

To alter the position of `hut2` to its place at the bottom-left of the yard, you call the `moveRect()` function with the coordinates of the required position as arguments. This roundabout way of getting the coordinates of `hut2` is totally unnecessary, and serves only to show how you can use a `struct` as an argument to a function.

IntelliSense Assistance with Structures

The editor in Visual C++ is quite intelligent — it knows the types of variables, for instance. This is because of the IntelliSense feature. If you hover the mouse cursor over a variable name in the editor window, it pops up a little box showing its type. It also can help a lot with structures (and classes, as you will see) because not only does it know the types of ordinary variables, it also knows the members that belong to a variable of a particular structure type. As you type the member selection operator following a structure variable name, the editor pops up a window showing the list of members. If you click one of the members, it shows the member definition including the comment that appeared in the original definition of the structure, so you know what it is. This is shown in Figure 7-2, using a fragment of the previous example.

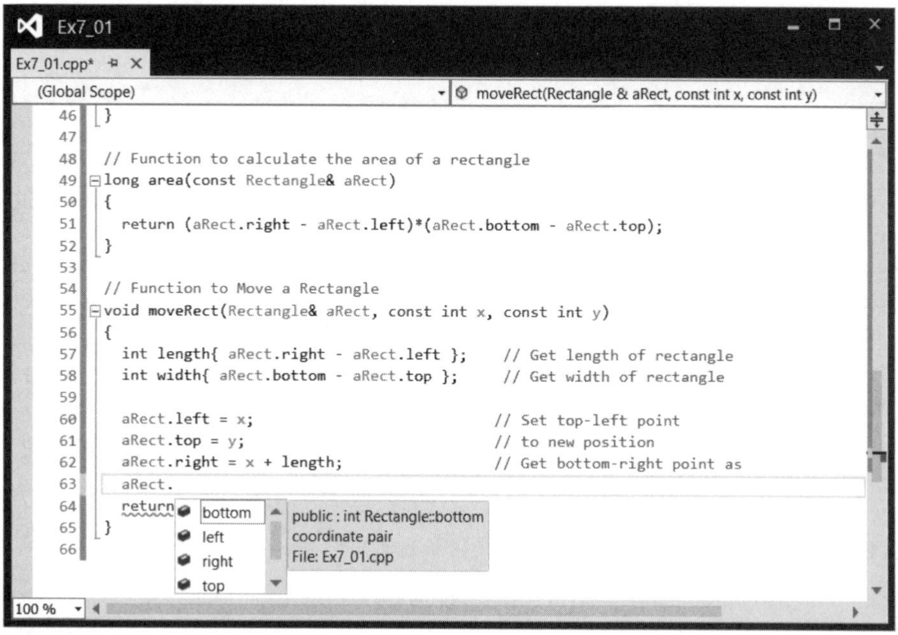

FIGURE 7-2

There's a real incentive to add comments, and to keep them short and to the point. If you double-click on a member in the list or press the Enter key when the item is highlighted, it is automatically inserted after the member selection operator, thus eliminating one source of typos in your code. Great, isn't it?

You can turn any or all of the IntelliSense features off. To turn the IntelliSense features on or off, first select Options from the Tools menu. Expand the Text Editor tree in the left pane of the dialog that displays by clicking the [unfilled] symbol, then click the unfilled symbol alongside C/C++. Click the Advanced option and you will see the IntelliSense options displayed in the right pane. Setting an option to false turns it off.

The editor also shows the parameter list for a function when you are typing the code to call it — it pops up as soon as you enter the left parenthesis for the argument list. This is particularly helpful with library functions, as it's tough to remember the parameter list for all of them. Of course, the `#include` directive for the header file must already be there in the source code for this to work. Without it, the editor has no idea what the library function is. Also, if you omit the `std` namespace prefix when you have also failed to include a `using` statement for a library function, the editor won't recognize the function. You will see more things that the editor can help with as you learn more about classes. After that interesting little diversion, let's get back to structures.

The RECT Structure

Rectangles are used a great deal in Windows programs. For this reason, there is a RECT structure predefined in the windef.h header file that is included in windows.h. Its definition is essentially the same as the structure that you defined in the last example:

```
struct RECT
{
  LONG left;                    // Top-left point
  LONG top;                     // coordinate pair

  LONG right;                   // Bottom-right point
  LONG bottom;                  // coordinate pair
};
```

Type LONG is a Windows type that is equivalent to the fundamental type long. This struct is usually used to define rectangular areas on your display for a variety of purposes. Because RECT is used so extensively, windows.h also contains prototypes for a number of functions to manipulate and modify rectangles. For example, it defines the InflateRect() function that increases the size of a rectangle, and the EqualRect() function that compares two rectangles.

The MFC defines a CRect class that is the equivalent of a RECT structure. After you understand classes, you will be using this rather than the RECT structure. The CRect class provides an extensive range of functions for manipulating rectangles, and you'll use many of these when you are writing Windows programs using the MFC.

Using Pointers with a struct

You can create a pointer to an object of a structure type. Many of the functions defined in windows.h that work with RECT objects require pointers to a RECT object as arguments, because this avoids the copying of the structure when a function is called. To define a pointer to a RECT object, the definition is what you might expect:

```
RECT* pRect {};              // Define a pointer to a RECT
```

Assuming that you have defined a RECT object, aRect, you can set the pointer to the address of this variable in the normal way:

```
pRect = &aRect;                     // Set pointer to the address of aRect
```

As you saw when I introduced the idea of a struct, a struct can't contain a member of the same type as the struct being defined, but it can contain a pointer to a struct, including a pointer to a struct of the same type. For example, you could define a structure like this:

```
struct ListElement
{
  RECT aRect;                   // RECT member of structure
  ListElement* pNext;           // Pointer to a list element
};
```

The first member of the ListElement structure is of type RECT, and the second member is a pointer to a structure of type ListElement — the same type as that being defined. This allows objects of type ListElement to be daisy-chained together, where each ListElement can contain the address of the next `ListElement` object in a chain, the last in the chain having the pointer as `nullptr`. This is illustrated in Figure 7-3.

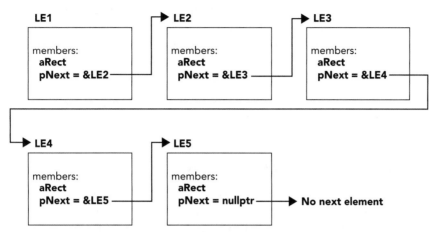

FIGURE 7-3

Each box in the diagram represents an object of type `ListElement`, and the `pNext` member of each object stores the address of the next object in the chain, except for the last object, where `pNext` is `nullptr`. This kind of arrangement is referred to as a *linked list*. It has the advantage that as long as you know the address of the first element in the list, you can find all the others. This is particularly useful when many objects are created dynamically, because you can use a linked list to keep track of them. Every time you create a new object, you can add it to the end of the list by storing its address in the `pNext` member of the last object in the chain.

Accessing Structure Members through a Pointer

Consider the following statements:

```
RECT aRect {0, 0, 100, 100};
RECT* pRect {&aRect};
```

The first defines the `aRect` object to be of type `RECT` with the first pair of members initialized to (0, 0) and the second pair to (100, 100). The second statement defines `pRect` as a pointer to type `RECT` and initializes it with the address of `aRect`. You can now access the members of `aRect` through the pointer with a statement such as this:

```
(*pRect).top += 10;                    // Increment the Top member by 10
```

The parentheses around the dereferenced pointer here are essential because the member access operator takes precedence over the dereferencing operator. Without the parentheses, you would be attempting to treat the pointer as a `struct` and trying to access the member, so the statement would not compile. After executing this statement, the `top` member will have the value 10 and, of course, the remaining members will be unchanged.

The syntax that you used to access the member of a `struct` through a pointer looks rather clumsy. Because this kind of operation crops up very frequently, C++ includes a special operator that expresses the same thing in a much more readable and intuitive form, so let's look at that next.

The Indirect Member Selection Operator

The *indirect member selection operator*, `->`, is specifically for accessing members of a `struct` or a class through a pointer; this operator is also referred to as the *indirect member access operator*. The operator looks like a little arrow (`->`) and is formed from a minus sign (`-`) followed by the symbol for greater than (`>`). You could use it to rewrite the statement to access the `top` member of `aRect` through the pointer `pRect`, as follows:

```
pRect->top += 10;                         // Increment the top member by 10
```

This is much more expressive of what is going on, isn't it? You'll see a lot more of the indirect member selection operator throughout the rest of the book.

TYPES, OBJECTS, CLASSES, AND INSTANCES

Before I get into the language, syntax, and programming techniques for classes, I'll first explain how your existing knowledge relates to the concept of classes. So far, you've learned that you can create variables that can be any of a range of fundamental data types: `int`, `long`, `double`, and so on. You have also seen how you can use the `struct` keyword to define a structure type that you can use as the type for a variable representing a composite of several other variables.

The variables of the fundamental types don't allow you to model real-world objects (or even imaginary objects) adequately. It's hard to model a box in terms of an `int`, for example; however, you can use the members of a `struct` to define a set of attributes for such an object. You could define variables `length`, `width`, and `height` to represent the dimensions of the box and bind them together as members of a `Box` structure, as follows:

```
struct Box
{
  double length;
  double width;
  double height;
};
```

With this definition of a new data type called `Box`, you can define variables of this type just as you did with variables of the basic types. You can then create, manipulate, and destroy as many `Box` objects as you need to in your program. This means that you can model objects using `struct`s and write your programs around them.

So — that's object-oriented programming all wrapped up, then? Well, not quite. Object-oriented programming (OOP) is based on three basic concepts relating to object types (*encapsulation*, *polymorphism*, and *inheritance*), and what you have seen so far doesn't quite fit the bill. Don't worry about what these terms mean for the moment — you'll explore that in the rest of this chapter and throughout the book.

The notion of a `struct` in C++ goes far beyond the original concept of a `struct` in C — it incorporates the object-oriented notion of a *class*. This idea of classes, from which you can create your own data types and use them just like the native types, is fundamental to C++, and the `class` keyword was introduced into the language to describe this concept. The keywords `struct` and `class` are almost identical in effect. They differ in the access control to the members, which you'll learn more about later in this chapter. The struct keyword is maintained in C++ for backwards compatibility with C, but everything that you can do with a struct, and more, you can achieve with a class.

Take a look at how you might define a class representing boxes:

```
class CBox
{
public:
  double m_Length;
  double m_Width;
  double m_Height;
};
```

When you define CBox as a class, you are essentially defining a new data type, similar to when you defined the Box structure. The only differences here are the use of the keyword class instead of struct, and the use of the public keyword followed by a colon that precedes the definition of the members of the class. The variables that you define as part of the class are called *data members* of the class, because they are variables that store data.

The public keyword is a clue as to the difference between a structure and a class. It just specifies that the members of the class that follow the keyword are generally accessible, in the same way as the members of a structure are. By default, the members of a class are not generally accessible and are said to be *private*, and to make members accessible, you must precede their definitions with the public keyword. The members of a struct, on the other hand, are public by default. The reason that class members are private by default is because, in general, an object of a class should be a self-contained entity such that the data that make the object what it is should be *encapsulated* and only changed under controlled circumstances. Public data members should be very much the exception. As you'll see a little later in the chapter, though, it's also possible to place other restrictions on the accessibility of members of a class.

I have also called the class CBox instead of Box. I could have called the class Box, but the MFC adopts the convention of using the prefix C for all class names, so you might as well get used to it. The MFC also prefixes data members of classes with m_ to distinguish them from other variables, so I'll use this convention, too. Remember, though, that in other contexts where you might use C++ without the MFC, this will not be the case; in some instances, the convention for naming classes and their members may be different, and in others, there may be no particular convention for naming entities.

You can define a variable, bigBox, which represents an instance of the CBox class type like this:

```
CBox bigBox;
```

This is exactly the same as declaring a variable for a struct, or, indeed, for any other variable type. After you have defined the CBox class, definitions for variables of this type are quite standard.

First Class

The notion of class was invented by an Englishman to keep the general population happy. It derives from the theory that people who know their place and function in society are much more secure and comfortable in life than those who do not. The famous Dane, Bjarne Stroustrup, who invented C++, undoubtedly acquired a deep knowledge of class concepts while at Cambridge University in England and appropriated the idea very successfully for use in his new language.

Class in C++ is similar to the English concept, in that each class usually has a very precise role and a permitted set of actions. However, it differs from the English idea because class in C++ has largely socialist overtones, concentrating on the importance of working classes. Indeed, in some ways it is the reverse of the English ideal because working classes in C++ often live on the backs of classes that do nothing at all.

Operations on Classes

You can define new data types as classes to represent whatever kinds of objects you like. Classes (and structures) aren't limited to just holding data; you can also define member functions or even operations that act on objects of your classes using the standard C++ operators. You can define the CBox class, for example, so that the following statements work and have the meanings you want them to have:

```
CBox box1;
CBox box2;

if(box1 > box2)          // Fill the larger box
  box1.fill();
else
  box2.fill();
```

You could also implement operations as part of the CBox class for adding, subtracting or even multiplying boxes — in fact, almost any operation to which you could ascribe a sensible meaning in the context of boxes.

I'm talking about incredibly powerful medicine here, and it constitutes a major change in the approach that you take to programming. Instead of breaking down a problem in terms of what are essentially computer-related data types (integers, floating-point numbers, and so on) and then writing a program, you can program in terms of problem-related data types, in other words, classes. These classes might be named CEmployee, or CCowboy, or CCheese, or CChutney, each defined specifically for the kind of problem that you want to solve, complete with the functions and operators that are necessary to manipulate instances of your new types.

Object-oriented program design starts with deciding what application-specific data types you need to solve the problem in hand, defining those as classes and writing the program in terms of operations on the specific types that the problem is concerned with, be they CCoffins or CCowpokes.

Terminology

I'll first summarize some of the terminology that I will be using when discussing classes:

➤ A *class* is a user-defined data type.

➤ *Object-oriented programming* (OOP) is the programming style based on the idea of defining your own data types as classes, where the data types are specific to the domain of the problem you intend to solve.

➤ Declaring an object of a class type is sometimes referred to as *instantiation* because you are creating an *instance* of a class.

➤ Instances of a class type are referred to as *objects*.

➤ The idea of an object containing the data implicit to its definition, together with the functions that operate on that data, is referred to as *encapsulation*.

When I get into the details of object-oriented programming, it may seem a little complicated in places, but getting back to the basics usually helps to make things clearer, so always keep in mind what objects are really about. They are about writing programs in terms of the objects that are specific to the domain of your problem. All the facilities around classes are there to make this as comprehensive and flexible as possible. Let's get down to the business of understanding classes.

UNDERSTANDING CLASSES

A class is a specification of a data type that you define. It can contain data elements that can either be variables of the fundamental types or of other user-defined types. The data elements may be single data items, arrays, pointers, arrays of pointers of almost any kind, or objects of other class types, so you have a lot of flexibility. A class typically contains functions that operate on objects of the class type by accessing the data elements that they include. So, a class combines both the definition of the elementary data that makes up an object and the means of manipulating the data that belongs to objects of the class type.

The data and functions within a class are called *members* of the class. Oddly enough, the members of a class that are data items are called *data members* and the members that are functions are called *function members* or *member functions*. The member functions are also sometimes referred to as *methods*; I will not use this term in general in this book, but it will turn up in Chapter 18.

When you define a class, you define a blueprint for objects of that type. This doesn't actually define any objects, but it does define what the class name means, that is, what an object of the class type will consist of and what operations can be performed on it. It's much the same as if you wrote a description of the basic type `double`. This wouldn't be an actual variable of type `double`, but a definition of how it's made up and what you can do with it. To create a variable of a fundamental type, you use a definition statement. It's exactly the same with a class type.

Defining a Class

Take a look again at the class example you saw earlier — a class of boxes. The `CBox` type was defined as:

```
class CBox
{
public:
  double m_Length;              // Length of a box in inches
  double m_Width;               // Width of a box in inches
  double m_Height;              // Height of a box in inches
};
```

The class type name follows the `class` keyword, and the three data members are defined between the curly braces. The data members are defined for the class using the definition statements that you already know and love, and the whole class definition is terminated with a semicolon. The names of all the members of a class are local to the class. You can, therefore, use the same names elsewhere in a program, including other class definitions.

Access Control in a Class

The `public` keyword determines the *access attributes* of the members of the class that follow it. Specifying members as `public` means that they can be accessed anywhere within the scope of the class object to which they belong. You can also specify the members of a class as `private` or `protected`, in which case the members cannot be accessed from outside the class. I'll explain these attributes in more detail later. If you omit the access specification, the members have the default access attribute, `private`. (This is the only difference between a class and a struct — the default access specifier for a struct is `public`.)

All you have defined so far is the `CBox` class, which is a type. You haven't created any objects. When I talk about accessing a class member, say `m_Height`, I'm talking about accessing the data member of a particular object, and that object needs to be defined somewhere.

Declaring Objects of a Class

You define objects of a class with exactly the same sort of definition that you use to define variables of fundamental types, so you could define objects of the `CBox` class type with these statements:

```
CBox box1;                          // Declare box1 of type CBox
CBox box2;                          // Declare box2 of type CBox
```

Both of these objects will, of course, have their own independent data members. This is illustrated in Figure 7-4.

The object name, `box1`, embodies the whole object, including its three data members. They are not initialized to anything — the data members of each object will contain junk values, so let's look at how you access them for the purpose of setting them to some specific values.

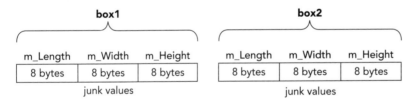

FIGURE 7-4

Accessing the Data Members of a Class

You can refer to the data members of a class object using the *direct member selection operator* that you used to access members of a struct. To set the value of the `m_Height` member of the object `box2` to 18.0, you can write this statement:

```
box2.m_Height = 18.0;               // Setting the value of a data member
```

You can access the data member in this way in a function that is outside the class because the `m_Height` member has `public` access. If it wasn't defined as `public`, this statement would not compile.

You'll see more about this shortly. Obviously, you could assign values to the other public data members of box2.

You can also copy the values of members of one object to another. For example:

```
CBox box1;
CBox box2;
box1.m_Length = box1.m_Width = box1.m_Height = 2;
box2 = box1;                        // Member-wise copying from box1 to box2
```

After creating two CBox objects, you set all the members of box1 to 2.0. The last statement copies the values of the box1 members to box2, so all the members of box2 will be 2.0. Member-wise copying from one object to another works regardless of the access specification of the data members.

TRY IT OUT Your First Use of Classes

This example shows that you can use your class in the same way as the structure:

```
// Ex7_02.cpp
// Creating and using boxes
#include <iostream>
using std::cout;
using std::endl;

class CBox                          // Class definition at global scope
{
public:
  double m_Length;                  // Length of a box in inches
  double m_Width;                   // Width of a box in inches
  double m_Height;                  // Height of a box in inches
};

int main()
{
  CBox box1;                        // Declare box1 of type CBox
  CBox box2;                        // Declare box2 of type CBox

  double boxVolume {};              // Stores the volume of a box

  box1.m_Height = 18.0;             // Define the values
  box1.m_Length = 78.0;            // of the members of
  box1.m_Width = 24.0;             // the object box1

  box2.m_Height = box1.m_Height - 10;   // Define box2
  box2.m_Length = box1.m_Length/2.0;    // members in
  box2.m_Width = 0.25*box1.m_Length;    // terms of box1

  // Calculate volume of box1
  boxVolume = box1.m_Height*box1.m_Length*box1.m_Width;

  cout << "Volume of box1 = " << boxVolume << endl;

  cout << "box2 has sides which total "
```

```
                << box2.m_Height+ box2.m_Length+ box2.m_Width
                << " inches." << endl;

        // Display the size of a box in memory
        cout << "A CBox object occupies "
                << sizeof box1 << " bytes." << endl;

        return 0;
    }
```

As you enter the code for main(), the editor prompts you with a list of member names whenever you enter a member selection operator following the name of a class object. You can then select the member you want from the list by double-clicking it. You can also use the arrow keys on the keyboard to move through the list and press Enter when you reach the one you want. Hovering the mouse cursor over any variable in your code will result in the type being displayed.

How It Works

Everything here works, as you would expect from your experience with structures. The class definition is outside of main() and therefore has global scope. This enables you to define CBox objects anywhere in the source file and the class shows up in the Class View tab.

You define two objects of type CBox within main(): box1 and box2. Of course, as with variables of the fundamental types, box1 and box2 are local to main(). Objects of a class type obey the same rules with respect to scope as variables of the fundamental types.

The first three assignment statements set the values of the data members of box1. You define the values of the data members of box2 in terms of the data members of box1 in the next three assignment statements.

You then have a statement that calculates the volume of box1 as the product of its three data members, and you output this value. Next, you output the sum of the data members of box2 by writing the expression for the sum directly in the output statement. The final action in the program is to output the number of bytes occupied by box1, which is produced by the sizeof operator.

If you run this program, you should get this output:

```
Volume of box1 = 33696
box2 has sides which total 66.5 inches.
A CBox object occupies 24 bytes.
```

The last line shows that box1 occupies 24 bytes, which is because it has three data members of 8 bytes each. The statement that produced the last line of output could equally well have been written like this:

```
    cout << "A CBox object occupies " << sizeof(CBox) << " bytes." << endl;
```

I have used the type name between parentheses as the operand for the sizeof operator, rather than a specific object name. You'll remember from Chapter 4 that this is standard syntax for the sizeof operator.

This example has demonstrated the mechanism for accessing the public data members of a class. It also shows that they can be used in exactly the same way as ordinary variables.

Memberwise Initialization of an Object

Because the data members of a CBox object are public, you can specify their values in an initializer list when you create the object. For example:

```
CBox box1 {2.5, 3.5, 4.5};
```

The members of box1 will be assigned values from the list in sequence so m_Length will be 2.5, m_Width will be 3.5, and m_Height will be 4.5. If you supply fewer initial values in the list than there are data members, the remainder will be set to zero. For example:

```
CBox box2 {2.5, 3.5};
```

m_Height for box2 here will be zero.

You can also supply an empty list to initialize all the members to zero:

```
CBox box3 {};              // All data members 0
```

You *cannot* do this if the data members are private. You also cannot use an initializing list in this way if the class includes a *constructor* definition. I'll explain what a constructor is a little later in this chapter.

Initializing Class Members

You can specify initial values for data members in the definition of a class type. The members of the CBox class store dimensions of a box, which should not be negative, so it would be sensible to make the initial values 1.0. Here's how you do this:

```
class CBox
{
public:
  double m_Length {1.0};              // Length of a box in inches
  double m_Width {1.0};               // Width of a box in inches
  double m_Height {1.0};              // Height of a box in inches
};
```

The syntax for initializing class members is the same as for ordinary variables. You use an initializer list. The initial values will apply for the members of any CBox object you create unless the member values are set by some other means.

You don't have to initialize every data member. The ones you don't provide initial values for will contain junk values. If you provide an initial value for one or more members, you cannot specify initial values when you create an object as I described in the previous section. If you try to do so the compiler will flag it as an error. To restore this capability you must include a *constructor* in the class. As I said, I'll explain class constructors a little later in this chapter.

Member Functions of a Class

A member function of a class is a function that has its definition or prototype within the class definition. It operates on any object of the class of which it is a member, and can access all the members of an object, regardless of the access specification. The names of the class members that you use in the body of a member function automatically refer to the members of the specific object used to call the function, and the function can only be called for a particular object of the class type. If you try to call a member function without specifying an object name, your program will not compile. Let's try it out.

TRY IT OUT   Adding a Member Function to CBox

This example extends the CBox class to include a member function that calculates the volume of a CBox object. This will demonstrate how you access the members of the class from within a member function.

```cpp
// Ex7_03.cpp
// Calculating the volume of a box with a member function
#include <iostream>
using std::cout;
using std::endl;

class CBox                             // Class definition at global scope
{
public:
  double m_Length{ 1.0 };              // Length of a box in inches
  double m_Width{ 1.0 };              // Width of a box in inches
  double m_Height{ 1.0 };             // Height of a box in inches

  // Function to calculate the volume of a box
  double volume()
  {
    return m_Length*m_Width*m_Height;
  }
};

int main()
{
  CBox box1;                           // Declare box1 of type CBox
  CBox box2;                           // Declare box2 of type CBox
  CBox box3;                           // Declare box3 of type CBox

  double boxVolume{ box1.volume() };   // Stores the volume of a box

  cout << "Default box1 volume : " << boxVolume << endl;

  box1.m_Height = 18.0;                // Define the values
  box1.m_Length = 78.0;                // of the members of
  box1.m_Width = 24.0;                 // the object box1

  boxVolume = box1.volume();           // Calculate new volume of box1
  cout << "Volume of box1 is now: " << boxVolume << endl;

  box2.m_Height = box1.m_Height - 10;  // Define box2
  box2.m_Length = box1.m_Length / 2.0; // members in
  box2.m_Width = 0.25*box1.m_Length;   // terms of box1
  cout << "Volume of box2 = " << box2.volume() << endl;

  box3 = box2;
  cout << "Volume of box3 = " << box3.volume() << endl;

  cout << "A CBox object occupies "
```

```
            << sizeof box1 << " bytes." << endl;

      return 0;
   }
```

If you execute this example, it produces this output:

```
Default box1 volume : 1
Volume of box1 is now: 33696
Volume of box2 = 6084
Volume of box3 = 6084
A CBox object occupies 24 bytes.
```

How It Works

The new code in the CBox class definition is the definition of the volume() member function. It has the same access attribute as the data members, public. Every class member that you define following an access attribute will have that attribute, until another access attribute specification appears within the class definition. The volume() function returns the volume of a CBox object as a value of type double. The expression in the return statement is just the product of the three data members.

There's no need to qualify the names of class members when you access them in member functions. The unqualified member names automatically refer to the members of the object for which the member function is called. You call a member function for a particular object by writing the name of the object, followed by a period, followed by the function name. The function automatically accesses the data members of the object for which it was called, so the first use of volume() calculates the volume of box1 and the value returned is used to initialize boxVolume. The output shows that the data members of box1 had the initial values you specified in the class definition when the volume() member was executed.

The member function is used a second time to produce the volume of box1 after new values have been set for the members of the object. Of course, the output reflects the volume of a box with the new dimensions. After computing values for the members of box2, you call the volume() member directly in the output statement so the return value is written to the stream. Using a member function of an object is no different from using an ordinary function.

The members of box3 are assigned the same values as box2 by an assignment statement. The output confirms that box3 has the same volume as box2.

Note that a CBox object still occupies the same number of bytes. Adding a function member to a class doesn't affect the size of the objects. Obviously, a member function has to be stored somewhere, but there's only one copy regardless of how many class objects you create. The memory occupied by member functions isn't counted when the sizeof operator produces the number of bytes that an object occupies.

You could try commenting out the public keyword. The code will no longer compile because all the members of the CBox class will be private by default.

> **NOTE** Adding a virtual function to a class, which you will learn about in Chapter 9, will increase the size of a class object.

Defining a Member Function Outside a Class

You can define a member function outside the class definition. In this case you just put the prototype inside the class. If you rewrite the CBox class definition with the function definition outside, the class definition looks like this:

```
class CBox                            // Class definition at global scope
{
public:
   double m_Length {1.0};             // Length of a box in inches
   double m_Width {1.0};              // Width of a box in inches
   double m_Height {1.0};             // Height of a box in inches
   double volume();                   // Member function prototype
};
```

Because the definition of the Volume() member will be outside the class, there has to be a way of telling the compiler that the function belongs to the CBox class. This is done by prefixing the function name with the name of the class and separating the two with the scope resolution operator. The function definition would look like this:

```
// Function to calculate the volume of a box
double CBox::volume()
{
   return m_Length*m_Width*m_Height;
}
```

The function produces the same output as the last example; however, the program isn't exactly the same. In the second case, all calls to the function are treated in the way that you're already familiar with. However, when you define a function within the class definition, as in Ex7_03.cpp, the compiler implicitly treats the function as an *inline function*.

Inline Functions

The compiler tries to expand the code in the body of an inline function in place of a call to the function. This avoids much of the overhead of calling the function and speeds up your code. This is illustrated in Figure 7-5.

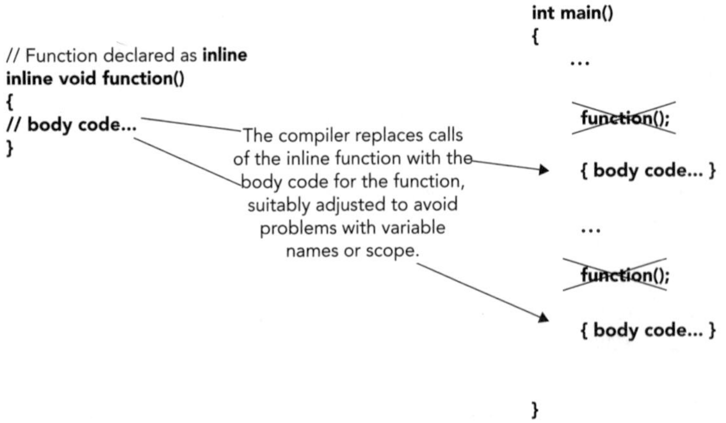

FIGURE 7-5

> **NOTE** *Of course, the compiler ensures that expanding a function inline doesn't cause any problems with variable name conflicts or scope.*

Specifying a function as inline does not guarantee the function will be inline. The compiler may not be able to insert the code for a function inline (such as with recursive functions or functions for which you have obtained an address), but generally, it will work. It's best used for very short, simple functions, such as our `volume()` function in the `CBox` class, because such functions will execute faster inline and inserting the body code in place of each call does not significantly increase the size of the executable module. When the compiler is not able to make a function inline, your code will still compile and run.

When you define a member function outside of a class, you can tell the compiler that you would like the function to be considered as inline by placing the keyword `inline` at the beginning of the function header:

```
// Function to calculate the volume of a box
inline double CBox::Volume()
{
   return m_Length*m_Width*m_Height;
}
```

With this function definition, the program is exactly the same as the original. Thus you can put the member function definitions outside of a class and still retain the execution performance benefits of inlining. You can apply the `inline` keyword to ordinary functions that have nothing to do with classes and get the same effect. Remember, however, that it's best used for short, simple functions.

Having said all that, it is not essential to use the `inline` keyword for functions to be inline. The compiler is sometimes smart enough to decide for itself whether inlining makes sense, even if the method is not marked as "inline".

Next I'll explain a little more about what happens when you define an object of a class.

CLASS CONSTRUCTORS

In the previous program, you defined the `CBox` objects, `box1` and `box2`, and then set values for members of each object explicitly. A major constraint on this approach arises when the data members of a class don't have the attribute `public` — you won't be able to access them from outside the class at all. There has to be a better way and of course there is — it's known as the class *constructor*.

What Is a Constructor?

A class constructor is a special function in a class that is responsible for creating new objects. A constructor can customize objects as they are created to ensure that data members have the values you want. Because a constructor is a member function, it can set the values for members regardless of their access attributes. A class can have several constructors, enabling you to create objects in various ways. A constructor can and often does include code to check the validity of the arguments passed to it to ensure that data members have legal values for the object type. A trivial example would be to ensure that the dimensions stored in a `CBox` object was not negative.

You have no leeway in naming constructors — they always have the same name as the class in which they are defined, even when there are two or more. CBox() for example, is a constructor for our CBox class. A constructor has no return type. It's wrong to specify a return type for a constructor; you must not even write it as void. The primary purpose of a constructor is to assign values to data members of the class, and no return type is necessary or permitted. If you specify a return type for a constructor, the compiler will report it as an error.

TRY IT OUT Adding a Constructor to the CBox class

Let's extend our CBox class to incorporate a constructor:

```cpp
// Ex7_04.cpp
// Using a constructor
#include <iostream>
using std::cout;
using std::endl;

class CBox                           // Class definition at global scope
{
public:
  double m_Length {1.0};             // Length of a box in inches
  double m_Width {1.0};              // Width of a box in inches
  double m_Height {1.0};             // Height of a box in inches

  // Constructor definition
  CBox(double lv, double wv, double hv)
  {
    cout << "Constructor called." << endl;
    m_Length = lv;                   // Set values of
    m_Width = wv;                    // data members
    m_Height = hv;
  }

  // Function to calculate the volume of a box
  double volume()
  {
    return m_Length* m_Width* m_Height;
  }

};

int main()
{
  CBox box1 {78.0,24.0,18.0};        // Declare and initialize box1
  CBox cigarBox {8.0,5.0,1.0};       // Declare and initialize cigarBox

  cout << "Volume of box1 = " << box1.volume() << endl;
  cout << "Volume of cigarBox = " << cigarBox.volume() << endl;
  return 0;
}
```

How It Works

The `CBox()` constructor has three parameters of type `double`, corresponding to the `m_Length`, `m_Width`, and `m_Height` members of an object. The first statement in the constructor outputs a message so that you can tell when it's been called. You wouldn't do this in production programs, but it's very helpful in showing when a constructor is called, so it's often used when testing a program. I'll use it regularly for the purposes of illustration. The code in the body of the constructor is very simple. It just assigns the arguments that you pass to the constructor when you call it to the corresponding data members. If necessary, you could also include checks that valid, non-negative arguments are supplied and in a real context you probably would do this, but our primary interest here is in seeing how the mechanism works.

Within `main()`, you define the `box1` object with values for the data members `m_Length`, `m_Width`, and `m_Height`, in sequence:

```
CBox box1 {78.0,24.0,18.0};          // Declare and initialize box1
```

The constructor arguments are in an initializer list following the object name. You can also use functional notation to call the constructor:

```
CBox box1(78.0,24.0,18.0);           // Declare and initialize box1
```

This is older syntax so you will still see it used, but it's better to use an initializer list because almost everything can be initialized in this way.

Note that calling a constructor is quite different from the statements earlier where you supplied an initializer list containing values for public data members. There you could have fewer values in the list and members would be initialized with zero. Here the initializer list contains the arguments for the constructor. There are three parameters so three values must appear in the list.

You create a second `CBox` object, called `cigarBox`, by calling the constructor.

The volume of `box1` is calculated by calling its `volume()` member as in the previous example, and is then output. You also output the value of the volume of `cigarBox`. The output from the example is:

```
Constructor called.
Constructor called.
Volume of box1 = 33696
Volume of cigarBox = 40
```

The first two lines are from the calls of the `CBox` constructor, once for each object created. The constructor that you have supplied is automatically called when a `CBox` object is defined, so the `CBox` objects have members with the values appearing in the initializer lists for the constructor calls. The values are passed to the constructor as arguments in the sequence that they are written in the list. As you can see, the volume of `box1` is the same as before and `cigarBox` has a volume looking suspiciously like the product of its dimensions, which is quite a relief.

The Default Constructor

Try modifying `Ex7_04.cpp` by adding this definition for `box2`:

```
CBox box2;                                // Define box2 of type CBox
```

When you rebuild this version of the program, you get the error message:

```
error C2512: 'CBox': no appropriate default constructor available
```

This means that the compiler is looking for a *default constructor* to create box2 (also referred to as the *noarg* constructor because it doesn't require arguments when it is called). The error message is because you haven't supplied an initializer list containing the arguments for the constructor defined in the class. The default constructor looks like this:

```
CBox()                          // Default constructor
{}                              // Totally devoid of statements
```

A default constructor can be either a constructor that has no parameters as here, or a constructor with all its parameters having default values specified. This statement worked perfectly well in Ex7_02.cpp, so why doesn't it work now?

The answer is that the previous example used a default constructor that was supplied by the compiler, and the compiler provided this constructor because you didn't supply any. In this example you *did* supply a constructor so the compiler assumes that you are taking care of everything needed to create CBox objects and it didn't supply the default. If you want to use definitions for CBox objects with no initializer list, you have to define the default constructor in the class. You don't have to write it as the previous fragment in the class. You can instruct the compiler to include the default constructor when it will otherwise be suppressed because you have defined other constructors for the class. Here's how you would do that for the CBox class:

```
class CBox                              // Class definition at global scope
{
public:
  double m_Length{ 1.0 };               // Length of a box in inches
  double m_Width{ 1.0 };                // Width of a box in inches
  double m_Height{ 1.0 };              // Height of a box in inches

  // Constructor definition
  CBox(double lv, double wv, double hv)
  {
    cout << "Constructor called." << endl;
    m_Length = lv;                      // Set values of
    m_Width = wv;                       // data members
    m_Height = hv;
  }

  CBox() = default;                     // Default constructor

  // Function to calculate the volume of a box
  double volume() {   return m_Length* m_Width* m_Height;   }
};
```

The default keyword after the = specifies that the CBox no-arg constructor should be included in the class. Specifying it this way shows clearly that the default constructor is included in the class. You can see such a constructor in action.

TRY IT OUT   Supplying a Default Constructor

Let's add a default constructor to the last example, along with the definition for box2, plus the original assignments for the data members of box2. You can enlarge the default constructor just enough to show that it is called. Here is the next version of the program:

```cpp
// Ex7_05.cpp
// Supplying and using a default constructor
#include <iostream>
using std::cout;
using std::endl;

class CBox                               // Class definition at global scope
{
public:
  double m_Length{ 1.0 };                // Length of a box in inches
  double m_Width{ 1.0 };                 // Width of a box in inches
  double m_Height{ 1.0 };                // Height of a box in inches

  // Constructor definition
  CBox(double lv, double wv, double hv)
  {
    cout << "Constructor called." << endl;
    m_Length = lv;                       // Set values of
    m_Width = wv;                        // data members
    m_Height = hv;
  }

  // Default constructor definition
  CBox()
  {
    cout << "Default constructor called." << endl;
  }

  // Function to calculate the volume of a box
  double volume()
  {
    return m_Length* m_Width* m_Height;
  }
};

int main()
{
  CBox box1{ 78.0, 24.0, 18.0 };         // Define and initialize box1
  CBox box2;                             // Define box2 - no initial values
  CBox cigarBox{ 8.0, 5.0, 1.0 };        // Define and initialize cigarBox

  cout << "Volume of box1 = " << box1.volume() << endl;;
  cout << "Volume of cigarBox = " << cigarBox.volume() << endl;;

  box2.m_Height = box1.m_Height - 10;    // Define box2
  box2.m_Length = box1.m_Length / 2.0;   // members in
  box2.m_Width = 0.25*box1.m_Length;     // terms of box1
  cout << "Volume of box2 = " << box2.volume() << endl;
  return 0;
}
```

How It Works

Now that you have included your own version of the default constructor, there are no error messages from the compiler and everything works. The program produces this output:

```
Constructor called.
Default constructor called.
Constructor called.
Volume of box1 = 33696
Volume of cigarBox = 40
Volume of box2 = 6084
```

The default constructor just displays a message. Evidently, it was called when you defined the object box2. You also get the correct value for the volumes of all three CBox objects, so the rest of the program is working as it should.

I included the full definition of the default constructor in the class so you can see when it is called. If you want to see it working using the default keyword, replace the definition with:

```
CBox() = default;
```

You now know that you can overload constructors just as you overloaded functions in Chapter 6. You have just executed an example with two constructors that differ only in their parameter list. One has three parameters of type double and the other has no parameters at all.

Default Parameter Values

You have seen how you can specify default values for the parameters to a function in the function prototype. You use the same syntax for class member functions, including constructors. If you put the definition of the member function inside the class, you can put the default values for the parameters in the function header. If you include only the prototype of a function in the class definition, the default parameter values should go in the prototype, not in the function definition.

You could use this technique as an alternative to specifying initial values for the data members of the CBox class. You could alter the class in the last example to this:

```
class CBox                              // Class definition at global scope
{
public:
  double m_Length;                      // Length of a box in inches
  double m_Width;                       // Width of a box in inches
  double m_Height;                      // Height of a box in inches

  // Constructor definition
  CBox(double lv = 1.0, double wv = 1.0, double hv = 1.0)
  {
    cout << "Constructor called." << endl;
    m_Length = lv;                      // Set values of
    m_Width = wv;                       // data members
    m_Height = hv;
  }
```

```
  // Default constructor definition
  CBox()
  {
    cout << "Default constructor called." << endl;
  }

  // Function to calculate the volume of a box
  double Volume()
  {
    return m_Length*m_Width*m_Height;
  }
};
```

If you make this change to the last example, what happens? You get another error message from the compiler, of course. Amongst a lot of other stuff, you get these useful comments from the compiler:

```
warning C4520: 'CBox': multiple default constructors specified
error C2668: 'CBox::CBox': ambiguous call to overloaded function
```

This is because the compiler can't work out which of the two constructors to call — the one for which you have set default parameter values or the constructor that doesn't accept any parameters. The definition of box2 requires a constructor without parameters and either constructor can now be called with no arguments. The obvious solution to this is to get rid of the constructor that has no parameters. This is actually beneficial. Without this constructor, any CBox object defined without being explicitly initialized will automatically have its members initialized to 1. Personally, I prefer to set up such default values as in-class member initializations, but let's see how it works with default constructor argument values anyway.

TRY IT OUT   Supplying Default Values for Constructor Arguments

You can demonstrate this with the following simplified example:

```
// Ex7_06.cpp
// Supplying default values for constructor arguments
#include <iostream>
using std::cout;
using std::endl;

class CBox                              // Class definition at global scope
{
public:
  double m_Length;                      // Length of a box in inches
  double m_Width;                       // Width of a box in inches
  double m_Height;                      // Height of a box in inches

  // Constructor definition
  CBox(double lv = 1.0, double wv = 1.0, double hv = 1.0)
  {
    cout << "Constructor called." << endl;
    m_Length = lv;                      // Set values of
    m_Width = wv;                       // data members
    m_Height = hv;
```

```
    }

    // Function to calculate the volume of a box
    double volume()
    {
      return m_Length*m_Width*m_Height;
    }
  };

  int main()
  {
    CBox box2;                              // Declare box2 - no initial values
    cout << "Volume of box2 = " << box2.volume() << endl;

    return 0;
  }
```

How It Works

You only define a single uninitialized CBox variable — box2 — because that's all you need for demonstration purposes. This version of the program produces the following output:

```
Constructor called.
Volume of box2 = 1
```

This shows that the constructor with default parameter values is doing its job of setting the values of objects that have no initializing values specified.

You should not assume from this that this is the only, or even the recommended, way of implementing the default constructor. There will be many occasions where you won't want to assign default values in this way, in which case, you'll need to write a separate default constructor. There will even be times when you don't want to have a default constructor operating at all, even though you have defined another constructor.

Using a Constructor Initialization List

You can initialize data members using a *constructor initialization list* within the header in a constructor definition. This is different from using an initializer list when you call a constructor; the initializer list just contains the arguments to be passed to the constructor. I can demonstrate this with an alternative CBox constructor:

```
    // Constructor definition using an initialization list
    CBox(double lv = 1.0, double wv = 1.0, double hv = 1.0):
                          m_Length {lv}, m_Width {wv}, m_Height {hv}
    {
      cout << "Constructor called." << endl;
    }
```

This definition is written assuming that it is within the class definition. The constructor initializing list is separated from the parameter list by a colon, and the initializers for class members are separated by commas. Values of the data members are not set in assignment statements in the body of the constructor. They each have an initial value defined in an initializer list that is part of the function header. The members are effectively created in the constructor initializer list. The member m_Length is initialized by the value of the argument passed for the parameter, lv, for example. Functional notation also works, but it's better to use the uniform initialization syntax. Initializing members in the constructor header is more efficient than using assignments as in the previous version. The member initialization list always executes before the body of the function so you can use the values of any members initialized in the list in the body of the constructor. If you substitute this constructor in Ex7_06.cpp, you will see that it works just as well.

With class members that are const or reference types, you have no choice as to how they are initialized. The *only* way is to use a member initializer list in a constructor. Assignment within the body of a constructor will not work. Note also that the members are not initialized in the order they are written in the constructor initializer list, but in the order in which they are defined in the class definition.

Making a Constructor Explicit

This discussion assumes that the CBox constructor with three parameters has no default parameter values specified. This is because the three-parameter constructor could function as a constructor with a single argument and as a constructor with two arguments because the parameters with no arguments specified would assume the default values.

If you define a constructor with a single parameter, the compiler will use this constructor for implicit conversions, which may not be what you want. For example, suppose you define a constructor for the CBox class like this:

```
CBox(double side): m_Length {side}, m_Width {side}, m_Height {side} {}
```

This constructor is handy when you want to define CBox objects that are cubes, where all three dimensions are the same. Because this constructor has a single parameter, the compiler will use it for implicit conversions from type double to type CBox when necessary. For example, consider the following:

```
CBox box;
box = 99.0;
```

The first statement calls the default constructor to create box, so a default constructor must be defined in the class. The second statement will call the constructor CBox(double) with the argument as 99.0, so you are getting an implicit conversion from a value of type double to type CBox. This may be what you want, but there will be many classes with single argument constructors where you don't want this to happen. In these situations, you can use the explicit keyword in the definition of the constructor to prevent it:

```
explicit CBox(double side): m_Length {side}, m_Width {side}, m_Height {side} {}
```

With the constructor defined as explicit, it will only be called when it is explicitly invoked; it will not be used for implicit conversions. With the constructor defined as explicit, the statement assigning 99.0 to box will not compile. In general, unless you want your single-parameter constructors to be used for implicit-type conversions, it is best to define them all as explicit.

With the explicit CBox constructor in the previous fragment, this will not compile:

```
CBox box = 4.0;
```

The statement requires an implicit conversion from the value, 4.0, of type `double`, to type `CBox` and the compiler will not allow it. This will compile though:

```
CBox box {4.0};
```

This is not a conversion. This is an explicit call for the constructor with a single parameter.

There's a more obscure way you can get accidental implicit conversions. In the previous version of the CBox class, the constructor has default values for all three parameters. This is how it looks using an initialization list in the header:

```
CBox(double lv = 1.0, double wv = 1.0, double hv = 1.0):
                        m_Length {lv}, m_Width {wv}, m_Height {hv}
{
  cout << "Constructor called." << endl;
}
```

Because there are default values for the second and third parameters, the following statements will compile:

```
CBox box;
box = 99.0;
```

This time, you get an implicit call to the constructor with the first argument as 99.0, and the other two arguments will have default values. This is unlikely to be what you want. To prevent this, make the constructor explicit:

```
explicit CBox(double lv = 1.0, double wv = 1.0, double hv = 1.0):
                        m_Length(lv), m_Width(wv), m_Height(hv)
{
  cout << "Constructor called." << endl;
}
```

Delegating Constructors

When a class has two or more constructors defined, one constructor can call another to help with creating an object, but only in the constructor initializer list in the constructor header, in which case there can be no other initializations within the list. Let's look at an example to see how this works. Suppose you have defined the CBox class constructor as:

```
explicit CBoxCbox(double lv, double wv, double hv):
                        m_Length{lv}, m_Width{wv}, m_Height{hv}     {}
```

You can now define a constructor with a single parameter like this:

```
explicit CBox(double side): CBox {side, side, side}
{}
```

This calls the previous constructor in the member initializing list. This technique can save repeating code in several constructors, where some of the members are always initialized in the same way, for example, but others are initialized uniquely, depending on which constructor is used.

The only way one constructor can call another in a given class is through the member initializing list. You cannot call a CBox constructor to assist with creating an object in the body of a CBox constructor. Calling a constructor in the body of a constructor, or any function for that matter, is creating an independent object.

PRIVATE MEMBERS OF A CLASS

Having a constructor that sets the values of the data members of a class object but still allows any part of a program to mess with what are essentially the guts of the object, is almost a contradiction in terms. To draw an analogy, after you have arranged for a brilliant surgeon with skills honed over years of training to do things to your insides with a sharp knife, letting the local plumber or bricklayer have a go is a bit risky, to say the least. You need protection for your class data members.

You can get the security you need by using the private keyword when you define the class members. Data and function members of a class that are private can, in general, be accessed only by member functions of a class. There's one exception, but we'll worry about that later. A normal function has no direct means of accessing the private members of a class. This is shown in Figure 7-6.

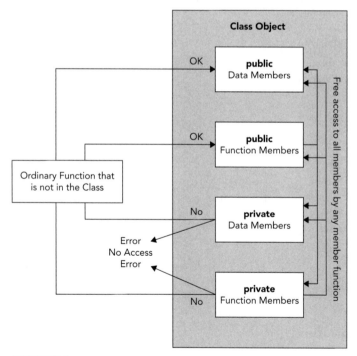

FIGURE 7-6

Having the possibility of specifying some class members as private enables you to separate the *interface* to the class from its internal implementation. The interface to a class consists of the public data members and the public member functions. Where necessary, public member functions can provide indirect access to any member of a class, including the `private` members. By keeping the internals of a class `private`, you can later modify them to improve performance for example, without requiring changes to code that uses the class through its public interface. To keep the data and function members of a class safe from unnecessary meddling, it's good practice to define those that don't need to be exposed as `private`. Only make `public` what is essential to the use of your class.

TRY IT OUT Private Data Members

You can rewrite the CBox class to make its data members `private`.

```cpp
// Ex7_07.cpp
// A class with private members
#include <iostream>
using std::cout;
using std::endl;

class CBox                              // Class definition at global scope
{
public:
  // Constructor definition using an initialization list
  explicit CBox(double lv = 1.0, double wv = 1.0, double hv = 1.0):
                          m_Length {lv}, m_Width {wv}, m_Height {hv}
  {
    cout << "Constructor called." << endl;
  }

  // Function to calculate the volume of a box
  double volume()
  {
    return m_Length*m_Width*m_Height;
  }

private:
  double m_Length;                     // Length of a box in inches
  double m_Width;                      // Width of a box in inches
  double m_Height;                     // Height of a box in inches
};

int main()
{
  CBox match {2.2, 1.1, 0.5};          // Declare match box
  CBox box2;                           // Declare box2 - no initial values

  cout << "Volume of match = " << match.volume() << endl;

// Uncomment the following line to get an error
// box2.m_Length = 4.0;

  cout << "Volume of box2 = " << box2.volume() << endl;

  return 0;
}
```

How It Works

The CBox constructor is explicit to prevent implicit conversions. The CBox class definition now has two sections. The first is the public section containing the constructor and the member function, volume(). The second section is specified as private and contains the data members. The data members can only be accessed by the member functions of the class. You don't have to modify any of the member functions — they can access all the data members of the class anyway. If you uncomment the statement in main() that assigns a value to the m_Length member of the box2 object, you'll get a compiler error message confirming that the data member is inaccessible. If you haven't already done so, take a look at the members of the CBox class in Class View; the icon alongside a member indicates its accessibility; a small padlock in the icon shows when a member is private.

A point to remember is that using a constructor or a member function is the only way to get a value into a private data member of an object. You have to make sure that all the ways in which you might want to set or modify private data members of a class are provided for through member functions.

You can put functions in the private section of a class. In this case, they can only be called by other member functions. If you put the volume() function in the private section, you will get compiler errors for the statements that attempt to use it in main(). If you put the constructor in the private section, you won't be able to create any objects of the class type.

The example generates this output:

```
Constructor called.
Constructor called.
Volume of match = 1.21
Volume of box2 = 1
```

The output demonstrates that the class is still working satisfactorily, with its data members defined as private. The major difference is that they are now completely protected from unauthorized access and modification.

If you don't specify otherwise, the default access attribute for class members is private. You could put all your private members at the beginning of the class definition and let them default to private. It's better, however, to explicitly state the access attribute in every case, so there is no doubt about what you intend.

Of course, you don't have to make all data members private. If the application for your class requires it, you can have some data members defined as private and some as public. It depends on what you're trying to do. If there's no reason to make members public, it's better to make them private because it makes the class more secure. Ordinary functions can't access the private members of your class.

Accessing private Class Members

On reflection, declaring the data members of a class as private is rather extreme. It's all very well protecting them from unauthorized modification, but that's no reason to keep their values a secret. What you need is a Freedom of Information Act for private members.

You don't have to start writing to your state senator to get it — it's already available. You can write a member function to return the value of a data member. Look at this member function for the CBox class:

```
inline double CBox::getLength()
{
   return m_Length;
}
```

Just to show how it looks, I have written this as a member function definition that is external to the class. I've specified it as `inline` because we'll benefit from the speed increase without increasing the size of the code much. As I said earlier, this is not strictly necessary with Visual C++. With the definition of the function in the `public` section of the class, you can use it like this:

```
double len {box2.getLength()};            // Obtain data member length
```

You can write a similar function for each data member that you want to make available to the outside world, and their values can be accessed without prejudicing the security of the class. Of course, if the function definitions are within the class, they will be `inline` by default.

The friend Functions of a Class

There will be circumstances when you want certain selected functions that are not members of a class to be able to access all the members of a class — a sort of elite group with special privileges. Such functions are called *friend functions* of a class and are defined using the keyword `friend`. You can either include the prototype of a `friend` function in the class definition, or you can include the whole function definition. Functions that are friends of a class and are defined within the class definition are also `inline` by default.

> **NOTE** *Friend functions are not members of the class, so the access attributes do not apply to them. They are just ordinary global functions with special privileges.*

Imagine that you want to implement a friend function in the CBox class to compute the surface area of a CBox object.

TRY IT OUT   Using a friend function to Calculate the Surface Area

You can see how a `friend` function works in the following example:

```
// Ex7_08.cpp
// Creating a friend function of a class
#include <iostream>
#include <iomanip>
using std::cout;
using std::endl;
using std::setw;

class CBox                                 // Class definition at global scope
```

```cpp
{
public:
  // Constructor definition
  Box(double lv, double wv, double hv) :
    m_Length{ lv }, m_Width{ wv }, m_Height{ hv }
          { cout << "3-arg Constructor called." << endl; }

  explicit CBox(double side) : CBox{ side, side, side }
          { cout << "1-arg Constructor called." << endl; }

  CBox() = default;

  // Function to calculate the volume of a box
  double volume()
  {
    return m_Length*m_Width*m_Height;
  }

private:
  double m_Length;                  // Length of a box in inches
  double m_Width;                   // Width of a box in inches
  double m_Height;                  // Height of a box in inches

  // Friend function
  friend double boxSurface(const CBox& aBox);
};

// friend function to calculate the surface area of a Box object
double boxSurface(const CBox& aBox)
{
  return 2.0*(aBox.m_Length*aBox.m_Width +
    aBox.m_Length*aBox.m_Height +
    aBox.m_Height*aBox.m_Width);
}

int main()
{
  CBox match{ 2.2, 1.1, 0.5 };            // match box using 3-arg constructor
  CBox cube{ 5.0 };                       // Define cube using 1-arg constructor
  CBox box;                               // Define box using default constructor

  cout << "Volume of match =" << setw(10) << match.volume()
        << "   Surface area = " << boxSurface(match) << endl;

  cout << setw(16) << "Volume of cube  =" << setw(10) << cube.volume()
     << "   Surface area = " << boxSurface(cube) << endl;

  cout << "Volume of box   =" << setw(10) << box.volume()
     << "   Surface area = " << boxSurface(box) << endl;

  return 0;
}
```

This example also calls a constructor in the member initializer list and specifies that the default constructor should be included using the `default` keyword. The output is something like:

```
3-arg Constructor called.
3-arg Constructor called.
1-arg Constructor called.
Volume of match =        1.21    Surface area = 8.14
Volume of cube  =         125    Surface area = 150
Volume of box   =-7.92985e+185    Surface area = 5.14037e+124
```

How It Works

You define the `boxSurface()` function as a friend of the `CBox` class by writing the function prototype in the class definition with the keyword `friend` at the front. The `boxSurface()` function is global, so it makes no difference where you put the `friend` definition within the class definition. It's a good idea to be consistent where you position this sort of definition, though. I chose to position it after all the `public` and `private` members of the class. Remember, a friend function isn't a class member, so access attributes don't apply.

The `friend` function definition follows that of the class. You specify access to the data members of the object within the definition of `boxSurface()`, using the `CBox` object specified by the parameter. Because a friend function isn't a class member, the data members can't be referenced just by their names. They each have to be qualified by an object name in exactly the same way as an ordinary function accesses public members. A friend function is the same as an ordinary function, except that it can access all the members of the class for which it is a friend, without restriction.

The output should be exactly what you would expect. The first line of output is from the constructor that creates the `match` object. The second line of output is from the call of the three-arg constructor in the constructor initializer list of the one-arg constructor. The third line of output is from the body of the one-arg constructor so this demonstrates that the member initializer list executes before the body of a constructor.

The friend function is computing the surface area of `CBox` objects from the values of the `private` data members. In the case of the `box` object created by the default constructor, the dimensions are junk values so the volume and surface area are also junk.

Placing friend Function Definitions Inside the Class

You could combine the definition of the function with its definition as a friend of the `CBox` class within the class definition, and the code would run as before. The function definition in the class would be:

```
friend double boxSurface(const CBox& aBox)
{
  return 2.0*(aBox.m_Length*aBox.m_Width +
              aBox.m_Length*aBox.m_Height +
              aBox.m_Height*aBox.m_Width);
}
```

However, this has a disadvantage. Although the function still has global scope, this might not be obvious to readers of the code, because the function is buried in the class definition.

The Default Copy Constructor

Suppose you define and initialize a CBox object like this:

```
CBox box1 {78.0, 24.0, 18.0};
```

You now want to create another CBox object, identical to box1. In other words you would like to initialize a new CBox object with box1. Let's try it.

TRY IT OUT   Copying Information Between Instances

The following example shows this in action:

```cpp
// Ex7_09.cpp
// Initializing an object with an object of the same class
#include <iostream>
using std::cout;
using std::endl;

class CBox                              // Class definition at global scope
{
public:
  // Constructor definition
  explicit CBox(double lv = 1.0, double wv = 1.0, double hv = 1.0) :
            m_Length {lv}, m_Width {wv}, m_Height {hv}
            {  cout << "Constructor called." << endl; }

  // Function to calculate the volume of a box
  double volume()
  {
    return m_Length*m_Width*m_Height;
  }

private:
  double m_Length;                      // Length of a box in inches
  double m_Width;                       // Width of a box in inches
  double m_Height;                      // Height of a box in inches
};

int main()
{
  CBox box1 {78.0, 24.0, 18.0};
  CBox box2 {box1};                     // Initialize box2 with box1

  cout << "box1 volume = " << box1.volume() << endl
       << "box2 volume = " << box2.volume() << endl;

  return 0;
}
```

This example produces the following output:

```
Constructor called.
box1 volume = 33696
box2 volume = 33696
```

How It Works

The program is working exactly as you would want, with both boxes having the same volume. However, as you can see from the output, our constructor was called only once — to create box1. So how was box2 created?

The mechanism is similar to when you had no constructor defined. The compiler supplied a default constructor to allow an object to be created. In this instance, the compiler generates a default version of what is referred to as a *copy constructor.*

A copy constructor does exactly what we're doing here — it creates a new object that is a copy of an existing object of the same type. The default version of the copy constructor creates a new object by copying the existing object, member by member.

This is fine for simple classes such as CBox, but for many classes — classes that have pointers as members, for example — the default copy constructor won't work as you would want. Indeed, with such classes the member-by-member copying that is done by the default copy constructor can create serious errors in your program. In these cases, you must create your own copy constructor, which will replace the default version. This requires a special approach that you'll look into more fully toward the end of this chapter and again in the next chapter.

THE POINTER THIS

You wrote the volume() member of the CBox class in terms of the class member names in the definition of the class. Of course, every CBox object that you create contains their own independent set of these members, so there has to be a mechanism for the function to refer to the members of the particular object for which it is called.

When any member function executes, it always contains a hidden pointer with the name this, which contains the address of the object used to call the function. Therefore when the m_Length member name appears in the body of the volume() function, it's actually this->m_Length, which is the fully specified reference to the member of the object that is used to call the function. The compiler takes care of adding this to the member names in the function.

You can use this explicitly within a member function if you need to — when you want to return a pointer to the current object, for example.

TRY IT OUT Explicit Use of this

You can add a public function to the CBox class that compares the volumes of two CBox objects:

```
// Ex7_10.cpp
// Using the pointer this
#include <iostream>
using std::cout;
using std::endl;
```

```
class CBox                              // Class definition at global scope
{
public:
  // Constructor definition
  explicit CBox(double lv = 1.0, double wv = 1.0, double hv = 1.0) :
            m_Length {lv}, m_Width {wv}, m_Height {hv}
  {
    cout << "Constructor called." << endl;
  }

  // Function to calculate the volume of a box
  double volume()
  {
    return m_Length*m_Width*m_Height;
  }

  // Function to compare two boxes which returns true
  // if the first is greater than the second, and false otherwise
  bool compare(CBox& xBox)
  {
    return this->volume() > xBox.volume();
  }

private:
  double m_Length;                      // Length of a box in inches
  double m_Width;                       // Width of a box in inches
  double m_Height;                      // Height of a box in inches
};

int main()
{
  CBox match {2.2, 1.1, 0.5};           // Define match box
  CBox cigar {8.0, 5.0, 1.0};           // Define cigar box

  if(cigar.compare(match))
    cout << "match is smaller than cigar" << endl;
  else
    cout << "match is equal to or larger than cigar" << endl;

  return 0;
}
```

How It Works

The compare() member returns true if the CBox object for which the member function is called has a greater volume than the CBox object passed as the argument, and false if it doesn't. The parameter to compare() is a reference type to avoid unnecessary copying of the argument. In the return statement, the prefixed object is referred to through the pointer this, using the indirect member access operator, ->.

Remember that you use the direct member access operator when accessing members through objects and the indirect member access operator when accessing members through pointers to objects. this is a pointer, so you use the -> operator.

The `->` operator works the same for pointers to class objects as it did when you were dealing with a `struct`. Using `this` here demonstrates that it exists and *does* work, but it's quite unnecessary to use it explicitly in this case. You could change the `return` statement in `compare()` to:

```
return volume() > xBox.volume();
```

You'll find that the program works just as well. Any references to unadorned member names are automatically the members of the object pointed to by `this`.

You use the `compare()` function in `main()` to check the relationship between the volumes of the objects `match` and `cigar`. The output is:

```
Constructor called.
Constructor called.
match is smaller than cigar
```

This confirms that the `cigar` object is larger than the `match` object.

It wasn't essential to define the `compare()` function as a class member. You could just as well have written it as an ordinary function with the objects as arguments. Note that this isn't true of the `volume()` function because it needs to access the `private` data members of the class. Of course, if you implemented `compare()` as an ordinary function, it wouldn't have access to the pointer `this`, but it would still be very simple:

```
// Comparing two CBox objects - ordinary function version
bool compare(CBox& box1, CBox& box2)
{
  return box1.volume() > box2.volume();
}
```

This has two `CBox` objects as arguments and returns `true` if the volume of the first is greater than the second. You could use this function to perform the same function as in the last example with this statement:

```
if(compare(cigar, match))
    cout << "match is smaller than cigar" << endl;
else
    cout << "match is equal to or larger than cigar" << endl;
```

If anything this looks slightly better and easier to read than the original; however, there's a much better way to do this, which you'll learn about in the next chapter.

CONST OBJECTS

The `volume()` function in the `CBox` class doesn't alter the object for which it is called; neither does a function such as `getHeight()` that returns the value of the `m_Height` member. Likewise, the `compare()` function in the previous example didn't change the class objects. This may seem at first sight to be a mildly interesting but largely irrelevant observation, but it isn't — it's quite important. Let's think about it.

You will undoubtedly want to create class objects that are fixed from time to time, just like values such as `pi` or `inchesPerFoot` that you might define as `const`. Suppose you wanted to define a `CBox` object as `const` — because it was a very important standard-sized box, for instance. You might define it with the following statement:

```
const CBox standard {3.0, 5.0, 8.0};
```

Now that you have defined your standard box having dimensions 3 × 5 × 8, you don't want it changed. In particular, you don't want to allow the values of its data members to be altered. How can you be sure they won't be?

Well, you already are. If you define an object as `const`, the compiler will not allow a member function to be called for it that might alter it. You can demonstrate this quite easily by modifying the definition for the object, `cigar`, in the previous example to:

```
const CBox cigar {8.0, 5.0, 1.0};              // Declare cigar box
```

If you try to compile the program with this change, you will see the error message:

```
error C2662: 'CBox::compare' : cannot convert 'this' pointer

from 'const CBox' to 'CBox &' Conversion loses qualifiers
```

This is caused by the `if` statement that calls the `compare()` member of `cigar`. An object that you define as `const` will always have a `this` pointer that is `const`, so the compiler will not allow any member function to be called that does not assume the `this` pointer is `const`. You need to find out how to make the `this` pointer `const` in a member function.

const Member Functions of a Class

To make `this` in a member function `const`, you must define the function as `const` in the class definition. Here's how you do that with the `compare()` and `volume()` members of `CBox`:

```
class CBox                              // Class definition at global scope
{
public:
  // Constructor definition
  explicit CBox(double lv = 1.0, double wv = 1.0, double hv = 1.0) :
          m_Length {lv}, m_Width {wv}, m_Height {hv}
  {
    cout << "Constructor called." << endl;
  }

  // Function to calculate the volume of a box
  double volume() const
  {
    return m_Length*m_Width*m_Height;
  }

  // Function to compare two boxes which returns true (1)
  // if the first is greater than the second, and false (0) otherwise
  bool compare(const CBox& xBox) const
  {
    return this->volume() > xBox.volume();
```

```
  }

private:
  double m_Length;                    // Length of a box in inches
  double m_Width;                     // Width of a box in inches
  double m_Height;                    // Height of a box in inches
};
```

You can find this code in the download as `Ex7_10A.cpp`. To specify that a member function is `const`, you append the `const` keyword to the function header. Note that you can only do this with functions that are class members. It does not apply to ordinary global functions. Declaring a function as `const` is only meaningful for a function that is a member of a class. The effect is to make the `this` pointer in the function `const`. This implies that a data member cannot appear on the left of an assignment within the function definition; it will be flagged as an error by the compiler. A `const` member function cannot call a non-const member function of the same class because this could potentially modify the object. This means that because `compare()` calls `volume()`, the `volume()` member must be defined as `const` too. With the `volume()` function defined as `const`, you can make the parameter to the `compare()` function `const`. When `volume()` was a non-const member of the class, making the `compare()` function parameter `const` would result in a C2662 error message from the compiler. When you define an object as `const`, the member functions that you call for it must be defined as `const`; otherwise, the program will not compile. The `compare()` function now works with `const` and non-const objects.

Member Function Definitions Outside the Class

When the definition of a `const` member function appears outside the class, the header for the definition must have the `const` keyword added, just as the definition within the class does. You should always define member functions that do not alter the class object for which they are called as `const`. With this in mind, the `CBox` class could be defined as:

```
class CBox                              // Class definition at global scope
{
public:
  // Constructor
  explicit CBox(double lv = 1.0, double wv = 1.0, double hv = 1.0);

  double volume() const;                // Calculate the volume of a box
  bool compare(const CBox& xBox) const; // Compare two boxes

private:
  double m_Length;                      // Length of a box in inches
  double m_Width;                       // Width of a box in inches
  double m_Height;                      // Height of a box in inches
};
```

This assumes that all function members, including the constructor, are defined outside the class. Both the `volume()` and `compare()` members have been defined as `const`. The `volume()` function is now defined as:

```
double CBox::volume() const
{
  return m_Length*m_Width*m_Height;
}
```

The compare() function definition is:

```
bool CBox::compare(const CBox& xBox) const
{
  return this->volume() > xBox.volume();
}
```

As you can see, the const modifier appears in both definitions. If you leave it out, the code will not compile. A function with a const modifier is a different function from one without, even though the name and parameters are exactly the same. Indeed, you can have both const and non-const versions of a function in a class, and sometimes this can be very useful.

With the class defined as shown, the constructor also needs to be defined separately, like this:

```
CBox::CBox(double lv, double wv, double hv):
              m_Length {lv}, m_Width {wv}, m_Height {hv}
{
  cout << "Constructor called." << endl;
}
```

ARRAYS OF OBJECTS

You create an array of objects in exactly the same way as you created an array of elements of a fundamental type. Each element of an array of objects that you don't initialize will cause the default constructor to be called.

TRY IT OUT   Arrays of Class Objects

The definition of CBox in this example includes a specific default constructor:

```
// Ex7_11.cpp
// Using an array of class objects
#include <iostream>
using std::cout;
using std::endl;

class CBox                           // Class definition at global scope
{
public:
  // Constructor definition
  explicit CBox(double lv, double wv = 1.0, double hv = 1.0) :
          m_Length{ lv }, m_Width{ wv }, m_Height{ hv }
  {
    cout << "Constructor called." << endl;
  }

  CBox()                             // Default constructor
  {
    cout << "Default constructor called." << endl;
    m_Length = m_Width = m_Height = 1.0;
  }

    // Function to calculate the volume of a box
    double volume() const
```

```
      {
        return m_Length*m_Width*m_Height;
      }
    private:
      double m_Length;                 // Length of a box in inches
      double m_Width;                  // Width of a box in inches
      double m_Height;                 // Height of a box in inches
  };
  int main()
  {
    CBox boxes[5];                     // Array of CBox objects defined
    CBox cigar(8.0, 5.0, 1.0);         // Define cigar box
    cout << "Volume of boxes[3] = " << boxes[3].volume()<< endl
         << "Volume of cigar = " << cigar.volume() << endl;

    return 0;
  }
```

The program produces this output:

```
Default constructor called.
Default constructor called.
Default constructor called.
Default constructor called.
Default constructor called.
Constructor called.
Volume of boxes[3] = 1
Volume of cigar = 40
```

How It Works

You have modified the constructor that accepts arguments so that only two default values are supplied, and you have added a default constructor that initializes the data members to 1 after displaying a message that it was called. You are now able to see *which* constructor was called *when*. The constructors now have quite distinct parameter lists, so there's no possibility of the compiler confusing them.

You can see from the output that the default constructor was called five times, once for each element of the boxes array. The other constructor was called to create the cigar object. It's clear from the output that the default constructor initialization is working satisfactorily, as the volume of the array element boxes[3] is 1.

Of course, you can initialize an array of objects when you define it. For example:

```
    CBox boxes[5] {CBox {1,2,3},CBox {1,3,2}};
```

The initial values are defined in an initializer list. The first two elements will be initialized by calling the constructor with three arguments. The remaining three elements will use the default constructor.

STATIC MEMBERS OF A CLASS

Both data members and function members of a class can be defined as static. Because the context is a class, there's a little more to it than the effect of the static keyword outside a class. We'll look at static data members first.

Static Data Members

When you define a data member of a class to be `static`, only one instance of the `static` member is created and this is shared between all objects of the class. Each object gets its own copy of each of the ordinary data members, but only one instance of each `static` data member exists, regardless of how many class objects have been defined. Figure 7-7 illustrates this.

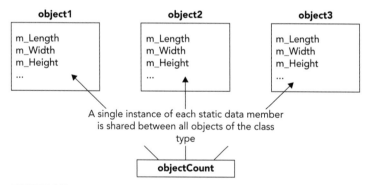

FIGURE 7-7

One use for a `static` data member is to count how many objects have been created. You could add a `static` data member to the `public` section of the `CBox` class by adding the following statement to the class definition:

```
static int objectCount;                 // Count of objects in existence
```

You now have a problem. How do you initialize the `static` data member?

You can't initialize a `static` data member in the class definition unless it is `const`, and then only when it is a numeric or enumeration type. You don't want to initialize `objectCount` in a constructor, because you want to increment it every time a constructor is called to accumulate the count of the number of objects created. You can't initialize it in another member function because a member function is associated with an object, and you want it initialized before any objects are created. You can initialize a `static` data member outside of the class definition though, like this:

```cpp
int CBox::objectCount {};          // Initialize static member of CBox class
```

Notice that the `static` keyword is not used in the initialization statement; however, you must qualify the member name by using the class name and the scope resolution operator so that the compiler understands that you are referring to a `static` member of the class. Otherwise, you would simply create a global variable that had nothing to do with the class.

TRY IT OUT   Counting Instances of a Class Type

Let's add the `static` data member and the object-counting capability to the previous example.

```cpp
// Ex7_12.cpp
// Using a static member to count objects
#include <iostream>
using std::cout;
using std::endl;

class CBox                          // Class definition at global scope
{
public:
  static int objectCount;          // Count of objects in existence

  // Constructor definition
  explicit CBox(double lv, double wv = 1.0, double hv = 1.0) :
            m_Length{ lv }, m_Width{ wv }, m_Height{ hv }
  {
    cout << "Constructor called." << endl;
    objectCount++;
  }

  CBox()                           // Default constructor
  {
    cout << "Default constructor called." << endl;
    m_Length = m_Width = m_Height = 1.0;
    objectCount++;
  }

  // Function to calculate the volume of a box
  double volume() const
  {
    return m_Length*m_Width*m_Height;
  }

private:
  double m_Length;                 // Length of a box in inches
  double m_Width;                  // Width of a box in inches
  double m_Height;                 // Height of a box in inches
};

int CBox::objectCount {};          // Initialize static member of CBox class

int main()
```

```
   {
     CBox boxes[5];                    // Array of CBox objects defined
     CBox cigar{ 8.0, 5.0, 1.0 };      // Declare cigar box

     cout << "Number of objects (accessed through class) = "
       << CBox::objectCount << endl;

     cout << "Number of objects (accessed through object) = "
       << boxes[2].objectCount << endl;

     return 0;
   }
```

This example produces the following output:

```
Default constructor called.
Default constructor called.
Default constructor called.
Default constructor called.
Default constructor called.
Constructor called.
Number of objects (through class) = 6
Number of objects (through object) = 6
```

How It Works

This code shows that it doesn't matter how you refer to the static member objectCount, whether through the class itself or any of the objects of that class. The value is the same and it is equal to the number of objects that have been created. The six objects are the five elements of the boxes array, plus the cigar object. It's interesting to note that static members of a class exist even though there may be no instances of the class defined. This is evidently the case, because you initialized the static member objectCount before any class objects were defined.

> **NOTE** Static data members are automatically created when your program begins, and they will be initialized with 0 or its equivalent unless you initialize them with some other value. Thus, you need only to initialize static data members of a class if you want them to start out with a value other than 0. However, you still need to define them. For example:
>
> ```
> int CBox::objectCount;
> ```
>
> This defines objectCount but does not initialize it explicitly so the value will be 0 by default.

Static Function Members of a Class

By declaring a function member as static, you make it independent of any objects of the class type. Consequently it does not have the pointer this. A static member function has the advantage that it exists, and can be called, even if no class objects exist. In this case, only static data members can be accessed because they are the only ones that exist. Thus, you can call a static function member of a class to examine static data members, even when you do not know for certain that any objects of the class exist. You could therefore use a static member function to determine whether any objects of the class have been created or how many have been created.

Here's an example of a prototype for a static function:

```
static void aFunction(int n);
```

A static function can be called in relation to a particular object by a statement such as the following:

```
aBox.aFunction(10);
```

The function has no access to the non-static members of aBox. The same function could also be called without reference to an object. In this case, the statement would be:

```
CBox::aFunction(10);
```

The class name qualifies the function. Using the class name and the scope resolution operator tells the compiler to which class aFunction() belongs.

POINTERS AND REFERENCES TO OBJECTS

Using pointers and references to class objects, is very important in object-oriented programming, particularly in the specification of function parameters. Class objects can involve considerable amounts of data, so using the pass-by-value mechanism for them can be very time-consuming and inefficient because each object that is passed to a function in this way will be copied. Using reference parameters avoids this overhead and reference parameters are essential to some operations with classes. As you'll see, it's not possible to write a copy constructor without using a reference parameter.

Pointers to Objects

You define a pointer to an object in the same way that you define other pointers. For example, a pointer to objects of type CBox is defined in this statement:

```
CBox* pBox {};            // Declare a pointer to CBox - initialized to nullptr
```

You can use this to store the address of a CBox object in an assignment in the usual way, using the address operator:

```
pBox = &cigar;            // Store address of CBox object cigar in pBox
```

As you saw when you used the this pointer in the compare() member function, you can call a function using a pointer to an object. You can call the volume() function for the pointer pBox like this:

```
cout << pBox->volume();    // Display volume of object pointed to by pBox
```

This uses the indirect member selection operator. This is the typical notation used for this kind of operation, *so from now on, I'll use it universally.*

TRY IT OUT   Pointers to Classes

Let's try exercising the indirect member access operator a little more. We will use the example `Ex7_10`
`.cpp` as a base, but change it a little:

```cpp
// Ex7_13.cpp
// Exercising the indirect member access operator
#include <iostream>
using std::cout;
using std::endl;

class CBox                                // Class definition at global scope
{
  public:
    // Constructor definition
    explicit CBox(double lv = 1.0, double wv = 1.0, double hv = 1.0) :
            m_Length{ lv }, m_Width{ wv }, m_Height{ hv }
    {
      cout << "Constructor called." << endl;
    }

    // Function to calculate the volume of a box
    double volume() const
    {
      return m_Length*m_Width*m_Height;
    }

    // Function to compare two boxes which returns true
    // if the first is greater than the second, and false otherwise
    bool compare(const CBox* pBox) const
    {
      if(!pBox)
        return false;
      return this->volume() > pBox->volume();
    }
  private:
    double m_Length;                      // Length of a box in inches
    double m_Width;                       // Width of a box in inches
    double m_Height;                      // Height of a box in inches
};
int main()
{
  CBox boxes[5];                          // Array of CBox objects defined
  CBox match {2.2, 1.1, 0.5};             // Declare match box
  CBox cigar {8.0, 5.0, 1.0};             // Declare cigar Box
  CBox* pB1 {&cigar};                     // Initialize pointer to cigar object address
  CBox* pB2 {};                           // Pointer to CBox initialized to nullptr
  cout << "Address of cigar is " << pB1 << endl     // Display address
       << "Volume of cigar is " << pB1->volume()    // Volume of object pointed to
       << endl;
  pB2 = &match;

  if(pB2->compare(pB1))                             // Compare via pointers
    cout << "match is greater than cigar" << endl;
```

```
    else
       cout << "match is less than or equal to cigar" << endl;

    pB1 = boxes;                           // Set to address of array
    boxes[2] = match;                      // Set 3rd element to match

    // Now access through pointer
    cout << "Volume of boxes[2] is " << (pB1 + 2)->volume() << endl;
    return 0;
}
```

When you run the example, the output looks something like this:

```
Constructor called.
Constructor called.
Constructor called.
Constructor called.
Constructor called.
Constructor called.
Constructor called.
Address of cigar is 00B3FA5C
Volume of cigar is 40
match is less than or equal to cigar
Volume of boxes[2] is 1.21
```

The address for cigar is likely to be different on your PC.

How It Works

The only change to the class isn't of great substance. I modified the compare() function to accept a pointer to a CBox object as an argument. You have an if statement in the function that guards against the possibility for the argument to be nullptr. compare() is defined as const because it doesn't alter the object. The main() function merely exercises pointers to CBox type objects in various, rather arbitrary, ways.

Within main(), you define two pointers to CBox objects after declaring an array, boxes, and the CBox objects cigar and match. The first, pB1, is initialized with the address of the cigar object, and the second, pB2, is initialized to nullptr. All of this uses the pointer in exactly the same way you would use a pointer to a basic type. The fact that you are using a pointer to a class type makes no difference.

You use pB1 with the indirect member access operator to generate the volume of the object pointed to, and the result is displayed. You then assign the address of match to pB2 and use both pointers in calling the compare function. Because the parameter for compare() is a pointer to a CBox object, the function uses the indirect member selection operator to call the volume() function for the argument.

To demonstrate that you can use address arithmetic on the pointer pB1 when using it to select a member function, you set pB1 to the address of the first element of the CBox array, boxes. In this case, you select the third element of the array and calculate its volume. This is the same as the volume of match.

You can see from the output that there were seven constructor calls, five for the boxes array, plus one each for the objects cigar and match. Overall, there's virtually no difference between using a pointer to a class object and using a pointer to a primitive type, such as double.

References to Class Objects

References really come into their own when they are used with classes. As with pointers, there is no difference between the way you define and use references to class objects and the way in which you have already defined and used references to variables of primitive types. To define a reference to the object cigar, for instance, you would write this:

```
CBox& rcigar {cigar};                 // Define reference to object cigar
```

To use a reference to calculate the volume of the object cigar, you would just use the reference name where the object name would otherwise appear:

```
cout << rcigar.volume();              // Output volume of cigar thru a reference
```

As you may remember, a reference acts as an alias for the object it refers to, so the usage is exactly the same as using the original object name.

Implementing a Copy Constructor

References are of major importance in the context of parameters and return values in functions, particularly class member functions. Let's return to the copy constructor as a first toe in the water. For the moment, I'll sidestep the question of *when* you need to write your own copy constructor and concentrate on the problem of *how* you write it. I'll use the CBox class to make the discussion more concrete.

The copy constructor is a constructor that creates a new object from an existing object of the same type. It therefore needs to accept an object of the class as an argument. You might consider writing the prototype like this:

```
CBox(CBox initB);
```

Now, think about what happens when this constructor is called. Suppose you write this definition:

```
CBox myBox {cigar};
```

This generates a call of the copy constructor. This seems to be no problem, until you realize that the argument is passed by value. So, before cigar can be passed to the constructor, the compiler needs to arrange to make a copy of it. Naturally, it calls the copy constructor to make a copy of the argument to the copy constructor. Unfortunately, since it is passed by value, this call also needs a copy of its argument to be made, so the copy constructor is called again, and so on and so on. You end up with an infinite number of calls to the copy constructor.

The solution, as I'm sure you'll have guessed, is to use a const reference parameter. You can write the prototype of the copy constructor like this:

```
CBox(const CBox& initB);
```

Now, the argument to the copy constructor doesn't need to be copied. The argument is used to initialize the reference parameter so no copying takes place. As you remember from the discussion on references, if a parameter to a function is a reference, no copying of the argument occurs when the function is called. The function accesses the argument in the caller function directly. The const qualifier ensures that the argument can't be modified by the function.

> **NOTE** This is another important use of the `const` qualifier. You should always define a reference parameter of a function as `const` unless the function will modify it.

You could implement the copy constructor as follows:

```
CBox::CBox(const CBox& initB) :
    m_Length {initB.m_Length}, m_Width {initB.m_Width}, m_Height {initB.m_Height}
{}
```

This definition assumes that it appears outside of the class definition. The constructor name is qualified with the class name using the scope resolution operator. Each data member of the object being created is initialized with the corresponding member of the object passed as the argument in the member initialization list.

The CBox class is not an example of when you need to write a copy constructor. As you have seen, the default copy constructor works perfectly well with CBox objects. I will get to *why* and *when* you need to write your own copy constructor in the next chapter.

SUMMARY

You now understand the basic ideas of classes. You're going to see more and more about using classes throughout the rest of the book.

EXERCISES

1. Define a struct `Sample` that contains two integer data items. Write a program that defines two objects of type `Sample`, called `a` and `b`. Set values for the data items that belong to `a` and then check that you can copy the values into `b` by simple assignment.

2. Add a `char*` member to the `Sample` struct in the previous exercise called `sPtr`. When you fill in the data for `a`, dynamically create a string buffer initialized with `"Hello World!"` and make `a.sPtr` point to it. Copy `a` into `b`. What happens when you change the contents of the character buffer pointed to by `a.sPtr` and then output the contents of the string pointed to by `b.sPtr`? Explain what is happening. How would you get around this?

3. Create a function that accepts a pointer to an object of type `Sample` as an argument and that outputs the values of the members of the object that is passed to it. Test this function by extending the program that you created for the previous exercise.

4. Define a class `CRecord` with two `private` data members that store a name up to 14 characters long and an integer item number. Define a `getRecord()` function member of the `CRecord` class that will set values for the data members by reading input from the keyboard, and a `putRecord()` function member that outputs the values of the data members. Implement the getRecord() function so that a calling program can detect when a zero item-number is entered. Test your CRecord class with a main() function that reads and outputs CRecord objects until a zero item-number is entered.

5. Define a class to represent a push-down stack of integers. A stack is a list of items that permits adding ("pushing") or removing ("popping") items only from one end and works on a last-in, first-out principle. For example, if the stack contained [10 4 16 20], pop() would return 10, and the stack would then contain [4 16 20]; a subsequent push(13) would leave the stack as [13 4 16 20]. You can't get at an item that is not at the top without first popping the ones above it. Your class should implement push() and pop() functions, plus a print() function so that you can check the stack contents. Store the list internally as an array, for now. Write a test program to verify the correct operation of your class.

6. What happens with your solution to the previous exercise if you try to pop more items than you've pushed, or save more items than you have space for? Can you think of a robust way to trap this? Sometimes, you might want to look at the number at the top of the stack without removing it; implement a peek() function to do this.

➤ WHAT YOU LEARNED IN THIS CHAPTER

TOPIC	CONCEPT
Classes	A class provides a means of defining your own data types. They can reflect whatever types of objects your particular problem requires.
Class members	A class can contain data members and function members. The function members of a class always have free access to the data members of the same class.
Class constructors	Objects of a class are created and initialized using member functions called constructors. A constructor is called automatically when you define an object. Constructors may be overloaded to provide different ways of initializing an object.
The default constructor	The compiler will supply a default constructor in a class that has no constructors defined. The default constructor has no parameters and does nothing. Defining any constructor in a class inhibits the insertion of the default constructor so if you need it, you must specify it.
Explicit constructors	Constructors specified using the `explicit` keyword can only be called explicitly, and therefore cannot be used for implicit conversions from another type. This is only relevant for one-arg constructors and constructors with multiple default arguments.
Member initializer list	Class members can be initialized in a member initializer list in the constructor header. Initializing members in this way is more efficient than using assignments in the body of the constructor.
Delegating constructors	A constructor can call another constructor in the same class, but only in its constructor initializer list. The constructor call must be the only thing in the initializer list.
Class member access	Members of a class can be specified as `public`, in which case, they are freely accessible by any function in a program. Members may be specified as `private`, in which case, they may only be accessed by member functions or friend functions of the class.
Static class members	Members of a class can be defined as `static`. Only one instance of each `static` data member of a class exists, which is shared amongst all instances of the class, no matter how many objects of the class are created. Static function members have no `this` pointer.
The pointer `this`	Every non-static function of a class contains the pointer `this`, which points to the object for which the function was called.

TOPIC	CONCEPT
`const` **member functions**	A member function that is defined as `const` has a `const this` pointer, and therefore cannot modify data members of the object for which it is called.
Calling `const` **member functions**	A member function that is defined as `const` cannot call another member function that is not `const`. You cannot call a non-`const` member function for a `const` object.
Passing objects to a function by reference	Using references to class objects as arguments to function calls can avoid substantial overhead in passing complex objects to a function.
The copy constructor	A copy constructor duplicates an existing object of the same class type. A copy constructor always has its parameter specified as a `const` reference.

More on Classes

WROX.COM CODE DOWNLOADS FOR THIS CHAPTER

You can find the wrox.com code downloads for this chapter on the Download Code tab at www.wrox.com/go/beginningvisualc. The code is in the Chapter 8 download and individually named according to the names throughout the chapter.

CLASS DESTRUCTORS

Although this section heading relates to destructors, it's also about dynamic memory allocation. When you allocate memory in the free store for class members, you are usually obliged to make use of a destructor, in addition to a constructor, of course. As you'll see, dynamically allocating memory for class members will also require you to write a copy constructor.

What Is a Destructor?

A *destructor* is a function that destroys objects when they are no longer required or when they go out of scope. The class destructor is called automatically when an object goes out of scope. Destroying an object involves freeing the memory occupied by the data members of the object (except for static members, which continue to exist even when there are no class objects in existence). The class destructor is a member function with a name that is a tilde (~) followed by the class name. A destructor doesn't return a value and doesn't have parameters. For example, the prototype for the CBox class destructor is:

```
~CBox();                  // Class destructor prototype
```

Because a destructor has a specific name and no parameters, there can only ever be one destructor in a class.

> **NOTE** It's an error to specify a return value or parameters for a destructor.

The Default Destructor

All the objects that you have been using up to now have been destroyed automatically by the *default destructor* for the class. The default destructor is always generated automatically by the compiler if you do not define your own destructor. The default destructor doesn't delete objects or object members that have been allocated in the free store. If space for class members has been allocated dynamically in a constructor, then you should define a destructor that will release the memory that has been allocated, just as you would with ordinary variables. You need some practice in writing destructors, so let's try it out.

> **NOTE** In Chapter 10 you'll learn about smart pointers that automatically release heap memory when it is no longer required. This can eliminate the need for a destructor in many instances.

TRY IT OUT A Simple Destructor

To get an appreciation of when the destructor for a class is called, you can include a destructor in the CBox class. Here's the example:

```
// Ex8_01.cpp
// Class with an explicit destructor
```

```cpp
#include <iostream>
using std::cout;
using std::endl;

class CBox                          // Class definition at global scope
{
public:
  // Destructor definition
  ~CBox()
  {
    cout << "Destructor called." << endl;
  }

  // Constructor definition
  explicit CBox(double lv = 1.0, double wv = 1.0, double hv = 1.0):
                                m_Length {lv}, m_Width {wv}, m_Height {hv}
  {
    cout << "Constructor called." << endl;
  }

  // Function to calculate the volume of a box
  double volume() const
  {
    return m_Length*m_Width*m_Height;
  }

  // Function to compare two boxes which returns true
  // if the first is greater than the second, and false otherwise
  bool compare(const CBox* pBox) const
  {
    if(!pBox)
      return false;
    return this->volume() > pBox->volume();
  }

  private:
    double m_Length;            // Length of a box in inches
    double m_Width;             // Width of a box in inches
    double m_Height;            // Height of a box in inches
};

// Function to demonstrate the CBox class destructor in action
int main()
{
  CBox boxes[5];                // Array of CBox objects defined
  CBox cigar {8.0, 5.0, 1.0};   // Declare cigar box
  CBox match {2.2, 1.1, 0.5};   // Declare match box
  CBox* pB1 {&cigar};           // Initialize pointer to cigar object address
  CBox* pB2 {};                 // Pointer to CBox initialized to nullptr

  cout << "Volume of cigar is " << pB1->volume() << endl;

  pB2 = boxes;                  // Set to address of array
  boxes[2] = match;             // Set 3rd element to match
```

```
        cout << "Volume of boxes[2] is " << (pB2 + 2)->volume() << endl;

        return 0;
}
```

How It Works

The CBox class destructor just displays a message showing that it was called. The output is:

```
Constructor called.
Constructor called.
Constructor called.
Constructor called.
Constructor called.
Constructor called.
Constructor called.
Volume of cigar is 40
Volume of boxes[2] is 1.21
Destructor called.
Destructor called.
Destructor called.
Destructor called.
Destructor called.
Destructor called.
Destructor called.
```

There's one destructor call for each of the objects that exist when main() ends. For each constructor call, there's a matching destructor call. You don't need to call the destructor explicitly here. The compiler arranges for the destructor to be called when an object needs to be destroyed. In our example, the destructor calls occur after main() has finished executing, so it's possible for an error in a destructor to cause a program to crash after main() has terminated.

Destructors and Dynamic Memory Allocation

You will often want to allocate memory for class data members dynamically. You can use the new operator in a constructor to allocate memory for an object member. In such a case, you are responsible for releasing the memory when the object is no longer required by providing a suitable destructor (or possibly use a smart pointer, which you will learn about in Chapter 10). Let's first define a simple class where we can do this.

Suppose you define a class where each object is a message of some description — for example, a text string. The class should be as memory-efficient as possible, so, rather than defining a data member as a char array big enough to hold the maximum length string that you might require, you'll allocate memory for the message when an object is created. Here's the class definition:

```
//Listing 08_02_1
class CMessage
{
  private:
    char* m_pMessage;              // Pointer to object text string

  public:
```

```
// Function to display a message
void showIt() const
{
  cout << m_pMessage << endl;
}

// Constructor definition
CMessage(const char* text = "Default message")
{
  size_t length {strlen(text) + 1};
  m_pMessage = new char[length + 1];        // Allocate space for text
  strcpy_s(m_pMessage, length + 1, text);   // Copy text to new memory
}

~CMessage();                                // Destructor prototype
};
```

The class has only one data member, m_pMessage, which is a pointer to a string. This is in the private section of the class, so it can't be accessed from outside the class.

In the public section, you have the showIt() function that outputs the string for a CMessage object. You also have a constructor definition and the prototype for the destructor, ~CMessage(), which I'll come to in a moment.

The constructor requires a string as an argument, but if none is passed, it uses the default string that is specified for the parameter. The constructor obtains the length of the argument string using the library function strlen() that is declared in the cstring header and allocates sufficient space for it in the free store. Of course, if the memory allocation fails, an exception will be thrown that will terminate the program. If you want to manage such a failure to provide a more graceful end to the program, you would catch the exception within the constructor code. Chapter 6 explained how you can handle out-of-memory conditions.

You use the strcpy_s() library function that is also declared in the cstring header file to copy the argument string to the memory allocated for it. strcpy_s() copies the string specified by the third argument to the address contained in the first argument. The second argument is the length of the destination location.

> **NOTE** The cstring header declares functions that are from the C runtime library, which is not defined within a namespace, so you can use the function names without qualifying them with a namespace name. Because they are also part of the C++ standard library, the names are also defined within the std namespace, so if you want to qualify them with std, you can. strcpy_s() is Microsoft-specific and not a standard library function so you must not qualify the name with std.

You need a destructor that will free the memory allocated for a message. If you don't provide a destructor, there's no way to delete the memory allocated for an object. If you use this class as it stands to create many CMessage objects, the free store will be gradually eaten away until the program fails. It's easy for this to occur in circumstances where it may not be obvious. For example, if you create a temporary CMessage object in a function that is called many times in a program, you might assume that the objects are being destroyed at the return from the function. You'd be right about that, but the free store memory will not be released. Thus, for each call of the function, more of the free store would be occupied by memory for discarded CMessage objects.

The code for the CMessage class destructor is:

```
// Listing 08_02_2
// Destructor to free memory allocated by new
CMessage::~CMessage()
{
  cout << "Destructor called." << endl;    // Just to track what happens
  delete[] m_pMessage;                      // Free memory assigned to pointer
}
```

Because you're defining the destructor outside the class, you must qualify the destructor name with the class name, CMessage. The destructor displays a message so that you can see when it is called, and then uses the delete operator to free the memory pointed to by m_pMessage. Note that you must include the square brackets with delete because you're deleting an array (of type char[]).

TRY IT OUT   Using the CMessage Class

You can exercise the CMessage class with a little example:

```
// Ex8_02.cpp
// Using a destructor to free memory
#include <iostream>          // For stream I/O
#include <cstring>           // For strlen() and strcpy()
using std::cout;
using std::endl;

// Put the CMessage class definition here (Listing 08_02_1)

// Put the destructor definition here (Listing 08_02_2)

int main()
{
  // Declare object
  CMessage motto {"A miss is as good as a mile."};

  // Dynamic object
  CMessage* pM {new CMessage {"A cat can look at a queen."}};

  motto.showIt();            // Display 1st message
  pM->showIt();              // Display 2nd message

  delete pM;                 // Manually delete object created with new
  return 0;
}
```

Replace the comments in the code with the `CMessage` class and destructor definitions from the previous section; it won't compile without this (the source code in the download contains all the code for the example).

How It Works

At the beginning of `main()`, you define an initialized `CMessage` object, `motto`, in the usual manner. In the second declaration, you define a pointer to a `CMessage` object, `pM`, and allocate memory for the `CMessage` object that is pointed to by using the operator `new`. The call to `new` invokes the `CMessage` class constructor, which has the effect of calling `new` again to allocate space for the message text pointed to by the data member `m_pMessage`. If you build and execute this example, it will produce the following output:

```
A miss is as good as a mile.
A cat can look at a queen.
Destructor called.
Destructor called.
```

You have two destructor calls recorded in the output, one for each of the two `CMessage` objects. I said earlier that the compiler doesn't take responsibility for objects created in the free store. The compiler arranged to call your destructor for the object `motto` because this is a normal, automatic object, even though the memory for the data member was allocated in the free store by the constructor. The object pointed to by `pM` is different. You allocated memory for the object in the free store, so you have to use `delete` to remove it. Try commenting out the statement that appears just before the `return` statement in `main()`:

```
    // delete pM;                    // Manually delete object created with new
```

If you run the code now, it will produce this output:

```
A miss is as good as a mile.
A cat can look at a queen.
Destructor called.
```

Now you get just one call of your destructor. This is surprising in a way. Clearly, `delete` is only dealing with the memory allocated by the call to `new` in the function `main()`. It only freed the memory pointed to by `pM`. Because your pointer `pM` points to a `CMessage` object (for which a destructor has been defined), `delete` also calls your destructor to allow you to release the memory for the members of the object. So when you use `delete` for an object created dynamically, it will always call the destructor for the object before releasing the memory that the object occupies. This ensures that any memory allocated dynamically for class members will also be freed.

IMPLEMENTING A COPY CONSTRUCTOR

When you allocate space for class members dynamically, there are demons lurking in the free store. For the `CMessage` class, the default copy constructor is woefully inadequate. Suppose you write these statements:

```
    CMessage motto1 {"Radiation fades your genes."};
    CMessage motto2 {motto1};      // Calls the default copy constructor
```

The default copy constructor will copy the address that is stored in the pointer member of the class from motto1 to motto2 because the copying process implemented by the default copy constructor just copies the values of the data members of the original object to the new object. Consequently, there will be only one text string shared between the two objects, as Figure 8-1 illustrates.

CMessage motto1{"Radiation fades your genes."};

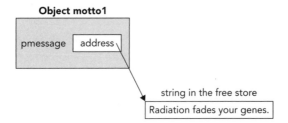

CMessage motto2{motto1}; // Calls the default copy constructor

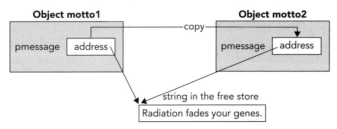

Both objects share the same string

FIGURE 8-1

If the string is changed for either object, it will be changed for the other object too, because both objects share the same string. If motto1 is destroyed, the pointer in motto2 will contain the address of memory that has been released, which may now be used for something else, so chaos will surely ensue. Of course, the same problem arises if motto2 is deleted; motto1 would contain a member pointing to a non-existent string.

The solution is to supply a copy constructor to replace the default version. You could implement this in the public section of the class as:

```
CMessage(const CMessage& aMess)
{
    size_t len {strlen(aMess.m_pMessage)+1};
    m_pMessage = new char[len];
    strcpy_s(m_pMessage, len, aMess.m_pMessage);
}
```

Remember from the previous chapter that the parameter must be specified as a const reference to avoid an infinite spiral of calls to a copy constructor. This copy constructor first allocates enough memory to hold the string from the aMess object, stores the address in the m_pMessage member of the new object, and then copies the string from the initializing object. Now the new object will be identical to the original, but quite independent of it.

Just because you don't explicitly initialize one CMessage class object with another, don't think that you're safe and need not bother with the copy constructor. Another monster lurks in the free store that can emerge to bite you when you least expect it. Consider the following statements:

```
CMessage thought {"Eye awl weighs yews my spell checker."};
displayMessage(thought);      // Call a function to output a message
```

Where the function displayMessage() is defined as:

```
void displayMessage(CMessage localMsg)
{
  cout << "The message is: " << endl;
  localMsg.showIt();
  return;
}
```

Looks simple enough, doesn't it? What could be wrong with that? A catastrophic error, that's what! What displayMessage() does is irrelevant. The problem lies with the parameter. The parameter is type CMessage, so the argument in a call is passed by value. With the default copy constructor, the sequence of events is as follows:

1. The object thought is created with the space for the message "Eye awl weighs yews my spell checker" allocated in the free store.

2. The function displayMessage() is called and, because the argument is passed by value, a copy, localMsg, is made using the default copy constructor. Now, the pointer in the copy points to the same string in the free store as the original object.

3. At the end of the function, the local object goes out of scope, so the destructor for the CMessage class is called. This deletes the local object (the copy) and releases the memory pointed to by m_pMessage.

4. On return from displayMessage(), the pointer in the original object, thought, still points to the memory that has just been deleted. Next time you use the original object, your program will behave in weird and mysterious ways.

Any call to a function that passes by value an object of a class that has a member defined dynamically will cause problems. So, out of this, you have an absolutely 100-percent, 24-carat golden rule:

If you allocate space for a member of a class dynamically, always implement a copy constructor. You should also implement a destructor unless you are using smart pointers that you'll learn about in Chapter 10.

OPERATOR OVERLOADING

Operator overloading is a very important capability. It enables you to make standard C++ operators, such as +, -, *, and so on, work with objects of your own data types. You can write a function that redefines an operator so that it performs a particular action when it's used with objects of a class type. For example, you could redefine the < operator to compare CBox objects and return true if the first CBox argument had a smaller volume than the second.

Operator overloading doesn't allow you to invent new operators. Nor can you change operator precedence, so your overloaded version of an operator will have the same priority in the sequence of evaluating an expression as the original operator. The operator precedence table is in Chapter 2 and in the MSDN Library.

Although you can't overload all the operators, the restrictions aren't particularly oppressive. These are the operators that you can't overload:

OPERATOR	DEFINITION
`::`	The scope resolution operator
`?:`	The conditional operator
`.`	The direct member selection operator
`sizeof`	The size-of operator
`.*`	The dereference pointer to class member operator

Anything else is fair game, which gives you quite a bit of scope. Obviously, it's a good idea to ensure that your versions of the operators are reasonably consistent with their original usage, or at least reasonably intuitive in their operation. It wouldn't be a very sensible approach to produce an overloaded + operator for a class that performed the equivalent of a multiplication on class objects. The best way to understand how operator overloading works is to work through an example, so let's implement what I just referred to, the less-than operator, <, for the CBox class.

Implementing an Overloaded Operator

A function defining an overloaded operator for a class must have a specific form. Assuming that it is a member of the CBox class, the declaration for the function to overload the < operator within the class definition will be as follows:

```
class CBox
{
  public:
    bool operator<(const CBox& aBox) const;  // Overloaded 'less than'

  // Rest of the class definition...
};
```

operator is a keyword. Combined with an operator symbol or name, in this case, <, it specifies an operator function name. The function name in this case is operator<. You can write an operator function with or without a space between the operator keyword and the operator itself, as long as there's no ambiguity. The ambiguity arises with operators with names rather than symbols such as new or delete. If you were to write operatornew and operatordelete without a space, they are legal names for ordinary functions, so for operator functions with these operators, you must leave a space between the keyword operator and the operator name. The strangest-looking name for an overloaded operator function is operator()(). This looks like a typing error, but it is, in fact, a function that overloads the function call operator, (). You declare operator<() as const because it doesn't modify the data members of the class.

The right operand of the operator<() function is specified by the argument. The left operand is defined implicitly by the pointer this. Suppose you have the following if statement:

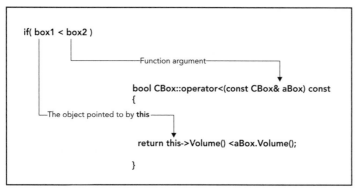

FIGURE 8-2

```
if(box1 < box2)
    cout << "box1 is less than box2" << endl;
```

The expression between the parentheses will call our operator function, so the statement is equivalent to:

```
if(box1.operator<(box2))
    cout << "box1 is less than box2" << endl;
```

The correspondence between the CBox objects in the expression and the operator function parameters is illustrated in Figure 8-2.

Let's look at how the code for the operator<() function works:

```
// Operator function for 'less than' which
// compares volumes of CBox objects.
bool CBox::operator<(const CBox& aBox) const
{
    return this->volume() < aBox.volume();
}
```

Using a reference parameter avoids copying of the argument when the function is called. Because the function does not alter the object for which it is called, you can declare the parameter as const. If you don't do this, you won't be able to use the operator with a const CBox object as the right operand. You also declare the function to be const because it doesn't modify the CBox object for which it is called.

The return expression uses the volume() member to calculate the volume of the object pointed to by this, and compares the result with the volume of aBox using the basic operator <.

Comparing CBox objects for equality is just as easy to implement:

```
bool CBox::operator==(const CBox& aBox) const
{
    return this->volume() == aBox.volume();
}
```

This implementation assumes two objects are equal if the volumes are the same. You might want to define equality differently though. A more stringent and perhaps more realistic implementation for equality might be that the objects had identical dimensions, but I'll leave that for you to explore.

Operator Overloading

You can exercise the operator functions for CBox objects with an example:

```cpp
// Ex8_03.cpp
// Exercising the overloaded 'less than' and equality operators
#include <iostream>                          // For stream I/O
using std::cout;
using std::endl;

class CBox                                   // Class definition at global scope
{
  public:
    // Constructor definition
    explicit CBox(double lv = 1.0, double wv = 1.0, double hv = 1.0):
                             m_Length(lv), m_Width(wv), m_Height(hv)
    {
      cout << "Constructor called." << endl;
    }

    // Function to calculate the volume of a box
    double volume() const
    {
      return m_Length*m_Width*m_Height;
    }

    bool operator<(const CBox& aBox) const;  // Overloaded 'less than'

    // Overloaded equality operator
    bool operator==(const CBox& aBox) const
    {
      return this->volume() == aBox.volume();
    }

    // Destructor definition
    ~CBox()
    {
      cout << "Destructor called." << endl;
    }
  private:
    double m_Length;                         // Length of a box in inches
    double m_Width;                          // Width of a box in inches
    double m_Height;                         // Height of a box in inches
};

// Operator function for 'less than' that
// compares volumes of CBox objects.
inline bool CBox::operator<(const CBox& aBox) const
{
  return this->volume() < aBox.volume();
}

int main()
{
  const CBox smallBox {4.0, 2.0, 1.0};
  const CBox mediumBox {10.0, 4.0, 2.0};
  CBox bigBox {30.0, 20.0, 40.0};
```

```
    CBox thatBox {4.0, 2.0, 10.0};

    if(mediumBox < smallBox)
      cout << "mediumBox is smaller than smallBox" << endl;

    if(mediumBox < bigBox)
      cout << "mediumBox is smaller than bigBox" << endl;
    else
      cout << "mediumBox is not smaller than bigBox" << endl;

    if(thatBox == mediumBox)
      cout << "thatBox is equal to mediumBox" << endl;
    else
      cout << "thatBox is not equal to mediumBox" << endl;

    return 0;
}
```

How It Works

The prototype of the operator<() function is in the public section of the class. The only reason the definition is outside the class here is to demonstrate the possibility. You could just as well have put the definition inside the class, like the operator==() function. Then you wouldn't need to qualify the function name with CBox.

The main() function has two if statements using the < operator with CBox objects. These automatically call the overloaded operator function. If you want to confirm this, add an output statement to the operator function. There is also a statement using the == operator. The output from this example is:

```
Constructor called.
Constructor called.
Constructor called.
Constructor called.
mediumBox is smaller than bigBox
thatBox is equal to mediumBox
Destructor called.
Destructor called.
Destructor called.
Destructor called.
```

The output demonstrates that the if statements work fine with our operator functions, and the operator overload works with const and non-const objects. Being able to express the solution to CBox problems directly in terms of CBox objects is beginning to be a realistic proposition.

Implementing Full Support for Comparison Operators

With the current version of operator<(), there are a lot of things that you can't do. Specifying a problem solution in terms of CBox objects might well involve statements such as this:

```
if(aBox < 20.0)
    // Do something...
```

Our class won't deal with that. If you use an expression comparing a CBox object with a numerical value, it won't compile. To support this capability, you would need to write another version of the operator<() function.

You can easily support the type of expression that you've just seen. The definition of the member function within the class would be:

```
// Function to compare a CBox object with a constant
bool CBox::operator<(const double value) const
{
  return this->volume() < value;
}
```

The right operand for the < operator corresponds to the function parameter. The CBox object that is the left operand will be passed as the implicit pointer this. This couldn't be much simpler, could it? But you still have a problem using the < operator with CBox objects. You may well want to write this:

```
if(20.0 < aBox)
    // do something...
```

You might argue that this could be done by implementing the operator>() operator function that accepted a right argument of type double, and rewriting the preceding statement to use it, which is true. Indeed, implementing the > operator is likely to be a requirement for comparing CBox objects, anyway, but an implementation of an operator for a type shouldn't artificially restrict the ways in which you can use it in an expression. The use of the operator should be as natural as possible. The problem is how to do it.

A member operator function always provides the left argument as the pointer this. Because the left argument is of type double in this case, you can't implement it as a member function. That leaves you with two choices: an ordinary function or a friend function. You don't need to access the private members of the class so it doesn't need to be a friend function. You can implement the overloaded < operator with a left operand of type double as an ordinary function, like this:

```
// Function comparing a constant with a CBox object
inline bool operator<(const double value, const CBox& aBox)
{
    return value < aBox.volume();
}
```

As you have seen, an ordinary function (and a friend function, too, for that matter) accesses the public members of an object by using the direct member selection operator and the object name. The volume() member is public, so there's no problem using it here.

If the class didn't have the public function volume(), you could either declare the operator function a friend function that could access the private data members directly, or you could provide a set of member functions to return the values of the private data members and use those to implement the comparison.

You still have quite a way to go yet. You still need the >, >=, <=, and != operators. You could plow on and implement all of these yourself. However, the standard library can save you the trouble. The utility header defines a set of templates for operator functions as follows:

```
template <class T> bool operator!=(const T& x, const T& y);   // Requires ==
template <class T> bool operator>(const T& x, const T& y);    // Requires <
template <class T> bool operator<=(const T& x, const T& y);   // Requires <
template <class T> bool operator>=(const T& x, const T& y);   // Requires <
```

These templates create comparison operator functions for any class. The comments indicate that you must implement operator<() and operator==() for all these templates to be usable with a class.

The templates are defined in the `std::rel_ops` namespace, so you can make the template function names available without qualification in your source file with the following `using` directive:

```
using namespace std::rel_ops;
```

With that in place, you will get the four additional operator functions in a class for free. Let's try it.

TRY IT OUT Complete Overloading of the Comparison Operators

We can put all this together in an example to show how it works:

```cpp
// Ex8_04.cpp
// Implementing the comparison operators
#include <iostream>                    // For stream I/O
#include <utility>                     // For operator overload templates
using std::cout;
using std::endl;
using namespace std::rel_ops;

class CBox                             // Class definition at global scope
{
  public:
    // Constructor definition
    explicit CBox(double lv = 1.0, double wv = 1.0, double hv = 1.0):
                          m_Length {lv}, m_Width {wv}, m_Height {hv}
    {
      cout << "Constructor called." << endl;
    }

    // Function to calculate the volume of a box
    double volume() const
    {
      return m_Length*m_Width*m_Height;
    }

    // Operator function for 'less than' that
    // compares volumes of CBox objects.
    bool operator<(const CBox& aBox) const
    {
      return this->volume() < aBox.volume();
    }
    // 'Less than' operator function to compare a CBox object volume with a constant
    bool operator<(const double value) const
    {
      return this->volume() < value;
    }
    // 'Greater than' function to compare a CBox object volume with a constant
    bool operator>(const double value) const
    {
      return this->volume() > value;
    }

    // Overloaded equality operator
    bool operator==(const CBox& aBox) const
    {
      return this->volume() == aBox.volume();
    }
```

```
    // Destructor definition
    ~CBox()
    { cout << "Destructor called." << endl; }

  private:
    double m_Length;              // Length of a box in inches
    double m_Width;               // Width of a box in inches
    double m_Height;              // Height of a box in inches
};

// Function comparing a constant with a CBox object
inline bool operator<(const double value, const CBox& aBox)
{
  return value < aBox.volume();
}

int main()
{
  CBox smallBox {4.0, 2.0, 1.0};
  CBox mediumBox {10.0, 4.0, 2.0};
  CBox otherBox {2.0, 1.0, 4.0};
  if(mediumBox != smallBox)
    cout << "mediumBox is not equal to smallBox" << endl;

  if(mediumBox > smallBox)
    cout << "mediumBox is bigger than smallBox" << endl;
  else
    cout << "mediumBox is not bigger than smallBox" << endl;

  if(otherBox >= smallBox)
    cout << "otherBox is greater than or equal to smallBox" << endl;
  else
    cout << "otherBox is smaller than smallBox" << endl;

  if(otherBox >= mediumBox)
    cout << "otherBox is greater than or equal to mediumBox" << endl;
  else
    cout << "otherBox is smaller than mediumBox" << endl;

  if(mediumBox > 50.0)
    cout << "mediumBox capacity is more than 50" << endl;
  else
    cout << "mediumBox capacity is not more than 50" << endl;

  if(10.0 < smallBox)
    cout << "smallBox capacity is more than 10"<< endl;
  else
    cout << "smallBox capacity is not more than 10"<< endl;

  return 0;
}
```

How It Works

Note the position of the definition for the ordinary function version of operator<(). It must follow the class definition, because it refers to a CBox object. If you place it before the class definition, the example will not compile because the CBox type has not been defined at that point.

There is a way you could place the function prototype at the beginning of the source file. You can use an *incomplete class declaration*, also called a *forward declaration* of the class type. This would precede the function definition and the code would look like this:

```
class CBox;                                        // Incomplete class declaration
inline bool operator<(const double value, const CBox& aBox); // Prototype
```

The forward declaration identifies CBox to the compiler as a class and is sufficient to allow the compiler to process the function prototype properly. It tells the compiler that CBox is a user-defined type to be specified later.

This mechanism is essential in circumstances where you have two classes, each of which has a pointer to an object of the other class type as a member. They will each require the other to be declared first. It is only possible to resolve such an impasse through the use of an incomplete class declaration.

> **NOTE** *You can have forward declarations for* enum *types as well as class types. For example:*
>
> ```
> enum class Suit;
> ```
>
> *This forward declaration allows you to use the* Suit *enum type to declare variables after this statement even though the* enum *type is not yet defined. However, you cannot refer to enumerators until you supply the complete definition for the type.*

The output from the example is:

```
Constructor called.
Constructor called.
Constructor called.
mediumBox is not equal to smallBox
mediumBox is bigger than smallBox
otherBox is greater than or equal to smallBox
otherBox is smaller than mediumBox
mediumBox capacity is more than 50
smallBox capacity is not more than 10
Destructor called.
Destructor called.
Destructor called.
```

Following the constructor messages due to the declarations of the CBox objects, you have the output lines from the if statements, each of which works as you would expect. The first of these calls the operator!=() function that is generated by the compiler from the template provided by the utility header. The template requires a definition for the == operator function in the class.

The output demonstrates that all of the template-generated operator functions are working. As it happens, you could have made both the operator functions that you defined as class member ordinary functions, because they only need access to the volume() function, which is public.

You can implement comparison operators for any class type in much the same way as you have implemented them here. They would only differ in the details that depend on the nature of the objects.

Overloading the Assignment Operator

If you don't provide an overloaded assignment operator function for your class, the compiler will provide a default. The default version implements member-by-member copying, similar to that of the default copy constructor. Don't confuse the default copy constructor with the default assignment operator. The copy constructor is called when you define an object that's initialized with another object of the same type. It will also be called when you pass an object to a function by value. The assignment operator is called when both sides of an assignment are objects of the same type.

The default assignment operator works with no problem for the CBox class but for any class that has space for members allocated dynamically, you must implement the assignment operator. There will be considerable potential for chaos if you omit the assignment operator in these circumstances.

Let's return to the CMessage class we used in the context of copy constructors. You'll remember it had a m_pMessage member that was a pointer to a string. Consider the effect that the default assignment operator could have with CMessage objects. Suppose you had two instances of the class, motto1 and motto2. You could set the members of motto2 equal to the members of motto1 using the default assignment operator, like this:

```
motto2 = motto1;
```

The effect of using the default assignment operator for this class is essentially the same as using the default copy constructor: disaster will result! Both objects will end up with a pointer to the same string; if the string is changed for one object, it's changed for both. There is also the problem that when one object is destroyed, its destructor will free the memory used for the string, so the other object will be left with a pointer to memory that may now be used for something else. What you need the assignment operator to do is to copy the text from the source object to a memory area owned by the destination object.

Fixing the Problem

You can fix this with your own assignment operator function, which I will assume is defined within the class definition. Here's a first stab at it, which I'll warn you now is not sufficient for proper operation:

```
// Overloaded assignment operator for CMessage objects
CMessage& operator=(const CMessage& aMess)
{
  // Release memory for 1st operand
  delete[] m_pMessage;
  size_t length { strlen(aMess.m_pMessage) + 1};
  m_pMessage = new char[length];
  // Copy 2nd operand string to 1st
  strcpy_s(this->m_pMessage, length, aMess.m_pMessage);

  return *this;                    // Return a reference to 1st operand
}
```

An assignment might seem very simple, but there are a couple of subtleties. First of all, note that you return a *reference* from the assignment operator function. It may not be immediately apparent why this is so — after all, the function does complete the assignment operation entirely, and the object on the right of the assignment will be copied to that on the left. Superficially, this would suggest that you don't need to return anything, but you need to consider in a little more depth how the operator might be used.

The result of an assignment operation can appear on the right-hand side of another assignment. Consider this statement:

```
motto1 = motto2 = motto3;
```

The assignment operator is right-associative so the assignment of `motto3` to `motto2` will be carried out first. The statement will translate into the following:

```
motto1 = (motto2.operator=(motto3));
```

The result of the operator function call is on the right of =, so the statement will finally become:

```
motto1.operator=(motto2.operator=(motto3));
```

If this is to work, you certainly have to return something from the `operator=()` function. The function call between the parentheses must return an object that can be used as the argument to the other `operator=()` function call. In this case, a return type of either `CMessage` or `CMessage&` would do it, so a reference is not mandatory for this situation, but you must at least return a `CMessage` object.

However, consider the following example:

```
(motto1 = motto2) = motto3;
```

This is perfectly legitimate code — the parentheses serve to make sure the leftmost assignment is carried out first. This translates into the following statement:

```
(motto1.operator=(motto2)) = motto3;
```

When you express the remaining assignment operation as the explicit overloaded function call, this ultimately becomes:

```
(motto1.operator=(motto2)).operator=(motto3);
```

Now, you have a situation where the object returned from the `operator=()` function is used to call the `operator=()` function. If the return type is just `CMessage`, this will not be legal because a temporary copy of the original object is returned which will be an rvalue, and the compiler will not allow a member function call using an rvalue. The only way to ensure this will compile and work correctly is to return a reference, which is an lvalue. The only possible return type if you want to allow fully flexible use of the assignment operator with your class objects is `CMessage&`.

Note that C++ does not enforce any restrictions on the accepted parameter or return types for the assignment operator, but it makes sense to declare the operator in the way I have just described if you want your assignment operator functions to support normal assignment usage.

Another subtlety is that each object already has memory for a string allocated, so the first thing that the operator function has to do is to delete the memory allocated to the first object and reallocate sufficient memory to accommodate the string from the second object. When this is done, the string from the second object can be copied to the new memory now owned by the first.

There's still a defect in this operator function. What if you were to write the following statement?

```
motto1 = motto1;
```

Obviously, you wouldn't do anything as stupid as this directly, but it could easily be hidden behind a pointer, as in the following statement:

```
motto1 = *pMessage;
```

If the pointer pMessage points to motto1, you essentially have the preceding assignment statement. In this case, the operator function as it stands will delete the memory for motto1, allocate some more memory based on the length of the string that has already been deleted, and try to copy the old memory, which, by then, could well have been corrupted. You can fix this by checking for identical left and right operands at the beginning of the function, so the definition of the operator=() function would become:

```
// Overloaded assignment operator for CMessage objects
CMessage& operator=(const CMessage& aMess)
{
  if(this != &aMess)                      // Check addresses are not equal
  {
    // Release memory for 1st operand
    delete[] m_pMessage;
    size_t length { strlen(aMess.m_pMessage) + 1};
    m_pMessage = new char[length];

    // Copy 2nd operand string to 1st
    strcpy_s(this->m_pMessage, length, aMess.m_pMessage);
  }

  return *this;                           // Return a reference to 1st operand
}
```

TRY IT OUT   Overloading the Assignment Operator

You can put the full operator=() function implementation in a working example. You'll add a reset() function to the CMessage class that just resets the message to a string of asterisks.

```
// Ex8_05.cpp
// Overloaded assignment operator working well
#include <iostream>
#include <cstring>
using std::cout;
using std::endl;

class CMessage
{
  private:
    char* m_pMessage;                     // Pointer to object text string

  public:
    // Function to display a message
    void showIt() const
    {
```

```
        cout << m_pMessage << endl;
      }

    //Function to reset a message to *
    void reset()
    {
      char* temp {m_pMessage};
      while(*temp)
        *(temp++) = '*';
    }
    // Overloaded assignment operator for CMessage objects
    CMessage& operator=(const CMessage& aMess)
    {
      if(this != &aMess)                        // Check addresses are not equal
      {
        // Release memory for 1st operand
        delete[] m_pMessage;
        size_t length {strlen(aMess.m_pMessage) + 1};
        m_pMessage = new char[length];

        // Copy 2nd operand string to 1st
        strcpy_s(this->m_pMessage, length, aMess.m_pMessage);
      }
      return *this;                             // Return a reference to 1st operand
    }

    // Constructor definition
    CMessage(const char* text = "Default message")
    {
      size_t length {strlen(text) + 1};
      m_pMessage = new char[length];            // Allocate space for text
      strcpy_s(m_pMessage, length, text);       // Copy text to new memory
    }

    // Copy constructor definition
    CMessage(const CMessage& aMess)
    {
      size_t length {strlen(aMess.m_pMessage)+1};
      m_pMessage = new char[length];
      strcpy_s(m_pMessage, length, aMess.m_pMessage);
    }

    // Destructor to free memory allocated by new
    ~CMessage()
    {
      cout << "Destructor called." << endl;     // Just to track what happens
      delete[] m_pMessage;                      // Free memory assigned to pointer
    }
};

int main()
{
  CMessage motto1 {"The devil takes care of his own."};
  CMessage motto2;
  cout << "motto2 contains:" << endl;
```

```
        motto2.showIt();
        motto2 = motto1;                              // Use new assignment operator
        cout << "motto2 contains:" << endl;
        motto2.showIt();

        motto1.reset();                               // Setting motto1 to * doesn't
                                                      // affect motto2
        cout << "motto1 now contains:" << endl;
        motto1.showIt();
        cout << "motto2 still contains:" << endl;
        motto2.showIt();

        return 0;
    }
```

You can see from the output that everything works exactly as required, with no linking between the messages of the two objects:

```
motto2 contains:
Default message
motto2 contains:
The devil takes care of his own
motto1 now contains:
******************************
motto2 still contains:
The devil takes care of his own
Destructor called.
Destructor called.
```

So you have another golden rule out of all of this:

Always implement an assignment operator function if you allocate space dynamically
for a data member of a class.

Having implemented the assignment operator, what happens with operations such as +=? Well, they don't work unless you implement them. For each form of op= that you want to use with your class objects, you need to write another operator function.

Overloading the Addition Operator

Let's look at overloading the addition operator for our CBox class. This is interesting because it involves creating and returning a new object. The new object will be the sum (whatever that means) of the CBox objects that are its operands.

So what do we want the sum of two boxes to mean? Well, there are quite a few legitimate possibilities, but we'll keep it simple here. Let's define the sum of two CBox objects as a CBox object that is large enough to contain the other two boxes stacked on top of each other. Ideally, you want to join the boxes by combining their shortest dimensions. You can do this by ensuring that the box height is always the smallest dimension. If you make the box length greater than or equal to the width, you can ensure the result of adding two boxes is not larger than it needs to be. A new object that results from addition will have an m_Length member that is the larger of the m_Length members of the operands and an m_Width member derived in a similar way. The m_Height member will be the sum of the m_Height members of the operands, so that the resultant CBox object can contain the other two CBox objects. This isn't necessarily optimal because one or other of the boxes could be rotated about its height axis for a more efficient combination, but it will be sufficient for our purposes. By altering the constructor, we'll also arrange that the length, width, and height of a CBox object are in descending magnitude.

Our version of the addition operation for boxes is easier to explain graphically, so it's illustrated in Figure 8-3.

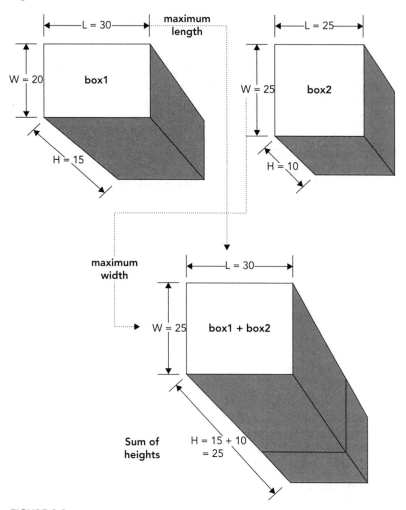

FIGURE 8-3

Because it needs to access the private members of a CBox object, the operator+() function will be a member of the class. The declaration of the function within the class definition will be:

```
CBox operator+(const CBox& aBox) const; // Function adding two CBox objects
```

You define the parameter as a reference to avoid copying of the right argument when the function is called, and you make it a const reference because the function doesn't modify the argument. The parameter must be const to allow a const object to be passed to the function, and the function must be declared as const to allow a const left operand.

The `algorithm` header defines function templates for `max()` and `min()` that return the maximum and minimum of two values respectively. You can use the first of these to define the `operator+()` function like this:

```
// Function to add two CBox objects
CBox CBox::operator+(const CBox& aBox) const
{
  // New object has larger length and width, and sum of heights
  return CBox(std::max(m_Length, aBox.m_Length),
          std::max(m_Width , aBox.m_Width) ,
          m_Height + aBox.m_Height);
}
```

You construct a local `CBox` object from the current object (`*this`) and the object that is passed as the argument. The return process will make a temporary copy of the local `CBox` object you create, and the temporary copy is passed back to the calling function, not the local object. The local object is destroyed on return from the function.

TRY IT OUT Exercising Our Addition Operator

You'll be able to see how the overloaded addition operator in the `CBox` class works in this example:

```
// Ex8_06.cpp
// Adding CBox objects
#include <iostream>              // For stream I/O
#include <algorithm>            // For min(), max() and swap()
#include <utility>             // For operator templates
using std::cout;
using std::endl;
using namespace std::rel_ops;

class CBox                        // Class definition at global scope
{
  public:
  // Constructor definition
  explicit CBox(double lv = 1.0, double wv = 1.0, double hv = 1.0):
    m_Length {std::max(lv, wv)}, m_Width{std::min(lv, wv)}, m_Height{hv}
  {
    // height is <= width
    // We need to ensure the height is <= width is <= length
    if (m_Height > m_Length)
    { // height greater than length, so swap them
      std::swap(m_Height, m_Length);
      std::swap(m_Width, m_Height);
    } else if (m_Height > m_Width)
    { // height less than or equal to length but greater than width so swap
      std::swap(m_Height, m_Width);
    }
  }

  // Function to calculate the volume of a box
  double volume() const
  {
    return m_Length*m_Width*m_Height;
  }

  // Operator function for 'less than' that
```

```cpp
    // compares volumes of CBox objects.
    bool operator<(const CBox& aBox) const
    {
      return this->volume() < aBox.volume();
    }

    // 'Less than' operator function to compare a CBox object volume with a constant
    bool operator<(const double value) const
    {
      return this->volume() < value;
    }

    // 'Greater than' function to compare a CBox object volume with a constant
    bool operator>(const double value) const
    {
      return this->volume() > value;
    }

    // Overloaded equality operator
    bool operator==(const CBox& aBox) const
    {
      return this->volume() == aBox.volume();
    }

    // Function to add two CBox objects
    CBox operator+(const CBox& aBox) const
    {
      // New object has larger length & width, and sum of heights
      return CBox(std::max(m_Length, aBox.m_Length),
                  std::max(m_Width , aBox.m_Width) ,
                  m_Height + aBox.m_Height);
    }

    // Function to show the dimensions of a box
    void showBox() const
    {
      cout << m_Length << " " << m_Width  << " " << m_Height << endl;
    }

private:
  double m_Length;                     // Length of a box in inches
  double m_Width;                      // Width of a box in inches
  double m_Height;                     // Height of a box in inches
};

// Function comparing a constant with a CBox object
inline bool operator>(const double value, const CBox& aBox)
{
  return value > aBox.volume();
}

int main()
{
  CBox smallBox {4.0, 2.0, 1.0};
  CBox mediumBox {10.0, 4.0, 2.0};
  CBox aBox;
  CBox bBox;
  cout << "smallBox dimensions are ";
```

```
    smallBox.showBox();
    cout << "mediumBox dimensions are ";
    mediumBox.showBox();
    aBox = smallBox + mediumBox;
    cout << "aBox dimensions are ";
    aBox.showBox();
    bBox = aBox + smallBox + mediumBox;
    cout << "bBox dimensions are ";
    bBox.showBox();
    return 0;
}
```

You'll be using the CBox class definition again a few pages down the road in this chapter, so note that you'll want to return to this point in the book.

How It Works

I changed the CBox class a little in this example. I deleted the destructor because the default is okay for this class, and I modified the constructor to ensure that the m_Length, m_Width, and m_Height members are in descending order of magnitude. This uses the max(), min(), and swap() template functions that are defined in the algorithm header. The swap() template function interchanges the values of its arguments.

I've also added the showBox() function to output the dimensions of an object. We can use this to verify that our overloaded addition operation is working.

The output from this program is:

```
    smallBox dimensions are 4 2 1
    mediumBox dimensions are 10 4 2
    aBox dimensions are 10 4 3
    bBox dimensions are 10 6 4
```

This seems to be consistent with the notion of adding CBox objects that we defined, and, as you can see, the operator works with multiple add operations in an expression. For the computation of bBox, the addition operator function is called twice. The result shows the combination is not optimum.

You could have implemented the addition operation as a friend function. Its prototype would then be:

```
    friend CBox operator+(const CBox& aBox, const CBox& bBox);
```

The process for producing the result would be much the same, except that you would use the direct member selection operator to obtain the members for both the arguments to the function.

> **NOTE** The algorithm *header defines many more template functions that are very useful when you are working with containers, which are covered in Chapter 10.*

Overloading the Increment and Decrement Operators

I'll briefly introduce the mechanism for overloading the increment and decrement operators in a class because they have some special characteristics that make them different from other unary operators. You need a way to deal with the fact that these operators come in a prefix and postfix form, and the effects differ between the two forms. The operator function is different for the prefix and postfix forms of the increment and decrement operators. Here's how they would be defined in a class with the name `Length`, for example:

```
class Length
{
  private:
    double m_Length;                  // Length value for the class

  public:
    Length& operator++();             // Prefix increment operator
    const Length operator++(int);     // Postfix increment operator

    Length& operator--();             // Prefix decrement operator
    const Length operator--(int);     // Postfix decrement operator

  // rest of the class...

};
```

This simple class assumes a length is stored just as a value of type `double`. You would probably make a length class more sophisticated than this but it will serve to illustrate how you overload these operators.

The prefix and postfix forms of the operator functions are differentiated by the parameter list; the prefix form has no parameters whereas there is a parameter of type `int` for the postfix form. The parameter in the postfix operator function is only there to distinguish it from the prefix form and is not used in the function implementation.

The prefix `++` and `--` operators increment or decrement the operand before its value is used in an expression, so you return a reference to the current object *after* it has been incremented or decremented. Here's how an implementation of the prefix `operator++()` function would look for the Length class:

```
inline Length& Length::operator++()
{
  ++(this->m_Length);
  return *this;
}
```

With the postfix forms, the operand is incremented after its value has been used in an expression. You achieve this by creating a copy of the current object before it has been incremented and you return the copy after you have modified the current object. Here's how you might implement the postfix `++` operator for the Length class:

```
inline const Length Length::operator++(int)
{
  Length length {*this};            // Copy the current object
  ++*this;                          // Increment the current object
  return length;                    // Return the copy
}
```

After copying the object, you increment it using the prefix `++` operator for the class. You return the un-incremented copy of the original object so it is this value that will be used in the expression in which the operator appears. Specifying the return value as `const` prevents expressions such as `data++++` from compiling.

Overloading the Function Call Operator

The function call operator is `()`, so the function to overload this for a class is `operator()()`. An object of a class that overloads the function call operator is referred to as a *function object* or *functor* because you can use an object name as though it is a function. Let's look at an example. Here's a class that overloads the function call operator:

```
class Area
{
  public:
    int operator()(int length, int width) { return length*width; }
};
```

The function call operator in this class calculates an area as the product of its integer arguments. To use this operator function, you just need to create an object of type `Area`, for example:

```
Area area;                                   // Create function object
int pitchLength {100}, pitchWidth {50};
int pitchArea {area(pitchLength, pitchWidth)};   // Execute function call overload
```

The first statement creates an `area` object. This object is used in the third statement to call its function call operator overload. This returns the area of a football pitch, in this case.

Of course, you can pass a function object to another function, just as you would any other object. Look at this function:

```
void printArea(int length, int width, Area& area)
{
  std::cout << "Area is " << area(length, width) << std::endl;
}
```

Here is a statement that uses this function:

```
printArea(20, 35, Area());
```

This statement calls the `printArea()` function with the first two arguments specifying the length and width of a rectangle. The third argument calls the default `Area` class constructor to create an object that is used in the function to calculate an area. Thus, you can use a function object to pass a function as an argument to another function that is simpler and easier to work with than using a pointer to a function.

Classes that define function objects typically do not need data members and do not have a constructor defined, so there is minimal overhead in creating and using function objects. Function object classes are usually defined as templates because this makes them very flexible.

> **NOTE** In Chapter 10 you'll learn about the `std::function<T>` template that provides more flexibility in passing functions around.

THE OBJECT COPYING PROBLEM

Copying is implicit in passing arguments by value to a function. This is not a problem when the argument is of a fundamental type, but for arguments that are objects of a class type, it can be. The overhead for copying an object can be considerable, especially when the object is large or owns memory that was allocated dynamically. The copy constructor copies an object so the efficiency of this function is critical to execution performance. As you saw with the CMessage class, the assignment operator also involves copying an object. However, there are circumstances where such copy operations are not really necessary, and if you can find a way to avoid them in such situations, execution time can be reduced. Rvalue reference parameters are the key to making this possible.

Avoiding Unnecessary Copy Operations

A modified version of the CMessage class from Ex8_05.cpp will provide a basis for seeing how this works. Here's a version of the class that implements the addition operator:

```
class CMessage
{
  private:
    char* m_pMessage;                       // Pointer to object text string

  public:
    // Function to display a message
    void showIt() const
    {
      cout << m_pMessage << endl;
    }

    // Overloaded addition operator
    CMessage operator+(const CMessage& aMess) const
    {
      cout << "Add operator function called." << endl;
      size_t len {strlen(m_pMessage) + strlen(aMess.m_pMessage) + 1};
      CMessage message;
      message.m_pMessage = new char[len];
      strcpy_s(message.m_pMessage, len, m_pMessage);
      strcat_s(message.m_pMessage, len, aMess.m_pMessage);
      return message;
    }

    // Overloaded assignment operator for CMessage objects
    CMessage& operator=(const CMessage& aMess)
    {
      cout << "Assignment operator function called." << endl;
      if(this != &aMess)                        // Check addresses are not equal
      {
        // Release memory for 1st operand
        delete[] m_pMessage;
        size_t length {strlen(aMess.m_pMessage) + 1};
        m_pMessage = new char[length];

        // Copy 2nd operand string to 1st
```

```
            strcpy_s(this->m_pMessage, length, aMess.m_pMessage);

          }
          return *this;                          // Return a reference to 1st operand
        }

        // Constructor definition
        CMessage(const char* text = "Default message")
        {
          cout << "Constructor called." << endl;
          size_t length {strlen(text) + 1};
          m_pMessage = new char[length];         // Allocate space for text
          strcpy_s(m_pMessage, length, text);    // Copy text to new memory
        }

        // Copy constructor definition
        CMessage(const CMessage& aMess)
        {
          cout << "Copy constructor called." << endl;
          size_t length {strlen(aMess.m_pMessage) + 1};
          m_pMessage = new char[length];
          strcpy_s(m_pMessage, length, aMess.m_pMessage);
        }

        // Destructor to free memory allocated by new
        ~CMessage()
        {
          cout << "Destructor called." << endl;   // Just to track what happens
          delete[] m_pMessage;                     // Free memory assigned to pointer
        }
    };
```

The changes from the version in Ex8_05.cpp are highlighted. There is now output from the constructor and the assignment operator functions to trace when they are called. There is also a copy constructor and the operator+() function for adding CMessage objects. You could add versions for concatenating a CMessage object with a string literal, but it's not needed here. Let's see how often copying occurs with some simple operations on CMessage objects.

TRY IT OUT   Tracing Object Copy Operations

Here's the code to exercise the CMessage class:

```
// Ex8_07.cpp
// How many copy operations?
#include <iostream>
#include <cstring>
using std::cout;
using std::endl;

// Insert CMessage class definition here...
```

```
int main()
{
  CMessage motto1 {"The devil takes care of his own. "};
  CMessage motto2 {"If you sup with the devil use a long spoon.\n"};
  CMessage motto3;
  cout << " Executing: motto3 = motto1 + motto2 " << endl;
  motto3 = motto1 + motto2;
  cout << " Done!! " << endl << endl;

  cout << " Executing: motto3 = motto3 + motto1 + motto2 " << endl;
  motto3 = motto3 + motto1 + motto2;
  cout << " Done!! " << endl << endl;

  cout << "motto3 contains:" << endl;
  motto3.showIt();

  return 0;
}
```

This example produces the following output:

```
Constructor called.
Constructor called.
Constructor called.
 Executing: motto3 = motto1 + motto2
Add operator function called.
Constructor called.
Copy constructor called.
Destructor called.
Assignment operator function called.
Destructor called.
 Done!!

 Executing: motto3 = motto3 + motto1 + motto2
Add operator function called.
Constructor called.
Copy constructor called.
Destructor called.
Add operator function called.
Constructor called.
Copy constructor called.
Destructor called.
Assignment operator function called.
Destructor called.
Destructor called.
 Done!!

motto3 contains:
The devil takes care of his own. If you sup with the devil use a long spoon.
The devil takes care of his own. If you sup with the devil use a long spoon.

Destructor called.
Destructor called.
Destructor called.
```

How It Works

The first statement of interest is:

```
motto3 = motto1 + motto2;          // Use new addition operator
```

This calls `operator+()` to add `motto1` and `motto2`, and the function calls the constructor to create the temporary object to be returned. The returned object is copied by the copy constructor and destroyed, as you can see from the destructor call. The returned copy is copied into `motto3` by the `operator=()` function. Finally, the temporary object — the copy — that was the right operand for the assignment is destroyed by calling the destructor. There are two operations that copy temporary objects, which are rvalues, as a result of this statement.

The second statement of interest is:

```
motto3 = motto3 + motto1 + motto2;
```

The `operator+()` function is called to concatenate `motto3` and `motto1`, and the function calls the constructor to create the result that is to be returned. The object to be returned is copied using the copy constructor, and after the original object that was created is destroyed by the destructor, the copy is concatenated with `motto2` by calling `operator+()` once more and the sequence of calls is repeated. Finally, the `operator=()` function is called to store the result. Thus, for this simple statement, we have three copy operations from temporary objects, two from copy constructor calls, and one from the assignment operator.

All of these copy operations could be expensive in elapsed time if `CMessage` objects were large or complex. If the copy operations could be avoided, you could improve execution efficiency. Let's look at how you can do this.

Applying Rvalue Reference Parameters

When the source `CMessage` object is a temporary object that is going to be destroyed immediately after a copy operation, the alternative to copying it is to steal the memory that belongs to the temporary object (the memory pointed to by its `m_pMessage` member) and transfer it to the destination object. If you can do this, you avoid the need to allocate memory for the destination object, you don't need to copy the data, and there will be no need to release the memory owned by the source object. The source object is going to be destroyed immediately after the operation, so there is no risk in doing this — just faster execution. The key to performing this trick is to detect when the source object in a copy operation is an rvalue. This is exactly what an rvalue reference parameter enables you to do.

You can create an additional overload for the `operator=()` function like this:

```
CMessage& operator=(CMessage&& aMess)
{
  cout << "Move assignment operator function called." << endl;
  delete[] m_pMessage;              // Release memory for left operand
  m_pMessage = aMess.m_pMessage;    // Steal string from rhs object
  aMess.m_pMessage = nullptr;       // Null rhs pointer
  return *this;                     // Return a reference to 1st operand
}
```

This function is called when the right operand of an assignment is an rvalue — a temporary object. When the right operand is an lvalue, the original function that has an lvalue reference parameter will be called. The rvalue reference version of the function deletes the string pointed to by the m_pMessage member of the destination object, and copies the address stored in the m_pMessage member of the source object. The m_pMessage member of the source object is then set to nullptr. It is essential that you do this; otherwise, the message would be deleted by the destructor call for the source object. Note that you must not specify the parameter as const in this case, because you are modifying it.

You can apply exactly the same logic to copy constructor operations by adding an overloaded copy constructor with an rvalue reference parameter:

```
CMessage(CMessage&& aMess)
{
  cout << "Move constructor called." << endl;
  m_pMessage = aMess.m_pMessage;
  aMess.m_pMessage = nullptr;
}
```

Instead of copying the message belonging to the source object to the object being constructed, you simply transfer the address of the message string from the source object to the new object so the copy is just a move operation. As before, you set m_pMessage for the source object to nullptr to prevent the message string from being deleted by the destructor. A copy constructor with an rvalue reference parameter is called a move constructor.

TRY IT OUT Efficient Object Copy Operations

You can create a new console application, Ex8_08, and copy the code from Ex8_07. You can then add the overloaded operator=() and copy constructor functions that I just discussed to the CMessage class definition. This example will produce the following output:

```
Constructor called.
Constructor called.
Constructor called.
 Executing: motto3 = motto1 + motto2
Add operator function called.
Constructor called.
Move constructor called.
Destructor called.
Move assignment operator function called.
Destructor called.
 Done!!

 Executing: motto3 = motto3 + motto1 + motto2
Add operator function called.
Constructor called.
Move constructor called.
Destructor called.
Add operator function called.
Constructor called.
Move constructor called.
Destructor called.
Move assignment operator function called.
```

```
Destructor called.
Destructor called.
 Done!!

motto3 contains:
The devil takes care of his own. If you sup with the devil use a long spoon.
The devil takes care of his own. If you sup with the devil use a long spoon.

Destructor called.
Destructor called.
Destructor called.
```

How It Works

You can see that all of the copying operations in the previous example now execute as move operations. The assignment operator function calls now use the version with the rvalue reference parameter, as do the move constructor calls . The output shows that motto3 ends up with the same string as before, so everything is working as it should.

For classes that define complex or large objects, implmenting a move assignment operator and move constructor in addition to the assignment operator and copy constructor can improve performance significantly.

> **WARNING** If you define the operator=() member function and the copy constructor in a class with the parameters as non-const rvalue references, make sure you also define the standard versions with const lvalue reference parameters. If you don't, the compiler will supply default versions of these that perform member-by-member copying. This will certainly not be what you want.

Named Objects Are Lvalues

When the move assignment operator in the CMessage class is called, you know for certain that the argument — the right operand — is an rvalue and is therefore a temporary object from which you can steal memory. However, the parameter, aMess, within the body of this operator function is an lvalue. This is because any expression that is a named variable is an lvalue. This can result in inefficiencies creeping back in, as I can demonstrate using a modified version of the CMessage class:

```
class CMessage
{
private:
  CText m_Text;                      // Object text string

public:
  // Function to display a message
  void showIt() const
  {
```

```cpp
    m_Text.showIt();
  }

  // Overloaded addition operator
  CMessage operator+(const CMessage& aMess) const
  {
    cout << "CMessage add operator function called." << endl;
    CMessage message;
    message.m_Text = m_Text + aMess.m_Text;
    return message;
  }

  // Copy assignment operator for CMessage objects
  CMessage& operator=(const CMessage& aMess)
  {
    cout << "CMessage copy assignment operator function called." << endl;
    if(this != &aMess)                    // Check addresses not equal
    {
      m_Text = aMess.m_Text;
    }
    return *this;                         // Return a reference to 1st operand
  }

  // Move assignment operator for CMessage objects
  CMessage& operator=(CMessage&& aMess)
  {
    cout << "CMessage move assignment operator function called." << endl;
    m_Text = aMess.m_Text;
    return *this;                         // Return a reference to 1st operand
  }

  // Constructor definition
  CMessage(const char* str = "Default message")
  {
    cout << "CMessage constructor called." << endl;
    m_Text = CText(str);
  }

  // Copy constructor definition
  CMessage(const CMessage& aMess)
  {
    cout << "CMessage copy constructor called." << endl;
    m_Text = aMess.m_Text;
  }

  // Move constructor definition
  CMessage(CMessage&& aMess)
  {
    cout << "CMessage move constructor called." << endl;
    m_Text = aMess.m_Text;
  }
};
```

The text for the message is now stored as an object of type CText, and the member functions of the class have been changed accordingly. Note that the class is kitted out with rvalue reference versions of the copy constructor and the assignment operator, so it should move rather than create new objects when it is feasible to do so. Here's the definition of the CText class:

```cpp
class CText
{
private:
  char* pText;

public:
  // Function to display text
  void showIt() const
  {
    cout << pText << endl;
  }

  // Constructor
  CText(const char* pStr="No text")
  {
    cout << "CText constructor called." << endl;
    size_t len {strlen(pStr)+1};
    pText = new char[len];                    // Allocate space for text
    strcpy_s(pText, len, pStr);               // Copy text to new memory
  }

  // Copy constructor definition
  CText(const CText& txt)
  {
    cout << "CText copy constructor called." << endl;
    size_t len {strlen(txt.pText)+1};
    pText = new char[len];
    strcpy_s(pText, len, txt.pText);
  }

  // Move constructor definition
  CText(CText&& txt)
  {
    cout << "CText move constructor called." << endl;
    pText = txt.pText;
    txt.pText = nullptr;
  }

  // Destructor to free memory allocated by new
  ~CText()
  {
    cout << "CText destructor called." << endl;   // Just to track what happens
    delete[] pText;                               // Free memory
  }

  // Assignment operator for CText objects
  CText& operator=(const CText& txt)
  {
    cout << "CText assignment operator function called." << endl;
```

```
  if(this != &txt)                              // Check addresses not equal
  {
    delete[] pText;                             // Release memory for 1st operand
    size_t length {strlen(txt.pText) + 1};
    pText = new char[length];

    // Copy 2nd operand string to 1st
    strcpy_s(this->pText, length, txt.pText);
  }
  return *this;                                 // Return a reference to 1st operand
}

// Move assignment operator for CText objects
CText& operator=(CText&& txt)
{
  cout << "CText move assignment operator function called." << endl;
  delete[] pText;                               // Release memory for 1st operand
  pText = txt.pText;
  txt.pText = nullptr;
  return *this;                                 // Return a reference to 1st operand
}

// Overloaded addition operator
CText operator+(const CText& txt) const
{
  cout << "CText add operator function called." << endl;
  size_t length {strlen(pText) + strlen(txt.pText) + 1};
  CText aText;
  aText.pText = new char[length];
  strcpy_s(aText.pText, length, pText);
  strcat_s(aText.pText, length, txt.pText);
  return aText;
}
};
```

It looks like a lot of code, but this is because the class has overloaded versions of the copy constructor and the assignment operator, and it has the `operator+()` function defined as well as a move constructor and move assignment operator. The CMessage class makes use of these in the implementation of its member functions. There are also output statements to trace when each function is called. Let's exercise these classes with an example.

TRY IT OUT   Creeping Inefficiencies

Here's a simple `main()` function that uses the CMessage copy constructor and assignment operator:

```
// Ex8_09.cpp Creeping inefficiencies
#include <iostream>
#include <cstring>
using std::cout;
using std::endl;

// Insert CText class definition here...
```

```
// Insert CMessage class definition here...

int main()
{
  CMessage motto1 {"The devil takes care of his own. "};
  CMessage motto2 {"If you sup with the devil use a long spoon.\n"};

  cout << endl << " Executing: CMessage motto3{motto1+motto2}; " << endl;
  CMessage motto3 {motto1+motto2};
  cout << " Done!! " << endl << endl << "motto3 contains:" << endl;
   motto3.showIt();
  CMessage motto4;
  cout << " Executing: motto4 = motto3 + motto2; " << endl;
  motto4 = motto3 + motto2;
  cout << " Done!! " << endl << endl << "motto4 contains:" << endl;
  motto4.showIt();

  return 0;
}
```

How It Works

It's a lot of output from relatively few statements in `main()`. I'll just discuss the interesting bits. Let's first consider the output arising from executing the statement:

```
CMessage motto3 {motto1+motto2};
```

The output looks like this:

```
CMessage add operator function called.
CText constructor called.
CMessage constructor called.
CText constructor called.
CText move assignment operator function called.
CText destructor called.
CText add operator function called.
CText constructor called.
CText move constructor called.
CText destructor called.
CText move assignment operator function called.
CText destructor called.
CText constructor called.
CMessage move constructor called.
CText assignment operator function called.
CText destructor called.
```

To see what is happening, you need to relate the output to the code in the functions that are called. First, `operator+()` for the `CMessage` class is called to concatenate `motto1` and `motto2`. In the body of this function, the `CMessage` constructor is called to create the message object, and within this process, the `CText` constructor is called. Everything is going swimmingly until we get to the second to last line of output, following the line indicating the `CMessage` move constructor is called. When this constructor executes, the argument must have been a temporary — an rvalue — so the assignment statement in the body of the function that stores the value of the `text` member should be a move assignment operation for `CText` objects, not a copy assignment. The problem arises because within the `CMessage` move constructor, the aMess parameter is an lvalue because it has a name, in spite of the fact that we know for certain that the argument passed to the function was an rvalue. This means that aMess.m_Text is also an lvalue. If it weren't, the CMessage copy constructor would be called.

The same problem arises with this statement:

```
motto4 = motto3 + motto2;
```

If you look at the output from this, you'll see that exactly the same problem arises when the move assignment operator for CMessage objects is called. The m_Text member of the argument is copied when really it could be moved.

To fix these inefficiencies you need a way to force aMess.m_Text to be an rvalue in the move assignment and move constructor functions in the CMessage class. The utility library header thoughtfully provides you with the std::move() function that will do precisely what you want. This function returns whatever argument you pass to it as an rvalue. You can change the CMessage move constructor like this:

```
CMessage(CMessage&& aMess)
{
  cout << "CMessage move constructor called." << endl;
  m_Text = std::move(aMess.m_Text);
}
```

Now, the right-hand side of the assignment that sets up the m_Text member of the new object is an rvalue so the move assignment operator function in the CText class will be called, not the copy assignment operator function.

You can modify the move assignment operator function in a similar way:

```
CMessage& operator=(CMessage&& aMess)
{
  cout << "CMessage move assignment operator function called." << endl;
  m_Text = std::move(aMess.m_Text);
  return *this;                    // Return a reference to 1st operand
}
```

The std::move() function is declared in the utility header, so you should add an #include directive for this to the example. This version is Ex8_09A.cpp in the download. If you compile the program and execute it once more, the output will show that you now get the CText move assignment operator function called from the two functions you have modified. Implementing a move constructor and a move assignment operator in a class is referred to as *move semantics*.

DEFAULT CLASS MEMBERS

It is useful to keep in mind everything that the compiler may supply by default for a class. Suppose you define a class like this:

```
class MyClass
{
public:
  int data {};
};
```

With just a single data member, you might imagine you can do very little with this class, but the compiler contributes some members. If you don't specify them, the compiler will supply definitions for:

➤ A default constructor:

```
MyClass(){}
```

➤ A copy constructor that does member-by-member copying:

```
MyClass(const MyClass& obj) {/* Copy members */}
```

➤ A destructor defined as:

```
~MyClass(){}
```

➤ A default assignment operator that does member-by-member copying:

```
MyClass& operator=(const MyClass& obj) {/* Copy members */}
```

If you define any constructor, the default constructor will not be supplied. If you don't want the default copy constructor and assignment operator to be in effect, you must define them. You can mark them with = delete if you don't want them to be included in the class. You can specify the inclusion of the members that are supplied by default using the default keyword, so you could define MyClass like this:

```
class MyClass
{
public:
  int data {};

  MyClass() = default;                                    // No-arg constructor
  MyClass(const MyClass& obj) = default;                  // Copy constructor
  MyClass& operator=(const MyClass& obj) = default;       // Assignment operator
  ~MyClass() = default;                                   // Destructor
};
```

Specifying these members like this demonstrates that their inclusion is what you intend.

> **WARNING** *Visual C++ does not currently implement the automatic provision of a default move constructor and move assignment operator in a class. You cannot use the* default *keyword to get these created for a class, so you must define them when you need them. This is not consistent with the latest language standard, which says that these members should be generated by default.*

CLASS TEMPLATES

You saw in Chapter 6 that you could define a function template that automatically generates functions from the type of arguments accepted, or from the type of values returned. There is a similar mechanism for classes. A *class template* is not a class, but a sort of "recipe" for a class that the compiler uses to generate a class definition. As Figure 8-4 shows, it's like a function template — you specify a class by supplying a type for the parameter (T, in this case) that appears between the angled brackets in the template. This generates a particular class that is referred to as an *instance* or a *specialization* of the template. Creating a class from a template is described as *instantiating* the template. Like function templates, class templates can have several parameters.

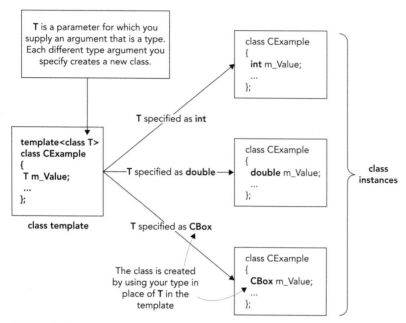

FIGURE 8-4

A class definition is generated when you instantiate a class template with a type argument for each template parameter, so you can generate any number of different classes from a single template. The principle use of class templates is in defining library classes, particularly container classes that organize and store collections of objects.

You would not normally define templates for a single application so you won't need to define your own class templates very often. However, the standard library uses class templates extensively and it's important to understand how templates are defined and how they work because there are potential pitfalls with their use. You'll learn about the templates that define container classes in Chapter 10. A good way to understand how a class template is defined and works in practice is by looking at an example.

Defining a Class Template

I'll choose a simple example, and I won't complicate things by worrying too much about errors that might arise if it's misused. Suppose you want to define classes that can store several data values of some type, and provide a `max()` function to return the maximum of the values stored. You could define a template to generate a `CSamples` class to store samples of any type:

```
template <class T>
class CSamples
{
```

```cpp
public:
  // Constructor definition to accept an array of samples
  CSamples(const T values[], int count)
  {
    m_Next = count < maxSamples ? count : maxSamples; // Don't exceed the array
    for(int i {}; i < m_Next; i++)                     // Store count samples
      m_Values[i] = values[i];
  }

  // Constructor to accept a single sample
  CSamples(const T& value)
  {
    m_Values[0] = value;                    // Store the sample
    m_Next = 1;                             // Next is free
  }

  CSamples() = default;                     // Default constructor

  // Function to add a sample
  bool add(const T& value)
  {
    bool OK {m_Next < maxSamples};          // Indicates there is a free place
    if(OK)
      m_Values[m_Next++] = value;           // OK true, so store the value
    return OK;
  }

  // Function to obtain maximum sample
  T max() const
  {
    // Set first sample as maximum
    T theMax {m_Values[0]};

    for(int i {1}; i < m_Next; i++)         // Check all the samples
      if(m_Values[i] > theMax)
        theMax = m_Values[i];               // Store any larger sample
    return theMax;
  }

private:
  static const size_t maxSamples {100};     // Maximum number of samples
  T m_Values[maxSamples];                   // Array to store samples
  int m_Next {};                            // Index of next free location
};
```

The `template` keyword indicates that you are defining a template. This is followed by the type parameter, T, between angled brackets, preceding the `class` keyword and the class name. This is essentially the same as the syntax you use for a function template. You can use `typename` instead of `class` to specify the parameters.

The compiler creates a definition for a `CSamples<T>` class for a specific T when you define an object of this type. Wherever T appears in the template definition, it will be replaced by the type that you specify in your object declaration; this creates a class definition corresponding to this type argument. You can specify any type (a fundamental data type or a class type) for T, but it has to make sense in the context of the template of course. A class type that you use to instantiate a template must have all the operators defined that the member functions of the template use with such objects. If your class hasn't implemented `operator>()`, for example, it will not work with the `CSamples<T>` class template.

In our class template the samples are stored in an array of type `T[]`. The array will be an array of elements of whatever type you specify for `T` when you define a `CSamples<T>` object. You use the type `T` in two of the constructors as well as in the `add()` and `max()` functions. Each occurrence of `T` will be replaced by your type when you instantiate the template.

The constructors support the creation of an empty object, an object with a single value, and an object initialized with an array of values. The `add()` function allows values to be added one at a time. You could overload this function to add an array of values. The template includes some elementary provision to prevent the capacity of the `m_Values` array being exceeded in the `add()` function and in the constructor that accepts an array of values.

In theory, you can create instances of a class template that will handle any data type: type `int`, type `double`, type `CBox`, or any other class type. In practice, an instance of a class template won't necessarily compile and work as you expect. It depends on what the template definition does and usually a template will only work for a particular range of types. Clearly, you'll usually be in the position of defining a template that works for some types but not others, but there's no easy way you can restrict what type is applied to a template.

Template Member Functions

You can place the definition of a member function for class template outside of the template. If you do, the definition must appear in the header file that contains the definition of the template, not in a separate `.cpp` file. The syntax for defining a member function outside a template isn't particularly obvious, so let's look at how you do it. First, you declare the function as a member of the class template in the normal way. For instance:

```
template <typename T>
class CSamples
{
  // Rest of the template definition...
  T max() const;                // Function to obtain maximum sample
  // Rest of the template definition...
}
```

This declares `max()` as a member of the template, but doesn't define it. You need a separate function template for `max()` and this must go in the header file. You use the template class name plus the parameters in angled brackets to identify the class template to which the function template belongs:

```
template<typename T>
T CSamples<T>::max() const
{
  // Set first sample as maximum
  T theMax {m_Values[0]};

  for(int i {1}; i < m_Next; i++)              // Check all the samples
```

```
      if(theMax < m_Values[i])
         theMax = m_Values[i];                  // Store any larger sample
   return theMax;
}
```

A function template for a member of a class template must have the same type parameters as the class template definition. There's just one in this case — T — but in general there can be several. If the class template had two or more parameters, then so would templates that define member functions.

Note how you qualify the function name with the template name followed by the parameter T between angled brackets. The combination of the template name and the parameters identify the class to which an instance of the function template belongs. The type will be CSamples<T>, with T replaced by the type argument you used to declare an object. Each class that's produced from the template will have its own definition for max(). This means that if you create ten different classes from the template, there will be ten copies of the max() function in memory.

You can define a constructor or a destructor outside of a class template in a similar way. You could write the definition of the constructor that accepts an array of samples as:

```
template<typename T>
CSamples<T>::CSamples(const T values[], int count)
{
   m_Next = count < maxSamples ? count : maxSamples; // Don't exceed the array

   for(int i {}; i < m_Next; i++)
      m_Values[i] = values[i];                  // Store count number of samples
}
```

You specify the class to which the constructor belongs in the template in the same way as for an ordinary member function. The constructor name doesn't require the type parameter specification — it is just CSamples, but it must be qualified by the class template type name CSamples<T>.

> **NOTE** Member functions that you define outside a class template definition must be in the header file that defines the class template. If they are not, the template won't compile.

Creating Objects from a Class Template

When you use a function defined by a template, the compiler can deduce the template type arguments from the types of the function arguments. The type parameters for a function template are implicitly defined by the specific use of a function. Class templates are different. To create an object based on a class template, you must specify the type parameters following the class name in the declaration.

For example, to define a CSamples<T> object to handle samples of type double, you could write the declaration as:

```
CSamples<double> myData {10.0};
```

This defines an object of type CSamples<double> that can store samples of type double. The object is created with one sample stored.

TRY IT OUT Using a Class Template

You could create an object from a slightly extended version of the CSamples<> template to store CBox objects. This will work because the CBox class implements the operator>() function to overload the greater-than operator. You could exercise the class template with the main() function in the following code:

```cpp
// Ex8_10.cpp
// Using a class template
#include <iostream>
#include <utility>                    // For operator overload templates
#include <algorithm>                  // For max(), swap() used in CBox
using std::cout;
using std::endl;
using namespace std::rel_ops;

// Put the CBox class definition from Ex8_06.cpp here...

// CSamples class template definition
template <typename T> class CSamples
{
  public:
    // Constructors
    CSamples(const T values[], int count);
    CSamples(const T& value);
    CSamples(T&& value);
    CSamples() = default;

    bool add(const T& value);             // Insert a value
    bool add(T&& value);                  // Insert a value with move semantics
    T max() const;                        // Calculate maximum

  private:
    static const size_t maxSamples {100};  // Maximum number of samples
    T m_Values[maxSamples];                // Array to store samples
    int m_Next {};                         // Index of free location in m_Values
};

// Constructor template definition to accept an array of samples
template<typename T> CSamples<T>::CSamples(const T values[], int count)
{
  m_Next = count < maxSamples ? count : maxSamples;      // Don't exceed the array
  for(int i {}; i < m_Next; i++)             // Store count of samples
    m_Values[i] = values[i];
}

// Constructor to accept a single sample
template<typename T> CSamples<T>::CSamples(const T& value)
{
  m_Values[0] = value;                  // Store the sample
  m_Next = 1;                           // Next is free
}

// Constructor to accept a temporary sample
template<typename T> CSamples<T>::CSamples(T&& value)
```

```
{
  cout << "Move constructor." << endl;
  m_Values[0] = std::move(value);          // Store the sample
  m_Next = 1;                              // Next is free
}

// Function to add a sample
template<typename T> bool CSamples<T>::add(const T& value)
{
  cout << "Add." << endl;
  bool OK {m_Next < maxSamples};           // Indicates there is a free place
  if(OK)
    m_Values[m_Next++] = value;            // OK true, so store the value
  return OK;
}

template<typename T> bool CSamples<T>::add(T&& value)
{
  cout << "Add move." << endl;
  bool OK {m_Next < maxSamples};           // Indicates there is a free place
  if(OK)
    m_Values[m_Next++] = std::move(value);   // OK true, so store the value
  return OK;
}

// Function to obtain maximum sample
template<typename T> T CSamples<T>::max() const
{
  T theMax {m_Values[0]};                  // Set first sample as maximum
  for(int i {1}; i < m_Next; i++)          // Check all the samples
    if(theMax < m_Values[i])
      theMax = m_Values[i];                // Store any larger sample
  return theMax;
}

int main()
{
  CBox boxes[]   {                         // Create an array of boxes
                   CBox { 8.0, 5.0, 2.0 },  // Initialize the boxes...
                   CBox { 5.0, 4.0, 6.0 },
                   CBox { 4.0, 3.0, 3.0 }
                 };

  // Create the CSamples object to hold CBox objects
  CSamples<CBox> myBoxes {boxes, _countof(boxes)};

  CBox maxBox {myBoxes.max()};             // Get the biggest box
  cout << "The biggest box has a volume of "// and output its volume
       << maxBox.volume() << endl;
  CSamples<CBox> moreBoxes {CBox { 8.0, 5.0, 2.0 }};
  moreBoxes.aAdd(CBox { 5.0, 4.0, 6.0 });
  moreBoxes.aAdd(CBox { 4.0, 3.0, 3.0 });
  cout << "The biggest box has a volume of "
```

```
                << moreBoxes.max().volume() << endl;
        return 0;
    }
```

Replace the comment with the CBox class and function definitions from Ex8_06.cpp. Except for the default constructor, all member functions of the template are defined by separate function templates, just to show you a complete example of how it's done. The CSamples<T> template includes a constructor and an add() function that have move semantics.

You create an array of three CBox objects in main() and use this array to initialize a CSamples<CBox> object. The declaration of the object is basically the same as it would be for an ordinary class, but with the addition of the template type parameter in angled brackets following the template name.

Next, you create the moreBoxes object but in a different way. This time the constructor and add() function with move semantics are called because the arguments are rvalues.

The program will generate the following output:

```
The biggest box has a volume of 120
Move constructor.
Add move.
Add move.
The biggest box has a volume of 120
```

When you create an instance of a class template, it does not follow that instances of the templates for function members will also be created. The compiler will only create instances of templates for member functions that you call in your program. In fact, as with templates for ordinary functions, your function templates can contain coding errors and, as long as you don't call the member function that belongs to the template, the compiler won't complain. You can test this out with the example. Try introducing an error into the template for the non-move add() member — maybe just delete a semicolon. The program will still compile and run because it doesn't call that version of the add() function.

You could try modifying the example to see what happens when you instantiate classes using various other types.

> **NOTE** You might be surprised at what happens if you add some output statements to the constructors. The constructors for CBox are called 103 times for the operations with myBoxes alone! Look at what happens in main(). First, you create an array of three CBox objects, so that's three calls. You then create a CSamples object to hold them, but a CSamples object contains an array of 100 CBox elements so you call the default constructor 100 times, once for each element. Of course, the maxBox object is created by the default copy constructor.

Class Templates with Multiple Parameters

Using multiple type parameters in a class template is a straightforward extension of using a single parameter. You can use each type parameter wherever you want in the template definition. For example, here's a template with two parameters:

```
template<typename T1, typename T2>
class CExampleClass
{
  // Class data members

  private:
    T1 m_Value1;
    T2 m_Value2;

  // Rest of the template definition...
};
```

The types of the class data members will be determined by the types you supply for the parameters when you instantiate an instance of the template. You can explicitly instantiate a template without defining any objects. For example, you can write the following statement after the definition of the CSamples<T> template:

```
template class CSamples<Foo>;
```

This explicitly instantiates CSamples for type Foo, but it doesn't instantiate any objects yet. The Foo class has to be available for this to compile. If Foo doesn't implement all the member functions required by the template, then the compiler will produce an error message with the explicit instantiation, just as it would when you define an object of the type.

The parameters in a class template aren't limited to types. You can specify parameters that require constants or constant expressions to be substituted in the class definition. In our CSamples<T> template, we arbitrarily defined the m_Values array with 100 elements. You could let the user of the template choose the size of the array when an object is instantiated by defining the template as:

```
template <typename T, size_t Size> class CSamples
{
  private:
    T m_Values[Size];            // Array to store samples
    int m_Next {};               // Index of free location in m_Values

  public:
    // Constructor definition to accept an array of samples
    CSamples(const T values[], int count)
    {
      m_Next = count < Size ? count : Size; // Don't exceed the array

      for(int i {}; i < m_Next; i++)
        m_Values[i] = values[i];            // Store count number of samples
    }
```

```
                // Constructor to accept a single sample
                CSamples(const T& value)
                {
                  m_Values[0] = value;                // Store the sample
                  m_Next = 1;                         // Next is free
                }

                CSamples() = default;

                // Function to add a sample
                int add(const T& value)
                {
                  int OK {m_Next < Size};             // Indicates there is a free place
                  if(OK)
                    m_Values[m_Next++] = value;       // OK true, so store the value
                  return OK;
                }

                // Function to obtain maximum sample
                T max() const
                {
                  // Set first sample as maximum
                  T theMax {m_Values[0]};

                  for(int i {1}; i < m_Next; i++)     // Check all the samples
                    if(m_Values[i] > theMax)
                      theMax = m_Values[i];           // Store any larger sample
                  return theMax;
                }
            };
```

The value supplied for `Size` when you create an instance of the template will replace all occurrences of the parameter in the template definition. Now you can define the `CSamples` object from the previous example as:

```
CSamples<CBox, 3> myBoxes {boxes, _countof(boxes)};
```

Because you can supply *any* constant expression for the `Size` parameter, you could also have written this as:

```
CSamples<CBox, _countof(boxes)> myBoxes {boxes, _countof(boxes)};
```

The example is a poor template, though — the original version was more flexible. A consequence of making `Size` a template parameter is that instances of the template that store the same type of objects but have different values for the `Size` parameter are different class types and cannot be mixed. For instance, an object of type `CSamples<double,10>` cannot be used in an expression with an object of type `CSamples<double,20>`.

You need to be careful with expressions that involve comparison operators when instantiating templates. Look at these statements:

```
CBox myBoxes[] = {CBox {1,2,3}, CBox {2,3,4},CBox {4,5,6}, CBox {5,7,8}};
CSamples<CBox, _countof(myBoxes) > 3 ? 3 : 2 > mySamples {myBoxes,4};// Wrong!
```

This will not compile correctly because the > following _countof(myBoxes) in the expression will be interpreted as the right angled bracket at the end of the argument list. You must write this statement as:

```
CSamples<CBox, (_countof(myBoxes) > 3 ? 3 : 2) > mySamples {myBoxes,4};
```

The parentheses ensure that the expression for the second template argument is evaluated first and doesn't get mixed up with the angled brackets.

Templates for Function Objects

A class that defines function objects is typically defined by a template, for the obvious reason that it allows you to define function objects that will work with a variety of argument types. Here's a template for the Area class that you saw earlier:

```
template<typename T> class Area
{
public:
  T operator()(const T length, const T width){ return length*width;  }
};
```

This template defines function objects to calculate areas with dimensions of any numeric type. You can define the printArea() function that you saw earlier as a function template:

```
template<typename T> void printArea(const T length, const T width, Area<T> area)
{  cout << "Area is " <<  area(length, width); }
```

Now, you can call the printArea() function like this:

```
printArea(1.5, 2.5, Area<double>());
printArea(100, 50, Area<int>());
```

You could avoid having to specify the third argument to instances of the printArea() function template by defining the template like this:

```
template<typename T>
void printArea(const T length, const T width, Area<T> area = Area<T>())
{  cout << "Area is " <<  area(length, width); }
```

Now you can use printArea() like this:

```
printArea(1.5, 2.5);          // 3rd argument deduced as Area<double>()
printArea(100, 50);           // 3rd argument deduced as Area<int>()
```

The compiler will deduce the correct type argument for the default specification for the third parameter as the type of the first two arguments, which must both be of the same type, of course.

There is a disadvantage to using templates like this. Each specialization of the template will have its own function definition. For example, if you use the Area template with type arguments, int, long, and long long, you will have generated three definitions for the function call operator overload, each occupying memory. You probably could manage with just one for type long long. It is easy to cause unnecessary code bloat with templates, so keep this in mind.

Function objects are applied extensively with the Standard Template Library that you will learn about in Chapter 10, so you will see practical examples of their use in that context.

PERFECT FORWARDING

Perfect forwarding is an important concept because it can significantly improve performance with large objects that take substantial time to copy or create. Perfect forwarding is only relevant in the context of a class or function template. At first sight it sounds a little complicated but once you grasp the idea, it is quite simple. So what is perfect forwarding?

Suppose you have a function, `fun1()`, that is parameterized by a class type, `T`. This could be a function template or be within a class template. Suppose also that `fun1()` is defined with an rvalue reference parameter of type `T&&`. You know from Chapter 6 that `fun1()` can be called with an argument that is an lvalue, an lvalue reference, or an rvalue. An lvalue or an lvalue reference argument results in the `fun1()` template instance having an lvalue reference parameter. Otherwise, it has an rvalue reference parameter.

Suppose further that `fun1()` calls another function, `fun2()`, that comes in two versions, one that has an lvalue reference parameter and the other with an rvalue reference parameter. `fun1()` passes the argument it receives as the argument to `fun2()`. Ideally, when the argument received by `fun1()` is an rvalue, you want it to call the version of `fun2()` that has an rvalue reference parameter so there is no moving or copying of the argument. When `fun1()` is called with an lvalue or an lvalue reference argument, you want it to call the version of `fun2()` that has an lvalue reference parameter. You want *perfect forwarding* of the argument to `fun1()`, in other words, so the code always maximizes efficiency.

To achieve this you need a way to convert the reference parameter in `fun1()` from an lvalue to an rvalue when the argument is an rvalue so you can pass it to `fun2()` as an rvalue. Then there will be no copying or moving of the argument. When the argument to `fun1()` is an lvalue or an lvalue reference, you want it left as it is in the call to `fun2()`. This is precisely what the `std::forward()` function template does. The template is defined in the `utility` header. If you pass an rvalue reference argument to `std::forward()`, it returns it as an rvalue. If you pass an lvalue reference to it, it returns it as an lvalue reference. Let's see it working.

TRY IT OUT   Perfect Forwarding

This example uses the `string` class that I'll discuss in detail at the end of this chapter. In addition to showing perfect forwarding in action, the example demonstrates defining a template function as a member of a non-template class, and using a template with two type parameters. The example defines a `Person` class like this:

```
class Person
{
public:
  // Constructor template
  template<typename T1, typename T2>
  Person(T1&& first, T2&& second) :
    firstname {std::forward<T1>(first)}, secondname {std::forward<T2>(second)} {}
//    firstname {first}, secondname {second} {}

  // Access the name
  string getName() const
  {
```

```
      return firstname.getName() + " " + secondname.getName();
    }

  private:
    Name firstname;
    Name secondname;
};
```

This is an ordinary class with the constructor defined by a template with two type parameters, T1 and T2. This allows the constructor arguments to be of different types — type string and type char*, for example. The data members that store the first and second name of a person are of type Name; I'll define the Name class in a moment. The Person constructor initializes the data members with the arguments after passing them to std::forward(). This ensures that an rvalue reference argument will remain as an rvalue reference when it is used to initialize a Person class data member. I'll come back to the commented-out line later. The getName() member returns a string representation of a Person object.

Here's the Name class definition:

```
class Name
{
public:
  Name(const string& aName) : name {aName}
  {  cout << "Lvalue Name constructor." << endl;  }

  Name(string&& aName) : name {std::move(aName)}
  {  cout << "Rvalue Name constructor." << endl;  }

  const string& getName() const { return name; }

private:
  string name;
};
```

This class encapsulates a single name as a string object. You can create a string object from a null-terminated string, or from another string object. The class has two constructors, one with an lvalue reference argument and the other with an rvalue reference argument. The latter will only be called when the argument is an rvalue reference. The reason for moving the rvalue reference argument is that the string class supports move semantics.

The program to use these classes is:

```
// Ex8_11.cpp
// Perfect forwarding
#include <iostream>
#include <utility>
#include <string>
using std::string;
using std::cout;
using std::endl;

// Put the Name class definition here...

// Put the Person class definition here...
```

```
int main()
{
  cout << "Creating Person{string{\"Ivor\"} , string{\"Horton\"}} - rvalue arguments:"
      << endl;
  Person me{string{"Ivor"} , string{"Horton"}};
  cout << "Person is " << me.getName() << endl << endl;
  string first{"Fred"};
  string second{"Fernackerpan"};
  cout << "Creating Person{first , second} - lvalue arguments:" << endl;
  Person other{first,second};
  cout << "Person is " << other.getName() << endl << endl;
  cout << "Creating Person{first , string{\"Bloggs\"}} - lvalue, rvalue arguments:"
      << endl;
  Person brother{first , string{"Bloggs"}};
  cout << "Person is " << brother.getName() << endl << endl;
  cout << "Creating Person{\"Richard\" , \"Horton\"} - rvalue const char* arguments:"
      << endl;
  Person another{"Richard", "Horton"};
  cout << "Person is " << another.getName() << endl << endl;
  return 0;
}
```

The output from this example is:

```
Creating Person{string{"Ivor"} , string{"Horton"}} - rvalue arguments:
Rvalue Name constructor.
Rvalue Name constructor.
Person is Ivor Horton
Creating Person{first , second} - lvalue arguments:
Lvalue Name constructor.
Lvalue Name constructor.
Person is Fred Fernackerpan
Creating Person{first , string{"Bloggs"}} - lvalue, rvalue arguments:
Lvalue Name constructor.
Rvalue Name constructor.
Person is Fred Bloggs
Creating Person{"Richard" , "Horton"} - rvalue const char* arguments:
Rvalue Name constructor.
Rvalue Name constructor.
Person is Richard Horton
```

How It Works

You can see from the output that the Name constructor with an lvalue reference parameter is called when the corresponding argument to the Person constructor is an lvalue reference, and the Name constructor that has an rvalue reference parameter is called when the Person constructor argument is an rvalue. Clearly the std::forward() function is working as advertised.

Now uncomment the commented-out line in the Person class and comment out the line above it. Now the constructor arguments are not being forwarded, and the output is:

```
Creating Person{string{"Ivor"} , string{"Horton"}} - rvalue arguments:
Lvalue Name constructor.
Lvalue Name constructor.
Person is Ivor Horton
```

```
Creating Person{first , second} - lvalue arguments:
Lvalue Name constructor.
Lvalue Name constructor.
Person is Fred Fernackerpan
Creating Person{first , string{"Bloggs"}} - lvalue, rvalue arguments:
Lvalue Name constructor.
Lvalue Name constructor.
Person is Fred Bloggs
Creating Person{"Richard" , "Horton"} - rvalue const char* arguments:
Rvalue Name constructor.
Rvalue Name constructor.
Person is Richard Horton
```

Everything looks consistent with forwarding not being applied, except for the last Person object. How come the Name constructors with an rvalue reference parameter were called without forwarding? The answer is that a literal is always an rvalue. If presenting a literal argument as an lvalue was permitted, you would be able to modify it, which is somewhat contrary to the notion of what a literal is.

There is a significant aspect to the use of a template for the constructor in the Person class. It allows you to create a Person object from two arguments where each argument can be a temporary string object, an lvalue string object, a temporary null-terminated string, or an lvalue null-terminated string. To provide for this without using a template you would need to write sixteen Person class constructors. With the template, the source code is much shorter and will result in a smaller executable module if you use less than the sixteen possible combinations of constructor arguments.

DEFAULT ARGUMENTS FOR TEMPLATE PARAMETERS

You can specify default arguments for parameters in function templates and class templates. You are likely to use them for class templates most. Parameter values for function templates can usually be deduced by the compiler, and therefore the parameters do not need default values to be specified. A default function template parameter value can be useful when you need flexibility in the return type because the return type cannot necessarily be deduced. Let's look at that first.

Default Function Template Arguments

Look at this function template:

```
template<typename T, typename R=double>
R sigma(T values[], size_t count)
{
  double mean {};
  for (size_t i {}; i < count; i++)
    mean += values[i];
  mean /= count;

  double deviation {};
  for (size_t i {}; i < count; i++)
    deviation += std::pow(values[i] - mean, 2);

  return static_cast<R>(std::sqrt(deviation/count));
}
```

This computes the *standard deviation* (denoted by the Greek letter sigma, σ) for an array of samples. It doesn't matter if you are not familiar with this, but if you are not and you'd like to get an idea, the standard deviation is a measure of how much the values in a set vary from the average. A low value σ means that the values are typically close to the average. A high σ value indicates they are widely dispersed. The type for the return value is specified by the second template parameter, R, which defaults to type double. You might use the template like this:

```
int heights[] {67, 72, 69, 74, 75, 66, 67, 78};            // In inches
std::cout << sigma(heights, _countof(heights)) << std::endl;   // Outputs 4.12311
```

No template parameter arguments are supplied, so the return value is the default type, double. You could also use the template like this:

```
std::cout << sigma<int, int>(heights, _countof(heights))       // Outputs 4
          << std::endl;
```

Both parameters values are supplied. The first parameter would be deduced to be int in any event, but you cannot omit it when you want to specify an argument for the second parameter.

Here's another example of using it:

```
int heights[] {52, 72, 53, 74, 75, 46, 67, 79};            // In inches
std::cout << sigma<int, float>(heights, _countof(heights)) << std::endl;
```

This outputs 11.7447 because these values are more widely dispersed. The function returns the result as type float.

It's conceivable that you might want the return type to be the same as the array element type by default, but still offer the possibility of choosing a return type. Defining the template like this does it:

```
template<class T, class R=T>
R sigma(T values[], size_t count)
{
  // Code as before…

  return static_cast<R>(std::sqrt(deviation/count));
}
```

The default for R is now T, so if you don't specify it, the default return type will be the element type.

Template parameters that have default values must come after parameters without defaults in a template definition. When you supply an argument for a parameter, all the preceding parameters in the list must have arguments specified.

Of course, a template is not really the best way to go for the sigma() function. Every unique combination of template arguments will cause the compiler to generate another function overload that occupies memory so a program may end up to be a lot larger than it needs to be.

> **NOTE** The sqrt() and pow() functions that are used in the sigma() template calculate square roots and powers respectively. They are declared along with many other functions in the cmath header.

Default Class Template Arguments

Any or all of the parameters for a class template can have default arguments. The same rules apply for defining default parameter values — all the parameters with defaults specified must be together at the end of the parameter list. If you supply a value for any parameter when you create an instance of a template then you must specify values for any preceding parameters in the list. Here's how you could specify defaults for the CSamples template you saw earlier:

```
template <class T=double, size_t Size=100> class CSamples
{
  public:
    // Constructors
    CSamples(const T values[], int count);
    CSamples(const T& value);
    CSamples(T&& value);
    CSamples() = default;

    bool add(const T& value);               // Insert a value
    bool add(T&& value);                    // Insert a value with move semantics
    T max() const;                          // Calculate maximum

  private:
    T m_Values[Size];                       // Array to store samples
    int m_Next {};                          // Index of free location in m_Values
};
```

Here's an example of how you can use this template:

```
double values[] { 2.5, 3.6, 4.7, -15.0, 6.8, 7.2, -8.1 };
CSamples<> data{ values, _countof(values) };
```

Neither template parameter has a value specified for it here so the defaults of double and 100 apply. Note that the angled brackets are essential, even though there are no parameter values. If you want to specify the Size parameter value, you must also specify a value for the first parameter — like this:

```
CSamples<double, _countof(values)> data{ values, _countof(values) };
```

If you omit the first parameter value here, the statement won't compile. Let's see it in action.

TRY IT OUT   Default Parameter Values in a Class Template

This example demonstrates the CSamples<> template with default parameter values. It uses the CBox class from Ex8_10:

```
// Ex8_12.cpp
// Default values for class template parameters
#include <iostream>
#include <utility>                          // For operator overload templates
#include <algorithm>                        // For max(), swap() used in CBox
using std::cout;
using std::endl;
using namespace std::rel_ops;

// Insert code for CBox class and its member from Ex8_10 here...
```

```cpp
// CSamples class template definition
template <typename T=double, size_t Size=100> class CSamples
{
public:
  // Constructors
  CSamples(const T values[], int count);
  CSamples(const T& value);
  CSamples(T&& value);
  CSamples() = default;

  bool add(const T& value);               // Insert a value
  bool add(T&& value);                     // Insert a value with move semantics
  T max() const;                           // Calculate maximum

private:
  T m_Values[Size];                        // Array to store samples
  int m_Next {};                           // Index of free location in m_Values
};

// Constructor template definition to accept an array of samples
template<typename T, size_t Size>
CSamples<T, Size>::CSamples(const T values[], int count)
{
  m_Next = count < Size ? count : Size;    // Don't exceed the array
  for (int i {}; i < m_Next; i++)          // Store count of samples
    m_Values[i] = values[i];
}

// Constructor to accept a single sample
template<typename T, size_t Size>
CSamples<T, Size>::CSamples(const T& value)
{
  m_Values[0] = value;                     // Store the sample
  m_Next = 1;                              // Next is free
}

// Constructor to accept a temporary sample
template<typename T, size_t Size>
CSamples<T, Size>::CSamples(T&& value)
{
  cout << "Move constructor." << endl;
  m_Values[0] = std::move(value);          // Store the sample
  m_Next = 1;                              // Next is free
}

// Function to add a sample
template<typename T, size_t Size>
bool CSamples<T, Size>::add(const T& value)
{
  cout << "Add." << endl;
  bool OK {m_Next < Size};                 // Indicates there is a free place
  if (OK)
    m_Values[m_Next++] = value;            // OK true, so store the value
  return OK;
}
```

```
template<typename T, size_t Size>
bool CSamples<T, Size>::add(T&& value)
{
  cout << "Add move." << endl;
  bool OK {m_Next < Size};              // Indicates there is a free place
  if (OK)
    m_Values[m_Next++] = std::move(value);  // OK true, so store the value
  return OK;
}

// Function to obtain maximum sample
template<typename T, size_t Size>
T CSamples<T, Size>::max() const
{
  T theMax {m_Values[0]};               // Set first sample as maximum
  for (int i {1}; i < m_Next; i++)      // Check all the samples
  if (theMax < m_Values[i])
    theMax = m_Values[i];               // Store any larger sample
  return theMax;
}

int main()
{
  CBox boxes[]  {                       // Create an array of boxes
      CBox { 8.0, 5.0, 2.0 },           // Initialize the boxes...
      CBox { 5.0, 4.0, 6.0 },
      CBox { 4.0, 3.0, 3.0 }
  };

  // Create the CSamples object to hold CBox objects
  CSamples<CBox> myBoxes { boxes, _countof(boxes) };

  CBox maxBox { myBoxes.max() };             // Get the biggest box
  cout << "The biggest box has a volume of "// and output its volume
    << maxBox.volume() << endl;

  double values[] { 2.5, 3.6, 4.7, -15.0, 6.8, 7.2, -8.1 };
  CSamples<> data{ values, _countof(values) };
  cout << "Maximum double value = " << data.max() << endl;

  // Uncomment next line for an error
  // CSamples <, _countof(values)> baddata{ values, _countof(values) };

  int counts[] { 21, 32, 444, 15, 6, 7, 8 };
  CSamples<int, _countof(counts)> dataset{ counts, _countof(counts) };
  cout << "Maximum int value = " << dataset.max() << endl;

  return 0;
}
```

This will produce the following output:

```
The biggest box has a volume of 120
Maximum double value = 7.2
Maximum int value = 444
```

How It Works

I defined the function members of the template outside its definition to show how it's done with multiple parameters with defaults specified. Note how each member function definition that appears outside the template definition has both class template parameters included, but without the default values.

The `main()` function first instantiates the template for an array of `CBox` objects, where the first template parameter has a value specified. The second parameter, `Size`, will have the default value, 100.

The `CSamples<>` template is used next with an array of `double` values. Neither template parameter is specified so the default values apply. You must supply the angled brackets when no parameter values are specified, unlike function templates. If you wanted to specify a value for the `Size` parameter, you must also specify a value for `T`. Uncomment the next line to show the compiler error message that you get if you don't.

The last use of `CSamples<>` is with an array of `int` values. Both template parameters have values specified. You could omit the `Size` value to use the default of 100, which would look like this:

```
CSamples<int> dataset{ counts, _countof(counts) };  // Default 2nd parameter value
```

Default template argument values are used frequently in the container class templates that you'll learn about in Chapter 10.

ALIASES FOR CLASS TEMPLATES

You can define an alias for a class template with values for some or all of its parameters specified. This can make your code easier to read. You use the `using` keyword for this. Here's an example:

```
using BoxSamples = CSamples<CBox>;
```

With this alias defined in `main()` in `Ex8_12`, you could define `myBoxes` like this:

```
BoxSamples myBoxes { boxes, _countof(boxes) };
```

`BoxSamples` can now be used whenever you want to specify the `CSamples<CBox>` type. This is especially useful if you have several uses of the template in this way because the code will look a lot less cluttered. When all the template parameters have default values, you could use an alias to get rid of the empty angled brackets when defining variables of the type:

```
using Samples = CSamples<>;                  // Default parameter values
Samples data { values, _countof(values) };
```

Thus `data` is a variable with a type specified by an instance of the `CSamples` template with `double` as the first parameter value and 100 as the value for the `Size` parameter so it is of type `CSamples<double,100>`.

Type aliases can be a great help in simplifying your code when you are working with the container class templates from the Standard Template Library that's in Chapter 10.

TEMPLATE SPECIALIZATION

Some parameter values for a function or class template may not work. Using the CBox type as an argument for the sigma() function template won't work, for example. Also, pointer types usually won't work for a template unless there is special provisioning for them. You can deal with such situations by defining a *template specialization*, which is an additional definition of a template for a specific set of parameter values. I'll illustrate how you define a template specialization with a very simple example. Suppose you have defined the following function template that computes an average:

```
template<typename T>
T average (T values[], size_t count)
{
  T mean {};
  for (size_t i {}; i < count; i++)
    mean += values[i];

  return mean/count;
}
```

I used typename instead of class to specify the parameter here to remind you that you can. Suppose you now want to use this with an array of CBox objects and you have defined an "average" CBox object to be one that has dimensions that are the average dimensions of a set of CBox objects. Given that the CBox class has members, getWidth(), getHeight(), and getLength() that return the dimensions of a box, you can define a specialization of the template for boxes like this:

```
template<>
CBox average(CBox boxes[], size_t count)
{
  double height {}, width {}, length {};
  for(size_t i {}; i<count; ++i)
  {
    height += boxes[i].getHeight();
    width += boxes[i].getWidth();
    length += boxes[i].getLength();
  }
  return CBox {length/count, width/count, height/count};
}
```

The first line with the empty angled brackets indicates to the compiler that this is a specialization of an existing template. The template argument will be deduced by the compiler from the type of the first argument. You could make the specialization argument explicit by defining it like this:

```
template<>
CBox average<CBox>(CBox boxes[], size_t count)
{
  // Code as above...
}
```

This form will be necessary when the template argument or arguments cannot be deduced by the compiler.

You could use the template specialization like this:

```
CBox boxes[] {CBox {8.0, 5.0, 2.0},CBox {5.0, 4.0, 6.0},CBox {4.0, 3.0, 3.0}};
average(boxes, _countof(boxes)).showBox();
```

With the `boxes` array as the first argument to `average()`, the compiler will generate the specialized version of the template and call it here. The `CBox` object that is returned is used to call the `show-Box()` member to output the dimensions.

Of course, you could define a function overload instead of a template specialization. So what difference would that make? If you use this function in a program, there is no difference between defining an overload and defining a specialization of the template. If you don't use it, there is a difference. A template will not be instantiated if you don't use it, whereas a function overload will always be compiled and included in the executable module. However, remember that templates are primarily intended for creating library facilities that will be reused in many applications, and not in one-off applications.

A specialization for a class template is defined in a similar manner. For example, you might specialize the `CSamples` class template with a single parameter to work with `CBox` objects like this:

```
template <>
class CSamples<CBox>
{
  public:
    // Constructor definition to accept an array of sample boxes
    CSamples(const CBox boxes[], int count)
    {
      m_Next = count < maxSamples ? count : maxSamples;   // Don't exceed the array
      for(int i {}; i < m_Next; i++)                      // Store count samples
        m_Boxes[i] = boxes[i];
    }

    // Constructor to accept a single sample
    CSamples(const CBox& box)
    {
      m_Boxes[0] = box;                      // Store the sample
      m_Next = 1;                            // Next is free
    }

    CSamples() = default;                    // Default constructor

    // Function to add a box
    bool add(const CBox& box))
    {
      bool OK {m_Next < maxSamples};         // Indicates there is a free place
      if(OK)
        m_Boxes[m_Next++] = box;             // OK true, so store the box
      return OK;
    }

    // Function to obtain maximum box
    CBox max() const
    {
      // Set first box as maximum
      CBox maxBox {m_Boxes[0]};

      for(int i {1}; i < m_Next; i++)        // Check all the boxes
```

```
        if(m_Boxes[i].volume() > maxBox.volume())
          maxBox = m_Boxes[i];                    // Store any larger box
      return maxBox;
    }

  private:
    static const size_t maxSamples {100};      // Maximum number of samples
    CBox m_Boxes[maxSamples];                  // Array to store boxes
    int m_Next {};                             // Index of next free location
};
```

The `template` keyword followed by the empty angled brackets indicates to the compiler that you are defining a template specialization. The specialized type appears between angled brackets following the template name, `CSamples`. When an instance of the `CSamples` template needs to be created with `CBox` as the parameter value, the compiler will use this specialization to create the class.

The preceding specialization is called a *complete specialization* because it only applies to a specific parameter value. A specialization of a template with multiple parameters with all parameters specified is also a complete specialization. You can define a template specialization that applies to a range of argument types, for any pointer type for example. This is called a *partial specialization*. The syntax is slightly different in this case. You could define a specialization of the `CSamples` template for pointers as something like this:

```
template <typename T>
class CSamples<T*>
{
  public:
    // Constructor definition to accept an array of pointers to samples
    CSamples(T* pSamples[], int count)
    {
      m_Next = count < maxSamples) ? count : maxSamples;   // Don't exceed the array
      for(int i {}; i < m_Next; i++)                        // Store count samples
        m_pSamples[i] = pSamples[i];
    }


    // Function to obtain address of maximum sample
    T* max() const
    {
      // Set first sample as maximum
      T* pMax {m_pSamples[0]};

      for(int i {1}; i < m_Next; i++)            // Check all the samples
        if(*m_pSamples[i] > *pMax)
          pMax = m_pSamples[i];                  // Store any larger sample
      return pMax;
    }

    // Plus other members adjusted for pointers...

  private:
    static const size_t maxSamples {100};      // Maximum number of samples
    T* m_pSamples[maxSamples];                 // Array to store pointers
    int m_Next {};                             // Index of next free location
};
```

The first line specifies that the template parameter is T and the type T* between angle brackets following the template type name; CSamples, is the form for which this template specialization applies, i.e., any pointer type. Thus this specialization will be used if T is double* or CBox*. Here's a fragment that will use this specialization:

```
CBox boxes[] { CBox {8.0, 5.0, 2.0},
               CBox {5.0, 4.0, 6.0},
               CBox {4.0, 3.0, 3.0}
             };
CBox* pBoxes[] {boxes, boxes + 1, boxes + 2};
CSamples<CBox*> pBoxSamples { pBoxes, _countof(pBoxes) };
pBoxSamples.max()->showBox();
```

The first statement creates an array of CBox objects, and the second statement creates an array of pointers to these objects. pBoxSamples is an object of type CSamples<CBox*> that is constructed using the array of pointers. The last line will output the dimensions of the largest CBox object pointed to.

When a template has more than one parameter, you can define a partial specialization that allows one or more of the parameters to remain variable. Here's how a partial specialization of the CSamples<T, Size> template would look:

```
template<size_t Size>
class CSamples<CBox, Size>
{
  // Code for a CBox version…
};
```

The type following the template keyword is still a variable and the types between the angled brackets following CSamples indicates that the first type parameter value for this specialization is fixed as CBox and the second is parameter Size and thus still variable.

USING CLASSES

I've touched on most of the basic aspects of defining a class, so maybe it's time to look at how you might use a class to solve a problem. The problem has to be simple in order to keep this book down to a reasonable number of pages, so I'll consider problems in which we can use an extended version of the CBox class.

The Idea of a Class Interface

The implementation of an extended CBox class should incorporate the notion of a *class interface*. You are going to provide a tool kit for anyone who wants to work with CBox objects, so you need to assemble a set of functions that represents the interface to the world of boxes. The interface will represent the only way to deal with CBox objects so it should provide everything one is likely to want do with a CBox object, and be implemented as far as possible in a way that protects against misuse or accidental errors.

The first question that you need to consider in designing a class is the nature of the problem you intend to solve, and, from that, determine the kind of functionality you need in the class interface.

Defining the Problem

The principal function of a box is to contain objects of one kind or another, so, in a word, the problem is *packaging*. We'll attempt to provide a class that eases packaging problems in general and then see how it might be used. We will assume that we'll always be packing CBox objects into other CBox objects; if you want to pack candy in a box, you can represent the pieces of candy as idealized CBox objects. The basic operations that you might want to provide in the CBox class include:

➤   Calculate the volume of a CBox. This is a fundamental characteristic of a CBox object, and you have an implementation of this already.

➤   Compare the volumes of two CBox objects. You probably should support a complete set of comparison operators for CBox objects.

➤   Compare the volume of a CBox object with a value, and vice versa.

➤   Add two CBox objects to produce a new object that will contain both original objects. The result will be at least the sum of the volumes but may be larger.

➤   Multiply a CBox object by an integer and vice versa to produce a new CBox object that will contain the specified number of original objects. This is effectively designing a carton.

➤   Determine how many of a given CBox object can be packed in another CBox object. This is effectively division, so you could implement this by overloading the / operator.

➤   Determine the volume of space remaining in a CBox object after packing it with the maximum number of CBox objects of a given size.

I had better stop right there! There are undoubtedly other functions that would be useful but, in the interest of saving trees, we'll consider the set to be complete, apart from ancillaries such as accessing box dimensions.

Implementing the CBox Class

You need to consider the degree of error protection that you want to build into the CBox class. The basic class that you defined to illustrate various aspects of classes is a starting point, but you should also consider some points a little more deeply. The constructor is weak in that it doesn't ensure that the dimensions are valid, so, perhaps the first thing is to ensure that you always have valid objects. You could redefine the basic class as follows to do this:

```
class CBox
{
public:
  CBox(const CBox& obj) = default;              // Copy constructor
  CBox& operator=(const CBox& obj) = default;   // Assignment operator
  ~CBox() = default;                            // Destructor

  explicit CBox(double lv = 1.0, double wv = 1.0, double hv = 1.0):
    m_Length {std::max(lv, wv)}, m_Width {std::min(lv, wv)}, m_Height {hv}
  {
    // height is <= width
    // We need to ensure the height is <= width is <= length
    if (m_Height > m_Length)
```

```
{ // height greater than length, so swap them
  std::swap(m_Height, m_Length);
  std::swap(m_Width, m_Height);
} else if (m_Height > m_Width)
{ // height less than or equal to length but greater than width so swap
  std::swap(m_Height, m_Width);
}
  }

  double volume() const                        // Calculate the volume of a box
  {  return m_Length*m_Width*m_Height;  }

  double getLength() const { return m_Length; }  // Return the length of a box
  double getWidth() const { return m_Width; }    // Return the width of a box
  double getHeight() const { return m_Height; }  // Return the height of a box

private:
  double m_Length;                             // Length of a box in inches
  double m_Width;                              // Width of a box in inches
  double m_Height;                             // Height of a box in inches
};
```

The constructor is now secure because any dimension that the user of the class tries to set to a value less than zero will cause an exception to be thrown.

The default copy constructor and assignment operator are satisfactory for the class, because you have no dynamic memory allocation for data members. The default destructor also works perfectly well. Next, you can consider what is required to support comparing CBox objects.

Comparing CBox Objects

You should support the operators >, >=, ==, !=, <, and <= so that they all work with both operands as CBox objects, as well as between a CBox object and a value of type double. This totals eighteen operator functions. You can get four of the ones with both operands as CBox objects for free, courtesy of the templates in the utility header, once you have defined the < and == operator functions. You saw how to do that in Ex8_06:

```
bool operator<(const CBox& aBox) const         // Less-than operator
{  return this->volume() < aBox.volume();  }

bool operator==(const CBox& aBox) const         // Compare for equality
{  return this->volume() == aBox.volume();  }
```

All the operator functions comparing a CBox left operand with a constant can be inside the class:

```
bool operator>(const double  value) const      // CBox > value
{  return volume() > value;  }

bool operator<(const double value) const       // CBox < value
{  return volume() < value;  }

bool operator>=(const double value) const      // CBox >= value
{  return volume() >= value;  }

bool operator<=(const double value) const      // CBox <= value
```

```
{   return volume() <= value;   }

bool operator==(const double value) const          // CBox ==   value
{   return volume() == value;   }

bool operator!=(const double value) const          // CBox != value
{   return volume() != value;   }
```

These will be `inline` by default.

You must define comparisons with a left operand of type `double` as ordinary functions outside the class:

```
inline bool operator>(const double value, const CBox& aBox)   // value > CBox
{   return value > aBox.volume();   }

inline bool operator<(const double value, const CBox& aBox)   // value < CBox
{   return value < aBox.volume();   }

inline bool operator>=(const double value, const CBox& aBox)  // value >= CBox
{   return value >= aBox.volume();   }

inline bool operator<=(const double value, const CBox& aBox)  // value <= CBox
{   return value <= aBox.volume();   }

inline bool operator==(const double value, const CBox& aBox)  // value == CBox
{   return value == aBox.volume();   }

inline bool operator!=(const double value, const CBox& aBox)  // value != CBox
{   return value != aBox.volume();   }
```

You now have a complete set of comparison operators. These will work with expressions as long as the expressions result in objects of the required type.

Combining CBox Objects

Now, you can implement overloads for the operators +, *, /, and % in the CBox class. I will take them in order. The add operation that you already have from Ex8_06.cpp has this prototype:

```
CBox operator+(const CBox& aBox) const;     // Function adding two CBox objects
```

Although the original implementation isn't ideal, let's use it anyway to avoid overcomplicating the class. A better version might examine whether the operands had any faces with the same dimensions and, if so, join along those faces, but coding that could get a bit messy. Of course, in a real application a better add operation could be developed later and substituted for this version; any programs written using the original would still run without change. The separation of the interface to a class from its implementation is crucial to good C++ programming.

I conveniently forgot about the subtraction operator. This is a judicious oversight to avoid the complications inherent in implementing this when the result is a CBox object. If you're really enthusiastic about it and think it's a sensible idea, you can give it a try — but you need to decide what to do when the result has a negative volume. If you allow the concept, you need to resolve which box dimension or dimensions are to be negative, and how such a box is to be handled in subsequent operations. A simpler concept might be that subtracting CBox objects resulted in a volume.

The multiply operation is easy. It represents the process of creating a box to contain n boxes, where n is the multiplier. A simple solution would be to take the width and length of the object to be packed and multiply the height by n to get the dimensions for the new CBox object. You can make it a little cleverer by checking whether or not the multiplier is even and in this case stack the boxes side by side by doubling the width and multiplying the height by half of n. This mechanism is illustrated in Figure 8-5 with examples of the CBox objects resulting from multiplying aBox by 3 and 6.

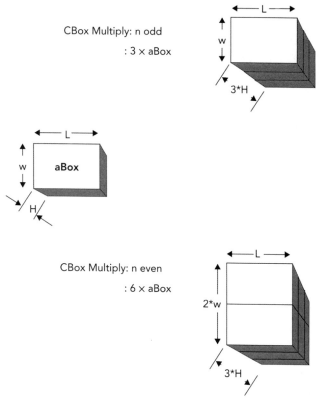

FIGURE 8-5

Of course, you don't need to check which is the larger of the length and width for the new object because the constructor sorts it out. You can write the operator*() function as a member function with the left operand as a CBox object like this:

```
// CBox multiply operator this*n
CBox operator*(int n) const
{
  if(n % 2)
    return CBox {m_Length, m_Width, n*m_Height};         // n odd
  else
    return CBox {m_Length, 2.0*m_Width, (n/2)*m_Height};  // n even
}
```

You use the % operator to determine whether n is even or odd. If n is odd, the value of n%2 is 1 and the if condition is true. If it's even, n%2 is 0 and the condition is false.

You can use the function you have just written in the implementation of the version with the left operand as an integer. You can write this as a non-member function:

```
// CBox multiply operator n*aBox
CBox operator*(int n, const CBox& aBox)
{
  return aBox*n;
}
```

This reverses the order of the operands so as to use the previous version of the function directly. That completes the arithmetic operators for CBox objects that we defined. You can now look at the analytical operator functions, operator/() and operator%().

Analyzing CBox Objects

The division operation will determine how many objects identical to the right operand can be contained in the CBox object specified by the left operand. To keep it simple I'll assume that all the objects are packed the right way up — that is, with their height dimension vertical. I'll also assume that they are all packed the same way round so that their lengths are aligned. Without these assumptions, it gets complicated.

The problem amounts to determining how many of the right-operand objects can be placed in a single layer inside the left-operand CBox, and then deciding how many layers you can get in it. You can code this as a member function like this:

```
int operator/(const CBox& aBox) const
{
  // Number of boxes in horizontal plane this way
  int tc1 {static_cast<int>((m_Length / aBox.m_Length))*
              static_cast<int>((m_Width / aBox.m_Width))};
  // Number of boxes in horizontal plane that way
  int tc2 {static_cast<int>((m_Length / aBox.m_Width))*
              static_cast<int>((m_Width / aBox.m_Length))};
  //Return best fit
  return static_cast<int>((m_Height/aBox.m_Height)*(tc1 > tc2 ? tc1 : tc2));
}
```

You first determine how many of the right-operand objects can fit in a layer with their lengths aligned with the length dimension of the left-operand. This is stored in tc1. You then calculate how many fit in a layer with the lengths of the right-operand objects lying in the width direction of the left-operand CBox. Finally, you multiply the larger of tc1 and tc2 by the number of layers you can pack in, and return that value. This process is illustrated in Figure 8-6.

Consider two possibilities: fitting bBox into aBox with its length aligned with that of aBox, and then with the length of bBox aligned with the width of aBox. You can see from Figure 8-6 that the best packing results from rotating bBox so that its width divides into the length of aBox.

The operator%() function for obtaining the free volume in a packed box is easier, because you can use the operator you have just written to implement it. It can be an ordinary global function because you don't need access to the private members of the class.

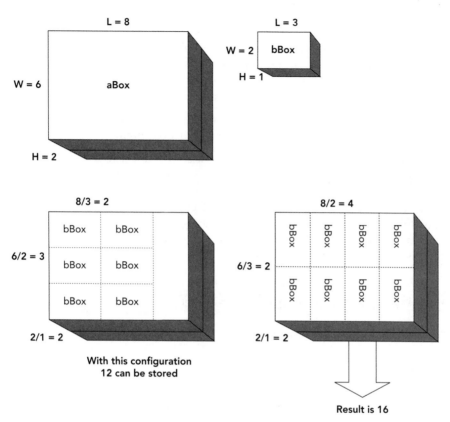

FIGURE 8-6

```cpp
// Operator to return the free volume in a packed box
inline double operator%(const CBox& aBox, const CBox& bBox)
{
   return aBox.volume() - ((aBox/bBox)*bBox.volume());
}
```

This computation falls out very easily using existing CBox class functions. The result is the volume of the big box, aBox, minus the total volume of the bBox boxes that can be stored in it. The number of bBox objects packed into aBox is given by the expression aBox/bBox, which uses the division operator function. You multiply this by the volume of a single bBox object to get the volume to be subtracted from the volume of the large box, aBox.

That completes the class interface. Clearly, there are many more functions that might be required for a production problem solver but, as an interesting working model demonstrating how you can produce a class for solving a particular kind of problem, it will suffice. Now you can try it out on a real problem.

TRY IT OUT A Multifile Project Using the CBox Class

Before you can actually start writing the code to *use* the CBox class and its overloaded operators, you need to assemble the definition for the class into a coherent whole. You're going to take a new approach in that you're going to create multiple files for the project. You're also going to start using the Visual C++ facilities for creating and maintaining classes. This will mean that you do rather less of the work, but it will also mean that the code will be slightly different in places.

Start by creating a new Win32 project for a console application called **Ex8_13** and check the Empty project application option and uncheck the Security Development Lifecycle option.

The Class View tab shows the classes in a project but of course there are none here yet. Although there are no classes defined — or anything else, for that matter — Visual C++ has made provisions for including some. You can create a skeleton for the CBox class, and the files that relate to it. Right-click Ex8_13 in Class View and select Add ⇨ Class from the pop-up menu. Select C++ from the class categories in the left pane of the dialog, select the C++ Class template in the right pane, and press Enter. (Ignore the Name and Location entry fields; they are disabled and not used.) You will then be able to enter the name of the class, CBox, as shown in Figure 8-7.

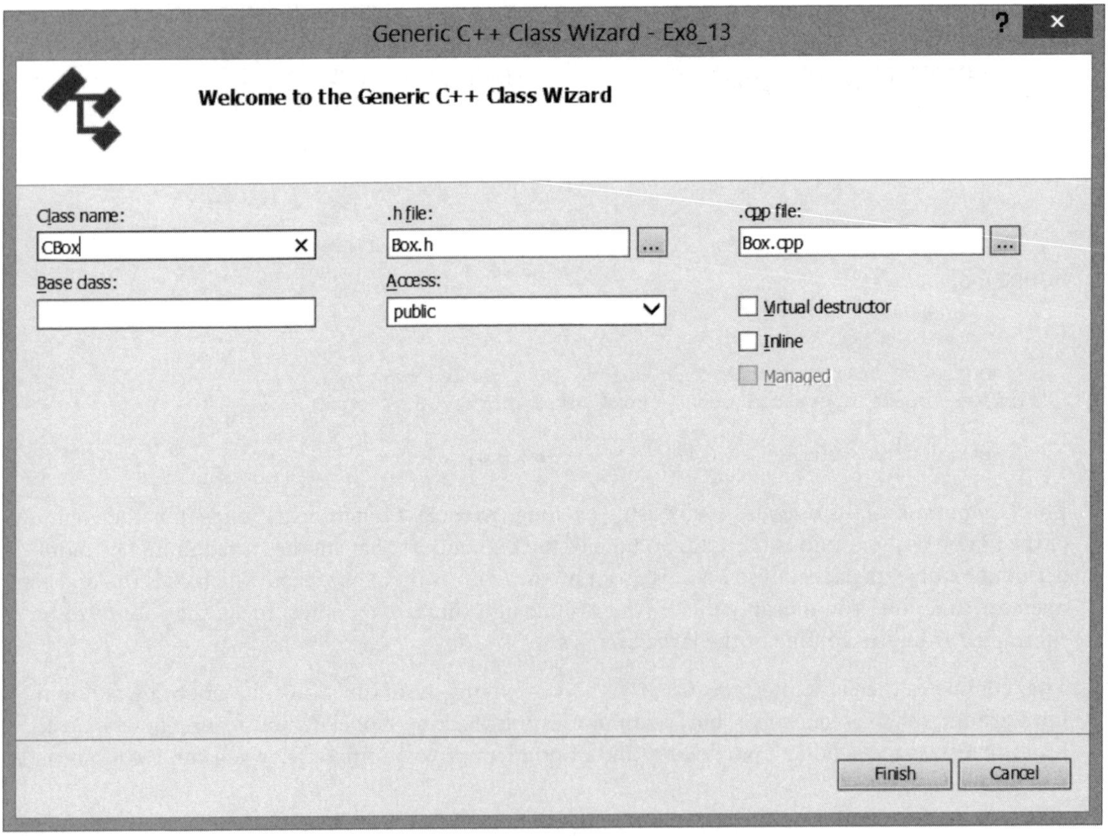

FIGURE 8-7

The Box.cpp file will contain the *class implementation*, which consists of the definitions for function members that are not in the class definition. This is the executable code for the class. You can change the name of this file if you want, but Box.cpp looks like a good name. The class definition will be stored in a file called Box.h. This is the standard way of structuring a program. Code that consists of class definitions is stored in files with the extension .h, and code that defines functions is stored in files with the extension .cpp. Usually, each class definition goes in its own .h file, and each class implementation goes in its own .cpp file.

When you click the Finish button, two things happen:

1. A Box.h file is created that contains a skeleton definition for the CBox class. This includes a no-arg constructor and a destructor.

2. A Box.cpp file is created that contains a skeleton implementation for the functions in the class with definitions for the constructor and the destructor — both bodies are empty of course.

The editor pane now displays the code for the class definition that is in Box.h. The second tab in the editor pane displays the contents of Box.cpp. Let's start developing the CBox class from what Visual C++ has provided automatically.

Defining the CBox Class

If you click the ⇨ to the left of Ex8_13 in the Class View, the tree will be expanded and you will see that CBox is now defined for the project. All the classes in a project are displayed in this tree. You can view the source code for a class definition by double-clicking the class name in the tree.

The CBox class definition that was generated starts with a preprocessor directive:

```
#pragma once
```

This prevents the file contents from being included in the source code more than once. Typically, a header file containing a given class definition may be included into several files in a project, including other header files, because each file that references the name of the class will need access to its definition. Thus the contents of a header file could potentially appear more than once in a source file. Having more than one definition of a class in a build is not allowed and will be flagged as an error. Putting the #pragma once directive at the start of every header file will ensure this cannot happen.

#pragma once may not be supported in other environments. If you are developing code that may need to be compiled in other environments, you can use the following directives in a header file to achieve the same effect:

```
// Box.h header file
#ifndef BOX_H
#define BOX_H
// Code that must not be included more than once
// such as the CBox class definition
#endif
```

The important lines are bolded and correspond to directives that are supported by any C++ compiler. The lines following the #ifndef directive down to the #endif directive will be included in a build as long as the symbol BOX_H is not defined. The line following #ifndef defines the symbol BOX_H, thus ensuring that the code in this header file will not be included a second time. Thus, this has the same effect as the #pragma once directive. Clearly, the #pragma once directive is simpler and less cluttered, so it's better to use that when you only expect to be using your code in Visual C++. You will sometimes see the #ifndef/#endif combination written as:

```
#if !defined BOX_H
#define BOX_H
// Code that must not be included more than once
// such as the CBox class definition
#endif
```

The Box.cpp file that Class Wizard generated contains the following code:

```
#include "Box.h"

CBox::CBox()
{
}

CBox::~CBox()
{
}
```

The first line is an #include directive that inserts the contents of Box.h— the class definition — into this file, Box.cpp. This is necessary because the code in Box.cpp refers to the CBox class, and the class definition needs to be available to assign meaning to the name CBox.

Adding Data Members

First, you can add the private data members m_Length, m_Width, and m_Height as type double. Right-click CBox in Class View and select Add ⇨ Add Variable from the pop-up menu. You can then specify the name, type, and access for the first data member that you want to add to the class in the Add Member Variable Wizard dialog. The way you specify a new data member in this dialog is quite self-explanatory. The upper and lower limits for variables only applies when you are defining an MFC variable attached to a control. You can add a comment in the lower input field, if you wish. Clicking the Finish button adds the variable to the class definition along with any comment you supplied. You can repeat the process for the other two class data members, m_Width and m_Height. The class definition in Box.h will then look like this:

```
#pragma once

class CBox
{
public:
  CBox();
  ~CBox();
private:
  double m_Length;
  double m_Width;
  double m_Height;
};
```

Of course, you could enter the declarations for these members manually. You always have the choice of whether or not you use the automation provided by the IDE. You can also delete anything manually that was generated automatically, but remember that both the .h and .cpp files will need to be changed sometimes. It's a good idea to save all the files whenever you make manual changes.

If you look in Box.cpp you'll see that the Wizard has also added an initialization list to the constructor definition for the data members you have added, with each variable initialized to 0 using the old syntax for the initial values. You could change this to the new syntax if you prefer. You'll modify the constructor to do what you want next.

Defining the Constructor

You need to change the declaration of the no-arg constructor in the class definition so that it has arguments with default values, so modify it to:

```
explicit CBox(double lv = 1.0, double wv = 1.0, double hv = 1.0);
```

Now, you're ready to implement it. Open the Box.cpp file, if it isn't open already, and modify the constructor definition to:

```
CBox::CBox(double lv, double wv, double hv) :
    m_Length {std::max(lv, wv)}, m_Width {std::min(lv, wv)}, m_Height {hv}
{
  if (lv < 0.0 || wv < 0.0 || hv < 0.0)
    throw "Negative dimension specified for CBox object.";
  // Ensure the height is <= width is <= length
  if (m_Height > m_Length)
  { // height greater than length, so swap them
    std::swap(m_Height, m_Length);
  }
  else if (m_Height > m_Width)
  { // height less than or equal to length but greater than width so swap
    std::swap(m_Height, m_Width);
  }
}
```

You'll need an #include directive for the algorithm header in Box.cpp. Remember that the default values for the parameters to a member function only appear in the member declaration in the class definition, not in the definition of the function. If you put them in the function definition, the code will not compile. You've seen this code already, so I won't discuss it again. It would be a good idea to save the file at this point by clicking the Save toolbar button. Get into the habit of saving the file you're editing before you switch to something else. If you need to edit the constructor again, you can get to it easily by double-clicking its entry in the lower pane on the Class View tab.

Clicking a class name in Class View will cause the members of the class to be displayed in the lower pane. You can get to a member function's definition in a .cpp file or to its declaration in an .h file directly by right-clicking its name in the Class View pane and selecting the appropriate item from the context menu that appears.

Adding Member Functions

You need to add the member functions you saw earlier to the CBox class. You defined several member functions within the class definition, so that these functions were automatically inline. First, add the #include directive for the utility header to Box.h and then add the following using declarations:

```
Using std::rel_ops::operator<=;
using std::rel_ops::operator>;
using std::rel_ops::operator>=;
using std::rel_ops::operator!=;
```

This makes the names of the templates for the comparison operators in the `std::rel_ops` namespace available. You should never add a "using namespace" to a header file so the only alternative to the declarations above would be to define the comparison operator functions yourself.

To add the `operator<()` function as inline, right-click `CBox` on the Class View tab and select Add ⇨ Add Function from the context menu. You then can enter the data defining the function in the dialog that is displayed, as Figure 8-8 shows.

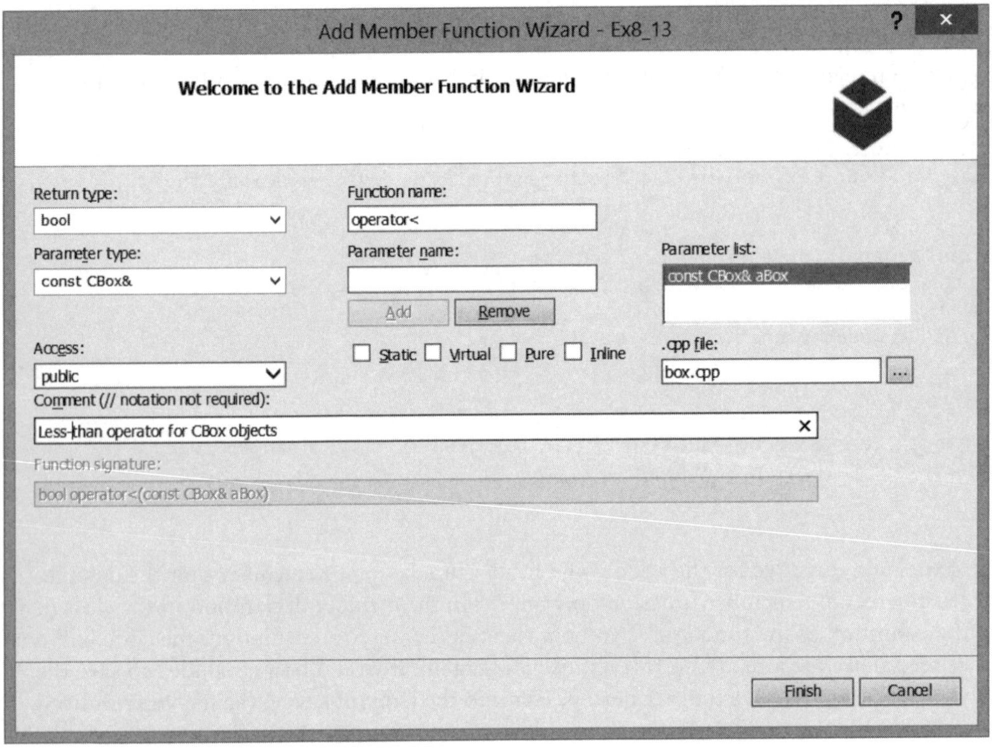

FIGURE 8-8

The drop-down lists for the Return Type and Parameter Type contain a limited range of types. If the type you want is not in the list, you just type it in. You must click the Add button to add the parameter. It will then appear in the parameter list to the right in the dialog. If you don't select the Inline option, the function definition will be in `Box.cpp`. Clicking Finish with Inline selected will create the skeleton for the function definition within the class definition. You must still edit the declaration in the `CBox` class definition to make the function const and to add the implementation to the function body. It should then look like this:

```
// Less-than operator for CBox objects
bool operator<(const CBox& aBox) const
{
  return volume() < aBox.volume();
}
```

You can add and implement the `operator==()` and `volume()` members that you saw earlier to the class definition in the same way:

```
// Operator function for == comparing CBox objects
bool operator==(const CBox& aBox) const
{
  return volume() == aBox.volume();
}

// Calculate the box volume
double volume() const
{
 return m_Length*m_Width*m_Height;
}
```

The templates in the `utility` header take care of the operator functions for `!=`, `>`, `<=`, and `>=`. I'll return to those that compare `CBox` objects with numerical values in a moment.

You can now add the `getHeight()`, `getWidth()`, and `getLength()` functions that you saw earlier as inline class members. I'll leave it to you whether you use the Add ⇨ Add Function menu option or enter them directly.

Enter the operator functions for add, multiply, and divide operations using the Add Member Function Wizard because the practice will be useful. Right-click `CBox` in the Class View tab and select the Add ⇨ Add Function menu item from the context menu, as before. You can then enter the details of the `operator+()` function in the dialog that appears, as Figure 8-9 shows.

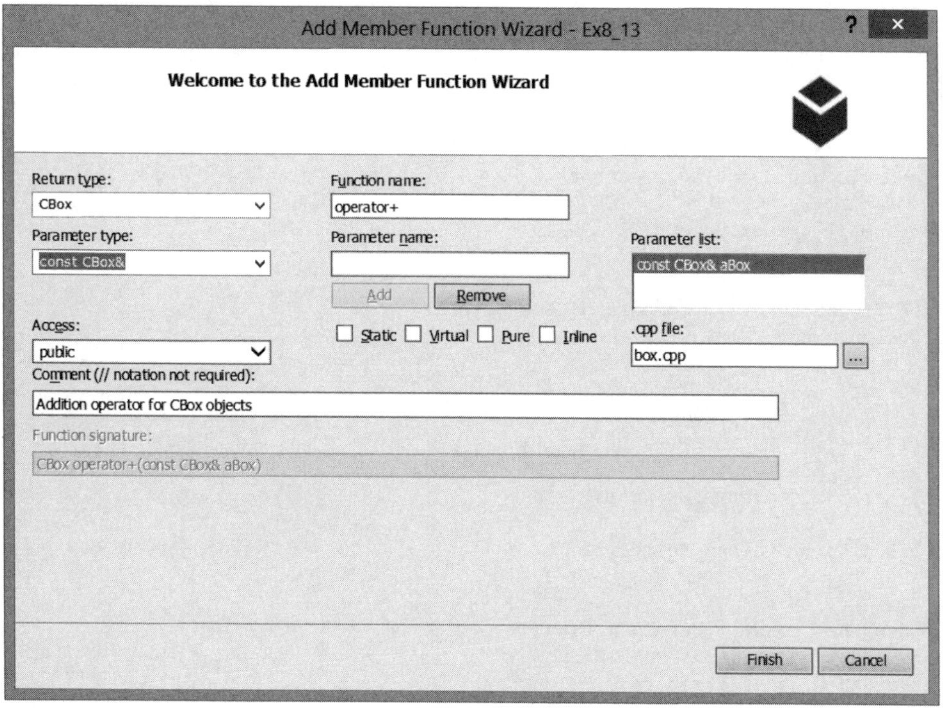

FIGURE 8-9

Figure 8-9 shows the dialog after the Add button has been clicked to add the parameter to the list. Inline is not selected in this instance. When you click Finish, the declaration for the function will be added to the class definition in the `Box.h` file and a skeleton definition for the function will be added to the `Box.cpp` file. The function needs to be declared as `const`, so you must add this keyword to the declaration of the `operator+()` function in the class definition, and to the function definition in `Box.cpp`. You must also add the code in the body of the function, like this:

```
CBox CBox::operator+(const CBox& aBox) const
{
    // New object has larger length and width and sum of the heights
    return CBox {std::max(m_Length, aBox.m_Length),
                 std::max(m_Width, aBox.m_Width),
                 m_Height + aBox.m_Height};
}
```

When you have repeated this process for the `operator*()` and `operator/()` functions that you saw earlier, the class definition in `Box.h` will look something like this:

```
#pragma once
#include <utility>                      // For operator overload templates
using namespace std::rel_ops;

class CBox
{
public:
    explicit CBox(double lv = 1.0, double wv = 1.0, double hv = 1.0);
    ~CBox();
private:
    double m_Length;
    double m_Width;
    double m_Height;
public:

    // Less-than operator for CBox objects
    bool operator<(const CBox& aBox) const
    {
        return volume() < aBox.volume();
    }

    // Operator function for == comparing CBox objects
    bool operator==(const CBox& aBox) const
    {
        return volume() == aBox.volume();
    }

    // Calculate the box volume
    double volume()@@@remove MG OK IH@@@) const
    {
        return m_Length*m_Width*m_Height;
    }

    double getLength() const { return m_Length; }
    double getWidth() const { return m_Width; }
    double getHeight() const { return m_Height; }
```

```
    CBox operator+(const CBox& aBox) const;    // Addition operator for CBox objects
    CBox operator*(int n) const;               // Multiply operator for CBox objects
    int operator/(const CBox& aBox) const;     // Division operator for CBox objects
};
```

I rearranged it a little. You can edit or rearrange the code in any way that you want — as long as it's still correct, of course.

If you look at Class View by clicking the tab, and then clicking the CBox class name, you'll see that all the members of the class are shown in the lower pane.

This completes the CBox class with its members, but you still need to define the global functions that implement operators that compare the volume of a CBox object with a numerical value. These are short and can be inline for efficiency.

Adding Global Functions

You might think that you put definitions for inline functions in a .cpp file like other function definitions, but this is not the case. Inline functions may not end up being "real" functions in the compiled code because the compiler may insert the code from the body of an inline function at each position it is called. The definitions for inline functions need to be available when a file containing calls to them is compiled. If they're not, you'll get linker errors and your program will not run. The .h files that you include into a .cpp file must contain everything the compiler needs to compile the code in the .cpp file. If you call an inline function in a .cpp file, the inline function definition *must* appear in an .h file that is included into the .cpp file. This also applies to inline member functions that you define outside the class definition.

The global functions that support operations on CBox objects will all be inline. You could put the global functions that support operations on CBox objects after the CBox class definition in Box.h, but to get the experience, you will add another .h file to the project to house them. Click the Solution Explorer tab to display it (you currently will have the Class View tab displayed) and right-click the Header Files folder. Select Add ⇨ New Item from the context menu. Choose the category as Code and the template as Header File (.h) in the right pane of the dialog, and enter the filename as **BoxOperators**.

You can now enter the following code in the editor pane:

```
// BoxOperators.h
// CBox object operations that don't need to access private members
#pragma once
#include "Box.h"

// Function for testing if a constant is > a CBox object
inline bool operator>(const double value, const CBox& aBox)
{ return value > aBox.volume(); }

// Function for testing if a constant is < CBox object
inline bool operator<(const double value, const CBox& aBox)
{ return value < aBox.volume(); }

// Function for testing if CBox object is > a constant
inline bool operator>(const CBox& aBox, const double value)
{ return aBox.volume() > value; }

// Function for testing if CBox object is < a constant
inline bool operator<( const CBox& aBox, const double value)
```

```
                 { return aBox.volume() < value; }

                 // Function for testing if a constant is >= a CBox object
                 inline bool operator>=(const double value, const CBox& aBox)
                 { return value >= aBox.volume(); }

                 // Function for testing if a constant is <= CBox object
                 inline bool operator<=(const double value, const CBox& aBox)
                 { return value <= aBox.volume(); }

                 // Function for testing if CBox object is >= a constant
                 inline bool operator>=( const CBox& aBox, const double value)
                 { return aBox.volume() >= value; }

                 // Function for testing if CBox object is <= a constant
                 inline bool operator<=( const CBox& aBox, const double value)
                 { return aBox.volume() <= value; }

                 // Function for testing if a constant is == CBox object
                 inline bool operator==(const double value, const CBox& aBox)
                 { return value == aBox.volume(); }

                 // Function for testing if CBox object is == a constant
                 inline bool operator==(const CBox& aBox, const double value)
                 { return aBox.volume() == value; }

                 // Function for testing if a constant is != CBox object
                 inline bool operator!=(const double value, const CBox& aBox)
                 {
                   return value != aBox.volume();
                 }

                 // Function for testing if CBox object is != a constant
                 inline bool operator!=(const CBox& aBox, const double value)
                 {
                   return aBox.volume() != value;
                 }

                 // CBox multiply operator n*aBox
                 inline CBox operator*(int n, const CBox& aBox)
                 { return aBox * n; }

                 // Operator to return the free volume in a packed CBox
                 inline double operator%( const CBox& aBox, const CBox& bBox)
                 { return aBox.volume() - (aBox / bBox) * bBox.volume(); }
```

The #pragma once directive ensures the contents of this cannot be included into another file more than once. You have an #include directive for Box.h because the functions refer to the CBox class. Save the file. When you have completed this, you can select the Class View tab. The Class View tab now includes a Global Functions and Variables folder that contains all the functions you have just added.

When you define global functions in a project that are not inline, you put their definitions in a .cpp file. You also need to put the prototypes for the functions in an .h file with a #pragma once directive at the beginning. You can then include the .h file into any .cpp file that calls any of the functions so the compiler knows what they are.

You're now ready to start applying these global functions along with the CBox class to a specific problem in the world of boxes.

Using the CBox Class

Suppose that you are packaging candies. The candies are on the big side, real jawbreakers, occupying an envelope 1.5 inches long by 1 inch wide by 1 inch high. You have access to a standard candy box that is 4.5 inches by 7 inches by 2 inches, and you want to know how many candies will fit in the box so that you can set the price. You also have a standard carton that is 2 feet, 6 inches long by 18 inches wide and 18 inches deep, and you want to know how many boxes of candy it can hold and how much space you're wasting when it has been filled.

In case the standard candy box isn't a good solution, you would also like to know what custom candy box would be suitable. You know that you can get a good price on boxes with a length from 3 inches to 7.5 inches, a width from 3 inches to 5 inches, and a height from 1 inch to 2.5 inches, where each dimension can vary in steps of half an inch. You also know that you need to have at least 30 candies in a box, because this is the minimum quantity consumed by your largest customers at a sitting. Also, the candy box should not have empty space; complaints go up because customers think they are being cheated when the box is not full. Further, ideally, you want to pack the standard carton completely so the candies don't rattle around. You don't want to be too stringent about this; otherwise, packing could become difficult, so let's say you have no wasted space if the free space in the packed carton is less than the volume of a single candy box.

With the CBox class, the problem becomes almost trivial; the solution is generated by the following main() function. Add a new source file, Ex8_13.cpp, to the project through the context menu you get when you right-click Source Files in the Solution Explorer pane, as you've done before. You can then type in the code shown here:

```
// Ex8_13.cpp
// A sample packaging problem
#include <iostream>
#include "Box.h"
#include "BoxOperators.h"
using std::cout;
using std::endl;

int main()
{
  CBox candy {1.5, 1.0, 1.0};          // Candy definition
  CBox candyBox {7.0, 4.5, 2.0};       // Candy box definition
  CBox carton {30.0, 18.0, 18.0};      // Carton definition

  // Calculate candies per candy box
  int numCandies {candyBox/candy};

  // Calculate candy boxes per carton
  int numCboxes {carton/candyBox};

  // Calculate wasted carton space
  double wasted {carton%candyBox};

  cout << "There are " << numCandies << " candies per candy box" << endl
```

```
                << "For the standard boxes there are " << numCboxes
                << " candy boxes per carton " << endl << "with "
                << wasted << " cubic inches wasted." << endl;

        cout << endl << "CUSTOM CANDY BOX ANALYSIS (No Waste)" << endl;
        const int minCandiesPerBox {30};

        // Try the whole range of custom candy boxes
        for (double length{3.0}; length <= 7.5; length += 0.5)
        {
          for (double width {3.0}; width <= 5.0; width += 0.5)
          {
            for (double height {1.0}; height <= 2.5; height += 0.5)
            {
              // Create new box each cycle
              CBox tryBox(length, width, height);

              if ((carton%tryBox < tryBox.volume()) && // Carton waste < a candy box
                  (tryBox%candy == 0.0) &&              // & no waste in candy box
                  (tryBox/candy >= minCandiesPerBox))   // & candy box holds minimum
              {
                cout << "Trial Box L = " << tryBox.getLength()
                     << " W = " << tryBox.getWidth()
                     << " H = " << tryBox.getHeight()
                     << endl;
                cout << "Trial Box contains " << tryBox / candy << " candies"
                     << " and a carton contains " << carton / tryBox
                     << " candy boxes." << endl;
              }
            }
          }
        }
        return 0;
}
```

Let's look at how the program is organized. You have divided it into a number of files, which is typical in C++. You can see the files in the Solution Explorer tab. Ex8_13.cpp contains main() and has #include directives for the iostream standard header, Box.h that contains the definition for CBox, and BoxOperators.h that contains the definitions for the inline nonmembers functions.

A console program is usually divided into a number of files that fall into one of three basic categories:

1. .h files containing library #include commands, global constants and variables, class definitions, and function prototypes — in other words, everything that is not executable code. They also contain inline function definitions. Where a program has several classes, the definitions are usually placed in separate .h files.

2. .cpp files containing the executable code for the program, plus #include directives for .h files that provide the definitions required by the executable code.

3. A .cpp file containing the function main().

The code in main() doesn't need a lot of explanation — it's almost a direct expression of the definition of the problem in words, because the operators in the class interface perform problem-oriented actions on CBox objects.

The solution to the question of the use of standard boxes is in the declaration statements, which also compute the required answers as initializing values. You output these values with some explanatory comments.

The second part of the problem is solved by the nested `for` loops that iterate over the possible ranges of m_Length, m_Width, and m_Height to evaluate all possible combinations. You could output them all, but this would involve 200 combinations of which you might only be interested in a few, so you have an `if` statement which identifies the options that you're interested in. The `if` expression is only `true` if there's no space wasted in the carton *and* the current trial candy box has no wasted space *and* it contains at least 30 candies.

How It Works

Here's the output from this program:

```
There are 42 candies per candy box
For the standard boxes there are 144 candy boxes per carton
with 648 cubic inches wasted.

CUSTOM CANDY BOX ANALYSIS (No Waste)
Trial Box L = 5 W = 4.5 H = 2
Trial Box contains 30 candies and a carton contains 216 candy boxes.
Trial Box L = 5 W = 4.5 H = 2
Trial Box contains 30 candies and a carton contains 216 candy boxes.
Trial Box L = 6 W = 3 H = 2.5
Trial Box contains 30 candies and a carton contains 216 candy boxes.
Trial Box L = 6 W = 4.5 H = 2
Trial Box contains 36 candies and a carton contains 180 candy boxes.
Trial Box L = 6 W = 4.5 H = 2.5
Trial Box contains 45 candies and a carton contains 144 candy boxes.
Trial Box L = 6 W = 5 H = 1.5
Trial Box contains 30 candies and a carton contains 216 candy boxes.
Trial Box L = 6 W = 5 H = 2
Trial Box contains 40 candies and a carton contains 162 candy boxes.
Trial Box L = 6 W = 5 H = 2.5
Trial Box contains 50 candies and a carton contains 129 candy boxes.
Trial Box L = 7.5 W = 3 H = 2
Trial Box contains 30 candies and a carton contains 216 candy boxes.
```

You have a duplicate solution because you evaluate boxes in the nested loop that have a length of 5 and a width of 4.5, and boxes that have a length of 4.5 and a width of 5. Because the CBox constructor ensures that the length is not less than the width, these are identical. You could include additional logic to avoid presenting duplicates, but it hardly seems worth the effort. You could treat it as an exercise if you like.

ORGANIZING YOUR PROGRAM CODE

In example Ex8_13, you distributed the code among several files for the first time. This is common practice with C++ applications generally and with Windows programming it is essential. The sheer volume of code involved in even the simplest Windows program necessitates dividing it into workable chunks.

As I discussed in the previous section, there are basically two kinds of source code files in a C++ program, .h files and .cpp files. This is illustrated in Figure 8-10.

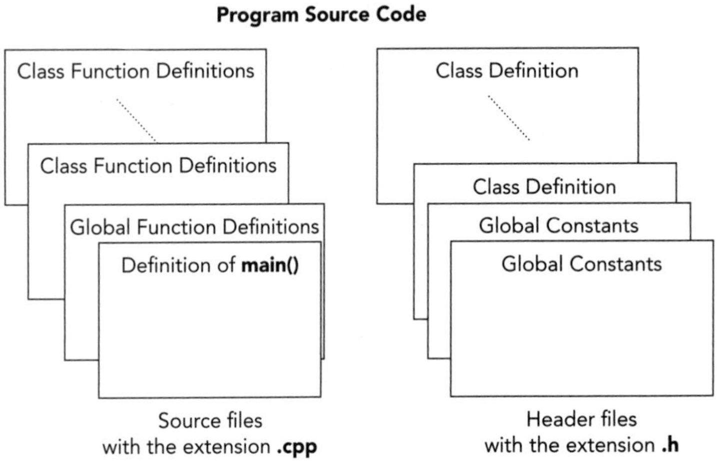

Program Source Code

FIGURE 8-10

From time to time, you might want to use code from existing files in a new project. In this case, you can add the files to the project, either by using the Project ➪ Add Existing Item menu option, or by right-clicking Source Files or Header Files in the Solution Explorer tab and selecting Add ➪ Existing Item from the context menu. You don't need to add .h files to your project, although you can if you want them shown in the Solution Explorer pane immediately. The code from .h files will be added at the beginning of the .cpp files that require them as a result of the #include directives that you specify. You need #include directives for header files containing standard library functions and other standard definitions, as well as for your own header files. Visual C++ automatically keeps track of all these files, and enables you to view them in the Solution Explorer tab. As you saw in the previous example, you can also view class definitions and global constants and variables in the Class View tab.

In a Windows program, there are other kinds of definitions for the specification of such things as menus and toolbar buttons. These are stored in files with extensions like .rc and .ico. These are created and tracked automatically by Visual C++.

Naming Program Files

As I have said, for classes of any complexity, it's usual to store the class definition in an .h file with a filename based on the class name, and to store the implementation of function members that are defined outside the class in a .cpp file with the same name. On this basis, the definition of our CBox class appeared in a file with the name Box.h. Similarly, the class implementation was stored in Box .cpp. We didn't follow this convention in the earlier examples because they were very short, and it was easier to reference the examples with names derived from the chapter number and the sequence number of the example within the chapter. With programs of any size though, it becomes essential to structure the code this way, so it would be a good idea to get into the habit of creating .h and .cpp files from now on.

Segmenting a program into .h and .cpp files is a very convenient approach, as it makes it easy to find the definition or implementation of any class, particularly if you're working in a development environment that doesn't have all the tools that Visual C++ provides. As long as you know the class name, you can go directly to the file you want. This isn't a rigid rule though. It's sometimes useful to group the definitions of a set of closely related classes together in a single file and assemble their implementations similarly. However you choose to structure your files, Class View still displays all the classes, as well as the members of each class. Double-clicking any of the entries in the Class View tree will take you directly to the relevant source code.

LIBRARY CLASSES FOR STRINGS

As I said in Chapter 4, the `string` header defines the `std::string` and `std::wstring` classes that represent character strings. They are both instances of the `std::basic_string<T>` class template. The `string` class is defined as `basic_string<char>`, and `wstring` is defined as `basic_string<wchar_t>`, so `string` objects are strings of characters of type `char`, and `wstring` represents strings of characters of type `wchar_t`.

These string types are much easier to use than null-terminated strings and bring with them a whole range of powerful functions. Because `string` and `wstring` are both instances of the `basic_string<T>` template, they provide the same functionality, so I'll only discuss their features and use in the context of the `string` type. The `wstring` type works in the same way, except that the strings contain Unicode UTF-16 character codes and you must use the `L` prefix for string literals. Subsequent code fragments assume that there is a `using` declaration for `std::string`.

Creating String Objects

Creating `string` objects is easy but you have a lot of choices as to how. First, you can create and initialize a `string` object like this:

```
string sentence {"This sentence is false."};
```

The `sentence` object is initialized with the literal that appears in the initializer list. A `string` object has no terminating null character, so the string length is the number of characters in the string, 23 in this instance. You can obtain the length of the string encapsulated by a `string` object by calling its `length()` member function. For example:

```
cout << "The string is of length " << sentence.length() << endl;
```

Executing the statement produces the output:

```
The string is of length 23
```

Incidentally, you can output a `string` object to `cout` in the same way as any other variable:

```
cout << sentence << endl;
```

This displays the `sentence` string on a line by itself. You can also read a string into a `string` object like this:

```
cin >> sentence;
```

Reading from `cin` in this way ignores leading whitespace until a non-whitespace character is found, and input ends when you enter a space after one or more non-whitespace characters. You will often want to read text into a `string` object that includes spaces and may span several lines. In this case, the `getline()` function template that is defined in the `string` header file is much more convenient. For example:

```
getline(cin, sentence, '*');
```

This template function is specifically for reading data from a stream into a `string` or `wstring` object. The first argument is the stream that is the source of input, which doesn't have to be `cin`; the second argument is the object that is to receive the input; and the third argument is the character that terminates input. Here, the terminating character is `'*'`, so this statement reads a string including any characters that are not `*` into `sentence` from `cin`. Input ends when an asterisk is read from the stream.

If you don't specify an initial string literal when you create a `string` object, the object will contain an empty string:

```
string astring;                    // Create an empty string
```

Calling `length()` for `astring` will return zero.

Another possibility is to initialize a `string` object with a single character repeated a number of times:

```
string bees(7, 'b');               // String is "bbbbbbb"
```

The first argument to the constructor is the number of repetitions of the character specified by the second argument. Note that you can't use uniform initialization here because of the rules for constructor selection with a constructor initialization list.

Finally, you can initialize a `string` object with all or part of another `string` object:

```
string letters {bees};
```

The `letters` object will be initialized with the string from `bees`.

To select part of a `string` object as initializer, you call the string constructor with three arguments; the first is the `string` object that is the source of the initializing string, the second is the index position of the first character to be selected, and the third argument is the number of characters to be selected. Here's an example:

```
string sentence {"This sentence is false."};
string part {sentence, 5, 11};
```

The `part` object will be initialized with 11 characters from `sentence` beginning with the sixth character (the first character is at index position 0). Thus, `part` will contain `"sentence is"`.

Of course, you can create arrays of `string` objects and initialize them using the usual notation. For example:

```
string animals[] { "dog", "cat", "horse", "donkey", "lion"};
```

This creates an array of five `string` objects initialized with the string literals between the braces.

Concatenating Strings

Perhaps the most common operation with strings is joining two strings to form a single string. You can use the + operator to join string objects or a `string` object with a string literal. Here are some examples:

```
string sentence1 {"This sentence is false."};
string sentence2 {"Therefore the sentence above must be true!"};
string combined;                     // Create an empty string
sentence1 = sentence1 + "\n";        // Append string containing newline
combined = sentence1 + sentence2;    // Join two strings
cout << combined << endl;            // Output the result
```

The first three statements create `string` objects. The next statement appends "\n" to `sentence1` and stores the result in `sentence1`. The next statement joins `sentence1` and `sentence2` and stores the result in `combined`. The last statement outputs `combined`. Executing these statements will result in the following output:

```
This sentence is false.
Therefore the sentence above must be true!
```

String concatenation using the + operator is possible because the `string` class implements `operator+()`. This implies that one of the operands must be a `string` object, so you can't use the + operator to join two string literals. Keep in mind that each time you use the + operator, you are creating a new `string` object, which involves a certain amount of overhead. However, the string class does use move semantics where possible.

You can use the + operator to join a character to a `string` object, so you could have written the fourth statement in the previous code fragment as:

```
sentence1 = sentence1 + '\n';        // Append newline character to string
```

The `string` class implements `operator+=()` such that the right operand can be a string literal, a `string` object, or a single character. You could write the previous statement as,

```
sentence1 += '\n';
```

or:

```
sentence1 += "\n";
```

There is a difference between using the += operator and using the + operator. As I said, the + operator creates a new `string` object containing the combined string. The += operator appends the string or character that is the right operand to the `string` object that is the left operand, so the `string` object is modified directly and no new object is created.

Let's exercise some of what I have described in an example.

TRY IT OUT Creating and Joining Strings

This is a simple example that reads names and ages from the keyboard and then lists what you entered. Here's the code:

```cpp
// Ex8_14.cpp
// Creating and joining string objects
#include <iostream>
#include <string>
using std::cout;
using std::endl;
using std::string;

// List names and ages
void listnames(string names[], string ages[], size_t count)
{
  cout << "The names you entered are: " << endl;
  for(size_t i {}; i < count && !names[i].empty(); ++i)
    cout << names[i] + " aged " + ages[i] + '.' << endl;
}

int main()
{
  const size_t count {100};
  string names[count];
  string ages[count];
  string firstname;
  string secondname;

  for(size_t i {}; i<count; ++i)
  {
    cout << "Enter a first name or press Enter to end: ";
    std::getline(cin, firstname, '\n');
    if(firstname.empty())
    {
      listnames(names, ages, i);
      cout << "Done!!" << endl;
      return 0;
    }

    cout << "Enter a second name: ";
    std::getline(std::cin, secondname, '\n');

    names[i] = firstname + ' ' + secondname;
    cout << "Enter " + firstname + "'s age: ";
    std::getline(std::cin, ages[i], '\n');
  }
  cout << "No space for more names." << endl;
  listnames(names, ages, count);
  return 0;
}
```

ages would usually be an array of integers but I made it an array of strings here just to use more strings. The example produces output similar to the following:

```
Enter a first name or press Enter to end: Marilyn
Enter a second name: Munroe
Enter Marilyn's age: 26

Enter a first name or press Enter to end: Tom
Enter a second name: Crews
Enter Tom's age: 45

Enter a first name or press Enter to end: Arnold
Enter a second name: Weisseneggar
Enter Arnold's age: 52

Enter a first name or press Enter to end:

The names you entered are:
Marilyn Munroe aged 26.
Tom Crews aged 45.
Arnold Weisseneggar aged 52.
Done!!
```

How It Works

The `listnames` function lists names and ages stored in arrays that are passed as the first two arguments. The third argument is a count of the number of elements in the arrays. Listing of the data occurs in a loop:

```
for(size_t i {}; i < count && !names[i].empty(); ++i)
  cout << names[i] + " aged " + ages[i] + '.' << endl;
```

The loop condition is a belt-and-braces control mechanism in that it not only checks that the index `i` is less than `count` that is passed as the third argument, but it also calls `empty()` for the current element to verify that it is not an empty string. The single statement in the body of the loop concatenates the current string in `names[i]` with the literal `" aged "`, the `ages[i]` string, and the character `'.'`, and it writes the resultant string to `cout`. The expression concatenating the strings is equivalent to:

```
((names[i].operator+(" aged ")).operator+(ages[i])).operator+('.')
```

Each call of the `operator+()` function returns a new `string` object. Thus, the expression demonstrates combining a `string` object with a string literal, a `string` object with another `string` object, and a `string` object with a character literal.

Although the preceding code demonstrates the `string::operator+()` function, for performance reasons, it would be better to use the following:

```
cout << names[i] << " aged " << ages[i] << '.' << endl;
```

This avoids the calls to the operator function and the creation of the `string` objects that result from that.

In `main()`, you create two arrays that can store `count` objects of type `string`:

```
const size_t count {100};
string names[count];
string ages[count];
```

The `names` and `ages` arrays store names and corresponding age values that are entered from the keyboard.

Within the `for` loop in `main()`, you read the first and second names separately using the `getline()` function template:

```
cout << "Enter a first name or press Enter to end: ";
std::getline(std::cin, firstname, '\n');
if(firstname.empty())
{
  listnames(names, ages, i);
  cout << "Done!!" << endl;
  return 0;
}

cout << "Enter a second name: ";
std::getline(std::cin, secondname, '\n');
```

The `getline()` function allows an empty string to be read, something you cannot do using the `>>` operator. The first argument to `getline()` is the stream that is the source of the input, the second argument is the destination for the input, and the third argument is the character that signals the end of the input. If you omit the third argument, the default is `'\n'`, so you could omit it here. You use the ability to read an empty string here because you test for an empty string in `firstname` by calling its `empty()` function. An empty string signals the end of input, so you call `listnames()` to output the data, and you end the program.

When `firstname` is not empty, you continue to read the second name into `secondname`, again using the `getline()` function template. You concatenate `firstname` and `secondname` using the `+` operator and store the result in `names[i]`, the currently unused element in the `names` array.

Finally in the loop, you read a string for the age of the person and store the result in `ages[i]`. The `for` loop limits the number of entries to `count`, which corresponds to the number of elements in the arrays. If you fall through the end of the loop, the arrays are full, so after displaying a message, you output the data that was entered.

Accessing and Modifying Strings

You can access any character in a `string` object to read it or overwrite it using the subscript operator, `[]`. Here's an example:

```
string sentence {"Too many cooks spoil the broth."};
for(size_t i {}; i < sentence.length(); i++)
{
  if(' ' == sentence[i])
    sentence[i] = '*';
}
```

This inspects each character in the `sentence` string in turn to see if it is a space, and if it is, replaces the character with an asterisk.

You can use the `at()` member function to achieve the same result:

```
string sentence {"Too many cooks spoil the broth."};
for(size_t i {}; i < sentence.length(); i++)
{
  if(' ' == sentence.at(i))
    sentence.at(i) = '*';
}
```

This does exactly the same as the previous fragment, so what's the difference between them? Well, subscripting is faster than using at () but the downside is that the validity of the index is not checked. If the index is out of range, the result of using the subscript operator is undefined. The at () function is a bit slower but it does check the index and if it is not valid, the function will throw an std::out_ of_range exception. You would use the at () function when there is the possibility of the index value being out of range, and in this situation you should put the code in a try block and handle the exception appropriately. If you are sure index out of range conditions cannot arise, then use the [] operator.

You can use the range-based for loop with a string object to iterate over all of the characters in the string:

```
string sentence {"Too many cooks spoil the broth."};
for(auto& ch : sentence)
{
  if(' ' == ch)
    ch = '*';
}
```

This replaces spaces with asterisks like the loop you saw earlier. This is much simpler. Using a reference type for ch enables you to change the string.

You can extract part of an existing object as a new string object. For example:

```
string sentence {"Too many cooks spoil the broth."};
string substring {sentence.substr(4, 10)};          // Extracts "many cooks"
```

The first argument to substr() is the first character of the substring to be extracted, and the second argument is the count of the number of characters in the substring.

By using the append() function for a string object, you can add one or more characters to the end of the string. This function comes in several versions. You can append one or more of a given character or a string literal or a string object to the object for which the function is called. For example:

```
string phrase {"The higher"};
string word {"fewer"};
phrase.append(1, ' ');          // Append one space
phrase.append("the ");          // Append a string literal
phrase.append(word);            // Append a string object
phrase.append(2, '!');          // Append two exclamation marks
```

After executing this sequence, phrase will contain "The higher the fewer!!". With the version of append() with two arguments, the first argument is the count of the number of times the character specified by the second argument is to be appended. When you call append(), the function returns a reference to the object for which it was called, so you could write the preceding four append() calls in a single statement:

```
phrase.append(1, ' ').append("the ").append(word).append(2, '!');
```

You can also use append() to append part of a string literal or part of a string object to an existing string:

```
string phrase {"The more the merrier."};
string query {"Any"};
query.append(phrase, 3, 5).append(1, '?');
```

After these statements `query` will contain `"Any more?"`. In the last statement, the first call to the `append()` function has three arguments:

➤ The first argument, `phrase`, is the `string` object from which characters are to be extracted and appended to `query`.

➤ The second argument, 3, is the index position of the first character to be extracted.

➤ The third argument, 5, is the count of the total number of characters to be appended.

Thus, the substring `" more"` is appended to `query` by this call. The second call for the `append()` function appends a question mark to `query`.

You could use the `push_back()` function as an alternative to `append()` when you want to append a single character, like this:

```
query.push_back('*');
```

This appends an asterisk to the end of the `query` string.

Sometimes, adding characters to the end of a string just isn't enough. There are occasions when you want to insert one or more characters into the interior of a string. Versions of the `insert()` function will do that for you:

```
string saying {"A horse"};
string word {"blind"};
string sentence {"He is as good as gold."};
string phrase {"a wink too far"};
saying.insert(1, " ");                  // Insert a space character
saying.insert(2, word);                 // Insert a string object
saying.insert(2, "nodding", 3);         // Insert 3 characters of a string literal
saying.insert(5, sentence, 2, 15);      // Insert part of a string at position 5
saying.insert(20, phrase, 0, 9);        // Insert part of a string at position 20
saying.insert(29, " ").insert(30, "a poor do", 0, 2);
```

I'm sure you'll be interested to know that after executing these statements, `saying` will contain the string `"A nod is as good as a wink to a blind horse"`. The parameters to the various versions of `insert()` are:

FUNCTION PROTOTYPE	DESCRIPTION

`string& insert(`
`  size_t index,`
`  const char* pstring)`
	Inserts the null-terminated string `pstring` at position index.

`string& insert(`
`  size_t index,`
`  const string& astring)`
	Inserts the `string` object `astring` at position index.

`string& insert(`
`  size_t index,`
`  const char* pstring,`
`  size_t count)`
	Inserts the first count characters from the null-terminated string `pstring` at position index.

FUNCTION PROTOTYPE	DESCRIPTION

`string& insert(`
  `size_t index,`
  `size_t count,`
  `char ch)`
	Inserts `count` copies of the character `ch` at position `index`.

`string& insert(`
  `size_t index,`
  `const string& astring,`
  `size_t start,`
  `size_t count)`
	Inserts `count` characters from the `string` object `astring`, beginning with the character at position `start`; the substring is inserted at position `index`.

These versions of `insert()` return a reference to the `string` object for which the function is called. This allows you to chain calls together, as in the last statement in the previous code fragment.

This is not the complete set of `insert()` functions, but you can do everything you need with those in the table. The other versions use *iterators* as arguments, and you'll learn about iterators in Chapter 10.

You can interchange the strings encapsulated by two `string` objects by calling the `swap()` member function. For example:

```
string phrase {"The more the merrier."};
string query {"Any"};
query.swap(phrase);
```

This results in `query` containing `"The more the merrier."` and `phrase` containing `"Any"`. Of course, executing `phrase.swap(query)` would have the same effect.

You can obtain the string in `string` object as a null-terminated string by calling its `c_str()` member. For example:

```
string phrase {"The higher the fewer"};
const char *pstring {phrase.c_str()};
```

The `c_str()` function returns a pointer to a null-terminated string with the same contents as the `string` object.

You can obtain the contents of a `string` object as an array of `char` elements by calling its `data()` member. Note that the array contains just the characters from the `string` object, without a terminating null.

You can replace part of a `string` object by calling its `replace()` function. This comes in several versions, as the table shows.

FUNCTION PROTOTYPE	DESCRIPTION

`string& replace(`
  `size_t index,`
  `size_t count,`
  `const char* pstring)`
	Replaces `count` characters, starting at position `index`, with the first `count` characters from `pstring`.

continues

(continued)

FUNCTION PROTOTYPE	DESCRIPTION

string& replace(
 	
  size_t index,
 	
  size_t count,
 	
  const string& astring)
	Replaces count characters, starting at position index, with the first count characters from astring.

string& replace(
 	
  size_t index,
 	
  size_t count1,
 	
  const char* pstring,
 	
  size_t count2)
	Replaces count1 characters, starting at position index, with up to count2 characters from pstring. This allows the replacement substring to be longer or shorter than the substring that is replaced.

string& replace(
 	
  size_t index1,
 	
  size_t count1,
 	
  const string& astring,
 	
  size_t index2,
 	
  size_t count2)
	Replaces count1 characters, starting at position index1, with count2 characters from astring, starting at position index2.

string& replace(
 	
  size_t index,
 	
  size_t count1,
 	
  size_t count2,
 	
  char ch)
	Replaces count1 characters, starting at index, with count2 occurrences of the character ch.

In each case, a reference to the string object for which the function is called is returned.

Here's an example:

```
string proverb {"A nod is as good as a wink to a blind horse"};
string sentence {"It's bath time!"};
proverb.replace(38, 5, sentence, 5, 3);
```

This uses the fourth version of replace() from the preceding table to substitute "bat" in place of "horse" in the string proverb.

Comparing Strings

You have a full complement of operators for comparing string objects or comparing a string object with a literal. Operator overloading has been implemented in the string class for the following operators:

```
==    !=    <    <=    >    >=
```

Here's an example of the use of these:

```
string dog1 {"St Bernard"};
string dog2 {"Tibetan Mastiff"};
if(dog1 < dog2)
  cout << dog1 << " comes first!" << endl;
else if(dog1 > dog2)
  cout << dog2 << " comes first!" << endl;
else
  cout << dog1 << " is equal to " << dog2 << "." << endl;
```

When you compare strings, corresponding characters are compared until either a pair of characters is found that differ, or the end of one or both strings is reached. When two corresponding characters differ, the character code values determine which string is less than the other. If no character pairs are different, the string with fewer characters is less than the other string. Two strings are equal if they contain the same number of characters and corresponding characters are identical.

TRY IT OUT Comparing Strings

This example illustrates the use of the comparison operators by implementing an extremely inefficient sorting method. Here's the code:

```
// Ex8_15.cpp
// Comparing and sorting words
#include <iostream>
#include <iomanip>
#include <string>
using std::cout;
using std::endl;
using std::string;

string* sort(string* strings, size_t count)
{
  bool swapped {false};
  while(true)
  {
    for(size_t i {}; i < count-1; i++)
    {
      if(strings[i] > strings[i+1])
      {
        swapped = true;
        strings[i].swap(strings[i+1]);
      }
    }
    if(!swapped)
      break;
    swapped = false;
  }
  return strings;
}

int main()
```

```
{
  const size_t maxstrings {100};
  string strings[maxstrings];
  size_t nstrings {};
  size_t maxwidth {};

  // Read up to 100 words into the strings array
  while(nstrings < maxstrings)
  {
    cout << "Enter a word or press Enter to end: ";
    std::getline(std::cin, strings[nstrings]);
    if(maxwidth < strings[nstrings].length())
      maxwidth = strings[nstrings].length();
    if(strings[nstrings].empty())
      break;
    ++nstrings;
  }

  // Sort the input in ascending sequence
  sort(strings,nstrings);
  cout << endl
       << "In ascending sequence, the words you entered are:"
       << endl
       << std::setiosflags(std::ios::left);       // Left-justify the output
  for(size_t i {}; i < nstrings; i++)
  {
    if(i % 5 == 0)
      cout << endl;
    cout << std::setw(maxwidth+2) << strings[i];
  }
  cout << endl;
  return 0;
}
```

Here's some typical output from this example:

```
Enter a word or press Enter to end: loquacious
Enter a word or press Enter to end: transmogrify
Enter a word or press Enter to end: abstemious
Enter a word or press Enter to end: facetious
Enter a word or press Enter to end: xylophone
Enter a word or press Enter to end: megaphone
Enter a word or press Enter to end: chauvinist
Enter a word or press Enter to end:

In ascending sequence, the words you entered are:

abstemious    chauvinist    facetious    loquacious    megaphone
transmogrify  xylophone
```

How It Works

The most interesting part is the `sort()` function that accepts two arguments, the address of a `string` array and the number of array elements. The function implements the bubble sort, which works by scanning through the array and comparing successive elements. All the work is done in the `while` loop:

```
bool swapped {false};
while(true)
{
  for(size_t i {}; i < count-1; i++)
  {
    if(strings[i] > strings[i+1])
    {
      swapped = true;
      strings[i].swap(strings[i+1]);
    }
  }
  if(!swapped)
    break;
  swapped = false;
}
```

Successive elements in the `strings` array are compared using the `>` operator. If any element is greater than its successor, the elements are swapped. Elements are interchanged by calling the `swap()` function for one `string` object with the second `string` object as argument. Comparing successive elements and swapping when necessary continues for the entire array. This process is repeated until there is a pass through all the elements where no elements are swapped. The elements are then in ascending sequence. `swapped` acts as an indicator for whether swapping occurreded on any pass. It is only set to `true` when two elements are swapped.

The `main()` function reads up to 100 words into the `strings` array in a loop:

```
while(nstrings < maxstrings)
{
  cout << "Enter a word or press Enter to end: ";
  std::getline(std::cin, strings[nstrings]);
  if(maxwidth < strings[nstrings].length())
    maxwidth = strings[nstrings].length();
  if(strings[nstrings].empty())
    break;
  ++nstrings;
}
```

`getline()` reads characters from `cin` until `'\n'` is read. The input is stored in the `string` object specified by the second argument, `strings[nstrings]`. Just pressing the Enter key will result in an `empty()` string, so the loop is terminated when calling `empty()` for a `string` object returns `true`. The `maxwidth` variable is used to record the length of the longest string entered. This is used in the output process after the input has been sorted.

Calling the `sort()` function sorts the contents of the `strings` array in ascending sequence. The result is output in a loop:

```
cout << endl
     << "In ascending sequence, the words you entered are:"
```

```
        << endl
        << std::setiosflags(ios::left);              // Left-justify the output
    for(size_t i {}; i < nstrings; i++)
    {
      if(i % 5 == 0)
        cout << endl;
      cout << std::setw(maxwidth+2) << strings[i];
    }
```

This outputs each element in a field of maxwidth+2 characters. Each word is left-justified in the field because of the call to the setiosflags() manipulator with the argument ios::left. Unlike setw(), the setiosflags() manipulator remains in effect until you reset it.

Searching Strings

You have four versions of the find() function that search a string object for a given character or substring, and they are described in the following table. All the find() functions are const.

FUNCTION PROTOTYPE	DESCRIPTION

size_t find(
 	
    char ch,
 	
    size_t offset=0)
	Searches a string object for ch, starting at index position offset. You can omit the second argument, in which case, the default value is 0.

size_t find(
 	
    const char* pstr,
 	
    size_t offset=0)
	Searches a string object for the null-terminated string pstr, starting at index position offset. You can omit the second argument, in which case, the default value is 0.

size_t find(
 	
    const char* pstr,
 	
    size_t offset,
 	
    size_t count)
	Searches a string object for the first count characters of the null-terminated string pstr, starting at index position offset.

size_t find(
 	
    const string& str,
 	
    size_t offset=0)
	Searches a string object for the string object str, starting at index position offset. You can omit the second argument, in which case, the default value is 0.

In each case, find() returns the index position where the character or first character of the substring was found, and returns string::npos if the item was not found. This is a constant defined in the string class that represents an illegal position in a string object; it is used generally to signal a search failure.

Here's a fragment showing some of the ways you might use find():

```
string phrase {"So near and yet so far"};
string str {"So near"};
```

```
cout << phrase.find(str) << endl;          // Outputs 0
cout << phrase.find("so far") << endl;     // Outputs 16
cout << phrase.find("so near") << endl;    // Outputs string::npos = 4294967295
```

The value of `string::npos` can vary with different compiler implementations, so you should always use `string::npos` to test for it, not the explicit value.

Here's another example that scans a string repeatedly, searching for occurrences of a particular substring:

```
string str {"Smith, where Jones had had \"had had\", \"had had\" had."
            " \"Had had\" had had the examiners' approval."};
string substr {"had"};

cout << "The string to be searched is:" << endl << str << endl;
size_t offset {};
size_t count {};
size_t increment {substr.length()};

while(true)
{
  offset = str.find(substr, offset);
  if(string::npos == offset)
    break;
  offset += increment;
  ++count;
}
cout << " The string \"" << substr
     << "\" was found " << count << " times in the string above."
     << endl;
```

This searches `str` to see how many times `"had"` appears. The search is done in the `while` loop, where `offset` records the position found, and is used as the start position for each search. The search starts at index position 0, the start of the string, and each time the substring is found, the starting position for the next search is set to the found position plus the length of the substring. This bypasses the substring that was found. Each time the substring is found, `count` is incremented. If `find()` returns `string::npos`, then the substring was not found and the search ends. Executing this fragment produces the output:

```
The string to be searched is:
Smith, where Jones had had "had had", "had had" had. "Had had" had had the
examiners' approval.
The string "had" was found 10 times in the string above.
```

`"Had"` is not a match for `"had"`, so 10 is the correct result.

The `find_first_of()` and `find_last_of()` member functions search a `string` object for any character from a given set. You could search a string to find spaces or punctuation characters, for example, to break a string into individual words. Both functions come in several flavors, as the following table shows. All functions in the table are `const` and return a value of type `size_t`.

FUNCTION PROTOTYPE	DESCRIPTION

`find_first_of(`
`  char ch,`
`  size_t offset=0)`
	Searches a `string` object for the first occurrence of the character, `ch`, starting at position `offset`, and returns the index position where the character is found as a value of type `size_t`. If you omit the second argument, the default value of `offset` is 0.

`find_first_of(`
`  const char* pstr,`
`  size_t offset=0)`
	Searches a `string` object for the first occurrence of any character in the null-terminated string, `pstr`, starting at position `offset`, and returns the index position where the character is found as a value of type `size_t`. If you omit the second argument, the default value of `offset` is 0.

`find_first_of(`
`  const char* pstr,`
`  size_t offset,`
`  size_t count)`
	Searches a `string` object for the first occurrence of any character in the first `count` characters of the null-terminated string, `pstr`, starting at position `offset`, and returns the index position where the character is found as a value of type `size_t`.

`find_first_of(`
`  const string& str,`
`  size_t offset=0)`
	Searches a `string` object for the first occurrence of any character in the string, `str`, starting at position `offset`, and returns the index position where the character is found as a value of type `size_t`. If you omit the second argument, the default value of `offset` is 0.

`find_last_of(`
`  char ch,`
`  size_t offset=npos)`
	Searches backward through a `string` object for the last occurrence of the character, `ch`, starting at position `offset`, and returns the index position where the character is found as a value of type `size_t`. If you omit the second argument, the default value of `offset` is npos, which is the end of the string.

`find_last_of(`
`  const char* pstr,`
`  size_t offset=npos)`
	Searches backward through a `string` object for the last occurrence of any character in the null-terminated string, `pstr`, starting at position `offset`, and returns the index position where the character is found as a value of type `size_t`. If you omit the second argument, the default value of `offset` is npos, which is the end of the string.

`find_last_of(`
`  const char* pstr,`
`  size_t offset,`
`  size_t count)`
	Searches backward through a `string` object for the last occurrence of any of the first `count` characters in the null-terminated string, `pstr`, starting at position `offset`, and returns the index position where the character is found as a value of type `size_t`.

`find_last_of(`
`  const string& str,`
`  size_t offset=npos)`
	Searches backward through a `string` object for the last occurrence of any character in the string, `str`, starting at position `offset`, and returns the index position where the character is found as a value of type `size_t`. If you omit the second argument, the default value of `offset` is npos, which is the end of the string.

All versions of `find_first_of()` and `find_last_of()` return `string::npos` if no matching character is found. With the same string as the previous fragment, you could see what the `find_last_of()` function does with the same search string, `"had"`.

```
string str {"Smith, where Jones had had \"had had\", \"had had\" had."
            " \"Had had\" had had the examiners' approval."};
string substr {"had"};

cout << "The string to be searched is:" << endl << str << endl;
size_t count {};
size_t offset {string::npos};
while(true)
{
  offset = str.find_last_of(substr, offset);
  if(string::npos == offset)
    break;
  --offset;
  ++count;
}
cout << " Characters from the string \"" << substr << "\" were found "
     << count << " times in the string above." << endl;
```

The default starting position is `string::npos`, the end of the string, because you will search the string backward. The output from this fragment is:

```
The string to be searched is:
Smith, where Jones had had "had had", "had had" had. "Had had" had had
the examiners' approval.
Characters from the string "had" were found 38 times in the string above.
```

The result should not be a surprise. You are searching for occurrences of *any* of the characters in `"had"` in the string `str`. There are 32 in the `"Had"` and `"had"` words, and 6 in the remaining words. Because you are searching backward, you decrement `offset` when you find a character.

The last set of search facilities are versions of the `find_first_not_of()` and `find_last_not_of()` functions. All of the functions in the following table are `const` and return a `size_t` value.

FUNCTION PROTOTYPE	DESCRIPTION
`find_first_not_of(` `char ch,` `size_t offset=0)`	Searches for the first occurrence of a character that is not `ch`, starting at position `offset`. The function returns the index position where the character is found as type `size_t`. If you omit the second argument, the default value of `offset` is 0.
`find_first_not_of(` `const char* pstr,` `size_t offset=0)`	Searches for the first occurrence of a character that is not in `pstr`, starting at `offset`, and returns the index where the character is found as type `size_t`. If you omit the second argument, the default value of `offset` is 0.
`find_first_not_of(` `const char* pstr,` `size_t offset,` `size_t count)`	Searches for the first occurrence of a character that is not in the first `count` characters of `pstr`, starting at `offset`. The function returns the index position where the character is found as type `size_t`.

continues

(continued)

FUNCTION PROTOTYPE	DESCRIPTION

`find_first_not_of(`
 	
`const string& str,`
 	
`size_t offset=0)`
	Searches for the first occurrence of any character that is not in `str`, starting at `offset`. The function returns the index where the character is found as type `size_t`. If you omit the second argument, the default value of `offset` is 0.

`find_last_not_of(`
 	
`char ch,`
 	
`size_t offset=npos)`
	Searches backward for the last occurrence of a character that is not `ch` starting at `offset`. The index where the character is found is returned as type `size_t`. If you omit the second argument, the default value of `offset` is `npos`, which is the end of the string.

`find_last_not_of(`
 	
`const char* pstr,`
 	
`size_t offset=npos)`
	Searches backward for the last occurrence of any character that is not in `pstr`, starting at `offset`. The index where a character is found is returned as type `size_t`. If you omit the second argument, the default value of `offset` is `npos`.

`find_last_not_of(`
 	
`const char* pstr,`
 	
`size_t offset,`
 	
`size_t count)`
	Searches backward for the last occurrence of a character that is not in the first `count` characters in `pstr` starting at `offset`. The function returns the index where a character is found as type `size_t`.

`find_last_not_of(`
 	
`const string& str,`
 	
`size_t offset=npos)`
	Searches backward for the last occurrence of any character not in `str` starting at `offset`. The function returns the index where a character is found as type `size_t`. If you omit the second argument, the default value of `offset` is `npos`.

As with previous search functions, `string::npos` is returned if the search does not find a character. These functions have many uses, typically finding tokens in a string that may be separated by characters of various kinds. For example, you could use these functions to find the words in a block of text that are separated by spaces or punctuation characters. Let's see that working in an example.

TRY IT OUT Sorting Words from Text

This example reads a block of text, and then extracts the words and outputs them in ascending sequence. I'll use the somewhat inefficient bubble sort function that you saw in `Ex8_14` here. In Chapter 10, you will use a library function for sorting that would be much better, but you need to learn about some other stuff before you can use that. The program will also figure out how many times each word occurs and output the count for each word. Such an analysis is called a *collocation*. Here's the code:

```cpp
// Ex8_16.cpp
// Extracting words from text
#include <iostream>
#include <iomanip>
#include <string>
using std::cout;
using std::endl;
using std::string;
```

```cpp
// Sort an array of string objects
string* sort(string* strings, size_t count)
{
  bool swapped {false};
  while(true)
  {
    for(size_t i {}; i < count-1; i++)
    {
      if(strings[i] > strings[i+1])
      {
        swapped = true;
        strings[i].swap(strings[i+1]);
      }
    }
    if(!swapped)
      break;
    swapped = false;
  }
  return strings;
}

int main()
{
  const size_t maxwords {100};
  string words[maxwords];
  string text;
  string separators {" \".,:;!?()\n"};
  size_t nwords {};
  size_t maxwidth {};

  cout << "Enter some text on as many lines as you wish."
    << endl << "Terminate the input with an asterisk:" << endl;

  std::getline(std::cin, text, '*');

  size_t start {}, end {}, offset {};   // Record start & end of word & offset
  while(true)
  {
    // Find first character of a word
    start = text.find_first_not_of(separators, offset);  // Find non-separator
    if(string::npos == start)              // If we did not find it, we are done
      break;
    offset = start + 1;                    // Move past character found


    // Find first separator past end of current word
    end = text.find_first_of(separators,offset);         // Find separator
    if(string::npos == end)                // If it's the end of the string
    {                                      // current word is last in string
      offset = end;                        // We use offset to end loop later
      end = text.length();                 // Set end as 1 past last character
    }
    else
      offset = end + 1;                    // Move past character found
```

```
      words[nwords] = text.substr(start, end-start);        // Extract the word

    // Keep track of longest word
    if(maxwidth < words[nwords].length())
      maxwidth = words[nwords].length();
    if(++nwords == maxwidths)                // Check for array full
    {
      cout << "Maximum number of words reached."
           << " Processing what we have." << endl;
      break;
    }

    if(string::npos == offset)               // If we reached the end of the string
      break;                                 // We are done
  }

  sort(words, nwords);

  cout << endl << "In ascending sequence, the words in the text are:" << endl;

  size_t count {1};                          // Count of duplicate words
  char initial {words[0][0]};                // First word character

  // Output words and number of occurrences
  for(size_t i {}; i<nwords; i++)
  {
    if(i < nwords-1 && words[i] == words[i+1])
    {
      ++count;
      continue;
    }

    if (initial != words[i][0])
    {                                        // New first character...
      initial = words[i][0];                 // ...so save it...
      cout << endl;                          // ...and start a new line
    }

    cout << std::setiosflags(std::ios::left)     // Output word left-justified
         << std::setw(maxwidth+2) << words[i];
    cout << std::resetiosflags(std::ios::right)  // and word count right-justified
         << std::setw(5) << count;
    count = 1;
  }
  cout << endl;
  return 0;
}
```

Here's an example of output from this program:

```
Enter some text on as many lines as you wish.
Terminate the input with an asterisk:
I sometimes think I'd rather crow
And be a rooster than to roost
And be a crow. But I dunno.
```

```
A rooster he can roost also,
Which don't seem fair when crows can't crow
Which may help some. Still I dunno.*

In ascending sequence, the words in the text are:
A         1    And      2
But       1
I         3    I'd      1
Still     1
Which     2
a         2    also     1
be        2
can       1    can't    1    crow      3    crows    1
don't     1    dunno    2
fair      1
he        1    help     1
may       1
rather    1    roost    2    rooster   2
seem      1    some     1    sometimes 1
than      1    think    1    to        1
when      1
```

How It Works

The input is read from `cin` using `getline()` with the termination character as an asterisk. This allows an arbitrary number of lines of input to be entered. Individual words are extracted from the input in the string object `text` and stored in the `words` array. This is done in the indefinite `while` loop.

The first step in extracting a word from `text` is to find the index position of the first character of the word:

```
start = text.find_first_not_of(separators, offset);  // Find non-separator
if(string::npos == start)              // If we did not find it, we are done
   break;
offset = start + 1;                    // Move past character found
```

The `find_first_not_of()` function returns the index of the first character that is not one of the characters in `separators` starting at `offset`. You could use the `find_first_of()` function here to search for any of A to Z, a to z, to achieve the same result. When the last word has been extracted, the search will reach the end of the string without finding a character, so you test for this by comparing the value returned with `string::npos`. If it is the end of the string, all words have been extracted, so you exit the loop. In any other instance, you set `offset` at one past the character that was found and continue with the next step.

The next search is for any separator character:

```
end = text.find_first_of(separators,offset);       // Find separator
if(string::npos == end)              // If it's the end of the string
{                                    // current word is last in string
   offset = end;                     // We use offset to end loop later
   end = text.length();              // Set end as 1 past last character
}
else
   offset = end + 1;                 // Move past character found
```

The search is from position `offset`, which is one past the first character of the word, so usually you will find the separator that is one past the last character of the word. When it's the last word in `text` and there is no separator following the last character of the word, the function returns `string::npos`, so you deal with this by setting `end` to one past the last character in the string and setting `offset` to `string::npos`. `offset` is tested later in the loop after the current word has been extracted to determine whether the loop should end.

Extracting a word is easy:

```
words[nwords] = text.substr(start, end-start);       // Extract the word
```

The `substr()` function extracts `end-start` characters from `text`, starting with the character at `start`. The length of the word is `end-start` because `start` is the first character and `end` is one past the last character.

The rest of the `while` loop keeps track of the maximum word length in the way you have seen before, checks for the end-of-string condition, and checks whether the `words` array is full.

The words are output in a `for` loop that iterates over all the elements in the `words` array. Before the loop you define `count` to record the number of identical words and `initial` as the first character of the first word. The second index to the `words` array accesses a character within the `string` element selected by the first element. You use the latter later in the `while` loop to output words with the same initial letter on the same line. The `if` statements deal with counting duplicate words:

```
if(i < nwords-1 && words[i] == words[i+1])
{
  ++count;
  continue;
}
```

The `count` variable records the number of duplicate words, so it is always a minimum of 1. `count` is set to 1 at the end of the loop body when a word and its count are written out.

The second `if` statement checks if the next word is the same as the current word, and if it is, `count` is incremented and the rest of the current loop iteration is skipped. This mechanism accumulates the number of times a word is duplicated in `count`. The loop condition also checks that the index, `i`, is less than `nwords-2`, because we don't want to check the next word when the current word is the last in the array. Thus, we only output a word and its count when the next word is different, or the current word is the last in the array.

After a sequence of duplicate words has been counted, the `if` statement checks whether the initial letter in the current word is different from that recorded in `initial`. If it is, `initial` is updated and a newline is written to the output stream.

The last step in the `for` loop is to output a word and its count:

```
cout << std::setiosflags(std::ios::left)          // Output word left-justified
     << std::setw(maxwidth + 2) << words[i];
cout << std::resetiosflags(std::ios::right)       // and word count right-justified
     << std::setw(5) << count;
count = 1;
```

A word is left-justified in a field width that is two greater than the longest word. The `count` is output right-justified in a field width of five.

SUMMARY

In this chapter, you have learned the basics of how you can define classes and how you create and use class objects. You have also learned about overloading operators to allow the operators to be applied to class objects. A class template is a parameterized specification of a class type that is used by the compiler to create class instances based on the arguments you supply for the template.

EXERCISES

1. Define a class to represent an estimated integer, such as "about 40." These are integers whose value may be regarded as exact or estimated, so the class needs to have as data members a value and an "estimation" flag. The state of the estimation flag affects arithmetic operations, so that "2 * about 40" is "about 80." The state of variables should be switchable between "estimated" and "exact."

Provide one or more constructors for such a class. Overload the + operator so that these integers can be used in arithmetic expressions. Do you want the + operator to be a global or a member function? Do you need an assignment operator? Provide a `print()` function member so that they can be printed out, using a leading "E" to denote that the "estimation" flag is set. Write a program to test the operation of your class, checking especially that the operation of the estimation flag is correct.

2. Implement a simple string class that holds a `char*` and an integer length as `private` data members. Provide a constructor that takes an argument of type `const char*`, and implement the copy constructor, assignment operator, and destructor functions. Verify that your class works. You will find it easiest to use the string functions from the `cstring` header file.

3. Modify your class from Exercise 2 to support move semantics. Are there other constructors that would be useful? If so code them up.

4. (Advanced) Does your class from Exercise 3 correctly deal with cases such as this?

```
string s1;
...
s1 = s1;
```

If not, how should it be modified?

5. (Advanced) Overload the + and += operators of your class for concatenating strings.

6. Modify the stack example from Exercise 5 in the previous chapter so that the size of the stack is specified in the constructor and dynamically allocated. What else will you need to add? Test the operation of your new class.

7. Write a program that uses the `string` class that is declared in the `string` header to read a text string of arbitrary length from the keyboard. The program should then prompt for entry of one or more words that appear in the input text. All occurrences of the chosen words in the input text, regardless of case, should be replaced, with as many asterisks as there are letters in the word. Only whole words should be replaced, so if the string is `"Our friend Wendy is at the end of the road."` and the chosen word is `"end"`, the result should be `"Our friend Wendy is at the *** of the road."`, not `"Our fri*** W***y is at the *** of the road."`.

8. Write a class called `CTrace` that you can use to show at run time when code blocks have been entered and exited, by producing output like this:

```
function 'f1' entry
'if' block entry
'if' block exit
function 'f1' exit
```

9. Can you think of a way to automatically control the indentation in the last exercise so that the output looks like this?

```
function 'f1' entry
 'if' block entry
 'if' block exit
function 'f1' exit
```

➤ WHAT YOU LEARNED IN THIS CHAPTER

TOPIC	CONCEPT
Destructors	Objects are destroyed using functions called *destructors*. It is essential to define a destructor in native C++ classes to destroy objects which contain members that are allocated on the heap, because the default constructor will not do this.
The default copy constructor	The compiler will supply a default copy constructor for a native C++ class if you do not define one. The default copy constructor will not deal correctly with objects of classes that have data members allocated on the free store.
Defining a copy constructor	When you define your own copy constructor in a native C++ class, you must use a reference parameter.
Operator overloading	Most basic operators can be overloaded to provide actions specific to objects of a class. You should only implement operator functions for your classes that are consistent with the normal interpretation of the basic operators.
The assignment operator in a class	If you do not define an assignment operator for a class, the compiler will supply a default version. As with the copy constructor, the default assignment operator will not work correctly with classes that have data members allocated on the free store.
Classes that allocate memory on the heap	It is essential that you provide a destructor, a copy constructor, and an assignment operator for classes that have members allocated by new. It is recommended that you add a move constructor and move assignment operator too.
The `string` class	The `string` class in the standard library provides a powerful and superior way to process strings in your programs.
Class templates	A class template is a pattern that you can use to create classes with the same structure, but which support different data types.
Class template parameters	You can define a class template that has multiple parameters, including parameters that can assume constant values rather than types.
Template specialization	You can redefine a general template to provide code unique to a particular template type argument or set of arguments. This enables you to accommodate situations where the general form of the template will not work with a given type or set of types. A partial specialization is a redefinition of a template for a set of types such as pointers, or with one or more template parameters unbound.

TOPIC	CONCEPT
Move semantics	You can use the `std::move()` function that is declared in the `utility` header to convert an lvalue or an rvalue to an rvalue without copying. This allows you to move rather than copy objects when it is appropriate to do so and avoid the unnecessary copying overhead.
Perfect forwarding	Perfect forwarding is enabled by the `std::forward<T>()` template function that is declared in the `utility` header. This allows you to avoid unnecessary copying in a template function that has an rvalue reference argument when the argument is passed to another function.
Organizing your code	You should put definitions for your programs in `.h` files, and executable code — function definitions — in `.cpp` files. You can then incorporate `.h` files into your `.cpp` files by using `#include` directives.

Class Inheritance and Virtual Functions

WROX.COM CODE DOWNLOADS FOR THIS CHAPTER

You can find the wrox.com code downloads for this chapter on the Download Code tab at www.wrox.com/go/beginningvisualc. The code is in the Chapter 9 download and individually named according to the names throughout the chapter.

OBJECT-ORIENTED PROGRAMMING BASICS

As you have seen, a class is a data type that you define to suit your own application requirements. Classes define the objects to which your program relates. You program the solution to a problem in terms of the objects that are specific to the problem, using operations that work directly with those objects. You can define a class to represent something abstract, such as a complex number, which is a mathematical concept, or a truck, which is decidedly physical (especially if you run into one on the highway). So, as well as being a data type, a class can also define a set of real-world objects of a particular kind, at least to the degree necessary to solve a given problem.

You can think of a class as defining the characteristics of a particular group of things that are identified by a common set of parameters or properties and share operations that may be performed on or between them. The operations for objects of a given class type are defined by the *class interface*, which corresponds to the `public` function members of the class. The CBox class in the previous chapter is a good example — it defined a box in terms of its dimensions plus a set of public functions that you could apply to CBox objects to solve a problem.

Of course, there are many different kinds of boxes in the real world: there are cartons, coffins, candy boxes, and cereal boxes, to name but a few, and you will certainly be able to come up with many others. You can differentiate boxes by the kinds of things they hold, the materials from which they are made, and in a multitude of other ways; but even though there are many different kinds of boxes, they share some common characteristics — the essence of *boxiness*, perhaps. Therefore, you can visualize all kinds of boxes as being related to one another because, even though they have many differentiating features, they share some fundamental characteristics. You could define a general kind of box as having the generic characteristics of all boxes — perhaps just a length, a width, and a height. You could then add additional characteristics to the basic box type to differentiate a particular kind of box from the rest. You may also find that there are things you can do with one specific type of box that you can't do with others.

It's also possible that some objects may be the result of combining a particular kind of box with some other type of object: a box of candy or a crate of beer, for example. To accommodate this, you could define one kind of box as a generic box with basic "boxiness" characteristics and then specify another sort of box as a further specialization of that. Figure 9-1 illustrates an example of the kinds of relationships you might define between different sorts of boxes.

The boxes become more specialized as you move down the diagram, and the arrows run from a given box type to the one on which it is based. Figure 9-1 defines three kinds of boxes based on the generic type, CBox. It also defines beer crates as a refinement of crates designed to hold bottles.

Thus, a good way to approximate the real world relatively well is to define classes that are interrelated. A candy box can be considered to be a box with all the characteristics of a basic box, plus a few characteristics of its own. This precisely illustrates the relationship between classes when one class is defined based on another. A more specialized class has all the characteristics of the class on which it is based, plus a few characteristics of its own that identify what makes it special. Let's look at how this works in practice.

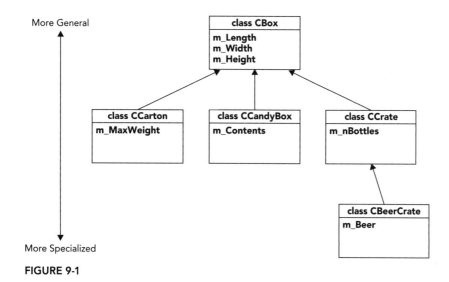

FIGURE 9-1

INHERITANCE IN CLASSES

When you define one class based on an existing class, the new class is called a *derived class*. A derived class automatically contains all the data members of the class that you used to define it and, with some restrictions, the function members too. The class *inherits* the members of the class on which it is based.

The only members of a base class that are not inherited in a derived class are the destructor, the constructors, and any member functions overloading the assignment operator. All other members are inherited by a derived class. Of course, the reason for certain base members not being inherited is that a derived class always has its own constructors and destructor. If the base class has an assignment operator, the derived class provides its own version. When I say these functions are not inherited, I mean that they don't exist as members of a derived class object. However, they still exist for the base class part of an object, as you will see.

What Is a Base Class?

A *base class* is any class that you use as a basis for defining another class. For example, if you define a class, B, directly in terms of a class, A, A is said to be a *direct base class* of B. In Figure 9-1, the CCrate class is a direct base class of CBeerCrate. When a class such as CBeerCrate is defined in terms of another class, CCrate, CBeerCrate is said to be derived from CCrate. Because CCrate is itself defined in terms of the class CBox, CBox is said to be an *indirect base class* of CBeerCrate. You'll see how this is expressed in the class definition in a moment. Figure 9-2 illustrates the way in which base class members are inherited in a derived class.

Just because member functions are inherited doesn't mean that you won't want to replace them by new versions in the derived class, and, of course, you can do that when necessary.

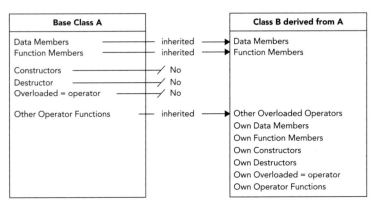

FIGURE 9-2

Deriving Classes from a Base Class

We can define a simple CBox class with public data members:

```
// Header file Box.h in project Ex9_01
#pragma once

class CBox
{
public:
  double m_Length;
  double m_Width;
  double m_Height;

  explicit CBox(double lv = 1.0, double wv = 1.0, double hv = 1.0):
                    m_Length {lv}, m_Width {wv}, m_Height {hv} {}
};
```

Create an empty Win32 console project with the name **Ex9_01** and save this code in a new header file in the project with the name Box.h. The #pragma once directive ensures the definition of CBox appears only once in a build. There's a constructor in the class so that you can initialize objects when you create them. Suppose you need another class, CCandyBox, that defines objects that have the same characteristics as CBox objects but also have another data member — a pointer to a string that identifies the contents of the box. I'll use a pointer here to demonstrate aspects of constructors and destructors in derived classes. In real-world code you should use std::string to store strings.

You can define CCandyBox as a derived class with CBox as the base class:

```
// Header file CandyBox.h in project Ex9_01
#pragma once
#include <cstring>                          // For strlen() and strcpy_s()
#include "Box.h"

class CCandyBox : CBox
{
public:
```

```
    char* m_Contents;

    explicit CCandyBox(const char* str = "Candy")          // Constructor
    {
      size_t length {strlen(str) + 1};
      m_Contents = new char[length];
      strcpy_s(m_Contents, length, str);
    }

    CCandyBox(const CCandyBox& box) = delete;
    CCandyBox& operator=(const CCandyBox& box) = delete;

    ~CCandyBox()                                           // Destructor
    { delete[] m_Contents; }
};
```

Add this header file to the project Ex9_01. You need the #include directive for Box.h because you refer to the CBox class in the code. If you were to leave this directive out, CBox would be unknown to the compiler, so the code would not compile. The base class name, CBox, appears after the name of the derived class, CCandyBox, and is separated from it by a colon. In all other respects, it looks like a normal class definition. The new member, m_Contents is a pointer to a string so you need a constructor to initialize it and a destructor to release the memory for it. You also need an assignment operator to prevent shallow assignments, and a copy constructor; or if you don't want them, define them as =delete. There's a default value for the string describing the contents of a CCandyBox object in the constructor. Objects of type CCandyBox contain all the members of the base class, CBox, plus the additional data member, m_Contents.

Note the use of the strcpy_s() function that you first saw in Chapter 6. Here, there are three arguments — the destination for the copy operation, the length of the destination buffer, and the source. If both arrays were static — that is, not allocated on the heap — you could omit the second argument and just supply the destination and source pointers. This is possible because the strcpy_s() function is also available as a template function that can infer the length of the destination string buffer automatically. You can therefore call the function with just the destination and source strings as arguments when you are working with static destination string buffers.

TRY IT OUT   Using a Derived Class

Now, you'll see how the derived class works in an example. Add the following code to the Ex9_01 project as the source file Ex9_01.cpp:

```
// Ex9_01.cpp
// Using a derived class
#include <iostream>                              // For stream I/O
#include "CandyBox.h"                            // For CBox and CCandyBox

int main()
{
  CBox myBox {4.0, 3.0, 2.0};                    // Create CBox object
  CCandyBox myCandyBox;
  CCandyBox myMintBox {"Wafer Thin Mints"};      // Create CCandyBox object

  std::cout << "myBox occupies " << sizeof myBox // Show how much memory
```

```
                   << " bytes" << std::endl               // the objects require
                   << "myCandyBox occupies " << sizeof myCandyBox
                   << " bytes" << std::endl
                   << "myMintBox occupies " << sizeof myMintBox
                   << " bytes" << std::endl;

  std::cout << "myBox length is " << myBox.m_Length << std::endl;

  myBox.m_Length = 10.0;

  // myCandyBox.m_Length = 10.0;          // uncomment this for an error

  return 0;
}
```

How It Works

You have an `#include` directive for the `CandyBox.h` header here, and because you know that contains an `#include` directive for `Box.h`, you don't need to add a directive to include `Box.h`. You could put an `#include` directive for `Box.h` in this file, in which case, the `#pragma once` directive in `Box.h` would prevent its inclusion more than once. This is important because each class can only be defined once in a program; two definitions for a class would be an error.

After defining a `CBox` object and two `CCandyBox` objects, you output the number of bytes that each object occupies. Let's look at the output:

```
myBox occupies 24 bytes
myCandyBox occupies 32 bytes
myMintBox occupies 32 bytes
myBox length is 4
```

The first line is what you would expect from the discussion in the previous chapter. A `CBox` object has three data members of type `double`, each of which is 8 bytes, making 24 bytes in all. Both `CCandyBox` objects are the same size — 32 bytes. The length of the string doesn't affect the size of an object because the memory to hold the string is allocated in the free store. The 32 bytes are made up of 24 bytes for the three `double` members inherited from the base class `CBox`, plus 4 bytes for the pointer, `m_Contents`, which makes 28 bytes. So where did the other 4 bytes come from? This is due to the compiler aligning members at addresses that are multiples of 8 bytes. You should be able to demonstrate this by adding an extra member of type `int`, say, to the class `CCandyBox`. You will find that the size of a class object is still 32 bytes.

You also output the value of the `m_Length` member of the `CBox` object, `myBox`. Even though you have no difficulty accessing this member of the `CBox` object, if you uncomment the following statement in the function `main()`,

```
  // myCandyBox.m_Length = 10.0;        // uncomment this for an error
```

the program no longer compiles. The compiler generates the following message:

```
error C2247: 'CBox::m_Length' not accessible because 'CCandyBox'
uses 'private' to inherit from 'CBox'
```

It says quite clearly that the `m_Length` member from the base class is not accessible because `m_Length` has become `private` in the derived class. This is because there is a default access specifier of `private` for a base class when you define a derived class — it's as if the first line of the derived class definition had been:

```
class CCandyBox : private CBox
```

There always has to be an access specification for a base class that determines the status of the inherited members in the derived class. If you omit the access specification for a base class, the compiler assumes that it's `private`. If you change the definition of the CCandyBox class in CandyBox.h to the following,

```
class CCandyBox : public CBox
{
public:
  char* m_Contents;

  explicit CCandyBox(const char* str = "Candy")           // Constructor
  {
    size_t length {strlen(str) + 1};
    m_Contents = new char[length];
    strcpy_s(m_Contents, length, str);
  }

  CCandyBox(const CCandyBox& box) = delete;
  CCandyBox& operator=(const CCandyBox& box) = delete;

  ~CCandyBox()                                             // Destructor
  { delete[] m_Contents; }
};
```

the m_Length member is inherited in the derived class as `public`, and is accessible in the function main(). With the access specifier `public` for the base class, all the inherited members originally specified as `public` in the base class have the same access level in the derived class.

ACCESS CONTROL UNDER INHERITANCE

The access to inherited members in a derived class needs to be looked at more closely. Let's consider the status of the `private` members of a base class in a derived class.

There was a good reason to choose the version of the class CBox with `public` data members in the previous example, rather than the more secure version with `private` data members. Although `private` data members of a base class are also members of a derived class, they remain `private` to the base class in the derived class, so function members defined in the derived class cannot access them. They are only accessible in the derived class through function members of the base class that are not `private`. You can demonstrate this very easily by changing all the CBox class data members to `private` and putting a volume() function in the derived class, CCandyBox:

```
// Version of the classes that will not compile
#include <cstring>                     // For strlen() and strcpy_s()

class CBox
{
public:
  explicit CBox(double lv = 1.0, double wv = 1.0, double hv = 1.0):
```

```
                                 m_Length {lv}, m_Width {wv}, m_Height {hv} {}

    private:
      double m_Length;
      double m_Width;
      double m_Height;
    };

    class CCandyBox : public CBox
    {
    public:
      char* m_Contents;

      // Function to calculate the volume of a CCandyBox object
      double volume() const               // Error - members not accessible
      { return m_Length*m_Width*m_Height; }

      // Rest of the code as before...
    };
```

A program using these classes does not compile. The `volume()` function in `CCandyBox` attempts to access the `private` members of the base class, which is not legal, so the compiler will flag each instance with error C2248.

TRY IT OUT   **Accessing Private Members of the Base Class**

However, it is legal to call a public function in the base class. If you move the definition of `volume()` from `CCandyBox` to the `public` section of the base class, `CBox`, not only will the program compile, but you can call the function to obtain the volume of a `CCandyBox` object. Create a new Win32 project, **Ex9_02**, with the `Box.h` contents as the following:

```
// Box.h in Ex9_02
#pragma once

class CBox
{
public:
  explicit CBox(double lv = 1.0, double wv = 1.0, double hv = 1.0):
                    m_Length {lv}, m_Width {wv}, m_Height{hv} {}

  //Function to calculate the volume of a CBox object
  double volume() const
  { return m_Length*m_Width*m_Height; }

private:
  double m_Length;
  double m_Width;
  double m_Height;
};
```

The `CandyBox.h` header in the project contains:

```
// Header file CandyBox.h in project Ex9_02
#pragma once
#include "Box.h"
```

```
#include <cstring>                          // For strlen() and strcpy_s()

class CCandyBox : public CBox
{
public:
  char* m_Contents;

  explicit CCandyBox(const char* str = "Candy")          // Constructor
  {
    size_t length {strlen(str) + 1};
    m_Contents = new char[length];
    strcpy_s(m_Contents, length, str);
  }

  CCandyBox(const CCandyBox& box) = delete;
  CCandyBox& operator=(const CCandyBox& box) = delete;

  ~CCandyBox()                                           // Destructor
  { delete[] m_Contents; }
};
```

The `Ex9_02.cpp` file in the project contains:

```
// Ex9_02.cpp
// Using a function inherited from a base class
#include <iostream>                    // For stream I/O
#include "CandyBox.h"                  // For CBox and CCandyBox

int main()
{
  CBox myBox {4.0, 3.0, 2.0};                       // Create CBox object
  CCandyBox myCandyBox;
  CCandyBox myMintBox {"Wafer Thin Mints"};         // Create CCandyBox object

  std::cout << "myBox occupies " << sizeof  myBox     // Show how much memory
            << " bytes" << std::endl                  // the objects require
            << "myCandyBox occupies " << sizeof myCandyBox
            << " bytes" << std::endl
            << "myMintBox occupies " << sizeof myMintBox
            << " bytes" << std::endl;
  std::cout << "myMintBox volume is " << myMintBox.volume()  // Get volume of a
            << std::endl;                                    // CCandyBox object
  return 0;
}
```

This example produces the following output:

```
myBox occupies 24 bytes
myCandyBox occupies 32 bytes
myMintBox occupies 32 bytes
myMintBox volume is 1
```

How It Works

The last line is the interesting additional output. It shows the value produced by the `volume()` function, which is now in the `public` section of the base class. Within the derived class, it operates on the members of the derived class that are inherited from the base. It is a full member of the derived class, so it can be used freely with objects of the derived class.

The volume of the derived class object is 1 because, in creating the CCandyBox object, the CBox() default constructor was called first to create the base class part of the object, and this sets default CBox dimensions to 1.

Constructor Operation in a Derived Class

Although I said that base class constructors are not inherited in a derived class, they still exist in the base class and are used to create the base part of a derived class object. This is because creating the base class part of a derived class object is really the business of a base class constructor, not the derived class constructor. After all, you have seen that private members of a base class are inaccessible in a derived class object, even though they are inherited, so responsibility for these has to lie with the base class constructors.

The default base class constructor was called by default in the last example to create the base part of a derived class object, but this doesn't have to be the case. You can call a particular base class constructor from a derived class constructor. This enables you to initialize the base class data members with a constructor other than the default, or, indeed, to choose to call a particular base class constructor, depending on the data supplied to the derived class constructor.

TRY IT OUT   Calling Constructors

You can see this in action through a modified version of the previous example. To make the class usable, you really need to provide a constructor for the derived class that allows you to specify the dimensions of the object. You can add an additional constructor in the derived class to do this, and call the base class constructor explicitly to set the values of the data members that are inherited from the base class.

In the Ex9_03 project, Box.h contains:

```
// Box.h in Ex9_03
#pragma once
#include <iostream>
class CBox
{
public:
  // Base class constructor
  explicit CBox(double lv = 1.0, double wv = 1.0, double hv = 1.0):
                     m_Length {lv}, m_Width {wv}, m_Height {hv}
  {  std::cout << "CBox constructor called" << std::endl;  }

  //Function to calculate the volume of a CBox object
  double volume() const
  { return m_Length*m_Width*m_Height; }

 private:
```

```
   double m_Length;
   double m_Width;
   double m_Height;
};
```

The `CandyBox.h` header file should contain:

```cpp
// CandyBox.h in Ex9_03
#pragma once
#include <cstring>                        // For strlen() and strcpy()
#include <iostream>
#include "Box.h"

class CCandyBox : public CBox
{
public:
  char* m_Contents;

  // Constructor to set dimensions and contents
  // with explicit call of CBox constructor
  CCandyBox(double lv, double wv, double hv, const char* str = "Candy")
                                              : CBox {lv, wv, hv}
  {
    std::cout << "CCandyBox constructor2 called" << std::endl;
    size_t length {strlen(str) + 1};
    m_Contents = new char[length];
    strcpy_s(m_Contents, length, str);
  }

  // Constructor to set contents
  // calls default CBox constructor automatically
  explicit CCandyBox(const char* str = "Candy")
  {
    std::cout << "CCandyBox constructor1 called" << std::endl;
    size_t length {strlen(str) + 1};
    m_Contents = new char[length];
    strcpy_s(m_Contents, length, str);
  }

  CCandyBox(const CCandyBox& box) = delete;
  CCandyBox& operator=(const CCandyBox& box) = delete;

  ~CCandyBox()                                  // Destructor
  { delete[] m_Contents; }
};
```

The `#include` directive for the `iostream` header is not strictly necessary here because `Box.h` contains the same code, but it does no harm to put them in. On the contrary, putting these statements in here also means that if you were to remove this code from `Box.h` because it was no longer required there, `CandyBox.h` would still compile.

The contents of `Ex9_03.cpp` are:

```cpp
// Ex9_03.cpp
// Calling a base constructor from a derived class constructor
#include <iostream>                     // For stream I/O
```

```
#include "CandyBox.h"                    // For CBox and CCandyBox

int main()
{
  CBox myBox {4.0, 3.0, 2.0};
  CCandyBox myCandyBox;
  CCandyBox myMintBox {1.0, 2.0, 3.0, "Wafer Thin Mints"};
  std::cout << "myBox occupies " << sizeof  myBox      // Show how much memory
            << " bytes" << std::endl                   // the objects require
            << "myCandyBox occupies " << sizeof myCandyBox
            << " bytes" << std::endl
            << "myMintBox occupies " << sizeof myMintBox
            << " bytes" << std::endl;

  std::cout << "myMintBox volume is "                  // Get volume of a
            << myMintBox.volume() << std::endl;        // CCandyBox object

  return 0;
}
```

How It Works

As well as adding a constructor to the derived class, you have added an output statement in each constructor so you know when either gets called. The explicit CBox constructor call appears after a colon in the function header of the derived class constructor. The notation is exactly the same as what you have been using for initializing members in a constructor:

```
// Calling the base class constructor
CCandyBox(double lv, double wv, double hv, const char* str= "Candy"):
                                            CBox {lv, wv, hv}
{
...
}
```

The notation for calling the base class constructor is perfectly consistent with initializing other members in the initializer list, because you are essentially initializing the CBox sub-object of a derived class object. Earlier, you were explicitly calling the default constructor for the double members m_Length, m_Width, and m_Height in the initialization list. Here, you are calling the constructor for CBox. This causes the specific CBox constructor you have chosen to be called before the CCandyBox constructor code is executed.

If you build and run this example, it produces the following output:

```
CBox constructor called
CBox constructor called
CCandyBox constructor1 called
CBox constructor called
CCandyBox constructor2 called
myBox occupies 24 bytes
myCandyBox occupies 32 bytes
myMintBox occupies 32 bytes
myMintBox volume is 6
```

The constructor calls are explained in the following table:

OUTPUT	OBJECT BEING CONSTRUCTED
CBox constructor called	myBox
CBox constructor called	myCandyBox
CCandyBox constructor1 called	myCandyBox
CBox constructor called	myMintBox
CCandyBox constructor2 called	myMintBox

The first line is due to the CBox constructor call, originating from the definition of the CBox object, myBox. The second line arises from the automatic call of the base class constructor caused by the definition of the CCandyBox object, myCandyBox. Notice how the base class constructor is always called before the derived class constructor. The base class is the foundation on which the derived class is built, so the base class must be created first.

The next line is due to your version of the default derived class constructor being called for the myCandyBox object. This constructor is invoked because the object is not initialized. The fourth line arises from the explicit call of the CBox class constructor in our new constructor for CCandyBox objects. The arguments for the dimensions of the CCandyBox object are passed to the base class constructor. Next comes the output from the new derived class constructor itself, so constructors are again called, first for the base class, then for the derived class.

It should be clear from what you have seen that when a derived class constructor executes, a base class constructor is always called to create the base part of the derived class object. If you don't specify the base class constructor, the compiler arranges for the default base constructor to be called. The last line in the table shows that the initialization of the base part of the myMintBox object is working as it should be, with the private members initialized by the CBox constructor.

Having the private members of a base class that are only accessible to member functions of the base class isn't always convenient. There will be many instances where you want to have private members of a base class that can be accessed from within the derived class. As you surely have anticipated by now, C++ provides a way to do this.

Declaring Protected Class Members

In addition to the public and private access specifiers for members of a class, you can also declare members as protected. The protected keyword has the same effect as the private keyword within a class: members that are protected can only be accessed by member functions of the class, and by friend functions of the class (also by member functions of a friend class — you will learn about friend classes later in this chapter). Base class members that are protected can be accessed from any derived class function. Using the `protected` keyword, you could redefine CBox as follows:

```
// Box.h in Ex9_04
#pragma once
#include <iostream>

class CBox
{
public:
  // Base class constructor
  explicit CBox(double lv = 1.0, double wv = 1.0, double hv = 1.0):
                        m_Length {lv}, m_Width {wv}, m_Height {hv}
  {  std::cout << "CBox constructor called" << std::endl;  }

  // CBox destructor - just to track calls
  ~CBox()
  { std::cout << "CBox destructor called" << std::endl; }

protected:
  double m_Length;
  double m_Width;
  double m_Height;
};
```

The data members are still effectively `private`, in that they can't be accessed by ordinary global functions, but they can still be accessed by member functions of a derived class.

TRY IT OUT   Using Protected Members

You can demonstrate the use of `protected` data members by using this version of CBox to derive a new version of the CCandyBox class that accesses the members of the base class through its own member function, `volume()`:

```
// CandyBox.h in Ex9_04
#pragma once
#include "Box.h"
#include <cstring>                          // For strlen() and strcpy()
#include <iostream>

class CCandyBox : public CBox
{
public:
  char* m_Contents;

  // Derived class function to calculate volume
  double volume() const
  { return m_Length*m_Width*m_Height; }

  // Constructor to set dimensions & contents with explicit CBox constructor call
  CCandyBox(double lv, double wv, double hv,
                  const char* str = "Candy") : CBox {lv, wv, hv}
  {
```

```
        std::cout <<"CCandyBox constructor2 called" << std::endl;
        size_t length{ strlen(str) + 1 };
        m_Contents = new char[length];
        strcpy_s(m_Contents, length, str);
    }

    // Constructor to set contents - calls default CBox constructor automatically
    explicit CCandyBox(const char* str = "Candy")
    {
        std::cout << "CCandyBox constructor1 called" << std::endl;
        size_t length{ strlen(str) + 1 };
        m_Contents = new char[length];
        strcpy_s(m_Contents, length, str);
    }

    CCandyBox(const CCandyBox& box) = delete;
    CCandyBox& operator=(const CCandyBox& box) = delete;

    ~CCandyBox()                                               // Destructor
    {
        std::cout << "CCandyBox destructor called" << std::endl;
        delete[] m_Contents;
    }
};
```

The code for `main()` in `Ex9_04.cpp` is:

```
// Ex9_04.cpp
// Using the protected access specifier
#include <iostream>              // For stream I/O
#include "CandyBox.h"            // For CBox and CCandyBox

int main()
{
    CCandyBox myCandyBox;
    CCandyBox myToffeeBox {2, 3, 4, "Stickjaw Toffee"};
    std::cout << "myCandyBox volume is " << myCandyBox.volume() << std::endl
              << "myToffeeBox volume is " << myToffeeBox.volume() << std::endl;

    // std::cout << myToffeeBox.m_Length;  // Uncomment this for an error

    return 0;
}
```

How It Works

In this example you calculate the volumes of the two `CCandyBox` objects by invoking the `volume()` function that is a member of the derived class. This function accesses the inherited members `m_Length`, `m_Width`, and `m_Height` to produce the result. The members are declared as `protected` in the base class and remain `protected` in the derived class. The program produces the output:

```
CBox constructor called
CCandyBox constructor1 called
CBox constructor called
CCandyBox constructor2 called
myCandyBox volume is 1
```

```
myToffeeBox volume is 24
CCandyBox destructor called
CBox destructor called
CCandyBox destructor called
CBox destructor called
```

The output shows that the volume is calculated properly for both CCandyBox objects. The first object has the default dimensions produced by calling the default CBox constructor so the volume is 1, and the second object has the dimensions defined as initial values in its definition.

The output also shows the sequence of constructor and destructor calls, and you can see how each derived class object is destroyed in two steps. Destructors for a derived class object are called in the reverse order of the constructors for the object. This is a general rule that always applies. Constructors are called starting with the base class constructor and then the derived class constructor, whereas the destructor for the derived class is called first when an object is destroyed, followed by the base class destructor.

You can demonstrate that the protected members of the base class remain protected in the derived class by uncommenting the statement preceding the return statement in main(). If you do this, you get this error message:

```
error C2248: 'CBox::m_Length': cannot access protected member declared in class 'CBox'
```

This indicates clearly that m_Length is inaccessible.

The Access Level of Inherited Class Members

If you have no access specifier for the base class in the definition of a derived class, the default specification is private. This has the effect of causing the inherited public and protected members of the base class to be private in the derived class. The private members of the base class remain private to the base and, therefore, inaccessible in the derived class. In fact they remain private to the base class regardless of how the base class is specified in the derived class definition.

Specifying a base class as public gives base class members the same access level in the derived class as they had in the base, so public members remain public, and protected members remain protected.

The last possibility is that you declare a base class as protected. This makes the inherited public members of the base protected in the derived class. The protected and private base members retain their original access level in the derived class. This is summarized in Figure 9-3, which shows classes CABox, CBBox, and CCBox derived from CBox.

This may look a little complicated, but you can reduce it to the following three rules for inherited members of a derived class:

➤ private members of a base class are never accessible in a derived class.

➤ Defining a base class as public doesn't change the access level of its members in a derived class.

➤ Defining a base class as protected changes its public members to protected in a derived class.

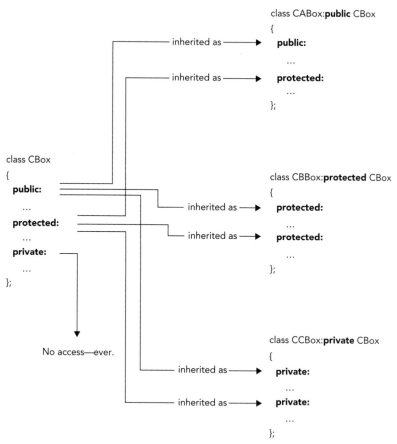

FIGURE 9-3

Being able to change the access level of inherited members in a derived class gives you a degree of flexibility, but don't forget that you cannot relax the level specified in the base class; you can only make the access level more stringent. This suggests that base classes need to have `public` members if you want to be able to vary the access level in derived classes. This may seem contrary to the idea of encapsulating data in a class in order to protect it from unauthorized access, but, as you'll see, it is often the case that you define base classes that only act as a base for other classes and aren't intended to be used for instantiating objects in their own right.

THE COPY CONSTRUCTOR IN A DERIVED CLASS

Remember that the copy constructor is called automatically when you define an object that is initialized with an object of the same class. Look at these statements:

```
CBox myBox {2.0, 3.0, 4.0};      // Calls constructor
CBox copyBox {myBox};            // Calls copy constructor
```

The first statement calls the constructor that accepts three arguments of type `double`, and the second calls the copy constructor. If you don't define a copy constructor, the compiler supplies one that copies the initializing object member by member to the corresponding members of the new object. So that you can see what is going on during execution, you can add your own version of a copy constructor to the `CBox` class. You can then use this class as a base for defining the `CCandyBox` class:

```cpp
// Box.h in Ex9_05
#pragma once
#include <iostream>

class CBox                      // Base class definition
{
public:
  // Base class constructor
  explicit CBox(double lv = 1.0, double wv = 1.0, double hv = 1.0):
                     m_Length {lv}, m_Width {wv}, m_Height {hv}
  {  std::cout << "CBox constructor called" << std::endl;  }

  // Copy constructor
  CBox(const CBox& initB)
  {
    std::cout << "CBox copy constructor called" << std::endl;
    m_Length = initB.m_Length;
    m_Width = initB.m_Width;
    m_Height = initB.m_Height;
  }

  // CBox destructor - just to track calls
  ~CBox()
  { std::cout << "CBox destructor called" << std::endl; }

protected:
  double m_Length;
  double m_Width;
  double m_Height;
};
```

Don't forget that a copy constructor must have its parameter specified as a reference to avoid the infinite number of calls to itself that would otherwise result from copying an argument by value. When the copy constructor in our example is called, it outputs a message, so you can see from the output when this is happening. You need to add a similar copy constructor to the `CCandyBox` class.

TRY IT OUT   The Copy Constructor in a Derived Class

Add the following code for the copy constructor to the `public` section of the derived `CCandyBox` class in `Ex9_04` in place of the deleted copy constructor:

```cpp
// Derived class copy constructor
CCandyBox(const CCandyBox& initCB)
{
```

```
        std::cout << "CCandyBox copy constructor called" << std::endl;
        size_t length {strlen(initCB.m_Contents) + 1};
        m_Contents = new char[length];                  // Get new memory
        strcpy_s(m_Contents, length, initCB.m_Contents);    // Copy string
    }
```

You can now run this new version (Ex9_05) of the last example with the following main() function to see how the new copy constructor works:

```
// Ex9_05
// Using the copy constructor in a derived class
#include <iostream>                              // For stream I/O
#include "CandyBox.h"                            // For CBox and CCandyBox

int main()
{
  CCandyBox chocBox {2.0, 3.0, 4.0, "Chockies"};  // Declare and initialize
  CCandyBox chocolateBox {chocBox};               // Use copy constructor

  std::cout << "Volume of chocBox is " << chocBox.volume() << std::endl
            << "Volume of chocolateBox is " << chocolateBox.volume() << std::endl;

  return 0;
}
```

How It Works

This example produces the following output:

```
CBox constructor called
CCandyBox constructor2 called
CBox constructor called
CCandyBox copy constructor called
Volume of chocBox is 24
Volume of chocolateBox is 1
CCandyBox destructor called
CBox destructor called
CCandyBox destructor called
CBox destructor called
```

Although this looks okay at first sight, there's something wrong. The third line of output shows that the default constructor is called for the CBox part of the chocolateBox object, rather than the copy constructor. As a consequence, the object has default dimensions rather than the dimensions of the initializing object, so the volume is incorrect. The reason for this is that when you write a constructor for an object of a derived class, you are responsible for ensuring that the members of the derived class object are properly initialized. This includes the inherited members.

The fix for this is to call the copy constructor for the base part of the class in the initialization list for the copy constructor for the CCandyBox class. The copy constructor then becomes:

```
// Derived class copy constructor
CCandyBox(const CCandyBox& initCB): CBox {initCB}
{
  std::cout << "CCandyBox copy constructor called" << std::endl;
  size_t length {strlen(initCB.m_Contents) + 1};
```

```
    m_Contents = new char[length];            // Get new memory
    strcpy_s(m_Contents, length, initCB.m_Contents);   // Copy string
}
```

The `CBox` copy constructor is called with the `initCB` object. This initializes the base part of the object that is being created so everything works out. If you modify the example by adding the base copy constructor call, the output is:

```
CBox constructor called
CCandyBox constructor2 called
CBox copy constructor called
CCandyBox copy constructor called
Volume of chocBox is 24
Volume of chocolateBox is 24
CCandyBox destructor called
CBox destructor called
CCandyBox destructor called
CBox destructor called
```

This shows that all the constructors and destructors are called in the correct sequence, and the copy constructor for the `CBox` part of `chocolateBox` is called before the `CCandyBox` copy constructor. The volume of the `chocolateBox` object is now the same as that of its initializing object, which is as it should be.

You have, therefore, another golden rule to remember.

If you write any kind of constructor for a derived class, you are responsible for the initialization of all members of the derived class object, including all its inherited members.

Of course, as you saw in the previous chapter, if you want to make a class that allocates memory on the heap as efficient as possible, you should overload the copy constructor with a version that uses an rvalue reference parameter. You could add the following to the `CCandyBox` class to take care of this:

```
// Move constructor
CCandyBox(CCandyBox&& initCB): CBox {std::move(initCB)}
{
    std::cout << "CCandyBox move constructor called"<< std::endl;
    m_Contents = initCB.m_Contents;
    initCB.m_Contents = 0;
}
```

You still have to call the base class move constructor to get the base members initialized.

PREVENTING CLASS DERIVATION

Circumstances can arise where you want to be sure that your class cannot be used as a base class. You can do this by specifying your class as `final`. Here's how you could prevent derivation from the `CBox` class:

```
class CBox final
{
    // Class details as before...
};
```

The final modifier following the class name tells the compiler that derivation from the CBox class is not to be allowed. If you modify the CBox class in Ex9_05 in this way, the code will not compile.

Note that final is not a keyword; it just has a special meaning in context. You are not allowed to use a keyword as a name, whereas you could use final as the name for a variable, for example.

CLASS MEMBERS AS FRIENDS

You saw in Chapter 7 how a function can be declared as a friend of a class. This gives the friend function the privilege of free access to any of the class members. Of course, there is no reason why a friend function cannot be a member of another class.

Suppose you define a CBottle class to represent a bottle:

```
// Bottle.h
#pragma once

class CBottle
{
public:
  CBottle(double height, double diameter) :
    m_Height {height}, m_Diameter {diameter} {}

private:
  double m_Height;                           // Bottle height
  double m_Diameter;                         // Bottle diameter
};
```

You now need a class to represent the packaging for a dozen bottles that automatically has custom dimensions to accommodate a particular kind of bottle. You might define this as the following — although this won't compile as it is:

```
// Carton.h
#pragma once
class CBottle;                             // Forward declaration

class CCarton
{
public:
  CCarton(const CBottle& aBottle)
  {
    m_Height = aBottle.m_Height;           // Bottle height
    m_Length = 4.0*aBottle.m_Diameter;     // Four rows of ...
    m_Width = 3.0*aBottle.m_Diameter;      // ...three bottles
  }

private:
  double m_Length;                         // Carton length
  double m_Width;                          // Carton width
  double m_Height;                         // Carton height
};
```

We now have two class definitions that each reference the other class type. The forward declaration for the CBottle class in Carton.h is essential; without it the compiler won't know what CBottle refers to. Forward declarations are always needed to resolve cyclic references between two or more classes. The CCarton constructor sets the height to be the same as that of the bottle it is to accommodate, and the length and width are set based on the diameter of the bottle so that 12 fit in the box. As you know by now, this won't work. The data members of the CBottle class are private, so the CCarton constructor can't access them. As you also know, a friend declaration in the CBottle class fixes it:

```
// Bottle.h
#pragma once;
class CCarton;                              // Forward declaration

class CBottle
{
public:
  CBottle(double height, double diameter) :
   m_Height {height}, m_Diameter {diameter} {}

private:
  double m_Height;                          // Bottle height
  double m_Diameter;                        // Bottle diameter

// Let the carton constructor in
friend CCarton::CCarton(const CBottle& aBottle);
};
```

The only difference between the friend declaration here and what you saw in Chapter 7 is that you must put the class name and the scope resolution operator with the friend function name to identify it. You must have a forward declaration for the CCarton class because the friend function refers to it.

You might think that this will compile correctly, but there's a problem. You have put a forward declaration of the CCarton class in the CBottle class and vice versa to resolve the cyclic dependency, but this still won't allow the classes to compile. The problem is with the CCarton constructor. This appears within the CCarton class definition and the compiler cannot compile this function without having first compiled the CBottle class. On the other hand, it can't compile the CBottle class without having compiled the CCarton class. The only way to resolve this is to put the CCarton constructor definition in a .cpp file, thus removing the need to compile it when the CCarton class is compiled. The header file holding the CCarton class definition will be:

```
// Carton.h
#pragma once
class CBottle;                              // Forward declaration

class CCarton
{
public:
  CCarton(const CBottle& aBottle);

private:
  double m_Length;                          // Carton length
```

```
    double m_Width;                            // Carton width
    double m_Height;                           // Carton height
};
```

The contents of the `Carton.cpp` file will be:

```
// Carton.cpp
#include "Carton.h"
#include "Bottle.h"

CCarton::CCarton(const CBottle& aBottle)
{
  m_Height = aBottle.m_Height;               // Bottle height
  m_Length = 4.0*aBottle.m_Diameter;         // Four rows of ...
  m_Width = 3.0*aBottle.m_Diameter;          // ...three bottles
}
```

Now, the compiler can compile both class definitions and the `carton.cpp` file.

Friend Classes

You can allow all the member functions of one class to have access to all the data members of another by declaring it as a *friend class*. You could define the CCarton class as a friend of the CBottle class by adding a friend declaration within the CBottle class definition:

```
friend CCarton;
```

With this declaration in the CBottle class, all function members of the CCarton class have free access to all the data members of the CBottle class.

Limitations on Class Friendship

Class friendship is not reciprocated. Making the CCarton class a friend of the CBottle class does not mean that the CBottle class is a friend of the CCarton class. If you want this to be so, you must add a friend declaration for the CBottle class to the CCarton class.

Class friendship is also not inherited. If you define another class with CBottle as a base, members of the CCarton class will not have access to its data members, not even those inherited from CBottle.

VIRTUAL FUNCTIONS

Let's look more closely at the behavior of inherited member functions and their relationship with derived class member functions. You could add a function to the CBox class to output the volume of a CBox object. The simplified class then becomes:

```
// Box.h in Ex9_06
#pragma once
#include <iostream>

class CBox                                   // Base class
```

```
{
public:
  // Function to show the volume of an object
  void showVolume() const
  { std::cout << "CBox usable volume is " << volume() << std::endl; }

  // Function to calculate the volume of a CBox object
  double volume() const
  { return m_Length*m_Width*m_Height; }

  // Constructor
  explicit CBox(double lv = 1.0, double wv = 1.0, double hv = 1.0)
                    :m_Length {lv}, m_Width {wv}, m_Height {hv} {}

protected:
  double m_Length;
  double m_Width;
  double m_Height;
};
```

Now, you can output the usable volume of a CBox object just by calling the showVolume() function for any object for which you require it. The constructor sets the data member values in the initialization list, so no statements are necessary in its body. The data members are protected so they are accessible to the member functions of any derived class.

Suppose you want to derive a class for a different kind of box called CGlassBox, to hold glassware. The contents are fragile, and because packing material is added to protect them, the capacity of the box is less than the capacity of a basic CBox object. You therefore need a different volume() function to account for this, so you add it to the derived class:

```
// GlassBox.h in Ex9_06
#pragma once
#include "Box.h"

class CGlassBox : public CBox              // Derived class
{
public:
  // Function to calculate volume of a CGlassBox
  // allowing 15% for packing
  double volume() const
  { return 0.85*m_Length*m_Width*m_Height; }

  // Constructor
  CGlassBox(double lv, double wv, double hv): CBox {lv, wv, hv} {}
};
```

There could be other members of the derived class, but we'll keep it simple and concentrate on how the inherited functions work for the moment. The constructor for the derived class calls the base constructor in its initialization list to set the data member values. No statements are necessary in its body. You have a new version of the volume() function to replace the version from the base class, the idea being that you can get the inherited function showVolume() to call the derived class version of the member function volume() when you call it for a CGlassBox object.

TRY IT OUT   Using an Inherited Function

You can see how the derived class works in practice very simply by creating objects of the base class and the derived class with the same dimensions and then verifying that the correct volumes are being calculated. The `main()` function to do this is as follows:

```
// Ex9_06.cpp
// Behavior of inherited functions in a derived class
#include <iostream>
#include "GlassBox.h"                    // For CBox and CGlassBox

int main()
{
  CBox myBox {2.0, 3.0, 4.0};           // Define a base box
  CGlassBox myGlassBox {2.0, 3.0, 4.0}; // Define derived box - same size

  myBox.showVolume();                    // Display volume of base box
  myGlassBox.showVolume();               // Display volume of derived box
  return 0;
}
```

How It Works

If you run this example, it produces the following output:

```
CBox usable volume is 24
CBox usable volume is 24
```

This isn't only dull and repetitive, but it's also disastrous. It isn't working the way you want at all, and the only interesting thing about it is why. Evidently, the fact that the second call is for an object of the derived class `CGlassBox` is not being taken into account. You can see this from the incorrect result for the volume in the output. The volume of a `CGlassBox` object should definitely be less than that of a basic `CBox` with the same dimensions.

The incorrect output is because the `volume()` function call in `showVolume()` is being set once and for all by the compiler as the version defined in the base class. `showVolume()` is a base class function and when `CBox` is compiled, the call to `volume()` is resolved at that time to the base class `volume()` function; the compiler has no knowledge of any other `volume()` function. This is called *static resolution* of the function call since the function call is fixed before the program is executed. This is also called *early binding* because the particular `volume()` function chosen is bound to the call from `showVolume()` during the compilation of the program rather than at execution time.

What we were hoping for was that the question of which `volume()` function call to use in any given instance would be resolved when the program was executed. This sort of operation is referred to as *dynamic binding*, or *late binding*. We want the version of `volume()` called by `showVolume()` to be determined by the kind of object being processed, and not arbitrarily fixed by the compiler before the program is executed.

No doubt, you'll be less than astonished that C++ does, in fact, provide you with a way to do this, because this whole discussion would have been futile otherwise! You need something called a *virtual function*.

What Is a Virtual Function?

A *virtual function* is a function in a base class that is declared using the keyword `virtual`. If you specify a function in a base class as `virtual` and the function is redefined in a derived class, it signals to the compiler that you don't want early binding for it. What you *do* want is the function to be called at any given point in the program to be chosen based on the kind of object for which it is called.

TRY IT OUT   Fixing the CGlassBox

To make this example work as originally hoped, you just need to add the `virtual` keyword to the definitions of the `volume()` function in the two classes. You can try this in a new project, `Ex9_07`. Here's how the definition of `CBox` should be:

```
// Box.h in Ex9_07
#pragma once
#include <iostream>

class CBox                                    // Base class
{
public:
  // Function to show the volume of an object
  void showVolume() const
  {
    std::cout << "CBox usable volume is " << volume() << std::endl;
  }

  // Function to calculate the volume of a CBox object
  virtual double volume() const
  { return m_Length*m_Width*m_Height; }

  // Constructor
  explicit CBox(double lv = 1.0, double wv = 1.0, double hv = 1.0) :
                         m_Length{ lv }, m_Width{ wv }, m_Height{ hv } {}

protected:
  double m_Length;
  double m_Width;
  double m_Height;
};
```

The `GlassBox.h` header file contents should be:

```
// GlassBox.h in Ex9_07
#pragma once
#include "Box.h"

class CGlassBox: public CBox                // Derived class
{
public:
  // Function to calculate volume of a CGlassBox allowing 15% for packing
  virtual double volume() const
```

```
        { return 0.85*m_Length*m_Width*m_Height; }

        // Constructor
        CGlassBox(double lv, double wv, double hv): CBox {lv, wv, hv} {}
    };
```

The Ex9_07.cpp file version of main() is the same as for the previous example.

How It Works

This version of the program with just the little word virtual added to the definitions of volume() produces this output:

```
    CBox usable volume is 24
    CBox usable volume is 20.4
```

This is now clearly doing what you wanted in the first place. The first call to showVolume() with the CBox object myBox calls the CBox class version of volume(). The second call with the CGlassBox object myGlassBox calls the version defined in the derived class.

Note that although you have put the keyword virtual in the derived class definition of the function volume(), it's not essential to do so. Specifying the base version of the function as virtual is sufficient. However, I recommend that you do specify the keyword for virtual functions in derived classes because it makes it clear to anyone reading the class definition that they are virtual functions and that they are selected dynamically.

For a function to behave as virtual, it must have the same name, parameter list, and return type in any derived class as the function in the base class, and if the base class function is const, the derived class function must be, too. If you try to use different parameters or return types, or declare one as const and the other not, the virtual function mechanism won't work.

The operation of virtual functions is an extraordinarily powerful mechanism. You may have heard the term *polymorphism* in relation to object-oriented programming, and this refers to the virtual function capability. Something that is polymorphic can appear in different guises, like Dr. Jekyll, or like a politician before and after an election. Calling a virtual function produces different effects depending on the kind of object for which it is being called.

Note that the volume() in the derived CGlassBox class hides the base class version from the view of derived class functions. If you wanted to call the base version of volume() from a derived class function, you would need to use the scope resolution operator and refer to the function as CBox::volume().

Ensuring Correct Virtual Function Operation

As I said in the previous section, for a function to behave as virtual, it must have the same name, parameter list, and return type in any derived class as a function in the base class. It's not difficult to make a mistake though. If you forget to specify volume() as const in CGlassBox in Ex9_07, the program will still compile — it just won't work correctly. When the function in the derived class has a different signature from the function in the base class it is supposed to be overriding, you are not overriding the base function at all. You can tell the compiler that a virtual function in a derived class is overriding a virtual function in a base class by using the `override` modifier. You could do this for the `volume()` function in `CGlassBox` in `Ex9_07` like this:

```
class CGlassBox : public CBox          // Derived class
{
public:
  // Function to calculate volume of a CGlassBox allowing 15% for packing
  virtual double volume() const override
  { return 0.85*m_Length*m_Width*m_Height; }

  // Constructor
  CGlassBox(double lv, double wv, double hv): CBox {lv, wv, hv} {}
};
```

Now the compiler will check that there is a base class `volume()` function with the same signature. If there isn't, you will get an error message. You can demonstrate this by changing the definition of `volume()` in `CGlassBox` by adding the `override` modifier and omitting the `const` keyword.

If you always use the `override` modifier with virtual functions in derived classes, you are guaranteed that any mistakes in specifying the overrides will be reported by the compiler. Note that like the `final` modifier, `override` is not a keyword. It just has special meaning in context.

Preventing Function Overriding

You may want to prevent a member function being overridden. This could be because you want to preserve a particular aspect of behavior. In this case you can specify a member function as `final`. For example, you could specify that the `volume()` member `CBox` class in `Ex9_07` is not to be overridden like this:

```
class CBox                              // Base class
{
public:
  // Class definition as before....

  // Function to calculate the volume of a CBox object
  virtual double volume() const final
  { return m_Length*m_Width*m_Height; }

  // Rest of the class as before...
};
```

The `final` modifier tells the compiler that the `volume()` function must not be overridden. With this amendment in `Ex9_07` the compiler will flag the `volume()` function in the derived class as an error.

Using Pointers to Class Objects

Using pointers to base class and derived class objects is an important technique. You can use a pointer to a base class type to store the address of a derived class object, as well as that of a base class object. Thus you can use a pointer of type "pointer to base" to obtain different behavior with virtual functions, depending on what type of object the pointer is pointing to. You'll see more clearly how this works by looking at an example.

TRY IT OUT Pointers to Base and Derived Classes

You'll use essentially the same classes as in the previous example, but make a small modification to main() so that it uses a pointer to a base class object. Create the Ex9_08 project with Box.h and GlassBox.h header files as in the previous example. You can copy the Box.h and Glassbox.h files from the Ex9_07 project to this project folder. Adding an existing file to a project is quite easy; you right-click Ex9_08 in the Solution Explorer tab, select Add ⇨ Existing Item from the pop-up menu, and then select a file to add it to the project. You can select multiple files to add, if you want. When you have added the headers, modify Ex9_08.cpp to the following:

```
// Ex9_08.cpp
// Using a base class pointer to call a virtual function
#include <iostream>
#include "GlassBox.h"                       // For CBox and CGlassBox

int main()
{
  CBox myBox {2.0, 3.0, 4.0};             // Define a base box
  CGlassBox myGlassBox {2.0, 3.0, 4.0};  // Define derived box of same size
  CBox* pBox {};                // A pointer to base class objects
  pBox = &myBox;                // Set pointer to address of base object
  pBox->showVolume();           // Display volume of base box
  pBox = &myGlassBox;           // Set pointer to derived class object
  pBox->showVolume();           // Display volume of derived box

  return 0;
}
```

In the code download for this example, you will find that I also added the override modifier to the volume() member of the CGlassBox class.

How It Works

The classes are the same as in Ex9_07 but main() now uses a pointer to call showVolume(). Because you are using a pointer, you use the indirect member selection operator, ->, to call the function. The showVolume() function is called twice, and both calls use the same pointer to base class objects, pBox. In the first call, the pointer contains the address of the base object, myBox, and in the second call, it contains the address of the derived class object, myGlassBox.

The output produced is:

```
CBox usable volume is 24
CBox usable volume is 20.4
```

This is exactly the same as that from the previous example, where you used explicit objects in the function calls. You can conclude from this that the virtual function mechanism works just as well through a pointer to a base class, and the function that is called is selected based on the type of object pointed to. This is illustrated in Figure 9-4.

This is an important result. You don't need to know the type of object pointed to by a base class pointer (when a pointer is passed to a function as an argument, for example); the virtual function mechanism will ensure that the correct function is called. This is an extraordinarily powerful capability, so make sure you understand it. Polymorphism is a fundamental mechanism that you will be using again and again.

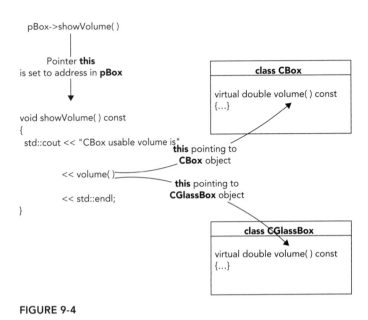

FIGURE 9-4

Using References with Virtual Functions

If you define a function with a parameter that is a reference to a base class type, you can pass an object of a derived class type to it. When the function executes, the appropriate virtual function for the object passed as the reference argument is selected automatically. You can see this happening by modifying main() in the previous example to call a function that has a reference parameter.

TRY IT OUT Using References with Virtual Functions

Let's move the call to showVolume() in main() into a separate function and call that separate function from main():

```
// Ex9_09.cpp
// Using a reference to call a virtual function
#include <iostream>
#include "GlassBox.h"                    // For CBox and CGlassBox

void output(const CBox& aBox);          // Function prototype

int main()
{
  CBox myBox {2.0, 3.0, 4.0};           // Define a base box
  CGlassBox myGlassBox {2.0, 3.0, 4.0}; // Define derived box of same size
  output(myBox);                        // Output volume of base class object
  output(myGlassBox);                   // Output volume of derived class object

  return 0;
```

```
    }

    void output(const CBox& aBox)
    {
      aBox.showVolume();
    }
```

`Box.h` and `GlassBox.h` for this example are the same as in the previous example.

How It Works

The `main()` function now consists of two calls of the `output()` function: the first with a base class object as the argument and the second with a derived class object. Because the parameter is a reference to the base class, the `output()` function will accept an object of any class derived from `CBox` as an argument, as well as a `CBox` object, of course. The appropriate version of the virtual function `volume()` will be called, depending on the object that initialized the reference parameter.

The program produces the same output as the previous example, demonstrating that the virtual function mechanism does indeed work through a reference parameter. You now know that polymorphism works with both pointers and references.

Pure Virtual Functions

It's possible that you'd want to include a virtual function in a base class so that it may be redefined in a derived class and thus get polymorphic behavior with derived class objects, but there is no meaningful definition for the function in the base class. For example, you might have a `CContainer` class, which could be a base for defining the `CBox` class, or a `CBottle` class, or even a `CTeapot` class. The `CContainer` class wouldn't have data members, but you might want to provide `volume()` as a virtual member function to allow it to be called polymorphically for any derived class object. Because `CContainer` has no data members and therefore no container dimensions, there is no sensible definition for the `volume()` function. However, you can still define the class including `volume()` like this:

```
// Container.h for Ex9_10
#pragma once
#include <iostream>

class CContainer          // Generic base class for specific containers
{
public:
  // Function for calculating a volume - no content
  // This is defined as a 'pure' virtual function, signified by '= 0'
  virtual double volume() const = 0;

  // Function to display a volume
  virtual void showVolume() const
  { std::cout << "Volume is " << volume() << std::endl; }
};
```

The statement for the virtual function volume() defines it as having no content by placing the equals sign and zero in the function header. This is called a *pure virtual function*. The class also contains the showVolume() function that displays the volume of derived class objects. Because this function is virtual, it can be replaced in a derived class but if it isn't, this inherited base class version is called for derived class objects.

Abstract Classes

A class that contains a pure virtual function is called an *abstract class*. It's called *abstract* because you can't define objects of a class that contains a pure virtual function. However, you can define pointers and references of an abstract class type. An abstract class exists only for the purpose of deriving classes from it. If a class that is derived from an abstract class does not define a pure virtual function that is inherited from the base class, then it is also an abstract class.

You should not conclude from the example of the CContainer class that an abstract class can't have data members. An abstract class can have both data members and member functions. The presence of a pure virtual function is the only condition that makes a class abstract. An abstract class can have several pure virtual functions. In this case a derived class must define every pure virtual function inherited from its base, otherwise it too will be an abstract class. If you forget to make the derived class version of the volume() function const, the derived class will still be abstract because it contains the pure virtual volume() function that is const, as well as the non-const version. const and non-const functions are always differentiated.

TRY IT OUT   **An Abstract Class**

You could implement a CCan class, representing beer or cola cans, perhaps, together with the original CBox class, and derive both from the CContainer class that you defined in the previous section. The definition of CBox as a subclass of CContainer is as follows:

```
// Box.h for Ex9_10
#pragma once
#include "Container.h"              // For CContainer definition
#include <iostream>

class CBox : public CContainer      // Derived class
{
public:

  // Function to show the volume of an object
  virtual void showVolume() const override
  { std::cout << "CBox usable volume is " << volume() << std::endl; }

  // Function to calculate the volume of a CBox object
  virtual double volume() const override
  { return m_Length*m_Width*m_Height; }

  // Constructor
  explicit CBox(double lv = 1.0, double wv = 1.0, double hv = 1.0)
                    :m_Length {lv}, m_Width {wv}, m_Height{hv} {}

protected:
```

```
    double m_Length;
    double m_Width;
    double m_Height;
};
```

The CBox class is essentially as you had it in the previous example, except that this time you have specified that it is derived from the CContainer class. The volume () function is fully defined within CBox (as it must be if this class is to be used to define objects). The only other option would be to specify it as a pure virtual function because it is pure in the base class but then you could not create CBox objects.

You can define the CCan class in the Can.h header file like this:

```
// Can.h for Ex9_10
#pragma once
#define _USE_MATH_DEFINES          // For constants in math.h
#include <math.h>
#include "Container.h"             // For CContainer definition

class CCan : public CContainer
{
public:
  // Function to calculate the volume of a can
  virtual double volume() const override
  { return 0.25*M_PI*m_Diameter*m_Diameter*m_Height; }

  // Constructor
  explicit CCan(double hv = 4.0, double dv = 2.0): m_Height {hv}, m_Diameter {dv} {}

protected:
  double m_Height;
  double m_Diameter;
};
```

The CCan class also defines a volume() function based on the formula $h\pi r^2$ where h is the height of a can and r is the radius of the cross-section. The constant, M_PI, is defined in math.h and becomes available when _USE_MATH_DEFINES is defined. The math.h header defines a wealth of other mathematical constants that you can see if you place the cursor in math.h in the code and press Ctrl+Shift+G. The volume is calculated as the height multiplied by the area of the base. Notice that the CBox class redefines the showVolume() function, but the CCan class does not. You will see the effect of this in the output.

You can exercise these classes with the following source file:

```
// Ex9_10.cpp
// Using an abstract class
#include "Box.h"                    // For CBox and CContainer
#include "Can.h"                    // For CCan (and CContainer)
#include <iostream>                 // For stream I/O

int main()
{
  // Pointer to abstract base class
  // initialized with address of CBox object
  CContainer* pC1 {new CBox {2.0, 3.0, 4.0}};

  // Pointer to abstract base class
```

```
      // initialized with address of CCan object
      CContainer* pC2 {new CCan {6.5, 3.0}};

      pC1->showVolume();                    // Output the volumes of the two
      pC2->showVolume();                    // objects pointed to

      delete pC1;                           // Now clean up ...
      delete pC2;                           // ... the free store

      return 0;
    }
```

How It Works

You define two pointers to the base class, CContainer. Although you can't define CContainer objects (because CContainer is an abstract class), you can still define pointers of type CContainer*, which you can use to store the address of any object whose type is a direct or indirect subclass of CContainer. The pointer pC1 is assigned the address of a CBox object created in the free store by the operator new. The second pointer is assigned the address of a CCan object in a similar manner.

Of course, because you created the derived class objects dynamically, you must use the delete operator to clean up the free store when you have finished with them. You learned about delete back in Chapter 4.

The output produced by this example is as follows:

```
    CBox usable volume is 24
    Volume is 45.9458
```

Because you defined showVolume() in the CBox class, the derived class version of the function is called for the CBox object. You did not define this function in the CCan class, so the base class version that CCan inherits is called for the CCan object. Because volume() is a virtual function that is implemented in both derived classes (necessarily, because it is a pure virtual function in the base class), the call to it is resolved when the program executes by selecting the version from the class of the object being pointed to. Thus, for the pointer pC1, the CBox version is called and for pC2 the CCan version is called. Therefore you obtain the correct result in each case.

You could equally well have used one pointer and assigned the address of the CCan object to it after calling the volume() function for the CBox object. A base class pointer can contain the address of any derived class object, even when several different classes are derived from the same base class, and so you can have automatic selection of the appropriate virtual function across a whole range of derived classes. Impressive stuff, isn't it?

Indirect Base Classes

At the beginning of this chapter, I said that a base class for a given class could, in turn, be derived from another, "more" base class. A small extension of the last example will illustrate this, as well as demonstrating the use of a virtual function across a second level of inheritance.

More Than One Level of Inheritance

All you need to do is to add the CGlassBox class to the classes you have from the previous example. The relationship between the classes you will then have is illustrated in Figure 9-5.

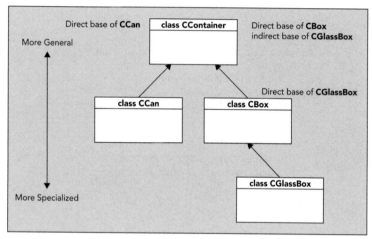

FIGURE 9-5

CGlassBox is derived from CBox exactly as before, but you omit the derived class version of show Volume() to show that the base class version still propagates through the derived classes. With the class hierarchy shown in Figure 9-5, CContainer is an indirect base of CGlassBox, and a direct base of the CBox and CCan classes.

The GlassBox.h header file for the example contains:

```
// GlassBox.h for Ex9_11
#pragma once
#include "Box.h"                    // For CBox

class CGlassBox: public CBox        // Derived class
{
public:

    // Function to calculate volume of a CGlassBox allowing 15% for packing
    virtual double volume() const override
    { return 0.85*m_Length*m_Width*m_Height; }

    // Constructor
    CGlassBox(double lv, double wv, double hv): CBox {lv, wv, hv} {}
};
```

The Container.h, Can.h, and Box.h header files contain the same code as those in the previous example, Ex9_10.

The main source file for the new example is as follows:

```cpp
// Ex9_11.cpp
// Using an abstract class with multiple levels of inheritance
#include "Box.h"                  // For CBox and CContainer
#include "Can.h"                  // For CCan (and CContainer)
#include "GlassBox.h"             // For CGlassBox (and CBox and CContainer)
#include <iostream>               // For stream I/O

int main()
{
  // Pointer to abstract base class initialized with CBox object address
  CContainer* pC1 {new CBox {2.0, 3.0, 4.0}};
  CCan myCan {6.5, 3.0};                     // Define CCan object
  CGlassBox myGlassBox {2.0, 3.0, 4.0};      // Define CGlassBox object
  pC1->showVolume();                          // Output the volume of CBox
  delete pC1;                                 // Now clean up the free store

  pC1 = &myCan;                               // Put myCan address in pointer
  pC1->showVolume();                          // Output the volume of CCan
  pC1 = &myGlassBox;                          // Put myGlassBox address in pointer
  pC1->showVolume();                          // Output the volume of CGlassBox

  return 0;
}
```

How It Works

You have the three-level class hierarchy shown in Figure 9-5 with CContainer as an abstract base class because it contains the pure virtual function, volume(). The main() function now calls showVolume() three times using the same base class pointer, but with the pointer containing the address of an object of a different type each time. Because showVolume() is not defined in either CCan or CGlassBox, the inherited version is called in each instance. A separate branch from the base CContainer defines the derived class CCan so CCan inherits showVolume() from CContainer and CGlassBox inherits the function from CBox.

The example produces this output:

```
CBox usable volume is 24
Volume is 45.9458
CBox usable volume is 20.4
```

The output shows that one of the three different versions of the function volume() is selected for execution according to the type of object involved.

Note that you must delete the CBox object from the free store before you assign another value to the pointer. If you don't do this, you won't be able to clean up the free store, because you would have no record of the address of the original object. This is an easy mistake to make when reassigning pointers and using the free store. You'll be able to avoid the possibility of this mistake by using smart pointers that you'll learn about in Chapter 10.

Virtual Destructors

A problem that arises when dealing with objects of derived classes using a pointer to a base class is that the correct destructor may not be called. You can see this happening by modifying the last example.

TRY IT OUT   Calling the Wrong Destructor

You need to add a public destructor that outputs a message to each of the classes in the example so that you can track which destructor is called when the objects are destroyed. The destructor for the CContainer class in the Container.h file for this example is:

```
~CContainer()
{ std::cout << "CContainer destructor called" << std::endl; }
```

The destructor for the CCan class in Can.h in the example is:

```
~CCan()
{ std::cout << "CCan destructor called" << std::endl; }
```

The CBox class destructor in Box.h should be:

```
~CBox()
{ std::cout << "CBox destructor called" << std::endl; }
```

The CGlassBox destructor in the GlassBox.h header file should be:

```
~CGlassBox()
{ std::cout << "CGlassBox destructor called" << std::endl; }
```

Finally, the source file Ex9_12.cpp for the program should be:

```
// Ex9_12.cpp
// Destructor calls with derived classes using objects via a base class pointer
#include "Box.h"                          // For CBox and CContainer
#include "Can.h"                          // For CCan (and CContainer)
#include "GlassBox.h"                     // For CGlassBox (and CBox, CContainer)
#include <iostream>                       // For stream I/O

int main()
{
  // Pointer to abstract base class initialized with CBox object address
  CContainer* pC1 {new CBox{2.0, 3.0, 4.0}};
  CCan myCan {6.5, 3.0};
  CGlassBox myGlassBox {2.0, 3.0, 4.0};
  pC1->showVolume();                      // Output the volume of CBox
  std::cout << "Delete CBox" << std::endl;
  delete pC1;                             // Now clean up the free store
  pC1 = new CGlassBox {4.0, 5.0, 6.0};    // Create CGlassBox dynamically
  pC1->showVolume();                      // ...output its volume...
  std::cout << "Delete CGlassBox" << std::endl;
  delete pC1;                             // ...and delete it
  pC1 = &myCan;                           // Get myCan address in pointer
  pC1->showVolume();                      // Output the volume of CCan
```

```
    pC1 = &myGlassBox;              // Get myGlassBox address in pointer
    pC1->showVolume();              // Output the volume of CGlassBox

    return 0;
}
```

How It Works

Apart from adding a destructor to each class that outputs a message to the effect that it was called, the only other change is a couple of additions to main(). There are additional statements that create a CGlassBox object dynamically, output its volume, and then delete it. There are messages displayed to indicate when the dynamically created objects are deleted. The output generated by this example is:

```
CBox usable volume is 24
Delete CBox
CContainer destructor called
CBox usable volume is 102
Delete CGlassBox
CContainer destructor called
Volume is 45.9458
CBox usable volume is 20.4
CGlassBox destructor called
CBox destructor called
CContainer destructor called
CCan destructor called
CContainer destructor called
```

You can see that when you delete the CBox object pointed to by pC1, the destructor for the base class CContainer is called, but there is no call of the CBox destructor. Similarly, when the CGlassBox object is deleted, the destructor for the base class CContainer is called but not the CGlassBox or CBox destructors. For the myCan and myGlassBox objects that are created statically, the correct destructor calls occur with the derived class destructor being called first, followed by the base class destructor. For the myGlassBox object, there are three destructor calls: first, the destructor for the derived class, then the direct base destructor, and finally the indirect base destructor.

All the problems are with objects created in the free store. In both cases, the wrong destructor is called. The reason for this is that the linkage to the destructors is resolved statically, at compile time. For the automatic objects, there is no problem — the compiler knows what they are and arranges for the correct destructors to be called. With objects created dynamically and accessed through a pointer, things are different. The only information that the compiler has when the delete operation is compiled is that the pointer type is a pointer to the base class. The type of object the pointer is pointing to is unknown to the compiler because this is determined when the program executes. The compiler, therefore, simply ensures that the delete operation is set up to call the base class destructor. In a real application, this can cause a lot of problems, with bits of objects left strewn around the free store and possibly more serious problems, depending on the nature of the objects.

The solution is simple. You need the calls to be resolved dynamically — as the program is executed. You can organize this by using *virtual destructors*. As I said when I first discussed virtual functions, it's sufficient to declare a base class function as virtual to ensure that all functions in any derived classes with the same name, parameter list, and return type are virtual as well. This applies to destructors just as it does to ordinary member functions. You need to add the keyword `virtual` to the definition of the destructor in the class `CContainer` in `Container.h`:

```
class CContainer                       // Generic base class for containers
{
 public:

   // Destructor
   virtual ~CContainer()
   { std::cout << "CContainer destructor called" << std::endl; }

   // Rest of the class as before
};
```

Now, the destructors in all the derived classes are automatically virtual, even though you don't explicitly specify them as such. Of course, you're free to specify them as virtual if you want the code to be absolutely clear.

If you rerun the example with this change, it produces the following output:

```
CBox usable volume is 24
Delete CBox
CBox destructor called
CContainer destructor called
CBox usable volume is 102
Delete CGlassBox
CGlassBox destructor called
CBox destructor called
CContainer destructor called
Volume is 45.9458
CBox usable volume is 20.4
CGlassBox destructor called
CBox destructor called
CContainer destructor called
CCan destructor called
CContainer destructor called
```

As you can see, all the objects are now destroyed with a proper sequence of destructor calls. Destroying the dynamic objects produces the same sequence of destructor calls as the automatic objects of the same type.

The question may arise in your mind at this point, can constructors be declared as virtual? The answer is no — only destructors and other member functions.

> **NOTE** It's a good idea to declare your base class destructor as virtual as a matter of course when using inheritance. There is a small overhead in the execution of the destructors but you won't notice it in the majority of circumstances. Using virtual destructors ensures that your objects will be properly destroyed and avoids potential program crashes that might otherwise occur.

CASTING BETWEEN CLASS TYPES

You have seen how you can store the address of a derived class object in a variable that is a pointer to a base class type, so a variable of type CContainer* can store the address of a CBox object for example. So if you have an address stored in a pointer of type CContainer*, can you cast it to type CBox*? Indeed, you can, and the dynamic_cast operator is specifically intended for this kind of operation. Here's how it works:

```
CContainer* pContainer {new CGlassBox {2.0, 3.0, 4.0}};
CBox* pBox {dynamic_cast<CBox*>(pContainer)};
CGlassBox* pGlassBox {dynamic_cast<CGlassBox*>(pContainer)};
```

The first statement stores the address of the CGlassBox object created on the heap in a base class pointer of type CContainer*. The second statement casts pContainer down the class hierarchy to type CBox*. The third statement casts the address in pContainer to its actual type, CGlassBox*.

You can apply the dynamic_cast operator to references as well as pointers. The difference between dynamic_cast and static_cast is that dynamic_cast checks the validity of a cast at run time, whereas the static_cast operator does not. If a dynamic_cast operation is not valid, the result is nullptr. The compiler relies on the programmer for the validity of a static_cast operation, so you should always use dynamic_cast for casting up and down a class hierarchy and check for a nullptr result if you want to avoid abrupt termination of your program.

Defining Conversion Operators

You can define operator functions in a class that convert an object to another type. The conversion can be to a fundamental type or a class type. For example, suppose you want to test whether a CBox object has dimensions other than the defaults of 1. You could provide for this by defining an operator function for CBox objects for conversion to type bool. For example, you could define the following member within the CBox class definition:

```
operator bool()
{  return m_Length == 1 && m_Width == 1 && m_Height == 1;  }
```

This defines the function operator bool(). The function returns true when all the dimensions of the CBox object are 1 and false otherwise. The name of an operator function for conversion is always the operator keyword followed by the destination type name. The destination type in the function name is the return type, so no return type needs to be specified in addition.

With the operator bool() function defined in the CBox class you could write this:

```
CBox box1;                         // Calls default constructor
if(box1)                           // Implicit conversion of box1 to bool
   std::cout << "box1 has default dimensions." << std::endl;
```

The if expression has to be type bool so the compiler will insert a call of the operator bool() function for box1 to make the if expression box1.operator bool().

You can also write the following:

```
CBox box2 {1, 2, 3};
bool isDefault {true};
isDefault = box2;                  // Implicit conversion to bool
```

Assigning the value of `box2` to `isDefault` also requires an implicit conversion so the operator function call will be inserted. Of course, you can write explicit conversions, too:

```
isDefault = static_cast<bool>(box1);    // Explicit conversion
```

This statement also calls `operator bool()` so it is equivalent to:

```
isDefault = box1.operator bool();
```

Explicit Conversion Operators

It may be that you do not want to allow implicit conversions that use a conversion operator function. This is particularly the case for conversions between class types. You can prevent this by prefixing the conversion operator function with the `explicit` keyword. Now compilation of any statement requiring an implicit type conversion will fail with an error message.

Only explicit conversion will compile correctly.

NESTED CLASSES

You can put the definition of one class inside the definition of another, in which case, you have defined a *nested class*. A nested class has the appearance of being a static member of the class that encloses it and is subject to the member access specifiers, just like any other member of the class. If you place a nested class definition in the private section of a class, the class can only be referenced from within the scope of the enclosing class. If you specify a nested class as `public`, the class is accessible from outside the enclosing class, but the nested class name must be qualified by the outer class name in such circumstances.

A nested class has free access to all the static members of the enclosing class. All the instance members can be accessed through an object of the enclosing class type, or a pointer or reference to an object. The enclosing class can only access the public members of the nested class, but in a nested class that is private in the enclosing class, the members are frequently declared as `public` to allow functions in the enclosing class free access to the entire nested class.

A nested class is particularly useful when you want to define a type that is only to be used within another type. In this case the nested class can be declared as `private`. Here's an example:

```
// A push-down stack to store CBox objects
#pragma once
class CBox;                               // Forward class declaration

class CStack
{
private:
  // Defines items to store in the stack
  struct CItem
  {
    CBox* pBox;                           // Pointer to the object in this node
    CItem* pNext;                         // Pointer to next item in the stack or null

    // Constructor
    CItem(CBox* pB, CItem* pN): pBox {pB}, pNext {pN} {}
```

```cpp
  };

  CItem* pTop {};                        // Pointer to item that is at the top

public:
  CStack()=default;                      // Constructor

  // Inhibit copy construction and assignment
  CStack(const CStack& stack) = delete;
  CStack& operator=(const CStack& stack) = delete;

  // Push a Box object onto the stack
  void push(CBox* pBox)
  {
    pTop = new CItem(pBox, pTop);        // Create new item and make it the top
  }

  // Pop an object off the stack
  CBox* pop()
  {
    if(!pTop)                            // If the stack is empty
      return nullptr;                    // return null

    CBox* pBox = pTop->pBox;             // Get box from item
    CItem* pTemp = pTop;                 // Save address of the top item
    pTop = pTop->pNext;                  // Make next item the top
    delete pTemp;                        // Delete old top item from the heap
    return pBox;
  }

  // Destructor
  virtual ~CStack()
  {
    CItem* pTemp {};
    while(pTop)                          // While pTop not null
    {
      pTemp = pTop;
      pTop = pTop->pNext;
      delete pTemp;
    }
  }
};
```

The CStack class defines a push-down stack for storing CBox objects. To be absolutely precise, it stores pointers to CBox objects so the objects pointed to are still the responsibility of the code using the CStack class. The nested struct, CItem, defines the items that are held in the stack. I chose to define CItem as a nested struct rather than a nested class because members of a struct are public by default. You could define CItem as a class and then specify the members as public so they can be accessed from the functions in CStack. The stack is implemented as a linked list of CItem objects, where each object stores a pointer to a CBox object plus the address of the next CItem object down in the stack. The push() function in CStack pushes a CBox object onto the stack, and the pop() function pops an object off the stack.

Pushing an object onto the stack creates a new CItem object holding the address of the object to be stored plus the address of the previous top item. The top item is nullptr initially. Popping an object off the stack returns the address of the object in pTop. The top item is deleted and the next item becomes the top of the stack.

Because a CStack object creates CItem objects on the heap, we need a destructor to delete any remaining CItem objects when a CStack object is destroyed. The process works down through the stack, deleting the top item after the address of the next item has been saved in pTop. Let's see if it works.

TRY IT OUT   Using a Nested Class

This example uses the CContainer, CBox, and CGlassBox classes from Ex9_12, so create an empty Win32 console project, **Ex9_13**, and add the header files containing those class definitions to it. Then add Stack.h to the project containing the definition of the CStack class from the previous section, and add Ex9_13.cpp to the project with the following contents:

```cpp
// Ex9_13.cpp
// Using a nested class to define a stack
#include "Box.h"            // For CBox and CContainer
#include "GlassBox.h"       // For CGlassBox (and CBox and CContainer)
#include "Stack.h"          // For the stack class with nested struct CItem
#include <iostream>         // For stream I/O

int main()
{
  CBox* pBoxes[] { new CBox{2.0, 3.0, 4.0},
                   new CGlassBox{2.0, 3.0, 4.0},
                   new CBox{4.0, 5.0, 6.0},
                   new CGlassBox{4.0, 5.0, 6.0}
                 };
  std::cout << "The boxes have the following volumes:\n";
  for (const CBox* pBox : pBoxes)
    pBox->showVolume();              // Output the volume of a box

  std::cout << "\nNow pushing the boxes on the stack...\n\n";
  CStack stack;                      // Create the stack
  for (CBox* pBox : pBoxes)          // Store box pointers in the stack
    stack.push(pBox);

  std::cout << "Popping the boxes off the stack presents them in reverse order:\n";
  CBox* pTemp {};
  while(pTemp = stack.pop())
    pTemp->showVolume();

  for (CBox* pBox : pBoxes)          // Delete the boxes
    delete pBox;
  return 0;
}
```

I removed the output statements from the `CContainer`, `CBox`, and `CGlassBox` class destructors. The output from this example is:

```
The boxes have the following volumes:
CBox usable volume is 24
CBox usable volume is 20.4
CBox usable volume is 120
CBox usable volume is 102

Now pushing the boxes on the stack...

Popping the boxes off the stack presents them in reverse order:
CBox usable volume is 102
CBox usable volume is 120
CBox usable volume is 20.4
CBox usable volume is 24
```

How It Works

An array of pointers to `CBox` objects can store addresses of `CBox` objects or addresses of any type that is derived from `CBox`. The `pBoxes` array is initialized with the addresses of four objects created on the heap:

```
CBox* pBoxes[] { new CBox{2.0, 3.0, 4.0},
                 new CGlassBox{2.0, 3.0, 4.0},
                 new CBox{4.0, 5.0, 6.0},
                 new CGlassBox{4.0, 5.0, 6.0}
               };
```

There are two `CBox` objects and two `CGlassBox` objects with the same dimensions as the `CBox` objects.

You list the volumes of the objects in the `pBoxes` array in a range-based `for` loop. You then create a `CStack` object and push the pointers to the objects onto the stack in another range-based `for` loop:

```
CStack stack;                     // Create the stack
for (CBox* pBox : pBoxes)         // Store box pointers in the stack
  stack.push(pBox);
```

Each element in the `pBoxes` array is pushed onto the stack by passing the element to the `push()` member for the `stack` object. This results in the first element from the array being at the bottom of the stack, and the last element at the top.

You pop the objects off the stack in a `while` loop:

```
CBox* pTemp {};
while(pTemp = stack.pop())
  pTemp->showVolume();
```

The `pop()` function returns the address of the element at the top of the stack, and you use this to call the `showVolume()` function for the object. The loop ends when the `pop()` function returns `nullptr`. Because the last element was at the top of the stack, the loop lists the volumes of the objects in reverse order. From the output, you can see that the `CStack` class does, indeed, implement a stack using a nested `struct` to define the items to be stored in the stack.

SUMMARY

This chapter covered the principal ideas involved in using inheritance.

You have now gone through all of the important language features of C++. It's important that you feel comfortable with the mechanisms for defining and deriving classes and the process of inheritance. Windows programming with Visual C++ involves extensive use of all these concepts.

EXERCISES

1. What's wrong with the following code?

```
class CBadClass
{
private:
    int len;
    char* p;
public:
    CBadClass(const char* str): p {str}, len {strlen(p)} {}
    CBadClass(){}
};
```

2. Suppose you have a CBird class that you want to use as a base class for deriving a hierarchy of bird classes:

```
class CBird
{
protected:
    int wingSpan {};
    int eggSize {};
    int airSpeed {};
    int altitude {};
public:
    virtual void fly() { altitude = 100; }
};
```

Is it reasonable to create a CHawk by deriving from CBird? How about a COstrich? Justify your answers. Derive an avian hierarchy that can cope with both of these birds.

3. Given the following class,

```
class CBase
{
protected:
    int m_anInt;
public:
    CBase(int n): m_anInt {n} { std::cout << "Base constructor\n"; }
    virtual void print() const = 0;
};
```

what sort of class is CBase and why? Derive a class from CBase that sets the value of m_anInt when an object is created and prints it on request. Write a test program to verify that your class is correct.

4. A binary tree is a structure made up of nodes, where each node contains a pointer to a "left" node and a pointer to a "right" node plus a data item, as shown in Figure 9-6.

The tree starts with a root node, and this is the starting point for accessing the nodes in the tree. Either or both pointers in a node can be nullptr. Figure 9-6 shows an ordered binary tree, which is a tree organized so that the value of each node is always greater than or equal to the left node and less than or equal to the right node.

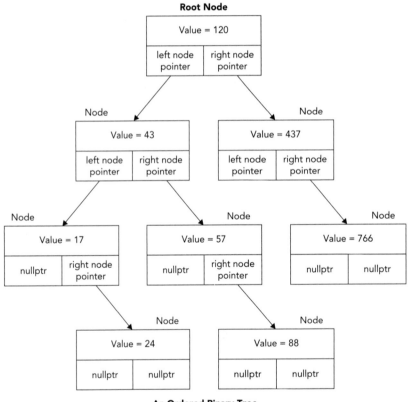

An Ordered Binary Tree

FIGURE 9-6

Define a class that defines an ordered binary tree that stores integer values. You also need to define a Node class, but that can be an inner class to the BinaryTree class. Write a program to test the operation of your BinaryTree class by storing an arbitrary sequence of integers in it and retrieving and outputting them in ascending sequence.

Hint: Don't be afraid to use recursion.

➤ WHAT YOU LEARNED IN THIS CHAPTER

TOPIC	CONCEPT
Inherited members of a class	A derived class inherits all the members of a base class except for constructors, the destructor, and the overloaded assignment operator.
Accessibility of inherited members of a class	Members of a base class declared as `private` in the base class are not accessible in any derived class. To obtain the effect of the keyword `private` but allow access in a derived class, you should use the keyword `protected` in place of `private`.
Access specifiers for a base class	A base class can be specified for a derived class with the keyword `public`, `private`, or `protected`. If none is specified, the default is `private`. Depending on the keyword specified for a base, the access level of the inherited members may be modified.
Constructors in derived classes	If you write a derived class constructor, you must arrange for data members of the base class to be initialized properly, as well as those of the derived class.
Virtual functions	A function in a base class may be declared as `virtual`. This allows other definitions of the function appearing in derived classes to be selected at execution time, depending on the type of object for which the function call is made.
Using `override`	When you define a virtual function in a derived class with the `override` modifier specified, the compiler will verify that a direct or indirect base class contains a virtual function with the same signature, and will issue an error message if this is not the case.
Final function members of a class	If a member function of a class is specified using the `final` modifier, a derived class cannot override the function. Any attempt to override the function will result in a compiler error message.
Final classes	A class that is `final` cannot be used as a base for another class. Attempting to use a `final` class as a base will result in a compiler error message.
Virtual destructors	You should declare class destructors as `virtual` in a class that can be a base for other classes. This ensures correct selection of a destructor for dynamically-created derived class objects.

TOPIC	CONCEPT
friend classes	A class may be designated as a `friend` of another class. In this case, all the member functions of the `friend` class may access all the members of the other class. If class A is a `friend` of B, class B is not a `friend` of A unless it has been declared as such.
Pure virtual functions	A virtual function in a base class can be specified as pure by placing `=0` at the end of the function declaration. The class then is an abstract class for which no objects can be created. In any derived class, all pure virtual functions inherited from the base class must be defined; if not, the derived class is abstract.

10

The Standard Template Library

WHAT IS THE STANDARD TEMPLATE LIBRARY?

As its name implies, the Standard Template Library is a library of standard class and function templates. You can use these templates to create a wide range of powerful general-purpose classes for organizing your data, as well as functions for processing that data in various ways. The STL is defined by the standard for C++ and is therefore always available with a conforming compiler. Because of its broad applicability, the STL can greatly simplify programming in many of your applications.

I'll first explain, in general terms, the kinds of resources the STL provides and how they interact with one another, before diving into the details of working examples. The STL contains six kinds of components: containers, container adapters, iterators, algorithms, function objects, and function adapters. Because they are part of the standard library, the names of the STL components are all defined within the std namespace.

The STL is a very large library, some of which is highly specialized, and to cover the contents fully would require a book in its own right. In this chapter, I'll introduce the fundamentals of how you use the STL and describe the more commonly used capabilities. Let's start with containers.

Containers

Containers are objects that you use to store and organize other objects. A class that implements a linked list is an example of a container. You create a container class from an STL template by supplying the type of the object that you intend to store. For example, vector<T> is a template for a container that is a linear array that automatically increases in size when necessary. T is the type parameter that specifies the type of objects to be stored. Here are a couple of statements that create vector<T> containers:

```
std::vector<std::string> strings;    // Stores object of type string
std::vector<double> data;            // Stores values of type double
```

The first statement creates the strings container class that stores objects of type string, while the second statement creates the data container that stores values of type double.

You can store items of a fundamental type, or of any class type, in a container. If your type argument for a container template is a class type, the container can store objects of that type, or potentially of any derived class type. However, storing objects of a derived class type in a container created for base class objects will cause object slicing. Object slicing results in the derived part of an object being sliced off and occurs when you pass a derived class object by value for a parameter of a base class type. The base class copy constructor will be called to copy the derived class object, and because this constructor has no knowledge of derived class data members, they will not be copied. You can avoid slicing of objects of a derived type by storing pointers in the container. You can store pointers to a derived class type in a container that stores base class pointers.

The templates for the STL container classes are defined in the standard headers shown in the following table:

HEADER FILE	CONTENTS
vector	A vector<T> container represents an array that stores elements of type T that automatically increases its size when required. You can only add new elements efficiently to the end of a vector container.
array	An array<T,N> container represents an array with a fixed number of elements, N, of type T. One advantage of this container over a normal array is that it is an object that knows its size, so when you pass an array<> container to a function it retains knowledge of the number of elements. An array<> container has an advantage over a vector<> in that it can be allocated entirely on the stack, whereas a vector<> needs heap access.

deque	A deque<T> container implements a double-ended queue of elements of type T. This is equivalent to a vector with the capability for adding elements to the beginning efficiently.
list	A list<T> container is a doubly-linked list of elements of type T.
forward_list	A forward_list<T> container is a singly linked list of elements of type T. Inserting and deleting elements in a forward_list<T> will be faster than in a list<T> as long as you are processing the list elements in a forward direction.
map	A map<K,T> is an associative container that stores each object (of type T) with an associated key (of type K). Key/object pairs are stored in the map as objects of type pair<K,T>, which is another STL template type. The key determines where the key/object pair is located and is used to retrieve an object. Each key must be unique. This header also defines the multimap<K,T> container where the keys in the key/object pairs need not be unique.
unordered_map	An unordered_map<K,T> container is similar to a map<K,T>, except that the key/object pairs are in no particular order in the container. Pairs are grouped into buckets based on hash values produced from the keys. The unordered_multimap<K,T> container is also in this header. This differs from an unordered_map<K,T> container in that the keys do not have to be unique.
set	A set<T> container is a map where each element serves as its own key. All elements in a set must be unique. A consequence of using an object as its own key is that you cannot change an object in a set; to change an object you must delete it and then insert the modified version. The elements in the container are ordered in ascending sequence by default but you can arrange to order them in any sequence you want. This header also defines the multiset<T> container, which is a set container where the elements need not be unique.
unordered_set	An unordered_set<T> container is similar to a set<T> except that the elements are not ordered in any particular way, but are organized into buckets depending on the hash values of the elements. Like set<T>, the elements must be unique. The unordered_multiset<T> container that is also in this header is similar to unordered_set<T>, except that the elements can be duplicated.
bitset	Defines the bitset<T> class template that represents a fixed number of bits. This is typically used to store flags that represent a set of states or conditions.

All the template names are defined within the std namespace. T is the template type parameter for the type of elements stored in a container; where keys are used, K is the type of key.

Allocators

Most of the STL containers grow their size automatically to accommodate however many elements you store. Additional memory for these containers is made available by an object called an allocator that allocates space when required. You can optionally supply your own allocator object type through an additional type parameter. For example, the vector<T> template for creating a vector is really a vector<T, Allocator=allocator<T>> template, where the second type parameter, Allocator, is the allocator type. The second type parameter has the default value allocator<T> so this allocator type is used when you don't specify your own.

Your allocator must be defined as a class template with a type parameter so that an instance of the allocator type can match the type of element stored in the container. For example, suppose you have defined your own class template, My_Allocator<T>, to provide memory to a container on request. You could then create a vector container that will use your allocator with the statement:

```
auto data = vector<CBox, My_Allocator<CBox>>();
```

This container stores elements of type CBox with additional memory being allocated to the container by an object of type My_Allocator<CBox>.

So why would you want to define your own allocator when you can always use the default? The primary reason is efficiency in particular circumstances. For example, your application may lend itself to allocating a large chunk of memory on the heap that your allocator can issue piecemeal to the container without further dynamic memory operations. You can then release the memory in one go when the container is no longer required. I won't be delving deeper into how you can define your own allocators. It's not that it's difficult — but I have to stop somewhere.

Comparators

Some containers use a comparator object that is used to determine the order of elements within the container. For example, the map<K, T> container template is really:

```
map<K, T, Compare=less<K>, Allocator=allocator<pair<K,T>> >
```

allocator<pair<K,T>> is an allocator type for key/object pairs and Compare is a function object type that acts as a comparator for keys of type K and determines the order in which the key/object pairs are stored. The last two type parameters have default values so you don't have to supply them. The default comparator type, less<K>, is a function object template defined in the STL that implements a "less than" comparison between objects of type K. I will discuss function objects later in this chapter.

It is quite likely that you will want to specify your own comparator for a map. You might want ordering based on "greater than" comparisons for the keys you are using. Supplying your own allocator type is much less likely. For this reason the allocator type parameter for the template comes last.

> **NOTE** *I won't be discussing allocators or comparators further. I will therefore ignore the optional template type parameters for these in all subsequent discussions of containers.*

Container Adapters

A *container adapter* is a template class that wraps an existing container class to provide a different, and typically more restricted, capability. The container adapters are defined in the headers in the following table.

HEADER FILE	CONTENTS
queue	A queue<T> container is defined by an adapter from a deque<T> container by default, but you could define it using a list<T> container. You can only access the first and last elements in a queue, and you can only add elements at the back and remove them from the front. Thus, a queue<T> container works more or less like the queue in your local coffee shop. This header also defines a priority_queue<T> container, which is a queue that orders the elements it contains so that the largest element is always at the front. Only the element at the front can be accessed or removed. A priority queue is defined by an adapter from a vector<T> by default, but you could use a deque<T> as the base container.
stack	A stack<T> container is defined by an adapter from a deque<T> container by default, but you could define it using a vector<T> or a list<T> container. A stack is a last-in first-out container, so adding or removing elements always occurs at the top, and you can only access the top element.

Iterators

Iterators are objects that behave like pointers and are very important for accessing the contents of all containers except for those defined by a container adapter; container adapters do not support iterators. You can obtain an iterator from a container, which you can use to access the objects you have stored in it. You can also create iterators that will allow input and output of objects, or data items of a given type from or to a stream. Although basically all iterators behave like pointers, not all iterators provide the same functionality. However, they do share a base level of capability. Given two iterators, iter1 and iter2, accessing the same set of objects, the comparison operations iter1 == iter2, iter1 != iter2, and the assignment iter1 = iter2 are always possible, regardless of the types of iter1 and iter2.

Iterator Categories

There are four categories of iterators, and each category supports a different range of operations. The operations described for each category in the following table are in addition to the three operations that I mentioned in the previous paragraph:

ITERATOR CATEGORY	DESCRIPTION

Input and output iterators	These iterators read or write a sequence of objects and may only be used once. To read or write a second time, you must obtain a new iterator. You can perform the following operations on these iterators:
	
	`++iter` or `iter++`
	
	`*iter`
	
	For the dereferencing operation, only read access is allowed in the case of an input iterator, and only write access for an output iterator.

Forward iterators	Forward iterators incorporate the capabilities of both input and output iterators, so you can apply the operations shown for the previous category to them, and you can use them for access and store operations. Forward iterators can also be reused to traverse a set of objects in a forward direction as many times as you want.
Bidirectional iterators	Bidirectional iterators provide the same capabilities as forward iterators and additionally allow the operations `--iter` and `iter--`. This means you can traverse backward as well as forward through a sequence of objects.

Random access iterators	Random access iterators have the same capabilities as bidirectional iterators but also allow the following operations:
	
	`iter+n` or `iter-n`
	
	`iter += n` or `iter -= n`
	
	`iter1 - iter2`
	
	`iter1 < iter2` or `iter1 > iter2`
	
	`iter1 <= iter2` or `iter1 >= iter2`
	
	`iter[n]`
	
	Being able to increment or decrement an iterator by an arbitrary value n allows random access to the set of objects. The last operation using the `[]` operator is equivalent to `*(iter + n)`.

Thus, iterators in the four successive categories provide a progressively greater range of functionality. Where an algorithm requires an iterator with a given level of functionality, you can use any iterator that provides the required level of capability. For example, if a forward iterator is required, you must use at least a forward iterator; an input or an output iterator will not do. On the other hand, you could use a bidirectional iterator or a random access iterator because they both have the capability provided by a forward iterator.

Note that when you obtain an iterator from a container, the kind of iterator you get will depend on the sort of container you are using. The types of some iterators can be complex, but as you'll see, in many instances the `auto` keyword can deduce the type for you.

SCARY Iterators

Visual C++ supports SCARY iterators, which in spite of the name, are nothing to be frightened of. SCARY is a strange acronym that is less than obvious, standing for "Seemingly erroneous (appearing Constrained by conflicting generic parameters), but Actually work with the Right implementation (unconstrained bY the conflicts due to minimized dependencies)." SCARY iterators are simply iterators that have a type that depends only on the type of element stored in a container, and not on other template parameters used to instantiate the container, such as the allocator and comparator types. In previous implementations of the STL, different containers created to store elements of a given type, but with different comparator or allocator types, would have iterators of different types. There is no necessity for an iterator type to be dependent on the type of comparator or allocator used by a container. With the current implementation of the STL, the iterators will have the same type, determined only by the element type. SCARY iterators can make the code faster and more compact.

Functions Returning Iterators

The `std::begin()` and `std::end()` functions return an iterator that points to the first element and one past the last element respectively of the container, `std::string` object or array that you pass as the argument. The `std::rbegin()` and `std::rend()` functions return reverse iterators that enable you to traverse backwards through a sequence. The `std::cbegin()`, `std::cend()`, `std::crbegin()` and `std::crend()` functions are similar to the first four I mentioned except that they return `const` iterators for the argument. These functions are included in the `iterator` header, the `string` header, and the headers for the majority of containers. You'll see these functions in action later in this chapter. In most situations you can use these functions without the `std` prefix. The compiler will deduce that the function is from the `std` namespace from the argument type.

SMART POINTERS

Smart pointers are objects of a template type that behave like pointers but are different — they are smart. They are intended for use with objects you allocate dynamically. If you use a smart pointer when you allocate heap memory, the smart pointer will take care of deleting it. Using smart pointers for objects you create dynamically means never having to use `delete`. This means that you avoid the possibility of memory leaks. You can store smart pointers in a container, as you'll see.

Smart pointers come in three flavors. The `memory` header defines the following template types for smart pointers in the `std` namespace:

➤ `unique_ptr<T>` defines a unique object that behaves as a pointer to `T`; i.e., there can be only one such object. Assigning or copying a `unique_ptr<T>` object is not possible. The address stored by one such object can be moved to another using `std::move()`. After such an operation the original object will be invalid.

➤ A `shared_ptr<T>` object stores an address of an object of type `T`, and several `shared_ptr<T>` objects can point to the same object. The number of `shared_ptr<T>` objects pointing to a given object is recorded. All `shared_ptr<T>` objects that point to the same object must be destroyed before the object that they point to can be deleted. When the last of the `shared_ptr<T>` objects pointing to a given object dies, the object to which it points will be destroyed and the memory released.

➤ weak_ptr<T> stores a pointer that is linked to a shared_ptr. A weak_ptr<T> does not increment or decrement the reference count of the linked shared_ptr so it does not prevent the object from being destroyed and its memory released when the last shared_ptr referencing it is destroyed.

The reference count for a shared_ptr<T> pointing to a given object, obj, is incremented each time a new one is created and is decremented each time one of the shared_ptr<T> objects is destroyed. When the last shared_ptr<T> object pointing to obj is destroyed, obj will also be destroyed.

It is possible to inadvertently create reference cycles with shared_ptr objects. Conceptually a reference cycle is where a shared_ptr object, pA, points to another shared_ptr object pB, and pB points to pA. With this situation, neither can be destroyed. In practice this occurs in a way that is a lot more complicated. weak_ptr objects are designed to avoid the problem of reference cycles. By using weak_ptr objects to point to an object that a single shared_ptr object points to, you avoid reference cycles. When the single shared_ptr object is destroyed, the object pointed to is also destroyed. Any weak_ptr objects associated with the shared_ptr will then not point to anything.

Using unique_ptr Objects

A unique_ptr object stores a pointer uniquely. No other unique_ptr object can contain the same address so the object pointed to is effectively owned by the unique_ptr object. When the unique_ptr object is destroyed, the object to which it points is destroyed too.

You can create and initialize a smart pointer like this:

```
unique_ptr<CBox> pBox {new CBox {2,2,2}};
```

pBox will behave just like an ordinary pointer and you can use it in the same way to call public member functions for the CBox object. The big difference is that you no longer have to worry about deleting the CBox object from the heap.

Here's a version of some code that you saw back in Chapter 5, modified to use a unique_ptr:

```
#include <iostream>
#include <memory>

std::unique_ptr<double> treble(double);      // Function prototype

int main()
{
   double num {5.0};
   std::unique_ptr<double> ptr {};
   ptr = treble(num);
   std::cout << "Three times num = " << 3.0*num << std::endl;
   std::cout << "Result = " << *ptr << std::endl;
}

std::unique_ptr<double> treble(double data)
{
   std::unique_ptr<double> result {new double {}};
   *result = 3.0*data;
   return result;
}
```

This produces the result you would expect. `ptr` points to a `double` value of 15.0 after the statement that calls `treble()` has executed. You cannot copy a `unique_ptr` object or pass it by value to a function. The `treble()` function creates a local `unique_ptr<double>` object, modifies the value that it points to, and returns it. How does the `treble()` function return a `unique_ptr<double>` object when it cannot be copied? When you return a `unique_ptr` object from a function, `std::move()` is used to move the pointer from the local `unique_ptr` object to the object that is received by the calling function. Moving the pointer from one `unique_ptr` to another transfers ownership of the object pointed to, so the source `unique_ptr` object will contain `nullptr`. This has implications when you store `unique_ptr` objects in a container. I'll show you how you can store smart pointers in an STL container later in this chapter.

The `make_unique<T>()` function template creates a new `T` object on the heap and then creates a `unique_ptr<T>` object that points to the `T`object. The arguments that you pass to `make_unique<T>()` are the arguments to the `T` class constructor. Here's how you could create a `unique_ptr` object holding the address of a `CBox` object:

```
auto pBox = std::make_unique<CBox>(2.0, 3.0, 4.0);
```

This creates a `CBox` object on the heap and stores its address in a new `unique_ptr<CBox>` object, `pBox`. Apart from the fact that it cannot be duplicated, you can use `pBox` just like an ordinary pointer.

Another version of `make_unique<>()` can create a `unique_ptr` object pointing to a new array in the free store. For example:

```
auto pBoxes = std::make_unique<CBox[]>(6);
```

This statement creates an array of six `CBox` objects on the heap and stores the address of the array in a `unique_ptr<CBox[]>` object. You put the array type as the function template argument and the array dimension as the argument to the function. You access the array elements by indexing the `unique_ptr` object, `pBoxes`. For example:

```
pBoxes[1] = CBox {1.0, 2.0, 3.0};
```

This sets the second element in the array to a `CBox` object with the dimensions you see. Thus the `unique_ptr` object acts just like the array name for a normal array.

Using shared_ptr Objects

You can define a `shared_ptr` object explicitly using the `shared_ptr<T>` constructor, but it is better to use the `make_shared<T>()` function that creates an object of type `T` on the heap and then returns a `shared_ptr<T>` object that points to it because the memory allocation is more efficient. Here's an example:

```
auto pBox = make_shared<CBox>(1.0, 2.0, 3.0);   // Points to a CBox object
```

This creates a `CBox` object on the heap with length, width, and height values as 1.0, 2.0, and 3.0 and stores the `shared_ptr<CBox>` object that points to it in `pBox`.

In contrast to `unique_ptr`, you can have multiple `shared_ptr` objects pointing to the same object. The object pointed to will survive until the last `shared_ptr` object that points to it is destroyed, then it too will be destroyed. A `shared_ptr` object will be copied when you return it from a function.

You can initialize a `shared_ptr` with another `shared_ptr`:

```
std::shared_ptr<CBox> pBox2 {pBox};
```

`pBox2` points to the same object as `pBox`.

Using a smart pointer works in the same way as an ordinary pointer:

```
std::cout << "Box volume = " << pBox->volume() << std::endl;
```

A smart pointer that you define with a base class type, can store a pointer to a derived class type. For example, given the CBox and CCandyBox classes that you saw in Chapter 9, you could define a shared_ptr like this:

```
shared_ptr<CBox> pBox {new CCandyBox {2,2,2}};
```

pBox points to a CCandyBox object so smart pointers work in the same way as ordinary pointers in this respect too.

If you use a local smart pointer in a function to point to an object on the heap, the memory for the object will be automatically released when the function returns — assuming that you are not returning the smart pointer from the function. You can use smart pointers as class members. If you are defining a class that uses smart pointers to keep track of heap objects, you won't need to implement a destructor to be sure that the memory for the objects is released when the class object is destroyed. The default constructor will call the destructor for each member that is a smart pointer.

Accessing the Raw Pointer in a Smart Pointer

You will sometimes need access to the address that a smart pointer contains; this is called a raw pointer. You will see later in the book that there are circumstances with the MFC where you need a raw pointer because MFC member functions do not accept smart pointers as arguments. Calling the get() memberof a smart pointer object returns the raw pointer, which you can then pass to a function that requires it.

Calling the reset() member of a smart pointer resets the raw pointer to nullptr. This will cause the object that is pointed to be destroyed when there are no other smart pointers that contain the same address.

Casting Smart Pointers

You cannot use the standard cast operators such as static_cast, dynamic_cast, and const_cast with smart pointers. When you need to cast a smart pointer, you must use static_pointer_cast, dynamic_pointer_cast, and const_pointer_cast instead of the standard operators. When you use dynamic_pointer_cast to cast a shared_ptr<T> object to a shared_ptr<Base> object, the result will be a shared_ptr containing nullptr if Base is not a base class for T. The cast operations for smart pointers are defined as function templates in the memory header.

ALGORITHMS

Algorithms are STL function templates that operate on a set of objects that are made available to them by an iterator. Because the objects are accessed through an iterator, an algorithm needs no knowledge of the source of the objects. The objects could be retrieved by the iterator from a container or even from a stream. Because iterators work like pointers, all STL functions that accept an iterator as an argument will work equally well with a regular pointer.

As you'll see, you will frequently use containers, iterators, and algorithms in concert, in the manner illustrated in Figure 10-1.

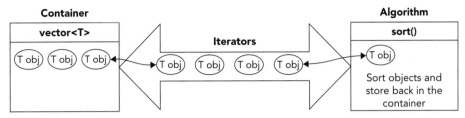

FIGURE 10-1

To apply an algorithm to the contents of a container, you supply iterators that point to objects within the container. The algorithm uses these iterators to access these objects in sequence and to write them back to the container when appropriate. For example, when you apply the sort() algorithm to a vector, you pass two iterators to the function. One points to the first element, and the other to one past the last element. The sort() function uses these iterators to access the objects for comparison, and to write them back to the container to establish the ordering. You'll see this working in an example later in this chapter.

Algorithms are defined in two standard header files, the algorithm header and the numeric header.

FUNCTION OBJECTS IN THE STL

Function objects are objects of a class type that overloads the () operator (the function call operator), which means that the class implements the operator()() function. The implementation of the operator()() member function in a function object can return a value of any type. Function objects are also called *functors*.

The STL defines a set of function templates object types that define functors in the functional header. For example, the STL defines the less<T> template that I mentioned in the context of the map container. If you instantiate the template as less<MyClass>, you have a type for function objects that implement operator()() to provide the less-than comparison for MyClass objects. For this to work, MyClass must implement the operator<() function.

Many algorithms make use of function objects to specify binary operations to be carried out, or to specify *predicates* that determine how or whether a particular operation is to be carried out. A predicate is a function that returns a value of type bool, and because a function object can implement the operator()() member function to return a value of type bool, a function object can be a predicate. For example, suppose you have defined a Comp class that implements operator()() to compare two objects and return a bool value. If you create an object obj of type Comp, the expression obj(a,b) returns a bool value that results from comparing a and b, and thus acts as a predicate.

Predicates come in two flavors, *binary predicates* that involve two operands, and *unary predicates* that require one operand. Comparisons such as less-than and equal-to, and logical operations such as AND and OR, are implemented as binary predicates that are members of function objects; logical negation, NOT, is implemented as a unary predicate member of a function object.

You can define your own function objects when necessary. You'll see function objects in action with algorithms and some container class functions later in this chapter. You can also define *lambda expressions*, which I'll also introduce later in this chapter. Lambda expressions are often easier to use than function objects.

FUNCTION ADAPTERS

Function adapters are function templates that allow function objects to be combined to produce a more complex function object. A simple example is the `not1` function adapter. This takes an existing function object that provides a unary predicate and inverts it. Thus, if the function object function returns `true`, the function that results from applying `not1` to it will be `false`. Function adapters are yet another topic I won't be discussing in depth, not because they are terribly difficult to understand — they aren't — but because there's a limit to how much I can cram into a single chapter.

THE RANGE OF STL CONTAINERS

You can apply the STL container templates in a wide range of applications. *Sequence containers* are containers in which you store objects of a given type in a linear fashion, either as a dynamic array or as a list. Elements are retrieved based on their position in the container. *Associative containers* store objects based on a key that you supply with each object to be stored; the key is used to locate the object within the container. Keys can be values of fundamental types or class objects. In a typical application, you might store phone numbers in an associative container, using names as the keys. You can retrieve a particular number from the container just by supplying the appropriate name. *Sets* are containers that hold elements that are stored and retrieved based on the elements themselves. They can be unordered, rather like objects rattling around in a bag, or they can be ordered, where a sequence is established within the container that depends on what the objects are. There are also sets that allow you to specify a comparator that will establish a particular order within the set. I won't be discussing sets in detail. I'll first introduce you to sequence containers, and then I'll delve into associative containers and what you can do with them.

SEQUENCE CONTAINERS

The class templates for the five basic sequence containers are `vector<T>`, `array<T,N>`, `list<T>`, `forward_list<T>`, and `deque<T>`.

Which template you choose in any particular instance depends on the application. These containers are differentiated by the operations they can perform efficiently, as Figure 10-2 shows.

If you need random access to the contents of a container with a variable size, and you are happy to always add or delete objects at the end of a sequence, then `vector<T>` is the container template to choose. It is possible to add or delete objects randomly within a vector, but the process will be somewhat slower than adding objects to the end because all the objects past the insertion or deletion point have to be moved. If you can manage with a fixed number of elements, the `array<T,N>` container will be faster than a `vector<T>` in store and retrieve operations because you don't have the overhead of providing for increasing the capacity of the container. An `array<T,N>` container can be allocated on the stack and is more flexible than a normal array.

A `deque<T>` container is similar to a `vector<T>` and supports the same operations, but it has the additional capability to add and delete elements at the beginning of the sequence. A `list<T>` container is a doubly-linked list, so adding and deleting at any position is efficient. The downside of a list is that there is no random access to the contents; the only way to access an object that is internal to the list is to traverse the contents from the beginning, or to run backward from the end.

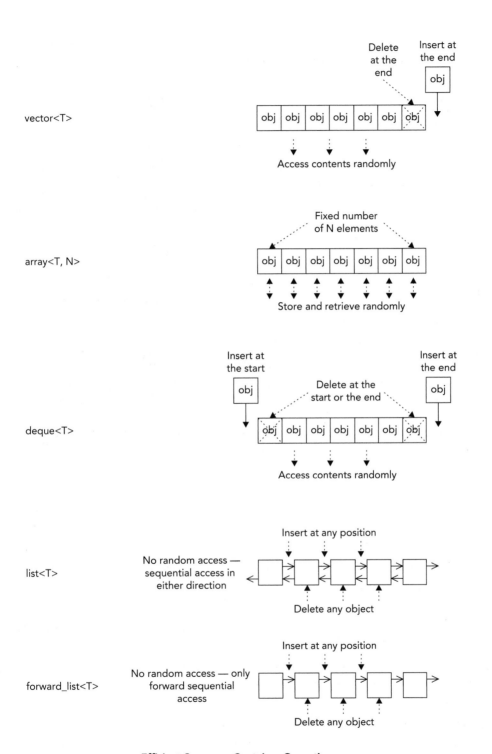

Efficient Sequence Container Operations

FIGURE 10-2

Let's look at sequence containers in more detail and try some examples. I'll be introducing the use of iterators, algorithms, and function objects along the way.

Creating Vector Containers

The simplest way to create a vector container is like this:

```
vector<int> mydata;
```

This creates a container that will store values of type int. The initial capacity is zero, so you will be allocating more memory right from the outset when you insert the first value.

The push_back() member function adds a new element to the end of a vector, so to store a value in this vector you would write:

```
mydata.push_back(99);
```

The argument to push_back() is the item to be stored. This statement stores 99 in the vector, so after executing this, the vector contains one element. The push_back() function is overloaded with an rvalue reference parameter version so it will move temporary objects into the vector rather than copy them.

Here's another way to create a vector to store integers:

```
vector<int> mydata(100);
```

This creates a vector that contains 100 elements that are all initialized to zero. Note that you must use parentheses here. If you put 100 between braces, the vector will contain one element with the value 100. If you add new elements, the memory allocated for the vector will be increased automatically, so obviously it's a good idea to choose a reasonably accurate value for the number of integers you are likely to store. This vector can be used just like an array. For example, to store a value in the third element, you can write:

```
mydata[2] = 999;
```

Of course, you can only use an index value to access elements that are within the range that exist in the vector. You can't add new elements in this way though. To add a new element, you can use the push_back() function.

You can initialize the elements in a vector to a different value, when you create it by using this statement:

```
vector<int> mydata(100, -1);
```

You must use parentheses here too. The second argument is the initial value to be used for elements, so all 100 elements will be set to -1.

If you don't want to create elements when you create a vector container, you can increase the capacity after you create it by calling its reserve() function:

```
vector<int> mydata;
mydata.reserve(100);
```

The argument to the reserve() function is the minimum number of elements to be accommodated. If the argument is less than the current capacity of the vector, then calling reserve() will have no effect. In this code fragment, calling reserve() causes the vector container to allocate sufficient memory for a total of 100 elements although the elements are not yet created.

When you want to specify a set of initial values for elements, you use an initializer list:

```
vector<int> values {100, 200, 300, 400);
```

This creates a vector containing four elements with the values from the list.

You can also create a vector with initial values for elements from an external array. For example:

```
double data[] {1.5, 2.5, 3.5, 4.5, 5.5, 6.5, 7.5, 8.5, 9.5, 10.5};
vector<double> mydata(data, data+8);
```

Here, the `data` array is created with 10 elements of type `double`, with the initial values shown. The second statement creates a vector storing elements of type `double`, with eight elements initially having the values corresponding to `data[0]` through `data[7]`. The arguments to the `vector<double>` constructor are pointers (and can also be iterators), where the first pointer points to the first initializing element in the array, and the second points to one past the last initializing element. Thus, the `mydata` vector will contain eight elements with initial values 1.5, 2.5, 3.5, 4.5, 5.5, 6.5, 7.5, and 8.5.

Because the constructor in the previous fragment can accept either pointer or iterator arguments, you can initialize a vector when you create it with values from another vector that contains elements of the same type. You just supply the constructor with an iterator pointing to the first element you want to use as an initializer, plus a second iterator pointing to one past the last element you want to use. Here's an example:

```
vector<double> values(begin(mydata), end(mydata));
```

After executing this statement, the `values` vector will have elements that are duplicates of the `mydata` vector. As Figure 10-3 illustrates, the `begin()` template function returns a random access iterator that points to the first element in the argument, and `end()` returns a random access iterator pointing to one past the last element. A sequence of elements is typically specified in the STL by two iterators, one pointing to the first element and the other pointing to one past the last element, so you'll see this time and time again.

> **NOTE** If you check the documentation, you'll see that the `vector` container and other sequence containers have `begin()` and `end()` member functions that you can call for a container object:
>
> ```
> vector<double> values(mydata.begin(),mydata.end());
> ```
>
> This does the same as the preceding statement, but I recommend that you use the non-member `begin()` and `end()` functions because they are more flexible. They work with arrays, strings and other containers. The `rbegin()`, `rend()`, `cbegin()`, and `cend()` template functions that I'll use later in this chapter also exist as members of container classes.
>
> You can usually use non-member `begin()`, `end()`, and etc. functions without qualifying them with `std` because the compiler can deduce that the function is from the `std` namespace from the argument.

Because `begin()` and `end()` return random access iterators, you can modify what they point to when you use them. For a `vector<T>`, the type of the iterators that `begin()` and `end()` return is `vector<T>::iterator`, where `T` is the type of object in the vector. Most of the time you can use the `auto` keyword to specify the iterator type.

Here's a statement that creates a vector that is initialized with the third through the seventh elements from the `mydata` vector:

```
vector<double> values(begin(mydata)+2, end(mydata)-1);
```

Adding 2 to the first iterator makes it point to the third element in `mydata`. Subtracting 1 from the second iterator makes it point to the last element in `mydata`; remember that the second argument to the constructor is an iterator that points to a position that is *one past* the element to be used as the last initializer, so the object that the second iterator points to is not included in the set.

As I said earlier, it is pretty much standard practice in the STL to indicate a sequence of elements in a container by a begin iterator that points to the first element and an end iterator that points to one past the last element. This allows you to iterate over all the elements in a sequence by incrementing the begin iterator until it equals the end iterator. This means that the iterators only need to support the equality operator to allow you to walk through the sequence.

Occasionally, you may want to access the contents of a vector in reverse order. Calling the `rbegin()` function for a vector returns an iterator that points to the last element, while `rend()` points to one before the first element (that is, the position preceding the first element), as Figure 10-4 illustrates.

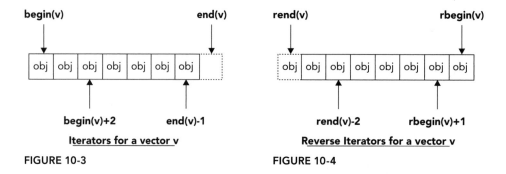

FIGURE 10-3

FIGURE 10-4

The iterators returned by `rbegin()` and `rend()` are called reverse iterators because they present the elements in reverse sequence. For a `vector<T>` container, reverse iterators are of type `vector<T>::reverse_iterator`. Figure 10-4 shows how adding a positive integer to the `rbegin()` iterator moves back through the sequence, and subtracting an integer from `rend()` moves forward through the sequence.

Here's how you could create a vector containing the contents of another vector in reverse order:

```
double data[] {1.5, 2.5, 3.5, 4.5, 5.5, 6.5, 7.5, 8.5, 9.5, 10.5};
vector<double> mydata(data, data+8);
vector<double> values(rbegin(mydata), rend(mydate));
```

Because you are using reverse iterators as arguments to the constructor in the last statement, the `values` vector will contain the elements from `mydata` in reverse order.

When you want to use iterators to access the elements in a vector but do not want to modify the elements you can use the `cbegin()` and `cend()` template functions that return `const` iterators. For example, suppose you want to list the squares of the integer values stored in a vector:

```
std::vector<int> mydata {1, 2, 3, 4, 5};
for(auto iter = std::cbegin(mydata) ; iter != std::cend(mydata) ; ++iter)
    std::cout << (*iter) << " squared is " << (*iter)*(*iter) << std::endl;
```

Using cbegin() and cend(), there is no possibility of modifying the elements in mydata accidentally within the loop. You also have the standalone template functions and container member functions crbegin() and crend() available that provide const reverse iterators.

The Capacity and Size of a Vector Container

The *capacity* of a vector is the maximum number of objects it can currently accommodate without allocating more memory. The *size* is the number of objects actually stored in the container. Obviously the size cannot be greater than the capacity.

You can obtain the size and capacity of the data container by calling the size() and capacity() member functions. For example:

```
std::cout << "The capacity of the container is: " << data.capacity() << std::endl
          << "The size of the container is: " << data.size() << std::endl;
```

Calling capacity() for a vector returns the current capacity, and calling its size() function returns the current size, both values being returned as type vector<T>::size_type. This is an implementation-defined integer type that is defined within the vector<T> class template. To create a variable to store the value returned from the size() or capacity() function, you can specify it as type vector<T>::size_type, where you replace T with the type of object stored in the container. The following fragment illustrates this:

```
vector<double> values;
vector<double>::size_type cap {values.capacity()};
```

Of course, the auto keyword makes it much easier:

```
auto cap = values.capacity();
```

> **NOTE** *The Visual C++ implementation of STL defines* vector<T>::size_type *as* size_t, *which is an unsigned integer type that is also the type for the result of the* sizeof *operator.*

If the value returned by the size() function is zero, then clearly the vector contains no elements; thus, you can use it as a test for an empty vector. You can also call the empty() function for a vector to test for this:

```
if(values.empty())
    std::cout << "No more elements in the vector.";
```

The empty() function returns a value of type bool that is true when the vector is empty and false otherwise.

You are unlikely to need it very often, but you can discover the maximum possible number of elements in a vector by calling its max_size() function. For example:

```
std::vector<std::string> strings;
std::cout << "Maximum length of strings vector: "
          << strings.max_size() << std::endl;
```

Executing this fragment produces the output:

```
Maximum length of strings vector: 153391689
```

The maximum length is returned as type `vector<string>::size_type`. Note that the maximum length of a vector will depend on the type of element stored. If you try this with a vector storing values of type `int`, you will get 1073741823 as the maximum length, and for a vector storing values of type `double` it is 536870911.

You can increase or decrease the size of a vector by calling its `resize()` function. If you specify a new size that is less than the current size, sufficient elements will be deleted from the end of the vector to reduce it to its new size. If the new size is greater than the old, new elements will be added to the end of the vector to increase its length to the new size. Here's code illustrating this:

```
vector<int> values(5, 66);   // Contains 66 66 66 66 66
values.resize(7, 88);        // Contains 66 66 66 66 66 88 88
values.resize(10);           // Contains 66 66 66 66 66 88 88 0 0 0
values.resize(4);            // Contains 66 66 66 66
```

The first argument to `resize()` is the new size. The second argument, when it is present, is the value to be used for new elements that need to be added to make up the new size. If you are increasing the size and you don't specify a value for new elements, the default value will be used. In the case of a vector storing objects of a class type, the default value will be the object produced by the no-arg constructor for the class.

TRY IT OUT   Exploring the Size and Capacity of a Vector

This example exercises some of the ways you have seen for creating a vector and shows how the capacity changes as you add elements:

```cpp
// Ex10_01.cpp
// Exploring the size and capacity of a vector

#include <iostream>
#include <vector>
using std::vector;

// Template function to display the size and capacity of any vector
template<class T>
void listInfo(const vector<T>& v)
{
  std::cout << "Container capacity: " << v.capacity()
            << " size: " << v.size() << std::endl;
}

int main()
{
  // Basic vector creation
  vector<double> data;
  listInfo(data);

  data.reserve(100);
```

```
            std::cout << "After calling reserve(100):" << std::endl;

            listInfo(data);


            vector<int> numbers(10,-1); // Create a vector with 10 elements and initialize it
            std::cout << "The initial values are: ";

            for(auto n : numbers)           // You can use the range-based for loop with a vector
                std::cout << " " << n;
            std::cout << std::endl << std::endl;

            // See how adding elements affects capacity increments
            auto oldC = numbers.capacity();   // Old capacity
            auto newC = oldC;                 // New capacity after adding element
            listInfo(numbers);
            for(int i {}; i<1000; i++)
            {
              numbers.push_back(2*i);
              newC = numbers.capacity();
              if(oldC < newC)                 // Only output when capacity increases
              {
                oldC = newC;
                listInfo(numbers);
              }
            }
          }
```

This example produces the following output:

```
Container capacity: 0 size: 0
After calling reserve(100):
Container capacity: 100 size: 0
The initial values are: -1 -1 -1 -1 -1 -1 -1 -1 -1 -1

Container capacity: 10 size: 10
Container capacity: 15 size: 11
Container capacity: 22 size: 16
Container capacity: 33 size: 23
Container capacity: 49 size: 34
Container capacity: 73 size: 50
Container capacity: 109 size: 74
Container capacity: 163 size: 110
Container capacity: 244 size: 164
Container capacity: 366 size: 245
Container capacity: 549 size: 367
Container capacity: 823 size: 550
Container capacity: 1234 size: 824
```

How It Works

The #include directive for the vector header adds the definition for the vector<T> template to the source file.

Following the using declaration you have a definition of the listInfo() function template:

```
template<class T>
void listInfo(const vector<T>& v)
{
  std::cout << "Container capacity: " << v.capacity()
            << " size: " << v.size() << std::endl;
}
```

This template outputs the current capacity and size of any vector. You will often find it convenient to write function templates when working with the STL. The example shows how easy it is. The T template parameter determines the parameter type for the function. You call this function with a vector container as the argument. Specifying the parameter as the reference type, const vector<T>&, enables the function body to access the container you pass as the argument to the function directly. If you specified the parameter as type const vector<T>, then the vector would be copied each time the function is called, which could be time-consuming for a large vector container.

The first action in main() is to create a vector and output its size and capacity:

```
vector<double> data;
listInfo(data);
```

You can see from the output that the size and the capacity are both zero. Adding an element requires more space to be allocated.

Next, you call the reserve() function for the container:

```
data.reserve(100);
```

You can see from the output that the capacity is now 100 and the size is zero. This means that the container contains no elements but has memory allocated to accommodate up to 100 elements. Only when you add the 101st element will the capacity be increased automatically.

Next, you create another container with this statement:

```
vector<int> numbers(10,-1);
```

This creates a vector that contains 10 elements, each initialized with -1. To demonstrate that this is indeed the case, you output the elements in the container with the following loop:

```
for(auto n : numbers)
  std::cout << " " << n;
```

This demonstrates that the range-based for loop works with a vector.

Alternatively, you could write the loop using a regular for loop:

```
for(vector<int>::size_type i {}; i<numbers.size(); ++i)
  std::cout << " " << numbers[i];
```

You could also use an iterator to access the elements in the loop:

```
for(auto iter = begin(numbers); iter != end(numbers); ++iter)
  std::cout << " " << *iter;
```

The loop variable, iter, is an iterator of type vector<int>::iterator, that you initialize with the iterator returned by the begin() function. This is incremented on each loop iteration, and the loop ends when it reaches end(numbers), which points to one past the last element. Note how you dereference the iterator just like a pointer to get at the value of the element.

The remaining statements in `main()` demonstrate how the capacity of a vector increases as you add elements. The first two statements create variables to store the current capacity and the new capacity after adding an element:

```
auto oldC = numbers.capacity();   // Old capacity
auto newC = oldC;                 // New capacity after adding element
```

After displaying the initial size and capacity, you execute the following loop:

```
for(int i {}; i<1000 ;i++)
{
  numbers.push_back(2*i);
  newC = numbers.capacity();
  if(oldC < newC)
  {
    oldC = newC;
    listInfo(numbers);
  }
}
```

This loop calls `push_back()` for the `numbers` vector to add 1,000 elements. The `if` condition ensures that we only display the capacity and size when the capacity increases.

The output shows an interesting pattern in the way additional space is allocated in the container. As you would expect with the initial size and capacity at 10, the first capacity increase occurs when you add the 11th element. The increase in this case is half the capacity, so the capacity increases to 15. The next capacity increase is when the size reaches 15, and the increase is to 22, so the increment is again half the capacity. This process continues with each capacity increase being half the current capacity. Thus, you automatically get larger chunks of memory space allocated when required, the more elements the vector contains. On the one hand, this mechanism ensures that once the initial memory allocation in the container is occupied, you don't cause more memory to be allocated every time you add a new element. On the other hand, this implies that you should take care when reserving space for a large number of elements in a vector. If you create a vector that provides for 100,000 elements initially, for example, exceeding this by one element will cause space for another 50,000 to be allocated. In this sort of situation you could check for reaching the capacity, and use `reserve()` to increase the available memory by a less extravagant amount.

Accessing the Elements in a Vector

You have already seen that you can access the elements in a vector by using the subscript operator, just as you would for an array. You can also use the `at()` member function where the argument is the index of the element you want to access. Here's how you could list the contents of the `numbers` vector in the previous example using `at()`:

```
for(vector<int>::size_type i {}; i<numbers.size() ;i++)
    std::cout << " " << numbers.at(i);
```

The operation of `at()` differs from the subscript operator, `[]`. If you use a subscript with the subscript operator that is outside the valid range, the result is undefined. If you do the same with `at()`, an exception of type `out_of_range` will be thrown. If there's the potential for subscript values outside the legal range to arise, it's better to use the `at()` function and catch the exception than to allow the possibility for undefined results.

> **NOTE** *The* `operator[]()` *member function of a vector does check for index out of bounds in debug builds, but not in release builds.*

Of course, when you want to access all the elements in a vector, the range-based `for` loop always provides a simpler mechanism:

```
for(auto number : numbers)
    std::cout << " " << number;
```

To access the first or last element in a vector you can call the `front()` or `back()` function, respectively:

```
std::cout << "The value of the first element is: " << numbers.front() << std::endl;
std::cout << "The value of the last element is: " << numbers.back() << std::endl;
```

Both functions come in two versions; one returns a reference to the element, and the other returns a `const` reference. The latter will be called when the vector object is const. If you call `front()` for a `const` vector, you cannot use the reference that is returned to modify the element and you cannot store the return value in a non-`const` variable.

Inserting and Deleting Elements in a Vector

In addition to the `push_back()` function you have seen, a vector container supports the `pop_back()` operation that deletes the last element. Both operations execute in constant time, that is, the time to execute will be the same, regardless of the number of elements in the vector. The `pop_back()` function is very simple to use:

```
vec.pop_back();
```

This statement removes the last element from the vector `vec` and reduces the size by 1. If you call `pop_back()` for an empty vector the behavior is undefined.

You could remove all the elements in a vector by calling the `pop_back()` function repeatedly, but the `clear()` function does this much more simply:

```
vec.clear();
```

This statement removes all the elements from `vec`, so the size will be zero. Of course, the capacity will be left unchanged.

Insert Operations

You can call the `insert()` function to insert one or more new elements anywhere in a vector. This operation will execute in linear time, which means that the time increases in proportion to the number of elements in the container. This is because inserting new elements involves moving the existing elements. The simplest version of `insert()` inserts a single element at a specific position; the first argument is an iterator specifying the insertion position and the second argument is the element to be inserted. For example:

```
vector<int> vec(5, 99);
vec.insert(begin(vec)+1, 88);
```

The first statement creates a vector with five integer elements, all initialized to 99. The second statement inserts 88 after the first element; so, after executing this, the vector will contain:

```
99 88 99 99 99 99
```

For a vector storing objects, an `insert()` function call will invoke the version with an rvalue reference parameter when the argument is a temporary object so a temporary object will be moved into the vector, not copied. If the second argument to `insert()` is an lvalue, the version with a normal reference parameter will be called.

You can insert several identical elements, starting from a given position:

```
vec.insert(begin(vec)+2, 3, 77);
```

The first argument is an iterator specifying the insertion position for the first element, the second argument is the number of elements to be inserted, and the third argument is the element to be inserted. After executing this statement, `vec` will contain:

```
99 88 77 77 77 99 99 99 99
```

You have yet another version of `insert()` that inserts a sequence of elements at a given position. The first argument is an iterator pointing to the insertion position for the first element. The second and third arguments are input iterators specifying the range of elements to be inserted from some source. Here's an example:

```
vector<int> newvec(5, 22);
newvec.insert(begin(newvec)+1, begin(vec)+1, begin(vec)+5);
```

The first statement creates a vector with five integer elements initialized to 22. The second statement inserts four elements from `vec`, starting with the second. After executing these statements, `newvec` will contain:

```
22 88 77 77 77 22 22 22 22
```

Don't forget that the second iterator in the interval specifies the position that is one past the last element, so the element it points to is not included.

Emplace Operations

The `emplace()` and `emplace_back()` member functions insert an object in a vector by creating it in place, rather than moving or copying it. This is useful when the object is constructed using two or more constructor arguments. The `emplace()` function inserts an object at a specified position. The first parameter is an iterator specifying the insertion position. This is followed by one or more rvalue reference parameters that will be used in a constructor call for type `T` to create the object in place. The `emplace_back()` function has one or more rvalue reference parameters that specify the object to be added at the end of the vector. For example, suppose you have defined a vector like this:

```
std::vector<CBox> boxes;
```

You could add `CBox` objects to the vector like this:

```
boxes.push_back(CBox {1, 2, 3});
boxes.push_back(CBox {2, 4, 6});
boxes.push_back(CBox {3, 6, 9});
```

This will create and append three `CBox` objects to the vector.

Alternatively you could write this:

```
boxes.emplace_back(1, 2, 3);
boxes.emplace_back(2, 4, 6);
boxes.emplace_back(3, 6, 9);
```

Each `emplace_back()` call selects the CBox constructor to create the object to be added to the end of the vector based on the arguments to the function. Using `emplace_back()` will result in fewer CBox objects being created than in the case of `push_back()`.

Erase Operations

The `erase()` member function deletes one or more elements from any position within a vector, but this also is a linear time function and will typically be slow. Here's how you erase a single element at a given position:

```
newvec.erase(end(newvec)-2);
```

The argument is an iterator that points to the element to be erased, so this statement removes the second to last element from `newvec`.

To delete several elements, you supply two iterator arguments specifying the interval. For example:

```
newvec.erase(begin(newvec)+1, begin(newvec)+4);
```

This will delete the second, third, and fourth elements from `newvec`. The element that the second iterator argument points to is not included in the operation.

As I said, both the `erase()` and `insert()` operations are slow, so you should use them sparingly.

Swap and Assign Operations

The `swap()` member function enables you to swap the contents of two vectors, provided, of course, the elements in the two vectors are of the same type. Here's a code fragment showing an example of how this works:

```
vector<int> first(5, 77);          // Contains 77 77 77 77 77
vector<int> second(8, -1);         // Contains -1 -1 -1 -1 -1 -1 -1 -1
first.swap(second);
```

After executing the last statement, the contents of the vectors `first` and `second` will have interchanged. Note that the capacities of the vectors are swapped as well as the contents and, of course, the size.

The `assign()` member function replaces the entire contents of a vector with another sequence, or replaces the contents with a given number of instances of an object. Here's how you could replace the contents of one vector with a sequence from another:

```
vector<double> values;
for(int i {1}; i <= 50 ;++i)
   values.emplace_back(2.5*i);
vector<double> newdata(5, 3.5);
newdata.assign(begin(values)+1, end(values)-1);
```

This creates the `values` vector and stores 50 elements that have the values 2.5, 5.0, 7.5, ... 125.0. The `newdata` vector is created with five elements, each having the value 3.5. The last statement calls the `assign()` member of `newdata`, which deletes all elements from `newdata`, and then inserts copies of all the elements from `values`, except for the first and the last. You specify the new sequence to be inserted by two iterators, the first pointing to the first element to be inserted and the second pointing to one past the last element to be inserted. Because you specify the new elements to be inserted by two iterators, the source of the data can be from any sequence, not just a vector. The `assign()` function will also work with regular pointers, so, for example, you could insert elements from an array of `double` elements.

Here's how you use `assign()` to replace the contents of a vector with a sequence of instances of the same element:

```
newdata.assign(30, 99.5);
```

The first argument is the count of elements in the replacement sequence, and the second argument is the element to be used. This statement will cause the contents of `newdata` to be deleted and replaced by 30 elements, each having the value 99.5.

Storing Class Objects in a Vector

You can store objects of any class type in a vector, but the class must meet certain minimum criteria. Here's a minimum specification for a given class `T` to be compatible with a vector or, in fact, any sequence container:

```
class T
{
public:
  T();                           // Default constructor
  T(const T& t);                 // Copy constructor
  ~T();                          // Destructor
  T& operator=(const T& t);      // Assignment operator
};
```

The compiler will supply default versions of these class members if you don't define them, so it's not difficult for a class to meet these requirements. The important thing to note is that they are required and are likely to be used, so when the default implementation that the compiler supplies will not suffice, you must provide your own implementation.

If you store objects of your own class types in a vector, it's highly recommended that you implement a move constructor and a move assignment operator for your class because the vector container fully supports move semantics. For example, if the vector needs to resize itself to allow more elements to be added, without move semantics the following sequence of events will occur:

1. A new vector with the new size is allocated.

2. All objects from the old vector are copied to the new vector.

3. All objects in the old vector are destroyed.

4. The old vector is deallocated.

With move semantics support in your class, this is what happens:

1. A new vector with the new size is allocated.

2. All objects from the old vector are moved to the new vector.

3. All objects in the old vector are destroyed.

4. The old vector is deallocated.

This will be significantly faster because no copying is necessary.

Let's try an example.

Storing Objects in a Vector

In this example you create `Person` objects that represent individuals by their name. Just to make it more interesting, we will pretend we have never heard of the `string` class, so we are stuck with using null-terminated strings to store names. This means you have to take care how you implement the class if you want to store objects in a `vector<Person>` container. In general, a `Person` class might have lots of data members relating to a person, but we will keep it simple with just their first and second names.

Here's the definition of the `Person` class:

```cpp
// Person.h in Ex10_02
// A class defining people by their names
#pragma once
#include <cstring>
#include <iostream>

class Person
{
  public:
  // Constructor, includes no-arg constructor
  Person (const char* first, const char* second)
  {
    initName(first, second);
  }

  // Copy constructor
  Person(const Person& p)
  {
    initName(p.firstname, p.secondname);
  }

  // Move constructor
  Person(Person&& p)
  {
  firstname = p.firstname;
  secondname = p.secondname;
    // Reset rvalue object pointers to prevent deletion
    p.firstname = nullptr;
    p.secondname = nullptr;
  }

  // Destructor
  virtual ~Person()
  {
    delete[] firstname;
    delete[] secondname;
  }

  // Copy assignment operator
```

```cpp
Person& operator=(const Person& p)
{
  // Deal with p = p assignment situation
  if(&p != this)
  {
    delete[] firstname;
    delete[] secondname;
    initName(p.firstname, p.secondname);
  }
  return *this;
}

// Move assignment operator
Person& operator=(Person&& p)
{
  // Deal with p = p assignment situation
  if(&p != this)
  {
    // Release current memory
    delete[] firstname;
    delete[] secondname;
    firstname = p.firstname;
    secondname = p.secondname;
    p.firstname = nullptr;
    p.secondname = nullptr;
  }
  return *this;
}
// Less-than operator
bool operator<(const Person& p) const
{
  int result {strcmp(secondname, p.secondname)};
  return (result < 0 || result ==  0 && strcmp(firstname, p.firstname) < 0);
}

// Output a person
void showPerson() const
{
  std::cout << firstname << " " << secondname << std::endl;
}

private:
char* firstname {};
char* secondname {};

// Private helper function to avoid code duplication
void initName(const char* first, const char* second)
{
  size_t length {strlen(first)+1};
  firstname = new char[length];
  strcpy_s(firstname, length, first);
  length = strlen(second)+1;
  secondname = new char[length];
  strcpy_s(secondname, length, second);
}
};
```

The private `initName()` function is there because the constructors and the assignment operator function need to carry out the same operations to initialize the data members. Using this helper function avoids repeating the same code.

Because the `Person` class allocates memory dynamically to store the first and second names of a person, you must implement the destructor to release the memory when an object is destroyed. You must also implement the assignment operator because this involves more memory allocation. Note the code at the beginning for dealing with the a = a assignment situation. Assigning an object to itself can arise in ways that are less than obvious, and can cause problems if you don't implement the `operator=()` function to take account of this.

The `showPerson()` function is a convenience function for outputting an entire name. It is declared as `const` to allow it to work with `const` and non-`const` `Person` objects. The `operator<()` function is there for use later.

The program to store `Person` objects in a vector looks like this:

```cpp
// Ex10_02.cpp
// Storing objects in a vector

#include <iostream>
#include <vector>
#include "Person.h"

using std::vector;

int main()
{
  vector<Person> people;                   // Vector of Person objects
  const size_t maxlength {50};
  char firstname[maxlength];
  char secondname[maxlength];

  // Input all the people
  while(true)
  {
    std::cout << "Enter a first name or press Enter to end: ";
    std::cin.getline(firstname, maxlength, '\n');
    if(strlen(firstname) == 0)
      break;
    std::cout << "Enter the second name: ";
    std::cin.getline(secondname, maxlength, '\n');
    people.emplace_back(Person(firstname, secondname));
  }

  // Output the contents of the vector using an iterator
  std::cout << std::endl;
  auto iter = cbegin(people);
  while(iter != cend(people))
  {
    iter->showPerson();
    ++iter;
  }
}
```

Here's an example of some output from this program:

```
Enter a first name or press Enter to end: Jane
Enter the second name: Fonda
Enter a first name or press Enter to end: Bill
Enter the second name: Cosby
Enter a first name or press Enter to end: Sally
Enter the second name: Field
Enter a first name or press Enter to end: Mae
Enter the second name: West
Enter a first name or press Enter to end: Oliver
Enter the second name: Hardy
Enter a first name or press Enter to end:

Jane Fonda
Bill Cosby
Sally Field
Mae West
Oliver Hardy
```

How It Works

You create a vector to store `Person` objects like this:

```
vector<Person> people;                  // Vector of Person objects
```

You then create two arrays of type `char[]` that you'll use as working storage when reading names from the standard input stream:

```
const size_t maxlength {50};
char firstname[maxlength];
char secondname[maxlength];
```

Each array accommodates up to `maxlength` characters, including the terminating null.

You read names from the standard input stream in an indefinite loop:

```
while(true)
{
  std::cout << "Enter a first name or press Enter to end: ";
  std::cin.getline(firstname, maxlength, '\n');
  if(strlen(firstname) == 0)
    break;
  std::cout << "Enter the second name: ";
  std::cin.getline(secondname, maxlength, '\n');
  people.emplace_back(firstname, secondname);
}
```

You read each name using the `getline()` member function for `cin`. This reads characters until a new-line is read, or until `maxlength-1` characters have been read. This ensures that you don't overrun the capacity of the input array because both arrays have `maxlength` elements, allowing for strings up to `maxlength-1` characters plus the terminating null. When an empty string is entered for the first name, the loop ends.

The `Person` object is created from the arguments to the `emplace_back()` function at the end of the vector.

The last step is to output the contents of the vector:

```
std::cout << std::endl;
auto iter = cbegin(people);
while(iter != cend(people))
{
  iter->showPerson();
  ++iter;
}
```

Here, you use an iterator of type `vector<Person>::const_iterator` to output the elements with the type deduced automatically from the initial value. Within the body of the loop, you output the element that the iterator points to and then increment the iterator. The loop continues as long as `iter` is not equal to the iterator returned by `cend()`.

This demonstrated the use of iterators but a range-based `for` loop would greatly simplify the code for the output:

```
for(const auto& p : people)
  p.showPerson();
```

The loop variable, `p`, will be of type `Person&`, which is a reference to the type of element stored in the vector.

Sorting Vector Elements

The `sort<T>()` function template that is defined in the `algorithm` header will sort a sequence of objects of any type as long as the required comparisons are supported. Objects are sorted in ascending sequence by default so the `<` operation must be supported. You identify the sequence by two random access iterators that point to the first and one-past-the-last objects. Note that random access iterators are essential; iterators with lesser capability will not suffice. The type parameter, `T`, specifies the type of random access iterator that the function will use. Thus, the `sort<T>()` template can sort the contents of any container that provides random access iterators, as long as the object type supports comparisons.

In the previous example, you implemented `operator <()` in the `Person` class, so you could sort a sequence of `Person` objects. Here's how you could sort the contents of the `vector<Person>` container:

```
std::sort(stdbegin(people), stdend(people));
```

This sorts the contents of the vector in ascending sequence. You can add an `#include` directive for `algorithm`, and put the statement in `main()` before the output loop, to see the sort in action. Note that you can use `sort<T>()` to sort arrays. The only requirement is that the `<` operator should work with the type of the elements. Here's a code fragment showing how you could use it to sort an array of integers:

```
const size_t N {100};
int data[N];
std::cout << "Enter up to " << N << " non-zero integers. Enter 0 to end:\n";
int value {};
size_t count {};
for(size_t i {} ;i<N ;i++)                    // Read up to N integers
```

```
{
  std::cin >> value;                   // Read a value
  if(!value)                           // If it is zero,
    break;                             // we are done
  data[count++] = value;
}
std::sort(data, data+count);           // Sort the integers
```

Note how the pointer marking the end of the sequence of elements to be sorted must still be one past the last element.

When you need to sort a sequence in descending order, you can use the version of the `sort<T>()` algorithm that accepts a third argument that is a function object that defines a binary predicate. The `functional` header defines a complete set of function object types for comparison predicates:

```
less<T>    less_equal<T>    equal<T>    greater_equal<T>    greater<T>
```

Each of these templates creates a class type for function objects that you can use with `sort()` and other algorithms for sorting objects of type T. The `sort()` function used in the previous fragment uses a `less<int>` function object by default. To specify a different function object to be used as the sort criterion, you add it as a third argument, like this:

```
std::sort(data, data+count, std::greater<int>());     // Sort the integers
```

The third argument to the function is an expression that calls the constructor for the `greater<int>` type, so you are passing an object of this type to the `sort()` function. This statement will sort the contents of the `data` array in descending sequence. If you are trying these fragments out, don't forget that you need the `functional` header to be included for the function object. The comparison predicates also come in the form of transparent operator functors. They are referred to as transparent because they perform perfect forwarding of the arguments. When you want to use the transparent form with an algorithm, you just omit the template type argument, like this:

```
std::sort(data, data+count, std::greater<>());
```

This sorts the container contents with perfect forwarding of the objects to be compared.

Storing Pointers in a Vector

A vector container, like other containers, makes a copy of the objects you add to it. This has tremendous advantages in many circumstances, but it could be very inconvenient in some situations. For example, if your objects are large, there could be considerable overhead in copying each object as you add it to the container. This is an occasion where you might be better off storing smart pointers to the objects in the container. You could create a new version of the `Ex10_02.cpp` example to store pointers to `Person` objects in a container.

TRY IT OUT Storing Pointers in a Vector

The `Person` class definition is exactly the same as before. Here's a revised version of the source file that defines `main()`:

```
// Ex10_03.cpp
// Storing pointers to objects in a vector
#include <iostream>
#include <vector>
```

```
#include <memory>
#include "Person.h"
using std::vector;
using std::unique_ptr;
using std::make_unique;

int main()
{
  vector<unique_ptr<Person>> people;           // Vector of Person object pointers
  const size_t maxlength {50};
  char firstname[maxlength];
  char secondname[maxlength];
  while(true)
  {
    std::cout << "Enter a first name or press Enter to end: ";
    std::cin.getline(firstname, maxlength, '\n');
    if(strlen(firstname) == 0)
      break;
    std::cout << "Enter the second name: ";
    std::cin.getline(secondname, maxlength, '\n');
    people.push_back(make_unique<Person>(firstname, secondname));
  }
  // Output the contents of the vector
  std::cout << std::endl;
  for( const auto& p : people)
    p->showPerson();
}
```

The output is essentially the same as before.

How It Works

There is an #include directive for the memory header and additional using declarations for the unique_ptr and the make_unique names. The first change in main() from Ex10_02 is in the definition of the container:

```
vector<unique_ptr<Person>> people;              // Vector of Person object pointers
```

The vector<T> template type parameter is now unique_ptr<Person>, which is a smart pointer to a Person object. We can use unique_ptr because there is not sharing of ownership in the example.

Within the input loop, each Person object is now created on the heap, and the address wrapped inside a unique_ptr is passed to the push_back() function for the vector:

```
people.push_back(make_unique<Person>(firstname, secondname));
```

The arguments to make_unique<Person>() are the arguments that it will use for the Person class constructor that will be pointed to by the uniqued_ptr<Person> object it will return. This is stored in the vector by the push_back() function.

You output the Person objects using the range-based for loop:

```
for(const auto& p : people)
  p->showPerson();
```

This time p is of type unique_ptr<Person>&, so you use the indirect member selection operator to call showPerson() for each Person object.

Finally, you empty the vector by calling its `clear()` function. This deletes everything stored in the container. There is no need to delete `Person` objects. This will be taken care of when the smart pointers are destroyed.

You could also store `shared_ptr<Person>` objects in the vector:

```
vector<shared_ptr<Person>> people;          // Vector of Person object pointers
```

The statement to store the pointers in the vector would be:

```
people.push_back(make_shared<Person>(firstname, secondname));
```

The loop to output the `Person` objects would be the same. However, there's a difference between using `unique_ptr` and `shared_ptr`. This rather less efficient loop would work with `shared_ptr` objects:

```
for(auto p : people)
  p->showPerson();
```

However, this will not compile with `unique_ptr` objects in the vector because they cannot be copied. You must use a reference to access the elements in this case.

These statements also would not compile:

```
auto pPerson = make_unique<Person>(firstname, secondname);
people.push_back(pPerson);
```

This involves copying the `unique_ptr` object so it's not allowed.

You could do this though:

```
people.push_back(std::move(pPerson));
```

This moves the pointer in `pPerson` to a `unique_ptr` in the vector. But now `pPerson` is not valid, so this statement would throw an exception:

```
pPerson->showPerson();
```

If you plan to retain a smart pointer for use after you have stored it in a container, use a `shared_ptr` and not a `unique_ptr`.

Array Containers

The `array<T,N>` template that is defined in the `array` header defines a container that is similar to an ordinary array in that it is of fixed length, `N`, and you can use the subscript operator to access the elements. You can also initialize an array container with an initializer list. For example:

```
std::array<double, 5> values {1.5, 2.5, 3.5, 4.5, 5.5};
```

If you supply fewer initializers than there are elements, the remaining elements will be initialized with the equivalent of zero. This means `nullptr` if the elements are pointers, and objects created by the default constructor if the elements are objects of a class type. If you supply too many initializers, the code won't compile.

You can define an array container without initializing it:

```
std::array<int, 4> data;
```

The size is fixed and the four elements of type int will be created containing junk values. Array container elements of a fundamental type will not be initialized by default, but elements of a class type will be initialized by calling the no-arg constructor. You could construct an array of Person objects where the Person class is as in Ex10_03:

```
std::array<Person, 10> people;
```

This container has 10 elements of type Person, all with the firstname and secondname members as nullptr.

An array container knows its size, so you can use the range-based for loop when it is passed to a function. For example, here's a function template that will list any array container of Person objects:

```
template<size_t N>
void listPeople(const std::array<Person, N>& folks)
{
  for(const auto& p : folks)
    p.showPerson();
}
```

Defining the function by a template with a parameter, N, allows it to be used to list an array of any number of Person objects. If your application classes use a standard function to display an object, you could add a template type parameter for the type of element stored and get a function that will list any of your arrays of any length or type. Remember, though, that each unique set of template parameter values will produce a separate instance of the template.

Because the elements of an array container are always created when you define it, you can reference an element using the subscript operator and use it as an lvalue. For example:

```
people[1] = Person("Joe", "Bloggs");
```

This stores a Person object in the second element in the array.

Here's a summary of some of the most useful members of an array container type:

➤ void fill(const T& arg) sets all the array elements to arg:

```
people.fill(Person("Ned", "Kelly"));    // Fill array with Ned Kellys
```

➤ size() returns the size of the array as an integer.

➤ back() returns a reference to the last array element:

```
people.back().showPerson();             // Output the last person
```

➤ begin() returns an iterator pointing to the first array element.

➤ end() returns an iterator pointing to one past the last array element.

➤ rbegin() returns a reverse iterator pointing to the last array element.

➤ rend() returns a reverse iterator pointing to before the first array element.

➤ `swap(array& right)` swaps the current array with `right`. The current array and `right` must store the same type of elements and have the same size.

```
array<int, 3> left = {1, 2, 3};
array<int, 3> right = {10, 20, 30};
left.swap(right);              // Swap contents of left and right
```

You can use any of the comparison operators, `<`, `<=`, `==`, `>=`, `>`, and `!=`, to compare two array containers as long as they store the same number of elements of the same type. Corresponding elements are compared in sequence to determine the result. For example, `array1<array2` will result in `true` if `array1` has the first occurring element that is less than the corresponding element in `array2`. Two arrays are equal if all corresponding elements are equal and unequal if any pair of corresponding elements differ.

Let's see an example of an array in use.

TRY IT OUT Using an Array

This example creates an interesting series of values in array containers:

```
// Ex10_04
// Using array containers
#include <iostream>
#include <iomanip>
#include <array>
#include <numeric>
using std::array;

// Lists array container contents
template<class T, size_t N>
void listValues(const array<T, N>& data)
{
  const int values_per_line {6};
  int count {};
  for(const auto& value: data)
  {
    std::cout << std::setw(14) << value;
    if(++count % values_per_line == 0)
      std::cout << std::endl;
  }
  std::cout << std::endl;
}

int main()
{
  // Create the famous Fibonacci series
  const size_t N {20};
  array<long, N> fibonacci {1L, 1L};
  for(size_t i {2} ;i<fibonacci.size() ;++i)
    fibonacci[i] = fibonacci[i-1] + fibonacci[i-2];
  std::cout << "Fibonacci series is:" << std::endl;
```

```
        listValues(fibonacci);

        array<long, N> numbers;
        numbers.fill(99L);
        fibonacci.swap(numbers);
        std::cout << std::endl << "After swap fibonacci contains:" << std::endl;
        listValues(fibonacci);

        // Create the series for pi/4
        array<double, 120> series;
        double factor {-1.0};
        for(size_t x {} ;x<series.size() ;++x)
        {
          factor *= -1.0;
          series[x] = factor/(2*x+1);
        }
        std::cout << std::endl << "Series for pi is:" << std::endl;
        listValues(series);
        double result {std::accumulate(cbegin(series), cend(series), 0.0)};
        std::cout << "The series sum converges slowly to pi/4. The sum x 4 is: "
                << 4.0*result << std::endl;
      }
```

I won't include the output here because there's quite a lot of it.

How It Works

You create the first array container with 20 elements of type `long` with the first two initialized to `1L`. In the Fibonacci series, each element is the sum of the two preceding elements and the `for` loop sets the values for the array from the third element onwards. You output the contents of the array using the `listValues()` template function. This lists values of elements from an array container of any size that contains elements of any type that can be written to the standard output stream.

Next, you create the `numbers` container storing the same number of `long` elements as `fibonacci`. The elements are all set to `99L` using the `fill()` member function. You use the `swap()` member function to swap the contents of `numbers` and `fibonacci`, and the output shows that `fibonacci` now contains elements that are all 99.

The third container, `series`, contains 120 elements of type `double`. The values are set in the `for` loop to those of the Leibnitz series that total $\pi/4$ if you sum an infinite number of them.

You sum the 120 elements using the `accumulate()` template function that is defined in the numeric header. The first argument is an iterator specifying the first container element, the second is an iterator specifying one past the last element, and the third argument is an initial value to which the values specified by the first two arguments are to be added. This function works with any sequence container that contains elements that support the + operator. There is another version of `accumulate()` that accepts a fourth argument that specifies the operation to be applied between elements if you don't want to add them. You specify the operation by a function object or lambda expression that defines a binary predicate.

You'll see from the output that the sum of the first 120 elements in the Leibnitz series is fairly close to $\pi/4$.

Double-ended Queue Containers

The double-ended queue container template, deque<T>, is defined in the deque header. A double-ended queue is very similar to a vector in that it can do everything a vector container can, and includes the same function members, but you can also add and delete elements efficiently at the beginning of the sequence as well as at the end. You could replace the vector in Ex10_02.cpp with a double-ended queue, and it would work just as well:

```
std::deque<Person> people;              // Double-ended queue of Person objects
```

The push_front() member function adds an element to the front of the container and you can delete the first element by calling pop_front(). There's also an emplace_front() member so if you were using a deque<Person> container in Ex10_02.cpp, you could add elements at the front instead of the back:

```
people.emplace_front(firstname, secondname);
```

Using this statement to add elements, the order of elements in the double-ended queue would be the reverse of those in the vector.

Here are examples of constructors for a deque<T> container:

```
deque<string> strings;                  // An empty container
deque<int> items(50);                   // 50 elements initialized to default value
deque<double> values(5, 0.5);           // 5 elements of 0.5
deque<int> data(cbegin(items), cend(items));  // Initialized with a sequence
deque<int> numbers {1, 3, 5, 7, 9, 11};
```

Although a double-ended queue is very similar to a vector and does everything a vector can do, it does have one disadvantage. Because of the additional capability, the memory management for a double-ended queue is more complicated than for a vector, so it will be slightly slower. Unless you need to add elements to the front of the container, a vector is a better choice. Let's see a double-ended queue in action.

TRY IT OUT   Using a Double-ended Queue

This example stores an arbitrary number of integers in a double-ended queue and then operates on them:

```
// Ex10_05.cpp
// Using a double-ended queue

#include <iostream>
#include <deque>
#include <algorithm>                   // For sort<T>()
#include <numeric>                     // For accumulate<T>()
#include <functional>                  // For transparent operator functors

int main()
{
  std::deque<int> data;

  // Read the data
  std::cout << "Enter a series of non-zero integers separated by spaces."
            << " Enter 0 to end." << std::endl;
  int value {};
```

```
    while(std::cin >> value, value != 0)
      data.push_front(value);

    // Output the data
    std::cout << std::endl << "The values you entered are:" << std::endl;
    for(const auto& n : data)
      std::cout << n << "  ";
    std::cout << std::endl;

    // Output the data using a reverse iterator
    std::cout << std::endl
              << "In reverse order the values you entered are:" << std::endl;
    for(auto riter = crbegin(data) ;riter != crend(data) ; ++riter)
      std::cout << *riter << "  ";
    std::cout << std::endl;

    // Sort the data in descending sequence
    std::cout << std::endl
              << "In descending sequence the values you entered are:" << std::endl;
    std::sort(begin(data), end(data), std::greater<>());   // Sort the elements
    for(const auto& n : data)
      std::cout << n << "  ";
    std::cout << std::endl;

    // Calculate the sum of the elements
    std::cout << std::endl << "The sum of the elements in the queue is: "
              << std::accumulate(cbegin(data), cend(data), 0)  << std::endl;

  }
```

Here is some sample output from this program:

```
Enter a series of non-zero integers separated by spaces. Enter 0 to end.
405 302 1 23 67 34 56 111 56 99 77 82 3 23 34 111 89 0

The values you entered are:
89  111  34  23  3  82  77  99  56  111  56  34  67  23  1  302  405

In reverse order the values you entered are:
405  302  1  23  67  34  56  111  56  99  77  82  3  23  34  111  89

In descending sequence the values you entered are:
405  302  111  111  99  89  82  77  67  56  56  34  34  23  23  3  1

The sum of the elements in the queue is: 1573
```

How It Works

You create the double-ended queue container at the beginning of `main()`:

```
std::deque<int> data;
```

The `data` container is empty to start with and the input is read in a `while` loop:

```
int value {};
while(std::cin >> value, value != 0)
  data.push_front(value);
```

The `while` loop condition makes use of the comma operator to separate two expressions, one that reads an integer from `cin` into `value` and another that tests whether the value read is non-zero. You saw in Chapter 2 that the value of a series of expressions separated by commas is the value of the rightmost, so the `while` loop continues as long as the expression `value != 0` is `true`, and the value read is non-zero. Within the loop you store the value in the queue using the `push_front()` function.

The next loop lists the values that you stored in the queue:

```
std::cout << std::endl << "The values you entered are:" << std::endl;
for(const auto& n : data)
  std::cout << n << "  ";
std::cout << std::endl;
```

This uses a range-based `for` loop to output the values. You could also write this as a `while` loop using an iterator:

```
auto iter = cbegin(data);
while(iter != cend(data))
  std::cout << *iter++ << "  ";
```

Here, you increment the iterator after the value it points to is written to `cout`. It's just for illustration — not a good alternative to the range-based `for`!

The next loop outputs the values in reverse order:

```
for(auto riter = crbegin(data) ;riter != crend(data) ;++riter)
  std::cout << *riter << "  ";
```

This uses a reverse iterator, so the loop starts with the last element and ends when `riter` is equal to the iterator returned by `crend()`. The `crbegin()` function returns an iterator pointing to the last element and the `crend()` function returns an iterator pointing to one before the first element. For vectors and double-ended queues, you get random access iterators. The `auto` keyword selects the type automatically; it will be `deque<int>::reverse_iterator`.

Next, you sort the elements in descending sequence and output them:

```
std::sort(begin(data), end(data), std::greater<>());   // Sort the elements
for(const auto& n : data)
  std::cout << n << "  ";
std::cout << std::endl;
```

By default, `sort<T>()` sorts in ascending sequence using a `less<T>()` function object as the comparator. When you supply the `greater<>()` object as the optional third argument, the integer elements will be sorted into descending sequence. The arguments will be forwarded to the comparator because omitting the template parameter selects the transparent version of the functor.

You could sort the queue elements in descending sequence like this:

```
std::sort(rbegin(data), rend(data));          // Sort into descending sequence
```

The default operation of the `sort()` algorithm is to sort the sequence passed to it by the iterator arguments in ascending sequence. Here, you pass reverse iterators to the function, so it sees the elements in reverse order and sorts the reversed sequence in ascending order. The result is that the elements end up in descending sequence when seen in the normal forward order.

The last operation in `main()` is to output the sum of the elements:

```
std::cout << std::endl << "The sum of the elements in the queue is: "
          << std::accumulate(cbegin(data), cend(data), 0)  << std::endl;
```

You could use a conventional loop to do this, but here you make use of the `accumulate()` algorithm from the numeric header that you saw in the previous example. The default addition operation applies here.

Using List Containers

The `list<T>` container template from the `list` header implements a doubly-linked list. The big advantage this has over a vector or a double-ended queue is that you can insert or delete elements anywhere in the sequence in constant time. The main drawback is that a list cannot directly access an element by its position. It's necessary to traverse the elements in a list from a known position when you want to do this, usually the first or the last. The range of constructors for a list container is similar to that for a vector or double-ended queue. This statement creates an empty list:

```
std::list<std::string> names;
```

You can also create a list with a given number of default elements:

```
std::list<std::string> sayings(20);                  // A list of 20 empty strings
```

Here's how you create a list containing a given number of identical elements:

```
std::list<double> values(50, 2.71828);
```

This creates a list of 50 values of type `double` equal to 2.71828.

You can also construct a list initialized with values from a sequence specified by two iterators:

```
std::list<double> samples(++cbegin(values), --cend(values));
```

This creates a list from the contents of the `values` list, omitting the first and last elements. The iterators returned by the `begin()` and `end()` functions for a list are bidirectional iterators, so you do not have the same flexibility as with a `vector` or a `deque` container that support random access iterators. You can only change the value of a bidirectional iterator using the increment or decrement operators.

Just like the other sequence containers, you can discover the number of elements in a list by calling its `size()` member. You can also change the number of elements by calling its `resize()` function. If the argument to `resize()` is less than the number of elements, elements will be deleted from the end; if the argument is greater, elements will be added using the default constructor for the type of elements stored.

Adding Elements to a List

You add an element to the beginning or end of a list by calling `push_front()` or `push_back()`, just as you would for a double-ended queue. To add elements to the interior of a list, you use the `insert()` function, which comes in three versions. Using the first version, you can insert a new element at a position specified by an iterator:

```
std::list<int> data(20, 1);          // List of 20 elements value 1
data.insert(++begin(data), 77);      // Insert 77 as the second element
```

The first argument to insert() is an iterator specifying the insertion position, and the second argument is the element to be inserted. Incrementing the bidirectional iterator returned by begin() makes it point to the second element. After executing this, the list contents will be:

```
1 77 1 1 1 1 1 1 1 1 1 1 1 1 1 1 1 1 1 1 1
```

You can see that the list now contains 21 elements, and that the elements from the insertion point on are simply displaced to the right.

You can insert a number of copies of the same element at a given position:

```
auto iter = begin(data);
   std::advance(iter, 9);      // Increment iterator by 9
data.insert(iter, 3, 88);      // Insert 3 copies of 88 starting at the 10th
```

iter will be of type list<int>::iterator. The first argument to the insert() function is an iterator specifying the insertion position, the second is the number of elements to be inserted, and the third is the element to be inserted repeatedly. To get to the tenth element you increment the iterator by caling the advance() template function. The advance() function increments the iterator specified by the first argument by the amount specified by the second. Using the advance() function is necessary because you cannot just add 9 to a bidirectional iterator. Thus, this fragment inserts three copies of 88 into the list, starting at the tenth element. Now the contents of the list will be:

```
1 77 1 1 1 1 1 1 88 88 88 1 1 1 1 1 1 1 1 1 1 1
```

Now the list contains 24 elements.

Here's how you can insert a sequence of elements into a list:

```
std::vector<int> numbers(10, 5);            // Vector of 10 elements with value 5
data.insert(--(--end(data)), cbegin(numbers), cend(numbers));
```

The first argument to insert() is an iterator pointing to the second-to-last element position. The sequence to be inserted is specified by the second and third arguments to the insert() function, so this will insert all the elements from the vector into the list, starting at the second to last element position. After executing this, the contents of the list will be:

```
1 77 1 1 1 1 1 1 88 88 88 1 1 1 1 1 1 1 1 1 1 5 5 5 5 5 5 5 5 5 5 1 1
```

Inserting the 10 elements from numbers in the second-to-last element position displaces the last two elements in the list to the right. The list now contains 34 elements.

There are three functions that will construct an element in place in the list: emplace(), which constructs an element at a position specified by an iterator; emplace_front(), which constructs an element at the beginning; and emplace_back(), which constructs an element at the end. Here are some examples of their use:

```
std::list<std::string> strings;
strings.emplace_back("first");
std::string second("second");
strings.emplace_back(std::move(second));
strings.emplace_front("third");
strings.emplace(++begin(strings), "fourth");
```

The fourth line of code uses the std::move() function to pass an rvalue reference to s to the emplace_back() function. After executing this operation, s will be empty because the contents will have been moved to the list. After executing these statements, strings will contain the elements:

```
third   fourth   first   second
```

Accessing Elements in a List

You can obtain a reference to the first or last element in a list by calling its `front()` or `back()` member. To access elements that are interior to the list you must use an iterator and increment or decrement it to get to the element you want. As you have seen, `begin()` and `end()` return a bidirectional iterator pointing at the first element, or one past the last element, respectively. The `rbegin()` and `rend()` functions return bidirectional iterators and enable you to iterate through the elements in reverse sequence. You can use the range-based `for` loop with a list so you don't have to use iterators when you want to process all the elements:

```
std::list<std::string> strings;
strings.emplace_back("first");
std::string second("second");
strings.emplace_back(std::move(second));
strings.emplace_front("third");
strings.emplace(++begin(strings), "fourth");
for(const auto& s : strings)
  std::cout << s << std::endl;
```

The loop variable, s, is a reference that will reference each list element in turn.

Sorting List Elements

Because a `list<T>` container does not provide random access iterators, you cannot use the `sort()` function that is defined in the `algorithm` header. This is why the `list<T>` template defines its own `sort()` member function. It comes in two versions. To sort a list in ascending sequence you call the `sort()` member with no arguments. Alternatively, you can specify a function object or a lambda expression that defines a different predicate for comparing members. For example:

```
strings.sort(std::greater<std::string>());      // Descending sequence
```

You can also use the transparent version of the predicate:

```
strings.sort(std::greater<>());                 // Perfect forwarding
```

This will be faster because the arguments to the comparison operation will be moved, not copied. Let's try out some of what we have seen in an example.

TRY IT OUT   Working with a List

In this example you read sentences from the keyboard and store them in a list:

```
// Ex10_06.cpp
// Working with a list
#include <iostream>
#include <list>
#include <string>
#include <functional>

using std::string;
```

```cpp
void listAll(const std::list<string>& strings)
{
  for (auto& s : strings)
    std::cout << s << std::endl;
}

int main()
{
  std::list<string> text;

  // Read the data
  std::cout << "Enter a few lines of text. Just press Enter to end:" << std::endl;
  string sentence;
  while (getline(std::cin, sentence, '\n'), !sentence.empty())
    text.push_front(sentence);

  std::cout << "Your text in reverse order:" << std::endl;
  listAll(text);

  text.sort();                          // Sort the data in ascending sequence
  std::cout << "\nYour text in  ascending sequence:" << std::endl;
  listAll(text);

  text.sort(std::greater<>());          // Sort the data in descending sequence
  std::cout << "\nYour text in  descending sequence:" << std::endl;
  listAll(text);
}
```

Here is some sample output:

```
Enter a few lines of text. Just press Enter to end:
This sentence contains three erors.
This sentence is false.
People who live in glass houses might as well answer the door.
If all else fails, read the instructions.
Home is where the mortgage is.

Your text in reverse order:
Home is where the mortgage is.
If all else fails, read the instructions.
People who live in glass houses might as well answer the door.
This sentence is false.
This sentence contains three erors.

Your text in ascending sequence:
Home is where the mortgage is.
If all else fails, read the instructions.
People who live in glass houses might as well answer the door.
This sentence contains three erors.
This sentence is false.

Your text in descending sequence:
This sentence is false.
This sentence contains three erors.
People who live in glass houses might as well answer the door.
If all else fails, read the instructions.
Home is where the mortgage is.
```

How It Works

There's a helper function, `listAll()`, that outputs the contents of the `list<string>` container that is passed to it. The parameter is a reference so the container won't be copied. You output the contents of a list in a loop in the `listAll()` function like this:

```
for(auto& s : strings)
    std::cout << s << std::endl;
```

This lists each element from the list on a separate line.

You create a list container in `main()` to hold strings:

```
std::list<string> text;
```

You then read an arbitrary number of input lines from the standard input stream:

```
string sentence;
while(getline(std::cin, sentence, '\n'), !sentence.empty())
    text.push_front(sentence);
```

This uses the same idiom for input as the previous example. The second expression in the `while` loop condition determines when the loop ends, which will be when calling `empty()` for `sentence` returns `true`. You add each input to the list using the `push_front()` function, but you could equally well use `push_back()`. The only difference would be that the order of elements in the list would be reversed.

A better way to code this would be to use an `emplace` function:

```
while(getline(std::cin, sentence, '\n'), !sentence.empty())
    text.emplace_front(std::move(sentence));
```

This would move the string from the sentence to the front of the list. This would avoid any copying and therefore would be faster to execute. The sentence object would be empty after each `emplace_front()` operation.

You output the contents of the list by calling the `listAll()` function. The output presents the input in reverse order because using `push_front()` creates the list in reverse sequence. If you used `push_back()`, elements would be in the sequence they were entered.

Next, you sort the contents of the list and output it:

```
text.sort();                            // Sort the data in ascending sequence
std::cout << "\nYour text in  ascending sequence:" << std::endl;
listAll(text);
```

This uses the `sort()` member of the `list<string>` object with no argument to sort the contents in ascending sequence. You sort the elements in descending sequence, like this:

```
text.sort(std::greater<>());            // Sort the data in descending sequence
```

This uses the transparent version of the functor to get perfect forwarding.

Other Operations on Lists

The `clear()` function deletes all the elements from a list. The `erase()` function allows you to delete either a single element specified by a single iterator, or a sequence of elements specified by a pair of iterators in the usual fashion — the first in the sequence and one past the last:

```
std::list<int> numbers {10, 22, 4, 56, 89, 77, 13, 9};
numbers.erase(++begin(numbers));        // Remove the second element

// Remove all except the first and the last two
numbers.erase(++begin(numbers), --(--end(numbers)));
```

Initially, the list contains all the values in the initializer list. The first `erase()` operation deletes the second element, so the list will contain:

```
10 4 56 89 77 13 9
```

For the second `erase()` operation, the first argument is the iterator returned by `begin()`, incremented by 1, so it points to the second element. The second argument is the iterator returned by `end()`, decremented twice, so it points to the second-to-last element. Of course, this is one past the end of the sequence, so the element that this iterator points to is not included in the set to be deleted. The list contents after this operation will be:

```
10 13 9
```

The `remove()` function removes elements from a list that match a particular value. With the `numbers` list defined as in the previous fragment, you could remove all elements equal to 22 with the following statement:

```
numbers.remove(22);
```

The `assign()` function removes all the elements from a list and copies either a single object into the list a given number of times, or copies a sequence of objects specified by two iterators. Here's an example:

```
std::list<int> numbers {10, 22, 4, 56, 89, 77, 13, 9};
numbers.assign(10, 99);         // Replace contents by 10 copies of 99
numbers.assign(data+1, data+4); // Replace contents by 22 4 56
```

The `assign()` function comes in the two overloaded versions illustrated here. The arguments to the first are the count of the number of replacement elements, and the replacement element value. The arguments to the second version are either two iterators or two pointers, specifying a sequence in the way you have already seen.

The `unique()` function will eliminate adjacent duplicate elements from a list, so if you sort the contents first, applying the function ensures that all elements are unique. Here's an example:

```
std::list<int> numbers {10, 22, 4, 10, 89, 22, 89, 10} ; // 10 22 4 10 89 22 89 10
numbers.sort();                                           // 4 10 10 10 22 22 89 89
numbers.unique();                                         // 4 10 22 89
```

The result of each operation is shown in the comments.

The `splice()` function removes all or part of one list and inserts it in another. Obviously, both lists must store elements of the same type. Here's the simplest way you could use the `splice()` function:

```
std::list<int> numbers {1, 2, 3};                 // 1 2 3
std::list<int> values {5, 6, 7, 8};               // 5 6 7 8
numbers.splice(++begin(numbers), values);         // 1 5 6 7 8 2 3
```

The first argument to `splice()` is an iterator specifying where the elements should be inserted, and the second argument is the list that is the source of the elements. This operation removes all the elements from the `values` list and inserts them immediately preceding the second element in the `numbers` list.

Here's another version of `splice()` that removes elements from a given position in a source list and inserts them at a given position in a destination list:

```
std::list<int> numbers {1, 2, 3};                              // 1 2 3
std::list<int> values {5, 6, 7, 8};                            // 5 6 7 8
numbers.splice(begin(numbers), values, --end(values));         // 8 1 2 3
```

In this version, the first two arguments to `splice()` are the same as the previous version of the function. The third argument is an iterator specifying the position of the first element to be selected from the source list; all elements, from this position to the end, are removed from the source and inserted in the destination list. After executing this code fragment, `values` will contain 5 6 7.

The third version of `splice()` requires four arguments and selects a range of elements from the source list:

```
std::list<int> numbers {1, 2, 3};                              // 1 2 3
std::list<int> values {5, 6, 7, 8};                            // 5 6 7 8
numbers.splice(++begin(numbers), values, ++begin(values),
                                 --end(values));// 1 6 7 2 3
```

The first three arguments to this version of `splice()` are the same as the previous version, and the last argument is one past the last element to be removed from the source. After executing this, `values` will contain:

```
5 8
```

The `merge()` function removes elements from the list that you supply as an argument and inserts them in the list for which the function is called. Both lists must be ordered in the same sense before you call `merge()`. The order of the second list argument determines the ordering of the final combined list. If the lists are not ordered in the same sense, the debug version of the code will assert; the release version will run but the result will not be correct. Here's a fragment showing how you might use it:

```
std::list<int> numbers {1, 2, 3};                              // 1 2 3
std::list<int> values {2, 3, 4, 5, 6, 7, 8};                   // 2 3 4 5 6 7 8
numbers.merge(values);                                         // 1 2 2 3 3 4 5 6 7 8
```

This merges the contents of `values` into `numbers`, so `values` will be empty after this operation. The `merge()` member function that accepts a single argument orders the result in the sequence corresponding to that of the argument. Because the values in both lists are already ordered here, you don't need to sort them. To merge the same lists in descending sequence, the code would be as follows:

```
numbers.sort(std::greater<>());                                // 3 2 1
values.sort(std::greater<>());                                 // 8 7 6 5 4 3 2
numbers.merge(values, std::greater<>());                       // 8 7 6 5 4 3 3 2 2 1
```

A `greater<>()` function object specifies that the lists should be sorted in descending sequence and then merged into the same sequence. The transparent version of the function object is used here where the type argument is deduced. The second argument to `merge()` is a function object specifying the ordering, which must be the same as that of the lists for correct operation. You can omit the second argument to `merge()`, in which case it will be deduced to be the same as `values`.

The `remove_if()` function removes elements based on the result of applying a unary predicate; I'm sure you'll recall that a unary predicate is a function object that applies to a single argument and returns a `bool` value, `true` or `false`. If the result of applying the predicate to an element is `true`, then the element will be deleted from the list. Typically, you would define your own predicate to do this. This involves defining your own class template for the function object or lambda expression that you want, while the STL defines the `unary_function<T, R>` base class template for use when you want to define your own class template. This template just defines types that will be inherited by the derived class that specifies your function object type. The base class template is defined as follows:

```
template<class _Arg, class _Result>
struct unary_function
{ // base class for unary functions
  typedef _Arg argument_type;
  typedef _Result result_type;
};
```

This defines `argument_type` and `result_type` for use in your definition of the `operator()()` function. You must use this base template if you want to use your predicates with function adapters. You'll see later in this chapter that lambda expressions provide a much easier way to define a predicate.

The way in which you can use the `remove_if()` function is best explained with a specific application, so let's try this in a working example.

TRY IT OUT **Defining a Predicate for Filtering a List**

Here's how you could define a template for a function object based on the helper template from the STL, which you could then use to remove negative values from a list:

```
// function_object.h
// Unary predicate to identify negative values
#pragma once
#include <functional>

template <class T> class is_negative : public std::unary_function<T, bool>
{
  public:
  result_type operator()(argument_type& value)
  {
    return value < 0;
  }
};
```

This predicate works with any type that supports a less-than comparison with the value 0. The base template is very useful in that it standardizes the representation of the argument and return types for the predicate, and this is required if you want your function object to be usable with function adapters. Function adapters allow function objects to be used in combination to provide more complex functions. You should be able to see how you could define unary predicates for filtering a list in other ways — selecting even or odd numbers for example, or multiples of a given number, or numbers falling within a given range.

If you are not concerned about the use of your predicate with function adapters, you could define the template without the base class template:

```
// Unary predicate to identify negative values
#pragma once

template <class T> class is_negative
```

```
{
  public:
  bool operator()(const T& value)
  {
    return value < 0;
  }
};
```

You don't need the `#include` directive for `functional` here because you are not using the base template. This definition is simple, and perhaps easier to understand, but I included the original version just to show how you use the base template. You will want to do this if you intend to use your predicate in a more general context. I'll create the example with the first version, but you can use either version, or perhaps try both.

To make the example more interesting, I'll include function templates for inputting data to a list and for writing out the contents of a list. Here's the program to make use of the predicate:

```cpp
// Ex10_07.cpp
// Using the remove_if() function for a list

#include <iostream>
#include <list>
#include "function_object.h"

// Template function to list the contents of a list
template <class T>
void listAll(const std::list<T>& data)
{
  for(const auto& t : data)
    std::cout << t << "  ";
  std::cout << std::endl;
}

// Template function to read data from cin and store it in a list
template<class T>
void loadList(std::list<T>& data)
{
  T value;
  while(std::cin >> value , value != T())   //Read non-zero values
    data.emplace_back(std::move(value));
}

int main()
{
  // Process integers
  std::list<int> numbers;
  std::cout << "Enter non-zero integers separated by spaces. Enter 0 to end."
            << std::endl;
  loadList(numbers);
  std::cout << "The list contains:" << std::endl;
  listAll(numbers);
  numbers.remove_if(is_negative<int>());
  std::cout << "After applying remove_if() the list contains:" << std::endl;
  listAll (numbers);

  // Process floating-point values
  std::list<double> values;
```

```
       std::cout << "\nEnter non-zero float values separated by spaces(some negative!)."
                  <<    "Enter 0 to end." << std::endl;
     loadList(values);
     std::cout << "The list contains:" << std::endl;
     listAll(values);
     values.remove_if(is_negative<double>());
     std::cout << "After applying remove_if() the list contains:" << std::endl;
     listAll(values);
   }
```

Here's some sample output from this program:

```
Enter non-zero integers separated by spaces. Enter 0 to end.
23 -4 -5 66 67 89 -1 22 34 -34 78 62 -9 99 -19 0
The list contains:
23   -4   -5   66   67   89   -1   22   34   -34   78   62   -9   99   -19
After applying remove_if() the list contains:
23   66   67   89   22   34   78   62   99

Enter non-zero float values separated by spaces(some negative!).Enter 0 to end.
2.5 -3.1 5.5 100 -99 -.075 1.075 13 -12.1 13.2 0
The list contains:
2.5   -3.1   5.5   100   -99   -0.075   1.075   13   -12.1   13.2
After applying remove_if() the list contains:
2.5   5.5   100   1.075   13   13.2
```

How It Works

The output shows that the predicate works for int and double values. The remove_if() function applies the predicate to each element in a list and deletes the elements for which the predicate returns true.

The body of the loadList<T>() template function that reads the input is:

```
T value;
while(std::cin >> value , value != T())   //Read non-zero values
  data.emplace_back(std::move(value));
```

The local variable value is defined as type T, the type parameter for the template, so this will be of whatever type you use to instantiate the function. The input is read in the while loop, and values continue to be read until you enter zero, in which case the last expression in the while loop condition will be false, thus ending the loop. Using emplace_back() with an rvalue reference to value moves value to the list, rather than copying it.

The body of the listAll<T>() function template is essentially the same as the function with the same name in the previous example. Note how you can use auto, even in a template. This deduces the type for the for loop control variable, t, which maps to the type required for the elements in the list container that is passed as the argument. If you wanted to try out the merge() function within this example, you could add the following code before the return statement in main():

```
// Another list to use in merge
std::list<double> morevalues;
std::cout << "\nEnter non-zero float values separated by spaces. Enter 0 to end."
          << std::endl;
loadlist(morevalues);
std::cout << "The list contains:" << std::endl;
listAll(morevalues);
```

```
        morevalues.remove_if(is_negative<double>());
        std::cout << "After applying the remove_if() function the list contains:"
                  << std::endl;
        listAll(morevalues);

        // Merge the last two lists
        values.sort(std::greater<>());
        morevalues.sort(std::greater<>());
        values.merge(morevalues, std::greater<>());
        std::cout << "\nSorting and merging two lists produces:" << std::endl;
        listAll(values);
```

The use of `std::greater<>()` requires that the `functional` header is included.

Using forward_list Containers

The `forward_list` header defines the `forward_list<T>` container template that implements a singly linked list of elements of type `T`, where each element contains a pointer to the next element. This means that, unlike a `list<T>` container, you can only traverse the elements forwards. Like the `list<T>` container, you cannot access an element by its position. The only way to access an element is to traverse the list from the beginning. Because the operations for a `forward_list<T>` container are similar to those for a `list<T>`, I'll just highlight a few of them.

The `front()` member function returns a reference to the first element in the list as long as the list is not empty and the reference will be const if the container object is const. You can test whether or not the list is empty using the `empty()` member, which returns `false` as long as there is at least one element in the list. The `remove()` function removes the element that matches the object you supply as the argument. There's also the `remove_if()` member for which you supply a predicate as an argument, which can be a function object or a lambda expression. All elements for which the predicate is true are removed.

Because it is a singly linked list, a `forward_list<T>` container only has forward iterators. You can use the global functions to obtain iterators such as `begin()` and `end()` with it, except for those that return reverse iterators.

You can add an element to a `forward_list` using either `push_front()` or `emplace_front()`. The `emplace_front()` function creates an object from the arguments that you supply and inserts it at the front of the list. The `push_front()` function inserts the object you supply as the argument at the front of the list.

For example:

```
        std::forward_list<std::string> words;
        std::string s1 {"first"};
        words.push_front(s1);
        words.emplace_front("second");
        std::string s2 {"third"};
        words.emplace_front(std::move(s2));
        words.emplace_front("fourth");
```

After executing this fragment, `words` will contain:

```
fourth  third  second  first
```

A `forward_list<T>` container also has a `before_begin()` function that returns an iterator pointing to the position before the first element. This is for use with the `insert_after()` and `emplace_after()` member functions. You can insert one or more objects after a given position in the list using the `insert_after()` function. There are several versions of this. Here are some examples:

```
std::forward_list<int> datalist;

// Returns an iterator pointing to the inserted element, 11
auto iter = datalist.insert_after(datalist.before_begin(), 11); // 11

// Inserts 3 copies of the 3rd argument after iter and increments iter
iter = datalist.insert_after(iter, 3, 15);                      // 11 15 15 15

// Insert a range following iter, and increments iter to point to 5
int data[] {1, 2, 4, 5};
iter = datalist.insert_after(
                iter, std::cbegin(data), std::cend(data)); // 11 15 15 15 1 2 4 5
```

`iter` will be of type `forward_list<int>::iterator`.

You can insert an element after a given position in the list using the `emplace_after()` function. The first argument is an iterator specifying the element after which the new element should be inserted. The second and subsequent arguments are passed to the constructor for the class type of the object to be inserted. For example:

```
words.emplace_after(std::cbegin(words), "fifth");
```

After executing this statement with `words` as it was left by the previous fragment adding elements, the list will contain:

```
fourth  fifth  third  second  first
```

The function created a `string("fifth")` object and stored it following the position pointed to by the first argument.

A `forward_list<T>` container provides better performance than a `list<T>` container. Having only one link to maintain makes it faster in operation and there is no size member keeping track of the number of elements. If you need to know the number of elements, you can obtain it using the `distance()` function from the `algorithm` header:

```
std::cout << "Size = " << std::distance(std::cbegin(words), std::cend(words));
```

The arguments are iterators specifying the first element and one past the last element to be counted.

Using Other Sequence Containers

The remaining sequence containers are implemented through container adapters that I introduced at the beginning of this chapter. I'll discuss each of them briefly and illustrate their operation with examples.

Queue Containers

A `queue<T>` container implements a first-in first-out storage mechanism through an adapter. You can only add to the end of the queue or remove from the front. Here's one way you can create a queue:

```
std::queue<std::string> names;
```

This creates a queue storing elements of type `string`. By default, the `queue<T>` adapter class uses a `deque<T>` container as the base, but you can specify a different sequence container as a base, as long as it supports the operations `front()`, `back()`, `push_back()`, and `pop_front()`. These four functions are used to operate the queue. Thus, a queue can be based on a list or a vector. You specify the alternate container as a second template parameter. Here's how you would create a queue based on a list:

```
std::queue<std::string, std::list<std::string>> names;
```

The second type parameter to the adapter template specifies the underlying sequence container to be used. The queue adapter class acts as a wrapper for the underlying container class and essentially restricts the range of operations you can carry out to those described in the following table.

FUNCTION	DESCRIPTION
`back()`	Returns a reference to the element at the back of the queue. There are two versions, one returning a `const` reference and the other returning a non-`const` reference. If the queue is empty, then the value returned is undefined.
`front()`	Returns a reference to the element at the front of the queue. There are two versions, one returning a `const` reference and the other returning a non-`const` reference. If the queue is empty, then the value returned is undefined.
`push()`	Adds the element specified by the argument to the back of the queue.
`pop()`	Removes the element at the front of the queue.
`size()`	Returns the number of elements in the queue.
`empty()`	Returns `true` if the queue is empty and `false` otherwise.

Note that there are no functions that make iterators available for a queue. The only way to access the contents of a queue is via the `back()` or `front()` functions.

TRY IT OUT Using a Queue Container

In this example you read a succession of one or more sayings, store them in a queue, and then retrieve and output them:

```
// Ex10_08.cpp
// Exercising a queue container
#include <iostream>
#include <queue>
#include <string>

int main()
{
  std::queue<std::string> sayings;
```

```
std::string saying;
std::cout << "Enter one or more sayings. Press Enter to end." << std::endl;
while(true)
{
  std::getline(std::cin, saying);
  if(saying.empty())
    break;
  sayings.push(saying);
}

std::cout << "There are " << sayings.size() << " sayings in the queue.\n"
          << std::endl;
std::cout << "The sayings that you entered are:" << std::endl;
while(!sayings.empty())
{
  std::cout << sayings.front() << std::endl;
  sayings.pop();
}
}
```

Here's an example of some output from this program:

```
Enter one or more sayings. Press Enter to end.
If at first you don't succeed, give up.
A preposition is something you should never end a sentence with.
The bigger they are, the harder they hit.
A rich man is just a poor man with money.
Wherever you go, there you are.
Common sense is not so common.

There are 6 sayings in the queue.

The sayings that you entered are:
If at first you don't succeed, give up.
A preposition is something you should never end a sentence with.
The bigger they are, the harder they hit.
A rich man is just a poor man with money.
Wherever you go, there you are.
Common sense is not so common.
```

How It Works

You first create a queue container that stores string objects:

```
std::queue< std::string> sayings;
```

You read sayings from the standard input stream and store them in the container in a `while` loop:

```
while(true)
{
  std::getline(std::cin, saying);
  if(saying.empty())
    break;
  sayings.push(saying);
}
```

This version of `getline()` reads text from `cin` into the `string` object, `saying`, until a newline is recognized. Newline is the default input termination character, and when you want to override this, you specify the termination character as the third argument to `getline()`. The loop continues until the `empty()` function for `saying` returns `true`, which indicates an empty line was entered. When the input in `saying` is not empty, you store it in the `sayings` queue container by calling its `push()` function.

When input is complete, you output the count of the number of sayings that were stored in the queue:

```
std::cout << "There are " << sayings.size() << " sayings in the queue.\n"
          << std::endl;
```

The `size()` function returns the number of elements in the queue.

You list the contents of the queue in another `while` loop:

```
while(!sayings.empty())
{
  std::cout << sayings.front() << std::endl;
  sayings.pop();
}
```

The `front()` function returns a reference to the object at the front of the queue, but the object remains in its place. Because you want to access each of the elements in the queue in turn, you have to call the `pop()` function, after listing each element, to remove it from the queue.

The process of listing the elements in the queue also deletes them, so after the loop ends, the queue will be empty. What if you wanted to retain the elements in the queue? Well, one possibility is that you could put each saying back in the queue after you have listed it. Here's how you could do that:

```
for(std::queue<std::string>::size_type i {} ;i < sayings.size() ;i++)
{
  saying = sayings.front();
  std::cout << saying << std::endl;
  sayings.pop();
  sayings.push(saying);
}
```

Here, you make use of the value returned by `size()` to iterate over the number of sayings in the queue. After writing each saying to `cout`, you remove it from the queue by calling `pop()`, and then you return it to the back of the queue by calling `push()`. When the loop ends, the queue will be left in its original state. Of course, if you don't want to remove the elements when you access them, you should use a different kind of container.

Priority Queue Containers

A `priority_queue<T>` container is a queue that always has the largest or highest priority element at the top. Think of a queue of people arranged from the tallest to the shortest. Here's one way to define a priority queue container:

```
std::priority_queue<int> numbers;
```

The default criterion for determining the relative priority of elements as you add them to the queue is a standard `less<T>()` function object. You add an element to the priority queue using the `push()` function:

```
numbers.push(99);                        // Add 99 to the queue
```

When you add an element, if the queue is not empty the function will use the less<T>() predicate to decide where to insert the new object. This will result in elements being ordered in ascending sequence from the back of the queue to the front. You cannot modify elements while they are in a priority queue, as this could invalidate the ordering that has been established.

The complete set of operations for a priority queue is shown in the following table.

FUNCTION	DESCRIPTION
top()	Returns a const reference to the element at the front of the priority queue, which will be the largest or highest priority element in the container. If the container is empty, then the value returned is undefined.
push()	Adds the element specified by the argument to the priority queue at a position determined by the predicate for the container, which by default is less<T>.
pop()	Removes the element at the front of the priority queue, which will be the largest or highest priority element in the container.
size()	Returns the number of elements in the priority queue.
empty()	Returns true if the container is empty and false otherwise.

There is a significant difference between the functions available for a priority queue and for a queue. With a priority queue, you have no access to the element at the back; only the element at the front is accessible.

By default, the base container for the priority queue adapter class is vector<T>. You can specify a different sequence container for the base, and an alternative function object for determining the priority of the elements. Here's how you could do that:

```
std::priority_queue<int, std::deque<int>, std::greater<>> numbers;
```

This statement defines a priority queue based on a deque<int> container, with elements being inserted using a transparent function object of type greater<>. The elements in this priority queue will be in descending sequence, with the smallest element at the top. The three template parameters are the element type, the type of the container to be used as a base, and the type for the predicate to be used for ordering the elements.

You could omit the third template parameter if you want the default predicate to apply, which will be less<int> in this case. If you want a different predicate but want to retain the default base container, you must explicitly specify it, like this:

```
std::priority_queue<int, std::vector<int>, std::greater<>> numbers;
```

This specifies the default base container as vector<int> and the predicate type greater<> to be used to determine element ordering.

TRY IT OUT   Using a Priority Queue Container

In this example you store Person objects in the container, with the Person class defined this time to hold the names as type string:

```
// Person.h
// A class defining a person
```

```
#pragma once
#include <iostream>
#include <string>

class Person
{
public:
  Person(const std::string first, const std::string second) :
                firstname {std::move(first)}, secondname {std::move(second)} {}


  Person()=default;


  // Less-than operator
  bool operator<(const Person& p)const
  {
    return (secondname < p.secondname ||
            ((secondname == p.secondname) && (firstname < p.firstname)));
  }

  // Greater-than operator
  bool operator>(const Person& p)const
  {
    return p < *this;
  }

  // Output a person
  void showPerson() const
  {
    std::cout << firstname << " " << secondname << std::endl;
  }

private:
  std::string firstname;
  std::string secondname;
};
```

The less-than and greater-than operators are implemented. This will allow objects to be placed in a priority queue that is ordered in either ascending or descending sequence.

Here's the program that stores `Person` objects in a priority queue:

```
// Ex10_09.cpp
// Exercising a priority queue container
#include <vector>
#include <queue>
#include <functional>
#include "Person.h"

int main()
{
  std::priority_queue<Person, std::vector<Person>, std::greater<>> people;
  std::string first, second;
  while(true)
  {
    std::cout << "Enter a first name or press Enter to end: " ;
```

```
      std::getline(std::cin, first);
      if(first.empty())
        break;

      std::cout << "Enter a second name: " ;
      std::getline(std::cin, second);
      people.push(Person {first,second});
    }

  std::cout << "\nThere are " << people.size() << " people in the queue."
            << std::endl;

  std::cout << "\nThe names that you entered are:" << std::endl;
  while(!people.empty())
  {
    people.top().showPerson();
    people.pop();
  }
}
```

Typical output from this example looks like this:

```
Enter a first name or press Enter to end: Oliver
Enter a second name: Hardy
Enter a first name or press Enter to end: Stan
Enter a second name: Laurel
Enter a first name or press Enter to end: Harold
Enter a second name: Lloyd
Enter a first name or press Enter to end: Mel
Enter a second name: Gibson
Enter a first name or press Enter to end: Brad
Enter a second name: Pitt
Enter a first name or press Enter to end:

There are 5 people in the queue.

The names that you entered are:
Mel Gibson
Oliver Hardy
Stan Laurel
Harold Lloyd
Brad Pitt
```

How It Works

The Person class is simpler than in the earlier version because the names are stored as string objects, and no dynamic memory allocation is necessary. You no longer need to define the assignment operato-ror copy constructor, as the defaults will be fine. Defining operator<() is sufficient to allow Person objects to be stored in a default priority queue, and operator>() permits Person objects to be ordered using a greater<> predicate.

You define the priority queue in main() like this:

```
std::priority_queue<Person, std::vector<Person>, std::greater<>> people;
```

Because you want to specify the third template type parameter, you must supply all three, even though the base container type is the default. Incidentally, don't confuse the type argument you are using in the template instantiation here, greater<>, with the object, greater<>(), that you might supply as an argument to the sort() algorithm.

Of course, the third parameter to the priority queue template does not have to be a template type. You could use your own function object type as long as it has a suitable implementation of operator()() in the class. For example:

```cpp
// function_object.h
#pragma once
#include <functional>
#include "Person.h"

class PersonComp : public std::binary_function<Person, Person, bool>
{
public:
  result_type operator()(const first_argument_type& p1,
                         const second_argument_type& p2) const
  {
    return p1 > p2;
  }
};
```

For function objects that work with the STL, a binary predicate must implement operator()() with two parameters, and if you want the predicate to work with function adapters, your function object type must have an instance of the binary_function<Arg1Type, Arg2Type, ResultType> template as a base. Although you will typically make both arguments to a binary predicate of the same type, the base class does not require it, so when it is meaningful, your predicates can apply to arguments of different types.

If you don't want to use your function objects with function adapters, you could define the type as:

```cpp
// function_object.h
#pragma once
#include "Person.h"

class PersonComp
{
public:
  bool operator()(const Person& p1, const Person& p2) const
  {
    return p1 > p2;
  }
};
```

With this function object type, you could define the priority queue object as:

```cpp
std::priority_queue<Person, std::vector<Person>, PersonComp> people;
```

You read names from the standard input stream in an indefinite while loop:

```cpp
while(true)
{
  std::cout << "Enter a first name or press Enter to end: " ;
```

```
      std::getline(std::cin, first);
      if(first.empty())
        break;

      std::cout << "Enter a second name: " ;
      std::getline(std::cin, second);
      people.push(Person {first, second});
    }
```

An empty first name will terminate the loop. After reading a second name, you create the `Person` object in the argument expression to the `push()` function that adds the object to the priority queue. It will be inserted at a position determined by a `greater<>` predicate. This will result in the objects being ordered with the smallest at the top. You can see from the output that the names are in ascending sequence based on the second name.

After outputting the number of objects in the queue using the `size()` function, you output the contents of the queue in a `while` loop:

```
    while(!people.empty())
    {
      people.top().showPerson();
      people.pop();
    }
```

The `top()` function returns a reference to the object at the front of the queue, and you use this reference to call `showPerson()` to output the name. You then call `pop()` to remove the element at the front of the queue; unless you do this, you can't access the next element.

When the loop ends, the priority queue will be empty. There's no way to access all the elements and retain them in the queue. If you want to keep them, you would have to put them somewhere else — perhaps in another priority queue.

Stack Containers

The `stack<T>` adapter template is defined in the `stack` header and implements a pushdown stack based on a `deque<T>` container by default. A pushdown stack is a last-in first-out storage mechanism where only the object that was added most recently is accessible.

Here's how you can define a stack:

```
    std::stack<Person> people;
```

This defines a stack to store `Person` objects.

The base container can be any sequence container that supports the operations `back()`, `push_back()`, and `pop_back()`. You could define a stack based on a list like this:

```
    std::stack<std::string, std::list<std::string>> names;
```

The first template argument is the element type as before, and the second is the container type to be used as a base for the stack.

There are only five operations available with a `stack<T>` container, and they are shown in the following table.

FUNCTION	DESCRIPTION
`top()`	Returns a reference to the element at the top of the stack. If the stack is empty, then the value returned is undefined. You can assign the reference returned to a `const` or non-`const` reference and if it is assigned to the latter, you can modify the object in the stack.
`push()`	Adds the element specified by the argument to the top of the stack.
`pop()`	Removes the element at the top of the stack.
`size()`	Returns the number of elements in the stack.
`empty()`	Returns `true` if the stack is empty and `false` otherwise.

As with the other containers provided through container adapters, you cannot use iterators to access the contents. Let's see a stack working.

TRY IT OUT Using a Stack Container

This example stores `Person` objects in a stack. The `Person` class is the same as in the previous example, so I won't repeat the code here.

```
// Ex10_10.cpp
// Exercising a stack container
#include <iostream>
#include <stack>
#include <list>
#include "Person.h"

int main()
{
  std::stack<Person, std::list<Person>> people;

  std::string first, second;
  while(true)
  {
    std::cout << "Enter a first name or press Enter to end: " ;
    std::getline(std::cin, first);
    if(first.empty())
      break;

    std::cout << "Enter a second name: " ;
    std::getline(std::cin, second);
    people.push(Person {first, second});
  }

  std::cout << "\nThere are " << people.size() << " people in the stack."
            << std::endl;
```

```
   std::cout << "\nThe names that you entered are:" << std::endl;
   while(!people.empty())
   {
     people.top().showPerson();
     people.pop();
   }
}
```

Here is an example of the output:

```
Enter a first name or press Enter to end: Gordon
Enter a second name: Brown
Enter a first name or press Enter to end: Harold
Enter a second name: Wilson
Enter a first name or press Enter to end: Margaret
Enter a second name: Thatcher
Enter a first name or press Enter to end: Winston
Enter a second name: Churchill
Enter a first name or press Enter to end: David
Enter a second name: Lloyd-George
Enter a first name or press Enter to end:

There are 5 people in the stack.

The names that you entered are:
David Lloyd-George
Winston Churchill
Margaret Thatcher
Harold Wilson
Gordon Brown
```

How It Works

The code in `main()` is more or less the same as in the previous example. Only the container definition is significantly different:

```
std::stack<Person, std::list<Person>> people;
```

The stack container stores `Person` objects and is based on a `list<T>` container in this instance. You could also use a `vector<T>`, and if you omit the second type parameter, the stack will use a `deque<T>` container as a base.

The output demonstrates that a stack is indeed a last-in first-out container, as the order of names in the output is the reverse of the input.

The tuple Class Template

The `tuple<>` class template that is defined in the tuple header is a useful adjunct to the `array<>` container, and to other sequence containers such as the `vector<>`. As its name suggests, a `tuple<>` object encapsulates a number of different items of different types. If you were working with fixed records from a file, or possibly from an SQL database, you could use a `vector<>` or an `array<>` container to store `tuple<>` objects that encapsulate the fields in a record. Let's look at a specific example.

Suppose you are working with personnel records that contain an integer employee number, a first name, a second name, and the age of the individual in years. You could define an alias for a `tuple<>` instance to encapsulate an employee record like this:

```
using Record = std::tuple<int, std::string, std::string, int>;
```

An alias is very useful for reducing the verbosity of the type specification. The `Record` type name is the equivalent of a `tuple<>` that stores values of type `int`, `string`, `string`, and `int`, corresponding to a person's ID, first name, second name, and age. You could now define an `array<>` container to store `Record` objects:

```
std::array<Record, 5> personnel { Record {1001, "Joan", "Jetson", 35},
                                  Record {1002, "Jim" , "Jones" , 26},
                                  Record {1003, "June", "Jello" , 31},
                                  Record {1004, "Jack", "Jester", 39} };
```

This defines the `personnel` container, which is an array that can store five `Record` objects. If you wanted flexibility in the number of tuples you were dealing with, you could use a `vector<>` or a `list<>`. Here, you initialize four of the five elements in `personnel` from the initializer list. Here's how you might store a fifth element:

```
personnel[4] = Record {1005, "Jean", "Jorell", 29};
```

This uses the index operator to access the fifth element in the array container. You also have the option of creating a `tuple<>` object using the `make_tuple()` function template:

```
personnel[4] = std::make_tuple(1005, "Jean", "Jorell", 29);
```

The `make_tuple()` function creates a `tuple<>` instance that is equivalent to our `Record` type because the deduced type parameters are the same.

To access the fields in a tuple, you use the `get()` template function. The template parameter is the index position of the field you want, indexed from zero. The argument to the function is the tuple that you are accessing. Here's how you could list the records in the `personnel` container:

```
std::cout << std::setiosflags(std::ios::left);      // Left align output
for (const auto& r : personnel)
{
  std::cout << std::setw(10) << std::get<0>(r) << std::setw(10) << std::get<1>(r)
            << std::setw(10) << std::get<2>(r) << std::setw(10) << std::get<3>(r)
            << std::endl;
}
```

You need to include `iomanip` to compile this fragment. This outputs the fields in each tuple in `personnel` on a single line, with the fields left-justified in a field width of 10 characters, so it looks tidy. Note that the type parameter to the `get()` function template must be a compile-time constant. This implies that you cannot use a loop index variable as the type parameter, so you can't iterate over the fields in a loop at runtime. It is helpful to define some integer constants that you can use to identify the fields in a tuple in a more readable way. For example, you could define the following constants:

```
const size_t ID {}, firstname {1}, secondname {2}, age {3};
```

Now you can use these variables as type parameters in `get()` function instantiations making it much clearer which field you are retrieving:

```
for (const auto& r : personnel))
{
  std::cout << std::setw(10) << std::get<ID>(r)
            << std::setw(10) << std::get<firstname>(r)
            << std::setw(10) << std::get<secondname>(r)
            << std::setw(10) << std::get<age>(r) << std::endl;
}
```

Let's put some of the fragments together into something you can compile and run.

TRY IT OUT Storing Tuples in an Array

Here's the code for the example:

```
// Ex10_11.cpp Using an array storing tuple objects
#include <array>
#include <tuple>
#include <string>
#include <iostream>
#include <iomanip>

const size_t maxRecords{ 100 };
using Record = std::tuple<int, std::string, std::string, int>;
using Records = std::array<Record, maxRecords>;

// Lists the contents of a Records array
void listRecords(const Records& people)
{
  const size_t ID{}, firstname{ 1 }, secondname{ 2 }, age{ 3 };
  std::cout << std::setiosflags(std::ios::left);
  Record empty;
  for (const auto& record : people))
  {
    if (record == empty) break;           // In case array is not full
    std::cout << "ID: " << std::setw(6) << std::get<ID>(record)
              << "Name: " << std::setw(25)
              << (std::get<firstname>(record) +" " + std::get<secondname>(record))
              << "Age: " << std::setw(5) << std::get<age>(record) << std::endl;
  }
}

int main()
{
  Records personnel { Record {1001, "Arthur", "Dent", 35},
                      Record {1002, "Mary", "Poppins", 55},
                      Record {1003, "David", "Copperfield", 34},
                      Record {1004, "James", "Bond", 44} };
  personnel[4] = std::make_tuple(1005, "Harry", "Potter", 15);
  personnel.at(5) = Record {1006, "Bertie", "Wooster", 28};

  listRecords(personnel);
}
```

This program produces the following output:

```
ID: 1001  Name: Arthur Dent           Age: 35
ID: 1002  Name: Mary Poppins          Age: 55
ID: 1003  Name: David Copperfield     Age: 34
ID: 1004  Name: James Bond            Age: 44
ID: 1005  Name: Harry Potter          Age: 15
ID: 1006  Name: Bertie Wooster        Age: 28
```

How It Works

To make the code easier to read, there are two aliases defined:

```
using Record = std::tuple<int, std::string, std::string, int>;
using Records = std::array<Record, maxRecords>;
```

The first defines Record as equivalent to the tuple<> type that stores four fields of type int, string, string, and int. The second defines Records as an array<> type, storing maxRecords elements of type Record. maxRecords is defined as a const value of type size_t. Aliases are a great help in simplifying code that uses the STL.

The listRecords() function outputs the elements in a Records array. The first statement in the function body defines constants for accessing the fields in a Record tuple. This enables meaningful names to be used, rather than numeric index values whose meaning would not be obvious. The next statement ensures that subsequent output to the output stream will be left-aligned. The range-based for loop runs through the elements in the Records array that has been passed to the function until an element that is the equivalent of zero is found. Elements that were not explicitly initialized will have been initialized using the no-arg constructor for the element type, Record. Fields in the tuple that each array element contains are accessed with the get<>() function using the constants that were defined for that purpose. The setw() manipulators set the width of the output field for the next item that is written to cout.

In main() you create the personnel array as type Records and initialize the first four elements with Record objects:

```
Records personnel    { Record {1001, "Arthur", "Dent", 35},
                        Record {1002, "Mary", "Poppins", 55},
                        Record {1003, "David", "Copperfield", 34},
                        Record {1004, "James", "Bond", 44} };
```

This is clearly a much more readable statement because of the aliases for Records and Record.

The next statement adds another Record to the array:

```
personnel[4] = std::make_tuple(1005, "Harry", "Potter", 15);
```

This uses the operator[]() function overload for the personnel array to access the element, and uses the make_tuple() function to create a tuple that is similar to the tuple of type Record to be stored in the array.

Curiously, the next statement uses a different technique to set the value for an array element:

```
personnel.at(5) = Record {1006, "Bertie", "Wooster", 28};
```

This uses the at() function for the array, and the argument value of 5 selects the sixth element in the array. Here, the tuple is created using the Record type name. Finally, you call listRecords() to list the contents of personnel. The output shows that everything works as it should.

ASSOCIATIVE CONTAINERS

I'll just discuss some of those available to give you an idea of how they work. The most significant feature of an associative container such as map<K,T> is that you can retrieve a particular object without searching. The location of an object of type T is determined from a key of type K that you supply along with the object when you add it to the container. You can retrieve any object rapidly just by supplying its key.

For `set<T>` and `multiset<T>` containers, objects act as their own keys. You might be wondering what the use of a container is, if before you can retrieve an object, you have to have the object available. After all, if you already have the object, why would you need to retrieve it? The point of set and multiset containers is not so much to store objects for later retrieval, but to create an aggregation of objects that you can test to see whether or not a given object is already a member.

I'll concentrate on map containers. The set and multiset containers are used somewhat less frequently, and their operations are very similar so you should have little difficulty using these after you have learned how to apply map containers.

Using Map Containers

When you create a `map<K,T>` container, K is the type of key you use to store an object of type T. Key/object pairs are stored as objects of type `pair<K,T>` that is defined in the `utility` header. The `utility` header is included into the `map` header so this type definition is automatically available. Here's an example of creating a map:

```
std::map<Person, std::string> phonebook;
```

This defines an empty map container that stores entries that are key/object pairs, with keys of type `Person` and objects of type `string`.

> **NOTE** *Although you use class objects here for both keys and objects in the map, the keys and objects can also be fundamental types such as* int, *or* double, *or* char.

You can also create a map that is initialized with a sequence of `pair<K,T>` objects from another container:

```
std::map<Person, std::string> phonebook {iter1, iter2};
```

`iter1` and `iter2` are a pair of iterators defining a series of key/object pairs from another container in the usual way, with `iter2` specifying a position one past the last pair to be included in the sequence. These iterators can be input iterators although the iterators you obtain from a map are bidirectional. You obtain iterators to access the contents of a map using the `begin()` and `end()` functions, just as you would for a sequence container.

The entries in a map are ordered based on a function object of type `less<Key>` by default, so they will be stored in ascending key sequence. You can change the type function object used for ordering entries by supplying a third template type parameter. For example:

```
std::map<Person, std::string, std::greater<>> phonebook;
```

This map stores entries that are `Person`/`string` pairs, where `Person` is the key with an associated string object. The ordering of entries will be determined by a function object of type `greater<>`, so the entries will be in descending key sequence.

Storing Objects

You can define a pair object like this:

```
auto entry = std::pair<Person, std::string>
                          {Person {"Mel", "Gibson"}, "213 345 5678"};
```

This creates the variable `entry` of type `pair<Person,string>` and initializes it to an object created from a `Person` object and a `string` object. I'm representing a phone number in a very simplistic way, just as a string, but of course it could be a class object identifying the components of the number, such as country code and area code. The `Person` class is the class from the previous example.

The `pair<K,T>` class template defines two constructors, a default constructor that creates an object from the default constructors for types `K` and `T`, and a constructor that defines an object from a key and its associated object. There are also constructor templates for copy constructors and constructors creating an object from rvalue references.

You can access the elements in a pair through the members `first` and `second`; thus, in the example, `entry.first` references the `Person` object and `entry.second` references the `string` object.

There is a helper template function, `make_pair()`, defined in the `utility` header that creates a pair object:

```
auto entry = std::make_pair(Person {"Nell", "Gwynne"}, "213 345 5678");
```

The `make_pair()` function automatically deduces the type for the pair, from the argument types. Note that in this case it will be a `pair<Person, const char*>` object but that will be converted to `pair<Person, string>` when you insert it into the phonebook map.

All of the comparison operators are overloaded for pair objects, so you can compare them with any of the operators `<`, `<=`, `==`, `!=`, `>=`, and `>`.

It's often convenient to define an alias to abbreviate the `pair<K,T>` type you are using. For example:

```
using Entry = std::pair<Person, std::string> ;
```

This defines `Entry` as the alias for the key/object pair type. Having defined `Entry`, you can use it to create objects. For example:

```
Entry entry1 {Person {"Jack", "Jones"}, "213 567 1234"};
```

This statement defines a pair of type `pair<Person, string>`, using `Person("Jack", "Jones")` as the `Person` argument and `"213 567 1234"` as the `string` argument.

You can insert one or more pairs in a map using the `insert()` function. For example, here's how you insert a single object:

```
phonebook.insert(entry1);
```

This inserts the `entry1` pair into the `phonebook` container, as long as there is no other entry in the map that uses the same key. This version of the `insert()` function returns a value that is also a pair, where the first object in the pair is an iterator and the second is a `bool` value. The `bool` value will be `true` if the insertion was made, and `false` otherwise. The iterator will point to the element if it was stored in the map, or the element that is already in the map for the `entry1` key if the insert failed. Therefore, you can check if the object was stored, like this:

```
auto checkpair = phonebook.insert(entry1);
if(checkpair.second)
   std::cout << "Insertion succeeded." << std::endl;
else
   std::cout << "Insertion failed." << std::endl;
```

The pair that `insert()` returns is stored in `checkpair`. The type for `checkpair` is `pair<map< Person,string>::iterator, bool>`, so `auto` is very helpful here. The type corresponds to a pair encapsulating an iterator of type `map<Person,string>::iterator` that you can access as `checkpair.first`; and a `bool` value that you access as `checkpair.second`. Dereferencing the iterator in the pair will give you access to the pair that is stored in the map; you can use the `first` and `second` members of that pair to access the key and object, respectively. This can be a little tricky, so let's see what it looks like for `checkpair` in the preceding code:

```
std::cout << "The key for the entry is:" << std::endl;
checkpair.first->first.showPerson();
```

The expression `checkpair.first` references the first member of `checkpair`, which is an iterator, so this expression accesses a pointer to the entry in the map. The entry in the map is another pair, so `checkpair.first->first` accesses the first member of that pair, the key, which is the `Person` object. You use this to call the `showPerson()` member to output the name. You could access the pair member that represents the phone number in a similar way, with the expression `checkpair.first->second`.

Another version of `insert()` inserts a series of pairs in a map. The pairs are defined by two iterators and the series would typically be from another map, although it could be from a different type of container.

A map defines the `operator[]()` member function, so you can use the subscript operator to insert an object. Here's how you could insert the `entry1` object in the `phonebook` map:

```
phonebook[Person {"Jack", "Jones"}] = "213 567 1234";
```

The subscript value is the key for the object that appears to the right of the assignment operator. This is perhaps a somewhat more intuitive way to store objects in a map. The disadvantage compared to `insert()` is that you lose the ability to discover whether the key was already in the map.

You can insert a pair that is constructed in place using the `emplace()` function template:

```
Entry him {Person {"Jack", "Spratt"}, "213 456 7899"};
auto checkpair = phonebook.emplace(std::move(him));
```

This creates the pair, `him`, and calls `emplace()` with an rvalue reference to `him` as the argument. The pair that is returned contains an iterator and a `bool` value, with the same significance as the pair returned by the `insert()` function.

Of course, you can also write:

```
auto checkpair = phonebook.emplace(Person {"Jack", "Spratt"}, "213 456 7899");
```

Accessing Objects

You can use the subscript operator to retrieve the object from a map that corresponds to a given key. For example:

```
string number {phonebook[Person{"Jack", "Jones"}]};
```

This initializes `number` with the object corresponding to the key `Person {"Jack", "Jones"}`. If the key is not in the map, then a pair entry will be inserted into the map for this key, with the object as the default for the object type. This implies that for the preceding statement, the no-arg `string` constructor will be called to create the object corresponding to this key if the entry is not there.

Of course, you may not want a default object inserted when you attempt to retrieve an object for a given key. In this case you can use the `find()` function to check whether there's an entry for a key, and then retrieve it if it's there:

```
std::string number;
Person key {"Jack", "Jones"};
auto iter = phonebook.find(key);

if(iter != phonebook.end())
{
  number = iter->second;
  std::cout << "The number is " << number << std::endl;
}
else
{
  std::cout << "No number for the key ";
  key.showPerson();
}
```

The `find()` function returns an iterator of type `map<Person,string>::iterator` that points to the object corresponding to the key if the key is present, or to one past the last map entry, which corresponds to the iterator returned by the `end()` function. Thus, if `iter` is not equal to the iterator returned by `end()`, the entry exists so you can access the object through the second member of the pair. If you want to prevent the object in the map from being modified, you could define the iterator type explicitly as `map<Person,string>::const_iterator`.

Calling `count()` for a map with a key as the argument will return a count of the number of entries found corresponding to the key. For a map, the value returned can only be 0 or 1, because each key must be unique. A multimap container allows multiple entries for a given key, so in this case other values are possible for the return value from `count()`.

Other Map Operations

The `erase()` function enables you to remove a single entry or a range of entries from a map. You have two versions of `erase()` that will remove a single entry. One requires an iterator as the argument pointing to the entry to be erased, and the other requires a key corresponding to the entry to be erased. For example:

```
Person key {"Jack", "Jones"};
auto count = phonebook.erase(key);
if(!count)
  std::cout << "Entry was not found." << std::endl;
```

When you supply a key to `erase()`, it returns a count of the number of entries that were erased. The value returned can only be `0` or `1` for a map. A multimap container can have several entries with the same key, in which case `erase()` may return a value greater than 1.

You can also supply an iterator as an argument to `erase()`:

```
Person key {"Jack", "Jones"};
auto iter = phonebook.find(key);
if(iter != phonebook.end())
  iter = phonebook.erase(iter);
if(iter == phonebook.end())
  std::cout << "End of the map reached." << std::endl;
```

In this case, `erase()` returns an iterator that points to the entry that remains in the map beyond the entry that was erased, or a pointer to one beyond the end of the map if no such element is present.

The following table shows other operations available with a map.

FUNCTION	DESCRIPTION
`begin()`	Returns a bidirectional iterator pointing to the first entry.
`end()`	Returns a bidirectional iterator pointing to one past the last entry.
`cbegin()`	Returns a `const` bidirectional iterator pointing to the first entry.
`cend()`	Returns a `const` bidirectional iterator pointing to one past the last entry.
`rbegin()`	Returns a reverse bidirectional iterator pointing to the last entry.
`rend()`	Returns a reverse bidirectional iterator pointing to one before the first entry.
`crbegin()`	Returns a `const` reverse bidirectional iterator pointing to the last entry in the map.
`crend()`	Returns a `const` reverse bidirectional iterator pointing to one before the first entry.
`at()`	Returns a reference to the data value corresponding to the key you supply as the argument.
`lower_bound()`	Accepts a key as an argument and returns an iterator pointing to the first entry with a key that is greater than or equal to (the lower bound of) the specified key. If the key is not present, the iterator pointing to one past the last entry will be returned.
`upper_bound()`	Accepts a key as an argument and returns an iterator pointing to the first entry with a key that is greater than (the upper bound of) the specified key. If the key is not present, the iterator pointing to one past the last entry will be returned.

continues

(continued)

FUNCTION	DESCRIPTION
`equal_range()`	Accepts a key as an argument and returns a pair containing two iterators. The first pair-member points to the lower bound of the specified key, and the second points to the upper bound of the specified key. If the key is not present, both iterators will point to one past the last entry.
`swap()`	Interchanges the entries you pass as the argument, with the entries for which the function is called.
`clear()`	Erases all entries in the map.
`size()`	Returns the number of entries in the map.
`max_size()`	Returns the maximum capacity of the map.
`empty()`	Returns `true` if the map is empty and `false` otherwise.

The `lower_bound()`, `upper_bound()`, and `equal_range()` functions are not very useful with a map container. However, they come into their own with a multimap when you want to find all elements with a given key. Let's see a map in action.

TRY IT OUT Using a Map Container

This example uses a map to store phone numbers and provides a mechanism for finding a phone number for a person. It uses a variation on the `Person` class:

```
// Person.h
// A class defining a person
#pragma once
#include <string>

class Person
{
public:
  Person(const std::string& first = "", const std::string& second = "") :
                                    firstname {first}, secondname {second} {}
  // Move constructor
  Person(std::string&& first, std::string&& second) :
                  firstname {std::move(first)}, secondname {std::move(second)}   {}

  // Move constructor
  Person(Person&& person) :
                        firstname {std::move(person.firstname)},
                        secondname {std::move(person.secondname)} {}

  // Move assignment operator
  Person& operator=(Person&& person)
  {
    firstname = std::move(person.firstname);
```

```
    secondname = std::move(person.secondname);
  }

  // Less-than operator
  bool operator<(const Person& p)const
  {
    return (secondname < p.secondname ||
                   ((secondname == p.secondname) && (firstname < p.firstname)));
  }

  // Get the name
  std::string getName()const
  {
    return firstname + " " + secondname;
  }

private:
  std::string firstname;
  std::string secondname;
};
```

The no-arg constructor is defined by providing default values for the constructor arguments. There is a move constructor for rvalue arguments for the data members and a move constructor for an rvalue Person argument. The new function getName() returns the complete name as a string.

The source file containing main() and some helper functions looks like this:

```
// Ex10_12.cpp
// Using a map container
#include <iostream>
#include <cstdio>
#include <iomanip>
#include <string>
#include <map>
#include "Person.h"

using std::string;
using PhoneBook = std::map<Person, string>;
using Entry = std::pair<Person, string>;

// Read a person from cin
Person getPerson()
{
  string first, second;
  std::cout << "Enter a first name: " ;
  getline(std::cin, first);
  std::cout << "Enter a second name: " ;
  getline(std::cin, second);
  return Person {std::move(first), std::move(second)};
}

// Read a phone book entry from standard input
Entry inputEntry()
{
```

```cpp
  Person person {getPerson()};

  string number;
  std::cout << "Enter the phone number for " << person.getName() << ": ";
  getline(std::cin, number);
  return std::make_pair(std::move(person), std::move(number));
}

// Add a new entry to a phone book
void addEntry(PhoneBook& book)
{
  auto pr = book.insert(inputEntry());

    if(pr.second)
      std::cout << "Entry successful." << std::endl;
    else
    {
      std::cout << "Entry exists for " << pr.first->first.getName()
                << ". The number is " << pr.first->second << std::endl;
    }
}

// List the contents of a phone book
void listEntries(const PhoneBook& book)
{
  if(book.empty())
  {
    std::cout << "The phone book is empty." << std::endl;
    return;
  }
  std::cout << setiosflags(std::ios::left);             // Left justify output
  for(const auto& entry : book)
  {
    std::cout << std::setw(30) << entry.first.getName()
              << std::setw(12) << entry.second << std::endl;
  }
  std::cout << resetiosflags(std::ios::right);          // Right justify output
}

// Retrieve an entry from a phone book
void getEntry(const PhoneBook& book)
{
  Person person {getPerson()};
  auto iter = book.find(person);
  if(iter == book.end())
    std::cout << "No entry found for " << person.getName() << std::endl;
  else
    std::cout << "The number for " << person.getName()
         << " is " << iter->second << std::endl;
}

// Delete an entry from a phone book
void deleteEntry(PhoneBook& book)
{
  Person person {getPerson()};
```

```cpp
  auto iter = book.find(person);
  if(iter == book.end())
    std::cout << "No entry found for " << person.getName() << std::endl;
  else
  {
    book.erase(iter);
    std::cout << person.getName() << " erased." << std::endl;
  }
}

int main()
{
  PhoneBook phonebook;
  char answer {};

  while(true)
  {
    std::cout << "Do you want to enter a phone book entry(Y or N): " ;
    std::cin >> answer;
    while(std::cin.get() != '\n');    // Ignore up to newline
    if(toupper(answer) == 'N')
      break;
    if(toupper(answer) != 'Y')
    {
      std::cout << "Invalid response. Try again." << std::endl;
      continue;
    }
    addEntry(phonebook);
  }

  // Query the phonebook
  while(true)
  {
    std::cout << "\nChoose from the following options:" << std::endl
        << "A  Add an entry   D Delete an entry   G  Get an entry" << std::endl
        << "L  List entries   Q  Quit" << std::endl;
    std::cin >> answer;
    while(std::cin.get() != '\n');    // Ignore up to newline

    switch(toupper(answer))
    {
      case 'A':
        addEntry(phonebook);
        break;
      case 'G':
        getEntry(phonebook);
        break;
      case 'D':
        deleteEntry(phonebook);
        break;
      case 'L':
        listEntries(phonebook);
        break;
      case 'Q':
        return 0;
```

```
        default:
          std::cout << "Invalid selection. Try again." << std::endl;
          break;
      }
    }
    return 0;
}
```

Here is some output from this program:

```
Do you want to enter a phone book entry(Y or N): y
Enter a first name: Jack
Enter a second name: Bateman
Enter the phone number for Jack Bateman: 312 455 6576
Entry successful.
Do you want to enter a phone book entry(Y or N): y
Enter a first name: Mary
Enter a second name: Jones
Enter the phone number for Mary Jones: 213 443 5671
Entry successful.
Do you want to enter a phone book entry(Y or N): y
Enter a first name: Jane
Enter a second name: Junket
Enter the phone number for Jane Junket: 413 222 8134
Entry successful.
Do you want to enter a phone book entry(Y or N): n

Choose from the following options:
A  Add an entry   D Delete an entry   G  Get an entry
L  List entries   Q  Quit
a
Enter a first name: Bill
Enter a second name: Smith
Enter the phone number for Bill Smith: 213 466 7688
Entry successful.

Choose from the following options:
A  Add an entry   D Delete an entry   G  Get an entry
L  List entries   Q  Quit
g
Enter a first name: Mary
Enter a second name: Miller
No entry found for Mary Miller

Choose from the following options:
A  Add an entry   D Delete an entry   G  Get an entry
L  List entries   Q  Quit
g
Enter a first name: Mary
Enter a second name: Jones
The number for Mary Jones is 213 443 5671

Choose from the following options:
A  Add an entry   D Delete an entry   G  Get an entry
L  List entries   Q  Quit
d
Enter a first name: Mary
```

```
Enter a second name: Jones
Mary Jones erased.

Choose from the following options:
A  Add an entry    D Delete an entry   G  Get an entry
L  List entries    Q  Quit
L
Jack Bateman                     312 455 6576
Jane Junket                      413 222 8134
Bill Smith                       213 466 7688

Choose from the following options:
A  Add an entry    D Delete an entry   G  Get an entry
L  List entries    Q  Quit
q
```

How It Works

You define aliases for the types for a `PhoneBook` container and its entries like this:

```
using PhoneBook = std::map<Person, string>;
using Entry = std::pair<Person, string>;
```

The object in an entry is a `string` containing a phone number, and the key is a `Person` object. These type aliases will make the code easier to read.

You load up the map initially in a `while` loop:

```
while(true)
{
  std::cout << "Do you want to enter a phone book entry(Y or N): " ;
  std::cin >> answer;
  while(std::cin.get() != '\n');     // Ignore up to newline
  if(toupper(answer) == 'N')
    break;
  if(toupper(answer) != 'Y')
  {
    std::cout << "Invalid response. Try again." << std::endl;
    continue;
  }
  addEntry(phonebook);
}
```

You check whether an entry is to be read by reading a character from the input stream. Reading a character from `cin` leaves at least a newline character in the buffer, and this can cause problems for subsequent input. The user might accidentally type additional characters to the response, too. The `while` loop skips everything up to the next newline by calling `get()` for `cin` repeatedly until a newline is reached. If `'n'` or `'N'` is entered, the loop is terminated. When `'y'` or `'Y'` is entered, an entry is created by calling the helper function `addEntry()` that is coded like this:

```
void addEntry(PhoneBook& book)
{
  auto pr = book.insert(inputEntry());
  if(pr.second)
    std::cout << "Entry successful." << std::endl;
  else
```

```
        {
          std::cout << "Entry exists for " << pr.first->first.getName()
                    << ". The number is " << pr.first->second << std::endl;

        }
      }
```

The parameter for addEntry() is a reference. The function modifies the container that is passed as the argument, so the function must have access to the original object. In any event, even if read-only access to the container argument was needed, it is important not to allow potentially very large objects, such as a map container, to be passed by value, because copying them can seriously degrade performance.

An entry is created by calling the inputEntry() helper function, which makes use of the getPerson() function that creates a Person object from keyboard input in the way you saw in the previous section. You then call insert() for the phonebook object, and store the object returned in pr. The pr object enables you to check that the entry was successfully inserted into the map, by testing its bool member. The pr variable is of type pair<map<Person,string>::iterator,bool>, but the auto keyword works that out for you. The first member of pr provides access to the entry, whether it's an existing entry or the new entry, and the second is the bool value. You use these to output a message.

After initial input is complete, a while loop provides the mechanism for querying and modifying the phone book. The switch statement decides the action to be taken, based on the character that is entered and stored in answer. Querying the phone book is managed by the getEntry() function:

```
      void getEntry(const PhoneBook& book)
      {
        Person person {getPerson()};
        auto iter = book.find(person);
        if(iter == book.end())
          std::cout << "No entry found for " << person.getName() << std::endl;
        else
          std::cout << "The number for " << person.getName()
                    << " is " << iter->second << std::endl;
      }
```

A Person object is created from a name that is read from the keyboard by calling the getPerson() function. The Person object is then used as the argument to the find() function for the map object. This returns an iterator of type map<Person,string>::const_iterator that either points to the required entry, or points to one past the last entry in the map. If an entry is found, accessing the second member of the pair pointed to by the iterator provides the number corresponding to the Person object key.

The deleteEntry() function deletes an entry from the map. The process is similar to that used in the getEntry() function, the difference being that when an entry is found by the find() function, the erase() function is called to remove it. You could use another version of erase() to do this, in which case the code would be like this:

```
      void deleteEntry(PhoneBook& book)
      {
        Person person getPerson();
        if(book.erase(person))
          std::cout << person.getName() << " erased." << std::endl;
        else
          std::cout << "No entry found for " << person.getName() << std::endl;
      }
```

The code turns out to be much simpler if you pass the key to the `erase()` function.

The `listEntries()` function lists the contents of a phone book. After an initial check for an empty map, the entries are listed in a range-based `for` loop. The output is left-justified by the `setiosflags` manipulator to produce tidy output. This remains in effect until the `resetiosflags` manipulator is used to restore right-justification.

Using a Multimap Container

A multimap works very much like the map container, in that it supports the same range of functions — except for the subscript operator, which you cannot use with a multimap. The principle difference between a map and a multimap is that you can have multiple entries with the same key in a multimap, and this affects the way some of the functions behave. Obviously, with the possibility of several keys having the same value, overloading `operator[]()` would not make much sense.

The `insert()` function flavors for a multimap are a little different from those for a map. The simplest version accepts a `pair<K,T>` object as an argument and returns an iterator pointing to the entry that was inserted. The equivalent function for a map returns a pair object because this provides an indication of when the key already exists in the map and the insertion is not possible; of course, this cannot arise with a multimap. A multimap also has a version of `insert()` with two arguments: the second being the pair object to be inserted, and the first being an iterator pointing to the position from which to start searching for an insertion point. This gives you some control over where a pair is inserted when the same key already exists. This version of `insert()` also returns an iterator pointing to the element that was inserted. A third version of `insert()` accepts two iterator arguments that specify a range of elements to be inserted from another source and this version doesn't return anything.

When you pass a key to `erase()` for a multimap, it erases all entries with the same key, and the value returned indicates how many were deleted. The significance of having a version of `erase()` that accepts an iterator as an argument should now be apparent — it allows you to delete a single element. You also have a version of `erase()` that accepts two iterators to delete a range of entries.

The `find()` member function can only find the first element with a given key. You really need a way to find several elements with the same key and the `lower_bound()`, `upper_bound()`, and `equal_range()` functions provide you with a way to do this. For example, given a `phonebook` object that is of type `multimap<Person, string>`, you could list the phone numbers corresponding to a given key like this:

```
Person person("Jack", "Jones");
auto iter = phonebook.lower_bound(person);
if(iter == phonebook.end())
  std::cout << "There are no entries for " << person.getName() << std::endl;
else
{
  std::cout << "The following numbers are listed for " << person.getName()
            << ":" << std::endl;
  auto upper = phonebook.upper_bound(person);
  for (; iter != upper; ++iter)
    std::cout << iter->second << std::endl;
}
```

It's important to check the iterator returned by `lower_bound()`. If you don't, you could end up referencing an entry one beyond the last entry.

MORE ON ITERATORS

The `iterator` header defines templates for stream iterators that transfer data from a source to a destination. These act as pointers to a stream for input or output, and they enable you to transfer data between a stream and any source or destination that works with iterators, such as an algorithm. Inserter iterators can transfer data into a basic sequence container. There are two stream iterator templates: `istream_iterator<T>` for input streams and `ostream_iterator<T>` for output streams, where `T` is the type of object to be extracted from, or written to, the stream. The header also defines three inserter templates, `insert_iterator<T>`, `back_insert_iterator<T>`, and `front_insert_iterator<T>`, where `T` is the type of sequence container in which data is to be inserted.

Let's explore some of these iterators in a little more depth.

Using Input Stream Iterators

Here's an example of how you create an input stream iterator:

```
std::istream_iterator<int> numbersInput {std::cin};
```

This creates the iterator `numbersInput` of type `istream_iterator<int>` that can point to objects of type `int` in a stream. The argument to the constructor specifies the stream to which the iterator relates, so this is an iterator that can read integers from `cin`, the standard input stream.

The default `istream_iterator<T>` constructor creates an end-of-stream iterator, which will be equivalent to the end iterator for a container that you have been obtaining by calling the `end()` function. Here's how you could create an end-of-stream iterator, complementing the `numbersInput` iterator:

```
std::istream_iterator<int> numbersEnd;
```

Now you have a pair of iterators that defines a sequence of values of type `int` from `cin`. You could use these to load values from `cin` into a `vector<int>` container:

```
std::vector<int> numbers;
std::cout << "Enter integers separated by spaces then a letter to end:"
          << std::endl;
std::istream_iterator<int> numbersInput {std::cin}, numbersEnd;
while(numbersInput != numbersEnd)
  numbers.push_back(*numbersInput++);
```

After defining the vector container to hold values of type `int`, you create two input stream iterators: `numbersInput` is an input stream iterator reading values of type `int` from `cin`, and `numbersEnd` is an end-of-stream iterator. The `while` loop continues as long as `numbersInput` is not equal to the end-of-stream iterator, `numbersEnd`. When you execute this fragment, input continues until end-of-stream is recognized for `cin`. But what produces that condition? The end-of-stream condition will arise if you enter `Ctrl+Z` to close the input stream, or if you enter an invalid character such as a letter.

Of course, you are not limited to using input stream iterators as loop control variables. You can use them to pass data to an algorithm, such as `accumulate()`, which is defined in the `numeric` header:

```
        std::cout << "Enter integers separated by spaces then a letter to end:"
                << std::endl;
    std::istream_iterator<int> numbersInput {std::cin}, numbersEnd;
    std::cout << "The sum of the input values that you entered is "
                << std::accumulate(numbersInput, numbersEnd, 0) << std::endl;
```

This fragment outputs the sum of however many integers you enter. You will recall that the arguments to accumulate() are an iterator pointing to the first value in the sequence, an iterator pointing to one past the last value, and the initial value for the sum. Here, you are transferring data directly from cin to the algorithm.

The sstream header defines the basic_istringstream<T> template that defines an object type that can access data from a stream buffer such as a string object. The header also defines the istringstream type as basic_istringstream<char>, which will be a stream of characters of type char. You can construct an istringstream object from a string object, which means you can read data from the string object, just as you read from cin. Because an istringstream object is a stream, you can pass it to an input iterator constructor and use the iterator to access the data in the underlying stream buffer. Here's an example:

```
    std::string data {"2.4 2.5 3.6 2.1 6.7 6.8 94 95 1.1 1.4 32"};
    std::istringstream input {data};
    std::istream_iterator<double> begin(input), end;
    std::cout << "The sum of the values from the data string is "
                << std::accumulate(begin, end, 0.0) << std::endl;
```

You create the istringstream object, input, from the string object, data, so you can read from data as a stream. You create two stream iterators that can access double values in the input stream, and you use these to pass the contents of the input stream to the accumulate() algorithm. Note that the type of the third argument to the accumulate() function determines the type of the result, so you must specify this as a value of type double to get the sum produced correctly. Let's try an example.

TRY IT OUT   Using an Input Stream Iterator

This example uses a stream iterator to read text from the standard input stream and transfer it to a map container to produce a word count for the text. Here's the code:

```
// Ex10_13.cpp
// A simple word collocation
#include <iostream>
#include <iomanip>
#include <string>
#include <map>
#include <iterator>

int main()
{
  std::map<std::string, int> words;             // Map to store words and word counts
  std::cout << "Enter some text, press Enter followed by Ctrl+Z"
            "then Enter to end:\n"
            << std::endl;

  std::istream_iterator<std::string> stream_begin {std::cin}; // Stream iterator
```

```
std::istream_iterator<std::string> stream_end;              // End stream iterator

while (stream_begin != stream_end)          // Iterate over words in the stream
  words[*stream_begin++]++;                 // Increment and store a word count

// Output the words and their counts
std::cout << "Here are the word counts for the text you entered:" << std::endl;
const int wordsPerLine {4};
int wordCount {};
std::cout << std::setiosflags(std::ios::left);        // Ouput left-justified
for (const auto& word : words)
{
  std::cout << std::setw(15) << word.first << " " << std::setw(5) << word.second;
  if (++wordCount % wordsPerLine == 0) std::cout << std::endl;
}
std::cout << std::endl;
}
```

Here's an example of some output from this program:

```
Enter some text and press Enter followed by Ctrl+Z then Enter to end:
Peter Piper picked a peck of pickled pepper
A peck of pickled pepper Peter Piper picked
If Peter Piper picked a peck of pickled pepper
Where's the peck of pickled pepper Peter Piper picked
^Z
Here are the word counts for the text you entered:
A               1   If              1   Peter           4   Piper           4
Where's         1   a               2   of              4   peck            4
pepper          4   picked          4   pickled         4   the             1
```

How It Works

You first define a map container to store the words and their counts:

```
std::map<std::string, int> words;          // Map to store words and word counts
```

This container stores each word count of type int, using the word of type string as the key. This will make it easy to accumulate the count for each word when you read from the input stream using stream iterators:

```
std::istream_iterator<std::string>  stream_begin{std::cin}; // Stream iterator
std::istream_iterator<std::string>  stream_end;             // End stream iterator
```

The begin iterator is a stream iterator for the standard input stream, and end is an end-of-stream iterator.

You read the words and accumulate the counts in a loop:

```
while(stream_begin != stream_end)           // Iterate over words in the stream
  words[*stream_begin++]++;                 // Increment and store a word count
```

This simple while loop does a great deal of work. The loop control expression will iterate over the words entered via the standard input stream until the end-of-stream state is reached. The stream iterator reads words from cin delimited by whitespace, just like the overloaded >> operator for cin. You use the subscript operator for the map to store a count with the word as the key; remember, the argument to the subscript operator for a map is the key. The expression *begin accesses a word, and the expression *stream_begin++ increments the iterator after accessing the word.

The first time a word is read, it will not be in the map, so the expression words[*stream_begin++] will store a new entry with the count having the default value 0, and increment the begin iterator to the next word, ready for the next loop iteration. The whole expression words[*stream_begin++]++ will increment the count for the entry, regardless of whether it is a new entry or not. Thus, an existing entry will just get its count incremented, whereas a new entry will be created and then its count incremented from 0 to 1.

Finally, you output the count for each word in a for loop:

```
for (const auto& word : words)
{
    std::cout << std::setw(15) << word.first << " " << std::setw(5) << word.second;
    if(++wordCount % wordsPerLine == 0) std::cout << std::endl;
}
```

Using Inserter Iterators

An inserter iterator can add new elements to the sequence containers vector<T>, deque<T>, and list<T>. There are three templates that create inserter iterators defined in the iterator header:

➤ back_insert_iterator<T> — Inserts elements at the end of a container of type T. The container must provide the push_back() member function for this to work.

➤ front_insert_iterator<T> — Inserts elements at the beginning of a container of type T. This depends on push_front() being available for the container so it won't work with a vector.

➤ insert_iterator<T> — Inserts elements starting at a specified position within a container of type T. The container must have an insert() member function that accepts an iterator as the first argument, and an item to be inserted as the second argument. This also works with sorted/ordered associative containers because they satisfy the requirements.

The constructors for the first two inserter iterator types expect a single argument specifying the container. For example:

```
std::list<int> numbers;
std::front_insert_iterator<std::list<int>> iter {numbers};
```

Here, you create an iterator that can insert data at the beginning of the list<int> container numbers.

Inserting a value into the container is very simple:

```
*iter = 99;                   // Insert 99 at the front of the numbers container
```

You could also use front_inserter() with the numbers container, like this:

```
std::front_inserter (numbers) = 99;
```

This creates a front inserter for the numbers list and uses it to insert 99 at the beginning of the list. The argument to front_inserter() is the container to which the iterator is to be applied.

The constructor for an `insert_iterator<T>` iterator requires two arguments:

```
std::vector<int> values;
std::insert_iterator<std::vector<int>> iter_anywhere {values, std::begin(values)};
```

The second argument is an iterator specifying where data is to be inserted — the start of the sequence in this instance. You can use this iterator in exactly the same way as the previous one. Here's how you could insert a series of values into the vector using this iterator:

```
for(int i {}; i < 100; i++)
    *iter_anywhere = i + 1;
```

This loop inserts the integers 1 to 100 in the `values` container at the beginning. After executing this, the first 100 elements will be 1, 2, and so on, through to 100.

You could also use `inserter()` to insert the elements in reverse order:

```
for(int i {}; i < 100; i++)
    std::inserter(values, std::begin(values)) = i + 1;
```

The first argument to `inserter()` is the container, and the second is an iterator identifying the position where data is to be inserted. The values will be in reverse order from 100 down to 1.

The inserter iterators can be used in conjunction with the `copy()` algorithm in a particularly useful way. Here's how you could read values from `cin` and transfer them to a `list<T>` container:

```
std::list<double> values;
std::cout << "Enter a series of values separated by spaces"
        << " followed by Ctrl+Z or a letter to end:" << std::endl;
std::istream_iterator<double> input {std::cin}, input_end;
std::copy(input, input_end, std::back_inserter<std::list<double>> {values});
```

You first create a list container that stores `double` values. After prompting for input, you create two input stream iterators for `double` values. The first iterator points to `cin`, and the second is an end-of-stream iterator created by the default constructor. You specify the input to the `copy()` algorithm with the two iterators; the destination for the copy operation is a back inserter iterator that you create in the third argument to the `copy()` function. The back inserter iterator adds the data transferred by the copy operation to the list container, `values`. This is quite powerful stuff. If you ignore the prompt, in two statements you read an arbitrary number of values from the standard input stream and transfer them to a list container.

Using Output Stream Iterators

Complementing the input stream iterator template, the `ostream_iterator<T>` template provides output stream iterators for writing objects of type `T` to an output stream. There are two constructors for output stream iterators. One creates an iterator that transfers data to the destination stream:

```
std::ostream_iterator<int> out {std::cout};
```

The template type argument, `int`, specifies the type of data to be handled, while the constructor argument, `cout`, specifies the stream that will be the destination for data, so the `out` iterator can write values of type `int` to the standard output stream. Here's how you might use this iterator:

```
int data[] {1, 2, 3, 4, 5, 6, 7, 8, 9};
std::copy(std::cbegin(data), std::cend(data), out);
```

The `copy()` algorithm that is defined in the `algorithm` header copies the sequence of objects specified by the first two iterator arguments to the output iterator specified by the third argument. Here, the function copies the elements from the `data` array to the `out` iterator, which will write the elements to `cout`. The result of executing this fragment will be:

```
123456789
```

As you can see, the values are written to the output stream with no spaces in between. The second constructor can improve on this:

```
std::ostream_iterator<int> out{std::cout, ", "};
```

The second argument is a string to be used as a delimiter for output values. If you use this iterator as the third argument to the `copy()` function in the previous fragment, the output will be:

```
1, 2, 3, 4, 5, 6, 7, 8, 9,
```

The delimiter string that you specify as a second constructor argument is written to the stream following each value.

Let's see how an output stream iterator works in practice.

TRY IT OUT Using an Output Stream Iterator

Suppose you want to read a series of integer values from `cin` and store them in a vector. You then want to output the values and their sum. Here's how you could do this with the STL:

```cpp
// Ex10_14.cpp
// Using stream and inserter iterators
#include <iostream>
#include <numeric>
#include <vector>
#include <iterator>

int main()
{
  std::vector<int> numbers;
  std::cout << "Enter a series of integers separated by spaces"
            << " followed by Ctrl+Z or a letter:" << std::endl;

  std::istream_iterator<int> input {std::cin}, input_end;
  std::ostream_iterator<int> out {std::cout, " "};

  std::copy(input, input_end, std::back_inserter<std::vector<int>> {numbers});

  std::cout << "You entered the following values:" << std::endl;
  std::copy(std::cbegin(numbers), std::cend(numbers), out);

  std::cout << "\nThe sum of these values is "
            << std::accumulate(std::cbegin(numbers), std::cend(numbers), 0)
            << std::endl;
}
```

Here's an example of some output:

```
Enter a series of integers separated by spaces followed by Ctrl+Z or a letter:
1 2 3 4 5 6 7 8 9 10 11 12 13 14 15 ^Z
```

```
You entered the following values:
1 2 3 4 5 6 7 8 9 10 11 12 13 14 15
The sum of these values is 120
```

How It Works

After creating the `numbers` vector to store integers and issuing a prompt for input, you create three stream iterators:

```
std::istream_iterator<int> input{std::cin}, input_end;
std::ostream_iterator<int> out {std::cout, " "};
```

The first statement creates two input stream iterators, `input` and `input_end`, for reading values of type `int` from the standard input stream; the latter is an end-of-stream iterator. The second statement creates an output stream iterator for transferring values of type `int` to the standard output stream, with a single space following each output value.

Data is read from `cin` and transferred to the vector container using the `copy()` algorithm:

```
std::copy(input, input_end, std::back_inserter<std::vector<int>> {numbers});
```

You specify the data source by two input stream iterators, `input` and `input_end`, and the destination is a back inserter iterator for the `numbers` container. Thus, the copy operation will transfer data from `cin` to the `numbers` container via the back inserter.

You output the values in the container using another copy operation:

```
std::copy(std::cbegin(numbers), std::cend(numbers), out);
```

The source for the copy is specified by the begin and end iterators for the container, and the destination is the output stream iterator, `out`. This operation writes the data from `numbers` to `cout`, with the values separated by a space.

Finally, you calculate the sum of the values in the `numbers` container in the output statement using the `accumulate()` algorithm:

```
std::cout << "\nThe sum of these values is "
          << std::accumulate(std::cbegin(numbers), std::cend(numbers), 0)
          << std::endl;
```

You specify the range of values to be summed by the begin and end iterators for the container, and the initial value for the sum is zero. If you wanted the average rather than the sum, this is easy too, using the statement:

```
std::cout << "\nThe average is "
   << std::accumulate(std::cbegin(numbers), std::cend(numbers), 0.0)/numbers.size()
   << std::endl;
```

MORE ON FUNCTION OBJECTS

I mentioned earlier that the `functional` header defines an extensive set of templates for creating function objects that you can use with algorithms and containers. I won't discuss them all in detail, but I'll summarize the most useful ones. The function objects for comparisons are:

FUNCTION OBJECT TEMPLATE	DESCRIPTION
less<T>	A binary predicate representing the < operation between objects of type T. For example, less<string>() defines a function object for comparing objects of type string.
less_equal<T>	A binary predicate representing the <= operation between objects of type T. For example, less_equal<double>() defines a function object for comparing objects of type double.
equal_to<T>	A binary predicate representing the == operation between objects of type T.
not_equal_to<T>	A binary predicate representing the != operation between objects of type T.
greater_equal<T>	A binary predicate representing the >= operation between objects of type T.
greater<T>	A binary predicate representing the > operation between objects of type T.

There is also the not2<>() template function that creates a binary predicate that is the negation of a binary predicate defined by a function object you pass as the argument. For example, not2(less<int>()) creates a binary predicate for comparing objects of type int that returns true if the left operand is not less than the right operand. You could use the not2() function template to define a binary predicate for use with the sort() algorithm to sort a container, v, with elements of type string:

```
std::sort(std::begin(v), std::end(v), std::not2(std::greater<std::string>()));
```

The argument to the not2 constructor is greater<string>(), so the sort() function will sort using "not greater than" as the comparison between the string objects in the container, v.

The functional header also defines function objects for performing arithmetic operations. You would typically use these to apply operations to sequences of numerical values using the transform() algorithm that is defined in the algorithm header. These function objects are described in the following table.

FUNCTION OBJECT TEMPLATE	DESCRIPTION
plus<T>	Calculates the sum of two elements of type T.
minus<T>	Calculates the difference between two elements of type T by subtracting the second operand from the first.
multiplies<T>	Calculates the product of two elements of type T.
divides<T>	Divides the first operand of type T by the second.
modulus<T>	Calculates the remainder after dividing the first operand of type T by the second.
negate<T>	Returns the negative of the operand of type T.

To make use of these, you need to apply the `transform()` function. I'll explain how this works in the next section.

MORE ON ALGORITHMS

The `algorithm` and `numeric` headers define a large number of algorithms. The algorithms in the `numeric` header are primarily devoted to processing arrays of numerical values, whereas those in the `algorithm` header are more general purpose and provide such things as the ability to search, sort, copy, and merge sequences of objects specified by iterators. There are far too many to discuss in detail in this introductory chapter, so I'll just introduce a few of the most useful algorithms from the `algorithm` header to give you a basic idea of how they can be used.

You have already seen the `sort()` and `copy()` algorithms in action. Let's take a brief look at a few others.

➤ **The `fill()` algorithm** — This algorithm is of this form:

```
fill(ForwardIterator begin, ForwardIterator end, const Type& value)
```

This fills the elements specified by the iterators begin and end with value. For example, given a vector v, containing more than 10 values of type string, you could write:

```
std::fill(std::begin(v), std::begin(v)+10, "invalid");
```

This would set the first 10 elements in v to `"invalid"`, the value specified by the last argument.

➤ **The `replace()` algorithm** — The `replace()` algorithm is of the form:

```
replace(ForwardIterator begin_it, ForwardIterator end_it,
                        const Type& oldValue, const Type& newValue)
```

This examines each element in the range specified by `begin_it` and `end_it`, and replaces each occurrence of `oldValue` by `newValue`. Given a vector v that stores `string` objects, you could replace occurrences of `"yes"` by `"no"` using the following statement:

```
std::replace(std::begin(v), std::end(v), "yes", "no");
```

Like all the algorithms that receive an interval defined by a couple of iterators, `replace()` will also work with pointers. For example:

```
char str[] = "A nod is as good as a wink to a blind horse.";
std::replace(str, str + strlen(str), 'o', '*');
std::cout << str << std::endl;
```

This will replace every occurrence of `'o'` in the null-terminated string `str` by `'*'`, so the result of executing this fragment will be:

```
A n*d is as g**d as a wink t* a blind h*rse.
```

➤ **The `find()` algorithm** — The `find()` algorithm is of the form:

```
InputIterator find(InputIterator begin, InputIterator end, const Type& value)
```

This searches the sequence specified by the first two arguments for the first occurrence of value. For example, given a vector v containing values of type int, you could write:

```
auto iter = std::find(std::cbegin(v), std::cend(v), 21);
```

By using iter as the starting point for a new search, you could use find() repeatedly to find all occurrences of a given value:

```
auto iter = std::cbegin(v);
const int value {21};
size_t count {};
while((iter = std::find(iter, std::cend(v), value)) != std::cend(v))
{
  ++iter;
  ++count;
}
std::cout << "The vector contains " << count << " occurrences of " << value
          << std::endl;
```

This searches the vector v for all occurrences of value. On the first iteration, the search starts at cbegin(v). On subsequent iterations, the search starts at one past the previous position that was found. The loop will accumulate the total number of occurrences of value in v.

➤ **The** transform() **algorithm** — transform() comes in two versions. The first applies an operation specified by a unary function object to a set of elements specified by a pair of iterators, and is of the form:

```
OutputIterator transform(InputIterator begin, InputIterator end,
                                OutputIterator result, UnaryFunction f)
```

This applies the unary function f to all elements in the range specified by the iterators begin and end, and stores the results, beginning at the position specified by the result iterator. The result iterator can be the same as begin, in which case the results will replace the original elements. The function returns an iterator that is one past the last result stored. Here's an example:

```
std::vector<double> data{ 2.5, -3.5, 4.5, -5.5, 6.5, -7.5};
std::transform(std::begin(data), std::end(data), std::begin(data),
                                std::negate<double>());
```

The transform() call applies a negate<double> predicate object to all the elements in the vector data. The results are stored back in data and overwrite the original values so after this operation the vector will contain:

```
-2.5, 3.5, -4.5, 5.5, -6.5, 7.5
```

Because the operation writes the results back to data, the transform() function will return the iterator std::end(data).

The second version of transform() applies a binary function, with the operands coming from two ranges specified by iterators. The function is of the form:

```
transform(InputIterator1 begin1, InputIterator1 end1, InputIterator2 begin2,
                                OutputIterator result, BinaryFunction f)
```

The range specified by `begin1` and `end1` defines the set of left operands for the binary function `f` that is specified by the last argument. The range defining the right operands starts at the position specified by the `begin2` iterator; an end iterator does not need to be supplied for this range because there must be the same number of elements as in the range specified by `begin1` and `end1`. The results will be stored in the range, starting at the `result` iterator position. The `result` iterator can be the same as `begin1` if you want the results stored back in that range, but it must not be any other position between `begin1` and `end1`. Here's an example:

```
double values[] { 2.5, -3.5, 4.5, -5.5, 6.5, -7.5};
std::vector<double> squares(_countof(values));
std::transform (std::begin(values), std::end(values), std::begin(values),
                        std::begin(squares), std::multiplies<double>());
std::ostream_iterator<double> out {std::cout, " "};
std::copy(std::cbegin(squares), std::cend(squares), out);
```

You create the `squares` vector with the same number of elements as `values` to store the results of the `transform()` operation. The `transform()` function uses the `multiplies<double>()` function object to multiply each element of `values` by itself. The results are stored in `squares`. The last two statements use an output stream iterator to list the contents of `squares`, which will be:

```
6.25 12.25 20.25 30.25 42.25 56.25
```

TYPE TRAITS AND STATIC ASSERTIONS

A static assertion enables you to detect usage errors at compile time. A static assertion is of the form:

```
static_assert(constant_expression, string_literal);
```

The `constant_expression` should result in a value that is convertible to type `bool`. If the result is `true`, the statement does nothing; if it is `false`, the string literal will be displayed by the compiler. A static assertion has no effect on the compiled code. Note that `static_assert` is a keyword.

The `type_traits` header defines a range of templates that enable you to create compile-time constants that you can use in conjunction with static assertions to cause the compiler to issue customized error messages. I don't have the space to describe the contents of `type_traits` in detail so I'll just give you one example and use type traits in the next section.

The `type_traits` header includes several templates for testing types that are particularly useful when you are defining your own templates. Suppose you define the following template:

```
template<class T>
T average(const std::vector<T>& data)
{
  T sum {};
  for(const auto& value : data)
    sum += value;
  return sum/data.size();
}
```

This template is intended to be used with a vector of values that are of an arithmetic type. It would be useful to be able to prevent the template from being used with non-arithmetic types — `Person` objects, for example. It would be useful if this can be caught at compile time. A `static_assert` in conjunction with the `is_arithmetic<T>` template from `type_traits` will do the trick:

```
template<class T>
T average(const std::vector<T>& data)
{
  static_assert(std::is_arithmetic<T>::value,
                       "Type parameter for average() must be arithmetic.");
  T sum {};
  for(auto& value : data)
    sum += value;
  return sum/data.size();
}
```

The `value` member of the `is_arithmetic<T>` template will be `true` if `T` is an arithmetic type and `false` otherwise. If it is `false` during compilation; that is, when the compiler processes the `average<T>()` template used with a non-arithmetic type, the error message will be displayed. An arithmetic type is a floating-point type or an integral type.

Other type testing templates include `is_integral<T>`, `is_signed<T>`, `is_unsigned<T>`, `is_floating_point<T>`, and `is_enum<T>`. There are many other useful templates in the `type_traits` header so it is well worth exploring the contents further.

LAMBDA EXPRESSIONS

A lambda expression provides you with an alternative programming mechanism to function objects. Lambda expressions are a C++ language feature and not specific to STL but they can be applied extensively in this context, which is why I chose to discuss them here. A lambda expression defines a function object without a name, and without the need for an explicit class definition. You would typically use a lambda expression as the means of passing a function as an argument to another function. A lambda expression is much easier to use and understand, and requires less code than defining and creating a function object. Of course, it is not a replacement for function objects in general.

Let's consider an example. Suppose you want to calculate the cubes (x3) of the elements in a vector containing numerical values. You could use the `transform()` operation for this, except that there is no function object to calculate cubes. You can easily create a lambda expression to do it, though:

```
double values[] { 2.5, -3.5, 4.5, -5.5, 6.5, -7.5};
std::vector<double> cubes(_countof(values));
std::transform(std::begin(values), std::end(values), std::begin(cubes),
                                [](double x){ return x*x*x;} );
```

The last statement uses `transform()` to calculate the cubes of the elements in the array, `values`, and store the result in the vector `cubes`. The lambda expression is the last argument to the `transform()` function:

```
[](double x){ return x*x*x;}
```

The opening square brackets are called the *lambda introducer*, because they mark the beginning of the lambda expression. There's a bit more to this, so I'll come back to it a little later in this chapter.

The lambda introducer is followed by the lambda parameter list between parentheses, just like a normal function. In this case, there's just a single parameter, x. There are restrictions on the lambda parameter list, compared to a regular function: You cannot specify default values for the parameters and the parameter list cannot be of a variable length.

Finally, you have the body of the lambda expression between braces, again just like a normal function. In this case the body is just a single return statement, but in general, it can consist of as many statements as you like, just like a normal function. I'm sure you have noticed that there is no return type specification. The return type defaults to that of the value returned. Otherwise, the default return type is void. Of course, you can specify the return type. To specify the return type you would write the lambda expression like this:

```
[](double x) -> double { return x*x*x; }
```

The type double following the arrow specifies the return type.

If you wanted to output the values calculated, you could do so in the lambda expression:

```
[](double x) {
            double result{x*x*x};
            std::cout << result << "  ";
            return result;
          }
```

This extends the body of the lambda to provide for writing the value that is calculated to the standard output stream. In this case, the return type is still deduced from the type of the value returned.

The Capture Clause

The lambda introducer can contain a *capture clause* that determines how the body of the lambda can access variables in the enclosing scope. In the previous section, the lambda expression had nothing between the square brackets, indicating that no variables in the enclosing scope can be accessed within the body of the lambda. A lambda that does not access anything from the enclosing scope is called a stateless lambda.

The first possibility is to specify a default capture clause that applies to all variables in the enclosing scope. You have two options for this. If you place = between the square brackets, the body has access to all automatic variables in the enclosing scope by value — that is, the values of the variables are made available within the lambda expression, but the original variables cannot be changed. If you put & between the square brackets, all the variables in the enclosing scope are accessible by reference, and therefore can be changed by the code in the body of the lambda. Look at this code fragment:

```
double factor {5.0};
double values[] { 2.5, -3.5, 4.5, -5.5, 6.5, -7.5};
std::vector<double> cubes(_countof(values));
std::transform(std::begin(values), std::end(values), std::begin(cubes),
                              [=](double x){ return factor*x*x*x;} );
```

In this fragment, the = capture clause allows all the variables in scope to be accessible by value from within the body of the lambda. Note that this is not quite the same as passing arguments by value.

The value of the variable `factor` is available within the lambda, but you cannot update the copy of `factor` because it is effectively `const`. The following statement will not compile, for example:

```
std::transform(std::begin(values), std::end(values),std::begin(cubes),
        [=](double x)  { factor += 10.0;           // Not allowed!
                         return factor*x*x*x;} );
```

If you want to modify the temporary copy of a variable in scope from within the lambda, adding the `mutable` keyword will enable this:

```
std::transform(std::begin(values), std::end(values),std::begin(cubes),
        [=](double x)mutable { factor += 10.0;           // OK
                               return factor*x*x*x;} );
```

Now you can modify the copy of any variable within the enclosing scope without changing the original variable. After executing this statement, the value of `factor` will still be 5.0. The lambda remembers the local value of `factor` from one call to the next, so for the first element `factor` will be 5 + 10 = 15, for the second element it will be 15 + 10 = 25, and so on.

If you want to change the original value of `factor` from within the lambda, just use `&` as the capture clause:

```
std::transform(std::begin(values), std::end(values),std::begin(cubes),
        [&](double x){ factor += 10.0;    // Changes original variable
                       return factor*x*x*x;} );
std::cout << "factor = " << factor << std::endl;
```

You don't need the `mutable` keyword here. All variables within the enclosing scope are available by reference, so you can use and alter their values. The result of executing this will be that `factor` is 65. If you thought it was going to be 15.0, remember that the lambda expression executes once for each element in `data`, and the cubes of the elements will be multiplied by successive values of `factor` from 15.0 to 65.0.

> **NOTE** *The use of a default capture clause is discouraged. It's recommended that you should explicitly state which variables you want to capture.*

Capturing Specific Variables

You can explicitly identify the variables in the enclosing scope that you want to access. You could rewrite the previous `transform()` statement as:

```
std::transform(std::begin(values), std::end(values),std::begin(cubes),
        [&factor](double x) { factor += 10.0;    // Changes original variable
                              return factor*x*x*x;} );
```

Now, `factor` is the only variable from the enclosing scope that is accessible, and it is available by reference. If you omit the `&`, `factor` would be available by value and not updatable. If you want to identify several variables in the capture clause, just separate them with commas. You could include = in the capture clause list, as well as explicit variable names. For example, with the capture clause `[=, &factor]` the lambda would have access to `factor` by reference and all other variables in the enclosing scope by value. Conversely, putting `[&, factor]` as the capture clause would capture `factor` by value and all other variables by reference. Note that in a function member of a class, you can include the `this` pointer in the capture clause for a lambda expression, which allows access to the other functions and data members that belong to the class.

A lambda expression can also include a `throw()` exception specification that indicates that the lambda does not throw exceptions. Here's an example:

```
std::transform(std::begin(values), std::end(values),std::begin(cubes),
        [&factor](double x)throw() { factor += 10.0;
                                     return factor*x*x*x;} );
```

If you want to include the `mutable` specification, as well as the `throw()` specification, the `mutable` keyword must precede `throw()` and must be separated from it by one or more spaces.

Templates and Lambda Expressions

You can use a lambda expression inside a template. Here's an example of a function template that uses a lambda expression:

```
template <class T>
T average(const vector<T>& vec)
{
  static_assert(std::is_arithmetic<T>::value,
                        "Type parameter for average() must be arithmetic.");
  T sum {};
  std::for_each(std::cbegin(vec), std::cend(vec),
    [&sum](const T& value){ sum += value; });
  return sum/vec.size();
}
```

This template generates functions for calculating the average of a set of numerical values stored in a vector. The `algorithm` header defines `for_each()`. The lambda expression uses the template type parameter in the lambda parameter specification, and accumulates the sum of all the elements in a vector. The `sum` variable is accessed from the lambda by reference, so it is able to accumulate the sum there. The last line of the function returns the average, which is calculated by dividing `sum` by the number of elements in the vector. Let's try an example.

Using Lambda Expressions

This example shows the use of a variety of lambda expressions:

```
// Ex10_15.cpp Using lambda expressions
#include <algorithm>
#include <iostream>
#include <iomanip>
#include <vector>
#include <random>

using namespace std; // Just to make the code easier  to read in the example...

// Template function to return the average of the elements in a vector
template <class T> T average(const vector<T>& vec)
{
```

```cpp
  static_assert(std::is_arithmetic<T>::value,
                        "Type parameter for average() must be arithmetic.");
  T sum {};
  for_each(cbegin(vec), cend(vec),
    [&sum](const T& value){ sum += value; });
  return sum/vec.size();
}

// Template function to set a vector to values beginning with start
// and incremented by increment
template <class T> void setValues(vector<T>& vec, T start, T increment)
{
  static_assert(std::is_arithmetic<T>::value,
                        "Type parameter for setValues() must be arithmetic.");
  T current {start};
  generate(begin(vec), end(vec),
    [increment, &current]() { T result {current};
                              current += increment;
                              return result;});
}

// Template function to set a vector to random values between min and max
template<class T> void randomValues(vector<T>& vec, T min_value, T max_value)
{
  static_assert(std::is_arithmetic<T>::value,
    "Type parameter for randomValues() must be arithmetic.");

  random_device engine;              // Random number source
  auto max_rand = engine.max();      // Maximum random value
  auto min_rand = engine.min();      // Minimum random value

  generate(begin(vec), end(vec),
    [&engine, max_rand, min_rand, min_value, max_value]
    {  return static_cast<T>(static_cast<double>(engine()) /
                        max_rand*(max_value - min_value) + min_value); } );
}

// Template function to list the values in a vector
template<class T> void listVector(const vector<T>& vec)
{
  int count {};        // Used to control outputs per line
  const int valuesPerLine {5};
  for_each(cbegin(vec), cend(vec),
    [&count, valuesPerLine](const T& n){
                              cout << setw(10) << n << "  ";
                              if(++count % valuesPerLine == 0)
                                cout << endl;});
}

int main()
{
  vector<int> integerData(50);
  randomValues(integerData, 1, 10);            // Set random integer values
  cout << "Vector contains random integers:" << endl;
  listVector(integerData);
```

```
        cout << "Average value is " << average(integerData) << endl;

        vector<double> realData(20);
        setValues(realData, 5.0, 2.5);    // Set real values starting at 5.0
        cout << "\nVector contains real values:" << endl;
        listVector(realData);
        cout << "Average value is " << average(realData) << endl;

        vector<double> randomData(20);
        randomValues(randomData, 5.0, 25.0);    // Set random values from 5.0 to 25
        cout << "\nVector contains random real values:" << endl;
        listVector(randomData);
        cout << "Average value is " << average(randomData) << endl;
    }
```

This example produces output similar to the following:

```
Vector contains random integers:
        2            9            9            2            8
        7            4            1            9            9
        7            3            3            2            4
        3            9            2            7            1
        4            6            6            8            9
        9            6            2            8            2
        9            3            1            5            8
        1            2            5            7            1
        4            2            8            4            2
        5            2            5            9            8
Average value is 5

Vector contains real values:
        5          7.5           10         12.5           15
     17.5           20         22.5           25         27.5
       30         32.5           35         37.5           40
     42.5           45         47.5           50         52.5
Average value is 28.75

Vector contains random real values:
   6.37904      19.0177      16.8027      10.6446       17.174
   12.1957      24.9999      10.8728      23.6502      16.9032
   16.7498      11.7784      17.3076      11.2226      15.8428
   8.52583      5.54059      10.3581       23.161      22.7069
Average value is 15.0917
```

Where the example uses random number generation, the values are likely to be different.

How It Works

There are four function templates that use lambda expressions in the implementation of the functions that operate on vectors. The first, `average()`, calculates the average value of the elements in a vector by passing the following lambda expression as the last argument to the `for_each()` function:

```
[&sum](const T& value){ sum += value; }
```

The `sum` variable that is defined in `average()` is accessed by reference in the lambda to accumulate the sum of all the elements. The parameter to the lambda is `value`, which is of type reference to `T`, so the lambda automatically deals with whatever element type is in the vector. The static assertion ensures that the template type argument is arithmetic.

The next function template is setValues(). This sets the elements of a vector in sequence with the first element set to start, the next to start+increment, the next to start+2*increment, and so on. Thus, the function will set the vector elements to any set of equi-spaced values. The function calls the generate() function that is defined in the algorithm header. This sets a sequence of elements, defined by the first two iterator arguments, to the value returned by the function object you specify as the third argument. In this case, the third argument is the lambda expression:

```
[increment, &current]() { T result {current};
                          current += increment;
                          return result; }
```

The lambda accepts no arguments, but it accesses increment by value and current by reference, the latter being used to store the next value to be set. This lambda has the side effect that current will be updated when generate is finished. The following lambda expression is similar, but without the side effect:

```
[=]()mutable { T result {current};
               current += increment;
               return result; }
```

The third function template is randomValues(), which stores random values of the appropriate type in the elements of a vector. The values will be in the range from min to max, the second and third arguments to the function. This uses a std::random_device function object from the random header for generating random numbers. The min() and max() member functions of std::random_device return the minimum and maximum values that it generates. The random header provides an extensive range of random number generators that are beyond the scope of this book but I encourage you to explore it if you need random number generators of any kind.

The randomValues() function calls generate() to store values produced by the following lambda expression in the vector:

```
[&engine, &max_rand, min_rand, min_value, max_value]
{  return static_cast<T>(static_cast<double>(engine()) /
                         max_rand*(max_value - min_value) + min_value); }
```

The engine functor is created in the outer scope, along with the values max_rand and min_rand. The four variables in the outer scope that are accessed by the lambda expression are identified in the capture clause. Only engine is accessed by reference; the other three are accessed by value. The arithmetic expression in the lambda scales the random value produced by engine() to the range min_value to max_value.

The last template function is listVector(), which outputs the values of the elements in a vector with the number of values per line specified by valuesPerLine. It uses the following lambda as the argument to the for_each() function to do this:

```
[&count, valuesPerLine](const T& n) {
                         cout << setw(10) << n << "  ";
                         if(++count % valuesPerLine == 0)
                           cout << endl; }
```

The capture clause captures the count variable that is defined in the listVector() function by reference, and this is used to record the number of values processed. valuesPerLine is captured by value. The parameter is a const reference to T, so any element type can be processed. The body of the lambda outputs the value of the current element, n, and the if statement ensures that after every fifth value, a newline is written to cout. The setw() manipulator ensures values are presented in the output in a field that is 10 characters wide, so we get nice neat columns of output.

You create a vector storing 50 integers and call randomValues() to set the elements to random values between 1 and 10:

```
vector<int> integerData(50);
randomValues(integerData, 1, 10);    // Set random integer values
cout << "Vector contains random integers:" << endl;
listVector(integerData);
cout << "Average value is "<< average(integerData) << endl;
```

The call to listVector() outputs the values, five to a line, as you see. The last statement calls the average() template function to calculate the average of the values in the vector. In all three template functions, the type is deduced from the vector<int> argument that is passed, and this also determines the type in the lambda that each function uses.

The next block of code in main() is:

```
vector<double> realData(20);
setValues(realData, 5.0, 2.5);    // Set real values starting at 5.0
cout << "\nVector contains real values:" << endl;
listVector(realData);
cout << "Average value is "<< average(realData) << endl;
```

This vector stores values of type double, and its elements are set using setValues(), which creates a sequence by incrementing from an initial value.

The last block of code stores random real values in a vector:

```
vector<double> randomData(20);
randomValues(randomData, 5.0, 25.0);    // Set random values from 5.0 to 25
cout << "\nVector contains random real values:" << endl;
listVector(randomData);
cout << "Average value is " << average(randomData) << endl;
```

The output shows that everything works as expected.

Naming a Lambda Expression

You can assign a stateless lambda — one that does not reference anything in an external scope — to a variable that is a function pointer, thus giving the lambda a name. You can then use the function pointer to call the lambda as many times as you like. For example:

```
auto sum = [](int a, int b){return a+b; };
```

The function pointer, sum, points to the lambda expression, so you can use it as many times as you like:

```
std::cout << "5 + 10 equals " << sum(5,10) << std::endl;
std::cout << "15 + 16 equals " << sum(15,16) << std::endl;
```

This is quite useful, but there's a much more powerful capability. An extension to the `functional` header defines the `function<>` class template that you can use to define a wrapper for a function object; this includes a lambda expression. The `function<>` template is referred to as a polymorphic function wrapper because an instance of the template can wrap a variety of function objects with a given parameter list and return type. I won't discuss all the details of the `function<>` class template, but I'll just show how you can use it to wrap a lambda expression. Using the `function<>` template to wrap a lambda effectively gives a name to the lambda, which not only provides the possibility of recursion within a lambda expression, it also allows you to use the lambda in multiple statements or pass it to several different functions. The same function wrapper could also wrap different lambda expressions at different times.

To create a wrapper object from the `function<>` template you need to supply information about the return type, and the types of any parameters, to a lambda expression. Here's how you could create an object of type `function` that can wrap a function object that has one parameter of type `double` and returns a value of type `int`:

```
std::function<int(double)> f = [](double x)->int{ return static_cast<int>(x*x); };
```

The type specification for the function template is the return type for the function object to be wrapped, followed by its parameter types between parentheses, and separated by commas. Let's try a working example that uses the basic capability that is built into the C++ language as well as the `function<T>` template.

TRY IT OUT Recursion in a Lambda Expression

This example will find the highest common factor (HCF) for a pair of integer values. The HCF is the largest number that will divide exactly into both integers. The HCF is also called the greatest common divisor (GCD). Here's the code:

```
// Ex10_16.cpp Wrapping a lambda expression
#include <iostream>
#include <functional>

// Global wrapper for lambda expression computing HCF
std::function<long long(long long,long long)> hcf =
                       [&](long long m, long long n) mutable ->long long{
                             if(m < n) return hcf(n,m);
                             long long remainder {m%n};
                             if(0 == remainder) return n;
                             return hcf(n, remainder);};
int main()
{
  // A lambda expression assigned to a function pointer
  // that outputs the highest common factor of the arguments
  auto showHCF = [](long long a, long long b) {
  std::cout << "For numbers " << a << " and " << b
          << " the highest common factor is " << hcf(a, b) << std::endl;
  };
  long long a {17719LL}, b {18879LL};
  showHCF(a,b);
  showHCF(103LL*53*17*97, 3LL*29*103);
  showHCF(53LL*941*557*43*29*229, 83LL*89*941*11*17*863*431);
}
```

This produces the output:

```
For numbers 17719 and 18879 the highest common factor is 29
For numbers 9001891 and 8961 the highest common factor is 103
For numbers 7932729108943 and 483489887381237 the highest common factor is 941
```

How It Works

You define a wrapper with the name hcf for a lambda expression that calculates the HCF at global scope:

```
std::function<long long(long long,long long)> hcf =
                    [&](long long m, long long n) mutable ->long long{
                        if(m < n) return hcf(n,m);
                        long long remainder {m%n};
                        if(0 == remainder) return n;
                        return hcf(n, remainder);};
```

The lambda needs to refer to hcf in order to work, and because this is defined outside the scope of the lambda, you cannot use a regular function pointer for hcf.

The lambda expression has two parameters of type long long and returns a value of type long long, so hcf is of type:

```
function<long long(long long, long long)>
```

The lambda expression uses Euclid's method for finding the highest common factor for two integer values. This involves dividing the larger number by the smaller number, and if the remainder is zero, the HCF is the smaller number. If the remainder is non-zero, the process continues by dividing the previous smaller number by the remainder, and this is repeated until the remainder is zero.

The code for the lambda expression assumes m is the larger of the two numbers that are passed as arguments, so if it isn't, it calls hcf() with the arguments reversed. If the first argument is the larger number, the remainder after dividing m by n is calculated. If the remainder is zero, then n is the highest common factor and is returned. If the remainder is not zero, hcf() is called with n and the remainder.

The first statement in main() assigns a stateless lambda to the showHCF pointer:

```
auto showHCF = [](long long a, long long b) {
std::cout << "For numbers " << a << " and " << b
            << " the highest common factor is " << hcf(a, b) << std::endl;
};
```

This lambda outputs the values for which the HCF is requested together with the HCF produced using the hcf object. The rest of main() calls this lambda through the showHCF function pointer three times to produce the results that you see. The results show that the lambda pointed to by hcf does indeed produce the highest common factor for its arguments.

You can use the function<> class template to specify the type for a function parameter. This enables you to define a function with a parameter for which you can supply an argument that can be a function object, a lambda expression, or a normal function pointer.

SUMMARY

This chapter introduced the capabilities of the STL. My objective in this chapter was to introduce enough of the details of the STL to enable you to explore the rest on your own. Even though this is a substantial chapter, I have barely scratched the surface of the STL's capabilities so I would encourage you to explore it further.

EXERCISES

1. Write a program that will read some text from the standard input stream, possibly involving several lines of input, and store the letters from the text in a `list<T>` container. Sort the letters in ascending sequence and output them.

2. Use a `priority_queue<T>` container to achieve the same result as in Exercise 1.

3. Modify `Ex10_12.cpp` so that it allows multiple phone numbers to be stored for a given name. The functionality in the program should reflect this: The `getEntry()` function should display all numbers for a given name, and the `deleteEntry()` function should delete a particular person/number combination.

4. Write a program to implement a phone book capability that will allow a name to be entered to retrieve one or more numbers, or a number to be entered to retrieve a name.

5. As you know, the Fibonacci series consists of the sequence of integers 0, 1, 1, 2, 3, 5, 8, 13, 21, … where each integer after the first two is the sum of the two preceding integers (note the series sometimes omits the initial zero). Write a program that uses a lambda expression to initialize a vector of integers with values from the Fibonacci series.

➤ WHAT YOU LEARNED IN THIS CHAPTER

TOPIC	CONCEPT
Standard Template Library	The STL includes templates for containers, iterators, algorithms, and function objects.
Containers	A container is a class object for storing and organizing other objects. Sequence containers store objects in a sequence, like an array. Associative containers store elements that are key/object pairs, where the key determines where the pair is stored in the container.
Iterators	Iterators are objects that behave like pointers. Iterators are used in pairs to define a set of objects by a semi-open interval, where the first iterator points to the first object in the series, and the second iterator points to a position one past the last object in the series.
Stream iterators	Stream iterators are iterators that allow you to access or modify the contents of a stream.
Iterator categories	There are four categories of iterators: input and output iterators, forward iterators, bidirectional iterators, and random access iterators. Each successive category of iterator provides more functionality than the previous one; thus, input and output iterators provide the least functionality, and random access iterators provide the most.
Smart pointers	Smart pointers are objects of template class types that encapsulate raw pointers. By using smart pointers instead of raw pointers you can often avoid the need to worry about deleting objects that you have allocated on the heap and thus avoid the risk of memory leaks.
Algorithms	Algorithms are template functions that operate on a sequence of objects specified by a pair of iterators.
Function objects	Function objects are objects of a type that overloads the `()` operator (by implementing `operator()()` in the class). The STL defines a wide range of standard function objects for use with containers and algorithms; you can also write your own classes to define function objects.
Lambda expressions	A lambda expression defines an anonymous function object without the need to explicitly define a class type. You can use a lambda expression as an argument to STL algorithms that expect a function object as an argument.
Stateless lambda expressions	A stateless lambda expression does not refer to any variables in an enclosing scope. You can store a pointer to a stateless lambda expression in a function pointer.
Polymorphic function wrappers	A polymorphic function wrapper is an instance of the `function<>` template that you can use to wrap a function object. You can also use a polymorphic function wrapper to wrap a lambda expression.

11

Windows Programming Concepts

WHAT YOU WILL LEARN IN THIS CHAPTER:

- ➤ The basic structure of a window

- ➤ The Windows API and how it is used

- ➤ Windows messages and how you deal with them

- ➤ The notation that is commonly used in Windows programs

- ➤ The basic structure of a Windows program

- ➤ How you create an elementary program using the Windows API and how it works

- ➤ Microsoft Foundation Classes

- ➤ The basic elements of an MFC-based program

WROX.COM CODE DOWNLOADS FOR THIS CHAPTER

You can find the wrox.com code downloads for this chapter on the Download Code tab at www.wrox.com/go/beginningvisualc. The code is in the Chapter 11 download and individually named according to the names throughout the chapter.

This chapter will take you on a tour of the basic ideas that are involved in every Windows program in C++. You'll first develop a simple example that uses the Windows operating system API directly. This will enable you to understand how a Windows application works behind the scenes, which will be useful when you are developing applications using the more sophisticated facilities provided by Visual C++. Next you will see what you get when you create a Windows program using the Microsoft Foundation Classes (MFC) that encapsulates Win32 capabilities.

WINDOWS PROGRAMMING BASICS

The Windows API is referred to as *WinAPI* or *Win32*, the latter being a slightly dated term since the availability of 64-bit versions of Windows. When you are developing an application with the Windows API, you are writing code at a relatively low level throughout — all the elements that make up the GUI for your application must be created programmatically by calling operating system functions. With MFC applications you are using a set of standard classes that insulate you from the Windows API and make coding much easier. There's also some help with GUI creation in that you can assemble controls on a dialog form graphically and just program the interactions with the user; however, you are still involved in a lot of coding.

Using the Windows API directly is the most laborious method for developing an application so I won't go into this in detail. However, you will put together a basic Windows API application so you'll have an opportunity to understand the mechanism that all Windows applications use under the covers to work with the operating system. Of course, it also is possible to develop applications in C++ that do not require the Windows operating system, and games sometimes take this approach. Many games use DirectX, which is a Windows specific graphics library. Although this is an interesting topic, it would require a whole book to do it justice, so I won't pursue it further.

Before getting to the examples I'll review the terminology that is used to describe an application window. You have already created a Windows program in Chapter 1 without writing a single line of code yourself, and I'll use the window generated by this example to illustrate the elements that go to make up a window.

Elements of a Window

You will inevitably be familiar with most, if not all, of the principal elements of the user interface to a Windows program. However, I will go through them anyway just to be sure we have a common understanding of what the terms mean. The best way to understand what the elements of a window can be is to look at one. An annotated version of the window displayed by the example that you saw in Chapter 1 is shown in Figure 11-1.

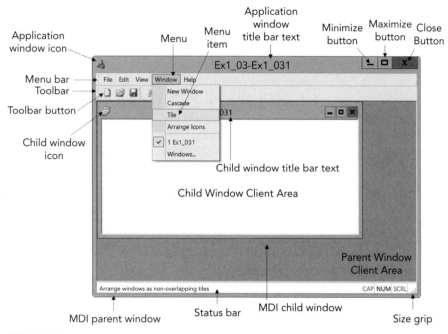

FIGURE 11-1

The example generated two windows. The larger window with the menu and the toolbars is the main application window, or *parent window*, and the smaller window is a *child window* of the parent. The child window can be closed without closing the parent window by double-clicking the title bar icon that is in the upper-left corner of the child window or by clicking the Close button in the upper-right corner of the child window. Closing the parent window automatically closes the child window. This is because the child window is owned by and dependent upon the parent window. In general, a parent window may have a number of child windows, as you'll see.

The most fundamental parts of a typical window are its *border*, the *title bar* that shows the name that you give to the window, the *title bar icon* that appears at the left end of the title bar, and the *client area*, which is the area in the center of the window not used by the title bar or borders. You can get all of these created for free in a Windows program. As you will see, all you have to do is provide some text for the title bar.

The border defines the boundary of a window and may be fixed or resizable. If the border is resizable, you can drag it to alter the size of the window. The window also may possess a size grip, which you can use to alter the size of a window. When you define a window, you can modify how the border behaves and appears if you want. Most windows will also have the maximize, minimize, and close buttons in the upper-right corner of the window. These allow the window to be increased to full screen size, reduced to an icon, or closed.

When you click the title bar icon, it provides a standard menu for altering or closing the window called the *system menu* or *control menu*. The system menu also appears when you right-click the title bar of a window. Although it's optional, it is always a good idea to include the title bar icon in any main windows that your program generates. Including the title bar icon provides you with a very convenient way of closing the program when things don't work during debugging, which is the process by which you find and eliminate errors in your code.

The client area is the part of the window where you usually want your program to write text or graphics. You can address the client area for this purpose in exactly the same way as the yard that you saw in Figure 7-1, in Chapter 7. The upper-left corner of the client area has the coordinates (0, 0), with x increasing from left to right, and y increasing from top to bottom.

The menu bar is optional in a window but is probably the most common way to control an application. Each menu in the menu bar displays a drop-down list of menu items when you click it. The contents of a menu and the physical appearance of many objects that are displayed in a window, such as the icons on the toolbar that appear in Figure 11-1, the cursor, and many others, are defined by a *resource file*. You will see many more resource files when we get to write some more sophisticated Windows programs.

A ribbon is an alternative to the menu bar. The latest editions of Microsoft Word and Microsoft Excel provide a ribbon as the primary mechanism for navigating around application functions. The MFC provides an extensive set of classes for creating a ribbon but I don't have the space to go into these.

The toolbar provides a set of icons that usually act as alternatives to the menu options that you use most often. Because they give a pictorial clue to the function provided, they can often make a program easier and faster to use.

I'll mention a caveat about terminology that you need to be conscious of. Users tend to think of a window as the thing that appears on the screen with a border around it, and, of course, it is, but it is only one kind of window. In Windows a window is a generic term covering a whole range of entities. Many entities that are displayed are windows — for example, a dialog is a window and each toolbar and dockable menu bar are also windows. I will generally use terminology to refer to objects that describe what they are, buttons, dialogs, and so on, but you need to have tucked in the back of your mind that many of them are windows too, because you can do things to them that you can do with a regular window — you can draw on a button, for instance.

Windows Programs and the Operating System

When you write a Windows program, your program is subservient to the operating system and Windows is in control. Your program cannot deal directly with the hardware, and all communications with the outside world must pass through Windows. When you use a Windows program, you are interacting primarily with Windows, which then communicates with the application program on your behalf. Your Windows program is the tail, Windows is the dog, and your program wags only when Windows tells it to.

There are a number of reasons why this is so. First and foremost, because your program is potentially always sharing the computer with other programs that may be executing at the same time, Windows has to have primary control to manage the sharing of machine resources. If one application were allowed to have primary control in a Windows environment, this would inevitably make programming more complicated because of the need to provide for the possibility of other programs, and information intended for other applications could be lost. A second reason is that Windows embodies a standard user interface and needs to be in charge to enforce that standard. You can only display information on the screen using the tools that Windows provides, and then only when authorized.

Event-Driven Programs

You have already seen in Chapter 1 that a Windows program is *event-driven*, so a Windows program essentially waits around for something to happen. A significant part of the code for a Windows application is dedicated to processing events that are caused by external actions of the user, but activities that are not directly associated with your application can nonetheless require that bits of your program code are executed. For example, if the operating system determines that your application window needs to be redrawn because it is no longer valid, it will send a message to you application to signal that your application must redraw the part of the application window that has been exposed.

Windows Messages

Events in a Windows application are occurrences such as the user clicking the mouse or pressing a key, or a timer reaching zero. The Windows operating system records each event in a *message* and places the message in a *message queue* for the program for which the message is intended. A Windows message is simply a record of the data relating to an event, and the message queue for an application is just a sequence of such messages waiting to be processed. By sending a message, Windows can tell your program that something needs to be done, or that some information has become available, or that an event such as a mouse click has occurred. If your program is properly organized, it will respond in the appropriate way to the message. There are many different kinds of messages and they can occur very frequently — several times per second when the mouse is being dragged for example.

A Windows program must contain a function specifically for handling these messages. The function is often called WndProc() or WindowProc(), although it doesn't have to have a particular name because Windows accesses the function through a pointer to a function that you supply. So the sending of a message to your program boils down to Windows calling a function that you provide that is typically called WindowProc(), and passing any necessary data to your program by means of arguments to this function. Within your WindowProc() function, it is up to you to work out what the message is from the data supplied and decide what to do about it.

Fortunately, you don't need to write code to process every message that Windows sends to your application. You can filter out those that are of interest, deal with those in whatever way you want, and pass the rest back to Windows. You pass a message back to Windows by calling a standard function called DefWindowProc(), which provides default message processing.

The Windows API

All of the communications between a Windows application and Windows itself use the Windows application programming interface, otherwise known as the *Windows API*. This consists of literally hundreds of functions that come as a standard with the Windows operating system that provide the means by which an application communicates with Windows, and vice versa. The Windows API was developed in the days when C was the primary language in use, long before the advent of C++, and for this reason structures rather than classes are frequently used for passing data between Windows and your application program.

The Windows API covers all aspects of the communications between Windows and your application. Because there is such a large number of functions in the API, using them in the raw can be very difficult — just understanding what they all are is a task in itself. This is where Visual C++ makes the life of the application developer very much easier. Visual C++ packages the Windows API in a way that structures the functions in an object-oriented manner, and provides an easier way to use the interface in C++ with more default functionality. This takes the form of the Microsoft Foundation Classes, MFC.

Visual C++ also provides Application Wizards that create basic applications of various kinds, including MFC applications. The Application Wizard can generate a complete working application that includes all of the boilerplate code necessary for a basic Windows application, leaving you just to customize this for your particular purposes. The example in Chapter 1 illustrated how much functionality Visual C++ is capable of providing without any coding effort at all on your part. I will discuss this in more detail when we get to write some more examples using the Application Wizard.

Windows Data Types

Windows defines a significant number of data types that are used to specify function parameter types and return types in the Windows API. These Windows-specific types also propagate through to functions that are defined in MFC. Each of these Windows types will map to some C++ type, but because the mapping between Windows types and C++ types can change over time, you should always use the Windows type where this applies. For example, in the past the Windows type WORD has been defined in one version of Windows as type unsigned short and in another Windows version as type unsigned int. On 16-bit machines these types are equivalent, but on 32-bit machines they are decidedly different so anyone using the C++ type rather than the Windows type could run into problems.

You can find the complete list of Windows data types in the documentation, but here are a few of the most common you are likely to meet:

BOOL or BOOLEAN	A Boolean variable can have the values TRUE or FALSE. Note that this is not the same as the C++ type bool, which can have the values true or false.
BYTE	An 8-bit byte.
CHAR	An 8-bit character.
DWORD	A 32-bit unsigned integer that corresponds to type unsigned long in C++.
HANDLE	A handle to an object — a handle being a 32-bit integer value that records the location of an object in memory, or 64-bit when compiling for 64-bit.

HBRUSH	A handle to a brush, a brush being used to fill an area with color.
HCURSOR	A handle to a cursor.
HDC	Handle to a device context — a device context being an object that enables you to draw on a window.
HINSTANCE	Handle to an instance.
LPARAM	A message parameter.
LPCTSTR	LPCWSTR if _UNICODE is defined, otherwise LPCSTR.
LPCWSTR	A pointer to a constant null-terminated string of 16-bit characters.
LPCSTR	A pointer to a constant null-terminated string of 8-bit characters.
LPHANDLE	A pointer to a handle.
LRESULT	A signed value that results from processing a message.
WORD	A 16-bit unsigned integer, so it corresponds to type unsigned short in C++.

I'll introduce any other Windows types we are using in examples as the need arises. All Windows types and the prototypes of the Windows API functions are contained in the header file windows.h, so you need to include this header file when you put your basic Windows program together.

Notation in Windows Programs

In many Windows programs, variable names have a prefix, which indicates what kind of value the variable holds and how it is used. There are quite a few prefixes and they are often used in combination. For example, the prefix lpfn signifies a long pointer to a function. A sample of the prefixes you might come across is:

PREFIX	MEANING
b	a logical variable of type BOOL, equivalent to int
by	type unsigned char; a **byte**
c	type char
dw	type DWORD, which is unsigned long
fn	a **fun**ction
h	a **h**andle, used to reference something
i	type int

continues

(continued)

PREFIX	MEANING
l	type `long`
lp	`long` **pointer**
n	type `unsigned int`
p	a **pointer**
s	a **string**
sz	a **z**ero terminated string
w	type `WORD`, which is `unsigned short`

The use of these prefixes is called *Hungarian notation*. It was introduced to minimize the possibility of misusing a variable by interpreting it differently from how it was defined or intended to be used. Such misinterpretation is easily done in the C language. With C++ and its stronger type checking you don't need to make such a special effort with your notation to avoid such problems. The compiler always flags an error for type inconsistencies in your program, and many of the kinds of bugs that plagued earlier C programs can't occur with C++.

On the other hand, Hungarian notation can still help to make programs easier to understand, particularly when you are dealing with a lot of variables of different types that are arguments to Windows API functions. Because Windows programs are still written in C, and, of course, because parameters for Windows API functions are still defined using Hungarian notation, the method is still used quite widely.

You can make up your own mind as to the extent to which you want to use Hungarian notation, as it is by no means obligatory. You may choose not to use it at all, but in any event, if you have an idea of how it works, you will find it easier to understand what the arguments to the Windows API functions are. There is a small caveat, however. As Windows has developed, the types of some of the API function arguments have changed slightly, but the variable names that are used remain the same. As a consequence, the prefix may not be quite correct in specifying the variable type.

THE STRUCTURE OF A WINDOWS PROGRAM

For a minimal Windows program that just uses the Windows API, you will write two functions. These are a `WinMain()` function, where execution of the program begins and basic program initialization is carried out, and a `WindowProc()` function that is called by Windows to pass messages to the application. The `WindowProc()` part of a Windows program is usually the larger portion because this is where most of the application-specific code is, responding to messages caused by user input of one kind or another.

Although these two functions make up a complete program, they are not directly connected. `WinMain()` does not call `WindowProc()`, Windows does. Windows also calls `WinMain()`. This is illustrated in Figure 11-2.

The `WinMain()` function communicates with Windows by calling Windows API functions. The same applies to `WindowProc()`. The integrating factor in your Windows desktop application is Windows itself, which links to both `WinMain()` and `WindowProc()`. After looking into what the pieces are that make up `WinMain()` and `WindowProc()` you will assemble them into a working example of a simple Windows program.

The WinMain( ) Function

The `WinMain()` function is the equivalent of `main()` in a console program. It's where execution starts and where the basic initialization for the program is carried out. To allow Windows to pass data to it, `WinMain()` has four parameters and a return value of type `int`. Its prototype is:

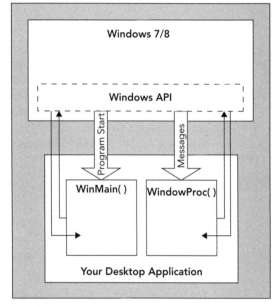

FIGURE 11-2

```
int WINAPI WinMain(HINSTANCE hInstance,
                   HINSTANCE hPrevInstance,
                   LPSTR lpCmdLine,
                   int nCmdShow
                   );
```

Following the return type specifier, `int`, you have a specification for the function, `WINAPI`. This is a Windows-defined macro that causes the function name and arguments to be handled in a special way that is specific to Windows API functions. This is different from the way functions are normally handled in C++. The precise details are unimportant — this is simply the way Windows requires things to be, so you need to put the `WINAPI` macro name in front of the names of functions called by Windows.

> **NOTE** *If you really want to know about calling conventions, they are described in the documentation that comes with Visual C++.* `WINAPI` *is defined as* `__stdcall`, *and putting this modifier before a function name indicates that the standard Windows calling convention is to be used. This requires that the parameters are pushed on the stack in reverse order and that the function that is called will clean up the stack when it ends. The* `CALLBACK` *modifier that you will see later in this chapter is also defined as* `__stdcall` *and is therefore the equivalent of* `WINAPI`. *The standard C++ calling convention is specified by the* `__cdecl` *modifier.*

The four arguments that are passed to your `WinMain()` function contain important data:

➤ `hInstance` is of type `HINSTANCE`, which is a handle to an instance — an instance here being a running program. A *handle* is an integer value that identifies an object of some kind — in this case, the instance of the application. The actual integer value of a handle is not important. There can be several programs in execution at any given instant. This raises the possibility of several copies of the same application being active at once, and this needs to be recognized. Hence, the `hInstance` handle identifies a particular copy. If you start more than one copy of a program, each one has its own unique `hInstance` value. As you will see, handles are used to identify all sorts of other things.

➤ `hPrevInstance` is a legacy from the old 16-bit versions of the Windows operating system, and you can safely ignore it. On current versions of Windows, it is always `nullptr`.

➤ `lpCmdLine` is a pointer to a string containing the command line that started the program. This pointer allows you to pick up any parameter values that may appear in the command line. The type `LPSTR` is another Windows type, specifying a 32-bit (long) pointer to a string, or 64-bit when compiling in 64-bit mode. There is also a version of `WinMain()` that accepts `LPWSTR` for Unicode builds.

➤ `nCmdShow` determines how the window is to look when it is created. It could be displayed normally or it might need to be minimized; for example, if the shortcut for the program specifies that the program should be minimized when it starts. This argument can take one of a fixed set of `int` values that are defined by symbolic constants such as `SW_SHOWNORMAL` and `SW_SHOWMAXIMIZED`. There are nine other constants like these that define the way a window is to be displayed, and they all begin with `SW_`. You don't usually need to examine the value of `nCmdShow`. You typically pass it directly to the Windows API function responsible for displaying your application window.

> **NOTE** *If you want to know what all the constants are that specify how a window displays, you can find a complete list of the possible values if you search for* `WinMain` *in the MSDN Library. You can access the MSDN library online at* `http://msdn.microsoft.com/en-us/library/default.aspx`.

The `WinMain()` function in your program needs to do four things:

➤ Tell Windows what kind of window the program requires

➤ Create the program window

➤ Initialize the program window

➤ Retrieve Windows messages intended for the program

We will take a look at each of these in turn and then create a complete `WinMain()` function.

Specifying a Program Window

The first step in creating a window is to define just what sort of window it is that you want to create. Windows defines a special `struct` type called `WNDCLASSEX` to contain the data specifying a window. The data that is stored in an instance of the `struct` defines a window class, which determines the type of window. You need to create a variable of type `WNDCLASSEX`, and give values to each of its members. After you've filled in the variables, you can pass it to Windows (via a function that you'll see later) to register the class. When that's been done, whenever you want to create a window of that class, you can tell Windows to look up the class that you have already registered.

The definition of the `WNDCLASSEX` structure is:

```
struct WNDCLASSEX
{
  UINT cbSize;             // Size of this object in bytes
  UINT style;             // Window style
  WNDPROC lpfnWndProc;     // Pointer to message processing function
  int cbClsExtra;         // Extra bytes after the window class
  int cbWndExtra;         // Extra bytes after the window instance
  HINSTANCE hInstance;     // The application instance handle
  HICON hIcon;             // The application icon
  HCURSOR hCursor;         // The window cursor
  HBRUSH hbrBackground;    // The brush defining the background color
  LPCTSTR lpszMenuName;    // A pointer to the name of the menu resource
  LPCTSTR lpszClassName;   // A pointer to the class name
  HICON hIconSm;           // A small icon associated with the window
};
```

You construct an object of type `WNDCLASSEX` in the way that you saw when I discussed structures, for example:

```
WNDCLASSEX WindowClass;                 // Create a window class object
```

You can now fill in values for the members of `WindowClass`. They are all `public` by default because `WindowClass` is a `struct`. Setting the value for the `cbSize` member of the `struct` is easy when you use the `sizeof` operator:

```
WindowClass.cbSize = sizeof(WNDCLASSEX);
```

The `style` member of the `struct` determines various aspects of the window's behavior, in particular, the conditions under which the window should be redrawn. You can select from a number of options for this member's value, each defined by a symbolic constant beginning with `CS_`.

> **NOTE** You'll find all the possible constant values for style if you search for "Window Class Styles" in the MSDN Library that you'll find at
> `http://msdn.microsoft.com/en-us/library/default.aspx`.

Where two or more options are required, the constants can be combined to produce a composite value using the bitwise OR operator, |. For example:

```
WindowClass.style = CS_HREDRAW | CS_VREDRAW;
```

The option `CS_HREDRAW` indicates to Windows that the window is to be redrawn if its horizontal width is altered, and `CS_VREDRAW` indicates that it is to be redrawn if the vertical height of the window is changed. In the preceding statement, you have elected to have the window redrawn in either case. As a result, Windows sends a message to your program indicating that you should redraw the window whenever the width or height of the window is altered by the user. Each of the possible options for the window style is defined by a unique bit in a 32-bit word being set to 1. That's why the bitwise OR is used to combine them. These bits indicating a particular style are usually called *flags*. Flags are used very frequently, not only in Windows but also in C++, because they are an efficient way of representing and processing features that are either there or not, or parameters that are either true or false.

The member `lpfnWndProc` stores a pointer to the function in your program that handles messages for the window you create. The prefix to the name signifies that this is a `long` pointer to a function. If you followed the herd and called the function to handle messages for the application `WindowProc()`, you would initialize this member with the statement:

```
WindowClass.lpfnWndProc = WindowProc;
```

The next two members, `cbClsExtra` and `cbWndExtra`, allow you to ask that extra space be provided internally to Windows for your own use. An example of this could be when you want to associate additional data with each instance of a window to assist in message handling for each window instance. Normally you won't need extra space allocated for you, in which case you set the `cbClsExtra` and `cbWndExtra` members to zero.

The `hInstance` member holds the handle for the current application instance, so you should set this to the `hInstance` value that was passed to `WinMain()` by Windows:

```
WindowClass.hInstance = hInstance;
```

The members `hIcon`, `hCursor`, and `hbrBackground` are handles that in turn reference objects that represent:

➤ The application when minimized

➤ The cursor the window uses

➤ The background color of the client area of the window

As you saw earlier, a handle is just a 32-bit integer (or 64-bit when compiled in 64-bit mode) used as an ID to represent something. These members are set using Windows API functions. For example:

```
WindowClass.hIcon = LoadIcon(nullptr, IDI_APPLICATION);
WindowClass.hCursor = LoadCursor(nullptr, IDC_ARROW);
WindowClass.hbrBackground = static_cast<HBRUSH>(GetStockObject(GRAY_BRUSH));
```

All three members are set to standard Windows values by these function calls. The icon is a default provided by Windows and the cursor is the standard arrow cursor used by the majority of Windows applications. A brush is a Windows object used to fill an area, in this case the client area of the window. The function GetStockObject() returns a generic type for all stock objects, so you need to cast it to type HBRUSH. In the preceding example, it returns a handle to the standard gray brush, and the background color for our window is thus set to gray. This function can also be used to obtain other standard objects for a window, such as fonts, for example. You could also set the hIcon and hCursor members to nullptr, in which case Windows would provide the default icon and cursor. If you set hbrBackground to nullptr, your program is expected to paint the window background, and messages are sent to your application whenever this becomes necessary.

The lpszMenuName member is set to the name of a resource defining the window menu, or to nullptr if there is no menu for the window:

```
WindowClass.lpszMenuName = nullptr;
```

You will look into creating and using menu resources when you use the AppWizard.

The lpszClassName member of the struct stores the name that you supply to identify this particular class of window. You would usually use the name of the application for this. You need to keep track of this name because you will need it again when a window is created. This member would therefore be typically set with the statements:

```
static LPCTSTR szAppName { _T("OFWin") };   // Define window class name
WindowClass.lpszClassName = szAppName;      // Set class name
```

I have defined szAppName using the _T() macro that is defined in the tchar.h header. The LPCTSTR type is defined as const wchar_t* if UNICODE is defined for the application, or const char* if it is not. The _T() macro will create a string of the correct type automatically.

The last member is hIconSm, which identifies a small icon associated with the window class. If you specify this as nullptr, Windows searches for a small icon related to the hIcon member and uses that.

Creating a Program Window

After you have set the members of your WNDCLASSEX structure to the values required, the next step is to tell Windows about it. You do this by calling the Windows API function RegisterClassEx(). Given that your WNDCLASSEX structure object is WindowClass, the statement to do this would be:

```
RegisterClassEx(&WindowClass);
```

Easy, isn't it? The address of the struct is passed to the function, and Windows extracts and squirrels away all the values that you have set in the structure members. This process is called *registering* the window class. Just to remind you, the term *class* here is used in the sense of classification and is not the same as the idea of a class in C++, so don't confuse the two. Each instance of the application must make sure that it registers the window classes that it needs.

After Windows knows the characteristics of the window that you want, and the function that is going to handle messages for it, you can go ahead and create it. You call the CreateWindow()

function for this. The window class that you have created determines the broad characteristics of the application window, and further arguments to `CreateWindow()` add additional characteristics. Because an application may have several windows in general, `CreateWindow()` returns a handle to the window it created that you can store to enable you to refer to that particular window later. There are many API calls that require you to specify the window handle as a parameter. Let's look at a typical use of `CreateWindow()`. This might be:

```
HWND hWnd;                                   // Window handle
...
hWnd = CreateWindow(
        szAppName,                           // the window class name
        _T("A Basic Window the Hard Way"),   // The window title
        WS_OVERLAPPEDWINDOW,                 // Window style as overlapped
        CW_USEDEFAULT,                       // Default screen position of upper left
        CW_USEDEFAULT,                       // corner of our window as x,y.
        CW_USEDEFAULT,                       // Default window size, width...
        CW_USEDEFAULT,                       // ...and height
        nullptr,                             // No parent window
        nullptr,                             // No menu
        hInstance,                           // Program Instance handle
        nullptr                              // No window creation data
      );
```

The `hWnd` variable of type `HWND` is a 32-bit integer handle to a window, or 64-bit in 64-bit mode. You use this variable to record the window handle that `CreateWindow()` returns. The first argument that you pass to `CreateWindow()` is the class name. This is used to identify the `WNDCLASSEX` object that you passed to the operating system previously in the `RegisterClassEx()` function call, so that information from this `struct` can be used in the window creation process.

The second argument to `CreateWindow()` defines the text that is to appear on the title bar. The third argument specifies the style that the window has after it is created. The option specified here, `WS_OVERLAPPEDWINDOW`, combines several options. It defines the window as having the `WS_OVERLAPPED`, `WS_CAPTION`, `WS_SYSMENU`, `WS_THICKFRAME`, `WS_MINIMIZEBOX`, and `WS_MAXIMIZEBOX` styles. This results in an overlapped window, which is a window intended to be the main application window, with a title bar and a thick frame, which has a title bar icon, system menu, and maximize and minimize buttons. A window that you specify as having a thick frame has borders that can be resized.

The next four arguments determine the position and size of the window on the screen. The first two are the screen coordinates of the upper-left corner of the window, and the second two define the width and height. The value `CW_USEDEFAULT` indicates that you want Windows to assign the default position and size for the window. This tells Windows to arrange successive windows in cascading positions down the screen. `CW_USEDEFAULT` only applies to windows specified as `WS_OVERLAPPED`.

The next argument value is `nullptr`, indicating that the window being created is not a child window (i.e., not a window that is dependent on a parent window). If you wanted it to be a child window, you would set this argument to the handle of the parent window. The next argument is also `nullptr`, indicating that no menu is required. You then specify the handle of the current instance of the program that was passed to the program by Windows. The last argument for window creation data is `nullptr` because you just want a simple window in the example. If you wanted to create a multiple-document interface (MDI) client window, the last argument would point to a structure related to this. You'll learn more about MDI windows later in the book.

> **NOTE** *The Windows API also includes a* `CreateWindowEx()` *function that you use to create a window with extended style information.*

After you call `CreateWindow()`, the window exists but is not yet displayed on the screen. You must call another Windows API function to get it displayed:

```
ShowWindow(hWnd, nCmdShow);                    // Display the window
```

Only two arguments are required here. The first identifies the window and is the handle returned by `CreateWindow()`. The second is the `nCmdShow` value that was passed to `WinMain()`, which indicates how the window is to appear on-screen.

Initializing the Program Window

After calling `ShowWindow()`, the window appears on-screen but still has no application content, so you need to get your program to draw in the client area of the window. You could just put together some code to do this directly in the `WinMain()` function, but this would be most unsatisfactory: in this case, the contents of the client area would not be permanent — if you want the client area contents to be retained, you can't just output what you want and forget about it. Any action on the part of the user that modifies the window in some way, such as dragging a border or dragging the whole window, typically requires that the window *and* its client area are redrawn.

When the client area needs to be redrawn for any reason, Windows sends a particular message to your program, and your `WindowProc()` function needs to respond by reconstructing the client area of the window. Therefore, the best way to get the client area drawn in the first instance is to put the code to draw the client area in the `WindowProc()` function and get Windows to send the message requesting that the client area be redrawn to your program. Whenever you know in your program that the window should be redrawn (when you change something, for example), you need to tell Windows to send a message back to get the window redrawn.

You can ask Windows to send your program a message to redraw the client area of the window by calling another Windows API function, `UpdateWindow()`. The statement to accomplish this is:

```
UpdateWindow(hWnd);                    // Cause window client area to be drawn
```

This function requires only one argument: the window handle `hWnd`, which identifies your particular program window. The result of the call is that Windows sends a message to your program requesting that the client area be redrawn.

Dealing with Windows Messages

The last task that `WinMain()` needs to address is dealing with the messages that Windows may have queued for your application. This may seem a bit odd because I said earlier that you needed the function `WindowProc()` to deal with messages, but let me explain a little further.

Queued and Non-Queued Messages

I oversimplified Windows messaging when I introduced the idea. There are, in fact, two kinds of Windows messages:

There are *queued messages* that Windows places in a queue, and the `WinMain()` function must extract these messages from the queue for processing. The code in `WinMain()` that does this is called the *message loop*. Queued messages include those arising from user input from the keyboard, moving the mouse, and clicking the mouse buttons. Messages from a timer and the Windows message to request that a window be redrawn are also queued.

There are *non-queued messages* that result in the `WindowProc()` function being called directly by Windows. A lot of the non-queued messages arise as a consequence of processing queued messages. What you are doing in the message loop in `WinMain()` is retrieving a message that Windows has queued for your application and then asking Windows to invoke your `WindowProc()` function to process it. Why can't Windows just call `WindowProc()` whenever necessary? Well, it could, but it just doesn't work this way. The reasons have to do with how Windows manages multiple applications executing simultaneously.

The Message Loop

As I said, retrieving messages from the message queue is done using a standard mechanism in Windows programming called the *message pump* or *message loop*. The code for this would be:

```
MSG msg;                                    // Windows message structure
while(GetMessage(&msg, nullptr, 0, 0) == TRUE)   // Get any messages
{
  TranslateMessage(&msg);                   // Translate the message
  DispatchMessage(&msg);                    // Dispatch the message
}
```

This involves three steps in dealing with each message:

➤ `GetMessage()` — Retrieves a message from the queue.

➤ `TranslateMessage()` — Performs any conversion necessary on the message retrieved.

➤ `DispatchMessage()` — Causes Windows to call the `WindowProc()` function in your application to deal with the message.

The operation of `GetMessage()` is important because it has a significant contribution to the way Windows works with multiple applications, so we should explore it in a little more detail.

The `GetMessage()` function retrieves a message queued for the application window and stores information about the message in the variable `msg`, pointed to by the first argument. The `msg` variable is a `struct` of type `MSG` that contains members that you are not accessing here. Still, for completeness, the definition of the structure looks like this:

```
struct MSG
{
  HWND    hwnd;              // Handle for the relevant window
  UINT    message;           // The message ID
  WPARAM  wParam;            // Message parameter (32-bits)
  LPARAM  lParam;            // Message parameter (32-bits)
  DWORD   time;              // The time when the message was queued
  POINT   pt;                // The mouse position
};
```

The `wParam` member is an example of a slightly misleading Hungarian notation prefix that I mentioned is now possible. You might assume that it was of type `WORD` (a 16-bit `unsigned integer`), which used to be true in earlier Windows versions, but now it is of type `WPARAM`, which is a 32-bit integer value.

The exact contents of the `wParam` and `lParam` members are dependent on what kind of message it is. The message ID in the member `message` is an integer value and can be one of a set of values that are predefined in the header file, `windows.h`, as symbolic constants. Message IDs for general windows all start with `WM_`; typical examples are shown in the following table. General windows messages cover a wide variety of events and include messages relating to mouse and menu events, keyboard input, and window creation and management.

ID	DESCRIPTION
WM_PAINT	The window should be redrawn.
WM_SIZE	The window has been resized.
WM_LBUTTONDOWN	The left mouse button is down.
WM_RBUTTONDOWN	The right mouse button is down.
WM_MOUSEMOVE	The mouse has moved.
WM_CLOSE	The window or application should close.
WM_DESTROY	The window is being destroyed.
WM_QUIT	The program should be terminated.

The function `GetMessage()` always returns `TRUE` unless the message is `WM_QUIT` to end the program, in which case the value returned is `FALSE`, or unless an error occurs, in which case the return value is `-1`. Thus, the `while` loop continues until a quit message is generated to close the application or until an error condition arises. In either case, you need to end the program by passing the `wParam` value back to Windows in a `return` statement.

> **NOTE** *There are prefixes other than* WM *for messages destined for other types of windows than a general window.*

The second argument in the call to GetMessage() is the handle of the window for which you want to get messages. This parameter can be used to retrieve messages for one application window separately from another. If this argument is nullptr, as it is here, GetMessage() retrieves all messages for an application. This is an easy way of retrieving all messages for an application regardless of how many windows it has. It is also the safest way because you are sure of getting all the messages for your application. When the user of your Windows program closes the application window for example, the window is closed before the WM_QUIT message is generated. Consequently, if you only retrieve messages by specifying a window handle to the GetMessage() function, you cannot retrieve the WM_QUIT message and your program is not able to terminate properly.

The last two arguments to GetMessage() are integers that hold minimum and maximum values for the message IDs you want to retrieve from the queue. This allows messages to be retrieved selectively. A range is usually specified by symbolic constants. Using WM_MOUSEFIRST and WM_MOUSELAST as these two arguments would select just mouse messages, for example. If both arguments are zero, as you have them here, all messages are retrieved.

Multitasking

If there are no messages queued, the GetMessage() function does not return control to your program. Windows allows execution to pass to another application, and you will only get a value returned from calling GetMessage() when a message appears in the queue.

This mechanism was fundamental in enabling multiple applications to run under older versions of Windows and is referred to as *cooperative multitasking* because it depends on concurrent applications giving up control of the processor from time to time. After your program calls GetMessage(), unless there is a message for it another application is executed and your program gets another opportunity to do something only if the other application releases the processor, perhaps by a call to GetMessage() when there are no messages queued for it, but this is not the only possibility.

With current versions of Windows, the operating system can interrupt an application after a period of time and transfer control to another application. This mechanism is called *pre-emptive multitasking* because an application can be interrupted at any time. With pre-emptive multitasking, however, you must still program the message loop in WinMain() using GetMessage() as before, and make provision for relinquishing control of the processor to Windows from time to time in a long-running calculation (this is usually done using the PeekMessage() API function). If you don't do this, your application may be unable to respond to messages to repaint the application window when these arise. This can be for reasons that are quite independent of your application — when an overlapping window for another application is closed, for example.

The conceptual operation of the GetMessage() function is illustrated in Figure 11-3.

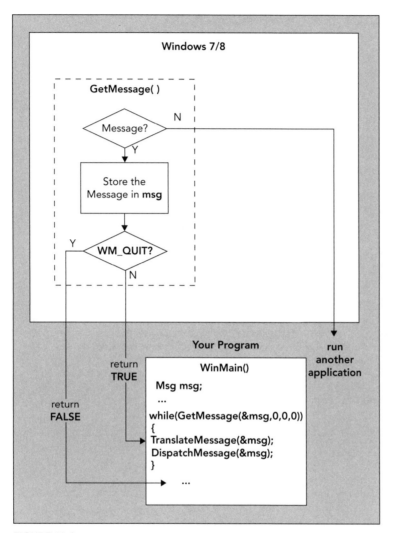

FIGURE 11-3

Within the `while` loop, the first call to `TranslateMessage()` requests Windows to do some conversion work for keyboard-related messages. Then the call to `DispatchMessage()` causes Windows to *dispatch* the message, which it does by calling the `WindowProc()` function in your program to process the message. The return from `DispatchMessage()` does not occur until `WindowProc()` has finished processing the message. A `WM_QUIT` message indicates that the program should end, so this results in `FALSE` being returned to the application, which stops the message loop.

A Complete WinMain( ) Function

You have looked at all the bits that need to go into `WinMain()` so now you can assemble them into a complete function:

```
// Listing OFWIN_1
int WINAPI WinMain(HINSTANCE hInstance, HINSTANCE hPrevInstance,
                   LPSTR lpCmdLine, int nCmdShow)
{
  WNDCLASSEX WindowClass;       // Structure to hold our window's attributes

  static LPCTSTR szAppName { _T("OFWin") };    // Define window class name
  HWND hWnd;                                    // Window handle
  MSG msg;                                      // Windows message structure

  WindowClass.cbSize = sizeof(WNDCLASSEX);     // Set structure size

  // Redraw the window if the size changes
  WindowClass.style   = CS_HREDRAW | CS_VREDRAW;

  // Define the message handling function
  WindowClass.lpfnWndProc = WindowProc;

  WindowClass.cbClsExtra = 0;     // No extra bytes after the window class
  WindowClass.cbWndExtra = 0;     // structure or the window instance

  WindowClass.hInstance = hInstance;            // Application instance handle

  // Set default application icon
  WindowClass.hIcon = LoadIcon(nullptr, IDI_APPLICATION);

  // Set window cursor to be the standard arrow
  WindowClass.hCursor = LoadCursor(nullptr, IDC_ARROW);

  // Set gray brush for background color
  WindowClass.hbrBackground = static_cast<HBRUSH>(GetStockObject(GRAY_BRUSH));

  WindowClass.lpszMenuName = nullptr;           // No menu
  WindowClass.lpszClassName = szAppName;        // Set class name
  WindowClass.hIconSm = nullptr;                // Default small icon

  // Now register our window class
  RegisterClassEx(&WindowClass);

  // Now we can create the window
  hWnd = CreateWindow(
          szAppName,                          // the window class name
          _T("A Basic Window the Hard Way"),  // The window title
          WS_OVERLAPPEDWINDOW,                // Window style as overlapped
          CW_USEDEFAULT,                      // Default position of upper left
          CW_USEDEFAULT,                      // corner of our window as x,y...
          CW_USEDEFAULT,                      // Default window size
          CW_USEDEFAULT,                      // ....
          nullptr,                            // No parent window
```

```
                nullptr,                            // No menu
                hInstance,                          // Program Instance handle
                nullptr                             // No window creation data
            );

        ShowWindow(hWnd, nCmdShow);                 // Display the window
        UpdateWindow(hWnd);                         // Redraw window client area

        // The message loop
        while(GetMessage(&msg, nullptr, 0, 0) == TRUE) // Get any messages
        {
          TranslateMessage(&msg);                   // Translate the message
          DispatchMessage(&msg);                    // Dispatch the message
        }

        return static_cast<int>(msg.wParam);        // End, so return to Windows
    }
```

You need a `WindowProc()` implementation to make this into a working Windows application. We will look at that after we explore how this code works.

How It Works

After declaring the variables that you need in `WinMain()`, all the members of the `WindowClass` structure are initialized and the window is registered. Next you call the `CreateWindow()` function to create the data for the physical appearance of the window based on the arguments and the data established in the `WindowClass` structure that was previously passed to Windows using the `RegisterClassEx()` function. The call to `ShowWindow()` causes the window to be displayed according to the mode specified by nCmdShow, and the `UpdateWindow()` function signals that a message to draw the window client area should be generated.

The message loop retrieves messages until a `WM_QUIT` message is issued for the application. When this occurs, the `GetMessage()` function returns `FALSE` and the loop ends. The value of the `wParam` member of the `msg` structure is passed back to Windows in the `return` statement.

Processing Windows Messages

The `WinMain()` function contains nothing that was application-specific beyond the general appearance of the application window. All of the code that makes the application behave in the way that you want is included in the message processing part of the program. This is the function `WindowProc()` that you identify to Windows in the `WindowClass` structure. Windows calls this function each time a message for your main application window is dispatched. Because you identify your `WindowProc()` function to Windows by a function pointer, you can use any name for the function that you like. I'll continue to call it `WindowProc()`.

This example is simple, so you will be putting all the code to process messages in the one function, `WindowProc()`. More generally, though, the `WindowProc()` function is responsible for analyzing what a given message is and which window it is destined for and then calling one of a whole range of functions, each of which would be geared to handling a particular message in the context of the window concerned. However, the overall sequence of operations and the way in which `WindowProc()` analyzes an incoming message is much the same in most application contexts.

The WindowProc( ) Function

The prototype of the `WindowProc()` function is:

```
LRESULT CALLBACK WindowProc(HWND hWnd, UINT message,
                            WPARAM wParam, LPARAM lParam);
```

The return type is `LRESULT`, which is a Windows type that is normally equivalent to type `long`. Because the function is called by Windows through a pointer (you set up the pointer with the address of `WindowProc()` in `WinMain()` in the `WNDCLASSEX` structure), you need to qualify the function as `CALLBACK`. I mentioned this specifier earlier, and its effect is the same as the `WINAPI` specifier that determines how the function arguments are handled. You could use `WINAPI` here instead of `CALLBACK`, although the latter expresses better what this function is about. The four arguments that are passed to `WindowProc()` provide information about the message causing the function to be called. The meaning of each argument is described in the following table:

ARGUMENT	MEANING
`HWND hWnd`	A handle to the window in which the event causing the message occurred.
`UINT message`	The message ID, which is a 32-bit value indicating the type of message.
`WPARAM wParam`	A 32-bit (or 64-bit in 64-bit mode) value containing additional information depending on what sort of message it is.
`LPARAM lParam`	A 32-bit (or 64-bit in 64-bit mode) value containing additional information depending on what sort of message it is.

The window that the incoming message relates to is identified by the first argument, `hWnd`. In this case, you have only one window, so you can ignore it.

Messages are identified by the `message` value that is passed to `WindowProc()`. You can test this value against predefined symbolic constants, each of which identifies a particular message. General windows messages begin with `WM_`, and typical examples are `WM_PAINT`, which corresponds to a request to redraw part of the client area of a window, and `WM_LBUTTONDOWN`, which indicates that the left mouse button was pressed. You can find the whole set of these by searching for `WM_` in the MSDN Library.

Decoding a Windows Message

Decoding the message that Windows sends is usually done using a `switch` statement in the `WindowProc()` function, based on the value of `message`. You select the message types that you want to process by putting a `case` statement for each message ID in the `switch`. The typical structure of such a `switch` statement is:

```
switch(message)
{
  case WM_PAINT:
    // Code to deal with drawing the client area
    break;

  case WM_LBUTTONDOWN:
    // Code to deal with the left mouse button being pressed
    break;

  case WM_LBUTTONUP:
    // Code to deal with the left mouse button being released
    break;

  case WM_DESTROY:
    // Code to deal with a window being destroyed
    break;

  default:
    // Code to handle any other messages
}
```

Every Windows program has something like this somewhere, although it will be hidden from sight in the Windows programs that you will write later using MFC. Each case corresponds to a particular message ID and provides suitable processing for that message. Any messages that a program does not want to deal with individually are handled by the default statement, which should hand the messages back to Windows by calling DefWindowProc(). This is the Windows API function that provides default message handling.

In a complex program dealing with a wide range of possible Windows messages, this switch statement can become large and rather cumbersome. When you get to use the Application Wizard to generate a Windows application that uses the MFC, you won't have to worry about this because it is all taken care of for you and you never see the WindowProc() function. You just need to supply the code to process the messages in which you are interested.

Drawing the Window Client Area

Windows sends a WM_PAINT message to the program to signal that the client area should be redrawn. So you need to draw the client area of the window in response to the WM_PAINT message.

You can't go drawing in the window willy-nilly. Before you can write to the application window, you need to tell Windows that you want to do so, and get Windows' authority to go ahead. You do this by calling the Windows API function BeginPaint(), which should only be called in response to a WM_PAINT message. It is used like this:

```
HDC hDC;                          // A display context handle
PAINTSTRUCT PaintSt;              // Structure defining area to be redrawn

hDC = BeginPaint(hWnd, &PaintSt); // Prepare to draw in the window
```

The HDC type represents a handle to a *display context*, or more generally a *device context*. A device context provides the link between the device-independent Windows API functions for outputting information to the screen or a printer, and the device drivers that support writing to the specific devices attached to your PC. You can also regard a device context as a token of authority that is handed to you on request by Windows and grants you permission to output some information. Without a device context, you simply can't generate any output.

The `BeginPaint()` function returns a handle to a display context. It requires two arguments. The first argument is a handle, `hWnd`, for the window to which you want to write. The second argument is the address of a `PAINTSTRUCT` variable `PaintSt`, in which Windows will place information about the area that is to be redrawn in response to the `WM_PAINT` message. I will ignore the details of this because you are not going to use it. You will just redraw the whole of the client area. You can obtain the coordinates of the client area in a `RECT` structure with the statements:

```
RECT aRect;                          // A working rectangle
GetClientRect(hWnd, &aRect);
```

The `GetClientRect()` function supplies the coordinates of the upper-left and lower-right corners of the client area for the window specified by the first argument. These coordinates are stored in the `RECT` structure `aRect` that you create, and you pass the address of this structure as the second argument. You can use `aRect` to identify the area in the client area where the text is to be written by the `DrawText()` function. Because your window has a gray background, you should alter the background of the text to be transparent, to allow the gray to show through; otherwise, the text appears against a white background. You can do this with this API function call:

```
SetBkMode(hDC, TRANSPARENT);         // Set text background mode
```

The first argument identifies the device context and the second sets the background mode. The default option is `OPAQUE`.

You can now write the text with the statement:

```
DrawText(hDC,                        // Device context handle
        _T("But, soft! What light through yonder window breaks?"),
        -1,                          // Indicate null terminated string
        &aRect,                      // Rectangle in which text is to be drawn
        DT_SINGLELINE|               // Text format - single line
        DT_CENTER|                   //              - centered in the line
        DT_VCENTER                   //              - line centered in aRect
    );
```

The first argument to the `DrawText()` function is your certificate of authority to draw on the window, the display context `hDC`. The next argument is the text string that you want to output. You could equally well have defined this in a variable and passed the pointer to the text as the second argument in the function call. The next argument, with the value `-1`, signifies that your string is terminated with a null character. If it weren't, you would put the count of the number of characters in the string here. The fourth argument is a pointer to a `RECT` structure defining a rectangle in which you want to write the text. In this case, it is the whole client area of the window defined in `aRect`. The last argument defines the format for the text in the rectangle. Here you have combined three specifications with a bitwise OR (|). The string is written as a single line, with the text centered on the line and the line centered vertically within the rectangle. This places it nicely in the center of the window. There are also a number of other options, which include the possibility to place text at the top or the bottom of the rectangle, and to left- or right-justify it.

After you have written all that you want to display, you must tell Windows that you have finished drawing the client area. For every `BeginPaint()` function call, there must be a corresponding `EndPaint()` function call. Thus, to end processing of the `WM_PAINT` message, you need the statement:

```
EndPaint(hWnd, &PaintSt);            // Terminate window redraw operation
```

The `hWnd` argument identifies your program window, and the second argument is the address of the `PAINTSTRUCT` structure that was filled in by the `BeginPaint()` function.

Ending the Program

You might assume that closing the window closes the application, but to get this behavior, you actually have to add some more code. The reason that the application won't close by default when the window is closed is that you may need to do some clearing up. It is also possible that the application may have more than one window. When the user closes the window by double-clicking the title bar icon or clicking the Close button, this causes a `WM_DESTROY` message to be generated. Therefore, to close the application, you need to process the `WM_DESTROY` message in `WindowProc()`. You do this by generating a `WM_QUIT` message:

```
PostQuitMessage(0);
```

The argument here is an exit code. This API function does exactly what its name suggests: it posts a `WM_QUIT` message in the message queue for your application. This results in the `GetMessage()` function that is called in `WinMain()` returning `FALSE` and ending the message loop, thus ending the program.

A Complete WindowProc( ) Function

You have covered all the elements necessary to assemble the complete `WindowProc()` function for the example. The code for the function is:

```
// Listing OFWIN_2
LRESULT CALLBACK WindowProc(HWND hWnd, UINT message,
                      WPARAM wParam, LPARAM lParam)
{

  switch(message)                    // Process selected messages
  {
    case WM_PAINT:                         // Message is to redraw the window
      HDC hDC;                             // Display context handle
      PAINTSTRUCT PaintSt;                 // Structure defining area to be drawn
      RECT aRect;                          // A working rectangle
      hDC = BeginPaint(hWnd, &PaintSt);// Prepare to draw the window

      // Get upper left and lower right of client area
      GetClientRect(hWnd, &aRect);
```

```
        SetBkMode(hDC, TRANSPARENT);      // Set text background mode

        // Now draw the text in the window client area
        DrawText(
            hDC,                          // Device context handle
            _T("But, soft! What light through yonder window breaks?"),
            -1,                           // Indicate null terminated string
            &aRect,                       // Rectangle in which text is to be drawn
            DT_SINGLELINE|                // Text format - single line
            DT_CENTER|                    //               - centered in the line
            DT_VCENTER);                  //               - line centered in aRect

        EndPaint(hWnd, &PaintSt);   // Terminate window redraw operation
        return 0;

      case WM_DESTROY:              // Window is being destroyed
        PostQuitMessage(0);
        return 0;
    }
    return DefWindowProc(hWnd, message, wParam, lParam);
}
```

How It Works

Apart from the last statement, the entire function body is just a `switch` statement. A particular `case` is selected based on the message ID that is passed to the function through the `message` parameter. Because this example is simple, you need to process only two types of message: `WM_PAINT` and `WM_DESTROY`. You hand all other messages back to Windows by calling the `DefWindowProc()` function after the `switch` statement. The arguments to `DefWindowProc()` are those that were passed to the function, so you are just passing them back as they are. Note the `return` statement at the end of processing each message type. For the messages that you handle, a zero value is returned.

TRY IT OUT   A Simple Windows API Program

Because you have written `WinMain()` and `WindowProc()` to handle messages, you have enough to create a complete Windows program using just the Windows API. Of course, you'll need to create a project for this program, but instead of choosing Win32 Console Application as you've done up to now, you should create this project using the Win32 Project template. You should elect to create it as an empty project with the name `Ex11_01` and add the `Ex11_01.cpp` file that will contain the following code:

```
// Ex11_01.cpp   Native windows program to display text in a window
#include <windows.h>
#include <tchar.h>
LRESULT CALLBACK WindowProc(HWND hWnd, UINT message,
                    WPARAM wParam, LPARAM lParam);

    // Insert code for WinMain() here (Listing OFWIN_1)

    // Insert code for WindowProc() here (Listing OFWIN_2)
```

If you build and execute the example, it produces the window shown in Figure 11-4.

Note that the window has a number of properties provided by the operating system that require no programming effort on your part to manage. The boundaries of the window can be dragged to resize it, and the whole window can be moved about on-screen. The maximize and minimize buttons also work. Of course, all of these actions do affect the program. Every time you modify the position or size of the window, a WM_PAINT message is queued and your program has to redraw the client area, but all the work of drawing and modifying the window itself is done by Windows.

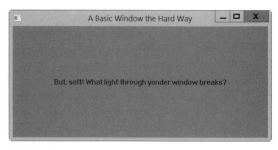

FIGURE 11-4

The system menu and Close button are also standard features of your window because of the options that you specified in the WindowClass structure. Again, Windows takes care of the management. The only additional effect on your program arising from this is the passing of a WM_DESTROY message if you close the window, as previously discussed.

THE MICROSOFT FOUNDATION CLASSES

The *Microsoft Foundation Classes (MFC)* are a set of predefined classes that make it easy to develop Windows desktop applications with Visual C++. These classes represent an object-oriented approach to Windows programming that encapsulates the Windows API. MFC does not adhere strictly to the object-oriented principles of encapsulation and data hiding, principally because much of the MFC code was written before such principles were well established.

The process of writing a Windows program involves creating and using MFC objects or objects of classes derived from MFC. In the main, you'll derive your own classes from MFC, with considerable assistance from the specialized tools in Visual C++ that make this easy. The objects of these MFC-based class types incorporate member functions for communicating with Windows, for processing Windows messages, and for sending messages to each other. Your derived classes inherit all of the members of their base classes. These inherited functions do practically all of the general grunt work necessary for a Windows application to work. All you need to do is to add data and function members to the classes to provide the application-specific functionality that you need in your program. In doing this, you'll apply most of the techniques that you've been grappling with in the preceding chapters, particularly those involving class inheritance and virtual functions.

MFC Notation

All the classes in MFC have names beginning with C, such as CDocument or CView. If you use the same convention when defining your own classes, or when deriving them from those in the MFC library, your programs will be easier to follow. Data members of an MFC class are prefixed with m_. I'll also follow this convention in the MFC examples.

You'll find that the MFC uses Hungarian notation for many variable names, particularly those that originate in the Windows API. As you recall, this involves using a prefix of p for a pointer, n for an unsigned int, l for long, h for a handle, and so on. The name m_lpCmdLine, for example, refers to a data member of a class (because of the m_ prefix) that is of type 'long pointer to a string'. Because C++ has strong type checking that picks up the sort of misuse that used to happen regularly in C, this kind of notation isn't essential, so I won't use it generally for variables in the examples in the book. I will, however, retain the p prefix for pointers and some of the other simple type denotations because this helps to make the code more readable.

How an MFC Program Is Structured

You know from Chapter 1 that you can produce a Windows program using the Application Wizard without writing a single line of code. Of course, this uses the MFC library, but it's quite possible to write a Windows program that uses MFC without using the Application Wizard. If you first scratch the surface by constructing the minimum MFC-based program, you'll get a clearer idea of the fundamental elements involved.

The simplest program that you can produce using MFC is slightly less sophisticated than the example that you wrote earlier in this chapter using the raw Windows API. The example you'll produce here has a window, but no text displayed in it. This is sufficient to show the fundamentals, so try it out.

TRY IT OUT   A Minimal MFC Application

Create a new project using the File ➪ New ➪ Project menu option, as you've done many times before. You won't use the Application Wizard that creates the basic code here, so select the template for the project as Win32 Project and choose Windows Application and the Empty project options in the second dialog. After the project is created, select Project ➪ Properties from the main menu, and on the General sub-page from Configuration Properties, click the Use of MFC property to set its value to Use MFC in a Shared DLL.

With the project created, you can create a new source file in the project as Ex11_02.cpp. So that you can see all the code for the program in one place, put the class definitions you need together with their implementations in this file. To achieve this, just add the code manually in the edit window — there isn't very much of it.

To begin with, add a statement to include the header file afxwin.h, as this contains the definitions for many MFC classes. This allows you to derive your own classes from MFC:

```
#include <afxwin.h>                    // For the class library
```

To produce the complete program, you'll only need to derive two classes from MFC: an *application class* and a *window class*. You won't even need to write a WinMain() function, as you did in the previous example in this chapter, because this is automatically provided by the MFC library behind the scenes. Take a look at how you define the two classes that you need.

The Application Class

The CWinApp class is fundamental to any Windows program written using the MFC. An object of this class type includes everything necessary for starting, initializing, running, and closing the application.

You need to derive your own application class from `CWinApp` to produce your application type. You will define a specialized version of the class to suit your application needs. The code for this is as follows:

```
class COurApp: public CWinApp

{
public:
  virtual BOOL InitInstance() override;

};
```

As you might expect for a simple example, there isn't a great deal of specialization necessary. You've only included one member in the definition of the class: the `InitInstance()` function. This function is defined as a virtual function in the base class, so it's an override in your derived class; you are simply redefining the base class function for your application class. All the other data and function members that you need in the class are inherited from `CWinApp`.

The application class is endowed with quite a number of data members, many of which correspond to variables that are used as arguments in Windows API function calls. For example, the `m_pszAppName` member stores a pointer to a string that defines the name of the application. The `m_nCmdShow` member specifies how the application window is to be shown when the application starts up. You don't need to go into all the inherited data members now. You'll see how they are used as the need arises in developing application-specific code.

In deriving your own application class from `CWinApp`, you must implement `InitInstance()`. Your version will be called by the version of `WinMain()` that's provided by the MFC, and you'll include code in the function to create and display your application window. However, before you write `InitInstance()`, I should introduce you to an MFC class that defines a window.

The Window Class

Your MFC application needs a window to provide the interface to the user; this is referred to as a *frame window*. You derive a window class for the application from the MFC class `CFrameWnd`, which is designed specifically for this purpose. Because `CFrameWnd` provides everything for creating and managing an application window, all you need to add to the derived class is a constructor. This will enable you to specify the title bar text for the window to suit the application context:

```
class COurWnd: public CFrameWnd
{
public:
  // Constructor
  COurWnd()
  {
    Create(nullptr, _T("Our Dumb MFC Application"));
  }
};
```

The `Create()` function that you call in the constructor is inherited from the base class. It creates the window and attaches it to the `COurWnd` object that is being created. Note that the `COurWnd` object is not the same thing as the window that is displayed by Windows — the class object and the physical window are distinct entities.

The first argument value for the Create() function, nullptr, specifies that you want to use the base class default attributes for the window — you'll recall that you needed to define window attributes in the previous example in this chapter that used the Windows API directly. The second argument specifies the text that is to be displayed in the window title bar. You won't be surprised to learn that there are other parameters to the function Create(), but they all have default values that are quite satisfactory so you can ignore them here.

Completing the Program

Having defined a window class for the application, you can implement the InitInstance() function in our COurApp class:

```
BOOL COurApp::InitInstance(void)
{
  m_pMainWnd = new COurWnd;                // Construct a window object...
  m_pMainWnd->ShowWindow(m_nCmdShow);      // ...and display it
  return TRUE;
}
```

This overrides the virtual function defined in the base class CWinApp, and as I said previously, it is called by the WinMain() function that's automatically supplied by the MFC library. The InitInstance() function constructs a main window object for the application in the free store by using the operator new. You store the address that is returned in the variable m_pMainWnd, which is an inherited member of your COurApp class. The effect of this is that the window object is owned by the application object. You don't even need to worry about freeing the memory for the object you have created — the supplied WinMain() function takes care of any cleanup necessary.

The only other item you need for a complete, albeit rather limited, program is to define an application object. An instance of our application class, COurApp, must exist before WinMain() is executed, so you must declare it at global scope with the statement:

```
COurApp AnApplication;       // Define an application object
```

The reason that this object needs to exist at global scope is that it encapsulates the application, and the application needs to exist before it can start executing. The WinMain() function that is provided by the MFC calls the InitInstance() member of the application object to construct the window object, which implies that the application object must already exist.

The Finished Product

Now that you've seen all the code, you can add it to the Ex11_02.cpp source file in the project. Classes are usually defined in .h files and the member functions that are not defined within the class definitions are defined in .cpp files. This application is so short that you may as well put it all in a single .cpp file. The merit of this is that you can view the whole lot together. The program code is:

```
// Ex11_02.cpp  An elementary MFC program
#include <afxwin.h>                       // For the class library

// Application class definition
class COurApp:publicCWinApp
{
```

```
public:
  virtual BOOL InitInstance() override;
};

// Window class definition
class COurWnd:publicCFrameWnd
{
public:
  // Constructor
  COurWnd()
  {
  Create(nullptr, _T("Our Dumb MFC Application"));
  }
};

// Function to create an instance of the main application window
BOOL COurApp::InitInstance(void)
{
  m_pMainWnd = new COurWnd;                 // Construct a window object...
  m_pMainWnd->ShowWindow(m_nCmdShow);       // ...and display it
  return TRUE;
}

// Application object definition at global scope
COurApp AnApplication;                              // Define an application object
```

That's all you need. It looks a bit odd because no `WinMain()` function appears, but as I noted previously, there is a `WinMain()` function supplied by the MFC library.

How It Works

Now you're ready to roll, so build and run the application. Select the Build ➪ Build Ex11_02 menu item, click the appropriate toolbar button, or just press F7 to build the solution. You should end up with a clean compile and link, in which case you can press Ctrl+F5 to run it. Your minimum MFC program appears as shown in Figure 11-5.

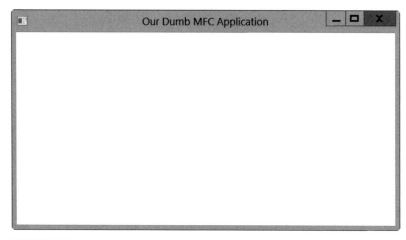

FIGURE 11-5

You can resize the window by dragging the border, move the whole thing around, and minimize or maximize it in the usual ways. The only other function that the program supports is "close," for which you can use the system menu, the Close button at the upper right of the window, or just key Alt+F4. It doesn't look like much, but considering that there are so few lines of code, it's quite impressive.

SUMMARY

In this chapter you've seen two ways of creating an elementary Windows application with Visual C++. You should now have a feel for the relationship between these two approaches. In subsequent chapters you'll be exploring in more depth how you develop applications using the MFC.

➤ WHAT YOU LEARNED IN THIS CHAPTER

TOPIC	CONCEPT
Windows API	The Windows API provides a standard programming interface by which a desktop application communicates with the Windows operating system.
Windows messages	Windows communicates with a desktop application by passing messages to it. A message typically indicates that an event of some kind has occurred that requires action on the part of the application.
Windows application structure	All Windows desktop applications must include two functions, `WinMain()` and `WindowProc()`, that will be called by the operating system. You can use any name you like for the `WindowProc()` function.
The `WinMain()` function	The `WinMain()` function is called by the operating system to begin execution of an application. The function includes code to set up the initial conditions required by the application, to specify the application window, and to retrieve messages from the operating system that are intended for the application.
The `WindowProc()` function	The Windows operating system calls a particular function that is usually called `WindowProc()` to process messages. A desktop application identifies the message processing function for each application window in `WinMain()` by passing a pointer to the message processing function to a Windows API function as part of a `WNDCLASSEX` structure.
The Microsoft Foundation Classes	The MFC consists of a set of classes that encapsulate the Windows API and greatly simplify the development of Windows desktop applications.

12

Windows Programming with the Microsoft Foundation Classes (MFC)

WHAT YOU WILL LEARN IN THIS CHAPTER:

➤ The basic elements of an MFC-based program

➤ The difference between Single Document Interface (SDI) applications and Multiple Document Interface (MDI) applications

➤ How to use the MFC Application Wizard to generate SDI and MDI programs

➤ The files generated by the MFC Application Wizard and what they contain

➤ How an MFC Application Wizard-generated program is structured

➤ The key classes in an MFC Application Wizard-generated program, and how they are interconnected

➤ How to customize an MFC Application Wizard-generated program

WROX.COM CODE DOWNLOADS FOR THIS CHAPTER

You can find the wrox.com code downloads for this chapter on the Download Code tab at www.wrox.com/go/beginningvisualc. The code is in the Chapter 11 download and individually named according to the names throughout the chapter.

THE MFC DOCUMENT/VIEW CONCEPT

When you write applications using the MFC, it implies acceptance of a specific structure for your program, with application data stored and processed in a particular way. This may sound restrictive, but it really isn't for the most part, and the benefits in speed and ease of implementation far outweigh any disadvantages. The structure of an MFC program incorporates two application-oriented entities — a document and a view — so let's look at what they are and how they're used.

What Is a Document?

A *document* is a collection of data in your application with which the user interacts. Although the word *document* seems to imply something of a textual nature, it isn't limited to text. It could be data for a game, a geometric model, a text file, a collection of data on the distribution of orange trees in California, or, indeed, anything you want. The term document is just a convenient label for the application data in your program, treated as a unit.

You won't be surprised to hear that a document is defined as an object of a document class. Your document class is derived from the CDocument class in the MFC library, and you add your own data members to store items that your application requires, and member functions to support processing of that data. Your application is not limited to a single document type; you can define multiple document classes when there are several different kinds of documents involved in your application.

Handling application data in this way enables standard mechanisms to be provided within the MFC for managing a collection of application data as a unit and for storing the data on disk. These mechanisms are inherited by your document class from CDocument, so you get a broad range of functionality built into your application automatically, without having to write any code.

Document Interfaces

You have a choice as to whether your program deals with just one document at a time, or with several. The *Single Document Interface (SDI)* is supported by the MFC for programs that require only one document to be open at a time. A program using this interface is an *SDI application*.

For programs needing several documents to be open at one time, you use the *Multiple Document Interface (MDI)*. With the MDI, as well as being able to open multiple documents of one type, your program can also be organized to handle documents of different types simultaneously with each document displayed in its own window. Of course, you need to supply the code to deal with processing all the types of documents you intend to use. In an MDI application, each document is displayed in a child window of the application window. You also have an application variant called the *multiple top-level document architecture* where each document window is a child of the desktop.

What Is a View?

A *view* always relates to a particular document object. A document object contains a set of application data, and a view is an object that provides a mechanism for displaying some or all of that data. A view defines how the data is to be displayed in a window and how the user can interact with it.

You define a view class by deriving it from the MFC class, CView. Note that a view object and the window, in which it is displayed, are distinct. The window in which a view appears is called a *frame window*. A view is displayed in its own window that exactly fills the client area of a frame window. Figure 12-1 illustrates how a document might be displayed in two views.

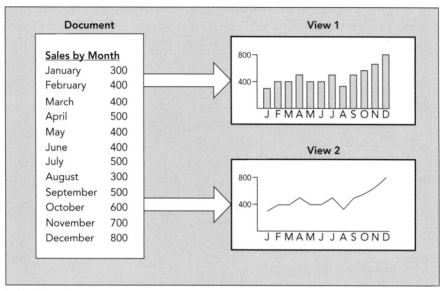

FIGURE 12-1

In Figure 12-1, each view displays all the data that the document contains in a different form, although a view could display just part of the data if that's what's required.

A document can have as many view objects associated with it as you want. Each view can provide a different presentation of the document data or a subset of the data. If you were dealing with text, for example, different views could display independent blocks of text from the same document. For a program handling graphical data, you could display the document data at different scales in separate windows, or in different formats, such as a textual representation of the elements that form the image. Figure 12-1 illustrates a document that contains numerical data — product sales data by month — where one view provides a bar chart representation of sales performance and a second view shows the data in the form of a graph.

Linking a Document and Its Views

The MFC incorporates a mechanism for integrating a document with its views, and each frame window with a currently active view. A document automatically maintains a list of pointers to its associated views, and a view object has a data member holding a pointer to the document to which it relates. Each frame window stores a pointer to the currently active view. The coordination between a document, a view, and a frame window is established by another MFC class of objects called document templates.

Document Templates

A *document template* manages the document objects in your program, as well as the windows and views associated with each of them. There is one document template for each type of document that you have in your application. If you have two or more documents of the same type, you need only one document template to manage them. A document template object creates document objects and frame window objects, and views for a document are created by a frame window object. The application object that is fundamental to every MFC application creates the document template object. Figure 12-2 shows a graphical representation of these interrelationships.

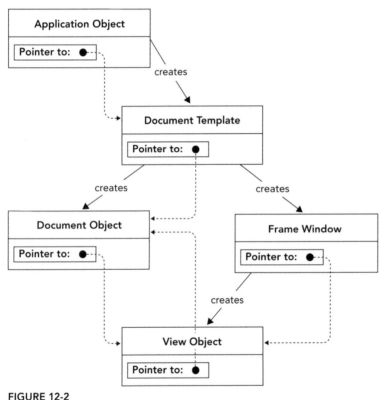

FIGURE 12-2

Figure 12-2 uses dashed arrows to show how pointers are used to relate objects. These pointers enable function members of one object to access the public data or function members in the interface of another object.

Document Template Classes

The MFC has two document template classes. CSingleDocTemplate is used for SDI applications. This is relatively straightforward because an SDI application has only one document and usually just one view. MDI applications are rather more complicated. They have multiple documents active at one time and the `CMultiDocTemplate` class defines the document template. You'll see more of these classes as you develop application code.

Your Application and MFC

Figure 12-3 shows the four basic classes that are going to appear in virtually all your MFC-based Windows applications:

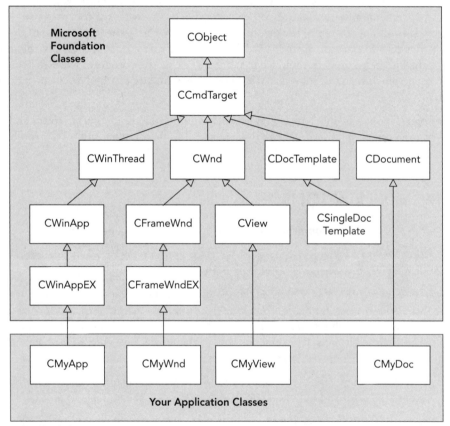

FIGURE 12-3

➤ The application class `CMyApp`

➤ The frame window class `CMyWnd`

➤ The view class `CMyView`, which defines how data contained in `CMyDoc` is to be displayed in the client area of a window created by a `CMyWnd` object

➤ The document class `CMyDoc`, defining a document to contain the application data

The names for these classes are specific to an application, but the derivation from the MFC is much the same, although there can be alternative base classes, particularly with the view class. The

MFC provides several variations of the view class that provide a lot of prepackaged functionality, saving you lots of coding. You normally don't need to extend the document template class so the standard `CSingleDocTemplate` class usually suffices in an SDI program. `CMultiDocTemplate` is the document template class in an MDI program and this is also derived from `CDocTemplate`. An MDI application also contains an additional class that defines a child window.

The arrows in Figure 12-3 point from a derived class to a base class. The MFC classes shown here form quite a complex inheritance structure, but these are just a very small part of the complete MFC structure. You need not be concerned about the details of the complete MFC hierarchy, but it is important to have a general appreciation of it if you want to understand what the inherited members of your classes are. You will not see any of the definitions of the base classes in your code, but the inherited members in a derived class are accumulated from the direct base class and each of the indirect base classes in the hierarchy. To determine what members one of your program's classes has, you need to know from which classes it inherits. After you know that, you can look up its members using the Help facility.

You don't need to worry about remembering which classes you need to have in your program and what base classes to use in their definition. As you'll see next, all of this is taken care of for you by Visual C++.

CREATING MFC APPLICATIONS

You use four primary tools in the development of your MFC-based Windows programs:

1. An *Application Wizard* for creating the basic application program code when you start. You use an Application Wizard whenever you create a project.

2. The *project context menu* in Class View enables you to add new classes and resources to a project. You display this menu by right-clicking the project name in the Class View pane and using the Add/Class menu item to add a new class. Resources are composed of non-executable data such as bitmaps, icons, menus, and dialog boxes. The Add/Resource menu item from the same menu helps you to add a new resource.

3. The *class context menu* in Class View enables you to extend and customize classes in your program. You use the Add/Add Function and Add/Add Variable menu items to do this.

4. You use a *Resource Editor* for creating or modifying resources such as menus and toolbars.

There are several resource editors; the one you use in any particular situation depends on the kind of resource that you're editing. You'll look at editing resources in the next chapter, but for now, let's jump in and create an MFC application.

Creating an MFC application is just as straightforward as creating a console program; there are just a few more choices along the way. As you have already seen, you start by creating a new project by selecting the File ⇨ New ⇨ Project menu item, or you can use the shortcut and press Ctrl+Shift+N. The New Project dialog box is displayed, where you can choose MFC as the project type and MFC Application as the template to be used. You also need to enter a name for the project, which can be anything you want — I've used `TextEditor`. You won't be developing this particular example into a serious application, so you can use any name you like.

The name that you assign to the project — TextEditor in this case — is used as the name of the folder that contains all the project files. It is also used as the basis for creating the names for classes that the Application Wizard generates for your project. When you click OK in the New Project dialog window, you'll see the MFC Application Wizard dialog, where you can choose options for the application, as shown in Figure 12-4.

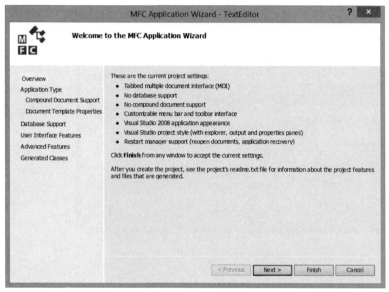

FIGURE 12-4

The dialog explains the project settings that are currently in effect, and in the left pane you have a range of options. You can choose any of these to have a look if you want — you can always get back to the base dialog by selecting the Overview option. Selecting any of the options on the left presents you with a range of further choices, so there are a lot of options in total. I won't discuss all of them — I'll just outline the ones that you are most likely to be interested in and leave you to investigate the others. Selecting Application Type enables you to choose from an SDI application, an MDI application that optionally can be tabbed, a dialog-based application, or an application with multiple top-level documents. Let's create an SDI application first and explore what some of the choices are.

Creating an SDI Application

Select the Application Type option from the list in the left dialog pane. The default option selected is Multiple documents with the tabbed option, which selects the MDI with each document in its own tabbed page; the appearance of this is shown at the top left in the dialog so that you'll know what to expect. Select the Single document Application type option, the MFC standard Project style option, and the Windows Native/Default option from the drop-down list of visual styles. The representation for the application that is shown top-left changes to a single window, as shown in Figure 12-5.

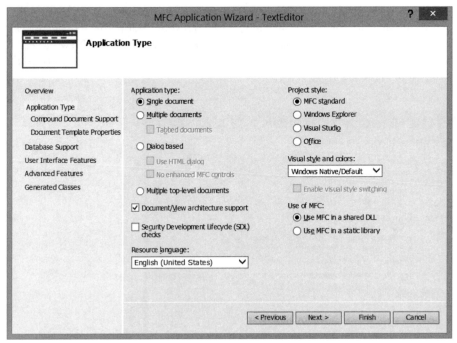

FIGURE 12-5

Some of the other options you have for the application type are:

OPTION	DESCRIPTION
Dialog based	The application window is a dialog window rather than a frame window.
Multiple top-level documents	Documents are displayed in child windows of the desktop rather than child windows of the application as they are with an MDI application.
Document/View architecture support	This option is selected by default so you get code built in to support the document/view architecture. If you uncheck this option, the support is not provided and it's up to you to implement whatever you want.
Resource language	The list box displays the choices available that apply to resources such as menus and text strings.
Project style	Here you can choose the visual appearance of the application window. Your choice will depend on the environment in which you want to run the application and the kind of application. For example, you would select the Office option for a Microsoft Office–related application.

If you hover the mouse cursor over any of the options, a tooltip will be displayed explaining the option.

You have several options for the Project style. I'll select the MFC Standard option and suggest that you do the same. I also selected Windows Native/Default from the Visual style and colors drop-down list. This makes the application appearance the same as your current operating system.

You can also choose how the MFC library is used in your project. The default choice of using the MFC library as a shared DLL (*Dynamic Link Library*) means that your program links to MFC routines at run time. This reduces the size of the executable file that you'll generate, but requires the MFC DLL to be on the machine that's running it. Your application's .exe module and the MFC .dll together may be bigger than if you statically link the MFC library. If you opt for static linking, the MFC library routines are included in the executable module for your program when it is built. If you keep the default option, several programs running simultaneously using the dynamic link library can all share a single copy of the library in memory.

If you select Document Template Properties in the left pane of the dialog, you can enter a file extension for files that the program creates in the right pane. The extension txt is a good choice for this example. You can also enter a Filter Name, which is the name of the filter that will appear in Open and Save As dialogs to filter the file list so only files with your file extension are displayed.

If you select User Interface Features from the list in the left pane, you get a further set of options that can be included in your application:

OPTION	DESCRIPTION
Thick Frame	Enables you to resize the application window by dragging a border. It is selected by default.
Minimize box	This is also selected by default and provides a minimize box at the top right of the application window.
Maximize box	This option is also selected by default and provides a maximize box at the top right of the application window.
Minimized	If you select this option, the application starts with the window minimized so it appears as an icon.
Maximized	With this option selected, the application starts with the window maximized.
System Menu	This provides the main application window with a control-menu box in the title bar.
About box	This provides your application with an About dialog.
Initial status bar	This adds a status bar at the bottom of the application window containing indicators for CAPS LOCK, NUM LOCK, and SCROLL LOCK and a message line that displays help strings for menus and toolbar buttons. It also adds menu commands to hide or show the status bar.
Split window	This provides a splitter bar for each of the application's main views.

In the Command bars sub-options you can choose whether you use a classic Windows menu with a docking toolbar, an Internet Explorer style toolbar, a menu bar and toolbar that you can customize at run time, or a ribbon. The User-defined toolbars and images sub-option allows the toolbar and images to be customized at run time. The Personalized menu behavior sub-option enables menus to display only the items used most frequently. You would typically use a ribbon with applications that complement Microsoft Office. In this example, we will use the classic menu with a classic docking toolbar.

You should be aware of a couple of features under the Advanced Features set of options. One is Printing and print preview, which is selected by default, and the other is the number of files on the recent file list. You can increase the latter to whatever you think is useful for the application. Printing and print preview add the standard Page Setup, Print Preview, and Print items to the File menu, and the Application Wizard also provides code to support these functions. You can uncheck all the other options for the example.

The Generated Classes option in the left pane of the dialog displays a list of the classes that will be generated, as shown in Figure 12-6.

You can highlight any class in the list by clicking it, and the boxes below show the class name, the header filename in which the class definition will be stored, the base class, and the name of the source file containing the implementation of the class. The class definition is always in an .h file, and the member function definitions are always in a .cpp file.

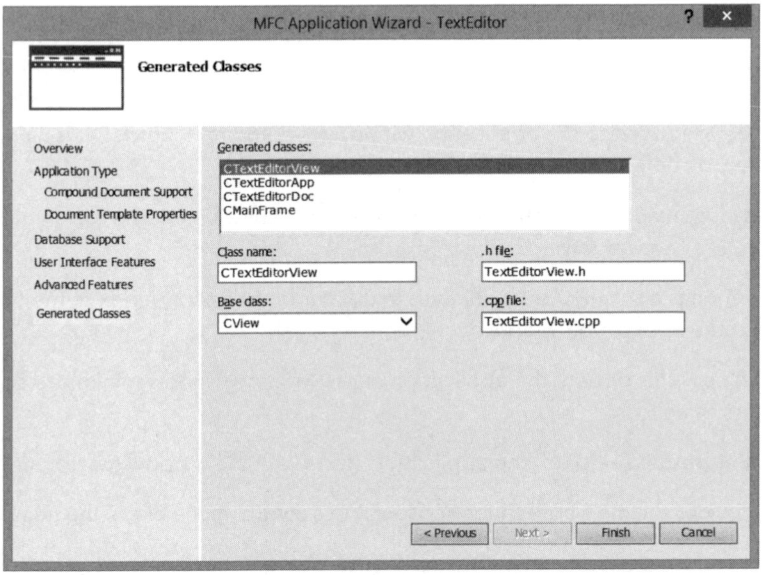

FIGURE 12-6

You can alter everything except the base class for the CTextEditorDoc class. The only thing you can change for CTextEditorApp is the class name. Try clicking the other classes in the list. For CMainFrame, you can alter everything except the base class, and for the CTextEditorView class shown in Figure 12-6, you can change the base class as well. Click the down arrow to display the list of other classes that you can have as a base class. The capability built into your view class depends on which base class you select:

BASE CLASS	VIEW CLASS CAPABILITY
`CEditView`	Provides simple multiline text-editing capability, including find and replace, and printing.
`CFormView`	Provides a view that is a form; a form is a dialog that can contain controls for displaying data and for input.
`CHtmlEditView`	Extends the `CHtmlView` class and adds the ability to edit HTML pages.
`CHtmlView`	Provides a view in which web pages and local HTML documents can be displayed.
`CListView`	Enables you to use the document-view architecture with list controls.
`CRichEditView`	Provides the capability to display and edit documents containing rich edit text.
`CScrollView`	Provides a view that automatically adds scrollbars when the data that is displayed requires them.
`CTreeView`	Provides the capability to use the document-view architecture with tree controls.
`CView`	Provides the basic capability for viewing a document.

Because you've called the application `TextEditor`, with the notion that it is able to edit text, choose `CEditView` to get basic text editing. You can now click Finish to generate the program files for a fully working base program using the options you've chosen. This will take a little while.

MFC Application Wizard Output

All the program files generated by the Application Wizard are stored in the `TextEditor` project folder, which is a subfolder to the solution folder with the same name. There are resource files in the `res` subfolder to the project folder. The IDE provides several ways for you to view the information relating to your project:

TAB/PANE	CONTENTS
Solution Explorer	Shows the files included in your project. The files are categorized in virtual folders with the names `Header Files`, `Resource Files`, and `Source Files`.
Class View	Displays the classes in your project and their members and any global entities. The classes are shown in the upper pane, and the lower pane displays the members for the class selected in the upper pane. By right-clicking entities in Class View, you can display a menu that you can use to view the definition of the entity or where it is referenced.
Resource View	Displays resources such as menu items and toolbar buttons used by your project. Right-clicking a resource displays a menu for editing the resource or adding new resources.

continues

(continued)

TAB/PANE	CONTENTS
Property Manager	Displays the versions you can build for your project. The debug version includes extra facilities to make debugging easier. The release version results in a smaller executable, and you build this version when your code is fully tested. By right-clicking a version you can display a context menu where you can add a property sheet or display the properties currently set for that version. A property sheet enables you to set options for the compiler and linker.

You can switch to view any of these by selecting from the View menu or clicking on a tab label. If you right-click TextEditor in the Solution Explorer pane and select Properties from the pop-up, the project properties window is displayed, as shown in Figure 12-7.

The left pane shows the property groups you can select to be displayed in the right pane. Currently, the General group of properties is displayed. You can change the value for a property in the right pane by clicking it and selecting a new value from the drop-down list box to the right of the property name or, in some cases, by entering a new value.

At the top of the property pages window, you can see the current project configuration and the target platform when the project is built. You can change these by selecting from the drop-down list for each. By selecting All Configurations you can change properties for both the Debug and Release configurations.

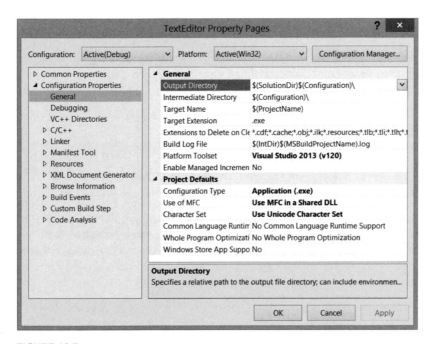

FIGURE 12-7

Viewing Project Files

The left pane in the IDE can display several tabs. The most useful are the Solution Explorer, Class View, and Resource View tabs. You can hide the currently visible tab by clicking the down arrow in the top right of the pane and selecting Hide from the menu. I'll just show the three interesting tabs in figures. I'll also show the pane as an undocked window, which you get by dragging its title bar away from the edge of the main window.

If you select the Solution Explorer tab and expand the list by clicking the arrow symbol for `TextEditor` files and then click the arrow symbol for each of the Source Files, Header Files, and Resource Files folders, you'll see the complete list of files for the project, as shown in Figure 12-8. To collapse any expanded branch of the tree, just click the arrow symbol.

There are a total of 18 files shown in the project, excluding `ReadMe.txt`. You can view the contents of any file by double-clicking the filename. The contents of the file selected are displayed in the Editor window. Try it out with the `ReadMe.txt` file. You'll see that it contains a brief explanation of the contents of each of the files that make up the project. I won't repeat the descriptions of the files here, because they are very clearly summarized in `ReadMe.txt`.

FIGURE 12-8

Viewing Classes

The Class View tab is often more convenient than the Solution Explorer tab because classes are the basis for the organization of the application. When you want to look at the code, it's typically a class definition or the implementation of a member function you want, and from Class View you can go directly to either. The Solution Explorer pane comes in handy when you want to check the `#include` directives in a `.cpp` file. From Solution Explorer you can open the file you're interested in directly.

In the Class View pane, you can expand the `TextEditor` classes item to show the classes defined for the application. Clicking the name of any class shows the members of that class in the lower pane. In the Class View pane shown in Figure 12-9, the `CTextEditorDoc` class has been selected.

The icons characterize the things that are displayed. You will find a key to what the icons indicate in the Class View documentation. Search for "Class View and Object Browser Icons." You can see that you have the four classes that I discussed earlier that are fundamental to an MFC application: `CTextEditorApp` for the application, `CMainFrame`

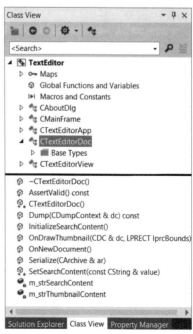

FIGURE 12-9

for the application frame window, `CTextEditorDoc` for the document, and `CTextEditorView` for the view. You also have a `CAboutDlg` class that defines objects that support the dialog box that appears when you select the menu item Help ➪ About in the application. If you select Global Functions and Variables, you'll see that it contains three items, as in Figure 12-10.

The application object, `theApp`, appears twice because there is an `extern` statement for `theApp` in `TextEditor.h` and a definition for it in `TextEditor.cpp`. If you double-click either of the appearances of `theApp`, it will take you to the corresponding statement. `indicators` is an array of four IDs for items that appear in the status bar: a separator, caps lock status, num lock status, and scroll lock status.

To view the code for a class definition double-click the class name in Class View. Similarly, to view the code for a member function, double-click the function name. Note that you can

FIGURE 12-10

drag the edges of any of the panes in an IDE window to view its contents or your code more easily. You can hide or show the set of panes by clicking the close button at the right end of the pane title bar.

The Class Definitions

I won't go into the application classes in complete detail here — you'll just get a feel for how they look and I'll highlight a few important aspects. The precise content of each class that is generated depends on the options you select when creating the project. If you double-click the name of a class in the Class View, the code defining the class is displayed.

The Application Class

Take a look at the application class, `CTextEditorApp`, first. The definition for this class is shown here:

```
// TextEditor.h : main header file for the TextEditor application
//
#pragma once

#ifndef __AFXWIN_H__
  #error "include 'stdafx.h' before including this file for PCH"
#endif

#include "resource.h"       // main symbols


// CTextEditorApp:
// See TextEditor.cpp for the implementation of this class
//
```

```
class CTextEditorApp : public CWinApp
{
public:
  CTextEditorApp();


// Overrides
public:
  virtual BOOL InitInstance();

// Implementation
  afx_msg void OnAppAbout();
  DECLARE_MESSAGE_MAP()
};

extern CTextEditorApp theApp;
```

The `CTextEditorApp` class derives from `CWinApp` and includes a constructor, a virtual function `InitInstance()`, a function `OnAppAbout()`, and a macro `DECLARE_MESSAGE_MAP()`.

> **NOTE** *A macro is not C++ code. It's a name defined by a `#define` pre-processor directive that will be replaced by some text that will normally be code but could also be constants or symbols of some kind.*

The `DECLARE_MESSAGE_MAP()` macro defines which Windows messages are handled by which member functions of the class. The macro appears in the definition of any class that can process Windows messages. Of course, our application class inherits a lot of functions and data members from the base class, and you will be looking further into these as you expand the program examples. If you look at the beginning of the code for the class definition, you will notice that the `#pragma once` directive prevents the file being included more than once. Following that is a group of preprocessor directives that ensure that the `stdafx.h` file is included before this file.

The Frame Window Class

The application frame window for our SDI program is created by an object of the class `CMainFrame`, which is defined by the following code:

```
// MainFrm.h : interface of the CMainFrame class
//

#pragma once

class CMainFrame : public CFrameWnd
{
```

```
protected: // create from serialization only
  CMainFrame();
  DECLARE_DYNCREATE(CMainFrame)

// Attributes
public:

// Operations
public:

// Overrides
public:
  virtual BOOL PreCreateWindow(CREATESTRUCT& cs);

// Implementation
public:
  virtual ~CMainFrame();
#ifdef _DEBUG
  virtual void AssertValid() const;
  virtual void Dump(CDumpContext& dc) const;
#endif

protected:  // control bar embedded members
  CToolBar          m_wndToolBar;
  CStatusBar        m_wndStatusBar;

// Generated message map functions
protected:
  afx_msg int OnCreate(LPCREATESTRUCT lpCreateStruct);
  DECLARE_MESSAGE_MAP()

};
```

This class is derived from CFrameWnd, which provides most of the functionality required for our application frame window. The derived class includes two protected data members — m_wndToolBar, and m_wndStatusBar, which are instances of the MFC classes CToolBar, and CStatusBar, respectively. The toolbar provides buttons to access standard menu functions, and the status bar appears at the bottom of the application window.

The Document Class

The definition of the CTextEditorDoc class that was created is:

```
// TextEditorDoc.h : interface of the CTextEditorDoc class
//


#pragma once


class CTextEditorDoc : public CDocument
{
protected: // create from serialization only
```

```
        CTextEditorDoc();
        DECLARE_DYNCREATE(CTextEditorDoc)

// Attributes
public:

// Operations
public:

// Overrides
public:
    virtual BOOL OnNewDocument();
    virtual void Serialize(CArchive& ar);
#ifdef SHARED_HANDLERS
    virtual void InitializeSearchContent();
    virtual void OnDrawThumbnail(CDC& dc, LPRECT lprcBounds);
#endif // SHARED_HANDLERS

// Implementation
public:
    virtual ~CTextEditorDoc();
#ifdef _DEBUG
    virtual void AssertValid() const;
    virtual void Dump(CDumpContext& dc) const;
#endif

protected:

// Generated message map functions
protected:
    DECLARE_MESSAGE_MAP()

#ifdef SHARED_HANDLERS
    // Helper function that sets search content for a Search Handler
    void SetSearchContent(const CString& value);
#endif // SHARED_HANDLERS

#ifdef SHARED_HANDLERS
private:
    CString m_strSearchContent;
    CString m_strThumbnailContent;
#endif // SHARED_HANDLERS
};
```

Most of the meat comes from the base class and is therefore not apparent here. The DECLARE_DYNCREATE() macro that appears after the constructor (and was also used in CMainFrame) enables an object of the class to be created dynamically by synthesizing it from data from a file. When you save an SDI document object, the frame window that contains the view is saved along with your data. This allows everything to be restored when you read it back. Reading and writing a document object to a file is supported by a process called *serialization*. You will see how to serialize your own documents and then read them back in the examples we will develop.

The document class also includes the DECLARE_MESSAGE_MAP() macro to enable Windows messages to be handled by class member functions.

The View Class

The view class in our SDI application is defined as:

```
// TextEditorView.h : interface of the CTextEditorView class
//

#pragma once


class CTextEditorView : public CEditView
{
protected: // create from serialization only
  CTextEditorView();
  DECLARE_DYNCREATE(CTextEditorView)

// Attributes
public:
  CTextEditorDoc* GetDocument() const;

// Operations
public:

// Overrides
public:
  virtual BOOL PreCreateWindow(CREATESTRUCT& cs);
protected:
  virtual BOOL OnPreparePrinting(CPrintInfo* pInfo);
  virtual void OnBeginPrinting(CDC* pDC, CPrintInfo* pInfo);
  virtual void OnEndPrinting(CDC* pDC, CPrintInfo* pInfo);

// Implementation
public:
  virtual ~CTextEditorView();
#ifdef _DEBUG
  virtual void AssertValid() const;
  virtual void Dump(CDumpContext& dc) const;
#endif

protected:

// Generated message map functions
protected:
  DECLARE_MESSAGE_MAP()
};

#ifndef _DEBUG  // debug version in TextEditorView.cpp
inline CTextEditorDoc* CTextEditorView::GetDocument() const
  { return reinterpret_cast<CTextEditorDoc*>(m_pDocument); }
#endif
```

As you specified in the Application Wizard dialog, the view class is derived from CEditView, which already includes basic text handling facilities. The GetDocument() function returns a pointer to the document object corresponding to the view, and you use this to access data in the document object when you add your own extensions to the view class that allow user interactions to add to or modify the document data.

There are two implementations for the `GetDocument()` member of the `CTextEditorView` class in the code generated by Application Wizard. The one in the `.cpp` file is used for the debug version of the program. You will normally use this during program development because it provides validation of the pointer value stored for the document. (This is stored in the inherited data member `m_pDocument` in the view class.) The version that applies to the release version of your program you can find after the class definition in `TextEditorView.h`. This version is declared as `inline` and it does not validate the document pointer. The `GetDocument()` function provides the view object with access to the document object. You can call any of the functions in the interface to the document class using the pointer to the document that the function returns.

By default, you have debug capability included. As well as the special version of `GetDocument()`, there are lots of checks in the MFC code that are included in this case. If you want to change this, you can use the drop-down list box in the Build toolbar to choose the release configuration, which doesn't contain the debug code.

Creating an Executable Module

To compile and link the program, you can click Build ➪ Build Solution, or press F7, or click the Build icon in the toolbar.

The first time you compile and link a program, it will take some time. The second and subsequent times should be quite a bit faster because of *precompiled headers*. During the initial compilation, the compiler saves the output from compiling header files included in stdafx.cpp. in a file with the extension `.pch`. On subsequent builds, if the source in a header has not changed, the compiler will skip compiling the header and use the precompiled code, thus saving the compilation time for the header.

You can determine whether or not precompiled headers are used and control how they are handled through the Properties dialog. Right-click `TextEditor` in Class View and select Properties from the menu. If you expand the C/C++ node, you can select Precompiled Headers to set or unset this property.

Running the Program

To execute the program, press Ctrl+F5. Because you chose `CEditView` as the base class for the `CTextEditorView` class, the program is a fully functioning, simple text editor. You can enter text in the window, as shown in Figure 12-11.

Note that the application has scroll bars for viewing text outside the visible area within the window, and, of course, you can resize the window by dragging the boundaries. All the items under all menus are fully operational so you can save and retrieve files, you can cut and paste text, and you can print the text in

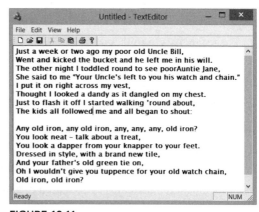

FIGURE 12-11

the window — and all that without writing a single line of code! As you move the cursor over the tool-bar buttons or the menu options, prompts appear in the status bar describing their functions, and if you let the cursor linger on a toolbar button, a tooltip is displayed showing its purpose. (You'll learn about tooltips in more detail in Chapter 13.)

How the Program Works

The application object is created at global scope. You can see this if you expand Global Functions and Variables in Class View and double-click the second `theApp`. In the Editor window, you'll see this statement:

```
CTextEditorApp theApp;
```

This declares `theApp` as an instance of our application class `CTextEditorApp`. The statement is in `TextEditor.cpp`, which also contains member function definitions for the application class, and the definition of the `CAboutDlg` class.

After `theApp` has been created, the MFC-supplied `WinMain()` function is called. This calls two member functions of the `theApp` object. First, it calls `InitInstance()`, which provides any initialization of the application that is necessary, and then the `Run()` function that is inherited from `CWinApp`, which provides initial handling for Windows messages. If you want to see the code for `CWinApp` functions, extend the tree for `CTextEditorApp` in Class View and extend `Base Types`. You can then click on `CWinApp` to see the members in the lower pane. `WinMain()` does not appear explicitly in the project source code, because it is supplied by the MFC class library and is called automatically when the application starts.

The InitInstance() Function

You can access the code for the `InitInstance()` function by double-clicking its entry in Class View after highlighting `CTextEditorApp` — or, if you're in a hurry, you can just look at the code immediately following the line defining the `theApp` object. There's a lot of code in the version created by the Application Wizard, so I just want to remark on a couple of fragments in this function. The first is:

```
SetRegistryKey(_T("Local AppWizard-Generated Applications"));
LoadStdProfileSettings(4);  // Load standard INI file options (including MRU)
```

The string passed to the `SetRegistryKey()` function defines a registry key under which program information is stored. You can change this to whatever you want. If I changed the argument to `"Horton"`, information about our program would be stored under the registry key:

```
HKEY_CURRENT_USER\Software\Horton\TextEditor\
```

All the application settings are stored under this key, including the most recently used files list. The call to `LoadStdProfileSettings()` loads the application settings that were saved last time around. Of course, the first time you run the program, there aren't any.

A document template object is created dynamically within `InitInstance()` by the statement:

```
pDocTemplate = new CSingleDocTemplate(
    IDR_MAINFRAME,
```

```
RUNTIME_CLASS(CTextEditorDoc),
RUNTIME_CLASS(CMainFrame),        // main SDI frame window
RUNTIME_CLASS(CTextEditorView));
```

The first parameter to the `CSingleDocTemplate` constructor is a symbol, `IDR_MAINFRAME`, which defines the menu and toolbar to be used with the document type. The following three parameters define the document, the mainframe window, and the View Class objects that are to be bound together within the document template. Because you have an SDI application here, there is only one of each in the program, managed through one document template object. `RUNTIME_CLASS()` is a macro that enables the type of a class object to be determined at run time.

There's a lot of other stuff here for setting up the application instance that you need not worry about. You can add any initialization of your own that you need for the application to the `InitInstance()` function.

The Run() Function

The `CTextEditorApp` class inherits the `Run()` function from `CWinApp`. Because the function is declared as *virtual*, you could replace the inherited version with your own, but this is not usually necessary. `Run()` receives all the messages from Windows destined for the application and ensures that each message is passed to the function designated to service it, if one exists. Therefore, this function continues executing as long as the application runs.

You can boil the operation of the application down to four steps:

1. Creating an application object, `theApp`.

2. Executing `WinMain()`, which is supplied by MFC.

3. `WinMain()` calling `InitInstance()`, which creates the document template, the mainframe window, the document, and the view.

4. `WinMain()` calling `Run()`, which executes the main message loop to acquire and dispatch Windows messages.

Creating an MDI Application

Now let's create an MDI application using the MFC Application Wizard. Press Ctrl+Shift+N and give the project the name **Sketcher** — and plan on keeping it. You'll be expanding this into a sketching program during subsequent chapters. You should have no trouble with this procedure, because there are only a few things that you need to do differently from creating the SDI application.

1. For the Application Type group of options:

   ➤ Leave the default option, Multiple documents, but opt out of Tabbed documents.

   ➤ Keep Document/View architecture support.

   ➤ Select MFC standard as the project style and Windows Native/Default as the Visual style and colors option.

2. Compound Document Support options should be the default selection, None.

3. For the Document Template Properties set of options in the dialog:

   ➤ Specify the file extension as ske. You'll see that you automatically get a filter for *.ske documents defined.

   ➤ Change the Doc type name to Sketch.

   ➤ Change the File new short name to Sketch.

4. Leave the Database Support options at the default settings, None.

5. For the User Interface Features options:

   ➤ Keep Use a classic menu, and the sub-option, Use a classic docking toolbar.

   ➤ Keep the other options that are selected by default: Thick frame, Minimize box, Maximize box, System menu, Initial status bar, Child minimize box and Child maximize box.

6. For the Advanced features set of options:

   ➤ Keep the Printing and print preview option.

   ➤ Deselect ActiveX controls, and Support Restart Manager.

7. Leave the Generated Classes options at the default settings so the base class for the CSketcherView class is CView.

You can see in the dialog with Generated Classes selected that you get an extra class for your application compared with the TextEditor example, the CChildFrame class, which is derived from CMDIChildWnd. This class provides a frame window for a view of the document that appears inside the application window created by a CMainFrame object. With an SDI application, there is a single document with a single view, so the view is displayed in the client area of the mainframe window. In an MDI application, you can have multiple documents open, and each document can have multiple views. To provide for this, each document view has its own child frame window created by a CChildFrame object. As you saw earlier, a view is displayed in a separate window, but one which exactly fills the client area of a frame window. Finally, click Finish to generate the project.

Running the Program

You can build and run the program by pressing Ctrl+F5. You get the application window shown in Figure 12-12.

In addition to the main application window, you have a separate document window with the caption Sketch1. Sketch1 is the default name for the initial document, and it has the extension .ske if you save it. You can create additional views for

FIGURE 12-12

the document by selecting the Window ⇨ New Window menu option. You can also create a new document by selecting File ⇨ New, so that there will be two active documents in the application. The situation with two views open for a document, is shown in Figure 12-13.

You can expand either sketch window to fill the client area. You can then switch between the sketch windows through the Window drop-down menu. You can't yet actually create any data in the application because we haven't added any code to do that, but all the code for creating documents and views has already been included by the Application Wizard.

FIGURE 12-13

SUMMARY

In this chapter, you've been concerned with the mechanics of using the MFC Application Wizard. You have seen the basic components of the MFC programs that the Application Wizard generates for both SDI and MDI applications. All our MFC examples are created by the MFC Application Wizard, so it's a good idea to keep the general structure and broad class relationships in mind. You probably won't feel comfortable with the details at this point, but don't worry about that. You'll find it becomes much clearer after you begin developing applications in the succeeding chapters.

EXERCISES

It isn't possible to give programming examples for this chapter, because it really just introduced the basic mechanics of creating MFC applications. There aren't solutions to all the exercises because you will either see the answer for yourself on the screen, or be able to check your answer with the text.

1. What is the relationship between a document and a view?

2. What is the purpose of the document template in an MFC Windows program?

3. Why do you need to be careful, and plan your program structure in advance, when using the Application Wizard?

4. Code up the simple text editor program. Build both debug and release versions, and examine the types and sizes of the files produced in each case.

5. Generate the text editor application several times, trying different project styles from the Application Type in Application Wizard.

➤ **WHAT YOU LEARNED IN THIS CHAPTER**

TOPIC	CONCEPT
The Application Wizard	The MFC Application Wizard generates a complete, working, framework Windows application for you to customize to your requirements.
SDI and MDI programs	The Application Wizard can generate single-document interface (SDI) applications that work with a single document and a single view, or multiple-document interface (MDI) programs that can handle multiple documents with multiple views simultaneously.
Classes in SDI programs	The four essential classes in an SDI application that are derived from the foundation classes are the application class, the frame window class, the document class, and the view class.
The application object	A program can have only one application object. This is defined automatically by the Application Wizard at global scope.
Document objects	A document class object stores application-specific data, and a view class object displays the contents of a document object.
Document templates	A document template class object is used to tie together a document, a view, and a window. For an SDI application, a `CSingleDocTemplate` class does this, and for an MDI application, the `CMultiDocTemplate` class is used. These are both foundation classes, and application-specific versions do not normally need to be derived.

13

Working with Menus and Toolbars

WHAT YOU WILL LEARN IN THIS CHAPTER:

➤ How an MFC-based program handles messages

➤ How you create and modify menu resources

➤ How you create and modify menu properties

➤ How to create functions to service menu messages

➤ How to add handlers to update menu properties

➤ How to add toolbar buttons associated with menu items

COMMUNICATING WITH WINDOWS

Windows communicates with your program by sending messages to it. Most of the drudgery of message handling is taken care of in an MFC application, so you don't have to worry about providing a `WndProc()` function. The MFC enables you to provide functions to handle the individual messages that you're interested in and to ignore the rest. These functions are referred to as *message handlers* or just *handlers*. In an MFC-based program, a message handler is always a member of one of your application's classes.

The association between a particular message and a function in your program that is to service it is established by a *message map*, and each class in your program that handles Windows messages will have one. A message map is a table of member functions that handle messages bounded by a couple of macros. The start of a message map is indicated by a BEGIN_MESSAGE_MAP() macro, and the end is marked by an END_MESSAGE_MAP() macro. Each entry in the message map associates a member function with a particular message; when a given message occurs, the corresponding function is called. Only the messages that are relevant to a class appear in its message map.

A message map for a class is created by the MFC Application Wizard when you create a project, or by Class Wizard when you add a class that handles messages. Additions to, and deletions from, a message map are mainly managed by Class Wizard, but there are circumstances in which you need to modify a message map manually. Let's look into how a message map operates using the Sketcher example.

Understanding Message Maps

A message map is established by the MFC Application Wizard for each class in your program. In Sketcher CSketcherApp, CSketcherDoc, CSketcherView, CMainFrame, and CChildFrame each have a message map. The message map for a class appears in the .cpp file. Of course, the functions that are in the message map are also declared in the class, but they are identified in the message map in a special way. Look at the definition for CSketcherApp in Sketcher.h:

```
class CSketcherApp : public CWinApp
{
public:
  CSketcherApp();


// Overrides
public:
  virtual BOOL InitInstance();
  virtual int ExitInstance();

// Implementation
  afx_msg void OnAppAbout();
  DECLARE_MESSAGE_MAP()
};
```

OnAppAbout() is the only message handler declared in the class. The afx_msg at the beginning of the line declaring the OnAppAbout() function identifies it as a message handler. afx_msg has no other purpose and is converted to white space by the preprocessor, so it has no effect when the program is compiled.

The DECLARE_MESSAGE_MAP() macro indicates that the class can contain members that are message handlers and therefore will have a message map in the .cpp file. Any class that has CCmdTarget as a direct or indirect base class can have message handlers, so such classes will always have this macro included as part of the class definition, either by the MFC Application Wizard or by the Add Class Wizard that you use to add a new class. The CSketcherApp class has CCmdTarget as an indirect base and therefore always includes the DECLARE_MESSAGE_MAP() macro. All the other application classes in Sketcher are ultimately derived from CCmdTarget too, so they all can handle messages.

When you add your own members directly to a class, it's best to leave the DECLARE_MESSAGE_MAP() macro as the last line in the class definition. If you do add members after DECLARE_MESSAGE_MAP(), you'll need to include an access specifier for them: public, protected, or private.

Message Handler Definitions

A class definition that includes the DECLARE_MESSAGE_MAP() macro will have the BEGIN_MESSAGE_MAP() and END_MESSAGE_MAP() macros in its .cpp file. If you look in Sketcher.cpp, you'll see the following code as part of the implementation of CSketcherApp:

```
BEGIN_MESSAGE_MAP(CSketcherApp, CWinApp)
  ON_COMMAND(ID_APP_ABOUT, &CSketcherApp::OnAppAbout)
  // Standard file based document commands
  ON_COMMAND(ID_FILE_NEW, &CWinApp::OnFileNew)
  ON_COMMAND(ID_FILE_OPEN, &CWinApp::OnFileOpen)
  // Standard print setup command
  ON_COMMAND(ID_FILE_PRINT_SETUP, &CWinApp::OnFilePrintSetup)
END_MESSAGE_MAP()
```

This is a message map. The BEGIN_MESSAGE_MAP() and END_MESSAGE_MAP() macros define its boundaries, and each message handler in the class appears between these macros. These message handlers are all dealing with the same type of message, WM_COMMAND messages. These are called *command messages*. A command message is generated when the user selects a menu option or enters an accelerator key. (There's another kind of WM_COMMAND message called a *control notification message*, which provides information about the activity of a control.)

The message map identifies the menu item or key press that will cause a handler to be called by an identifier (ID) that's included in the message handler macro. There are four ON_COMMAND macros in the preceding code, one for each of the command messages to be handled by the CSketcherApp object. The first argument to an ON_COMMAND macro is an ID identifying a particular command source, and the macro ties the address of a function (i.e., a pointer to a function) to commands originating from the source specified by the ID. Thus, when a command message corresponding to the identifier ID_APP_ABOUT is received, the OnAppAbout() function is called. Similarly, for a command message corresponding to the ID_FILE_NEW identifier, OnFileNew() is called. This handler is inherited from the base class, CWinApp, as are the two remaining handlers.

The BEGIN_MESSAGE_MAP() macro has two arguments. The first identifies the class name for which the message map is defined, and the second identifies the base class that will be searched for a message handler when a handler isn't found in the class that defined the message map.

Command IDs for messages from standard menu items and toolbar buttons such as ID_APP_ABOUT are defined in the MFC. The ID_ prefix identifies a command as associated with a menu item or a toolbar button, as you'll see when I discuss resources later. For example, ID_FILE_NEW is the ID that corresponds to the selection of the File ⇨ New menu item, and ID_APP_ABOUT corresponds to Help ⇨ About.

The WM_ prefix for message IDs stands for "Windows message." There are many other identifiers for Windows messages and these are defined in Winuser.h along with a lot of other stuff. This header is included in Windows.h. If you want to look at the message IDs, you'll find Winuser.h in the C:\ Program Files (x86)\Windows Kits\8.1\Include\um folder.

> **NOTE** *There's a nice shortcut for viewing any* .h *file that appears in an* #include *directive in the editor window — you can right-click the name and select Open Document "Filename.h" from the menu. This works with standard library header files as well as those you have created.*

Windows messages often have additional data values that refine the identification of a particular message specified by a given ID. The WM_COMMAND message, for instance, is sent for a range of commands, including those originating from the selection of a menu item or a toolbar button.

When you are adding message handlers manually, you should not map a message (or, in the case of command messages, a command ID) to more than one message handler. If you do, it won't break anything, but the second message handler is never called. Normally, you add message handlers through the Properties window for a class, and in this case you will not be able to map a message to more than one handler. To see the Properties window for a class such as CSketcherApp, right-click its name in Class View and select Properties from the menu. You add a message handler by selecting the Messages button at the top of the Properties window that is displayed (see Figure 13-1). To determine which button is the Messages button, simply hover the cursor over each button until the tooltip displays.

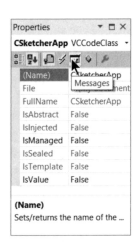

FIGURE 13-1

Clicking the Messages button brings up a list of message IDs; however, before I go into what you do next, I'll explain a little more about the types of messages you may be handling.

Message Categories

Many Windows messages are identified by an ID with the prefix WM_. There are many categories, and the category to which a message belongs determines how it is handled. The categories of Windows messages that your program may be dealing with include:

MESSAGE CATEGORY	DESCRIPTION
Standard Windows messages	These are Windows messages that begin with the WM_ prefix other than WM_COMMAND messages. Examples of these messages are WM_PAINT, which indicates that you need to redraw the client area of a window, and WM_LBUTTONUP, which signals that the left mouse button has been released.

MESSAGE CATEGORY	DESCRIPTION
Control notification messages	These are WM_COMMAND messages sent from controls (such as a list box) to the window that created the control or from a child window to a parent window. Parameters associated with a WM_COMMAND message enable messages from the controls in your application to be differentiated.
Command messages	These are WM_COMMAND messages that originate from user interface elements such as menu items and toolbar buttons. MFC defines unique identifiers for standard menu and toolbar command messages.

You'll be writing handlers for standard Windows messages in the first category in the next chapter. The messages in the second category are a group of WM_COMMAND messages that you'll see in Chapter 16 when you work with dialogs. You'll deal with command messages originating from menus and toolbars in this chapter. In addition to the message IDs defined by the MFC for standard menus and toolbars, you can define your own message IDs for menus and toolbar buttons that you create. If you don't supply IDs for these, MFC generates IDs based on the menu text.

Handling Messages in Your Program

You can't put message handlers anywhere you like. The classes where you can implement a handler depend on the kind of message. The first two categories in the previous section — standard Windows messages and control notification messages — are always handled by objects of classes that are ultimately derived from CWnd. Frame window classes and view classes, for example, have CWnd as an indirect base class, so they can handle Windows messages and control notification messages. Application classes, document classes, and document template classes are not derived from CWnd, so they can't handle these messages.

Using the Properties window for a class to add a handler solves the problem of remembering where to place handlers, because it only offers you the IDs allowed for the class. For example, you won't be offered any of the WM_ messages in the Properties window for the CSketcherDoc class.

The CWnd class provides default message handling for standard Windows messages. If your class doesn't include a handler for one of these, it will be processed by the default handler in CWnd. If you do provide a handler you sometimes still need to call the base class handler from your handler to ensure that the message is processed properly. When you're creating your own handler through the Properties window for a class, a skeleton implementation is provided that includes a call to the base handler where necessary.

You have much more flexibility with handling command messages than you have with standard Windows messages. You can put handlers for command messages in the application class, the document and document template classes, and in the window and view classes. So what happens when a command message is sent to your application, bearing in mind that there are a lot of options as to where it is handled?

How Command Messages Are Processed

All command messages are sent to the main frame window for the application. The main frame window then tries to get the message handled by routing it in a specific sequence to the classes in your program. If one class can't process the message, the main frame window passes it on to the next.

For an SDI program, the sequence in which classes are offered an opportunity to handle a command message is:

1. The view object
2. The document object
3. The document template object
4. The main frame window object
5. The application object

The view object is given the opportunity to handle a command message first, and, if no handler has been defined, the next class object has a chance to process it. If none of the classes has a handler defined, default Windows processing takes care of it, essentially throwing the message away.

For an MDI program, things are only a little more complicated. Although you have the possibility of multiple documents, each with multiple views, only the active view and its associated document are involved in the routing of a command message. The sequence for routing a command message in an MDI program is:

1. The active view object
2. The document object associated with the active view
3. The document template object for the active document
4. The frame window object for the active view
5. The main frame window object
6. The application object

It's possible to alter the sequence for routing messages, but this is so rarely necessary that I won't go into it in this book.

EXTENDING THE SKETCHER PROGRAM

You're going to add code to the Sketcher program you created in the previous chapter to implement the functionality you need to create sketches. You'll provide code for drawing lines, circles, rectangles, and curves with various colors and line thicknesses, and for adding annotations to a sketch. The data for a sketch will be stored in a document object, and you'll allow multiple views of the same document at different scales.

It will take several chapters to learn how to add everything that I've described. A good starting point would be to add menu items to enable you to choose the type of element that you want to draw, and to select a drawing color. You'll make the element type and color selection persistent, which means that once a color and an element type has been selected, they will remain in effect until you choose another color or element type.

You'll work through the following steps to add menus to Sketcher:

1. Define the menu items that will appear on the main menu bar and the items in each of the corresponding drop-down menus.

2. Decide which class will handle messages for each menu item.

3. Add message handling functions to the class for the menu messages.

4. Add functions to the class that update the appearance of the menus to show the current selection in effect.

5. Add a toolbar button complete with tooltips for each menu item.

ELEMENTS OF A MENU

You'll look at two aspects of dealing with menus: the creation and modification of the menu as it appears in your application, and the processing necessary when a menu item is selected — the definition of a message handler for it. Let's look first at how you create new menu items.

Creating and Editing Menu Resources

Menus and other user interface elements are defined separately from the program code in a *resource file*, and the specification of an interface element is referred to as a *resource*. You can include many kinds of resources in your application: typical examples are menus, icons, dialogs, toolbars, and toolbar buttons. You'll be seeing more on these as you extend Sketcher.

Having a menu defined by a resource allows you to change the physical appearance of the menu without affecting the code that processes menu messages. For example, you could change your menu items from English to French, or Norwegian or whatever, without having to modify or recompile the program code. The code to handle a message doesn't need to be concerned with how the menu looks, only with the fact that it was selected. Of course, if you do add items to a menu, you must add code to handle messages for each of them to ensure that they actually do something!

Sketcher already has a menu, which means that it already has a resource file and menu resources. You can access the resource file contents for Sketcher by selecting the Resource View pane, or, if you have the Solution Explorer pane displayed, you can double-click `Sketcher.rc`. This switches you to the Resource View, which displays the resources. If you display the menu resources by double-clicking `Menu`, you'll see that it includes menus with the identifiers `IDR_MAINFRAME` and `IDR_SketchTYPE`. The `IDR_MAINFRAME` menu will be displayed when there are no documents open in the application, and the `IDR_SketchTYPE` menu will be displayed when you have a document open. The `IDR_` prefix identifies a resource that defines a complete menu for a window.

You're only going to modify the menu that has the identifier IDR_SketchTYPE. You don't need to change IDR_MAINFRAME, because your new menu items will be relevant only when a document is open. You can open a resource editor for a menu by double-clicking its menu ID in Resource View. If you do this for IDR_SketchTYPE, the Resource Editor pane appears, as shown in Figure 13-2, where I show it as a floating window.

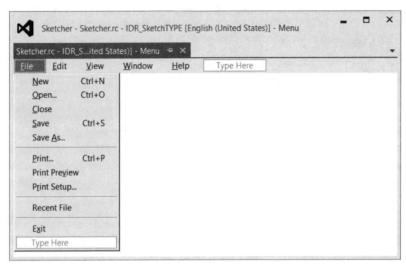

FIGURE 13-2

Adding a Menu Item to the Menu Bar

To add a new menu item to the menu bar, click the menu box on the menu bar with the text "Type Here" to select it, and then type in your menu name. If you insert an ampersand (&) in front of a letter in the menu item, that letter will be a shortcut key to invoke the menu from the keyboard. Type the first menu item as **E&lement**. This selects l as the shortcut letter, so you will be able to select the menu item and display its pop-up by typing Alt+L. You can't use E as the shortcut letter because it's already used by Edit. When you finish typing the name, you can right-click the menu item and select Properties from the pop-up to display its properties, as shown in Figure 13-3.

Properties are parameters with values that determine how the menu item will appear and behave. Figure 13-3 displays the properties grouped by category. If you want them displayed in alphabetical sequence, click the second button from the left. Note that the Popup property is set to True by default because the new Element menu item is at the top level on the menu bar, so it would normally present a pop-up menu when it is selected. Clicking a property in the left column enables you to modify its value in the right column. In this case, you want to leave everything as it is, so you can just close the Properties window. No ID is necessary for a pop-up menu item, because selecting

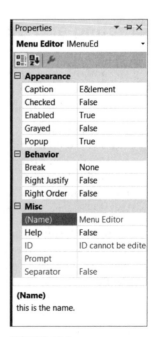

FIGURE 13-3

it just displays the menu beneath and there's no event for your code to handle. Note that you get a new blank menu box for the first item in the pop-up menu, as well as one on the main menu bar.

It would be better if the Element menu appeared between the View and Window menus, so place the mouse cursor on the menu item and, keeping the left mouse button pressed, drag it to a position between the View and Window menu items. After positioning the new menu item, the next step is to add items to its pop-up menu.

Adding Items to the Element Menu

Select the first item (currently labeled "Type Here") in the Element pop-up by clicking it; then, type **Line** as the caption and press Enter. You can see the properties for this item by right-clicking it and selecting Properties; the properties for this item are shown in Figure 13-4.

The properties determine the appearance of the menu item and specify the ID of the message passed to your program when the item is selected. Here, you have the ID already specified as ID_ELEMENT_LINE, but you can change it to something else if you want. Sometimes it's convenient to specify the ID yourself, such as when the generated ID is too long or its meaning is unclear. If you define your own ID, you should use the MFC convention of prefixing it with ID_ to indicate that it's a command ID for a menu item.

The Popup property is False here. When the Popup property for a menu item is True, clicking the item displays a pop-up menu. As you see in Figure 13-4, you can display the possible values for the Popup property by selecting the down arrow. Don't you love the way pop-ups pop up all over the place?

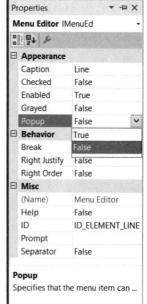

FIGURE 13-4

You can enter a text string for the value of the Prompt property that will appear in the status bar for Sketcher when the menu item is highlighted. If you leave it blank, nothing is displayed. I suggest you enter Draw lines as the value for the Prompt property. You get a brief indication of the purpose of a selected property at the bottom of the Properties window. The Break property can alter the appearance of the pop-up by shifting the item into a new column. You don't need that here, so leave it as it is. Close the Properties window and click the Save icon in the toolbar to save the values you have set.

Modifying Existing Menu Items

If you make a mistake and want to change an existing menu item, or even if you just want to verify that you set the properties correctly, it's very easy to go back to an item. Just double-click the item you're interested in, and the Properties window for that item is displayed. If the Properties pane is already open, just single-clicking an item will display its properties. You can then change the properties in any way you want. If the item you want to access is in a pop-up menu that isn't displayed, just click the item on the menu bar to display the pop-up.

Completing the Menu

Now, you can create the remaining Element pop-up menu items that you need: Rectangle, Circle, and Curve. You can accept the default IDs, ID_ELEMENT_RECTANGLE, ID_ELEMENT_CIRCLE, and ID_ELEMENT_CURVE, respectively. You could also set the values for the Prompt property value to Draw rectangles, Draw circles, and Draw curves.

You also need a Color menu on the menu bar, with pop-up menu items for Black, Red, Green, and Blue. You can create these, starting at the empty menu entry on the menu bar, using the same procedure that you just went through. You can use the default IDs (ID_COLOR_BLACK, etc.) as the IDs for the menu items. You can also add the status bar prompt for each as the value of the Prompt property. After you've finished, if you drag Color so that it's just to the right of Element, the menu should be as in Figure 13-5.

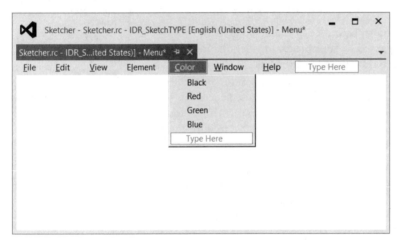

FIGURE 13-5

You need to take care not to use the same shortcut letter more than once in the main menu. There's no check made as you create menu items, but if you right-click on the menu bar when you've finished editing it, you'll get a pop-up containing Check Mnemonics. Selecting this checks for duplicate shortcut keys. It's a good idea to do this every time you edit a menu, because it's easy to create duplicates by accident.

That completes extending the menu for elements and colors. Don't forget to save the file to make sure that the additions are safely stored away. Next, you'll decide which classes will deal with messages from your menu items, and add member functions to handle them. For that, you'll be using the Event Handler Wizard.

ADDING MENU MESSAGE HANDLERS

To create an event handler for a menu item, right-click the item and select Add Event Handler from the pop-up displayed. If you try this with the Black menu item in the Color menu pop-up, you'll see the dialog shown in Figure 13-6.

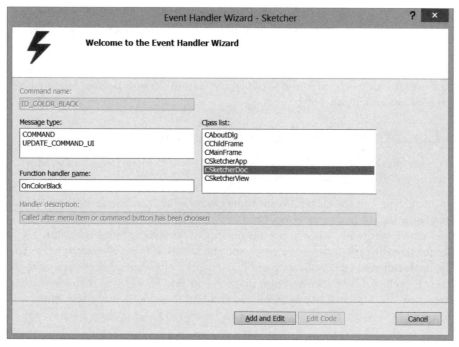

FIGURE 13-6

The wizard has already chosen a name for the handler function. You could change it, but OnColorBlack seems like a good name to me.

You obviously need to specify the message type as one of the choices shown in the dialog. The "Message type:" box in the window in Figure 13-6 shows the two kinds of messages that can arise for a particular menu ID. Each type of message serves a distinct purpose in dealing with a menu item.

MESSAGE TYPE	DESCRIPTION
COMMAND	This is issued when a menu item has been selected. The handler should provide the action appropriate to the menu item such as setting the current color object or setting the element type.
UPDATE_COMMAND_UI	This is issued when the menu should be updated — checked or unchecked, for example — depending on its status. This message occurs before a pop-up menu is displayed so you can set the appearance of the menu item before the user sees it.

The way these messages work is quite simple. When you click a menu item in the menu bar, an UPDATE_COMMAND_UI message is sent for each item in that menu before the menu is displayed. This provides the opportunity to do any necessary updating of the menu items' properties before the user sees it. When these messages are handled and any changes to the items' properties are completed, the menu is drawn. When you then click an item in the menu, a COMMAND message for that menu item is sent. I'll deal with the COMMAND messages now, and come back to the UPDATE_COMMAND_ UI messages a little later in this chapter.

Because events for menu items result in command messages, you can choose to handle them in any of the classes that are currently defined in the Sketcher application. So how do you decide where you should process a message for a menu item?

Choosing a Class to Handle Menu Messages

Before you can decide which class should handle the messages for the menu items you've added, you need to decide what you want to do with the messages.

You want the element type and the element color to be modal — that is, whatever is set for the element type and color should remain in effect until it is changed. This enables you to create as many blue circles as you want, and when you want red circles, you just change the color. You have two possibilities for handling the setting of a color and the selection of an element type: setting them by view or by document. You could set them by view, in which case, if there's more than one view of a document, each will have its own color and element set. This means that you might draw a red circle in one view, switch to another view, and find that you're drawing a blue rectangle. This would be confusing and in conflict with how you would probably want your tools to work.

It would be better to have the current color and element selection apply to a document. You can then switch from one view to another and continue drawing the same element in the same color. There might be other differences between the views such as the scale at which the document is displayed, perhaps, but the drawing operation will be consistent across multiple views.

This suggests that you should store the current color and element in the document object. These could then be accessed by any view associated with the document. Of course, if you had more than one document active, each document would have its own color and element type settings. It would therefore be sensible to handle the messages for your new menu items in the CSketcherDoc class and to store information about the current selections in an object of this class. I think you're ready to dive in and create a handler for the Black menu item.

Creating Menu Message Handlers

Highlight the CSketcherDoc class name in the Event Handler Wizard dialog by clicking it. You'll also need to select the COMMAND message type. You can then click the Add and Edit button. This closes the dialog, and the code for the handler you have created in the CSketcherDoc class is displayed in the edit window. The function looks like this:

```
void CSketcherDoc::OnColorBlack()
{
  // TODO: Add your command handler code here
}
```

The highlighted line is where you'll put your code that handles the event that results from the user selecting the Black menu item. The wizard also has updated the CSketcherDoc class definition:

```
class CSketcherDoc : public CDocument
{
  ...

// Generated message map functions
protected:
  DECLARE_MESSAGE_MAP()

#ifdef SHARED_HANDLERS
  // Helper function that sets search content for a Search Handler
  void SetSearchContent(const CString& value);
#endif // SHARED_HANDLERS
public:
  afx_msg void OnColorBlack();
};
```

The OnColorBlack() method has been added as a public member of the class, and the afx_msg prefix marks it as a message handler.

You can now add COMMAND message handlers to CSketcherDoc for the other color menu items and all the Element menu items in exactly the same way. You can create each of the handler functions with just five mouse clicks. Right-click the menu item, click the Add Event Handler menu item, click the CSketcherDoc class name in the dialog for the Event Handler Wizard, click the COMMAND message type, and click the Add and Edit button for the dialog.

The Event Handler Wizard should now have added the handlers to the CSketcherDoc class, which now looks like this:

```
class CSketcherDoc: public CDocument
{
  ...

// Generated message map functions
protected:
  DECLARE_MESSAGE_MAP()

#ifdef SHARED_HANDLERS
  // Helper function that sets search content for a Search Handler
  void SetSearchContent(const CString& value);
#endif // SHARED_HANDLERS
public:
  afx_msg void OnColorBlack();
  afx_msg void OnColorRed();
  afx_msg void OnColorGreen();
  afx_msg void OnColorBlue();
  afx_msg void OnElementLine();
  afx_msg void OnElementRectangle();
  afx_msg void OnElementCircle();
  afx_msg void OnElementCurve();
};
```

A declaration has been added for each handler that you've created using the Event Handler Wizard dialog. Each function declaration is prefixed with `afx_msg` to indicate that it is a message handler.

The Event Handler Wizard automatically updates the message map in your `CSketcherDoc` class implementation with the new message handlers. If you look in `SketcherDoc.cpp`, you'll see the message map:

```
BEGIN_MESSAGE_MAP(CSketcherDoc, CDocument)
    ON_COMMAND(ID_COLOR_BLACK, &CSketcherDoc::OnColorBlack)
    ON_COMMAND(ID_COLOR_RED, &CSketcherDoc::OnColorRed)
    ON_COMMAND(ID_COLOR_GREEN, &CSketcherDoc::OnColorGreen)
    ON_COMMAND(ID_COLOR_BLUE, &CSketcherDoc::OnColorBlue)
    ON_COMMAND(ID_ELEMENT_LINE, &CSketcherDoc::OnElementLine)
    ON_COMMAND(ID_ELEMENT_RECTANGLE, &CSketcherDoc::OnElementRectangle)
    ON_COMMAND(ID_ELEMENT_CIRCLE, &CSketcherDoc::OnElementCircle)
    ON_COMMAND(ID_ELEMENT_CURVE, &CSketcherDoc::OnElementCurve)
END_MESSAGE_MAP()
```

The Event Handler Wizard has added an `ON_COMMAND()` macro for each handler. This associates the pointer to a handler function with the message ID, so, for example, `OnColorBlack()` will be called to service a `COMMAND` message for the menu item with the `ID_COLOR_BLACK` ID.

Each handler generated by the Event Handler Wizard is just a skeleton. For example, look at the code provided for `OnColorBlue()`. This also appears in `SketcherDoc.cpp` so you can scroll down to find it, or go directly to it by switching to the Class View, clicking `CSketcherDoc` in the upper pane and double-clicking the function name in the lower pane.

```
void CSketcherDoc::OnColorBlue()
{
    // TODO: Add your command handler code here
}
```

The function takes no arguments and returns nothing. It also does nothing at the moment, but this is hardly surprising. The Event Handler Wizard has no way of knowing what you want to do with these messages!

Implementing Menu Message Handlers

Now let's consider what you should do with the `COMMAND` messages for the new menu items. I said earlier that you want to record the current element and color in the document, so you need to add data members to the `CSketcherDoc` class to store these.

Adding Members to Store Color and Element Mode

You could add the data members to `CSketcherDoc` just by editing the class definition directly, but let's use the Add Member Variable Wizard to do it. Display the dialog for the wizard by right-clicking the `CSketcherDoc` class name in the Class View and then selecting Add ⇨ Add Variable from the pop-up menu that appears. You then see the dialog for the wizard, as shown in Figure 13-7.

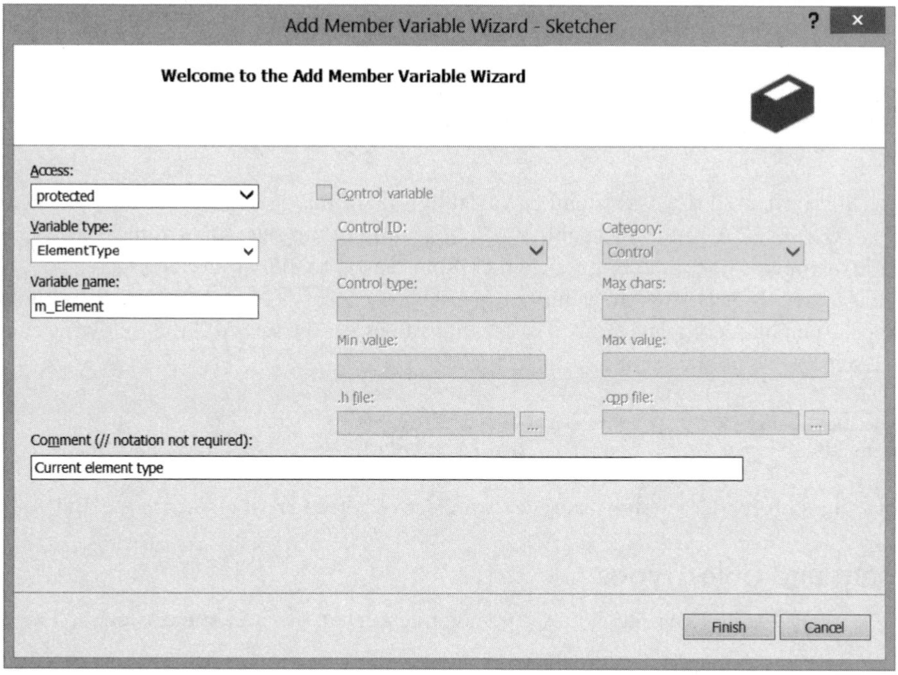

FIGURE 13-7

I've already entered the information in the dialog for the m_Element variable that stores the current element type to be drawn. I have selected protected as the access because it should not be accessible directly from outside the class. I have also entered the type as ElementType. You will define this type in the next section. When you click the Finish button, the variable is added to the class definition in the SketcherDoc.h file.

Add the CSketcherDoc class member to store the element color manually just to show that you can. Its name is m_Color and its type is ElementColor, which we will define in the next section. You can add the declaration for the m_Color member to the CSketcherDoc class like this:

```
class CSketcherDoc : public CDocument
{
...
// Generated message map functions
protected:
  DECLARE_MESSAGE_MAP()
...
public:
  afx_msg void OnColorBlack();
  afx_msg void OnColorRed();
  afx_msg void OnColorGreen();
  afx_msg void OnColorBlue();
  afx_msg void OnElementLine();
  afx_msg void OnElementRectangle();
  afx_msg void OnElementCircle();
```

```
afx_msg void OnElementCurve();

protected:
  ElementType m_Element;         // Current element type
  ElementColor m_Color;          // Current drawing color
};
```

Of course, you could have used the Add Member Variable Wizard dialog as you did for m_Element; you would type ElementColor in the "Variable type" box, rather than selecting from the drop-down list. The m_Color member is protected, because there's no reason to allow public access. You can add functions to access or change the values of protected or private class members, with the advantage that you then have complete control over what values can be set. Add the following functions to CSketcherDoc in a public section of the class:

```
ElementType GetElementType()const { return m_Element; }
ElementColor GetElementColor()const { return m_Color; }
```

Now an external class object, a view for instance, can discover the current element type and color.

Defining Element and Color Types

You can define ElementType as an enum class type in a new header file, ElementType.h. The definition is:

```
#pragma once

// Standard Sketcher element type identifiers
enum class ElementType{LINE, RECTANGLE, CIRCLE, CURVE};
```

Because it's an enum type, each of the possible values is automatically defined as a unique integer value, type int by default. Because it's an enum class type, the enumerators are type safe and must be prefixed with the type name to access them. If you need to add further types in the future, it will be very easy to add them here. You can add an #include directive for ElementType.h to SketcherDoc.h.

You can define another enum class type for the standard drawing colors in Sketcher in ElementColor.h:

```
#pragma once

// Standard Sketcher drawing colors
enum class ElementColor : COLORREF{BLACK = RGB(0,0,0),    RED = RGB(255,0,0),
                                   GREEN = RGB(0,255,0), BLUE = RGB(0,0,255)};
```

You can define enumerators to be of any integer type. A color in Windows is of type COLORREF, which is an unsigned 32-bit integer, so the enumerators in ElementColor can be specified as this type. A color value is composed of three 8-bit unsigned integer values, packed into the 32-bit word, that correspond to the intensities of the red, green, and blue components of the color. The values are stored as 0x00bbggrr, where bb, gg, and rr are hexadecimal color component values.

Each `ElementColor` enumerator is initialized by the `RGB()` macro, which is used to define `COLORREF` values. The macro is defined in the `Wingdi.h` header file that is included as part of `Windows.h`, so you can add an `#include` for `windows.h` to `ElementColor.h` after the `#pragma once` directive. The three arguments to the macro define the red, green, and blue components of the color value, respectively. Each argument must be an integer between 0 and 255, 0 being no color component and 255 being the maximum color component. `RGB(0,0,0)` corresponds to black because there are no components of red, green, or blue. `RGB(255,0,0)` creates a color value with a maximum red component and no green or blue contribution. `RGB(0,255,0)` and `RGB(0,0,255)` correspond to green and blue with maximum intensity. You can create other colors by combining red, green, and blue components with other intensities. Add an `#include` for `ElementColor.h` to `SketcherDoc.h`. The `ElementType` and `ElementColor` types should now be visible in Class View.

Initializing the Color and Element Type Members

It's important to make sure that the data members you have added to the `CSketcherDoc` class are initialized appropriately when a document is created. You can modify the code in the class definition in `SketcherDoc.h`, as shown here:

```
ElementType m_Element {ElementType::LINE};          // Current element type

ElementColor m_Color {ElementColor::BLACK};         // Current drawing color
```

`enum class` types require that enumerators are explicitly qualified by the class name.

Implementing Menu Command Message Handlers

Now, you're ready to add the code for the handler functions that you created for the Element and Color menu items. You can do this from the Class View. Double-click the name of the first handler function, `OnColorBlack()`. You just need to add one line to the function, so the code for it becomes:

```
void CSketcherDoc::OnColorBlack()
{
    m_Color = ElementColor::BLACK;        // Set the drawing color to black
}
```

The only job that the handler has to do is to set the appropriate color. In the interest of conciseness, the new line replaces the comment provided originally. You can go through and add one line to each of the Color menu handlers setting the appropriate color value.

The Element menu handlers are much the same. The handler for the Element ➤ Line menu item is:

```
void CSketcherDoc::OnElementLine()
{
    m_Element = ElementType::LINE;        // Set element type as a line
}
```

With this model, it's not too difficult to write the other handlers for the Element menu. That's eight message handlers completed. You can now build the example and see how it works.

Running the Extended Example

Assuming that there are no typos, the compiled and linked program should run without error. When you run the program, you should see the window shown in Figure 13-8.

The new menus are in place on the menu bar, and you can see that the items you have added to the menu are all there and you should see the prompt message in the status bar that you provided in the properties box when the mouse cursor is over a menu item. You can also verify that Alt+C and Alt+L work. Ideally, the currently selected items in the Color and Element menus should be

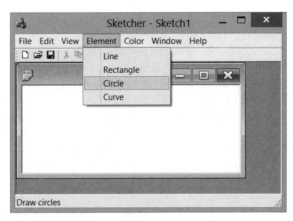

FIGURE 13-8

checked as a cue to the current state. Let's look at how you can arrange for that to happen.

Adding Menu Update Message Handlers

To set the checkmark correctly for the new menus, you need to add the second kind of message handler, UPDATE_COMMAND_UI (signifying "update command user interface") for each of the menu items. These handlers are intended for updating the properties of the menu items before the menu is displayed.

Go back to viewing the IDR_SketchTYPE menu in the editor window. Right-click the Black item in the Color menu and select Add Event Handler. You can then select CSketcherDoc as the class and UPDATE_COMMAND_UI as the message type, as shown in Figure 13-9.

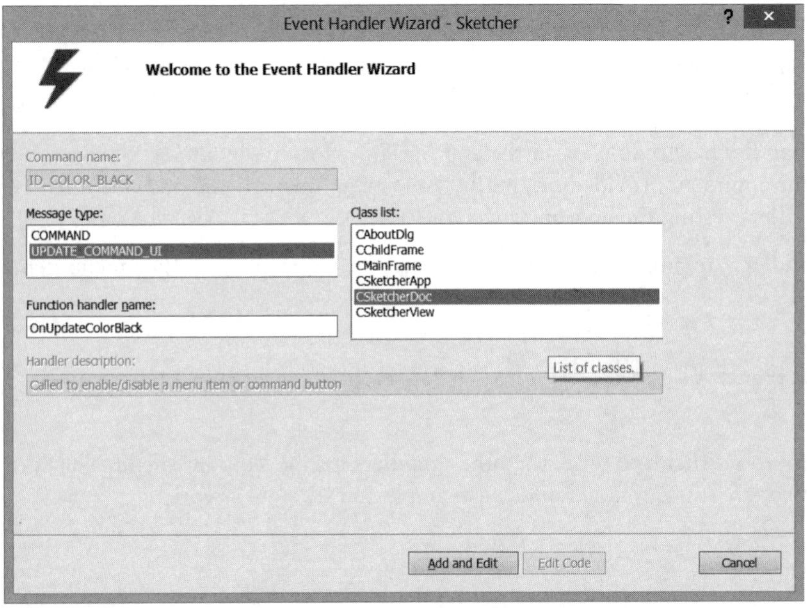

FIGURE 13-9

The name for the update function has been generated as `OnUpdateColorBlack()`. This seems a reasonable name so click the Add and Edit button and have the Event Handler Wizard generate it. The skeleton function definition is added in `SketcherDoc.cpp` and its declaration is added to the class definition. An entry for it is also made in the message map in the `SketcherDoc.cpp` that looks like this:

```
ON_UPDATE_COMMAND_UI(ID_COLOR_BLACK, &CSketcherDoc::OnUpdateColorBlack)
```

This uses the `ON_UPDATE_COMMAND_UI()` macro that identifies the function you have just generated as the handler to deal with update messages corresponding to the `ID_COLOR_BLACK` ID. You can now enter the code for the new handler, but before you do that, add command update handlers for each of the menu items for both the Color and Element menus first.

Coding a Command Update Handler

You can access the code for the `OnUpdateColorBlack()` handler in `CSketcherDoc` by selecting the function in Class View. This is the skeleton code for the function:

```
void CSketcherDoc::OnUpdateColorBlack(CCmdUI* pCmdUI)
{
    // TODO: Add your command update UI handler code here

}
```

The argument passed to the handler is a pointer to an object of type `CCmdUI`. This is an MFC class type that is used only with update handlers, and it applies to toolbar buttons as well as menu items. `pCmdUI` points to an object that identifies the item that originated the message, so you use this to operate on the item to update it before it is displayed. The `CCmdUI` class has five member functions that act on user interface items. The operations that these provide are:

FUNCTION	DESCRIPTION
`ContinueRouting()`	Passes the message on to the next priority handler.
`Enable()`	Enables or disables the relevant interface item.
`SetCheck()`	Sets a checkmark for the relevant interface item.
`SetRadio()`	Sets a button in a radio group on or off.
`SetText()`	Sets the text for the relevant interface item.

We'll use `SetCheck()` as that seems to do what we want. The function is declared in the `CCmdUI` class as:

```
virtual void SetCheck(int nCheck = 1);
```

This function sets a menu item as checked if you pass 1 as the argument, and unchecked if you pass 0 as the argument. The parameter has a default value of 1, so if you just want to set a checkmark for an item, you call this function without an argument.

For Sketcher, you want to set a Color menu item as checked if it corresponds with the current color. You can, therefore, write the update handler for OnUpdateColorBlack() as:

```
void CSketcherDoc::OnUpdateColorBlack(CCmdUI* pCmdUI)
{
    // Set menu item Checked if the current color is black
    pCmdUI->SetCheck(m_Color == ElementColor::BLACK);
}
```

This calls SetCheck() for the Color ⇨ Black menu item with the argument m_Color==Element Color::BLACK. This results in true if m_Color is ElementColor::BLACK, which will convert to 1, or false, which will convert to 0. The effect is to check the menu item only if the current color in m_Color is ElementColor::BLACK, which is precisely what you want. You can implement the update handlers for the other Color menu items in the same way. Update handlers for menu items are always called before the menu is displayed, so the items are always displayed reflecting their current state.

A typical Element menu item update handler is coded as follows:

```
void CSketcherDoc::OnUpdateElementLine(CCmdUI* pCmdUI)
{
    // Set Checked if the current element is a line
    pCmdUI->SetCheck(m_Element==ElementType::LINE);
}
```

You can now code all the other update handlers for items in the Element menu in a similar manner.

Exercising the Update Handlers

When you've added the code for the update handlers, you can build and execute the Sketcher application again. Now, when you change a color or an element type selection, this is reflected in the menu, as shown in Figure 13-10.

You have completed all the code that you need for the menu items. Make sure that you have saved everything before embarking on the next stage. Toolbars are a must in any Windows program of consequence, so the next step is to look at how you add toolbar buttons to support the new menus.

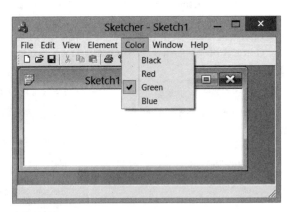

FIGURE 13-10

ADDING TOOLBAR BUTTONS

Select the Resource View and extend the toolbar resource. You'll see that the toolbar resource has the same ID as the main menu, IDR_MAINFRAME. This provides you with toolbar icons that have four-bit color pixels (16 colors).

If you double-click IDR_MAINFRAME, the editor window shown in Figure 13-11 appears.

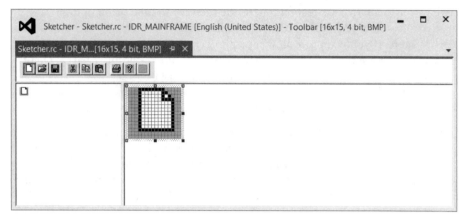

FIGURE 13-11

A toolbar button is a 16 × 15 (width × height) array of pixels that contains a pictorial representation of the function it initiates. Each pixel in this toolbar is a 4-bit color, so a button is a 16-color bitmap. You can see in Figure 13-11 that the resource editor provides an enlarged view of a toolbar button so that you can see and manipulate individual pixels. It also provides you with a color palette to the right (not shown in Figure 13-11), from which you can choose the current working color. If it is not already visible, you can display the palette from which you can choose a color by right-clicking a toolbar button icon and selecting Show Colors Window from the menu.

If you click the new button icon at the right end of the row, you'll be able to draw this icon. Before starting editing, drag the new icon about half a button-width to the right on the toolbar. This separates the button from its neighbor on the left to start a new block. You should keep toolbar buttons in the same sequence as the items on the menu bar, so you'll create the buttons corresponding to the Element menu first. You'll probably want to use the editing buttons provided by the resource editor, which appear in the IDE application window toolbar and include:

> ➤ Pencil for drawing individual pixels

> ➤ Eraser for erasing individual pixels

> ➤ Fill an area with the current color

> ➤ Zoom the view of the button

> ➤ Draw a line

> ➤ Draw a rectangle

> ➤ Draw an ellipse

> ➤ Draw a curve

You select a foreground color by left-clicking a color from the palette, and a background color by right-clicking.

The first icon will be for the button corresponding to the Element ⇨ Line menu option. You can let your creative juices flow and draw whatever you like here to depict the act of drawing a line, but I'll keep it simple. If you want to follow my approach, make sure that black is selected as the foreground color and use the line tool to draw a diagonal line in the enlarged image of the new toolbar button icon. In fact, if you want the icon to appear a bit bigger, you can use the Magnification Tool editing button to make it up to eight times its actual size: just click the down arrow alongside the button and select the magnification you want. I drew a double black line.

If you make a mistake, you can select the Undo button or you can change to the Erase Tool editing button and use that, but in the latter case, you need to make sure that the color selected corresponds to the background color for the button you are editing. You can also erase individual pixels by clicking them using the right mouse button, but again, you need to be sure that the background color is set correctly when you do this. After you're happy with what you've drawn, the next step is to edit the toolbar button properties.

Editing Toolbar Button Properties

Right-click your new button icon in the toolbar and select Properties from the pop-up to bring up its Properties window, as shown in Figure 13-12.

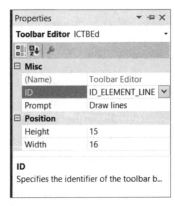

The Properties window shows a default ID for the button, but you want to associate the button with the menu item Element ⇨ Line that you have already defined, so click ID and then click the down arrow to display alternative values. You can then select ID_ELEMENT_LINE from the drop-down list. If you look at the Prompt property, you'll find that the same prompt value appears because the prompt is recorded along with the ID. You can click Save to complete the button definition.

FIGURE 13-12

You can now move on to designing the other three element buttons. You can use the rectangle editing button to draw a rectangle and the ellipse button to draw a circle. You can draw a curve using the pencil to set individual pixels, or use the curve button. You need to associate each button with the ID for the equivalent menu item that you defined earlier.

Now add the buttons for the colors. You should also drag the first button for selecting a color to the right, so that it starts a new group of buttons. You could keep the color buttons very simple and just color the whole button with the color it selects. You can do this by selecting the appropriate foreground color, then selecting the Fill editing button and clicking on the enlarged button image. Again, you need to use ID_COLOR_BLACK, ID_COLOR_RED, and so on as IDs for the buttons. The toolbar editing window should look like the one shown in Figure 13-13.

That's all you need for the moment, so save the resource file and give Sketcher another spin.

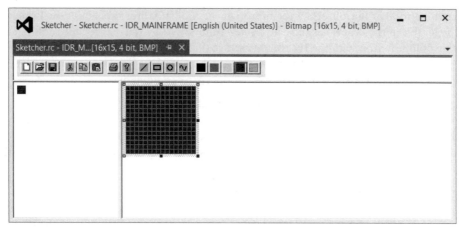

FIGURE 13-13

Exercising the Toolbar Buttons

Build the application once again and execute it. You should see the application window shown in Figure 13-14.

There are some amazing things happening here. The toolbar buttons you added already reflect the default settings that you defined for the new menu items, and the selected button is shown depressed. If you let the cursor linger over one of the buttons, the prompt for the button appears in the status bar. The new buttons work as a complete substitute for the menu items, and any new selection made, with either the menu or the toolbar, is reflected by the toolbar button being shown depressed.

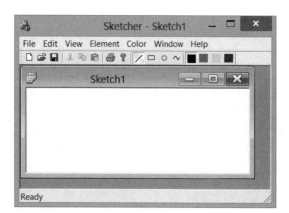

FIGURE 13-14

If you close the document view window, Sketch1, you'll see that your toolbar buttons are automatically grayed and disabled and your menu items disappear. If you open a new document window, the toolbar buttons are automatically enabled once again and your menu items reappear. You can also drag the toolbar using the grip at the left. You can move the toolbar to either side of the application window, or have it free-floating. You got all this toolbar functionality without writing a single additional line of code!

Adding Tooltips

There's one further tweak that you can add that is remarkably easy: tooltips. A tooltip is a small box that appears adjacent to the toolbar button when you let the cursor linger on the button. The tooltip contains a text string that is an additional clue to the purpose of the toolbar button.

To add a tooltip for a toolbar button, select the button in the toolbar editor tab. Select the Prompt property for the button in the Properties pane and enter \n followed by the text for the tooltip. For example, for the toolbar button with the ID ID_ELEMENT_LINE, you could enter the Prompt property value as \nDraw lines. The tooltip text will be displayed when you hover the mouse cursor over the toolbar button but you won't get the status bar text for the corresponding menu item.

You can have status bar text displayed for the menu item and different tooltip text for the toolbar button, though. Set the value for the Prompt property for the Line menu item as Draw lines\nLines. This will display "Draw lines" in the status bar when you hover the mouse cursor over the menu item. When you hover the mouse over the toolbar button, the status bar text will be displayed and the tooltip text will appear a short while afterwards.

You can change the Prompt property text for each of the toolbar buttons corresponding to the Element and Color menus in a similar way. That's all you have to do. After saving the resource file, you can build the application and execute it. Hovering the cursor over a toolbar button causes the prompt text to appear in the status bar and the tooltip to be displayed.

SUMMARY

In this chapter, you learned how MFC connects a message with a class member function to process it, and you wrote your first message handlers. Much of the work in writing a Windows program is writing message handlers, so it's important to have a good grasp of what happens in the process. When we consider other message handlers, you'll see that the process for adding them is the same.

You have also extended the standard menu and the toolbar in the MFC Application Wizard–generated program, which provides a good base for the application code that you add in the next chapter. Although there's no functionality under the covers yet, the menu and toolbar operation looks very professional, courtesy of the Application Wizard–generated framework and the Event Handler Wizard.

In the next chapter, you'll add the code necessary to draw elements in a view, and use the menus and toolbar buttons that you created here to select what to draw and in which color. This is where the Sketcher program begins to live up to its name.

EXERCISES

1. Add an Ellipse menu item to the Element menu.

2. Implement the command and command update handlers for the Ellipse menu item in the document class.

3. Add a toolbar button corresponding to the Ellipse menu item, and add status bar text and a tooltip for the button.

4. Modify the command update handlers for the color menu items so that the currently selected menu item displays in uppercase, and the others in lowercase.

➤ WHAT YOU LEARNED IN THIS CHAPTER

TOPIC	CONCEPT
Message maps	MFC defines the message handlers for a class in a message map that appears in the `.cpp` file for the class.
Handling command messages	Command messages that arise from menus and toolbars can be handled in any class that's derived from `CCmdTarget`. These include the application class, the frame and child frame window classes, the document class, and the view class.
Handling non-command messages	Messages other than command messages can be handled only in a class derived from `CWnd`. This includes frame window and view classes, but not application or document classes.
Identifying a message handler for command messages	MFC has a predefined sequence for searching the classes in your program to find a message handler for a command message.
Adding message handlers	You should always use the Event Handler Wizard to add message handlers to your program.
Resource files	The physical appearances of menus and toolbars are defined in resource files, which are edited by the built-in resource editor.
Menu IDs	Items in a menu that can result in command messages are identified by a symbolic constant with the prefix `ID_`. These IDs are used to associate a handler with the message from the menu item.
Relating toolbar buttons to menu items	To associate a toolbar button with a particular menu item, give it the same ID as the menu item.
Adding tooltips	To add a tooltip to a toolbar button corresponding to a menu item in your MFC application, select the Prompt property for the button in the Properties pane and enter `\n`, followed by the text for the tooltip as the property value.

14

Drawing in a Window

WHAT YOU WILL LEARN IN THIS CHAPTER:

➤ The coordinate systems you use to draw in a window

➤ How to use a device context to draw shapes

➤ How and when your program draws in a window

➤ How to define handlers for mouse messages

➤ How to define your own shape classes

➤ How to program the mouse to draw shapes

➤ How to capture the mouse

WROX.COM CODE DOWNLOADS FOR THIS CHAPTER

You can find the wrox.com code downloads for this chapter on the Download Code tab at www.wrox.com/go/beginningvisualc. The code is in the Chapter 14 download and individually named according to the names throughout the chapter.

BASICS OF DRAWING IN A WINDOW

When you draw in the client area of a window, you must obey the rules. You must redraw the client area whenever a WM_PAINT message is sent to your application. This is because there are many external events that require that your application window is redrawn — the user resizing the window for example or moving another window to expose part of your window that was hidden. Windows sends information along with the WM_PAINT message that enables you to determine which part of the client area needs to be re-created. This means that you don't have to draw all the client area in response to a WM_PAINT message, just the area identified as the *update region*. In an MFC application, the MFC intercepts the WM_PAINT message and redirects it to a function in one of your classes. I'll explain how you handle this message later in this chapter.

The Window Client Area

A window doesn't have a fixed position on-screen, or even a fixed visible area, because the user can drag a window around and resize it by dragging its borders. How, then, do you know where to draw on-screen?

Fortunately, you don't. Windows provides a consistent way of drawing in a window that is independent of where it is on-screen; without this, drawing in a window would be inordinately complicated. Windows does this by maintaining a coordinate system for the client area of a window that is local to the window. It always uses the upper-left corner of the client area as its reference point. All points within the client area are defined relative to this point, as shown in Figure 14-1.

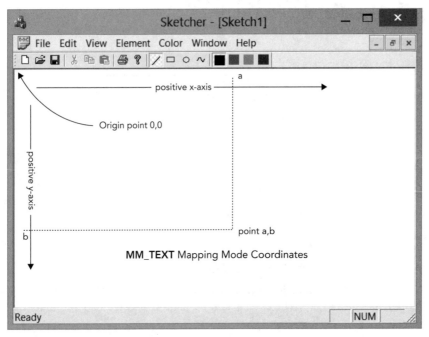

FIGURE 14-1

The horizontal and vertical distances of a point in the client area from the upper-left corner will always be the same, regardless of where the window is on-screen or how big it is. Of course, Windows keeps track of where the window is, and when you draw something at a point in the client area, it has to figure out where that point actually is on-screen.

The Windows Graphical Device Interface

You don't write data to the screen in any direct sense. All output to your display is graphical, regardless of whether it is lines and circles or text. Windows insists that you define this output using the *Graphical Device Interface (GDI)*. The GDI enables you to program graphical output in a way that is independent of the hardware on which it is displayed, meaning that your program will work on different machines with different display hardware without change. The GDI also supports printers and plotters, so outputting data to those involves essentially the same mechanism as writing to the screen.

Working with a Device Context

When you draw something on an output device such as a display, you must use a *device context*. A device context is a Windows data structure that contains information that allows Windows to translate your output requests in the form of device-independent GDI function calls, into actions on the physical device. The MFC class, CDC, encapsulates a device context so you do all drawing by calling functions for an object of this type. A pointer to a CDC object is supplied to the OnDraw() member of your view class object and you implement this to draw in the client area represented by the view. You also use a device context when you want to send output to other graphical devices.

A device context provides you with a choice of coordinate systems called *mapping modes*, which are automatically converted to client area coordinates. You can alter parameters (called *attributes*) that affect the output to a device context by calling functions for a CDC object. Examples of attributes that you can change are the drawing color, the background color, the line thickness to be used when drawing, and the font for text output.

Mapping Modes

Each mapping mode in a device context is identified by an ID, much like a Windows message. Each ID has the prefix MM_ to indicate that it defines a mapping mode. The mapping modes are:

MAPPING MODE	DESCRIPTION
MM_TEXT	A logical unit is one device pixel with positive x from left to right, and positive y from top to bottom of the window client area.
MM_LOENGLISH	A logical unit is 0.01 inches with positive x from left to right, and negative y from top to bottom of the client area.
MM_HIENGLISH	A logical unit is 0.001 inches with the x and y directions as in MM_LOENGLISH.
MM_LOMETRIC	A logical unit is 0.1 millimeters with the x and y directions as in MM_LOENGLISH.
MM_HIMETRIC	A logical unit is 0.01 millimeters with the x and y directions as in MM_LOENGLISH.
MM_ISOTROPIC	A logical unit is of arbitrary length, but the same along both axes. The x and y directions are as in MM_LOENGLISH.

continues

(continued)

MAPPING MODE	DESCRIPTION
MM_ANISOTROPIC	This is similar to MM_ISOTROPIC, but allows the length of a logical unit on the x-axis to be different from that of a logical unit on the y-axis.
MM_TWIPS	A logical unit is a TWIP, which is a twentieth of an inch point and a point is 1/72 of an inch. Thus, a TWIP corresponds to 1/1440 of an inch, or 6.9×10^{-4} of an inch. (A point is a font size measurement unit). The axes are as in MM_LOENGLISH.

You will not use all these mapping modes with this book; however, the ones you will use form a good cross-section of those available, so you should not have any problem using the others when you need to.

MM_TEXT is the default mapping mode for a device context. If you need to use a different mapping mode, you have to change it. Note that the direction of the positive y-axis in the MM_TEXT mode is the opposite of what you saw in high-school coordinate geometry, as Figure 14-1 shows.

By default, the origin point with the coordinates (0,0) is at the upper-left corner of the client area in every mapping mode, although it's possible to move it. For example, an application that presents data in graphical form might move the origin to the center of the client area to make plotting the data easier. You might also define shapes relative to (0,0) and then move the origin to the position where a shape is to be drawn. This means that a shape can be drawn using the same code, regardless of where it is.

With the default origin position in MM_TEXT mode, a point 50 pixels from the left border and 100 pixels down from the top of the client area has the coordinates (50,100). Because the units are pixels, the physical distance of the point from the upper-left corner of the client area on your screen depends on the resolution of your monitor. If the resolution is set to 1280 × 1024 the point will be nearer to the origin than if it's set to 1024 × 768 because the pixels are smaller. An object drawn in this mapping mode will be smaller at the 1280 × 1024 resolution than at 1024 × 768. Note that the DPI setting for your display also affects presentation in all mapping modes. The default settings assume 96 DPI, so if the DPI for your display is different, this affects how things look. Coordinates are always 32-bit signed integers. The maximum physical size of the area you can draw varies with the length of a coordinate unit, which depends on the mapping mode.

The directions of the coordinate axes in all mapping modes other than MM_TEXT are the same, but different from MM_TEXT in that the y-coordinate axis is in the opposite direction. The coordinate system for MM_LOENGLISH is shown in Figure 14-2. Although the positive y-direction is consistent with what you learned in high school (y-values increase as you move up the screen), MM_LOENGLISH is still slightly odd because the origin is at the upper-left corner of the client area, so y is always negative for points within the visible client area.

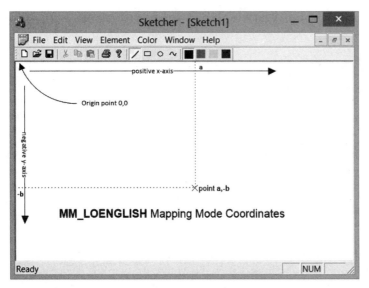

FIGURE 14-2

In the MM_LOENGLISH mapping mode, the units along the axes are 0.01 inches, so a point at the position (50, −100) is half an inch from the left border and one inch down from the top of the client area. An object is the same size in the client area and the same distance from the origin, regardless of the resolution of the monitor on which it's displayed. Anything you draw in MM_LOENGLISH mode with negative x- or positive y-coordinates will be outside the client area and therefore not visible. You can move the origin by calling the SetViewportOrg() member of the CDC object that encapsulates a device context, which I'll discuss shortly.

THE MFC DRAWING MECHANISM

The MFC encapsulates the Windows interface to your screen and printer and relieves you of the need to worry about much of the details involved in programming graphical output. As you saw in the last chapter, an Application Wizard-generated program already contains a class derived from CView that's specifically designed to display document data.

The View Class in Your Application

The primary purpose of the Application Wizard-generated CSketcherView class is to display information from a document object in the client area of a document window. The class definition includes overrides for several virtual functions, but the one of particular interest here is the OnDraw() function. This is called whenever the client area of the document window needs to be redrawn. It's the function that's called by the application framework when a WM_PAINT message is received by your program.

The OnDraw() Member Function

The implementation of the OnDraw() function looks like this:

```
void CSketcherView::OnDraw(CDC* /*pDC*/)
{
    CSketcherDoc* pDoc = GetDocument();
    ASSERT_VALID(pDoc);
    if(!pDoc)
      return;

    // TODO: add draw code for native data here
}
```

A pointer to a CDC class object is passed to the OnDraw() member of the view class. This object has member functions that call Windows API functions that enable you to draw in the device context. The parameter name is commented out: you must uncomment it or substitute your own name before you can use the pointer.

Because you'll put all the code to draw a document in this function, the Application Wizard includes a declaration for the pDoc pointer and initializes it using the GetDocument() function that returns the address of the document object for the current view:

```
CSketcherDoc* pDoc = GetDocument();
```

The GetDocument() function in CSketcherView retrieves the pointer to the document from m_pDocument, an inherited member of the view object. The function performs the important task of casting the pointer stored in this member to the type corresponding to the document class in the application, CSketcherDoc. This is so you can use the pointer to access the members of the document class that you've defined; otherwise, you could use the pointer only to access the members of the base class. Thus pDoc points to the document object in your application that is associated with the current view, and you use it to access the data that you've stored in the document.

The next line is:

```
ASSERT_VALID(pDoc);
```

This macro ensures that pDoc contains a valid address, and the if statement that follows verifies that pDoc is not nullptr. ASSERT_VALID is ignored in a release version of the application.

The parameter name, pDC, for the OnDraw() function stands for "pointer to device context." The CDC object pointed to by pDC is the key to drawing in a window. It provides a device context for the client area of the view, plus the tools you need to write graphics and text to it, so you need to look at this in more detail.

The CDC Class

You should do all the drawing in your program using members of the CDC class. All objects of this class and classes derived from it contain a device context and the member functions you need for sending graphics and text to your display or your printer. There are also member functions for retrieving information about the physical output device you are using.

Because a CDC object provides almost everything you're likely to need in the way of graphical output, there are a lot of member functions of this class — in fact, well over a hundred. You'll look only at the ones you're going to use in the Sketcher program in this chapter; I'll go into others as you need them later on.

The MFC includes more specialized classes for graphics output that are derived from CDC. For example, you will be using CClientDC objects. The CClientDC class has the advantage over CDC that it always contains a device context that represents only the client area of a window, and this is precisely what you want in most circumstances.

Displaying Graphics

You draw entities such as lines, circles, and text relative to the *current position* in a device context. The current position is a point in the client area that was set either by the previous entity that was drawn or by you calling a function to set it. For example, you could extend the OnDraw() function to set the current position like this:

```
void CSketcherView::OnDraw(CDC* pDC)
{
   CSketcherDoc* pDoc = GetDocument();
   ASSERT_VALID(pDoc);
   if(!pDoc)
     return;

   pDC->MoveTo(50, 50);    // Set the current position as 50,50
}
```

The first line is bolded because I changed it. You must uncomment the parameter name if the code is to compile. The second bolded line calls the MoveTo() function for the CDC object pointed to by pDC. This function sets the current position to the x- and y-coordinates you specify as arguments. The default mapping mode is MM_TEXT so the coordinates are in pixels. The current position will be set to a point 50 pixels to the right from the inside-left border of the window, and 50 pixels down from the top of the client area.

The CDC class overloads the MoveTo() function to provide flexibility as to how you specify the current position. There are two versions declared in the CDC class as:

```
CPoint MoveTo(int x, int y);    // Move to position x,y
CPoint MoveTo(POINT aPoint);    // Move to position defined by aPoint
```

The first version accepts the x- and y-coordinates as separate arguments. The second accepts one argument of type POINT. This is a structure that is defined as:

```
typedef struct tagPOINT
{
    LONG x;
    LONG y;
} POINT;
```

The coordinates are the x and y members of the struct and are of type LONG, which is a type defined in the Windows API as a 32-bit signed integer. You may prefer to use a class instead of a structure, in which case, you can use a CPoint object anywhere that a POINT object can be used. The CPoint class has data members x and y of type LONG, and using CPoint objects has the advantage that the class also defines functions that operate on both CPoint and POINT objects. This may seem weird because CPoint would seem to make POINT objects obsolete, but remember that the Windows API was built before the MFC was around, and POINT objects are used in the Windows API and have to be dealt with sooner or later. I'll use CPoint objects in examples, so you'll see some of the functions in action.

The MoveTo() function returns a CPoint object that specifies the current position as it was *before* the move. You might think this is a little odd, but consider the situation in which you want to move to a new position, draw something, and then move back. You may not know the current position before the move, and it is lost after the move occurs, so returning the position as it was before the move makes sure it's available if you need it.

Drawing Lines

You can follow the call to MoveTo() in the OnDraw() function with a call to the LineTo() function, which draws a line in the client area from the current position to the point specified by the arguments, as illustrated in Figure 14-3.

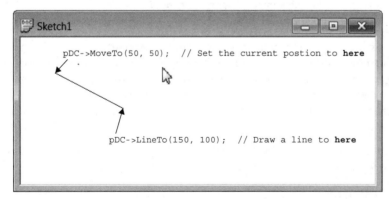

FIGURE 14-3

The CDC class defines two versions of the LineTo() function that have the following prototypes:

```
BOOL LineTo(int x, int y);    // Draw a line to position x,y
BOOL LineTo(POINT aPoint);    // Draw a line to position defined by aPoint
```

This offers you the same flexibility for the arguments as `MoveTo()`. You can use a `CPoint` object as the argument to the second version. The function returns `TRUE` if the line is drawn and `FALSE` otherwise.

When the `LineTo()` function executes, the current position is changed to the point at the end of the line. This enables you to draw a series of connected lines by just calling the `LineTo()` function for each line. Look at the following version of the `OnDraw()` function:

```
void CSketcherView::OnDraw(CDC* pDC)
{
   CSketcherDoc* pDoc = GetDocument();
   ASSERT_VALID(pDoc);
   if(!pDoc)
     return;

   pDC->MoveTo(50,50);         // Set the current position
   pDC->LineTo(50,200);        // Draw a vertical line down 150 units
   pDC->LineTo(150,200);       // Draw a horizontal line right 100 units
   pDC->LineTo(150,50);        // Draw a vertical line up 150 units
   pDC->LineTo(50,50);         // Draw a horizontal line left 100 units
}
```

If you plug this code into the Sketcher program and execute it, it will display the document window shown in Figure 14-4. Don't forget to uncomment the parameter name.

The four calls to `LineTo()` draw the rectangle counterclockwise starting with the upper-left corner. The first uses the current position set by the `MoveTo()` function; the succeeding calls use the current position set by the previous `LineTo()` function call. You can use this method to draw any figure consisting of a sequence of lines, each connected to the previous line. Of course, you can use `MoveTo()` to change the current position at any time.

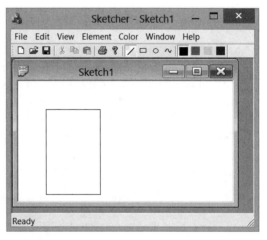

FIGURE 14-4

Drawing Circles

You have a choice of several `CDC` member functions for drawing circles, but they're all designed to draw ellipses. As you know from high-school geometry, a circle is a special case of an ellipse that has its major and minor axes equal. You can, therefore, use the `Ellipse()` member to draw a circle. Like other closed shapes supported by the `CDC` class, the `Ellipse()` function fills the interior of the shape with a color that you set. The interior color is determined by a *brush* that is selected into the device context. A brush is one example of a GDI object that is used to draw in a window and is encapsulated by the MFC `CBrush` class. The current brush in the device context determines how any closed shape is filled. There are two versions of the `Ellipse()` function:

```
BOOL Ellipse(int x1, int y1, int x2, int y2);
BOOL Ellipse(LPCRECT lpRect);
```

The first draws an ellipse bounded by the rectangle defined by the points x1,y1, and x2,y2. The second version defines the ellipse by a RECT object that is pointed to by the argument. The function also accepts a pointer to an object of the MFC CRect class, which has four public data members: left, top, right, and bottom. These correspond to the x- and y-coordinates of the upper-left and lower-right points of the rectangle. CRect provides member functions that operate on CRect objects, and you will be using some of these later. Ellipse() returns TRUE if the operation is successful and FALSE if it is not. With either function, the ellipse that is drawn extends up to, but does not include, the right and bottom sides of the rectangle. This means that the width and height of the ellipse are x2-x1 and y2-y1, respectively.

You can set the color of a CBrush object and also define a pattern to be produced when you are filling a closed shape such as an ellipse. If you want to draw a closed shape that isn't filled, you can select a null brush into the device context, which leaves the interior of the shape empty. I'll come back to brushes a little later in this chapter.

Another way to draw circles that aren't filled is to use the Arc() function, which doesn't involve brushes. This is because the curve drawn by the Arc() function is not closed, and therefore cannot be filled. Arc() has the advantage that you can draw any arc of an ellipse. There are two versions of this function in the CDC class:

```
BOOL Arc(int x1, int y1, int x2, int y2, int x3, int y3, int x4, int y4);
BOOL Arc(LPCRECT lpRect, POINT ptStart, POINT ptEnd);
```

In the first version, (x1,y1) and (x2,y2) define the upper-left and lower-right corners of a rectangle enclosing the complete curve. If these coordinates are the corners of a square, the curve drawn is a segment of a circle. The points (x3,y3) and (x4,y4) define the start and end points of the segment to be drawn. The segment is drawn counterclockwise from (x3,y3) to (x4,y4). If you make (x4,y4) identical to (x3,y3), you'll generate a complete ellipse, although it will not be a closed curve.

In the second version of Arc(), the enclosing rectangle is defined by a RECT object, and a pointer to this object is passed as the first argument. The POINT objects startPt and endPt define the start and end of the arc to be drawn, respectively.

Here's some code that calls the Ellipse() and Arc() functions:

```
void CSketcherView::OnDraw(CDC* pDC)
{
   CSketcherDoc* pDoc = GetDocument();
   ASSERT_VALID(pDoc);
   if(!pDoc)
     return;

   pDC->Ellipse(50,50,150,150);                 // Draw the 1st (large) circle

   // Define the bounding rectangle for the 2nd (smaller) circle
   CRect rect {250,50,300,100};
   CPoint start {275,100};                       // Arc start point
```

```
        CPoint end {250,75};                    // Arc end point
        pDC->Arc(&rect, start, end);            // Draw the second circle
}
```

You use a `CRect` class object instead of a `RECT` structure to define the bounding rectangle, and you use `CPoint` objects instead of `POINT` structures. You'll be using `CRect` objects again later, and they have some limitations, as you'll see. The `Arc()` and `Ellipse()` functions do not require a current position to be set because the position and extent of the curve are completely defined by the arguments you supply. The current position is unaffected by the drawing of an arc or an ellipse — it remains exactly wherever it was before the shape was drawn. Now, try running Sketcher with this code in the `OnDraw()` function. You should get the results shown in Figure 14-5.

Try moving the borders of the window. The client area is automatically redrawn as you cover or uncover the arcs. Remember that screen resolution affects the scale of what is displayed. The lower the screen resolution, the larger and farther from the upper-left corner of the client area the arcs will be.

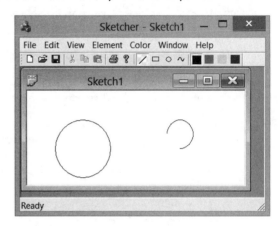

Drawing in Color

Everything that you've drawn so far has appeared on the screen in black. Drawing always uses a *pen object* that specifies the color, thickness, and line type (solid, dotted, dashed, and so on) that is drawn. A pen is another GDI object. You have been using the default pen object that is provided in a device context up to now. You're not obliged to do this, of course — you can create your own pen with a given thickness, color, and line type. MFC defines the class `CPen` to help you do this.

FIGURE 14-5

Creating a Pen

The simplest way to create a pen is first to define an object of the `CPen` class using the default class constructor:

```
CPen aPen;              // Define a pen object
```

This object must be initialized with the properties you want and you do this by calling the `CreatePen()` function for the object. This function is declared in the `CPen` class as:

```
BOOL CreatePen(int aPenStyle, int aWidth, COLORREF aColor);
```

The function returns TRUE as long as the pen is successfully initialized and FALSE otherwise. The first argument defines the line style, which must be one of the following symbolic values:

PEN STYLE	DESCRIPTION
PS_SOLID	The pen draws a solid line.
PS_DASH	The pen draws a dashed line. This line style is valid only when the pen width is 1.
PS_DOT	The pen draws a dotted line. This line style is valid only when the pen width is 1.
PS_DASHDOT	The pen draws a line with alternating dashes and dots. This line style is valid only when the pen width is 1.
PS_DASHDOTDOT	The pen draws a line with alternating dashes and double dots. This line style is valid only when the pen width is 1.
PS_NULL	The pen doesn't draw anything.
PS_INSIDEFRAME	The pen draws a solid line but, unlike with PS_SOLID, the points that specify the line occur on the edge of the pen rather than in the center, so that the drawn object never extends beyond the defining rectangle for closed shapes such as ellipses.

> **NOTE** There is another CPen class constructor that enables you to create your own line styles. You specify a line style by an array of values that specify the lengths of the dashes and spaces in the line.

The second argument to CreatePen() defines the line width. If aWidth is 0, the line is one pixel wide, regardless of the mapping mode in effect. For values of 1 or more, the pen width is in units determined by the mapping mode. For example, a value of 2 for aWidth in MM_TEXT mode is two pixels; in MM_LOENGLISH mode, the pen width is 0.02 inches.

The last argument specifies the line color, so you could initialize a pen with the following statement:

```
aPen.CreatePen(PS_SOLID, 2, RGB(255,0,0));  // Create a red solid pen
```

If the mapping mode is MM_TEXT, this pen draws a solid red line that is two pixels wide. RGB is the macro that you met in Chapter 13. It creates a 24-bit color value composed from three unsigned byte integer values that are the intensities of the red, green, and blue components of the color.

You can also create a pen object with specified line type, width, and color using the constructor:

```
CPen aPen{PS_SOLID, 2, RGB(0, 255, 0)};     // Create a green solid pen
```

When you create a pen of your own in this way, you are creating a Windows GDI PEN object that is encapsulated by the CPen object. When the CPen object is destroyed, the CPen destructor will delete the GDI pen object automatically. If you create a GDI PEN object explicitly, you must delete the object by calling DeleteObject() with the PEN object as the argument.

Using a Pen

To use a pen, you must select it into the device context. You call the SelectObject() function for the CDC object to do this. To select a pen, you call this function with the address of the pen object as the argument. The function returns a pointer to the previous pen object, so that you can save the old pen and restore it when you have finished drawing. A typical statement selecting a pen is:

```
CPen* pOldPen {pDC->SelectObject(&aPen)}    // Select aPen as the pen
```

You must always return a device context to its original state once you have finished with whatever you have selected into it. To restore the old pen when you're done, you call SelectObject() again, passing the pointer returned from the original call as the argument:

```
pDC->SelectObject(pOldPen);                 // Restore the old pen
```

You can see all this in action if you amend the previous version of the OnDraw() function in CSketcherView to the following:

```
void CSketcherView::OnDraw(CDC* pDC)
{
    CSketcherDoc* pDoc = GetDocument();
    ASSERT_VALID(pDoc);
    if(!pDoc)
      return;

    // Declare a pen object and initialize it as
    // a red solid pen drawing a line 2 pixels wide
    CPen aPen;
    aPen.CreatePen(PS_SOLID, 2, RGB(255, 0, 0));

    CPen* pOldPen {pDC->SelectObject(&aPen)}; // Select aPen as the pen
    pDC->Ellipse(50,50,150,150);              // Draw the 1st (large) circle

    // Define the bounding rectangle for the 2nd (smaller) circle
    CRect rect {250,50,300,100};
    CPoint start {275,100};                   // Arc start point
    CPoint end {250,75};                      // Arc end point
    pDC->Arc(&rect,start, end);               // Draw the second circle
    pDC->SelectObject(pOldPen);               // Restore the old pen

}
```

If you build and execute Sketcher with this version of OnDraw(), you get the same curves drawn as before, but this time, the lines will be thicker and they'll be red. You could usefully experiment with this example by trying different combinations of arguments to the `CreatePen()` function and seeing their effects. Note that we have ignored the value returned from the `CreatePen()` function, so you run the risk of the function failing and not detecting it in the program. It doesn't matter here, as the program is trivial, but as you develop the program, it is important to check for failures of this kind.

Creating a Brush

An object of the `CBrush` class encapsulates a Windows brush. You can define a brush to be solid, hatched, or patterned. A brush is an eight-by-eight block of pixels that's repeated over the region to be filled.

To define a brush with a solid color, you just specify the color when you create the object. For example:

```
CBrush aBrush {RGB(255,0,0)};              // Define a red brush
```

This defines a red brush. The value passed to the `CBrush` constructor must be of type `COLORREF`, which is the type produced by the `RGB()` macro so this is a good way to specify the color.

Another constructor defines a hatched brush. It requires two arguments: the first defines the type of hatching, and the second specifies the color. The hatching argument can be any of the following:

HATCHING STYLE	DESCRIPTION
HS_HORIZONTAL	Horizontal hatching
HS_VERTICAL	Vertical hatching
HS_BDIAGONAL	Downward hatching from left to right at 45 degrees
HS_FDIAGONAL	Upward hatching from left to right at 45 degrees
HS_CROSS	Horizontal and vertical crosshatching
HS_DIAGCROSS	Crosshatching at 45 degrees

To obtain a red, 45-degree crosshatched brush, you could define the `CBrush` object with the following statement:

```
CBrush aBrush {HS_DIAGCROSS, RGB(255,0,0)};
```

You can initialize a `CBrush` object much as you do a `CPen` object, by calling the `CreateSolidBrush()` member for a `CBrush` object to initialize it as a solid brush, and the `CreateHatchBrush()` member for a hatched brush. They require the same arguments as the equivalent constructors. For example, you could create the same hatched brush as before with the following statements:

```
CBrush aBrush;                         // Define a brush object
aBrush.CreateHatchBrush(HS_DIAGCROSS, RGB(255,0,0));
```

Using a Brush

To use a brush, you select the brush into the device context by calling the `SelectObject()` member of the `CDC` object much as you did for a pen. This member function is overloaded to support selecting brush objects into a device context. This selects the brush defined previously:

```
CBrush* pOldBrush {pDC->SelectObject(&aBrush)};     // Select the brush into the DC
```

`SelectObject()` returns a pointer to the old brush, or `nullptr` if the operation fails. You use the pointer that is returned to restore the old brush in the device context when you are done.

There are seven standard brushes available that are identified by predefined constants. They are:

GRAY_BRUSH	LTGRAY_BRUSH	DKGRAY_BRUSH
BLACK_BRUSH	WHITE_BRUSH	
HOLLOW_BRUSH	NULL_BRUSH	

The names are quite self-explanatory. To use one, call the `SelectStockObject()` member of the `CDC` object, with the symbolic name for the brush that you want to use as the argument. To select the null brush that leaves the interior of a closed shape unfilled, you would write this:

```
CBrush* pOldBrush {dynamic_cast<CBrush*>(pDC->SelectStockObject(NULL_BRUSH))};
```

`pDC` is a pointer to the `CDC` object, as before. You can also select one of a range of standard pens with the `SelectStockObject()` function. The symbols for standard pens are `BLACK_PEN`, `NULL_PEN` (which doesn't draw anything), and `WHITE_PEN`. `SelectStockObject()` works with a variety of object types. You've seen pens and brushes in this chapter but it also works with fonts. The return type for `SelectStockObject()` is `CGdiObject*`. `CGdiObject` is a base class for all the GDI object classes, so a pointer to this class type can store the address of any GDI object. You can store the pointer returned by `SelectObject()` or `SelectStockObject()` as type `CGdiObject*` and pass that to `SelectObject()` when you want to restore it. However, it is better to `dynamic_cast` the pointer value to the appropriate type so that you can keep track of the types of objects you are restoring.

The typical coding pattern for using a stock brush and later restoring the old brush when you're done is this:

```
CBrush* pOldBrush {dynamic_cast<CBrush*>(pDC->SelectStockObject(NULL_BRUSH))};

// draw something...

pDC->SelectObject(pOldBrush);                  // Restore the old brush
```

You'll be using this pattern in an example later in the chapter.

DRAWING GRAPHICS IN PRACTICE

You now know how to draw lines and arcs, so it's about time to consider how a user is going to draw in Sketcher. In other words, you need to decide how the user interface is going to work.

Because Sketcher is to be a sketching tool, you don't want the user to worry about coordinates. The easiest mechanism for drawing is using just the mouse. To draw a line for instance, users could position the mouse cursor where the line is to start and press the left mouse button; they could then define the end of the line by moving the cursor to where they want with the button held down, then releasing it. It would be ideal if you could arrange for the line to be continuously drawn as the cursor is moved with the button down (this is known as "rubber-banding"). The line would be fixed when the mouse button is released. Figure 14-6 illustrates this process.

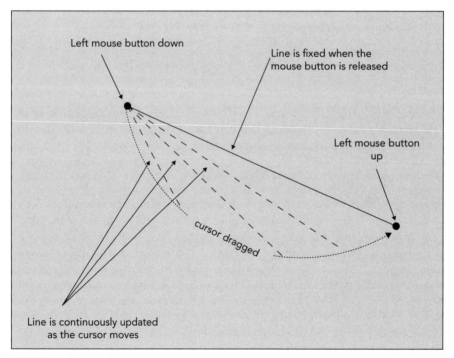

FIGURE 14-6

Circles can be drawn in a similar fashion. The point where the mouse button is pressed defines the center, and as the cursor is dragged with the button down, the program tracks and redraws the circle continuously with the cursor position defining a point on the circumference. Like the line, the circle is fixed when the button is released. Figure 14-7 shows this process.

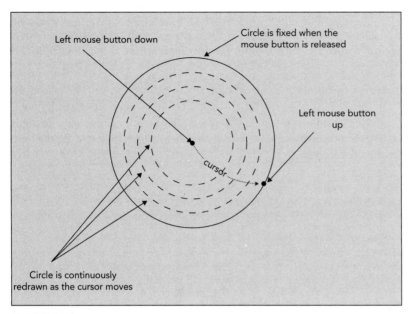

FIGURE 14-7

You can draw a rectangle as easily as you draw a line, as illustrated in Figure 14-8.

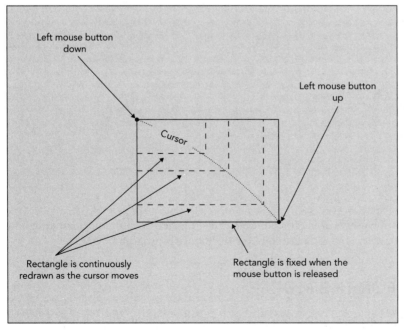

FIGURE 14-8

The first point is defined by the cursor position when the left mouse button is pressed. This is one corner of the rectangle. The cursor position when the mouse is moved with the button held down defines the diagonally opposite corner of the rectangle. The rectangle stored is the one defined when the button is released.

A curve is somewhat different. An arbitrary number of points may define a curve. The mechanism you'll use is illustrated in Figure 14-9. As with the other shapes, the first point is defined by the cursor position when the left mouse button is pressed. Successive cursor positions that are recorded as the mouse cursor is moved are connected by straight line segments to form the curve, so the mouse cursor track defines the curve to be drawn.

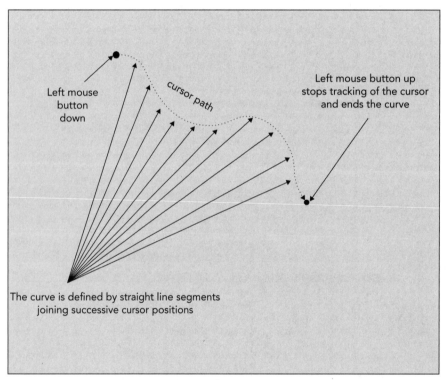

FIGURE 14-9

Now that you know how the user is going to define elements, the next step in understanding how you can implement this process is to get a grip on how the mouse is programmed.

PROGRAMMING FOR THE MOUSE

To program the drawing of Sketcher elements in the way that I have discussed, you need to identify how the mouse will be used:

➤ Pressing a mouse button signals the start of a drawing operation.

➤ The location of the cursor when the mouse button is pressed provides a first defining point for the shape.

➤ A mouse movement after detecting that a mouse button has been pressed is a cue to draw a shape, and the cursor position provides a second defining point for the shape.

➤ Releasing the mouse button signals the end of the drawing operation and that the final version of the shape should be drawn using the last cursor position.

As you may have guessed, all the information about what is happening with the mouse and its buttons is provided by Windows in the form of messages sent to your program. The implementation of the process for drawing lines, rectangles, circles, and curves consists almost entirely of writing message handlers.

Messages from the Mouse

When the users of your program are drawing an element, they will interact with a particular document view. The view class is, therefore, the obvious place to put the message handlers for the mouse. Right-click the `CSketcherView` class name in Class View and then display its properties window by selecting Properties from the menu. If you then click the messages button (wait for the button tooltips to display if you don't know which it is) you'll see the list of IDs for the standard Windows messages that are sent to the class, which are prefixed with `WM_` (see Figure 14-10).

You need to know about three mouse messages at the moment:

FIGURE 14-10

MESSAGE	DESCRIPTION
WM_LBUTTONDOWN	Occurs when the left mouse button is pressed
WM_LBUTTONUP	Occurs when the left mouse button is released
WM_MOUSEMOVE	Occurs when the mouse is moved

These messages are quite independent of one another and are sent to the document views in your program even if you haven't supplied handlers for them. It's quite possible for a window to receive a WM_LBUTTONUP message without having previously received a WM_LBUTTONDOWN message. This can happen if the button is pressed with the cursor over another window and the cursor is then moved to your view window before being released, so you must keep this in mind when coding handlers for these messages.

If you look at the list in the Properties window, you'll see there are other mouse messages that can occur. You can choose to process any or all of these, depending on your application. Let's define in general terms what we want to do with the three messages we are currently interested in, based on the process we have defined for drawing lines, rectangles, and circles.

WM_LBUTTONDOWN

This message starts the process of drawing an element. You should do the following:

1.   Record that the element-drawing process has started.

2.   Store the current cursor position as the first defining point for an element.

WM_MOUSEMOVE

This message is an intermediate stage in drawing an element in which you want to create and draw a temporary version of it, but only if the left mouse button is down. Complete the following steps:

1.   Verify that the left button is down.

2.   If the left button is down, delete any previous version of the current element that was drawn.

3.   If the left button isn't down, then exit the element creation operation.

4.   Record the current cursor position as the second defining point for the current element.

5.   Cause the current element to be drawn using the two defining points.

WM_LBUTTONUP

This message indicates that the element drawing process is finished. You need to do the following:

1.   Store the final version of the element defined by the first point recorded, together with the last cursor position when the button was released for the second point.

2.   Record the end of the process of drawing an element.

Now you are ready to generate handlers for these messages.

Mouse Message Handlers

Display the Properties for the CSketcherView class and click the Messages icon to display the messages this class can handle. You can create a handler for a mouse message by clicking its ID in the Properties window to select it and then selecting from the list that is displayed when you click the down arrow in the adjacent column position. Try selecting <add> OnLButtonUp for the WM_LBUTTONUP message, for example. Repeat the process for the WM_LBUTTONDOWN and WM_MOUSEMOVE messages. The functions generated in CSketcherView are OnLButtonDown(), OnLButtonUp(), and OnMouseMove(). You don't get the option of changing the names of these, because you're adding overrides for versions already defined in the base class. Now, we'll look at how you implement these handlers.

You can start with the WM_LBUTTONDOWN message handler. This is the skeleton code that's generated:

```
void CSketcherView::OnLButtonDown(UINT nFlags, CPoint point)
{
  // TODO: Add your message handler code here and/or call default

  CView::OnLButtonDown(nFlags, point);
}
```

There is a call to the base class handler in the skeleton version. This ensures that the base handler is called if you don't add any code. You don't need to call the base class handler when you handle this message yourself, although you can if you want to. Whether you need to call a base class message handler depends on the circumstances.

Generally, the comment in the implementation of your handler that indicates where you should add your code is a good guide. Where it suggests, as in the present instance, that calling the base class handler is optional, you can omit it when you add your own code. The position of the comment in relation to the base class handler call is also important, because sometimes you must call the base class handler before your code, and sometimes afterwards. The comment indicates where your code should appear in relation to the base class handler call.

The WM_LBUTTONDOWN handler is passed two arguments:

➤ nFlags is of type UINT and contains a number of status flags indicating which keys and/or mouse buttons are down. The UINT type is defined in the Windows API and corresponds to a 32-bit unsigned integer.

➤ The CPoint object, point, defines the cursor position when the left mouse button was pressed.

The value of nFlags can be any combination of the following values:

FLAG	DESCRIPTION
MK_CONTROL	The control key is pressed.
MK_LBUTTON	The left mouse button is down.
MK_MBUTTON	The middle mouse button is down.
MK_RBUTTON	The right mouse button is down.
MK_XBUTTON1	The first extra mouse button is down.
MK_XBUTTON2	The second extra mouse button is down.
MK_SHIFT	The shift key is pressed.

Being able to detect if a key is pressed enables you to support different actions for the message, depending on the states of the key. nFlags may contain more than one of these flags, each of which corresponds to a unique single bit in the word. You can test if a particular flag bit is 1 using the bit-wise AND operator. For example, to test if the control key is pressed you could write:

```
if(nFlags & MK_CONTROL)
  // Do something...
```

The expression `nFlags & MK_CONTROL` will be a non-zero value that converts to `true` only if `nFlags` has the `MK_CONTROL` bit set. In this way, you can perform different actions when the left mouse button is pressed, depending on whether or not the control key is pressed. You use the bitwise AND operator here, which ANDs corresponding bits together. Don't confuse this with the logical AND, `&&`, which would not do what you want.

The arguments passed to the other two message handlers are the same as those for `OnLButtonDown()`; the code generated for them is:

```
void CSketcherView::OnLButtonUp(UINT nFlags, CPoint point)
{
  // TODO: Add your message handler code here and/or call default

  CView::OnLButtonUp(nFlags, point);
}

void CSketcherView::OnMouseMove(UINT nFlags, CPoint point)
{
  // TODO: Add your message handler code here and/or call default

  CView::OnMouseMove(nFlags, point);
}
```

The skeleton code is more or less the same for each.

If you look at the end of the code for the `CSketcherView` class definition, you'll see that three function declarations have been added:

```
// Generated message map functions
protected:
  DECLARE_MESSAGE_MAP()
public:
  afx_msg void OnLButtonDown(UINT nFlags, CPoint point);
  afx_msg void OnLButtonUp(UINT nFlags, CPoint point);
  afx_msg void OnMouseMove(UINT nFlags, CPoint point);
};
```

These identify the functions that you added as message handlers. Now that you understand the information that is passed to the mouse message handlers, you can add your own code to make them do what you want.

Drawing Using the Mouse

For the `WM_LBUTTONDOWN` message, you want to record the cursor position as the first defining point for an element. You also want to record the cursor position after a mouse move. The obvious place to store these positions is in the `CSketcherView` class, so you can add data members for these. Right-click the `CSketcherView` class name in Class View and select Add ➪ Add Variable from the pop-up. You'll then be able to add details of the variable to be added to the class, as Figure 14-11 shows.

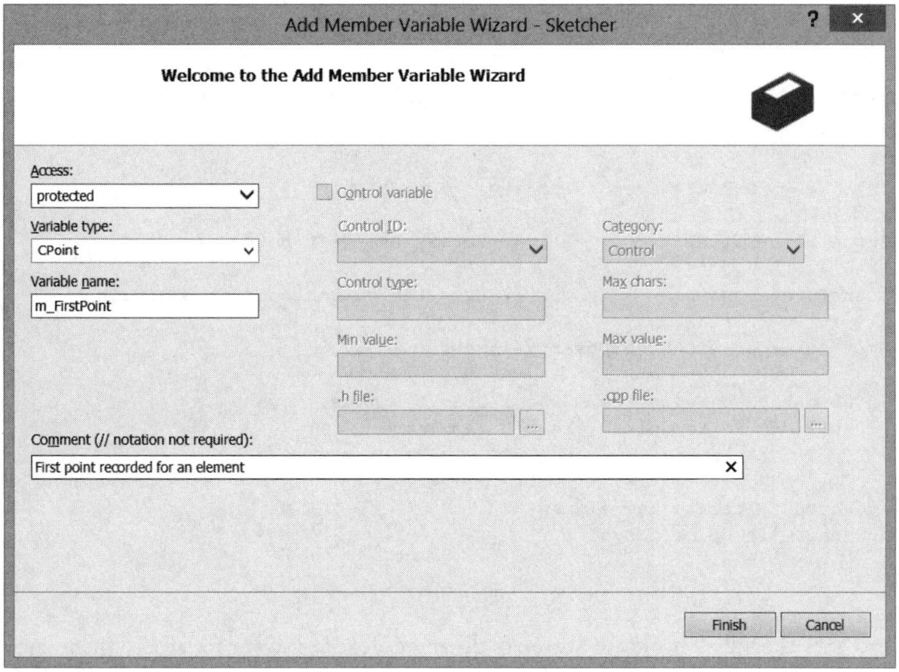

FIGURE 14-11

The drop-down list of types includes only fundamental types, so you must enter the variable type as CPoint. The new data member should be protected to prevent direct modification of it from outside the class so change the Access value to that from the list. Enter the name as m_FirstPoint. When you click the Finish button, the variable will be created and an initial value will be set arbitrarily as 0 in the constructor initializer.

```
CSketcherView::CSketcherView(): m_FirstPoint {CPoint {}}
{
    // TODO: add construction code here
}
```

The MSDN documentation for the CPoint class says that the default constructor does not initialize the data members but this is not correct. The code for the default CPoint constructor initializes both members to zero. This has been the case since Visual Studio 2010 but the documentation hasn't caught up yet. This means that if you are happy with (0,0) as the default for a CPoint object you don't need to worry about initializing it explicitly. I have removed the initialization from the code in SketcherView.cpp.

You can now implement the handler for the WM_LBUTTONDOWN message as follows:

```
void CSketcherView::OnLButtonDown(UINT nFlags, CPoint point)
{
    m_FirstPoint = point;                   // Record the cursor position
}
```

All the handler does is record the point passed by the second argument. You can ignore the first argument in this situation altogether.

You can't complete the WM_MOUSEMOVE message handler yet, but you can have a stab at outlining the code for it:

```
void CSketcherView::OnMouseMove(UINT nFlags, CPoint point)
{
   if(nFlags & MK_LBUTTON)              // Verify the left button is down
   {
      m_SecondPoint = point;            // Save the current cursor position

      // Test for a previous temporary element
      {
         // We get to here if there was a previous mouse move
         // so add code to delete the old element
      }

      // Add code to create new element
      // and cause it to be drawn
   }
}
```

It's important to verify that the left mouse button is down because you want to handle the mouse move only when this is the case. Without the check, you would be processing the event when the right button was down or when the mouse was moved with no buttons pressed.

If the left mouse button is down, you save the current cursor position. This is the second defining point for an element. The rest of the logic is clear in general terms, but you need to establish a few more things before you can complete the function. You have no means of defining an element — you'll want to define an element as a class object, so you must define some classes. You must also devise a way to delete an element and get one drawn when you create a new one. A brief digression is called for.

Getting the Client Area Redrawn

Drawing or erasing elements involves redrawing all or part of the client area of a window. As you've already discovered, the client area gets drawn by the OnDraw() member function of the CSketcherView class, and this function is called when a WM_PAINT message is received by the Sketcher application. Along with the basic message to repaint the client area, Windows supplies information about the area that needs to be redrawn. This can save a lot of time when you're displaying complicated images because only the area specified needs to be redrawn, and this may be a very small proportion of the total area.

You can tell Windows that a particular area should be redrawn by calling the InvalidateRect() member of your view class. The function requires two arguments. The first is a pointer to a RECT or CRect object that defines the rectangle in the client area to be redrawn. Passing nullptr causes the whole client area to be redrawn. The second argument is a BOOL value, which is TRUE if the background to the rectangle is to be erased and FALSE otherwise. This argument has a default value of TRUE, because you normally want the background erased before the rectangle is redrawn, so you don't need to supply it most of the time.

A typical situation in which you will want to cause an area to be redrawn will be where something has changed in a way that makes it necessary — moving something displayed in the client area entity is one example. In this case, you want to erase the background to remove the old representation of what was displayed before you draw the new version. When you want to draw over an existing background, you pass FALSE as the second argument to InvalidateRect().

Calling InvalidateRect() doesn't directly cause any part of the window to be redrawn; it just communicates the rectangle that you would like to have redrawn to Windows. Windows maintains a cumulative update region — actually, a rectangle — that identifies the total area that needs to be redrawn, and this may be due to several InvalidateRect() calls. The area specified in your call to InvalidateRect() is added to the current update region, so the new update region encloses the old region plus the new rectangle you have identified. When a WM_PAINT message is sent to a view, the update region is passed to the view object along with the message. When processing of the WM_PAINT message is complete, the update region is reset to the empty state. Calling the UpdateWindow() function that is inherited in the view class causes a WM_PAINT message to be sent to the view.

Thus, to get a newly created element drawn you need to:

1. Make sure that the OnDraw() function in your view includes the newly created element when it redraws the window.

2. Call InvalidateRect() with a pointer to the rectangle bounding the element to be redrawn as the first argument.

3. Cause a WM_PAINT message to be sent to the view by calling the inherited UpdateWindow() function for the view.

Similarly, if you want an element removed from the client area of a window, you need to do the following:

1. Remove the element from the items that the OnDraw() function will draw.

2. Call InvalidateRect() with the first argument pointing to the rectangle bounding the element that is to be removed.

3. Cause a WM_PAINT message to be sent to the view by calling the inherited UpdateWindow() function for the view.

Because the background to the update region is automatically erased, the element disappears as long as the OnDraw() function doesn't draw the element again. Of course, this means that you need to be able to obtain the rectangle bounding any element that you create, so you'll include a function to return this rectangle as a member of the classes that define Sketcher elements.

Defining Element Classes

Thinking ahead a bit, as well as storing sketch elements in a document in some way, you will want to store the document in a file for subsequent retrieval if a sketch is to have any permanence. I'll deal with the details of file operations later on, but for now, it's enough to know that the MFC class CObject includes the tools for you to do this, so you'll use CObject as a base class for the classes that define sketch elements.

You don't know in advance what sequence of element types a user will create, so Sketcher must be able to handle any sequence of elements. This suggests that using a base class pointer to store the address of the latest element that was created might simplify things a bit. You'll be able to call element class functions without knowing precisely what kind of element it is. For example, you don't need to know what an element is to draw it. As long as you are accessing the element through a base class pointer, you can always get an element to draw itself by calling a `virtual` function. All you must do to achieve this is to make sure that the classes that define elements share a common base class and that you declare all the functions you want to be called polymorphically at run time as `virtual` in the base class. You could organize the element classes as shown in Figure 14-12.

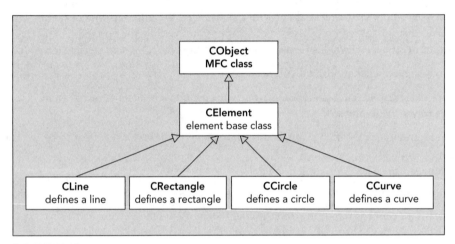

FIGURE 14-12

Each arrow in the diagram points toward a base class. If you need to add another type of element, you derive another class from `CElement`.

You can create the `CElement` class by right-clicking Sketcher in Class View and selecting Add ⇨ Class from the pop-up. Select MFC from the list of installed templates, and then select MFC Class in the center pane. When you click the Add button in the dialog, another dialog displays in which you can specify the class name and select the base class, as shown in Figure 14-13.

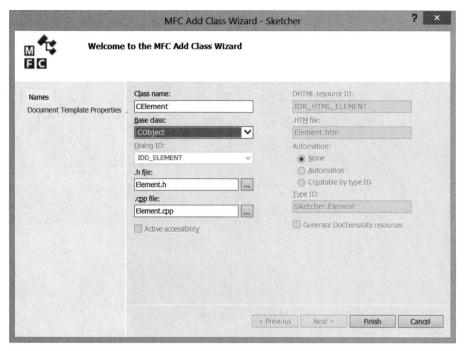

FIGURE 14-13

I have already filled in the class name as CElement and selected CObject from the drop-down list as the base class. When you click the Finish button, the code for the class definition is generated:

```
#pragma once


// CElement command target

class CElement : public CObject
{
public:
  CElement();
  virtual ~CElement();
};
```

The only members that have been declared for you are a constructor and a virtual destructor, and skeleton definitions for these appear in the Element.cpp file. You can see that the Class Wizard has included a #pragma once directive to ensure that the contents of the header file cannot be included into another file more than once.

You can add the other element classes using essentially the same process. Because the other element classes have CElement rather than an MFC class as the base class, you should set the class category as C++ and the template as C++ class. Select the Virtual destructor option. For the CLine class, the Class Wizard dialog should look like Figure 14-14.

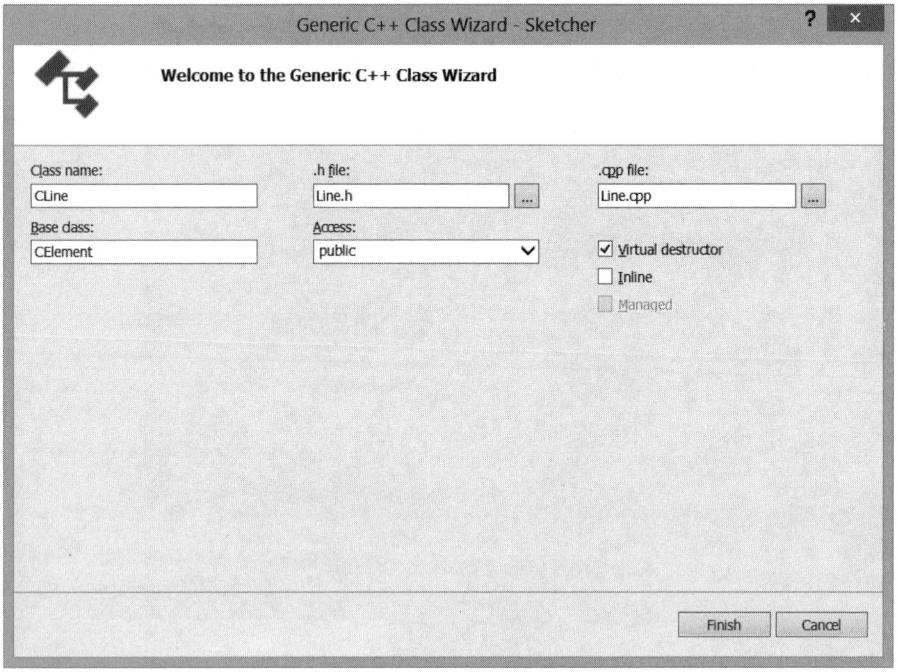

FIGURE 14-14

The Class Wizard supplies the names of the header file and `.cpp` file as `Line.h` and `Line.cpp` by default, but you can change these to different names or have the code added to existing files. You get an `#include` directive for `Element.h` for the base class definition. When you have created the `CLine` class, do the same for `CRectangle`, `CCircle`, and `CCurve`. When you are done, you should have `.h` files containing the definitions of all four subclasses of `CElement`, each with a constructor and a virtual destructor.

Storing a Temporary Element in the View

When I discussed how sketch elements would be drawn, it was evident that as the mouse was dragged with the left mouse button down, a series of temporary element objects would be created and drawn. The base class for all elements is `CElement`, so you can add a smart pointer of type `std::shared_ptr<CElement>` to the view class to store the address of a temporary element. You could consider `unique_ptr` as a candidate for this but eventually you will need access to a pointer to an element in the mouse event handler functions, while the same pointer is stored in a container in the document object. A `unique_ptr` would not allow this.

First, you can add `#include` directives for the `memory` header and `Element.h` following the `#pragma once` directive. Next, right-click `CSketcherView` and select the Add ➪ Add Variable option. The `m_pTempElement` variable will be of type `std::shared_ptr<CElement>`, and it should be `protected` like the previous two data members that you added. You'll be able to use the `m_pTempElement` pointer in the `WM_MOUSEMOVE` message handler as a test for whether a previous temporary element exists because it will be `nullptr` when there are none.

The CElement Class

You'll be developing the element class definitions incrementally as you increase the functionality of Sketcher — but what do you need right now? Some data items, such as color and position, are common to all types of elements, so you can put those in the CElement base class so that they are inherited in the derived classes. Other data members that define specific element properties will be declared in the derived class to which they belong.

The CElement class will contain virtual functions that will be implemented in the derived classes, plus data and function members that are common to all the derived classes. The virtual functions will be those that are selected polymorphically for a particular object through a CElement* pointer. You could use the Add Member Wizard to add these members to the CElement class, but modify the class manually for a change. For now, you can modify the CElement class definition to the following:

```
class CElement: public CObject
{
protected:
  CPoint m_StartPoint;          // Element position
  int m_PenWidth;               // Pen width
  COLORREF m_Color;             // Color of an element
  CRect m_EnclosingRect;        // Rectangle enclosing an element

public:
  virtual ~CElement();
  virtual void Draw(CDC* pDC) {}  // Virtual draw operation

  // Get the element enclosing rectangle
  const CRect& GetEnclosingRect() const {  return m_EnclosingRect;  }

protected:
  // Constructors protected so they cannot be called outside the class
  CElement();
  CElement(const CPoint& start, COLORREF color, int penWidth = 1);
};
```

I have made the constructors protected to prevent them from being called from outside the class. The new constructor will only be called from a derived class. It has three parameters with a default value for the pen width because most of the time the pen width will be 1. At the moment, the data members to be inherited in the derived classes store the position, the color, and the pen width for an element, and the enclosing rectangle that identifies the area occupied by an element.

There are two member function definitions within the class:

➤   GetEnclosingRect() returns m_EnclosingRect. This will be used when the area an element occupies needs to be invalidated.

➤   A virtual Draw() function that will be implemented in the derived classes to draw an element. The Draw() function needs a pointer to a CDC object passed to it to provide access to the functions that you need to draw in a device context.

You might be tempted to declare the `Draw()` member as a pure virtual function in the `CElement` class and leave it to the derived classes to define — after all, it can have no meaningful content here. Normally, you would do this, but `CElement` inherits a facility from `CObject` called *serialization* that you'll use later to store element objects in a file. Serialization requires that `CElement` is not abstract so an object of this type can be created. If you want to use MFC's serialization capability, your classes must not be abstract and they must have a no-arg constructor.

> **NOTE** *Serialization is a general term for writing objects to a file.*

You can add the definition for the new constructor to `Element.cpp`:

```
CElement::CElement(const CPoint& start, COLORREF color, int penWidth) :
                   m_StartPoint {start}, m_PenWidth {penWidth}, m_Color {color} {}
```

All members are initialized in the constructor initializer list so there is no code required for the body of the constructor.

The CLine Class

You can amend the definition of the `CLine` class to the following:

```
class CLine: public CElement
{
public:
  virtual ~CLine(void);
  virtual void Draw(CDC* pDC) override; // Function to display a line

  // Constructor for a line object
  CLine(const CPoint& start, const CPoint& end, COLORREF aColor);

protected:
  CPoint m_EndPoint;                    // End point of line

protected:
  CLine();                              // Default constructor should not be used
};
```

A line is defined by two points, `m_StartPoint` that is inherited from `CElement` and `m_EndPoint`. The class has a `public` constructor that has parameters for the values that define a line, and the no-arg default constructor has been moved to the `protected` section of the class to prevent its use externally. The constructor parameters are `const` references to avoid copying the arguments. Using the `override` keyword with the `Draw()` member declaration ensures that the compiler will verify that it overrides the base class function correctly.

Implementing the CLine Class

You put the implementations of the `CLine` member functions in the `Line.cpp` file that was created by the Class Wizard. The `stdafx.h` file that is included into this file makes the standard system header files available and the contents of stdafx.h will be precompiled. Any of your headers that you do not anticipate changing can be included in stdafx.h to have them precompiled too. You can now add the basic code for the CLine constructor to Line.cpp.

The CLine Constructor

The code for the constructor is as follows:

```
// CLine class constructor
CLine::CLine(const CPoint& start, const CPoint& end, COLORREF color) :
                          CElement {start, color}, m_EndPoint {end} {}
```

You initialize the inherited m_StartPoint and m_Color members by calling the CElement base class constructor. The pen width is set to 1 by default in this constructor when you omit the third argument. The m_EndPoint member of CLine is initialized in the initialization list for the constructor. You'll add a bit more code to this later.

Drawing a Line

The CPen object you need to draw lines will be the same for all elements. You could usefully add a function within the CElement class definition to create it:

```
// Create a pen
void CreatePen(CPen& aPen)
{
  if(!aPen.CreatePen(PS_SOLID, m_PenWidth, m_Color))
  {
    // Pen creation failed
    AfxMessageBox(_T("Pen creation failed."), MB_OK);
    AfxAbort();
  }
}
```

This will only be called by derived class objects so you can put the definition in a protected section of the class. Defining the function within the class definition will make it inline. The reference parameter allows the function to modify the aPen object that is defined in the calling function. Calling CreatePen() for a CPen object creates a pen and attaches it to the object. You create a pen of the appropriate color and with a line thickness specified by m_PenWidth, and you make sure that the creation works. In the unlikely event that it doesn't, the most likely cause is that you're running out of memory, which is a serious problem. This is almost invariably caused by an error in the program, so you have written the function to call AfxMessageBox(), which is an MFC global function to display a message box, and then call AfxAbort() to terminate the program. The first argument to AfxMessageBox() specifies the message, and the second specifies that it should have an OK button. You can get more information on these functions by placing the cursor within the function name in the Editor window and pressing F1.

Without this function in the base class, you would have to repeat this code in the Draw() function in every derived class.

> **WARNING** *Device contexts, pens, brushes, fonts, and other objects you use to draw in a window are GDI objects. You must not attempt to copy or assign GDI objects. If you do, your code will not compile. This has implications. It means, for example, that you cannot pass a GDI object by value to another function.*

The `Draw()` function for the `CLine` class isn't too difficult, although you do need to take account of the color that is to be used when the line is drawn:

```
// Draw a CLine object
void CLine::Draw(CDC* pDC)
{
  // Create a pen for this object and initialize it
  CPen aPen;
  CreatePen(aPen);

  CPen* pOldPen {pDC->SelectObject(&aPen)};        // Select the pen

  // Now draw the line
  pDC->MoveTo(m_StartPoint);
  pDC->LineTo(m_EndPoint);

  pDC->SelectObject(pOldPen);                      // Restore the old pen
}
```

Calling the inherited `CreatePen()` function sets up the pen in `aPen`. After selecting the pen into the device context, you move the current position to the start of the line, defined in `m_StartPoint`, and then draw the line from this point to `m_EndPoint`. Finally, you restore the old pen in the device context and you are done.

Creating Enclosing Rectangles

At first sight, obtaining the enclosing rectangle for an element looks trivial. For example, a line is always a diagonal of a rectangle, and a circle is defined by a rectangle, but there are a couple of slight complications. The element must lie *completely* inside the enclosing rectangle; otherwise, part of the element may not be drawn or erased. You must take account of how the element is drawn in relation to its defining parameters and allow for the thickness of the line used to draw it. How you work out adjustments to the coordinates that define the enclosing rectangle depends on the mapping mode, so you must take that into account too.

Different mapping modes only affect how you adjust the y-coordinates of the corners of a defining rectangle to obtain the enclosing rectangle; adjustment of the x-coordinate is the same for all mapping modes; you subtract the line thickness from the x-coordinate of the top-left corner and add it to the x-coordinate of the bottom-right corner. To adjust the y-coordinate of the top-left corner of the defining rectangle in the MM_TEXT mapping mode, you *subtract* the line thickness from it. However, in MM_LOENGLISH (and all the other mapping modes), the y-axis increases in the opposite direction, so you need to *add* the line thickness to the y-coordinate of the upper-left corner of the defining rectangle. You'll create the enclosing rectangle for an element in the constructor for each element type.

> **WARNING** *The data members of a* CRect *object are* left *and* top *storing the x- and y-coordinates of the top-left corner, and* right *and* bottom *storing the coordinates of the bottom-right corner. These are all public members, so you can access them directly. A mistake often made, especially by me, is to write the coordinate pair as (*top, left*) instead of the correct order: (*left, top*).*

Normalized Rectangles

A *normalized rectangle* is a rectangle where the value of the left coordinate is less than the right, and the top coordinate is less than the bottom. If a rectangle is not normalized, functions that operate on CRect objects won't work correctly. For example, the InflateRect() member of the CRect class works by subtracting the argument values from the top and left members of the rectangle and adding them to the bottom and right. This means that you may find that your rectangle decreases in size when you apply InflateRect() to it if you don't make sure that the rectangle is normalized. As long as your rectangles are normalized, InflateRect() will work correctly whatever the mapping mode. You can normalize a CRect object by calling its NormalizeRect() member.

Calculating the Enclosing Rectangle for a Line

You can add code in the CLine constructor to calculate the enclosing rectangle:

```
CLine::CLine(const CPoint& start, const CPoint& end, COLORREF color):
        CElement {start, color}, m_EndPoint {end}
{
  // Define the enclosing rectangle
  m_EnclosingRect = CRect {start, end};
  m_EnclosingRect.NormalizeRect();
  m_EnclosingRect.InflateRect(m_PenWidth, m_PenWidth);
}
```

You ensure that the enclosing rectangle has left and top values that are less than its right and bottom values, regardless of the relative positions of the start and end points of the line, by calling the NormalizeRect() member of the m_EnclosingRect object. Calling InflateRect() enlarges the rectangle by the pen width. The first argument is the adjustment for the left and right sides and the second is the adjustment for the top and bottom. One overload of InflateRect() has a single parameter of type SIZE, which also accepts a CSize object that encapsulates the SIZE struct. A CSize object defines a size by public members cx and cy of type long.

The CRectangle Class

You'll be defining a rectangle object with the same data that you use to define a line; the points define opposite corners. You can define the class as:

```
class CRectangle: public CElement
{
public:
  virtual ~CRectangle();
  virtual void Draw(CDC* pDC) override; // Function to display a rectangle

  // Constructor for a rectangle object
```

```
    CRectangle(const CPoint& start, const CPoint& end, COLORREF color);

protected:
    CPoint m_BottomRight;           // Bottom-right point for the rectangle
    CRectangle();                   // Default constructor - should not be used
};
```

The no-arg constructor is `protected` to prevent its use externally. The definition of the rectangle class is very simple — just a constructor, the virtual `Draw()` function, plus the no-arg constructor in the `protected` section of the class.

The CRectangle Constructor

The code for the new `CRectangle` class constructor is a little more complicated than that for `CLine`:

```
// CRectangle constructor
CRectangle::CRectangle (
                const CPoint& start, const CPoint& end, COLORREF color) :
                CElement {start, color}
{
  // Normalize the rectangle defining points
  m_StartPoint = CPoint {(std::min)(start.x, end.x),(std::min)(start.y, end.y)};
  m_BottomRight = CPoint {(std::max)(start.x, end.x), (std::max)(start.y, end.y)};

  // Ensure width and height between the points is at least 2
  if((m_BottomRight.x - m_StartPoint.x) < 2)
    m_BottomRight.x = m_StartPoint.x + 2;
  if((m_BottomRight.y - m_StartPoint.y) < 2)
    m_BottomRight.y = m_StartPoint.y + 2;

  // Define the enclosing rectangle
  m_EnclosingRect = CRect {m_StartPoint, m_BottomRight};
  m_EnclosingRect.InflateRect(m_PenWidth, m_PenWidth);
}
```

You call the `CElement` constructor in the initialization list to get the color and pen width initialized. The `CElement` constructor also initializes `m_StartPoint`, but you will replace this. You can only draw a `CRect` object that has a width and height of at least 2, so you adjust the coordinates of the two defining points if necessary, after arranging that the points define a normalized rectangle. Because you adjusted the points, there's no need to call `NormalizeRect()`. `std::min()` and `std::max()` are template functions defined in the `algorithm` header that return the minimum and maximum of their arguments, respectively. Add an `#include` directive for the `algorithm` header to `Rectangle.cpp`.

> **WARNING** The parentheses around `std::min` and `std::max` in the code are essential. This is not typical with other C++ compilers but is a peculiarity of Visual C++. The `windows.h` header defines macros for `min` and `max` and without the parentheses, the preprocessor will make the substitution for these macros before compilation starts. This will cause the compiler to generate error messages. The parentheses prevent the preprocessor macro substitutions.

Drawing a Rectangle

The `Rectangle()` member of the `CDC` class draws a rectangle. This function draws a closed figure and fills it with the current brush. You want to draw rectangles as outlines and selecting a `NULL_BRUSH` into the device context will do that. Just so you know, there's also a `PolyLine()` member of `CDC` that draws shapes consisting of multiple line segments from an array of points. You could also use `LineTo()` to draw the four sides of the rectangle, but the easiest approach is to use the `Rectangle()` function:

```
// Draw a CRectangle object
void CRectangle::Draw(CDC* pDC)
{
  // Create a pen for this object and initialize it
  CPen aPen;
  CreatePen(aPen);

  // Select the pen and the null brush
  CPen* pOldPen {pDC->SelectObject(&aPen)};
  CBrush* pOldBrush {dynamic_cast<CBrush*>(pDC->SelectStockObject(NULL_BRUSH))};

  // Now draw the rectangle
  pDC->Rectangle(m_StartPoint.x, m_StartPoint.y,
              m_BottomRight.x, m_BottomRight.y);

  pDC->SelectObject(pOldBrush);      // Restore the old brush
  pDC->SelectObject(pOldPen);        // Restore the old pen
}
```

After setting up the pen and the brush, you call the `Rectangle()` function to draw the rectangle element. The arguments are the coordinates of the top-left and bottom-right corners. There's an overload of this function that accepts a `CRect` object to specify the rectangle. All that remains to do is to restore the device context's old pen and brush.

The CCircle Class

The `CCircle` class interface is similar to that of the `CRectangle` class. You draw a circle using the `Ellipse()` member of the `CDC` class, which draws an ellipse bounded by a rectangle. As long as the defining rectangle is square, the ellipse will be a circle. You will define a circle from its two defining points, the center and a point on the circumference, so the class definition is:

```
class CCircle : public CElement
{
public:
  virtual ~CCircle();
  virtual void Draw(CDC* pDC) override;      // Function to display a circle

  // Constructor for a circle object
  CCircle(const CPoint& start, const CPoint& end, COLORREF color);

protected:
  CPoint m_BottomRight;              // Bottom-right point for defining circle
  CCircle();                         // Default constructor - should not be used
};
```

You have defined a public constructor that creates a circle from two points and its drawing color, and the no-arg constructor is `protected` to prevent its use externally. You have also added a declaration for the draw function override to the class that will draw a circle.

Implementing the CCircle Class

When you create a circle, the point at which you press the left mouse button will be the center, and the point at which you release the button will be a point on the circumference. The job of the constructor is to obtain the corner points of the defining rectangle from these points.

The CCircle Class Constructor

The point at which you release the left mouse button can be anywhere on the circumference, so the coordinates of the points specifying the defining rectangle need to be calculated in the way I've illustrated in Figure 14-15.

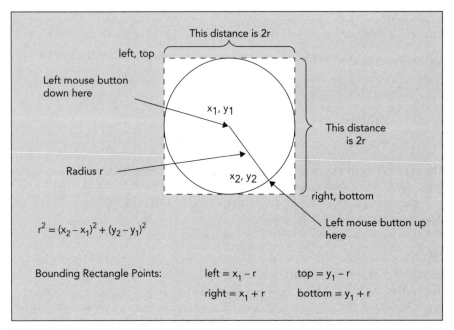

FIGURE 14-15

From Figure 14-15, you can see that you can calculate the coordinates of the upper-left and lower-right points of the enclosing rectangle relative to the center of the circle (x_1, y_1). Assuming that the mapping mode is MM_TEXT, you get the (left, top) point by subtracting the radius from each of the coordinates of the center. Similarly, you obtain the (right, bottom) point by adding the radius to the coordinates of the center. You can calculate the radius as the square root of the expression in Figure 14-15. Based on this you can code the constructor as follows:

```
// Constructor for a circle object
CCircle::CCircle(const CPoint& start, const CPoint& end, COLORREF color) :
               CElement {start, color}
```

```
{
  // Calculate the radius using floating-point values
  // because that is required by sqrt() function (in cmath)
  long radius {static_cast<long> (sqrt(
                static_cast<double>((end.x-start.x)*(end.x-start.x)+
                                    (end.y-start.y)*(end.y-start.y)))))};
  if(radius < 1L) radius = 1L;        // Circle radius must be >= 1

  // Define left-top and right-bottom points of rectangle for MM_TEXT mode
  m_StartPoint = CPoint {start.x - radius, start.y - radius};
  m_BottomRight = CPoint {start.x + radius, start.y + radius};

  // Define the enclosing rectangle
  m_EnclosingRect = CRect {m_StartPoint.x, m_StartPoint.y,
                           m_BottomRight.x, m_BottomRight.y};
  m_EnclosingRect.InflateRect(m_PenWidth, m_PenWidth);
}
```

To use the `sqrt()` function, you need an `#include` directive for the `cmath` header at the beginning of the `Circle.cpp` file. The maximum point coordinate values are 32 bits, and the `CPoint` members x and y are declared as `long`, so converting the value returned from `sqrt()` to type `long` should produce accurate results. The result of the square root calculation is of type `double`, so you cast it to type `long` to use it as an integer. The radius must be at least 1, otherwise nothing will be drawn by the `Ellipse()` member of `CDC`.

You store a `CPoint` object in `m_StartPoint` with the coordinates of the top left of the defining rectangle that you obtain by subtracting `radius` from the coordinates of the center. The `m_BottomRight` point is produced by adding `radius` to the coordinates of the center.

Drawing a Circle

The implementation of the `Draw()` function in the `CCircle` class is:

```
// Draw a circle
void CCircle::Draw(CDC* pDC)
{
  // Create a pen for this object and initialize it
  CPen aPen;
  CreatePen(aPen);

  CPen* pOldPen {pDC->SelectObject(&aPen)};   // Select the pen

  // Select a null brush
  CBrush* pOldBrush {dynamic_cast<CBrush*>(pDC->SelectStockObject(NULL_BRUSH))};

  // Now draw the circle
  pDC->Ellipse(m_StartPoint.x, m_StartPoint.y,
               m_BottomRight.x, m_BottomRight.y);

  pDC->SelectObject(pOldPen);                 // Restore the old pen
  pDC->SelectObject(pOldBrush);               // Restore the old brush
}
```

After selecting a pen of the appropriate color and a null brush into the device context, you draw the circle by calling the `Ellipse()` function. The arguments are the coordinates of the corner points of the defining rectangle. An overload of `Ellipse()` accepts a `CRect` argument.

The CCurve Class

The `CCurve` class is different from the others in that it needs to deal with a variable number of defining points. A curve is defined by two or more points, and you can store these in an STL container. It won't be necessary to remove points from a curve, so a `vector<CPoint>` container is a good candidate. You looked at the `vector<T>` template in some detail back in Chapter 10. However, before you can complete the `CCurve` class definition, you need to explore how a curve will be created and drawn by a user.

Drawing a Curve

Drawing a curve is different from drawing a line, a rectangle, or a circle. With these elements, as you move the cursor with the left button down you are creating a succession of different elements that share a common reference point — the point at which the left mouse button was pressed. This is not the case when you draw a curve, as shown in Figure 14-16.

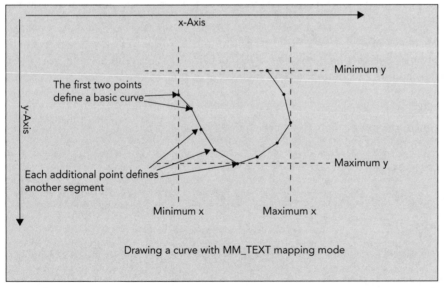

FIGURE 14-16

When you move the mouse cursor drawing a curve, you're not creating a sequence of new curves, but extending the same curve. Each new cursor position after the first adds a segment to the curve. Therefore, you must create a `CCurve` object as soon as you have the two points from the `WM_LBUTTONDOWN` message and the first `WM_MOUSEMOVE` message. Points that are defined with subsequent mouse move messages should add segments to the initial `CCurve` object. To make this possible you can add an `AddSegment()` function to the `CCurve` class that will extend a curve.

A further point to consider is how you are to calculate the enclosing rectangle. You can define this by getting the minimum-x and minimum-y pair from all the defining points to establish the upper-left corner of the rectangle, and the maximum-x and maximum-y pair for the bottom right. The easiest way of generating the enclosing rectangle is to compute it initially in the constructor based on the first two points and then re-compute it incrementally in the AddSegment() function as points are added to the curve.

Add an #include directive for the vector header to Curve.h. You can modify the CCurve class definition to the following:

```
class CCurve : public CElement
{
public:
  virtual ~CCurve();
  virtual void Draw(CDC* pDC) override;    // Function to display a curve

  // Constructor for a curve object
  CCurve(const CPoint& first, const CPoint& second, COLORREF color);

  void AddSegment(const CPoint& point);    // Add a segment to the curve

protected:
  std::vector<CPoint> m_Points;            // Points defining the curve
  CCurve();                          // Default constructor - should not be used
};
```

You can add the definition for the constructor in Curve.cpp:

```
// Constructor for a curve object
CCurve::CCurve(const CPoint& first, const CPoint& second, COLORREF color) :
              CElement {first, color}
{
  // Store the second point in the vector
  m_Points.push_back(second);
  m_EnclosingRect = CRect {
              (std::min)(first.x, second.x), (std::min)(first.y, second.y),
              (std::max)(first.x, second.x), (std::max)(first.y, second.y)};
  m_EnclosingRect.InflateRect(m_PenWidth, m_PenWidth);
}
```

The constructor receives the first two defining points as arguments so it defines a curve with only one segment. The first point is stored in the m_StartPoint member by the CElement constructor. The second point is stored in the vector, m_Points. I'm sure you recall that the push_back() function adds an element to the end of a vector. You use the std::min() and std::max() template functions in the creation of the enclosing rectangle so you'll need an #include directive for the algorithm header in Curve.cpp.

You can define the Draw() function for a curve like this:

```
// Draw a curve
void CCurve::Draw(CDC* pDC)
{
```

```
    // Create a pen for this object and initialize it
    CPen aPen;
    CreatePen(aPen);

    CPen* pOldPen {pDC->SelectObject(&aPen)};   // Select the pen

    // Now draw the curve
    pDC->MoveTo(m_StartPoint);
    for(const auto& point : m_Points)
      pDC->LineTo(point);

    pDC->SelectObject(pOldPen);                 // Restore the old pen
}
```

The Draw() function has to provide for a curve with an arbitrary number of points. Once the pen has been set up, the first step is to move the current position in the device context to m_StartPoint. Line segments for the curve are drawn in the for loop, one segment for each point in the vector. A LineTo() operation moves the current position to the end of the line it draws, so each function call draws a line from the current position to the next point in the vector. In this way, you draw all the segments that make up the curve.

You can implement the AddSegment() function like this:

```
// Add a segment to the curve
void CCurve::AddSegment(const CPoint& point)
{
    m_Points.push_back(point);                  // Add the point to the end

    // Modify the enclosing rectangle for the new point
    m_EnclosingRect.DeflateRect(m_PenWidth, m_PenWidth);
    m_EnclosingRect = CRect {(std::min)(point.x, m_EnclosingRect.left),
                             (std::min)(point.y, m_EnclosingRect.top),
                             (std::max)(point.x, m_EnclosingRect.right),
                             (std::max)(point.y, m_EnclosingRect.bottom) };
    m_EnclosingRect.InflateRect(m_PenWidth, m_PenWidth);
}
```

You add point to the vector and adjust the enclosing rectangle by ensuring the top-left point is the minimum x and y, and the bottom-right is the maximum x and y. The enclosing rectangle for the complete curve is the rectangle corresponding to the minimum x and y of all the defining points for the left-top corner, and the maximum of all the point coordinates for bottom right. You then want to inflate the resulting rectangle by the pen width. For this reason, you must reduce m_EnclosingRect by the pen width before you find the coordinates of the top-left and bottom right-corners. Otherwise you will not end up with the correct rectangle. Calling the DeflateRect() member of CRect does the opposite of InflateRect(), so this is just what you want.

Completing the Mouse Message Handlers

You can now return to the WM_MOUSEMOVE message handler and fill out the details. You can get to it through selecting CSketcherView in Class View and double-clicking the handler name, OnMouseMove().

Except when creating a CCurve element, this handler is concerned with drawing a succession of temporary elements as you move the cursor, and the final element is created when you release the mouse button. You can therefore treat the drawing of temporary elements as being entirely local to this function, leaving the final version of an element to be drawn by the OnDraw() member of the view. With this approach, drawing the temporary elements will be reasonably efficient because it won't involve the OnDraw() member of CSketcherView that draws the entire document.

You can implement this very easily with the help of a CDC class member that is particularly useful in rubber-banding operations: the SetROP2() function.

Setting the Drawing Mode

Calling SetROP2() sets the *drawing mode* for all subsequent output operations in the device context associated with a CDC object. The "ROP" bit of the function name stands for **R**aster **OP**eration, because the setting of drawing modes applies to raster displays. In case you're wondering what SetROP1() is — it doesn't exist. The whole function name stands for **Set R**aster **OP**eration **to**, not **Set R**aster **OP**eration 2!

The drawing mode determines how the color of the pen combines with the background color in the window to produce the color of the entity that you will see. You specify the drawing mode with a single argument to the SetROP2() function that can be any of the following values:

DRAWING MODE	EFFECT
R2_BLACK	All drawing is in black.
R2_WHITE	All drawing is in white.
R2_NOP	Drawing operations do nothing.
R2_NOT	Drawing is in the inverse of the screen color. This ensures that the output is always visible because it draws in the inverse color to the background.
R2_COPYPEN	Drawing is in the pen color. This is the default drawing mode if you don't set a mode.
R2_NOTCOPYPEN	Drawing is in the inverse of the pen color.
R2_MERGEPENNOT	Drawing is in the color produced by OR-ing the pen color with the inverse of the background color.
R2_MASKPENNOT	Drawing is in the color produced by AND-ing the pen color with the inverse of the background color.
R2_MERGENOTPEN	Drawing is in the color produced by OR-ing the background color with the inverse of the pen color.
R2_MASKNOTPEN	Drawing is in the color produced by AND-ing the background color with the inverse of the pen color.

continues

(continued)

DRAWING MODE	EFFECT
R2_MERGEPEN	Drawing is in the color produced by OR-ing the background color with the pen color.
R2_NOTMERGEPEN	Drawing is in the color that is the inverse of the R2_MERGEPEN color.
R2_MASKPEN	Drawing is in the color produced by AND-ing the background color with the pen color.
R2_NOTMASKPEN	Drawing is in the color that is the inverse of the R2_MASKPEN color.
R2_XORPEN	Drawing is in the color produced by exclusive OR-ing the pen and background colors. The result is a color composed of the RGB components that are in the pen and background colors but not in both.
R2_NOTXORPEN	Drawing is in the color that is the inverse of the R2_XORPEN color.

These symbols are predefined values of type int. There are a lot of options here, but the one that can work some magic for us is the last of them, R2_NOTXORPEN.

When you set the mode as R2_NOTXORPEN, the first time you draw on the default white background, the element is drawn normally in the pen color. If you draw the same element overwriting the first, the element disappears. This is because the color for the element as it appears on the screen is produced by exclusive OR-ing the pen color with itself, which results in a white element on a white background. You can see more clearly why this happens by working through an example.

White is formed from equal proportions of the maximum intensities for red, green, and blue, 255,255,255, so each component value has all bits 1. For simplicity I'll represent this as 1,1,1 — the three values represent the RGB components of the color. In the same scheme, I'll define red as 1,0,0 instead of 255,0,0. These combine as follows:

	R	G	B
Background—white, the window background color	1	1	1
Pen—red	1	0	0
XOR-ed—produces the complement of red	0	1	1
NOT XOR—produces red, the drawing color	1	0	0

So, the first time you draw a red line on a white background, it comes out red, as the last line in the table indicates. If you now draw the same line a second time, overwriting the existing line, the background pixels you are writing over are red. The resultant drawing color works out as follows:

	R	G	B
Background—red, the pixels that you drew last time	1	0	0
Pen—red	1	0	0
XOR-ed—produces black	0	0	0
NOT XOR—produces white, the window background color	1	1	1

As the last line indicates, the line appears in white, and because the window background is white, the line disappears.

You need to choose the right background color for this technique to work. You should be able to see that drawing with a white pen on a red background is not going to work too well, as the first time you draw something, it is red and, therefore, invisible. The second time, it appears as white. If you draw on a black background, things appear and disappear as on a white background, but they are not drawn in the pen color you choose.

Coding the OnMouseMove() Handler

You can now add the code to create an element after a mouse move message. Because you are going to draw the element in the handler function, you need to create a device context that you can draw in. The most convenient class to use for this is `CClientDC`, which is derived from `CDC`. An object of this type automatically takes care of destroying the device context for you when you are done, so you can create a `CClientDC` object, use it, and forget it. You can create a `CClientDC` object by passing a pointer to the window for which you want a device context to the `CClientDC` constructor. The device context that it creates corresponds to the client area of the window, so if you pass a pointer to the view, you'll get exactly what you want.

The logic for drawing an element is a little complicated. You can draw a shape using the `R2_NOTXORPEN` mode as long as the shape is not a curve. When a curve is being created, you don't want to draw a new curve each time the mouse moves. You just want to extend the curve by adding a new segment. This means you must treat creating a curve as a special case. You also want to delete any previous temporary element, but only when it is not a curve. Here's how you can implement that:

```
void CSketcherView::OnMouseMove(UINT nFlags, CPoint point)
{
  // Define a Device Context object for the view
  CClientDC aDC {this};                 // DC is for this view
  if(nFlags & MK_LBUTTON)               // Verify the left button is down
  {
    m_SecondPoint = point;              // Save the current cursor position
    if(m_pTempElement)
    {
      // An element was created previously
      if(ElementType::CURVE == GetDocument()->GetElementType())    // A curve?
      { // We are drawing a curve so add a segment to the existing curve
        std::dynamic_pointer_cast<CCurve>(m_pTempElement)->
                                           AddSegment(m_SecondPoint);
```

```
        m _ pTempElement->Draw(&aDC);       // Now draw it
        return;                              // We are done
      }
      else
      {
        // If we get to here it's not a curve so
        // redraw the old element so it disappears from the view
        aDC.SetROP2(R2 _ NOTXORPEN);        // Set the drawing mode
        m _ pTempElement->Draw(&aDC);       // Redraw the old element to erase it
      }
    }

    // Create a temporary element of the type and color that
    // is recorded in the document object, and draw it
    m _ pTempElement = CreateElement();
    m _ pTempElement->Draw(&aDC);
  }
}
```

The first line of code creates a local `CClientDC` object. The `this` pointer that you pass to the constructor identifies the current view object, so the `CClientDC` object is a device context that corresponds to the client area of the current view. This object has all the drawing functions you need because they are inherited from the `CDC` class.

A previous temporary element exists if `m_pTempElement` is not `nullptr`. You want to do different things depending on whether or not `m_pTempElement` points to a curve, so you need to check for this. The `shared_ptr<T>` type supports conversion to type `bool` so you can use it in an `if` expression. You call the `GetElementType()` function for the document object to get the current element type. If the current element type is `ElementType::CURVE`, you cast `m_pTempElement` to type `shared_ptr<CCurve>` so you can call the `AddSegment()` function for the object to add the next segment to the curve. You must use a special conversion, to convert a smart pointer. This can be `static_pointer_cast`, `dynamic_pointer_cast` or `const_pointer_cast`, which are equivalent to `static_cast`, `dynamic_cast`, and `const_cast` for ordinary pointers. `dynamic_pointer_cast` checks that the cast is valid at runtime. These operations are defined by function templates in the `memory` header and in the `std` namespace. Finally, you draw the curve and return. You must add an `#include` for `Curve.h` to `SketcherView.cpp`. You'll be referring to the other element classes in the view class eventually so you can include the headers for the other three element classes too.

When the current element exists, but is not a curve, you redraw the old element after calling the `SetROP2()` function of the `aDC` object to set the mode to `R2_NOTXORPEN`. This erases the old element on the display. There is no need to reset `m_pTempElement` because you will replace the pointer it contains after the `if` statement.

The code after the `if` statement is executed when there is a temporary element that is not a curve, or when there is no temporary element. In either case you want to create a new element of the current type and color and draw it normally. You create the new element and store its address in `m_pTempElement` by calling the `CreateElement()` member of `CSketcherView`. This replaces the current smart pointer that `m_pTempElement` contains. In our case, the smart pointer to the previous element will be destroyed along with the element object to which it points. If `m_pTempElement` contains `nullptr`, then that will be replaced by the new smart pointer. Even though our object representing

Sketcher is created on the heap we never need to worry about deleting it; this is automatically taken care of by smart pointers. The code automatically rubber-bands the element being created, so it will appear to be attached to the mouse cursor as it moves.

Using the smart pointer to the new element, you call its `Draw()` member to get the object to draw itself. The address of the `CClientDC` object is passed as the argument. Because you defined the `Draw()` function as `virtual` in the `CElement` base class, the function for whatever type of element `m_pTempElement` is pointing to is automatically selected. The new element is drawn normally with the `R2_NOTXORPEN` mode, because you are drawing it for the first time on a white background.

Creating an Element

Add the `CreateElement()` function declaration as a `protected` member in the Implementation section of the `CSketcherView` class:

```
class CSketcherView: public CView
{
   // Rest of the class definition as before...

   // Implementation
   // Rest of the class definition as before...

protected:
  std::shared_ptr<CElement> CreateElement() const;
  // Create a new element on the heap

   // Rest of the class definition as before...

};
```

You can either amend the class definition directly by adding the bolded line, or you can right-click on the class name, `CSketcherView`, in Class View, select Add ⇨ Add Function from the context menu, and add the function through the dialog. The function is `protected` because it is called only from within the view class.

If you added the declaration to the class definition manually, you'll need to add the complete definition for the function to the `.cpp` file. This is as follows:

```
// Create an element of the current type
std::shared_ptr<CElement> CSketcherView::CreateElement() const
{
   // Get a pointer to the document for this view
   CSketcherDoc* pDoc = GetDocument();
   ASSERT_VALID(pDoc);                     // Verify the pointer is good

   // Get the current element color
   COLORREF color {static_cast<COLORREF>(pDoc->GetElementColor())};

   // Now select the element using the type stored in the document
   switch(pDoc->GetElementType())
   {
```

```
        case ElementType::RECTANGLE:
            return std::make_shared<CRectangle>(m_FirstPoint, m_SecondPoint, color);

        case ElementType::CIRCLE:
            return std::make_shared<CCircle>(m_FirstPoint, m_SecondPoint, color);

        case ElementType::CURVE:
            return std::make_shared<CCurve>(m_FirstPoint, m_SecondPoint, color);

        case ElementType::LINE:
            return std::make_shared<CLine>(m_FirstPoint, m_SecondPoint, color);

        default:
            // Something's gone wrong
            AfxMessageBox(_T("Bad Element code"), MB_OK);
            AfxAbort();
            return nullptr;
    }
}
```

You first get a pointer to the document object by calling `GetDocument()`, as you've seen before. For safety, you use the `ASSERT_VALID()` macro to ensure that a good pointer is returned. In the debug version of your application, this macro calls the `AssertValid()` member of the object, which is specified as the argument to the macro. This checks the validity of the current object, and if the pointer is `nullptr` or the object is defective in some way, an error message is displayed. In the release version of your application, the `ASSERT_VALID()` macro does nothing.

You cannot use the `ElementColor` enumerator that the `GetElementColor()` function returns as a color value when you create an element because it's the wrong type. However, the numerical value of each enumerator is a `COLORREF` color value so you can cast an enumerator to type `COLORREF` to get the color value. The `switch` statement selects the element to be created based on the type returned by `GetElementType()`. In the unlikely event that the type is not an `ElementType` enumerator, you display a message box and end the program.

Dealing with WM_LBUTTONUP Messages

The `WM_LBUTTONUP` message completes the process of creating an element. The job of this handler is to pass the final version of the element to the document object, and then to clean up the view object data members. You can add an STL container object in the `CSketcherDoc` class to store elements. You will also need a document class function that you can call when you want to add an element. It's likely that you will want to delete elements from the document at some point. A `vector<T>` would be faster but I'll use a list container here for the experience because you use a vector container to store the points for a curve. Add the following `protected` data member to `CSketcherDoc`:

```
std::list<std::shared_ptr<CElement>> m_Sketch;    // A list containing the sketch
```

Sketch elements are created on the heap so you can store smart pointers to elements rather than the elements themselves. Add #include directives for the `list` and `memory` headers and `Element.h` to

`SketcherDoc.h`. When the document object is destroyed, `m_Sketch` will also be destroyed along with all the elements pointed to by the smart pointers it contains.

Add the following function definitions to the Implementation section of the `CSketcherDoc` class as `public` members:

```
// Add a sketch element
void AddElement(std::shared_ptr<CElement>& pElement)
{
  m_Sketch.push_back(pElement);
}

// Delete a sketch element
void DeleteElement(std::shared_ptr<CElement>& pElement)
{
  m_Sketch.remove(pElement);
}
```

The first function adds the smart pointer for an element that you pass as the argument to the list, `m_Sketch`. The second removes the pointer from the list, which will also delete the element from the heap. You will implement the UI mechanism for deleting sketch elements in the next chapter.

You can now implement the `OnLButtonUp()` handler. Add the following lines to the function definition in `SketcherView.cpp`:

```
void CSketcherView::OnLButtonUp(UINT nFlags, CPoint point)
{
  // Make sure there is an element
  if(m_pTempElement)
  {
    // Add the element pointer to the sketch
    GetDocument()->AddElement(m_pTempElement);
    InvalidateRect(&m_pTempElement->GetEnclosingRect());
    m_pTempElement.reset();                 // Reset the element pointer
  }
}
```

The `if` statement verifies that `m_pTempElement` is not `nullptr` before processing it. It's always possible that the user could press and release the left mouse button without moving the mouse, in which case, no element would have been created. As long as there is an element, the pointer to the element is passed to the document object function that adds it to the sketch. Finally, the `m_pTempElement` pointer is reset, ready for the next time the user draws an element.

DRAWING A SKETCH

All the elements that make up a sketch are safely stored in the document object. You now need a way to display the sketch in the view. The `OnDraw()` function in `CSketcherView` will do this. Obviously, it will need access to the data for a sketch that is owned by the document object, and ideally this should happen without the document object exposing it to external modification. One way to achieve this is for the document object to make `const` iterators available. The iterator type name for a sketch is a little long-winded and you can economize on typing by adding a type alias definition to SketcherDoc.h after the #include directives:

```
using SketchIterator = std::list<std::shared_ptr<CElement>>::const_iterator;
```

You can now use SketchIterator to specify the type for a const iterator for the sketch list container. By adding the following functions to the CSketcherDoc class definition you will enable the view object to obtain the iterators it needs to draw a sketch:

```
// Provide a begin iterator for the sketch
SketchIterator begin() const { return std::begin(m_Sketch);  }

// Provide an end iterator for the sketch
SketchIterator end() const { return std::end(m_Sketch);  }
```

These should be public, and you can put them in the Operations section of CSketcherDoc. A const iterator can be incremented and dereferenced but it cannot be used to modify what it points to.

You can use these functions to implement the OnDraw() member of CSketcherView:

```
void CSketcherView::OnDraw(CDC* pDC)
{
  CSketcherDoc* pDoc = GetDocument();
  ASSERT_VALID(pDoc);
  if (!pDoc)
    return;

  // Draw the sketch
  for(auto iter = pDoc->begin() ; iter != pDoc->end() ; ++iter)
  for (const auto& pElement : *pDoc)
  {
    if (pDC->RectVisible(pElement->GetEnclosingRect()))
      pElement->Draw(pDC);
  }
}
```

Because the document object defines begin() and end() functions that return iterators for the elements in the sketch, we can use the range-based for loop directly with it. You only want to draw an element when it is visible in the client area of the view. Drawing elements that do not appear in the view just consumes processor time to no effect. The RectVisible() member of a CDC object returns TRUE if any part of the rectangle that you pass as the argument is within the client area, otherwise it returns FALSE. Calling this in the if statement ensures that only visible elements are drawn. You draw a sketch element by calling its Draw() member with the pointer to the device context as the argument.

Running the Example

After making sure that you have saved all the source files, build the program. If you haven't made any mistakes entering the code, you'll get a clean compile and link, so you can execute the program.

You can draw lines, circles, rectangles, and curves in any of the four colors the program supports. A typical window is shown in Figure 14-17.

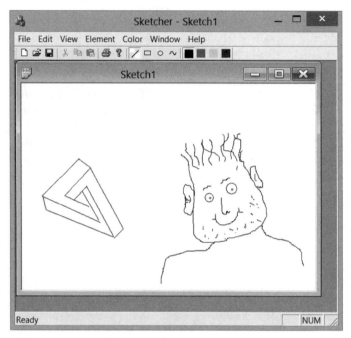

FIGURE 14-17

Try experimenting with the user interface. Note that you can move the window around and that the elements are drawn automatically if you expose them after they are hidden. However, all is not as it should be. If you try drawing a shape while dragging the cursor outside the client view area, you'll notice some peculiar effects. Outside the view window, you lose track of the mouse, which stops the rubber-banding mechanism from working while the cursor is not in the client area. What's going on?

Capturing Mouse Messages

The problem is caused by Windows sending the mouse messages to the window under the cursor. As soon as the cursor leaves the client area of the application view, the WM_MOUSEMOVE messages are being sent elsewhere. You can fix this with the aid of some inherited members of the CSketcherView class.

The view class inherits the SetCapture() function from CWnd. You call this function to tell Windows that you want your view window to receive all mouse messages until such time as you say otherwise. This is referred to as *capturing the mouse*. You can stop capturing the mouse by calling another inherited function, ReleaseCapture().

You can capture the mouse as soon as the left button is pressed by modifying the handler for the WM_LBUTTONDOWN message:

```
// Handler for left mouse button down message
void CSketcherView::OnLButtonDown(UINT nFlags, CPoint point)
{
    m_FirstPoint = point;           // Record the cursor position
    SetCapture();                   // Capture subsequent mouse messages
}
```

Now, you must call ReleaseCapture() in the WM_LBUTTONUP handler. If you don't do this, other programs cannot receive any mouse messages as long as your program continues to run. Of course, you should release the mouse only if you've captured it earlier. The GetCapture() function that the view class inherits returns a pointer to the window that has captured the mouse, and this gives you a way of telling whether or not you have captured mouse messages. You just need to add the following to the handler for WM_LBUTTONUP:

```
void CSketcherView::OnLButtonUp(UINT nFlags, CPoint point)
{
    if(this == GetCapture())
        ReleaseCapture();                    // Stop capturing mouse messages

    // Make sure there is an element
    if(m_pTempElement)
    {
        GetDocument()->AddElement(m_pTempElement);
        InvalidateRect(&m_pTempElement->GetEnclosingRect());
        m_pTempElement.reset();              // Reset the element pointer
    }
}
```

If the pointer returned by GetCapture() is equal to the pointer this, your view has captured the mouse, so you release it.

The final alteration you should make is to modify the WM_MOUSEMOVE handler so that it deals only with messages that have been captured by the view. You can do this with one small change:

```
void CSketcherView::OnMouseMove(UINT nFlags, CPoint point)
{
    // Define a Device Context object for the view
    CClientDC aDC {this};                    // DC is for this view

    // Verify the left button is down and mouse messages are captured
    if((nFlags & MK_LBUTTON) && (this == GetCapture()))
    {
        // Code as before...
    }
}
```

The handler now processes the message only if the left button is down *and* the mouse has been captured by your view window.

If you build Sketcher with these additions you'll find that the problems that arose earlier when the cursor was dragged off the client area no longer occur.

SUMMARY

After completing this chapter, you should have a good grasp of how to write message handlers for the mouse, and how to organize drawing operations in your Windows programs. You have seen how using polymorphism with the shape classes makes it possible to operate on any shape in the same way, regardless of its actual type.

EXERCISES

1. Add a menu item and Toolbar button to Sketcher for an ellipse element. Add an element type for ellipses and define a class to support drawing ellipses defined by two points on opposite corners of their enclosing rectangle.

2. Which functions must you modify to support drawing ellipses? Modify the program to draw ellipses.

3. Which functions must you modify in the example from the previous exercise so that the first point defines the center of the ellipse, and the current cursor position defines a corner of the enclosing rectangle? Modify the example to work this way. (Hint: look up the CPoint class members in Help.)

4. Add a new Pen Style menu to the menu bar to allow solid, dashed, dotted, dash-dotted, and dash-dot-dotted lines to be specified.

5. Which parts of the program need to be modified to support the operation of the menu, and the drawing of elements in the line types listed in the previous exercise?

6. Implement support for the new menu and drawing all elements in any of the line types.

➤ **WHAT YOU LEARNED IN THIS CHAPTER**

TOPIC	CONCEPT
The client coordinate system	By default, Windows addresses the client area of a window using a client coordinate system with the origin in the upper-left corner of the client area. The positive x-direction is from left to right, and the positive y-direction is from top to bottom.
Drawing in the client area	You can draw in the client area of a window only by using a device context.
Device contexts	A device context provides a range of logical coordinate systems called mapping modes for addressing the client area of a window.
Mapping modes	The default origin position for a mapping mode is the upper-left corner of the client area. The default mapping mode is MM_TEXT, which provides coordinates measured in pixels. The positive x-axis runs from left to right in this mode, and the positive y-axis from top to bottom.
Drawing in a window	Your program should always draw the permanent contents of the client area of a window in response to a WM_PAINT message, although temporary entities can be drawn at other times. All the drawing for your application document should be controlled from the OnDraw() member function of a view class. This function is called when a WM_PAINT message is received by your application.
Redrawing a window	You can identify the part of the client area you want to have redrawn by calling the InvalidateRect() member function of your view class. The area passed as an argument is added by Windows to the total area to be redrawn when the next WM_PAINT message is sent to your application.
Mouse messages	Windows sends standard messages to your application for mouse events. You can create handlers to deal with these messages by using the Class Wizard.
Capturing mouse messages	You can cause all mouse messages to be routed to your application by calling the SetCapture() function that is inherited in your view class. You must release the mouse when you're finished with it by calling the ReleaseCapture() function. If you fail to do this, other applications are unable to receive mouse messages.

TOPIC	CONCEPT
Rubber-banding	You can implement rubber-banding during the creation of geometric entities by drawing them in the message handler for mouse movements.
Selecting a drawing mode	The `SetROP2()` member of the `CDC` class enables you to set drawing modes. Selecting the right drawing mode greatly simplifies rubber-banding operations.
Adding event handlers	The Properties window for a GUI component also enables you to add event handler functions automatically.
Casting smart pointers	You can cast a smart pointer to another smart pointer type using `static_pointer_cast`, `dynamic_pointer_cast`, and `const_pointer_cast`.

15

Improving the View

WHAT YOU WILL LEARN IN THIS CHAPTER:

➤ How to draw and update multiple views

➤ How to implement scrolling in a view

➤ How to create a context menu at the cursor

➤ How to highlight the element nearest the cursor to provide feedback to the user

➤ How to program the mouse to move and delete elements

WROX.COM CODE DOWNLOADS FOR THIS CHAPTER

You can find the wrox.com code downloads for this chapter on the Download Code tab at www.wrox.com/go/beginningvisualc. The code is in the Chapter 15 download and individually named according to the names throughout the chapter.

SKETCHER LIMITATIONS

There are still some limitations in Sketcher. For instance:

1. You can open another view window for the current sketch by using the Window ⇨ New Window menu option. This capability is built into an MDI application. However, if you draw in one window the elements are not drawn in the other window. Elements never appear in windows other than the one in which they were created unless the area they occupy is redrawn for some other reason.

2. You can draw only in the client area you can see. It would be nice to be able to scroll the view and draw over a bigger area.

3. Even though the document object can delete an element from the sketch, you have no user interface mechanism for deleting an element. If you make a mistake, you either live with it or start over with a new document.

4. You can't view a sketch window at different scales. Being able to view a sketch at a larger scale would make it easier to add fine detail.

5. You can't print a sketch. If you want to show your artistic capabilities to someone, you have to bring your computer along.

6. You can't save a sketch in a file so it has no permanence at all.

These are quite serious deficiencies that limit the usability of the program. You'll overcome the first three before the end of this chapter. You'll remove the remaining limitations before the end of the book.

IMPROVING THE VIEW

The first item that you can fix is the updating of all the document view windows when an element is drawn. The problem arises because only the view in which you draw an element knows about it. Each view is acting independently of the others, and there is no communication between them. If you can arrange for all the views to be notified when an element is added to the document, they can take the appropriate action.

Updating Multiple Views

The document class contains the `UpdateAllViews()` function to help with this particular problem. The function provides a means for the document to send a message to all its views. You just need to call it from the `AddElement()` function in `CSketcherDoc` that adds a new element:

```
void AddElement(std::shared_ptr<CElement>& pElement)
{
  m_Sketch.push_back(pElement);
  UpdateAllViews(nullptr, 0, pElement.get());      // Tell all the views
}
```

The inherited `UpdateAllViews()` function is called whenever an element is added to the document. This communicates with the views by calling the `OnUpdate()` member of each view. The `UpdateAllViews()` function has three parameters, two of which have default values. The arguments that you can supply are:

1. A pointer to the current view object. This identifies the view for which the `OnUpdate()` function should not be called. This is a useful feature when the current view is up to date and you have a pointer to it. You could arrange for this if you needed to by adding an extra parameter of type `CSketcherView*` to `AddElement()` and passing the `this` pointer for the view to it when it was called. Another possibility is that you could call `UpdateAllViews()` from a view object when an element is created. When you specify `nullptr` as the argument

as in this instance, OnUpdate() will be called for all views. This will be passed on as the first argument in all OnUpdate() function calls.

2. A long integer value that has a default value of zero. This is intended to provide a hint about the region to be updated. If you supply a value for this, it will be passed as the second argument in the call to the OnUpdate() function for each view object.

3. A pointer of type CObject* with a default value of nullptr. If you supply this argument, it will be passed as the third argument in the OnUpdate() function call for each view. It should point to an object that provides information about the region to be updated. In our case it should be a pointer to the new element; a smart pointer cannot be used. Calling get() for the smart pointer, pElement, returns the CElement* pointer that pElement contains.

To process the information passed to the UpdateAllViews() function, you must add an override for the OnUpdate() member of the view class. You can do this through the Properties window for CSketcherView. Just to remind you, you display the properties for a class by right-clicking the class name in Class View and selecting Properties from the menu. If you click the Overrides button in the Properties window, you'll be able to find OnUpdate in the list of functions. Click the function name, then the <Add> OnUpdate option that shows in the drop-down list in the adjacent column. You'll be able to edit the code for the OnUpdate() override you have added in the Editor pane. You only need to add the following highlighted code to the function definition:

```
void CSketcherView::OnUpdate(CView* pSender, LPARAM lHint, CObject* pHint)
{
    // Invalidate the area corresponding to the element pointed to
    // by the third argument, otherwise invalidate the whole client area
    if(pHint)
    {
        InvalidateRect(dynamic_cast<CElement*>(pHint)->GetEnclosingRect());
    }
    else
    {
        InvalidateRect(nullptr);
    }
}
```

Note that you must uncomment the parameter names; otherwise, it won't compile with the additional code. The three arguments passed to OnUpdate() correspond to the arguments that you passed in the UpdateAllViews() function call. Thus, pHint contains the address of the new element. However, you can't assume that this is always the case. The OnUpdate() function is also called when a view is first created, but with nullptr for the third argument. Therefore, the function verifies that pHint isn't nullptr and only then calls GetEnclosingRect() to obtain the rectangle enclosing the element. It invalidates this area in the client area of the view by passing the rectangle to the InvalidateRect() function. This area is redrawn by the OnDraw() function in this view when the next WM_PAINT message is sent to the view. If pHint is nullptr, the whole client area is invalidated.

You might be tempted to consider redrawing the new element in the OnUpdate() function. This isn't a good idea. You should do permanent drawing only in response to a Windows WM_PAINT message. This means that the OnDraw() function in the view should be the only thing that's initiating any drawing operations for document data. This ensures that the view is drawn correctly whenever Windows deems it necessary.

Come to think of it, the views ought to be notified when an element is deleted from the document. You can modify the `DeleteElement()` member of the document class to take care of it:

```
void DeleteElement(std::shared_ptr<CElement>& pElement)
{
  m_Sketch.remove(pElement);
  UpdateAllViews(nullptr, 0, pElement.get());    // Tell all the views
}
```

Calling `remove()` for the list removes the element that matches the argument by calling its destructor. This will cause the smart pointer that was in the list to be destroyed. The element to which it points will not be destroyed because there is another `shared_ptr` referencing it, namely the object that was passed to `DeleteElement()`. You use this to pass the element pointer to `UpdateAllViews()`. The smart pointer is passed by reference, so the element will ultimately be destroyed when the smart pointer on the calling site is destroyed.

If you build and execute Sketcher with the new modifications, you should find that you can create multiple views of the document and draw in any of them. All the views get updated to reflect the contents of the document.

Scrolling Views

Adding scrolling to a view looks remarkably easy at first sight, but the water is, in fact, deeper and murkier than it at first appears. We will jump in anyway. The first step is to change the base class for `CSketcherView` from `CView` to `CScrollView`. This new base class has the scrolling functionality built in, so you can alter the definition of the `CSketcherView` class to this:

```
class CSketcherView : public CScrollView
{
    // Class definition as before...
};
```

You must also modify two lines of code at the beginning of the `SketcherView.cpp` file that refer to the base class for `CSketcherView`. You need to replace `CView` with `CScrollView` as the base class:

```
IMPLEMENT_DYNCREATE(CSketcherView, CScrollView)

BEGIN_MESSAGE_MAP(CSketcherView, CScrollView)
```

However, this is still not quite enough. The new view class needs to know some things about the area you are drawing on and want to scroll, such as its size and how far the view is to be scrolled when you use the scroller. This information must be supplied before the view is drawn. You can put the code to do this in the `OnInitialUpdate()` function in the view class because this will be called after the view is attached to the document but before the view is displayed.

You supply the information required for scrolling by calling the `SetScrollSizes()` function that is inherited from the `CScrollView` class. The arguments to this function are explained in Figure 15-1.

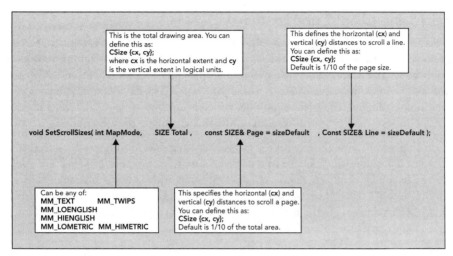

This is the total drawing area. You can define this as:
CSize {cx, cy};
where **cx** is the horizontal extent and **cy** is the vertical extent in logical units.

This defines the horizontal (**cx**) and vertical (**cy**) distances to scroll a line. You can define this as:
CSize {cx, cy};
Default is 1/10 of the page size.

void SetScrollSizes(int MapMode,   SIZE Total ,   const SIZE& Page = sizeDefault   , Const SIZE& Line = sizeDefault);

Can be any of:
**MM_TEXT   MM_TWIPS
MM_LOENGLISH
MM_HIENGLISH
MM_LOMETRIC MM_HIMETRIC**

This specifies the horizontal (**cx**) and vertical (**cy**) distances to scroll a page. You can define this as:
CSize {cx, cy};
Default is 1/10 of the total area.

FIGURE 15-1

Scrolling a distance of one line occurs when you click on the up or down arrow on the scroll bar; a page scroll occurs when you click the scrollbar itself. You have an opportunity to change the mapping mode here. MM_LOENGLISH would be a good choice for the Sketcher application, but we will first get scrolling working with the MM_TEXT mapping mode because there are still some difficulties to be uncovered.

To add the code to call SetScrollSizes(), you need to override the default version of the OnInitialUpdate() function in the view. You access this in the same way as for the OnUpdate() function override — through the Properties window for CSketcherView. After you have added the override, add the code to the function where indicated by the comment:

```
void CSketcherView::OnInitialUpdate()
{
  CScrollView::OnInitialUpdate();

  CSize DocSize {20000,20000};                        // The document size

  // Set mapping mode and document size
  SetScrollSizes(MM_TEXT, DocSize, CSize {500,500}, CSize {20,20};
}
```

This maintains the mapping mode as MM_TEXT and defines the total extent that you can draw on as 20,000 pixels in each direction. It also specifies a page scroll increment as 500 pixels in each direction and a line scroll increment as 20 pixels, because the defaults would be too large.

This is enough to get scrolling working after a fashion. Build Sketcher and execute it with these additions. You'll be able to draw a few elements and then scroll the view. However, although the window scrolls OK, if you try to draw more elements with the view scrolled, things don't work as they should. The elements appear in a different position from where you draw them and they're not displayed properly. What's going on?

Logical Coordinates and Client Coordinates

The problem is because of the coordinate systems you're using — and that plural is deliberate. You have been using *two* coordinate systems in all the examples up to now, although you may not have noticed because they were coincident. When you call a function such as `LineTo()` for a CDC object it assumes that the arguments you pass to it are *logical coordinates*. The device context has its own system of logical coordinates. The mapping mode, which is a property of the device context, determines what the unit of measurement is for the coordinates when you draw something.

The coordinate data that you receive along with the mouse messages has nothing to do with the device context or the CDC object — and outside of a device context, logical coordinates don't apply. The points passed to the `OnLButtonDown()` and `OnMouseMove()` handlers have coordinates that are always in device units — that is, pixels — and are measured relative to the upper left corner of the client area. These are referred to as *client coordinates*. Similarly, when you call `InvalidateRect()`, the rectangle is assumed to be defined in terms of client coordinates.

In `MM_TEXT` mode, client coordinates and the logical coordinates in the device context are both in pixels, and so they are the same — *as long as you don't scroll the window*. In all the previous examples, there was no scrolling, so everything worked without any problems. With the latest version of Sketcher, it all works well until you scroll the view, whereupon the logical coordinates origin (the 0,0 point) is moved by the scrolling mechanism, so it's no longer in the same place as the client coordinates origin. The *units* for logical coordinates and client coordinates are the same, but the *origins* for the coordinates systems are different. This situation is illustrated in Figure 15-2.

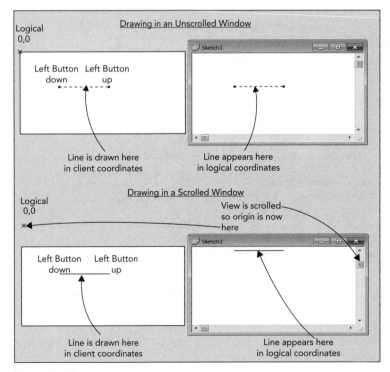

FIGURE 15-2

The left side of Figure 15-2 shows the position in the client area where you draw, and the points that are the mouse cursor positions defining the line. These are recorded in client coordinates. The right side shows where the line is actually drawn. Drawing is in logical coordinates, but you have been using client coordinate values as arguments to the drawing functions. When the view is scrolled, the line appears displaced because the logical origin has been relocated.

This means that you are using the wrong values to define elements in Sketcher. When you invalidate areas of the client area to get them redrawn, the enclosing rectangles you pass to the function are also wrong — hence, the weird behavior of the program. With other mapping modes, it gets worse. Not only are the units of measurement in the two coordinate systems different, but the y-axes may be in opposite directions!

Dealing with Client Coordinates

Let's consider what needs to be done to fix the problem. There are two things you have to address:

➤   You must convert the client coordinates that you got with mouse messages to logical coordinates before you use them to create elements.

➤   You must convert a bounding rectangle that you created in logical coordinates back to client coordinates if you want to use it in a call to InvalidateRect().

These amount to making sure that you always use logical coordinates with device context functions, and always use client coordinates for other communications about the window. The functions that will do the conversions between client coordinates and logical coordinates are members of a device context object, so you need to obtain a device context whenever you want to convert from logical coordinates to client coordinates or vice versa. The coordinate conversion functions are defined in the CDC class and inherited by CClientDC so you can use an object of this type to do the work.

The revised version of the OnLButtonDown() handler incorporating this is as follows:

```
// Handler for left mouse button down message
void CSketcherView::OnLButtonDown(UINT nFlags, CPoint point)
{

    CClientDC aDC {this};        // Create a device context
    OnPrepareDC(&aDC);           // Get origin adjusted
    aDC.DPtoLP(&point);          // Convert point to logical coordinates
    m_FirstPoint = point;        // Record the cursor position
    SetCapture();                // Capture subsequent mouse messages
}
```

You obtain a device context for the current view by creating a CClientDC object and passing the pointer this to the constructor. As you're using CScrollView, the inherited OnPrepareDC() member function must be called to set the origin for the logical coordinate system in the device context to correspond with the scrolled position. After you have set the origin by this call, you call the DPtoLP() function that converts from **Device Points to Logical Points**. This converts the point value that was passed to OnLButtonDown() and is in client coordinates to logical coordinates. You then store the point in logical coordinates in m_FirstPoint, ready for creating an element in the OnMouseMove() handler.

The new code for the `OnMouseMove()` handler is as follows:

```
void CSketcherView::OnMouseMove(UINT nFlags, CPoint point)
{
  CClientDC aDC {this};            // Device context for the current view
  OnPrepareDC(&aDC);               // Get origin adjusted
  aDC.DPtoLP(&point);              // Convert point to logical coordinates

  // Verify the left button is down and mouse messages captured
  if((nFlags&MK_LBUTTON)&&(this==GetCapture()))
  {
    m_SecondPoint = point;         // Save the current cursor position

    // Rest of the function as before...
  }
}
```

The code for converting `point` is essentially the same as in the previous handler, and that's all you need here for the moment. The last function that you must change is easy to overlook: the `OnUpdate()` function in the view class. This needs to be modified to the following:

```
void CSketcherView::OnUpdate(CView* pSender, LPARAM lHint, CObject* pHint)
{
  // Invalidate the area corresponding to the element pointed to
  // if there is one, otherwise invalidate the whole client area
  if(pHint)
  {
    CClientDC aDC {this};          // Create a device context
    OnPrepareDC(&aDC);             // Get origin adjusted

    // Get the enclosing rectangle and convert to client coordinates
    CRect aRect {dynamic_cast<CElement*>(pHint)->GetEnclosingRect()};
    aDC.LPtoDP(aRect);
    InvalidateRect(aRect);         // Get the area redrawn
  }
  else
  {
    InvalidateRect(nullptr);       // Invalidate the client area
  }
}
```

The function now creates a `CClientDC` object and uses an overloaded version of the `LPtoDP()` member to convert the enclosing rectangle for the element to client coordinates.

You must do the same thing in `OnLButtonUp()` when you invalidate the enclosing rectangle for the element:

```
void CSketcherView::OnLButtonUp(UINT nFlags, CPoint point)
{
  if(this == GetCapture())
    ReleaseCapture();              // Stop capturing mouse messages

  // Make sure there is an element
```

```
if(m_pTempElement)
{
    CRect aRect {m_pTempElement->GetEnclosingRect()}; // Get enclosing rectangle

    GetDocument()->AddElement(m_pTempElement);      // Add element pointer to sketch

    CClientDC aDC {this};                           // Create a device context
    OnPrepareDC(&aDC);                              // Get origin adjusted
    aDC.LPtoDP(aRect);                              // Convert to client coordinates
    InvalidateRect(aRect);                          // Get the area redrawn
    m_pTempElement.reset();                         // Reset pointer to nullptr
}
}
```

If you now compile and execute Sketcher with these modifications and are lucky enough not to have introduced any typos, it will work correctly, regardless of the scroller position. If you have a mouse wheel, you can scroll a view using that.

Using MM_LOENGLISH Mapping Mode

The advantage of using the MM_LOENGLISH mapping mode is that it provides drawings in logical units of 0.01 inches, which ensures that the drawing size is the same on displays at different resolutions. This makes the application much more satisfactory from the user's point of view.

You can set the mapping mode in the call to SetScrollSizes() made from the OnInitialUpdate() function in the view class. You also need to specify the total drawing area: if you define it as 3,000 by 3,000, this provides a drawing area of 30 inches by 30 inches, which should be adequate. The default scroll distances for a line and a page are satisfactory, so you don't need to specify those. You can use the Class View to get to the OnInitialUpdate() function and then change it to the following:

```
void CSketcherView::OnInitialUpdate(void)
{
    CScrollView::OnInitialUpdate();

    CSize DocSize {3000,3000};                  // Document 30x30ins in MM_LOENGLISH
    SetScrollSizes(MM_LOENGLISH, DocSize);      // Set mapping mode and document size
}
```

That's all you need to enable the view to work in MM_LOENGLISH. Note that you are not limited to setting the mapping mode once and for all. You can change the mapping mode in a device context at any time and draw different parts of a view using different mapping modes. A function, SetMapMode(), is used to do this, but I won't be going into this any further here. Whenever you create a CClientDC object for the view and call OnPrepareDC(), the device context that it owns has the mapping mode you've set in the OnInitialUpdate() function. That should do it for the program as it stands. If you build Sketcher, you should have scrolling working, with support for multiple views.

DELETING AND MOVING ELEMENTS

Being able to delete shapes is a fundamental requirement in a drawing program. The document object already has the facility for deleting a sketch element but you still have to decide on the user interface mechanism for this. How are you going to select the element you want to delete? Of course, after you decide on a mechanism for selecting an element, this will apply equally well to selecting an element to move it. This suggests that you can treat moving and deleting elements as related problems. But first, let's consider how you might initiate move and delete operations in the user interface.

A neat way of providing these functions would be to have a *context menu* popup at the cursor position when you click the right mouse button. You could then include Move and Delete as items on the menu. A pop-up menu that works like this is a very handy facility in lots of situations.

> **NOTE** Context menus are also referred to as pop-up menus *or as* shortcut menus.

How should the context menu work? The standard way is that the user moves the mouse over a particular element that is displayed and right-clicks it. This selects the element and pops up a menu containing a list of menu items offering actions that can be performed on that element. The element provides the context for the menu. Naturally, different elements can have different context menus. You have seen this in action in the IDE for Visual C++. When you right-click a class name in Class View, you get a menu that applies to the class, and that's different from the one you get if you right-click a filename in Solution Explorer. You have two contexts to consider in Sketcher. You could right-click with the mouse cursor over a sketch element, or you could right-click when there is no element under the cursor.

How can you implement this functionality in Sketcher? First you need to create two menus, one for when you have an element under the cursor and one for when you don't. You can check if there's an element under the cursor when the user clicks the right mouse button. If there *is* an element under the cursor, you can highlight it by changing its color so that the user knows exactly the element to which the context menu relates.

First, I'll explain how you can create and display a menu at the mouse cursor position in response to a right-click, then I'll discuss how you can implement the details of the move and delete operations.

IMPLEMENTING A CONTEXT MENU

You need two menus for the context menu: one for when there is an element under the mouse cursor and another for when there isn't. Change to Resource View and expand the list of resources. Right-click the Menu folder to bring up a context menu — another demonstration of what you are now trying to create in the Sketcher application. Select Insert Menu to create a new menu resource.

This has a default ID IDR_MENU1 assigned, but you can change this. Select the name of the new menu in the Resource View and display the Properties window for the resource by pressing Alt+Enter (this is a shortcut to the View ⇨ Other Windows ⇨ Properties Window menu item). You can then edit the resource ID in the Properties window by clicking the value for the ID. You could change it to something more suitable, such as IDR_CONTEXT_MENU, in the right column. Note that the name for a menu resource must start with IDR. Pressing the Enter key saves the new name.

The next step is to create a drop-down menu containing Move and Delete as menu items that will apply when an element is under the cursor. The other drop-down menu will contain menu items from the Element and Color menus to allow the current selections to be changed. You can enter a name for the new item on the menu bar in the Editor pane. This can have any old caption because it won't actually be seen by the user; the caption "element" will be OK. Now you can add the Move and Delete items to this menu. The default IDs of ID_ELEMENT_MOVE and ID_ELEMENT_DELETE will do fine, but you can change them if you want in the Properties window for each item.

Create a second drop-down menu with the menu name "no element". Figure 15-3 shows how the element menu looks with the no element menu added.

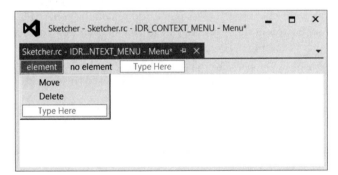

FIGURE 15-3

The no element menu is going to contain menu items for the available element types and colors, identical to those on the Element and Color menus. The IDs you use for these items will be the same as the ones for the IDR_SketchTYPE menu items. The handler for a menu item is associated with the menu ID. Messages for menu items with the same ID will call the same handler, so the same handler will be called for a Line menu item regardless of whether the message originates from an item in the main Element menu or from the no element context menu.

There is a shortcut that saves you from having to re-create all these menu items. If you display the IDR_SketchTYPE menu and extend the Element menu, you can select all the menu items by clicking the first item and then clicking the last item while holding down the Shift key. You can then right-click the selection and select Copy from the pop-up or simply press Ctrl+C. If you then return to the IDR_CONTEXT_MENU and right-click the first item on the no element menu, you can insert the complete contents of the Element menu by selecting Paste from the pop-up or by pressing Ctrl+V. The copied menu items will have the same IDs as the originals. To insert a separator before you add the color menu items, right-click the empty menu item and select Insert Separator from the menu.

Add the items from the Color menu to the no element menu after the separator and you're done. Close the properties box and save the resource file. At the moment, all you have is the definition of the context menus in a resource file. It isn't connected to the code in the Sketcher program. You now need to associate these menus and their IDs with the view class. You also must create command handlers for the menu items in the pop-up corresponding to the IDs ID_ELEMENT_MOVE and ID_ELEMENT_DELETE.

To choose the appropriate menu to display when the right mouse button is clicked, you'll need to know whether or not there is an element under the cursor. You can add a protected shared_ptr<CElement> member to the view class to track this:

```
std::shared_ptr<CElement> m_pSelected;        // Records element under the cursor
```

You'll store the address of the element under the cursor in this member, when there is one; otherwise, it will contain nullptr.

Associating a Menu with a Class

To associate the context menu with the view class, go to the Class View pane and display the Properties window for CSketcherView by right-clicking the class name and selecting Properties from the pop-up. If you click the Messages button in the Properties window, you'll be able to add a handler for the WM_CONTEXTMENU message by selecting <Add>OnContextMenu from the adjacent cell in the right column. This handler is called when the user right-clicks in the view. The first argument passed to the handler is a pointer to the window in which the user right-clicked, and the second argument is the cursor position in screen coordinates.

Add the following code to the handler:

```
void CSketcherView::OnContextMenu(CWnd* pWnd, CPoint point)
{
  CMenu menu;
  menu.LoadMenu(IDR_CONTEXT_MENU);                  // Load the context menu
  CMenu* pContext {menu.GetSubMenu(m_pSelected ? 0 : 1)};
  ASSERT(pContext != nullptr);                      // Ensure it's there

  pContext->TrackPopupMenu(TPM_LEFTALIGN | TPM_RIGHTBUTTON,
                                            point.x, point.y, this);
}
```

Don't forget to uncomment the parameter names. This handler displays the first menu in the context menu when m_pSelected points to an element, and the second menu when it does not. Calling the LoadMenu() function for the menu object loads the menu resource corresponding to the ID supplied as the argument and attaches it to the CMenu object. The GetSubMenu() function returns a pointer to the context menu corresponding to the integer argument that specifies the position of the context menu in the CMenu object, with 0 being the first, 1 being the second, and so on. After ensuring the pointer returned by GetSubMenu() is not nullptr, you display the context menu by calling TrackPopupMenu(). The ASSERT macro only operates in the debug version of the program. It produces no code in the release version.

The first argument to the `TrackPopupMenu()` function consists of two flags ORed together. One flag specifies how the pop-up menu should be positioned and can be any of the following values:

`TPM_CENTERALIGN` centers the pop-up horizontally relative to the x-coordinate supplied as the second argument to the function.

`TPM_LEFTALIGN` positions the pop-up so that the left side of the menu is aligned with the x-coordinate supplied as the second argument to the function.

`TPM_RIGHTALIGN` positions the pop-up so that the right side of the menu is aligned with the x-coordinate supplied as the second argument to the function.

This is just a selection of the options. There are more options available which you can find in the documentation.

The other flag specifies the mouse button and can be either of the following values:

`TPM_LEFTBUTTON` specifies that the pop-up only tracks the left mouse button.

`TPM_RIGHTBUTTON` specifies that the pop-up tracks either the left or the right mouse button.

The next two arguments to `TrackPopupMenu()` specify the x- and y-coordinates of the context menu in screen coordinates. The y-coordinate determines the position of the top of the menu. The fourth argument specifies the window that owns the menu and that should receive all `WM_COMMAND` messages from the menu.

Now you can add the handler for the item in the context menu for moving elements. Return to the Resource View and double-click on `IDR_CONTEXT_MENU`. Right-click the Move menu item and then select Add Event Handler from the menu. It's a `COMMAND` handler and you create it in the `CSketcherView` class. Click the Add and Edit button to create the handler function. You can follow the same procedure to create the handler for the Delete menu item.

Checking Context Menu Items

You don't have to do anything for `COMMAND` events for the no element menu items, as you already have handlers for them in the document class. These will automatically take care of the messages from the pop-up items. However, the menu items are in a separate resource, and the menu items will not get checked to reflect the currently selected element type and color. You can fix this in the `OnContextMenu()` handler, before the context menu is displayed.

The `CMenu` class has a `CheckMenuItem()` member that checks a menu item. This function checks or unchecks any item in the menu. The first argument selects which item in the menu is to be checked or unchecked; the second argument is a combination of two flags, one of which determines how the first argument specifies which item is to be checked, and the other specifies whether the menu item is to be checked or unchecked. Because each flag is a single bit in a `UINT` value, you combine the two using the bitwise OR. The second argument can contain the flag `MF_BYCOMMAND` if the first parameter is a menu ID or it can contain the flag `MF_BYPOSITION` which implies the first argument is an index. You can use the former because you know the element IDs. If the second argument contains the MF_CHECKED flag, the item will be checked; the MF_UNCHECKED flag indicates the opposite. Here's how you can implement checking for the no element menu items:

```
void CSketcherView::OnContextMenu(CWnd* pWnd, CPoint point)
{
  CMenu menu;
  menu.LoadMenu(IDR_CONTEXT_MENU);                    // Load the context menu
  CMenu* pContext {};
  if(m_pSelected)
  {
    pContext = menu.GetSubMenu(0);
  }
  else
  {
    pContext = menu.GetSubMenu(1);

    // Check color menu items
    ElementColor color {GetDocument()->GetElementColor()};
    menu.CheckMenuItem(ID_COLOR_BLACK,
        (ElementColor::BLACK == color ? MF_CHECKED : MF_UNCHECKED)| MF_BYCOMMAND);
    menu.CheckMenuItem(ID_COLOR_RED,
         (ElementColor::RED == color ? MF_CHECKED : MF_UNCHECKED)| MF_BYCOMMAND);
    menu.CheckMenuItem(ID_COLOR_GREEN,
        (ElementColor::GREEN == color ? MF_CHECKED : MF_UNCHECKED)| MF_BYCOMMAND);
    menu.CheckMenuItem(ID_COLOR_BLUE,
         (ElementColor::BLUE == color ? MF_CHECKED : MF_UNCHECKED)| MF_BYCOMMAND);

    // Check element menu items
    ElementType type {GetDocument()->GetElementType()};
    menu.CheckMenuItem(ID_ELEMENT_LINE,
         (ElementType::LINE == type ? MF_CHECKED : MF_UNCHECKED) | MF_BYCOMMAND);
    menu.CheckMenuItem(ID_ELEMENT_RECTANGLE,
      (ElementType::RECTANGLE == type? MF_CHECKED : MF_UNCHECKED) | MF_BYCOMMAND);
    menu.CheckMenuItem(ID_ELEMENT_CIRCLE,
         (ElementType::CIRCLE == type? MF_CHECKED : MF_UNCHECKED) | MF_BYCOMMAND);
    menu.CheckMenuItem(ID_ELEMENT_CURVE,
         (ElementType::CURVE == type? MF_CHECKED : MF_UNCHECKED) | MF_BYCOMMAND);
  }
  ASSERT(pContext != nullptr);                        // Ensure it's there

  pContext->TrackPopupMenu(TPM_LEFTALIGN | TPM_RIGHTBUTTON,
                                          point.x, point.y, this);
}
```

That's the context menu finished. You need to identify when an element is under the cursor next.

IDENTIFYING AN ELEMENT UNDER THE CURSOR

It will be a very simple mechanism for identifying the element under the mouse cursor. A sketch element will be under the cursor whenever the cursor is within the enclosing rectangle for the element. For this to be effective, Sketcher must track whether or not there is an element under the cursor at all times.

You can add code to the `OnMouseMove()` handler in the `CSketcherView` class to determine which element is under the cursor. This handler is called every time the mouse cursor moves, so all you have to do is add code to determine whether there's an element under the current cursor position and set `m_pSelected` accordingly. The test for whether a particular element is under the cursor is simple: if the cursor position is inside the enclosing rectangle for an element, that element is under the cursor. Here's how you can modify the `OnMouseMove()` handler to determine whether there's an element under the cursor:

```
void CSketcherView::OnMouseMove(UINT nFlags, CPoint point)
{
  // Define a Device Context object for the view
  CClientDC aDC {this};              // DC is for this view
  OnPrepareDC(&aDC);                 // Get origin adjusted
  aDC.DPtoLP(&point);                // Convert point to logical coordinates

  // Verify the left button is down and mouse messages captured
  if((nFlags & MK_LBUTTON) && (this == GetCapture()))
  {
    // Code as before...
  }
  else
  { // We are not creating an element, so select an element
    m_pSelected = GetDocument()->FindElement(point);
  }
}
```

The new code is one statement that is executed only when you are not creating a new element. The `else` clause calls the `FindElement()` function for the document object that you'll add shortly and stores the smart pointer that is returned in `m_pSelected`. The `FindElement()` function has to search the document for the first element that has an enclosing rectangle that encloses `point`. You can add `FindElement()` to the `CSketcherDoc` class definition as a `public` member and implement it like this:

```
// Finds the element under the point
std::shared_ptr<CElement> FindElement(const CPoint& point) const
{
  for(const auto& pElement : m_Sketch)
  {
    if(pElement->GetEnclosingRect().PtInRect(point))
      return pElement;
  }
  return nullptr;
}
```

You use a range-based `for` loop to search the list from the beginning. Because elements are added to the back of the list, the most recently created element will be tested last. The `GetEnclosingRect()` member of a sketch element object returns its enclosing rectangle. The `PtInRect()` member of the `CRect` class returns `TRUE` if the point you pass as the argument lies within the rectangle, and `FALSE` otherwise. You use this function to test whether or not `point` lies within any enclosing rectangle for a sketch element. The function returns the address of the first element for which this is true, or `nullptr` if no element in the sketch is found. You can now test the context menus.

Exercising the Context Menus

You have added all the code you need to make the context menus operate, so you can build and execute Sketcher to try them out. When you right-click the mouse a context menu will be displayed. If there are no elements under the cursor, the second context pop-up appears, enabling you to change the element type and color. These options work because they generate exactly the same messages as the main menu options for which you have already written handlers.

If there is an element under the cursor, the first context menu will appear with Move and Delete on it. It won't do anything at the moment, as you've yet to implement the handlers for the messages. Try right-button clicks outside the view window. Messages for these are not passed to the view window in your application, so the pop-up is not displayed.

Highlighting Elements

Ideally, the user will want to know which element is under the cursor *before* right-clicking to get the context menu. When you intend to delete an element, you want to be sure which element you are operating on. If there are concentric circles displayed, only one will be selected but you won't know which. Equally, when you want to use the other context menu — to change the drawing color for example — you must be sure no element is under the cursor when you right-click the mouse, otherwise you'll get the Move/Delete menu displayed. To show which element is under the cursor, you need to highlight it in some way before a right-button click occurs.

You can change the Draw() member function for each element type to accommodate this. You can pass an extra argument to the Draw() function to indicate when the element should be highlighted. If you pass the address of the currently selected element that you save in the m_pSelected member of the view to the Draw() function for an element, you can pass it on to the CreatePen() function, which can compare it to the this pointer to decide the color of the pen.

Highlighting will work in the same way for all element types, so let's take the CLine member as an example. You can add similar code to each of the classes for the other element types. Before you start changing CLine, you must first amend the definition of the base class CElement:

```
static const COLORREF SELECT_COLOR{RGB(255,0,180)};      // Highlight color

class CElement : public CObject
{
protected:
  CPoint m_StartPoint;                      // Element position
  int m_PenWidth;                           // Pen width
  COLORREF m_Color;                         // Color of an element
  CRect m_EnclosingRect;                    // Rectangle enclosing an element


public:
  virtual ~CElement();
  // Virtual draw operation
  virtual void Draw(CDC* pDC, std::shared_ptr<CElement> pElement=nullptr) {}

  // Get the element enclosing rectangle
```

```
      const CRect& GetEnclosingRect() const
      {
        return m_EnclosingRect;
      }

  protected:
      // Constructors protected so they cannot be called outside the class
      CElement();
      CElement(const CPoint& start, COLORREF color, int penWidth = 1);

      // Create a pen
      void CreatePen(CPen& aPen, std::shared_ptr<CElement> pElement)
      {
        if(!aPen.CreatePen(PS_SOLID, m_PenWidth,
          this == pElement.get()? SELECT_COLOR : m_Color))
        {
          // Pen creation failed
          AfxMessageBox(_T("Pen creation failed"), MB_OK);
          AfxAbort();
        }
      }
  };
```

You need an `#include` directive for the `memory` header in `Element.h`. `SELECT_COLOR` is the highlight color for all elements and this is a static constant that is defined and initialized at a global scope. A second parameter has been added to the virtual `Draw()` function. This is a pointer to an element and it will be used when an element is to be highlighted because it is under the mouse cursor. With the second parameter initialized to `nullptr`, the function can still be called with just one argument; the second argument will be `nullptr` by default.

The `CreatePen()` function also has an additional argument that is a pointer to an element. When `pElement` contains the address of the current element, the pen is created using the highlight color.

You need to modify the declaration of the `Draw()` function in each of the definitions for the classes derived from `CElement` in exactly the same way. For example, you should change the `CLine` class definition to:

```
  class CLine :
    public CElement
  {
  public:
    virtual ~CLine(void);
    // Function to display a line
    virtual void Draw(CDC* pDC, std::shared_ptr<CElement> pElement=nullptr)
                                                                override;

        // Rest of the class as before...
  };
```

The implementations for the `Draw()` functions for the derived classes also need to be extended in the same way. For the `CLine` class it is:

```
void CLine::Draw(CDC* pDC, std::shared_ptr<CElement> pElement)
{
  // Create a pen for this object and initialize it
  CPen aPen;
  CreatePen(aPen, pElement);

  // Rest of the function body as before...
}
```

This is a very simple change. The second argument to the `CreatePen()` function call is the `pElement` smart pointer that is passed as the second argument to the `Draw()` function.

You have nearly implemented element highlighting. The derived classes of the `CElement` class are now able to draw themselves as highlighted when required — you just need a mechanism to cause an element to *be* selected. So where should you create this? You can determine which element, if any, is under the cursor in the `OnMouseMove()` handler in the `CSketcherView` class, so that's obviously the place to expedite the highlighting.

The amendments to the `OnMouseMove()` handler are as follows:

```
void CSketcherView::OnMouseMove(UINT nFlags, CPoint point)
{
  // Define a Device Context object for the view
  CClientDC aDC {this};                  // DC is for this view
  OnPrepareDC(&aDC);                     // Get origin adjusted
  aDC.DPtoLP(&point);                    // Convert point to logical coordinates

  // Verify the left button is down and mouse messages captured
  if((nFlags & MK_LBUTTON) && (this == GetCapture()))
  {
    // Code as before...
  }
  else
  { // We are not creating an element, so do highlighting
    auto pOldSelected = mp_Selected;                  // Copy previous
    m_pSelected = GetDocument()->FindElement(point);
    if(m_pSelected != pOldSelected)
    {
      if(m_pSelected)
        GetDocument()->UpdateAllViews(nullptr, 0, m_pSelected.get());
      if(pOldSelected)
        GetDocument()->UpdateAllViews(nullptr, 0, pOldSelected.get());
    }
  }
}
```

You must keep track of any previously highlighted element before you store the address of a new one. If there's a new element to be highlighted, you must un-highlight the old one. To do this, you save a copy of m_pSelected in pOldSelected before you check for a selected element. You then store the smart pointer returned by the FindElement() function for the document object in m_pSelected.

If pOldSelected and m_pSelected are equal, then either they both contain the address of the same element or they are both nullptr. If they both contain a valid address, the element will already have been highlighted last time around. If they are both nullptr, nothing is highlighted and nothing needs to be done. Thus, in either case, you do nothing.

Thus, you want to do something only when m_pSelected is not equal to pOldSelected. If m_pSelected is not nullptr, you need to get it redrawn, so you call UpdateAllViews() with the first argument as nullptr to get all views updated, and the third argument as m_pSelected.get() identify the region to be updated. If pOldSelected is also not nullptr, you must un-highlight the old element by updating its area in the same way. The updating of each view will be done by its OnUpdate() member, which will invalidate the rectangle enclosing the element. Only the currently active view will have element highlighting active.

Drawing Highlighted Elements

You still need to arrange that the highlighted element is actually drawn highlighted. Somewhere, the m_pSelected pointer must be passed to the draw function for each element. The only place to do this is in the OnDraw() function for the view object:

```
void CSketcherView::OnDraw(CDC* pDC)
{
  CSketcherDoc* pDoc = GetDocument();
  ASSERT_VALID(pDoc);
  if (!pDoc)
    return;

  // Draw the sketch
  for (const auto& pElement : *pDoc)
  {
    if (pDC->RectVisible(pElement->GetEnclosingRect())) // Element visible?
      pElement->Draw(pDC, m_pSelected);                 // Yes, draw it.
  }
}
```

You need to change only one line. The second argument to the Draw() function call for an element is the address of the element to be highlighted.

Exercising the Highlights

This is all that's required for the highlighting to work all the time. It wasn't trivial but, on the other hand, it wasn't terribly difficult. You can build and execute Sketcher to try it out. Any time there is an element under the cursor, the element is drawn in magenta. This makes it obvious which element the context menu is going to act on before you right-click the mouse, and means that you know in advance which context menu will be displayed.

Implementing Move and Delete

The next step is to provide code in the bodies of the handlers in the view class for the Move and Delete menu items that you added earlier. You can add the code for Delete first because that's the simpler of the two.

Deleting an Element

The code that you need in the OnElementDelete() handler in the CSketcherView class to delete the currently selected element is simple:

```
void CSketcherView::OnElementDelete()
{
  if(m_pSelected)
  {
    GetDocument()->DeleteElement(m_pSelected);          // Delete the element
    m_pSelected.reset();
  }
}
```

The code to delete an element is executed only if m_pSelected is not nullptr, indicating that there is an element to be deleted. You get a pointer to the document and call the function DeleteElement() for the document object. You have already added this function to CSketcherDoc. When the element has been removed from the document, you call reset() for the smart pointer to change its pointer to nullptr.

That's all you need in order to delete elements. You should now have a Sketcher program in which you can draw in multiple scrolled views, and delete any of the elements in your sketch from any of the views.

Moving an Element

Moving the selected element is a bit more involved. The element should move along with the mouse cursor, so you need to add code to the OnMouseMove() method to provide for this behavior. Because this message handler is also used to draw elements, you need a mechanism for indicating when you're in "move" mode. The easiest way to do this is to have a flag in the view class, which you can call m_MoveMode. You can define it as type bool, with the value false indicating that move mode is not in effect.

You'll also have to keep track of the cursor during the move, so you can add another data member in the view class for this. You can call it m_CursorPos, and it will be of type CPoint. Another thing you should provide for is the possibility of aborting a move. For this you must remember the position of the cursor when the move operation started, so you can move the element back when necessary. This is another member of type CPoint, and it is called m_FirstPos. Add the three new members to the protected section of the view class:

```
class CSketcherView: public CScrollView
{
  // Rest of the class as before...

protected:
  CPoint m_FirstPoint;          // First point recorded for an element
  CPoint m_SecondPoint;         // Second point recorded for an element
  CPoint m_CursorPos;           // Cursor position
  CPoint m_FirstPos;            // Original position in a move
  std::shared_ptr<CElement> m_pTempElement;
  std::shared_ptr<CElement> m_pSelected;   // Records element under the cursor
  bool m_MoveMode {false};      // Move element flag

  // Rest of the class as before...
};
```

The element move process starts when the Move menu item from the context menu is selected. You can add the code to the message handler for the Move menu item to set up the conditions necessary for the operation:

```
void CSketcherView::OnElementMove()
{
    CClientDC aDC {this};
    OnPrepareDC(&aDC);                 // Set up the device context
    GetCursorPos(&m_CursorPos);        // Get cursor position in screen coords
    ScreenToClient(&m_CursorPos);      // Convert to client coords
    aDC.DPtoLP(&m_CursorPos);          // Convert to logical
    m_FirstPos = m_CursorPos;          // Remember first position
    m_MoveMode = true;                 // Start move mode
}
```

You are doing four things in this handler:

1. You get the coordinates of the current mouse cursor position because the move operation starts from this reference point.

2. You convert the cursor position to logical coordinates because your elements are defined in logical coordinates.

3. You record the initial cursor position in case the user wants to abort the move later.

4. You set m _ MoveMode to true. This is a flag for the OnMouseMove() handler to recognize move mode.

The GetCursorPos() function is a Windows API function that stores the current cursor position in m_CursorPos. Note that you pass a pointer to this function. The cursor position is in screen coordinates (i.e., coordinates measured in pixels relative to the upper-left corner of the screen). All operations with the mouse cursor are in screen coordinates. You want the cursor position in logical coordinates, so you must do the conversion in two steps. The ScreenToClient() function is inherited from CWnd in the view class. It converts a CPoint or CRect argument from screen to client coordinates. You apply the DPtoLP() function member of the aDC object to m_CursorPos, which is now in client coordinates, to convert it to logical coordinates. Now that you have set the move mode flag, you can update the mouse move message handler to deal with moving an element.

Modifying the WM_MOUSEMOVE Handler to Move an Element

Moving an element only occurs when move mode is on and the cursor is being moved. Therefore, all you need in OnMouseMove() is a block of code to handle moving an element that gets executed only when m_MoveMode is true. The new code to do this is as follows:

```
void CSketcherView::OnMouseMove(UINT nFlags, CPoint point)
{
  CClientDC aDC {this};               // DC is for this view
  OnPrepareDC(&aDC);                  // Get origin adjusted

  aDC.DPtoLP(&point);                 // Convert point to logical coordinates

  // If we are in move mode, move the selected element
  if(m_MoveMode)
  {
    MoveElement(aDC, point);          // Move the element
  }
  else if((nFlags & MK_LBUTTON) && (this == GetCapture()))
  {
   // Rest of the mouse move handler as before...
  }
}
```

This addition doesn't need much explaining, really, does it? When m_MoveMode is true you're in move mode so you call the MoveElement() function that does what is necessary for the move. If m_MoveMode is false, everything continues as before. All you have to do now is implement MoveElement().

Add the declaration for MoveElement() as a protected member of CSketcherView by adding the following at the appropriate point in the class definition:

```
    void MoveElement(CClientDC& aDC, const CPoint& point); // Move an element
```

As always, you can also right-click the class name in Class View to do this. The function needs access to the device context object for the view, aDC, and the current cursor position, point, so both of these are reference parameters. The basic implementation of the function in the SketcherView .cpp file is:

```
void CSketcherView::MoveElement(CClientDC& aDC, const CPoint& point)
{
  CSize distance {point - m_CursorPos};   // Get move distance
  m_CursorPos = point;                    // Set current point as 1st for
                                          // next time

  // If there is an element selected, move it
  if(m_pSelected)
  {
    aDC.SetROP2(R2_NOTXORPEN);
    m_pSelected->Draw(&aDC, m_pSelected); // Draw element to erase it
    m_pSelected->Move(distance);          // Now move the element
    m_pSelected->Draw(&aDC, m_pSelected); // Draw the moved element
  }
}
```

The distance to move the element that is currently selected is stored locally as a CSize object, distance. The CSize class is designed to represent a relative coordinate position and has two public data members, cx and cy, which correspond to *x* and *y* increments. These are calculated as the difference between the current cursor position, stored in point, and the previous cursor position, saved in m_CursorPos. This uses the subtraction operator, which is overloaded in the CPoint class. The version you are using here returns a CSize object, but there is also a version that returns a CPoint object. You can usually operate on CSize and CPoint objects combined. You save the current cursor position in m_CursorPos for use the next time this function is called, which occurs if there is a further mouse move message during the current move operation.

You implement moving an element in the view using the R2_NOTXORPEN drawing mode, because it's easy and fast. This is exactly the same as what you have been using during the creation of an element. You call Draw() for the selected element in its current color (SELECT_COLOR because it is selected) to reset it to the background color, and then call the Move() member of the element object to relocate it by the distance specified by distance. You'll add this function to the element classes in a moment. When the element has moved itself, you call its Draw() function once more to display it highlighted at the new position. The color of the element will revert to normal when the move operation ends, because the OnLButtonUp() handler will redraw all the views normally.

Updating Other Views

There's something we must not overlook. The view in which you are moving an element may not be the only view. If there are other views, then the element should move in those too. You can call UpdateAllViews() for the document object in MoveElement() and pass this as the first argument so that it doesn't update the current view. You need to do this before and after you move an element. Here's how that looks:

```
void CSketcherView::MoveElement(CClientDC& aDC, const CPoint& point)
{
  CSize distance {point - m_CursorPos};   // Get move distance
  m_CursorPos = point;                    // Set current point as 1st for
                                          // next time

  // If there is an element selected, move it
```

```
      if(m_pSelected)
      {
         CSketcherDoc* pDoc {GetDocument()};               // Get the document pointer

         pDoc->UpdateAllViews(this, 0L, m_pSelected.get()); // Update all except this

         aDC.SetROP2(R2_NOTXORPEN);
         m_pSelected->Draw(&aDC, m_pSelected);             // Draw element to erase it
         m_pSelected->Move(distance);                      // Now move the element
         m_pSelected->Draw(&aDC, m_pSelected);             // Draw the moved element

         pDoc->UpdateAllViews(this, 0 , m_pSelected.get()); // Update all except this
      }
   }
```

By passing m_pSelected as the third argument to UpdateAllViews(), only the region occupied by the element pointed to will be redrawn. The first call to UpdateAllViews() invalidates the area occupied by the element before the move in each of the other views. The second call invalidates the area after the move.

Getting the Elements to Move Themselves

Add the Move() function as a virtual member of the base class, CElement. Modify the class definition to the following:

```
class CElement : public CObject
{
protected:
  CPoint m_StartPoint;                         // Element position
  int m_PenWidth;                              // Pen width
  COLORREF m_Color;                            // Color of an element
  CRect m_EnclosingRect;                       // Rectangle enclosing an element

public:
  virtual ~CElement();
  virtual void Draw(CDC* pDC, std::shared_ptr<CElement> pElement=nullptr) {}
  virtual void Move(const CSize& aSize){}      // Move an element

  // Rest of the class as before...

};
```

As I discussed earlier in relation to the Draw() member, although an implementation of Move() has no meaning here, you can't make it a pure virtual function because of the requirements of serialization.

You can now add a declaration for the Move() function as a public member of each of the classes derived from CElement. It is the same in each:

```
   virtual void Move(const CSize& aSize) override; // Function to move an element
```

Next, you can add the implementation of `Move()` for the `CLine` class to `Line.cpp`:

```
void CLine::Move(const CSize& aSize)
{
  m_StartPoint += aSize;           // Move the start point
  m_EndPoint += aSize;             // and the end point
  m_EnclosingRect += aSize;        // Move the enclosing rectangle
}
```

The overloaded `+=` operators in the `CPoint` and `CRect` classes make this easy. They all work with `CSize` objects, so you just add the relative distance specified by `aSize` to the start and end points for the line and to the enclosing rectangle.

Moving a `CRectangle` object is just as easy:

```
void CRectangle::Move(const CSize& aSize)
{
  m_StartPoint += aSize;           // Move the start point
  m_BottomRight += aSize;          // Move the bottom right point
  m_EnclosingRect += aSize;        // Move the enclosing rectangle
}
```

Because the rectangle is defined by the opposite corner points, the code to move it is essentially the same as that for moving a line.

The `Move()` member of the `CCircle` class is identical:

```
void CCircle::Move(const CSize& aSize)
{
  m_StartPoint += aSize;           // Move the start point
  m_BottomRight += aSize;          // Move the bottom right point
  m_EnclosingRect += aSize;         // Move the enclosing rectangle
}
```

Moving a `CCurve` object is a little more complicated, because it's defined by an arbitrary number of points. You can implement the function as:

```
void CCurve::Move(const CSize& aSize)
{
  m_EnclosingRect += aSize;        // Move the rectangle
  m_StartPoint += aSize;           // Move the start point
  // Now move all the other points
  for(auto& p : m_Points)
    p += aSize;
}
```

There's still not a lot to it. You first move the enclosing rectangle stored in `m_EnclosingRect`, using the overloaded `+=` operator for `CRect` objects. You then move the first point. You move the remaining points by using a range-based `for` loop to iterate over the points in the `m_Points` vector.

Dropping the Element

Once you have clicked on the Move menu item, the element under the cursor will move around as you move the mouse. All that remains is to add the capability to drop the element in position once the user has finished moving it, or to abort the whole move. To drop the element in its new position, the user will click the left mouse button, so you can manage this operation in the OnLButtonDown() handler. To abort the operation, the user will click the right mouse button — so you can add the code to the OnRButtonDown() handler to deal with this.

You can take care of dropping the element in OnLButtonDown() first. You'll have to provide for this as a special action when move mode is on. The changes are highlighted:

```
void CSketcherView::OnLButtonDown(UINT nFlags, CPoint point)
{
  CClientDC aDC {this};            // Create a device context
  OnPrepareDC(&aDC);               // Get origin adjusted
  aDC.DPtoLP(&point);              // convert point to logical coordinates

  if(m_MoveMode)
  {
    // In moving mode, so drop the element
    m_MoveMode = false;            // Kill move mode
    auto pElement(m_pSelected);    // Store selected address
    m_pSelected.reset();           // De-select the element
    GetDocument()->UpdateAllViews(nullptr, 0,
                              pElement.get());  // Redraw all the views
  }
  else
  {
    m_FirstPoint = point;          // Record the cursor position
    SetCapture();                  // Capture subsequent mouse messages
  }
}
```

The code is pretty simple. You first check for move mode. If this is the case, you just set the move mode flag back to false. You save the address of the selected element in a local pointer because you want to use it to identify the area to be redrawn in the views. You then deselect the element and call the document's UpdateAllViews() function, causing all the views to be redrawn. This is all that's required because you've been moving the element along with the mouse cursor, so it's already in the right place.

Add a handler for the WM_RBUTTONDOWN message to CSketcherView using the Properties window for the class. The implementation for aborting a move must do two things. It must move the element back to where it was and turn off move mode. You can move the element back in the right-button-down handler, but you must leave switching off move mode to the right-button-up handler to allow the context menu to be suppressed. The code to move the element back is as follows:

```
void CSketcherView::OnRButtonDown(UINT nFlags, CPoint point)
{
  if(m_MoveMode)
  {
    // In moving mode, so drop element back in original position
```

```
            CClientDC aDC {this};
            OnPrepareDC(&aDC);                      // Get origin adjusted
            MoveElement(aDC, m_FirstPos);           // Move element to original position
            m_pSelected.reset();                    // De-select element
            GetDocument()->UpdateAllViews(nullptr); // Redraw all the views
        }
    }
```

You first create a `CClientDC` object for use in the `MoveElement()` function. You then call the `MoveElement()` function to move the currently selected element the distance from the current cursor position to the original cursor position that we saved in `m_FirstPos`. After the element has been repositioned, you just deselect the element and get all the views redrawn.

The last thing you must do is switch off move mode in the right-button-up handler so add it and implement it like this:

```
    void CSketcherView::OnRButtonUp(UINT nFlags, CPoint point)
    {
      if(m_MoveMode)
      {
        m_MoveMode = false;
      }
      else
      {
          CScrollView::OnRButtonUp(nFlags, point);
      }
    }
```

This switches move mode off if it is on. The default handler was calling the `OnContextMenu()` handler every time. Now the context menu gets displayed only when it is not move mode.

Exercising the Application

Everything is now complete for the context pop-ups to work. If you build Sketcher, you can select the element type and color from the context menu when the cursor is not over an element. When it is over an element, you can move or delete that element using the other context menu.

DEALING WITH MASKED ELEMENTS

There's still a limitation that you ought to overcome. If the element you want to move or delete is enclosed by the bounding rectangle of another element that is drawn earlier in sequence, you won't be able to highlight it because Sketcher always finds the older element first. The older element completely masks the element it encloses. This is a result of the sequence of elements in the list. You add new elements to the back so the elements are ordered in the list from oldest to newest. You could fix this by adding a Send to Back item to the context menu that would move an element to the end of the list.

Add a separator and a menu item to the element menu in the `IDR_CONTEXT_MENU` resource, as shown in Figure 15-4.

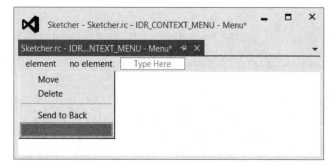

FIGURE 15-4

The default ID will be ID_ELEMENT_SENDTOBACK, which is fine. You can try a different technique to add the message handler for the new item. You can add the handler for the item to the view class through the Properties window for the CSketcherView class. It's best to handle it in the view because that's where you record the selected element. Select the Events toolbar button in the Properties window for the class and double-click the message ID ID_ELEMENT_SENDTOBACK. You'll then be able to select COMMAND and <Add>OnElementSendtoback in the right column. You can implement the handler as follows:

```
void CSketcherView::OnElementSendtoback()
{
   GetDocument()->SendToBack(m_pSelected);   // Move element to end of list
}
```

You'll get the document to do the work by passing the currently selected element pointer to a public function, SendToBack(), that you will implement in the CSketcherDoc class. Add it to the class definition with a void return type and a parameter of type shared_ptr<CElement>&. You can implement this function within the class definition as:

```
void SendToBack(std::shared_ptr<CElement>& pElement)
{
   if(pElement)
   {
     m_Sketch.remove(pElement);             // Remove the element from the list
     m_Sketch.push_back(pElement);          // Put it back at the end of the list
   }
}
```

After checking that the parameter is not nullptr, you remove the element from the list by calling remove(). You add the smart pointer back at the end of the list, using the push_back() function.

With the element moved to the end of the list, it cannot mask any of the others because you search for an element to highlight from the beginning. You will always find one of the other elements first if the applicable enclosing rectangle contains the current cursor position. The Send to Back menu option can always resolve any element masking problem in the view, although you may have to apply it to more than one masking element.

SUMMARY

You have improved the view capability in Sketcher in several ways. You've added scrolling to the views using the MFC class CScrollView, and you've introduced a pop-up at the cursor for moving and deleting elements. You have also implemented an element-highlighting feature to provide the user with feedback during the moving or deleting of elements.

EXERCISES

1. Implement element highlighting so that the line type changes for the element under the cursor as well as the element color.

2. Change the Sketcher program so that it uses a vector container to store a sketch instead of a list.

➤ WHAT YOU LEARNED IN THIS CHAPTER

TOPIC	CONCEPT
Windows coordinate systems	When you draw in a device context using the MFC, coordinates are in logical units that depend on the mapping mode set. Points in a window that are supplied along with Windows mouse messages are in client coordinates. The two coordinate systems are usually not the same.
Screen coordinates	Coordinates that define the position of the cursor are in screen coordinates that are measured in pixels relative to the upper-left corner of the screen.
Converting between coordinate systems	Functions to convert between client coordinates and logical coordinates are available in the CDC class.
Updating multiple views	To get multiple views updated when you change the document contents, you can call the UpdateAllViews() member of the document object. This causes the OnUpdate() member of each view object to be called.
Updating efficiently	You can pass information to the UpdateAllViews() function to indicate which area in the view needs to be redrawn. This makes redrawing the views faster.
Creating a context menu	You create a context menu as a menu resource. The resource can then be loaded into a CMenu object in the handler function for the context menu event.
Displaying a context menu	You can display a context menu at the cursor position in an MFC application in response to a right mouse button click by implementing the OnContextMenu() handler for a view. The menu is created as a normal pop-up at the cursor position.

16

Working with Dialogs and Controls

WHAT YOU WILL LEARN IN THIS CHAPTER:

- ➤ How to create dialog resources
- ➤ How to add controls to a dialog
- ➤ The basic varieties of controls available
- ➤ How to create a dialog class to manage a dialog
- ➤ How to program the creation of a dialog box, and how to get information back from the controls in it
- ➤ What are modal and modeless dialogs
- ➤ How to implement and use direct data exchange and validation with controls
- ➤ How to implement view-scaling
- ➤ How to use the status bar in an application

WROX.COM CODE DOWNLOADS FOR THIS CHAPTER

You can find the wrox.com code downloads for this chapter on the Download Code tab at www.wrox.com/go/beginningvisualc. The code is in the Chapter 16 download and individually named according to the names throughout the chapter.

UNDERSTANDING DIALOGS

Of course, dialogs are not new to you. Most Windows programs of consequence use dialogs to manage some of their data input. You click a menu item and up pops a *dialog* with various *controls* that you use for entering information. Just about everything that appears in a dialog is a control. A dialog is actually a window and each control in a dialog is also a specialized window. Come to think of it, an application window under Microsoft Windows is composed almost entirely of windows within windows.

You need two things to create and display a dialog in an MFC program: the physical appearance of the dialog, which you define as a resource, and a dialog class object that you use to manage the operation of the dialog and its controls. MFC provides the CDialog and CDialogEx classes for you to use once you have defined your dialog resource.

UNDERSTANDING CONTROLS

Many different standard controls are available and in most cases there's flexibility to how they look and operate. Most of them fall into one of the categories shown in the following table.

CONTROL TYPE	WHAT THEY DO
Static controls	These are used to provide titles or descriptive information.
Button controls	Buttons provide a single-click input mechanism. There are basically three flavors of button controls: simple push buttons, radio buttons (of which only one may be in a selected state at any one time), and checkboxes (of which several may be in a selected state at one time).
Scrollbars	You have already seen scrollbars in Sketcher. Scrollbars are typically used to scroll text or images, either horizontally or vertically, within another control.
List boxes	These present a list of choices from which one or more selections can be made.
Edit controls	An edit control allows text input or editing of text that is displayed by the control.
Combo boxes	Combo boxes present a list of choices from which you can select, combined with the option of entering text yourself.

A control may or may not be associated with a class object. Static controls don't do anything directly, so an associated class object may seem superfluous; however, there's an MFC class, CStatic, that provides functions to enable you to alter the appearance of static controls. Button controls can also be handled by the dialog object in many cases, but again, MFC provides the CButton class for when you need a class object to manage a control. MFC also provides a full complement of classes to support the other controls. All controls are windows so the MFC classes for controls are all derived from CWnd.

COMMON CONTROLS

The set of standard controls supported by the MFC and the Resource editor are called *common controls*. Common controls include all the controls I have just described, as well as other more complex controls such as the *animate control*, which can play an AVI (Audio Video Interleaved) file, and the *tree control*, which can display a hierarchy of items in a tree.

Another useful control in the set of common controls is the *spin button*. You can use this to increment or decrement values in an associated edit control. To go into all of the possible controls that you might use is beyond the scope of this book, so I'll just take a few examples (including one that uses a spin button) and show you how to implement them in Sketcher.

CREATING A DIALOG RESOURCE

Here's a concrete example. You could add a dialog to Sketcher to provide a choice of pen widths for drawing elements. This ultimately involves storing and modifying the current pen width in the document, as well as adding capability in the element classes to allow variable pen widths. You'll deal with all that, though, after you've gotten the dialog together.

Display the Resource View, expand the resource tree for Sketcher, and right-click the Dialog folder; then click Insert Dialog from the pop-up to add a new dialog resource to Sketcher. This results in the Dialog Resource editor swinging into action and displaying the dialog in the Editor pane, and the Toolbox showing a list of controls that you can add; if the Toolbox is not displayed, click Toolbox in the right-hand sidebar or press Ctrl+Alt+X.

The dialog has OK and Cancel button controls already in place. Adding more controls to the dialog is simplicity itself: you can just drag the control from the list in the Toolbox window to the position at which you want to place it in the dialog. Alternatively, you can click a control from the list to select it, and then click in the dialog where you want the control to be positioned. When it appears you'll still be able to move it around to set its exact position, and you'll also be able to resize it by dragging handles on the boundaries.

The dialog has a default ID assigned, IDD_DIALOG1, but it would be better to have an ID that's a bit more meaningful. You can edit the ID by right-clicking the dialog name in the Resource View pane and selecting Properties from the pop-up; this displays the properties for the dialog. Change the ID to something that relates to the purpose of the dialog, such as IDD_PENWIDTH_DLG. You can also display the properties for the dialog itself by right-clicking the dialog in the Dialog Editor pane and selecting Properties. Here you can change the Caption property value that appears in the title bar of the dialog to Set Pen Width.

Adding Controls to a Dialog

To provide a mechanism for entering a pen width, you will add controls to the basic dialog that is displayed initially until it looks like the one shown in Figure 16-1. You place a control on the dialog by dragging it with the mouse from the Toolbox to the dialog. The figure shows a grid that you can use to position controls. If the grid is not displayed, you can select the appropriate toolbar button to display it; the button toggles the grid on and off.

Alternatively, you can display rules along the side and top of the dialog, which you can use to create guide lines, by clicking the Toggle Guides button. You create a horizontal guide by clicking in the appropriate rule where you want the guide to appear. Controls placed in contact with a guide will be attached to it and move with the guide. You can reposition a guide line by dragging the arrow for it along the rule. You can use one or more guides when positioning a control. You can toggle guides on and off by clicking the Toggle Guides toolbar button.

The dialog shown has six *radio buttons* that provide the pen width options. These are enclosed within a *group box* with the caption Pen Widths. The group box serves to enclose the radio buttons and make them operate as a group, for which only one member of the group can be checked at any given time. Each radio button has an appropriate label to identify the pen width that is set when it is selected. There are also the default OK and Cancel buttons that close the dialog. Each of the controls in the dialog has its own set of properties that you can access and modify, just as for the dialog itself. Let's press on with putting the dialog together.

The next step in the creation of the dialog shown in Figure 16-1 is to add the group box. As I said, the group box serves to associate the radio buttons in a group from an operational standpoint, and to provide a caption and a boundary for the group of buttons. Where you need more than one set of radio buttons, a means of grouping them is essential if they are to work properly. You can select the button corresponding to the group box from the common controls palette by clicking it; then click the approximate position in the dialog where you want to place the center of the group box. This places a group box of default size onto the dialog. You can then drag the borders of the group box to enlarge it to accommodate the six radio buttons that you add. To set the caption for the group box, type the caption you want while the group box is selected (in this case, type **Pen Widths**).

The last step is to add the radio buttons. Select the radio button control by clicking it, and then clicking the position in the dialog where you want to place a radio button within the group box. Do the same for all six radio buttons. You can select each button by clicking it; then type in the caption to change it. You can also drag the border of the button to set its size, if necessary. To display the Properties window for a control, select it by right-clicking it; then select Properties from the pop-up. You can change the ID for each radio button in the Properties window for the control, in order to make the ID correspond better to its purpose: IDC_PENWIDTH0 for the one-pixel-width

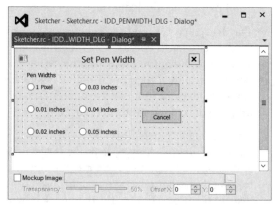

FIGURE 16-1

pen, IDC_PENWIDTH1 for the 0.01-inch-width pen, IDC_PENWIDTH2 for the 0.02-inch-pen, and so on.

You can position individual controls by dragging them around with the mouse. You can select a group of controls by selecting successive controls with the Shift key pressed, or by dragging the cursor with the left button pressed to create an enclosing rectangle for a group. To align a group of controls, or to space them evenly horizontally or vertically, select the appropriate button from the

Dialog Editor toolbar. If the Dialog Editor toolbar is not visible, you can show it by right-clicking in the toolbar area and selecting it from the list of toolbars that is displayed. You can also align controls in the dialog by selecting from the Format menu.

Testing the Dialog

The dialog resource is now complete. You can test it by selecting the toolbar button that appears at the left end of the Dialog Editor toolbar or by pressing Ctrl+T. This displays the dialog with the basic operations of the controls available, so you can try clicking on the radio buttons. When you have a group of radio buttons, only one can be selected at a time. As you select one, any other that was selected is reset. Click either the OK or Cancel button, or even the close icon in the title bar of the dialog, to end the test. After you save the dialog resource, you're ready to add code to support it.

PROGRAMMING FOR A DIALOG

There are two aspects to programming for a dialog: getting it displayed, and handling user interactions with its controls. Before you can display the dialog corresponding to the resource you've just created, you must define a dialog class for it. The Class Wizard helps with this.

Adding a Dialog Class

Right-click in the Resource Editor pane for the dialog and then select Add Class from the pop-up to display the Class Wizard dialog. You'll define a new dialog class derived from the MFC class `CDialogEx`, so select that class name from the "Base class" drop-down list if it's not already selected. You can enter the class name as **CPenDialog**. The Class Wizard dialog should look like Figure 16-2. Click the Finish button to create the new class.

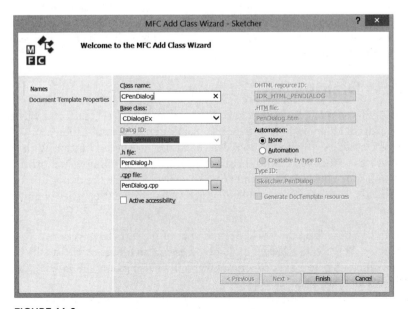

FIGURE 16-2

The `CDialogEx` class is a window class (derived from `CWnd`) that's specifically for displaying and managing dialogs. The dialog resource will be automatically associated with a `CPenDialog` object because the `IDD` class member is initialized with the dialog resource ID:

```
class CPenDialog : public CDialogEx
{
  DECLARE_DYNAMIC(CPenDialog)

public:
  CPenDialog(CWnd* pParent = NULL);   // standard constructor
  virtual ~CPenDialog();

// Dialog Data
  enum { IDD = IDD_PENWIDTH_DLG };

protected:
  virtual void DoDataExchange(CDataExchange* pDX);     // DDX/DDV support

  DECLARE_MESSAGE_MAP()
};
```

The boldfaced statement defines `IDD` as a symbolic name for the dialog ID in the enumeration. Incidentally, using an enumeration used to be the only way to get an initialized data member into a class definition. Another way is to define a static `const` integral member of the class, so the Class Wizard could have used the following in the class definition:

```
static const int IDD = {IDD_PENWIDTH_DLG};
```

As you saw in Chapter 7, with latest C++ standard supported in Visual C++ you can put an initial value for any regular non-static data member declaration in a class.

Having your own dialog class derived from `CDialogEx` means that you get all the functionality that that class provides. You can customize the dialog class by adding data members and functions to suit your particular needs. You'll often handle messages from controls within the dialog class, although you can also choose to handle them in a view or a document class.

Modal and Modeless Dialogs

There are two types of dialogs, *modal* and *modeless*, and they work in completely different ways. While a modal dialog is displayed, all operations in the other windows in the application are suspended until the dialog is closed, usually by the user clicking an OK or Cancel button. With a modeless dialog you can move the focus back and forth between the dialog window and other windows in your application just by clicking them, and you can continue to use the dialog at any time until you close it. The Class Wizard is an example of a modal dialog; the Properties window is a modeless dialog.

You can create a modeless dialog by calling the `Create()` member of the `CDialogEx` class in your dialog class constructor. You create a modal dialog by creating an object on the stack from your dialog class and calling its `DoModal()` function. You will be using only modal dialogs in Sketcher.

Displaying a Dialog

Where you put the code to display a dialog in your program depends on the application. In Sketcher it will be convenient to add a menu item that results in the pen width dialog being displayed. You can put this item in the `IDR_SketchTYPE` menu bar. The pen width and the drawing color are both associated with a pen, so you can rename the Color menu as Pen. You do this by clicking the Color menu item in the Resource Editor pane to open its Properties window and changing the `Caption` property value to &Pen.

When you add the Width menu item to the Pen menu, it would be a good idea to separate it from the colors in the menu. Add a separator after the last color menu item by right-clicking the empty menu item and selecting Insert Separator. You can then enter the new Width... item as the next menu item. The Width... menu item ends with an ellipsis (three periods) to indicate that it displays a dialog; this is a standard Windows convention. Click the menu item to display its properties as in Figure 16-3.

The default ID, `ID_PEN_WIDTH`, is fine, so you don't need to change that. You can add a status bar prompt for the menu item, and because you'll add a toolbar button, you can include text for the tooltip as well. Remember, you just put the tooltip text after the status bar prompt text, separated from it by \n. Here, the value for the `Prompt` property is "Change pen width\nShow pen width options."

You need to add a toolbar button corresponding to the Width... menu item to the toolbar resource. To add the toolbar button, double-click the `IDR_MAINFRAME` toolbar resource in Resource View. You can add a toolbar button to represent a pen width. The one shown in Figure 16-4 tries to represent a pen drawing a line.

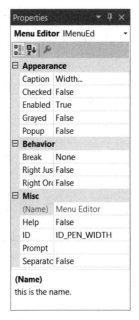

FIGURE 16-3

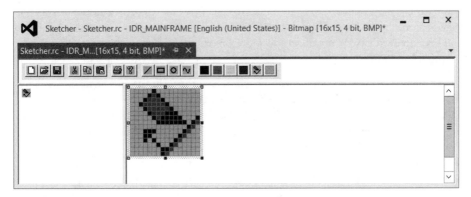

FIGURE 16-4

To associate the new button with the menu item that you just added, open the Properties box for the button and specify its ID as `ID_PEN_WIDTH`, the same as that for the menu item.

Displaying the Dialog

The code to display the dialog goes in the handler for the Pen ⇨ Width menu item. So, in which class should you implement this handler? The CSketcherView class is a candidate for dealing with pen widths, but following the logic for dealing with element color and type, it would be sensible to have the pen width selection in the document, so the handler should go in the CSketcherDoc class.

Right-click the Width... menu item in the Resource Editor pane for the IDR_SketchTYPE menu and select Add Event Handler from the pop-up. You can then create a function for the COMMAND message handler corresponding to ID_PEN_WIDTH in the CSketcherDoc class. Now edit this handler and enter the following code:

```
// Handler for the pen width menu item
void CSketcherDoc::OnPenWidth()
{
    CPenDialog aDlg;                    // Create a local dialog object
    aDlg.DoModal();                     // Display the dialog as modal
}
```

There are just two statements at the moment. The first creates a dialog object that is automatically associated with your dialog resource. The second displays the dialog by calling the DoModal() function for the aDlg object.

Because the handler creates a CPenDialog object, you must add an #include directive for PenDialog.h to the beginning of SketcherDoc.cpp. After you've done that, you can build Sketcher and try out the dialog. It should appear when you click the pen-width toolbar button. Of course, if the dialog is to do anything, you still have to add the code to support the operation of the controls; to close the dialog, you can use either of the buttons or the close icon in the title bar.

Code to Close the Dialog

The OK and Cancel buttons (and the close icon on the title bar) already close the dialog. The handlers to deal with the BN_CLICKED event handlers for the OK and Cancel button controls have been implemented for you in the base class. However, it's useful to know how the action of closing the dialog is implemented, in case you want to do more before the dialog is closed, or if you are working with a modeless dialog.

The CDialog base class for CDialogEx defines the OnOK() method that is called when you click the default OK button; this has IDOK as its ID. This function closes the dialog and causes the DoModal() method to return the ID of the default OK button, IDOK. The OnCancel() function is called when you click the default Cancel button in the dialog; this closes the dialog and DoModal() returns the button ID, which is IDCANCEL. You can override either or both of these functions in your dialog class to do what you want. You need to make sure that you call the corresponding base class function at the end of your function implementation. You'll probably remember by now that you can add an override to a class by clicking the Overrides button in the Properties window for the class. For example, you could implement an override for the OnOK() function as follows:

```
void CPenDialog::OnOK()
{
  // Your code for data validation or other actions...
  CDialogEx::OnOK();                        // Close the dialog
}
```

In a complicated dialog, you might want to verify that the options selected or the data that has been entered is valid. You could put code here to check the state of the dialog and fix up the data, or even to leave the dialog open if there are problems.

Calling the base class OnOK() function closes the dialog and causes DoModal() to return IDOK. Thus, you can use the value returned from DoModal() to detect when the dialog was closed via the OK button.

As I said, you can override the OnCancel() function in a similar way if you need to do extra cleanup operations before the dialog closes. Be sure to call the base class function at the end of your function implementation.

When you are using a modeless dialog you must implement the OnOK() and OnCancel() function overrides so that they call the inherited DestroyWindow() function to terminate the dialog. In this case you must not call the base class OnOK() or OnCancel() functions because they do not destroy the dialog window, but merely render it invisible.

SUPPORTING THE DIALOG CONTROLS

For the pen dialog you'll store the selected pen width in a data member, m_PenWidth, of the CPenDialog class. You can either add the data member by right-clicking the CPenDialog class name and selecting from the context menu, or you can add it directly to the class definition as follows:

```
class CPenDialog : public CDialogEx
{
// Construction
public:
    CPenDialog(CWnd* pParent = NULL);    // standard constructor
    virtual ~CPenDialog();
// Dialog Data
    enum { IDD = IDD_PENWIDTH_DLG };

    int m_PenWidth;                        // Record the current pen width

// Plus the rest of the class definition....

};
```

> **NOTE** *If you use the context menu for the class to add* m_PenWidth, *be sure to add a comment to the member variable definition. This is a good habit to get into, even when the member name looks self-explanatory.*

You'll use the m_PenWidth data member to set the radio button corresponding to the current pen width in the document as checked. You'll also arrange for the pen width that is selected in the dialog to be stored in this member, so that you can retrieve it when the dialog closes. At this point you can initialize m_PenWidth to 0 in the CPenDialog class constructor:

```
CPenDialog::CPenDialog(CWnd* pParent /*=NULL*/)
                    : CDialogEx(CPenDialog::IDD, pParent), m_PenWidth {}
{
}
```

Initializing Dialog Controls

You can initialize the radio buttons by overriding the OnInitDialog() function that is inherited from the CDialog base class. This is called in response to a WM_INITDIALOG message, which is sent during the execution of DoModal() just before the dialog is displayed. You can add the function to the CPenDialog class by selecting OnInitDialog in the list of overrides in the Properties window for the class. The implementation for the new version of OnInitDialog() is:

```
BOOL CPenDialog::OnInitDialog()
{
  CDialogEx::OnInitDialog();

  // Check the radio button corresponding to the pen width value
  switch(m_PenWidth)
  {
    case 1:
      CheckDlgButton(IDC_PENWIDTH1,BST_CHECKED);
      break;
    case 2:
      CheckDlgButton(IDC_PENWIDTH2,BST_CHECKED);
      break;
    case 3:
      CheckDlgButton(IDC_PENWIDTH3,BST_CHECKED);
      break;
    case 4:
      CheckDlgButton(IDC_PENWIDTH4,BST_CHECKED);
      break;
    case 5:
      CheckDlgButton(IDC_PENWIDTH5,BST_CHECKED);
      break;
    default:
      CheckDlgButton(IDC_PENWIDTH0,BST_CHECKED);
  }
  return TRUE;  // return TRUE unless you set the focus to a control
                // EXCEPTION: OCX Property Pages should return FALSE
}
```

You should leave the call to the base class function there because it does some essential setup for the dialog. The switch statement checks one of the radio buttons, depending on the value set in the m_PenWidth data member. This implies that you must arrange to set m_PenWidth to a suitable value before you execute DoModal() because the DoModal() function causes the WM_INITDIALOG message to be sent, resulting in your version of OnInitDialog() being called.

The CheckDlgButton() function is inherited indirectly from CWnd. The first argument identifies the button, and the second argument of type UINT sets its check status. If the second argument is BST_CHECKED it checks the button corresponding to the ID you specify in the first argument. If it's BST_UNCHECKED, the button is unchecked. This function works with checkboxes and radio buttons.

Handling Radio Button Messages

After the dialog is displayed, every time you click a radio button a message is generated and sent to the application. You can add handlers to the CPenDialog class to deal with these messages. Return to the dialog resource that you created, right-click each of the radio buttons in turn, and select Add Event Handler from the menu to create a handler for the BN_CLICKED message. Figure 16-5 shows the event handler dialog window for the button that has IDC_PENWIDTH0 as its ID. Note that I have edited the name of the handler, as the default name was a little cumbersome.

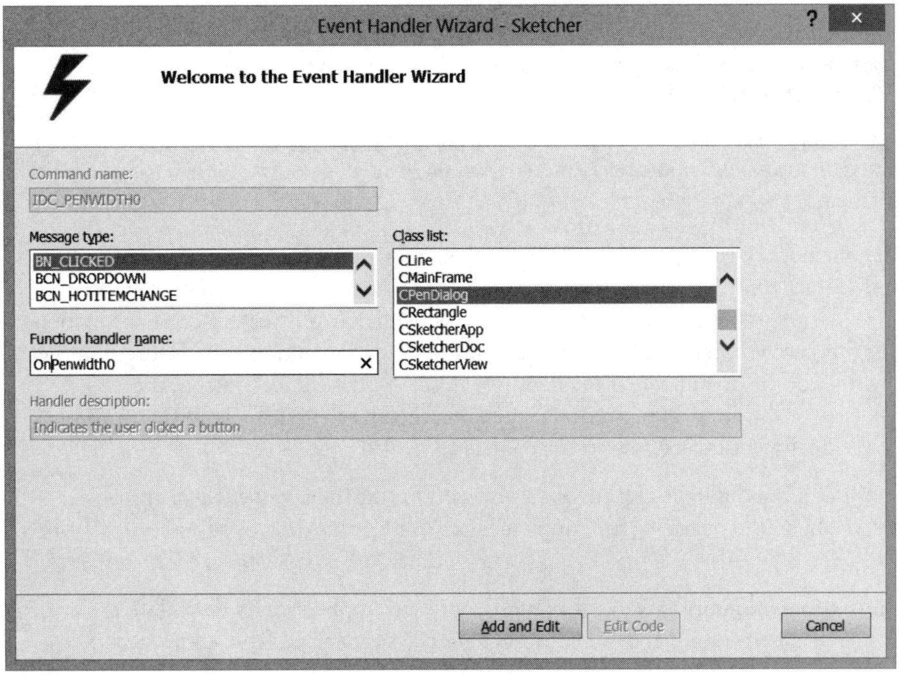

FIGURE 16-5

The implementations of the BN_CLICKED event handlers for all of these radio buttons are similar because each just sets the pen width in the dialog object. As an example, the handler for IDC_PENWIDTH0 is as follows:

```
void CPenDialog::OnPenwidth0()
{
  m_PenWidth = 0;
}
```

You need to add the code for all six handlers to the CPenDialog class implementation, setting m_PenWidth to 1 in OnPenwidth1(), to 2 in OnPenwidth2(), and so on.

COMPLETING DIALOG OPERATIONS

You must now modify the OnPenWidth() handler in CSketcherDoc to make the dialog effective. Add the following code to the function:

```
// Handler for the pen width menu item
void CSketcherDoc::OnPenWidth()
{
  CPenDialog aDlg;                      // Create a local dialog object

  // Set pen width in the dialog to that in the document
  aDlg.m_PenWidth = m_PenWidth;

  if(aDlg.DoModal() == IDOK)            // Display the dialog as modal
    m_PenWidth = aDlg.m_PenWidth;       // When closed with OK, get the pen width
}
```

The m_PenWidth member of the aDlg object is set to the pen width stored in the m_PenWidth member of the document; you still have to add this member to CSketcherDoc. The DoModal() function call now occurs in the if statement condition, which is true if the DoModal() function returns IDOK. In this case you retrieve the pen width stored in the aDlg object and store it in the m_PenWidth member of the document. If the dialog is closed by the Cancel button, the keyboard escape key, or the close icon, IDOK won't be returned by DoModal() and the value of m_PenWidth in the document object will not be changed.

Note that even though the dialog is closed when DoModal() returns a value, the aDlg object still exists, so you can call its member functions. The aDlg object is destroyed on return from OnPenWidth().

All that remains to do to support variable pen widths in your application is to update the affected classes: CSketcherDoc, CElement, and the four element classes derived from CElement.

Adding Pen Widths to the Document

You need to add the m_PenWidth member to the document class, and the GetPenWidth() function to allow external access to the value stored. You should add the following bolded statements to the CSketcherDoc class definition:

```
class CSketcherDoc : public CDocument
{
// the rest as before...

// Operations
public:
// the rest as before...
  int GetPenWidth() const { return m_PenWidth; }   // Get current pen width

// the rest as before...

protected:
// the rest as before...
  int m_PenWidth {}                                // Current pen width

// the rest as before...
};
```

Because it's trivial, you can define the GetPenWidth() function in the definition of the class and gain the benefit of it being implicitly inline. You don't need to add initialization for m_PenWidth to the constructor for CSketcherDoc. The initial value is set in the declaration for the m_PenWidth value in CSketcherDoc.

Adding Pen Widths to the Elements

You have a little more work in the element classes. You already have a member m_PenWidth in CElement to store the pen width and the constructor has a parameter for a pen width. You must extend each of the derived class constructors to accept a pen width argument and set the member accordingly. The members that create or modify the enclosing rectangle for an element must be altered to deal with a pen width of 0.

Each of the constructors for CLine, CRectangle, CCircle, and CCurve must be modified to accept a pen width argument. In the CLine class, the constructor declaration becomes:

```
CLine(const CPoint& start, const CPoint& end, COLORREF aColor, int penWidth);
```

And the constructor implementation should be modified to this:

```
CLine::CLine(const CPoint& start, const CPoint& end,
             COLORREF color, int penWidth) :
               CElement {start, color, penWidth}, m_EndPoint {end}
{
  // Define the enclosing rectangle
  m_EnclosingRect = CRect {start, end};
  m_EnclosingRect.NormalizeRect();
  int width {penWidth == 0 ? 1 : penWidth};   // Inflate rect by at least 1
  m_EnclosingRect.InflateRect(width, width);
}
```

The enclosing rectangle is now produced by inflating the defining rectangle by at least 1.

The CRectangle constructor implementation is:

```
CRectangle::CRectangle (const CPoint& start, const CPoint& end,
                        COLORREF color, int penWidth) :
                            CElement {start, color, penWidth}
{
  // Normalize the rectangle defining points
  m_StartPoint = CPoint {(std::min)(start.x, end.x)},
                        (std::min)(start.y, end.y)};
  m_BottomRight = CPoint {(std::max)(start.x, end.x)},
                        (std::max)(start.y, end.y)};

  // Ensure width and height between the points is at least 2
  if((m_BottomRight.x - m_StartPoint.x) < 2)
    m_BottomRight.x = m_StartPoint.x + 2;
  if((m_BottomRight.y - m_StartPoint.y) < 2)
    m_BottomRight.y = m_StartPoint.y + 2;

  // Define the enclosing rectangle
  m_EnclosingRect = CRect {m_StartPoint, m_BottomRight};
  int width{penWidth == 0 ? 1 : penWidth}; // Inflate rect by at least 1
  m_EnclosingRect.InflateRect(width, width);
}
```

Don't forget to add the pen width parameter to the constructor declaration in the class definition here and in the other element classes.

The CCircle constructor definition becomes:

```
CCircle::CCircle(const CPoint& start, const CPoint& end,
                COLORREF color, int penWidth) :
                                    CElement {start, color, penWidth}
{
  // Code as before...

  // Define the enclosing rectangle
  m_EnclosingRect = CRect {m_StartPoint.x, m_StartPoint.y,
                          m_BottomRight.x, m_BottomRight.y};
  int width{penWidth == 0 ? 1 : penWidth}; // Inflate rect by at least 1
  m_EnclosingRect.InflateRect(width, width);
}
```

You must modify the constructor and the AddSegment() member of the CCurve class. Here's the revised constructor definition:

```
CCurve::CCurve(const CPoint& first, const CPoint& second,
              COLORREF color, int penWidth) :
                                  CElement {first, color, penWidth}
{
  // Store the second point in the vector
  m_Points.push_back(second);
  m_EnclosingRect = CRect {
                  (std::min)(first.x, second.x),
```

```
                    (std::min)(first.y, second.y),
                    (std::max)(first.x, second.x),
                    (std::max)(first.y, second.y)};
  int width {penWidth == 0 ? 1 : penWidth};        // Inflate rect by at least 1
  m_EnclosingRect.InflateRect(width, width);
}
```

The `AddSegment()` member implementation should be changed to:

```
void CCurve::AddSegment(const CPoint& point)
{
  m_Points.push_back(point);                       // Add the point to the end

  // Modify the enclosing rectangle for the new point
  int width {m_PenWidth == 0 ? 1 : m_PenWidth};    // Deflate rect by at least 1

  m_EnclosingRect.DeflateRect(width, width);
  m_EnclosingRect = CRect {(std::min)(point.x, m_EnclosingRect.left),
                           (std::min)(point.y, m_EnclosingRect.top),
                           (std::max)(point.x, m_EnclosingRect.right),
                           (std::max)(point.y, m_EnclosingRect.bottom)};
  m_EnclosingRect.InflateRect(width, width);
}
```

That's got the element classes covered. Now you must alter the rest of Sketcher to use the new element constructors.

Creating Elements in the View

The last change you need to make is to the `CreateElement()` member of `CSketcherView`. Because you have added the pen width as an argument to the constructors for each of the shapes, you must update the calls to the constructors to reflect this. Change the definition of `CSketcherView::CreateElement()` to the following:

```
std::shared_ptr<CElement> CSketcherView::CreateElement() const
{
    // Get a pointer to the document for this view
    CSketcherDoc* pDoc = GetDocument();
    ASSERT_VALID(pDoc);                            // Verify the pointer is good

    // Get the current element color
    COLORREF color {static_cast<COLORREF>(pDoc->GetElementColor())}

    int penWidth{pDoc->GetPenWidth()};             // Get current pen width

    // Now select the element using the type stored in the document
    switch(pDoc->GetElementType())
    {
        case ElementType::RECTANGLE:
            return std::make_shared<CRectangle>(m_FirstPoint, m_SecondPoint,
                                                color, penWidth);
```

```
            case ElementType::CIRCLE:
                return std::make_shared<CCircle>(m_FirstPoint, m_SecondPoint,
                                                          color, penWidth);
            case ElementType::CURVE:
                return std::make_shared<CCurve>(m_FirstPoint, m_SecondPoint,
                                                          color, penWidth);
            case ElementType::LINE:
                return std::make_shared<CLine>(m_FirstPoint, m_SecondPoint,
                                                          color, penWidth);
            default:                        // Something's gone wrong
                AfxMessageBox(_T("Bad Element code"), MB_OK);
                AfxAbort();
                return nullptr;
        }
    }
```

Each constructor call now passes the pen width as an argument. This is retrieved from the document with the GetPenWidth() function that you added to the document class.

Exercising the Dialog

You can now build and run the latest version of Sketcher to see how the pen dialog works out. Selecting the Pen ➪ Width menu option or the associated toolbar button displays the dialog so that you can select the pen width. The screen shown in Figure 16-6 is typical of what you might see when the Sketcher program is executing.

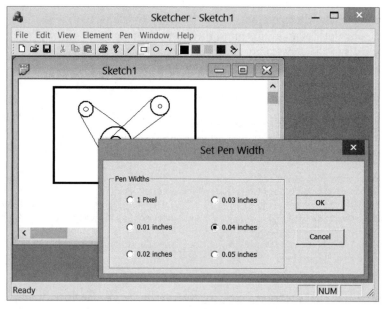

FIGURE 16-6

Note that the dialog is a completely separate window. You can drag it around to position it where you want. You can even drag it outside the Sketcher application window.

USING A SPIN BUTTON CONTROL

Now you can look at how the spin button can help in Sketcher. The spin button is particularly useful when you want to constrain an input within a given integer range. It's normally used in association with another control, called a *buddy control*, that displays the value that the spin button modifies. The associated control is usually an edit control, but it doesn't have to be.

It would be nice to be able to draw at different viewing scales in Sketcher. If you had a way to change the scale, you could scale up whenever you wanted to fill in the fine detail in your masterpiece, and scale down again when working across the whole vista. You could apply the spin control to managing scaling in a document view. A drawing scale would be a view-specific property, and you would want the element drawing functions to take the current scale of a view into account. Altering the existing code to deal with view-scaling requires rather more work than setting up the control, so first look at how you create a spin button and make it work.

Adding a Scale Menu Item and Toolbar Button

The first step is to provide a means of displaying the scale dialog. Go to Resource View and open the IDR_SketchTYPE menu. You are going to add a Scale menu item to the end of the View menu. Enter the caption for the unused menu item in the View menu as **Scale. . . .** This item will bring up the scale dialog, so you end the caption with an ellipsis to indicate this. The default ID is ID_VIEW_SCALE. You can add a separator before the new menu item by right-clicking it and selecting Insert Separator. The menu should now look as shown in Figure 16-7. Add a suitable Prompt property value for the menu item.

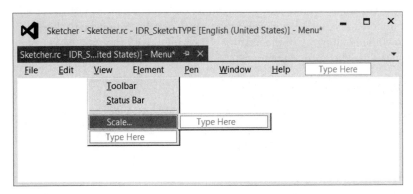

FIGURE 16-7

You can also add a toolbar button for this menu item with a bitmap image to represent scaling. Make sure that the ID for the button is also set to ID_VIEW_SCALE.

Creating the Spin Button

You've got the menu item; you need a dialog to go with it. In Resource View, add a new dialog by right-clicking the Dialog folder and selecting Insert Dialog. Change the ID for the resource to IDD_SCALE_DLG and the Caption property for the dialog to Set Drawing Scale.

FIGURE 16-8

Click the spin control in the Toolbox, and then click on the position in the dialog where you want it to be placed. Next, right-click the spin control to display its properties. Change its ID to something more meaningful than the default, such as IDC_SPIN_SCALE. Now take a look at the properties for the spin button. They are shown in Figure 16-8.

The Arrow Keys property is already set to True, enabling you to operate the spin button by using arrow keys on the keyboard. You should also set to True the value for both the Set Buddy Integer property that specifies the buddy control value as an integer, and Auto Buddy that provides for automatic selection of the buddy control. The effect of the latter is that the control selected as the buddy is automatically the previous control defined in the dialog. At the moment this is the Cancel button, which is not exactly ideal, but you'll see how to change this in a moment. The Alignment property determines how the spin button is displayed in relation to its buddy. You should set this to Right Align so that the spin button is attached to the right edge of its buddy control.

Next, add an edit control at the left side of the spin button by selecting the edit control from the Toolbox pane and clicking in the dialog where you want it positioned. Change the ID for the edit control to IDC_SCALE. You can change its Align Text property value to Center.

To make the contents of the edit control quite clear, you could add a static control just to the left of the edit control in the dialog and enter **View Scale:** as the caption. You can select all three controls by clicking them while holding down the Shift key. Pressing the F9 function key aligns the controls tidily, or you can use the Format menu.

The Controls' Tab Sequence

Controls in a dialog have what is called a *tab sequence*. This is the sequence in which the focus shifts from one control to the next when you press the Tab key, and it is determined initially by the sequence in which you add controls to the dialog. You can see the tab sequence for the current dialog by selecting Format ⇨ Tab Order from the main menu, or by pressing Ctrl+D. Figure 16-9 shows the tab order required for the spin control to work with its buddy control.

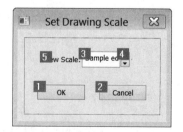

FIGURE 16-9

If the tab order you see is different, you have to change it. You really want the edit control to precede the spin button in the tab sequence, so you need to select the controls by clicking them in the order in which you want them to be numbered: OK button; Cancel button; edit control; spin button; and finally the static control. So, the tab order will be as in Figure 16-9. Now the edit control is selected as the buddy to the spin button.

Generating the Scale Dialog Class

After saving the resource file, you can right-click the dialog in the Resource Editor pane and select Add Class. You'll then be able to define the new class associated with the dialog resource that you have created. You should name the class CScaleDialog and leave the base class as the default, CDialogEx. Clicking the Finish button adds the class to the Sketcher project.

You need a variable in the dialog class to store the value returned from the edit control, so right-click the CScaleDialog class name in Class View and select Add ⇨ Add Variable. The new data member is a special kind, called a *control variable*, so first check the "Control variable" box in the Add Member Variable Wizard dialog. A control variable is a variable that is to be associated with a control in the dialog. Select IDC_SCALE as the ID from the Control ID drop-down list and Value from the Category list box. Enter the variable name as m_Scale. You'll be storing an integer scale value, so select int as the variable type. The Add Member Variable Wizard displays edit boxes in which you can enter maximum and minimum values for the variable m_Scale. For our application, a minimum of 1 and a maximum of 8 would be good values. Note that this constraint applies only to the edit box with the ID IDC_SCALE; the spin control is independent of it.

Figure 16-10 shows how the window for the Add Member Variable Wizard should look when you are done.

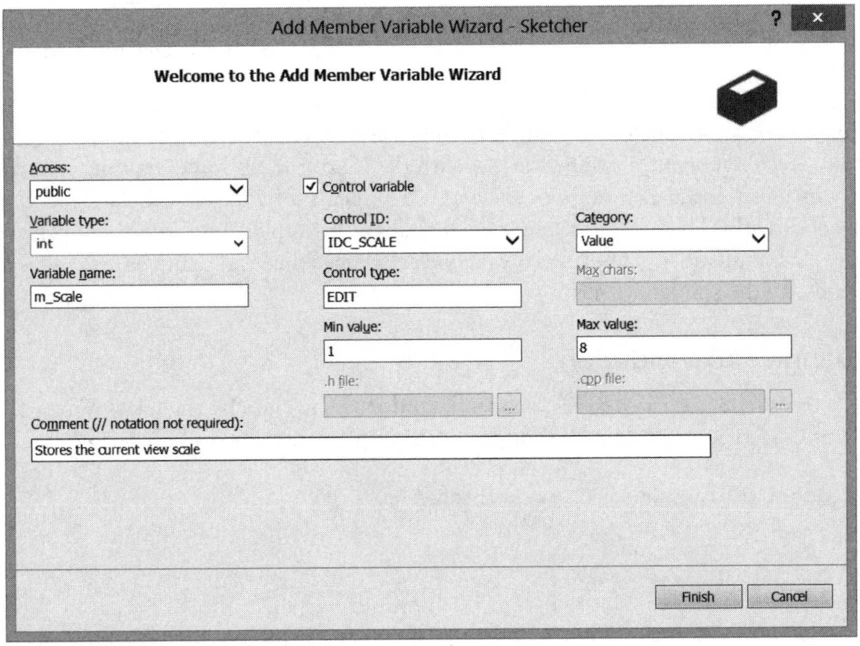

FIGURE 16-10

When you click the Finish button, the wizard takes care of entering the code necessary to support your new control variable.

You will also need to access the spin control in the dialog class and you can use the Add Member Variable Wizard to create that, too. Right-click `CScaleDialog` in Class View once again, select Add variable..., and click the Control variable checkbox in the dialog. Leave the Category selection as Control and select `IDC_SPIN_SCALE` as the control ID: this corresponds to the spin control. The type will be automatically selected as `CSpinButtonCtrl`. You can now enter the variable name as `m_Spin`, select protected for the Access value and add a suitable comment. When you click the Finish button, the new variable will be added to the `CScaleDialog` class.

The class definition you'll end up with after the wizard has added the new members is as follows:

```cpp
class CScaleDialog : public CDialogEx
{
  DECLARE_DYNAMIC(CScaleDialog)

public:
  CScaleDialog(CWnd* pParent = NULL);         // standard constructor
  virtual ~CScaleDialog();

// Dialog Data
  enum { IDD = IDD_SCALE_DLG };

protected:
  virtual void DoDataExchange(CDataExchange* pDX); // DDX/DDV support

  DECLARE_MESSAGE_MAP()
public:
  int m_Scale;                                // Stores the current view scale
protected:
  CSpinButtonCtrl m_Spin;                     // Spin control for view scale
};
```

The interesting bits of the class definition are bolded. The class is associated with the dialog resource through the enum statement, initializing IDD with the ID of the resource. It contains the variable `m_Scale`, which is a `public` member of the class so you can set and retrieve its value in a `CScaleDialog` object directly. There's also some special code in the implementation of the class to deal with the new `m_Scale` member. The `m_Spin` variable references the `CSpinButtonCtrl` object so you can call functions for the spin control.

Dialog Data Exchange and Validation

A virtual function called `DoDataExchange()` has been included in the class by the Class Wizard. If you look in the `ScaleDialog.cpp` file, you'll find that the implementation looks like this:

```cpp
void CScaleDialog::DoDataExchange(CDataExchange* pDX)
{
  CDialogEx::DoDataExchange(pDX);
  DDX_Text(pDX, IDC_SCALE, m_Scale);
  DDV_MinMaxInt(pDX, m_Scale, 1, 8);
  DDX_Control(pDX, IDC_SPIN_SCALE, m_Spin);
}
```

This function is called by the framework to carry out the exchange of data between variables in a dialog and the dialog's controls. This mechanism is called *dialog data exchange*, usually abbreviated to *DDX*. This is a powerful mechanism that can provide automatic transfer of information between a dialog and its controls in most circumstances, thus saving you the effort of programming to get the data yourself, as you did with the radio buttons in the pen width dialog.

DDX handles data transfers between the edit control and the variable m_Scale in the CScaleDialog class. The variable pDX that is passed to the DoDataExchange() function controls the direction in which data is transferred. After the base class DoDataExchange() function is called, the DDX_Text() function is called. The latter moves data between the m_Scale variable and the edit control.

The call to the DDV_MinMaxInt() function verifies that the value transferred is within the limits specified. This mechanism is called *dialog data validation*, or *DDV*. The DoDataExchange() function is called automatically before the dialog is displayed to pass the value stored in m_Scale to the edit control. When the dialog is closed with the OK button, it is automatically called again to pass the value in the control back to the variable m_Scale in the dialog object. All this is taken care of for you. You need only to ensure that the right value is stored in m_Scale before the dialog is displayed, and arrange to collect the result when the dialog closes.

Initializing the Dialog

You'll use an override of the inherited OnInitDialog() function to initialize the dialog, just as you did for the pen width dialog. This time you'll use it to set up the spin control. You'll initialize the m_Scale member a little later when you create the dialog in the message handler for the Scale menu item, because it should be set to the value of the scale that is stored in the view. For now, add an override for the OnInitDialog() function to the CScaleDialog class, using the class properties pane as you did for the previous dialog, and add code to initialize the spin control:

```
BOOL CScaleDialog::OnInitDialog()
{
  CDialogEx::OnInitDialog();


  m_Spin.SetRange(1, 8);                    // Set the spin control range

  return TRUE;  // return TRUE unless you set the focus to a control
                // EXCEPTION: OCX Property Pages should return FALSE
}
```

There is only one line of code to add. This sets the upper and lower limits for the spin button object by calling its SetRange() member. Although you have set the range limits for the edit control, this doesn't affect the spin control directly. If you don't limit the values in the spin control here, you allow the spin control to insert values outside the limits in the edit control, and there will be an error message from the edit control. You can demonstrate this by commenting out the statement that calls SetRange() here and trying out Sketcher without it.

If you want to set the buddy control using code, rather than by setting the value of Auto buddy in the spin button's properties to `True`, the `CSpinButtonCtrl` class has a function member to do this. You would add the following statement following the `OnInitDialog()` call:

```
m_Spin.SetBuddy(GetDlgItem(IDC_SCALE));
```

> **NOTE** *You can access controls in a dialog programmatically. The* `GetDlgItem()` *function is inherited from* `CWnd` *via* `CDialog` *and* `CDialogEx`, *and you can use this member to retrieve the address of any control identified by the ID you pass as the argument. Thus, calling* `GetDlgItem()` *with* `IDC_SPIN_SCALE` *as the argument would return the address of the spin control. As you saw earlier, a control is just a specialized window, so the pointer returned is of type* `CWnd*`. *You have to cast it to the type appropriate to the particular control if you want to call member functions. The type would be* `CSpinButtonCtrl*` *in this case.*

Displaying the Spin Button

The dialog is to be displayed when the Scale menu item or its associated toolbar button is selected. Add a COMMAND event handler to `CSketcherView` corresponding to the `ID_VIEW_SCALE` event through the Properties window for the class. You can then add code as follows:

```
void CSketcherView::OnViewScale()
{
  CScaleDialog aDlg;                // Create a dialog object
  aDlg.m_Scale = m_Scale;          // Pass the view scale to the dialog
  if(aDlg.DoModal() == IDOK)
  {
    m_Scale = aDlg.m_Scale;        // Get the new scale
    InvalidateRect(nullptr);       // Invalidate the whole window
  }
}
```

You create the dialog as a modal dialog, just as you did with the pen width dialog. Before the dialog is displayed by the `DoModal()` function call, you store the scale value from the `m_Scale` member of `CSketcherView` in the dialog member with the same name; this ensures that the control displays the current scale value when the dialog is displayed. If the dialog is closed with the OK button, you store the new scale from the `m_Scale` member of the dialog object in the view member with the same name. Because you have changed the view scale, you need to get the view redrawn with the new scale value applied. The call to `InvalidateRect()` does this. Don't forget to add an `#include` directive for `ScaleDialog.h` to `SketcherView.cpp`.

Of course, you must not forget to add the m_Scale data member to the definition of CSketcherView, so add the following line at the end of the other protected data members in the class definition:

```
int m_Scale {1};                         // Current view scale
```

This defines the m_Scale member and initializes it to 1. This results in a view always starting out with a scale of 1 to 1. That's all you need to get the scale dialog and its spin control operational. You can build and run Sketcher to give it a trial spin before you add the code to use a view scale factor in the drawing process.

USING THE SCALE FACTOR

Scaling with Windows usually involves using one of the scalable mapping modes, MM_ISOTROPIC or MM_ANISOTROPIC. By using one of these mapping modes you can get Windows to do most of the work. Unfortunately, it's not as simple as just changing the mapping mode, because neither is supported by CScrollView. If you can get around that, however, you're home and dry. You'll use MM_ANISOTROPIC for reasons that you'll see in a moment, so let's first understand what's involved in using this mapping mode.

Scalable Mapping Modes

There are two mapping modes that allow the mapping between logical coordinates and device coordinates to be altered, and these are the MM_ISOTROPIC and MM_ANISOTROPIC modes. The MM_ISOTROPIC mode forces the scaling factor for both the x- and y-axes to be the same, which has the advantage that your circles will always be circles. The disadvantage is that you can't map a document to fit into a rectangle of a different aspect ratio. The MM_ANISOTROPIC mode, on the other hand, permits scaling of each axis independently. Because it's the more flexible mode of the two, you'll use MM_ANISOTROPIC for scaling operations in Sketcher.

Just to remind you:

> ➤ *Logical coordinates* (also referred to as *page coordinates*) are determined by the mapping mode. For example, the MM_LOENGLISH mapping mode has logical coordinates in units of 0.01 inches, with the origin in the upper-left corner of the client area, and the positive y-axis direction running from bottom to top. These are used by the device context drawing functions.

> ➤ *Device coordinates* (also referred to as *client coordinates* in a window) are measured in pixels in the case of a window, with the origin at the upper-left corner of the client area, and with the positive y-axis direction from top to bottom. These are used outside a device context — for example, for defining the position of the cursor in mouse message handlers.

> ➤ *Screen coordinates* are measured in pixels and have the origin at the upper-left corner of the screen, with the positive y-axis direction from top to bottom. These are used for getting or setting the cursor position.

The way in which logical coordinates are transformed to device coordinates in the MM_ISOTROPIC and MM_ANISOTROPIC mapping modes is dependent on the following parameters that you can set:

PARAMETER	DESCRIPTION
Window Origin	The logical coordinates of the upper-left corner of the window. You set this by calling CDC::SetWindowOrg().
	For example, calling SetWindowOrg(50,50) sets the window origin at the point (50,50).
Window Extent	The size of the window specified in logical coordinates. You set this by calling CDC::SetWindowExt().
	For example, calling SetWindowExt(250,350) sets the window extent 250 in the x-direction and 350 in the y-direction.
Viewport Origin	The coordinates of the upper-left corner of the window in device coordinates (pixels). You set this by calling CDC::SetViewportOrg().
	For example, calling SetViewportOrg(10,10) sets the viewport origin at the point (10,10).
Viewport Extent	The size of the viewport in device coordinates (pixels). You set this by calling CDC::SetViewportExt().
	For example, calling SetViewportExt(150,150) sets the viewport extent to 150 in both the x-direction and y-direction.

The *viewport* referred to here has no physical significance by itself; it only has meaning in relation to the window extent. The viewport extent together with the window extent determines how coordinates are transformed from logical coordinates to device coordinates. To put it another way, the SetWindowExt() and SetViewportExt() functions define corresponding rectangles that determine the transformation between logical coordinates and device coordinates. When you call SetWindowExt(), you are defining a rectangle in logical coordinates that corresponds to the rectangle in device coordinates that you define when you call SetViewportExt().

The formulae used by Windows to convert from logical coordinates to device coordinates are:

$$x_{Device} = (x_{Logical} - x_{WindowOrigin}) \times \frac{x_{ViewportExtent}}{x_{WindowExtent}} + x_{ViewportOrigin}$$

$$y_{Device} = (y_{Logical} - y_{WindowOrigin}) \times \frac{y_{ViewportExtent}}{y_{WindowExtent}} + y_{ViewportOrigin}$$

With coordinate systems other than those provided by the MM_ISOTROPIC and MM_ANISOTROPIC mapping modes, the window extent and the viewport extent are fixed by the mapping mode and can't be changed. Calling SetWindowExt() or SetViewportExt() in the CDC object to change them has no effect, although you can still move the position of (0,0) in your logical reference frame by calling SetWindowOrg() or SetViewportOrg(). However, with the MM_ISOTROPIC or MM_ANISOTROPIC mapping modes, for a given document size that is expressed by the window extent in logical coordinate units, you can adjust the scale at which elements are displayed by setting the viewport extent appropriately. By setting the window and viewport extents, you can get the scaling done automatically.

Setting the Document Size

You need to define the size of the document in logical units in the document object. You can add a protected data member, m_DocSize, to the CSketcherDoc class definition to store the size of the document implementation of CSketcherDoc() to:

```
CSize m_DocSize {CSize {3000, 3000}};                    // Document size
```

This defines the extent of the document as 3000 logical units in both the x and y directions. CSize is an MFC class that is the equivalent of the Windows SIZE structure. It has public data members cx and cy. The class overloads the +, -, +=, -=, ==, and != operators so you can add, subtract and compare CSize objects for equality or inequality. The physical extent of a dimension in logical units will be determined by the window extent and the viewport extent that is in effect. Either or both extents can be changed with the scaleable mapping modes, which will alter the physical extent of a given number of logical units. You will want to access the m_DocSize data member from the view class, so add a public function to the CSketcherDoc class definition as follows:

```
CSize GetDocSize() const { return m_DocSize; }    // Retrieve the document size
```

You don't need to initialize the m_DocSize member in the constructor for the document because an initial value has been specified for it.

You'll be using notional MM_LOENGLISH coordinates, so a logical unit is 0.01 inches, and the value for the document size gives you an area of 30 inches square to draw on.

Setting the Mapping Mode

You can set the mapping mode to MM_ANISOTROPIC in an override of the inherited OnPrepareDC() function in the CSketcherView class. This function is always called for any WM_PAINT message that is sent to the view and it allows you to set up the device context to your liking before the OnDraw() member is called. You have to do a little more than just set the mapping mode to get view-scaling working. You must figure out what you should set the viewport extent to, so that the sketch will be drawn at the scale that is set in the view.

You'll need to create the function override for OnPrepareDC() in CSketcherView before you can add the code. Open the Properties window for the CSketcherView class and click the Overrides button. Add the override by selecting OnPrepareDC from the list and clicking <Add>

OnPrepareDC in the adjacent column. You can now type the code directly into the Editor pane. The implementation of OnPrepareDC() is:

```
void CSketcherView::OnPrepareDC(CDC* pDC, CPrintInfo* pInfo)
{
  CScrollView::OnPrepareDC(pDC, pInfo);
  CSketcherDoc* pDoc {GetDocument()};
  pDC->SetMapMode(MM_ANISOTROPIC);        // Set the map mode
  CSize DocSize {pDoc->GetDocSize()};     // Get the document size

  pDC->SetWindowExt(DocSize);             // Now set the window extent

  // Get the number of pixels per inch in x and y
  int xLogPixels {pDC->GetDeviceCaps(LOGPIXELSX)};
  int yLogPixels {pDC->GetDeviceCaps(LOGPIXELSY)};

  // Calculate the viewport extent in x and y for the current scale
  int xExtent {(DocSize.cx*m_Scale*xLogPixels)/100};
  int yExtent {(DocSize.cy*m_Scale*yLogPixels)/100};

  pDC->SetViewportExt(xExtent,yExtent); // Set viewport extent
}
```

The implementation of the override of OnPrepareDC() is unusual here in that you have left in the call to CScrollView::OnPrepareDC() and added the modifications after it, rather than where the comment in the default code suggests. If the class was derived from CView, you would replace the call to the base class version because it does nothing, but in the case of CScrollView, this isn't the case. You need the base class function to set some attributes before you set the mapping mode. Don't make the mistake of calling the base class function after your code — if you do, scaling won't work.

The window extent is set to the document size, which is in logical coordinate units. The CDC member function GetDeviceCaps() supplies information about the device with which the device context is associated. You can get various kinds of information about the device, depending on the argument you pass to the function. Here the arguments LOGPIXELSX and LOGPIXELSY cause the function to return the number of pixels per logical inch in the x- and y-directions, respectively. These values are the number of pixels in 100 units (1 inch) in your logical coordinates.

You use these values to calculate the x- and y-values for the viewport extent for the current scale, which you store in the local variables xExtent and yExtent. The document extent along an axis in logical units, divided by 100, gives the document extent in inches. When you multiply this by the number of logical pixels per inch for the device, you get the number of pixels for the document extent. If you were to use this value as the viewport extent, you would get the elements displayed at a scale of 1 to 1. When the window origin and the viewport origin are both (0,0), the equations for converting between device and logical coordinates are very simple:

$$x_{Device} = x_{Logical} \times \frac{x_{ViewportExtent}}{x_{WindowExtent}}$$

$$y_{Device} = y_{Logical} \times \frac{y_{ViewportExtent}}{y_{WindowExtent}}$$

If you multiply the viewport extent values by the view scale, m_Scale, the elements are drawn scaled by a factor of m_Scale. This logic is exactly represented by the expressions for the x- and y-viewport extents in your code. The simplified equations, with the scale included, are as follows:

$$x_{Device} = x_{Logical} \times \frac{m\_Scale \times x_{ViewportExtent}}{x_{WindowExtent}}$$

$$y_{Device} = y_{Logical} \times \frac{m\_Scale \times y_{ViewportExtent}}{y_{WindowExtent}}$$

You should be able to see from this that a given point (x,y) in device coordinates varies in proportion to the scale value. The coordinates at a scale of three are three times the coordinates at a scale of one. Of course, as well as making elements larger, increasing the scale also moves them away from the origin.

Unfortunately, at the moment scrolling won't work with scaling, so you need to see what you can do about that.

Implementing Scrolling with Scaling

CScrollView just won't work with the MM_ANISOTROPIC mapping mode, so clearly you must use another mapping mode to set up the scrollbars. The easiest way to do this is to use MM_TEXT, because in this case the units of logical coordinates are the same as the client coordinates — pixels, in other words. All you need to do, then, is figure out how many pixels are equivalent to the logical document extent for the scale at which you are drawing, which is easier than you might think. You can add a function to CSketcherView to take care of the scrollbars and implement it to work out the number of pixels corresponding to the logical document extent. Right-click the CSketcherView class name in Class View and add a public function, ResetScrollSizes(), with a void return type and no parameters. Add the code to the implementation, as follows:

```
void CSketcherView::ResetScrollSizes()
{
  CClientDC aDC {this};
  OnPrepareDC(&aDC);                            // Set up the device context
  CSize DocSize {GetDocument()->GetDocSize()};  // Get the document size
  aDC.LPtoDP(&DocSize);                         // Get the size in pixels
  SetScrollSizes(MM_TEXT, DocSize);             // Set up the scrollbars
}
```

After creating a local CClientDC object for the view, you call OnPrepareDC() to set up the MM_ANISOTROPIC mapping mode. Because this takes scaling into account, the LPtoDP() member of the aDC object converts the document size stored in the local variable DocSize to the correct number of pixels for the current logical document size and scale. The total document size in pixels defines how large the scrollbars must be in MM_TEXT mode — remember, MM_TEXT logical coordinates are in pixels. You can then get the SetScrollSizes() member of CScrollView to set up the scrollbars based on this by specifying MM_TEXT as the mapping mode.

It may seem strange that you can change the mapping mode in this way, but it's important to keep in mind that the mapping mode is nothing more than a definition of how logical coordinates are to be converted to device coordinates. Whatever mode (and therefore coordinate conversion algorithm) you've set up applies to all subsequent device context functions until you change it, and you can change it whenever you want. When you set a new mode, subsequent device context function calls just use the conversion algorithm defined by the new mode. You figure out how big the document is in pixels with MM_ANISOTROPIC because this is the only way you can get the scaling into the process; you then switch to MM_TEXT to set up the scrollbars because you need units for this in pixels for it to work properly. Simple really, when you know how.

Setting Up the Scrollbars

You must set up the scrollbars initially for the view in the OnInitialUpdate() member of CSketcherView. Change the previous implementation of the function to the following:

```
void CSketcherView::OnInitialUpdate()
{
    ResetScrollSizes();                 // Set up the scrollbars
    CScrollView::OnInitialUpdate();
}
```

All you do is call the ResetScrollSizes() function that you just added to the view. This takes care of everything — well, almost. The CScrollView object needs an initial extent to be set in order for OnPrepareDC() to work properly, so you need to add one statement to the CSketcherView constructor:

```
CSketcherView::CSketcherView()
{
    SetScrollSizes(MM_TEXT, CSize {};    // Set arbitrary scrollers
}
```

The additional statement just calls SetScrollSizes() with an arbitrary extent to get the scrollbars initialized before the view is drawn. When the view is drawn for the first time, the ResetScrollSizes() function call in OnInitialUpdate() sets up the scrollbars properly. There is nothing else the view constructor needs to do. All the CPoint members are initialized by default and the m_MoveMode and m_Scale members have initial values specified in the class.

Of course, each time the view scale changes, you need to update the scrollbars before the view is redrawn. This is because changing the view scale has the effect of changing the document extent in device coordinates. You can take care of this in the OnViewScale() handler in the CSketcherView class:

```
void CSketcherView::OnViewScale()
{
    CScaleDialog aDlg;                   // Create a dialog object
    aDlg.m_Scale = m_Scale;             // Pass the view scale to the dialog
    if(aDlg.DoModal() == IDOK)
```

```
    {
        m_Scale = aDlg.m_Scale;        // Get the new scale
        ResetScrollSizes();            // Adjust scrolling to the new scale
        InvalidateRect(nullptr);       // Invalidate the whole window
    }
}
```

With the ResetScrollSizes() function, taking care of the scrollbars isn't complicated. Everything is covered by the one additional line of code.

Now you can build the project and run the application. You'll see that the scrollbars work just as they should. Note that each view maintains its own scale factor, independently of the other views.

That's all you need in order to scale the view. You can have multiple scrolled views, all at different scales, and what you draw in one view displays at the appropriate scales in the other views.

WORKING WITH STATUS BARS

With each view now being scaled independently, there's a real need to have some indication of what the current scale in a view window is. A convenient way to do this would be to display the scale in the status bar for each view window. A status bar was created by default in the Sketcher main application window, but not in the view windows. Usually, a status bar appears at the bottom of a window, below the horizontal scrollbar, although you can arrange for it to be at the top of the client area. A status bar is divided into segments called *panes*; the status bar in the main application window in Sketcher has four panes. The one on the left contains the text "Ready," and the other three are the areas on the right that are used as indicators to record when Caps Lock, Num Lock, and Scroll Lock are in effect.

It's possible for you to write to the status bar that the Application Wizard supplied by default, but you need access to the m_wndStatusBar member of the CMainFrame object for the application, as this represents it. It's a protected member of the class, so you must either add a public member function that you can call from outside the class to modify the status bar, or add a member to return a reference to m_wndStatusBar.

You may well have several views of a sketch, each with its own view scale, so you really want each view window to display its own scale. A good approach would be to give each child window its own status bar. The m_wndStatusBar object in CMainFrame is an instance of the CStatusBar class. You can use the same class to implement your own status bars in the view windows.

Adding a Status Bar to a Frame

The CStatusBar class defines a control bar with multiple panes in which you can display information. The first step to using CStatusBar is to add a data member for the status bar to the definition of CChildFrame, which is the frame window for a view. Add the following declaration to the public section of the class:

```
    CStatusBar m_StatusBar;            // Status bar object
```

> **NOTE** *A status bar should be part of the frame, not part of the view. You don't want to scroll a status bar or draw over it. It should just remain anchored to the bottom of the window. If you were to add a status bar to the view, it would appear inside the scrollbars and would be scrolled whenever you scrolled the view. Drawing over the part of the view containing the status bar would cause the bar to be redrawn, leading to an annoying flicker. Having the status bar as part of the frame avoids all these problems.*

Creating Status Bar Panes

To create panes in a status bar, you call the `SetIndicators()` function for the status bar object. This function requires two arguments, a `const` array of indicators of type `UINT` and the number of elements in the array. Each element in the array is a resource symbol that will be associated with a pane in the status bar, and each resource symbol must have an entry in the *resource string table* that will define the default text in the pane. The IDs for status panes start with `ID_INDICATOR_` and there are standard resource symbols, such as `ID_INDICATOR_CAPS` and `ID_INDICATOR_NUM`, which are used to identify indicators for the Caps Lock and Num Lock keys, respectively. You can see these in use if you look at the implementation of the `OnCreate()` function in the `CMainFrame` class. The standard symbols appear in the MFC string table resource so you should take a look at that. Double-click the `String Table` resource in Resource View and double-click the String Table entry to display the table. The string table for Sketcher is shown in Figure 16-11 as a floating window.

ID	Value	Caption
IDR_MAINFRAME	128	Sketcher
IDR_SketchTYPE	130	\nSketch\nSketch\nSketcher Files (*.ske)\n.ske\nSketcher.Document\nSketcher.Document
ID_ELEMENT_LINE	32771	Draw lines\nLines
ID_ELEMENT_RECTANGLE	32772	Draw rectangles\nRectangles
ID_ELEMENT_CIRCLE	32773	Draw circles\nCircles
ID_ELEMENT_CURVE	32774	Draw curves\nCurves
ID_COLOR_BLACK	32775	Draw in black\nBlack
ID_COLOR_RED	32776	Draw in red\nRed
ID_COLOR_GREEN	32777	Draw in green\nGreen
ID_COLOR_BLUE	32778	Draw in blue\nBlue
ID_PEN_WIDTH	32794	Change pen width\nShow pen width options.
ID_VIEW_SCALE	32797	Set drawing scale\nDrawing scale
AFX_IDS_APP_TITLE	57344	Sketcher
AFX_IDS_IDLEMESSAGE	57345	Ready
ID_FILE_NEW	57600	Create a new document\nNew
ID_FILE_OPEN	57601	Open an existing document\nOpen
ID_FILE_CLOSE	57602	Close the active document\nClose
ID_FILE_SAVE	57603	Save the active document\nSave

FIGURE 16-11

Figure 16-11 shows string table entries for our menu items. Each entry consists of three parts: the ID, the value for the ID, which is a unique integer value, and the string. If you scroll the string table down, you will find the status pane entries for the application window; the first has the ID `ID_INDICATOR_EXT`. Incidentally, clicking a column-heading in the string table pane will sort the entries in ascending order of that column.

You can create your own entries in the string table for indicator resource symbols. Right-click any entry in the string table and select New String from the menu. Alternatively, just press the Insert key. If you right-click the new entry and select Properties from the menu, you will be able to change its default ID to ID_INDICATOR_SCALE and the caption to View Scale : 1.

You should initialize the m_StatusBar member before the visible view window is displayed. Using the Properties window for the CChildFrame class, you can add a message handler to the class that will be called in response to the WM_CREATE message that is sent to the application when the window is to be created. Add the following code to the OnCreate() handler:

```
int CChildFrame::OnCreate(LPCREATESTRUCT lpCreateStruct)
{
  if(CMDIChildWnd::OnCreate(lpCreateStruct) == -1)
    return -1;

  // Create the status bar
  m_StatusBar.Create(this);
  static UINT indicators[] {ID_SEPARATOR, ID_INDICATOR_SCALE};
  m_StatusBar.SetIndicators(indicators, _countof(indicators));
  return 0;
}
```

The generated code isn't bolded. There's a call to the base class version of OnCreate(), which takes care of creating the definition of the view window. It's important that you don't delete this function call; otherwise, the window is not created.

Calling the Create() function for the CStatusBar object creates the status bar. You pass the this pointer for the current CChildFrame object to the Create() function, setting up a connection between the status bar and the window that owns it. The indicators that define the panes in the status bar are typically defined as an array of UINT elements. Here you define indicators as an array that is initialized just with the ID for a separator and the symbol for your status pane. When you want to add more panes to a status bar, you can separate them by including ID_SEPARATOR symbols between your symbols in the indicators array. You call the SetIndicators() function for the status bar object with the address of indicators as the first argument and a count of the number of elements in the array as the second argument. Here, this creates a single pane to the right in the status bar.

When the first pane indicator is ID_SEPARATOR, the pane is automatically stretched to align subsequent panes to the right in the status bar. You can call SetPaneStyle() for a pane referenced by its index in the indicators array to set the pane style. The first argument to SetPaneStyle() is the pane index and the second a UINT value specifying the style or styles to be set. Only one pane can have the SBPS_STRETCH style, which stretches the pane to fill the available space in the status bar. Other styles you can set for a pane are as follows:

SBPS_NORMAL	No stretch, borders, or pop-out styles set.
SBPS_POPOUT	Border reversed, so text pops out.
SBPS_NOBORDERS	No 3D borders.
SBPS_DISABLED	No text drawn in the pane.

You just OR the styles together when you want to set more than one style for a pane.

Updating the Status Bar

If you build and run the code now, the status bars appear, but they show only a scale factor of one, no matter what scale factor is actually being used — not very useful. This is because there is no mechanism in place for updating the status bar. You need to add code somewhere to change the text in the status bar pane each time a different scale is chosen. The obvious place to do this is in the CSketcherView class because that's where the current view scale is recorded.

You can update a pane in the status bar by adding an UPDATE_COMMAND_UI handler that is associated with the indicator symbol for the pane. Right-click CSketcherView in Class View, and select Class Wizard from the pop-up. This will display the MFC Class Wizard dialog. As you can see, this enables you to create and edit a whole range of functions in a class and provides an alternative way to access any class member.

If it is not already visible, select the Commands tab in the dialog: this enables you to add command handlers to the class. Select ID_INDICATOR_SCALE in the Object IDs pane; this ID identifies the status bar pane you want to update. Then, select UPDATE_COMMAND_UI in the Messages pane. The dialog should look like Figure 16-12.

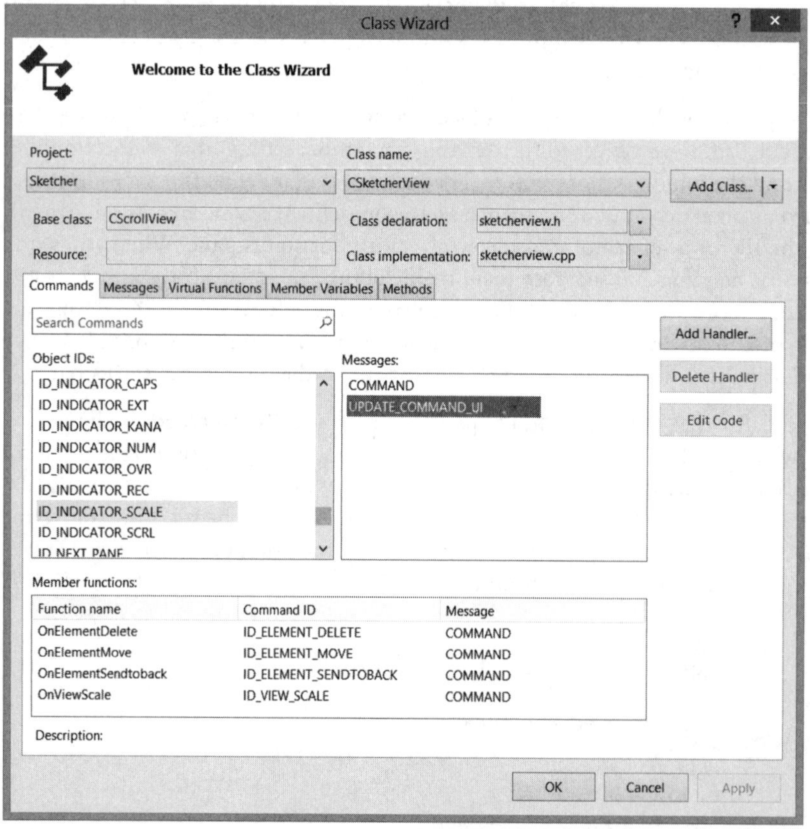

FIGURE 16-12

Click the Add Handler button to add the command handler to the class. Another dialog will be displayed that gives you the opportunity to change the handler function name to OnUpdateScale, which is a little more concise than the default. You can then click OK to close the dialog, and OK again to close the MFC Class Wizard dialog.

All you need is to complete the definition for the handler that was added, so add the following code to the function in SketcherView.cpp:

```
void CSketcherView::OnUpdateScale(CCmdUI *pCmdUI)
{
    pCmdUI->Enable();
    CString scaleStr;
    scaleStr.Format(_T(" View Scale : %d"), m_Scale);
    pCmdUI->SetText(scaleStr);
}
```

The parameter is a pointer to a CCmdUI object that encapsulates the status bar pane as a command target. You create a CString object and call its Format() function to generate the text string to be displayed in the pane. The first argument to Format() is a format control string in which you can embed conversion specifiers for subsequent arguments. The format string with the embedded specifiers is the same as for the C function, printf(). Each of the subsequent arguments is converted according to the corresponding format specifier in the first argument, so there must be one format specifier in the format string for each argument after the first. Here the %d specifier converts the value of m_Scale to a decimal string, and this is incorporated into the format string. Other common specifiers you can use are %f for floating point values and %s for string values. Calling SetText() for the CCmdUI object sets the string you supply as the argument in the status bar pane. Calling Enable() for the CCmdUI object causes the pane text to be displayed normally because the BOOL parameter has a default value of TRUE. An explicit argument of FALSE would make the pane text grayed out.

That's all you need for the view status bar. If you build Sketcher again, you should have multiple, scrolled windows, each at different scales, with the scale displayed in the status bar in each view.

THE CString CLASS

You used a CString object in the previous section, and there's more to it than you have seen so far. The CString class provides a convenient and easy-to-use mechanism for handling strings that you can use just about anywhere a string is required. To be more precise, you can use a CString object in place of strings of type const TCHAR*, or of type LPCTSTR, which is a type that comes up in Windows API functions. If you are using the DDX mechanism for strings, then you must use CString, otherwise DDX won't work.

The CString class provides the overloaded operators shown in the following table.

OPERATOR	USAGE

=	Copies one string to another, as in:
	`str1 = str2;`
	`str1 = _T("A normal string");`

+	Concatenates two or more strings, as in: `str1 = str2 + str3 + _T(" more");`
+=	Appends a string to an existing `CString` object, as in: `str1 += str2;`
==	Compares two strings for equality, as in: `if(str1 == str2) //do something...`
<	Tests if one string is less than another.
<=	Tests if one string is less than or equal to another.
>	Tests if one string is greater than another.
>=	Tests if one string is greater than or equal to another.

The variables `str1` and `str2` in the preceding table are `CString` objects.

`CString` objects automatically grow as necessary, such as when you add an additional string to the end of an existing object. For example:

```
CString str {_T("A fool and your money")};
str += _T(" are soon partners.");
```

The first statement declares and initializes the object `str`. The second statement appends an additional string to `str`, so the length of `str` automatically increases.

USING AN EDIT BOX CONTROL

An edit box control is for managing text entry to an application. You will use an edit box control to add annotations to a sketch in Sketcher. You'll need a new Sketcher element type, `CText`, that encapsulates a text string, and a menu item in the Element menu to set TEXT mode for creating elements. Because a text element needs only one reference point, you can create it in the `OnLButtonDown()` handler in the view class. You'll add this text capability to Sketcher in the following sequence:

1. Create a dialog resource and its associated class with an edit box control for input.

2. Add the new menu item.

3. Add the code to open the dialog for creating a `CText` element.

4. Add support for creating `CText` elements.

Creating an Edit Box Resource

Create a new dialog resource in Resource View by right-clicking the Dialog folder and selecting Insert Dialog. Change the ID for the new dialog to `IDD_TEXT_DLG`, and the Caption property value for the dialog to Enter Text.

To add an edit box, select the Edit Control icon in the Toolbox pane and click the position in the dialog where you want to place it. You can adjust the size of the edit control by dragging its borders, and you can alter its position in the dialog by dragging the whole thing around. You can display the properties for the edit box by right-clicking it and selecting Properties from the pop-up. You could first change its ID to `IDC_EDIT_TEXT`, as shown in Figure 16-13.

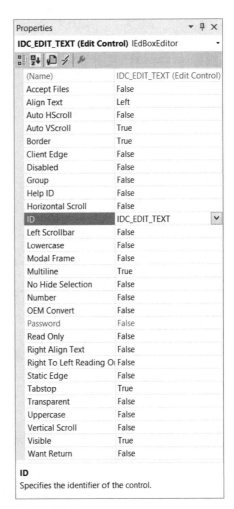

FIGURE 16-13

Some of the properties for this control are of interest at this point. First, select the `Multiline` property. Setting the value for this as `True` creates a multiline edit box in which the text you enter can span more than one line. This enables you to enter a long line of text that will still remain visible in its entirety in the edit box. The `Align text` property determines how the text is to be positioned in the multiline edit box. The value `Left` is fine here, but you also have the options for `Center` and `Right`.

If you were to change the value for the `Want return` property to `True`, pressing Enter on the keyboard while entering the text in the control would insert a return character into the text string. This enables you to analyze the string if you want to break it into multiple lines for display. You don't want this effect, so leave the property value as `False`. In this state, pressing Enter has the effect of selecting the default control (which is the OK button), which closes the dialog.

If you set the value of the `Auto HScroll` property to `False`, there is an automatic spill to the next line in the edit box when you reach the edge of the control while entering text. However, this is just for visibility in the edit box — it has no effect on the contents of the string. You could also change the value of the `Auto VScroll` property to `True` to allow text to continue beyond the number of lines that are visible in the control. If you set the `Vertical Scroll` property to `True`, the edit control will be supplied with a scrollbar that will allow you to scroll the text.

When you've finished setting the properties for the edit box, close its Properties window. Make sure that the edit box is first in the tab order by selecting the Format ➪ Tab Order menu item or by pressing Ctrl+D. You can then test the dialog by selecting the Test Dialog menu item or by pressing Ctrl+T. The dialog is shown in Figure 16-14. You can even enter text into the dialog in test mode to see how it works. Clicking the OK or Cancel button closes the dialog.

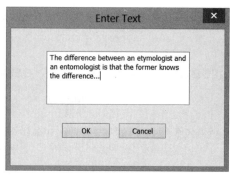

FIGURE 16-14

Creating the Dialog Class

After saving the dialog resource, you can create a suitable dialog class corresponding to the resource, which you could call CTextDialog. To do this, right-click the dialog in the Editor pane and select Add Class. The base class should be CDialogEx. Next you can add a control variable to the CTextDialog class by right-clicking the class name in Class View and selecting Add ➪ Add Variable. Select IDC_EDIT_TEXT as the control ID and Value as the category. Call the new variable m_TextString and leave its type as CString. You can also specify a maximum length for it in the Max chars edit box, as shown in Figure 16-15.

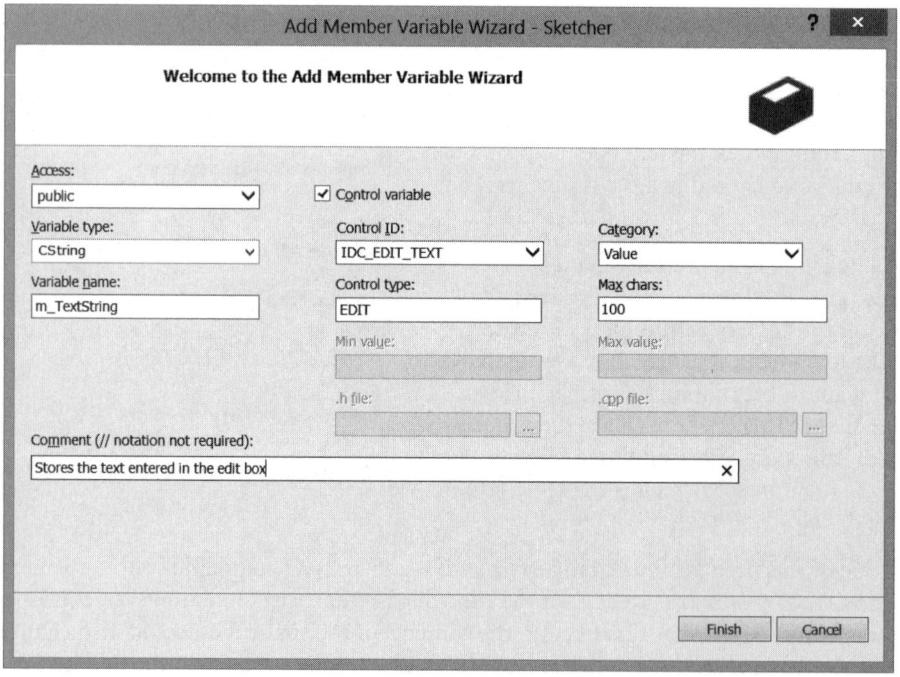

FIGURE 16-15

A length of 100 is more than adequate for your needs. The variable that you have added here is automatically updated from the data entered into the control by the DDX mechanism. You can click Finish to create the variable in the CTextDialog class, and close the Add Member Variable wizard.

> **NOTE** As I said earlier, the DDX mechanism does not support strings of type std::string so you must use type CString here.

Adding the Text Menu Item

Adding a new menu item should be easy by now. You just need to open the menu resource with the ID IDR_SketchTYPE in Resource View by double-clicking it, and add a new menu item, Text, to the Element menu. The default ID, ID_ELEMENT_TEXT, that appears in the Properties window for the item is fine, so you can leave that as it is. You can add a prompt to be displayed on the status bar corresponding to the menu item, and because you'll also want to add an additional toolbar button corresponding to this menu item, you can add a tooltip to the end of the prompt line, using \n to separate the prompt and the tooltip.

Don't forget the context menu. You can copy the menu item from IDR_SketchTYPE. Right-click the Text menu item and select Copy from the pop-up. Open the menu IDR_CONTEXT_MENU, right-click the empty item at the bottom of the no element menu, and select Paste. All you need to do then is drag the item to the appropriate position — above the separator — and save the resource file.

Add the toolbar button to the IDR_MAINFRAME toolbar and set its ID to the same as that for the menu item, ID_ELEMENT_TEXT. You can drag the new button so that it's positioned at the end of the block defining the other types of elements. When you've saved the resources, you can add an event handler for the new menu item.

You need a new type for CText elements so add a TEXT enumerator to the ElementType enum:

```
enum class ElementType{LINE, RECTANGLE, CIRCLE, CURVE, TEXT};
```

In the Class View pane, right-click CSketcherDoc and display its Properties window. Add a COMMAND handler for the event corresponding to the ID_ELEMENT_TEXT ID and add code to it as follows:

```
void CSketcherDoc::OnElementText()
{
  m_Element = ElementType::TEXT;
}
```

Only one line of code is necessary to set the element type in the document to ElementType::TEXT.

You also need to add a function to check the menu item if it is the current mode, so add an `UPDATE_COMMAND_UI` handler corresponding to the event for the `ID_ELEMENT_TEXT` ID, and implement the code for it as follows:

```
void CSketcherDoc::OnUpdateElementText(CCmdUI* pCmdUI)
{
  // Set checked if the current element is text
  pCmdUI->SetCheck(m_Element == ElementType::TEXT);
}
```

This operates in the same way as the other Element menu items. Of course, you could also have added both of these handlers through the Class Wizard dialog that you display by selecting Class Wizard from the context menu in Class View.

Don't forget that the context menu needs updating too. Add code to the `OnContextMenu()` member of `CSketcherView` to check the Text menu item. The next step is to define the `CText` class for an element of type `TEXT`.

Defining a Text Element

You can derive the `CText` class from the `CElement` class as follows:

```
#pragma once
#include <memory>
#include "Element.h"

// Class defining a text element
class CText : public CElement
{
public:
  // Constructor for a text element
  CText(const CPoint& start, const CPoint& end,
                     const CString& aString, COLORREF color);

  virtual void Draw(CDC* pDC,
              std::shared_ptr<CElement> pElement=nullptr) override;
  virtual void Move(const CSize& aSize) override;  // Move a text element
  virtual ~CText() {}

protected:
    CString m_String;                              // Text to be displayed
    CText(){}
};
```

I added this manually but I'll leave it to you to decide how you want to do it. This class definition declares the virtual `Draw()` and `Move()` functions, as the other element classes do. The data member `m_String` of type `CString` stores the text to be displayed.

The `CText` constructor declaration defines four parameters: the two points defining the rectangle in which the text is to be displayed, the string to be displayed, and the color. The pen width doesn't apply to text, because the appearance is determined by the font.

Implementing the CText Class

You have three functions to implement for the CText class:

➤ The constructor for a CText object

➤ The virtual Draw() function to display it

➤ The virtual Move() function to support moving a text object by dragging it with the mouse

I added these directly to the Text.cpp file.

The CText Constructor

The constructor for a CText object needs to initialize the class and base class data members:

```
// CText constructor
CText::CText(const CPoint& start, const CPoint& end,
            const CString& aString, COLORREF color) :
                                    CElement {start, color}
{
  m_String = aString;                   // Store the string

  m_EnclosingRect = CRect {start, end};
  m_EnclosingRect.NormalizeRect();
  m_EnclosingRect.InflateRect(m_PenWidth, m_PenWidth);
}
```

The base class constructor call stores the start point and the color and initializes the pen width to 1 by default. You calculate the rectangle that will enclose the string when it is displayed from the start and end points.

Creating a Text Element

If the element type has been set to ElementType::TEXT, a text object should be created at the cursor position whenever you click the left mouse button and enter the text you want to display. You therefore need to display the dialog that permits text to be entered in the OnLButtonDown() handler, but only when the element type is ElementType::TEXT. Add the following code to this handler in the CSketcherView class:

```
void CSketcherView::OnLButtonDown(UINT nFlags, CPoint point)
{
  CClientDC aDC {this};                    // Create a device context
  OnPrepareDC(&aDC);                       // Get origin adjusted
  aDC.DPtoLP(&point);                      // convert point to Logical
  CSketcherDoc* pDoc {GetDocument()};      // Get a document pointer

  if(m_MoveMode)
  { // In moving mode, so drop the element
    m_MoveMode = false;                    // Kill move mode
    auto pElement(m_pSelected);            // Store selected address
    m_pSelected.reset();                   // De-select the element
```

```
       pDoc->UpdateAllViews(nullptr, 0, pElement.get());   // Redraw all the views
   }
   else if(pDoc->GetElementType() == ElementType::TEXT)
   {
     CTextDialog aDlg;
     if(aDlg.DoModal() == IDOK)
     { // Exit OK so create a text element
       CSize textExtent {aDC.GetOutputTextExtent(aDlg.m_TextString)};
       textExtent.cx *= m_Scale;
       textExtent.cy *= m_Scale;
       std::shared_ptr<CElement> pTextElement
           {std::make_shared<CText>(point, point + textExtent, aDlg.m_TextString,
                                 static_cast<COLORREF>(pDoc->GetElementColor()))};

       pDoc->AddElement(pTextElement); // Add the element to the document
       pDoc->UpdateAllViews(nullptr, 0, pTextElement.get());   // Update all views
     }
   }
   else
   {
     m_FirstPoint = point;              // Record the cursor position
     SetCapture();                      // Capture subsequent mouse messages
   }
}
```

The code to be added is bolded. It creates a CTextDialog object and then opens the dialog using the DoModal() function call. The m_TextString member of aDlg is automatically set to the string entered in the edit box via the DDX mechanism, so you can use this data member to pass the string entered back to the CText constructor if the OK button was used to close the dialog. The color is obtained from the document using the GetElementColor() member that you have used previously.

You need to determine the corners of the rectangle that bounds the text in the client area of the view and this is a bit more complicated than with the geometric elements. The size of the rectangle that will enclose a string when you display it depends on the font used in the device context, as well as the number of characters in the string. You need the help of the device context object to figure this out. The GetOuputTextExtent() member of the CClientDC object, aDC, returns a CSize object that defines what the width and height of the string you pass as the argument will be. This is calculated using characters from the current font for the device context. The dimensions are in logical coordinates, which is just what you need. You store the CSize object that is returned in textExtent.

The drawing scale adds a further complication. The text will be drawn at a given font size that is not affected by the scale. If the current drawing scale is greater than one, you must adjust textExtent in the same proportion, otherwise the enclosing rectangle for the text will not be large enough at lower scales. You do this by multiplying the cx and cy members of textExtent by the scale.

The left-top corner of the rectangle enclosing the string will be point, which is already in logical coordinates. You get the right-bottom corner by adding the dimensions in textExtent to point.

The CText object is created using the make_shared<T>() function because the list in the document stores shared_ptr<CElement> pointers to the elements. You can store a pointer of type shared_ptr<CText> in a shared_ptr<CElement> variable because CText is derived from CElement. You add the new element to the document by calling the AddElement() member of CSketcherDoc, with the pointer to the new text element as an argument. Finally, UpdateAllViews() is called with the first argument nullptr, which specifies that all views are to be updated. Don't forget that you need #include directives for TextDialog.h and Text.h in SketcherView.cpp.

Drawing a CText Object

Drawing text in a device context is different from drawing a geometric figure. The implementation of the Draw() function for a CText object is:

```
void CText::Draw(CDC* pDC, std::shared_ptr<CElement> pElement)
{
  // Set the text color and output the text
  pDC->SetTextColor(this == pElement.get() ? SELECT_COLOR : m_Color);
  pDC->SetBkMode(TRANSPARENT);              // Transparent background for text
  pDC->ExtTextOut(m_StartPoint.x, m_StartPoint.y, 0,
                                        nullptr, m_String, nullptr);
}
```

You don't need a pen to display text. You have a choice of several functions in the CDC class that output text and in our case the simplest to use is ExtTextOut(). With this function you can specify a rectangle in which the text is to be displayed as well as other options that affect character spacing and the way in which the text is displayed in the rectangle. These are the parameters in sequence for one of the two versions of this function:

PARAMETER	DESCRIPTION
int x	Logical x-coordinate of the first character in the string.
int y	Logical y-coordinate of the first character in the string.
UINT options	Either, neither, or both of the flags: ETO_CLIPPED: string is clipped to pRect. ETO_OPAQUE: current background color fills pRect.
LPCRECT pRect	Rectangle that determines the dimensions of the rectangle in which the text is displayed (It's location is specified by x and y). This can be nullptr.
const CString& str	The string to be displayed.
LPINT widths	Pointer to an array of integers specifying distances between characters in the string. nullptr will select default spacing.

We have ignored all these options and just supplied the coordinates of where the text is to be displayed and the CString object that contains the text.

Before calling ExtTextOut(), you specify the text color using the SetTextColor() member function of the CDC object. You also call SetBkMode() to ensure the background to the string is transparent. An OPAQUE argument value would make the background opaque.

Moving a CText Object

The Move() function for a CText object is simple:

```
void CText::Move(const CSize& size)
{
  m_EnclosingRect += size;           // Move the rectangle
  m_StartPoint += size;              // Move the reference point
}
```

All you need to do is alter the enclosing rectangle by the distance specified in the size parameter and adjust the m_StartPoint member by the same amount.

Because the ExtTextOut() function for a CDC object doesn't use a pen, it isn't affected by setting the drawing mode of the device context. This means that the raster operations (ROP) method that you use to move geometric elements leaves trails behind when applied to text. You used the SetROP2() function to specify the way in which the pen would logically combine with the background. By choosing R2_NOTXORPEN as the drawing mode, you could cause a previously drawn element to disappear by redrawing it. Fonts aren't drawn with a pen, so it won't work properly with the text elements.

To fix the trails problem when moving a text element, you can treat it as a special case in the MoveElement() function in CSketcherView. Providing an alternative move mechanism for text elements requires that you can discover when the m_pSelected pointer contains the address of a CText object. The typeid operator that you met back in Chapter 2 can help with this.

By comparing the expression typeid(*(m_pSelected.get())) with typeid(CText), you can determine whether or not m_pSelected points to a CText object. Here's how you can update MoveElement() to eliminate the trails when moving text:

```
void CSketcherView::MoveElement(CClientDC& aDC, const CPoint& point)
{
  CSize distance {point - m_CursorPos};              // Get move distance
  m_CursorPos = point;              // Set current point as 1st for next time

  // If there is an element selected, move it
  if(m_pSelected)
  {
    CSketcherDoc* pDoc {GetDocument()};              // Get the document pointer
    pDoc->UpdateAllViews(this, 0 , m_pSelected.get());

    if (typeid(*(m_pSelected.get())) == typeid(CText))
    { // The element is text so use this method...
      CRect oldRect {m_pSelected->GetEnclosingRect()};  // Get old bound rect
```

```
          aDC.LPtoDP(oldRect);                          // Convert to client coords
          m_pSelected->Move(distance);                 // Move the element
          InvalidateRect(&oldRect);

          UpdateWindow();                               // Redraw immediately
          m_pSelected->Draw(&aDC,m_pSelected);         // Draw highlighted
        }
        else
        { // ...it is not text so use the ROP method
          aDC.SetROP2(R2_NOTXORPEN);
          m_pSelected->Draw(&aDC, m_pSelected);        // Draw the element to erase it
          m_pSelected->Move(distance);                 // Now move the element
          m_pSelected->Draw(&aDC, m_pSelected);        // Draw the moved element
        }
        pDoc->UpdateAllViews(this, 0 , m_pSelected.get());
      }
    }
```

You use the `typeid` operator to check whether or not `m_pSelected` points to a `CText` element.
If `m_pSelected` does not point to a `CText` element, the code proceeds as before. When `m_pSelected`
does point to a `CText` element, you obtain the bounding rectangle in the current view for the position
of the element before moving it to its new position. You convert the rectangle to client coordinates
because that's what `InvalidateRect()` expects as an argument. You call `InvalidateRect()` and
`UpdateWindow()` after the move to erase the element from its old position. Finally, you call `Draw()` for
the text element to draw the element in its new position. The other views are taken care of by the
calls to `UpdateAllViews()` for the document object, as before. You should now be able to produce
annotated sketches using multiple scaled and scrolled views, such as the ones shown in Figure 16-16.

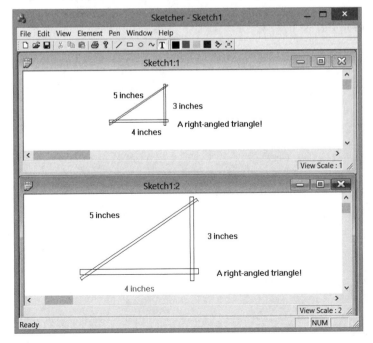

FIGURE 16-16

You can see that the text does not scale along with the shapes. You could scale the text by adjusting the font size in the device context based on the scale. This would involve creating a font of the appropriate point size based on the scale, and doing this whenever a CText element was drawn or redrawn. However, it's probably better to leave text elements at the font size with which they were created.

SUMMARY

In this chapter you've seen several different dialogs using a variety of controls. Although you haven't created dialogs involving several different controls at once, the mechanism for handling them is the same as what you have seen, because each control can operate independently of the others. Dialogs are a fundamental tool for managing user input in an application. They provide a way for you to manage the input of multiple related items of data. You can easily ensure that an application only receives valid data. Judicious choice of the controls in a dialog can force the user to choose from a specific set of options. You can also check the data after it has been entered in a dialog and prompt the user when it is not valid.

EXERCISES

1. Implement the scale dialog in Sketcher using radio buttons.

2. Implement the pen width dialog in Sketcher using a list box.

3. Implement the pen width dialog in Sketcher as a combo box with the drop list type selected as the Type property. (The drop list type allows the user to select from a drop-down list but not to enter alternative entries in the list.)

➤ WHAT YOU LEARNED IN THIS CHAPTER

TOPIC	CONCEPT
Status bars	The `CStatusBar` class encapsulates a status bar that can have multiple panes. You add a status bar to a window by adding it to the frame.
Dialogs	A dialog involves two components: a resource defining the dialog window and its controls, and a class that is used to display and manage the dialog. Dialog classes are typically derived from `CDialogEx`.
Extracting data from a dialog	Information can be extracted from controls in a dialog by means of the DDX mechanism. The data can also be validated with the DDV mechanism. To use DDX/DDV you need only to select the Control Variable option for the Add Member Variable wizard to define a variable in the dialog class that is associated with a control. The associated control is identified by its ID.
Modal dialogs	A modal dialog retains the focus in the application until the dialog is closed. As long as a modal dialog is displayed, all other windows in an application are inactive.
Modeless dialogs	A modeless dialog allows the focus to switch from the dialog to other windows in the application and back again. A modeless dialog can remain displayed as long as the application is executing, if required.
Common controls	Common controls are a set of standard Windows controls supported by MFC and the resource editing capabilities of Visual Studio.
Adding controls	Although controls are usually associated with a dialog, you can add controls to any window.
Displaying a dialog	You can display a dialog as modal by calling its `DoModal()` function.
Edit boxes	An edit box control allows entry of one or more lines of text. The text can be optionally scrolled vertically and/or horizontally.

17

Storing and Printing Documents

WHAT YOU WILL LEARN IN THIS CHAPTER:

➤ How serialization works

➤ How to make objects of a class serializable

➤ The role of a `CArchive` object in serialization

➤ How to implement serialization in your own classes

➤ How to implement serialization in the Sketcher application

➤ How printing works with MFC

➤ Which view class functions support printing

➤ What a `CPrintInfo` object contains and how it's used in the printing process

➤ How to implement multipage printing in Sketcher

WROX.COM CODE DOWNLOADS FOR THIS CHAPTER

You can find the wrox.com code downloads for this chapter on the Download Code tab at www.wrox.com/go/beginningvisualc. The code is in the Chapter 17 download and individually named according to the names throughout the chapter.

UNDERSTANDING SERIALIZATION

A document in an MFC-based program is not a simple entity — it's a class object that can be very complicated. It typically contains a variety of objects, each of which may contain other objects, each of which may contain still more objects and that structure may continue for a number of levels.

You want to be able to save a document in a file, but writing a class object to a file represents something of a problem because it isn't the same as a basic data item like an integer or a character string. A basic data item consists of a known number of bytes, so to write it to a file only requires that the appropriate number of bytes be written. Conversely, if you know a value of type int was written to a file, to get it back, you just read the appropriate number of bytes.

Writing objects to a file is different. Even if you write all the data members of an object to a file, that's not enough to be able to get the original object back. Class objects contain members function as well as data members, and all the members, both data and functions, have access specifiers; therefore, to record an object in an external file, the information that is written to the file must contain complete specifications of all the class structures involved. The read process must also be clever enough to synthesize the original objects completely from the data in the file. MFC supports a mechanism called *serialization* to help you to implement input and output of your class objects with a minimum of time and effort.

The basic idea behind serialization is that any class that's serializable should take care of storing and retrieving itself. This means that for your classes to be serializable — in the case of the Sketcher application, this will include the CElement class and the element classes you have derived from it — they must be able to write themselves to a file. This implies that for a class to be serializable, all the class types that are used to declare data members of the class must be serializable too.

SERIALIZING A DOCUMENT

This all sounds rather tricky, but the basic capability for serializing your document was built into the application by the Application Wizard right at the outset. The handlers for the File ➪ Save, File ➪ Save As, and File ➪ Open menu items all assume that you want serialization implemented for your document, and already contain the code to support it. Take a look at the parts of the definition and implementation of CSketcherDoc that relate to creating a document using serialization.

Serialization in the Document Class Definition

The code in the definition of CSketcherDoc that enables serialization of a document object is shown shaded in the following fragment:

```
class CSketcherDoc : public CDocument
{
protected: // create from serialization only
    CSketcherDoc();
    DECLARE_DYNCREATE(CSketcherDoc)

// Rest of the class...

// Overrides
public:
    virtual BOOL OnNewDocument();
    virtual void Serialize(CArchive& ar);

// Rest of the class...

};
```

There are three things here that relate to serializing a document object:

1. The DECLARE_DYNCREATE() macro.

2. The Serialize() member function.

3. The default class constructor.

DECLARE_DYNCREATE() is a macro that enables objects of the CSketcherDoc class to be created dynamically by the application framework during the serialization input process. It's matched by a complementary macro, IMPLEMENT_DYNCREATE(), in the class implementation. These macros apply only to classes derived from CObject, but as you will see shortly, they aren't the only pair of macros that can be used in this context. For any class that you want to serialize, CObject must be a direct or indirect base because it adds the functionality that enables serialization to work. This is why the CElement class was derived from CObject. Almost all MFC classes are derived from CObject and are serializable.

> **NOTE** The Hierarchy Chart in the Microsoft Foundation Class Reference for Visual C++ shows those classes, that are not derived from CObject. Note that CArchive is in this list.

The CSketcherDoc class definition also includes a declaration for a virtual function Serialize(). Every class that's serializable must include this function. It's called to perform both input and output serialization operations on the data members of the class. The object of type CArchive that's passed as an argument determines whether the operation that is to occur is input or output. You'll explore this in more detail when considering the implementation of serialization for the document class.

Note that the class explicitly defines a default constructor. This is also essential for serialization to work because the default constructor is used by the framework to synthesize an object when reading it from a file. The synthesized object produced by the no-arg constructor is filled out with the data from the file to set the values of the data members of the object.

Serialization in the Document Class Implementation

There are two bits of the SketcherDoc.cpp file that relate to serialization. The first is the IMPLEMENT_DYNCREATE() macro that complements the DECLARE_DYNCREATE() macro:

```
// SketcherDoc.cpp : implementation of the CSketcherDoc class
//

#include "stdafx.h"
// SHARED_HANDLERS can be defined in an ATL project implementing preview,
// thumbnail and search filter handlers and allows sharing of document code
// with that project.
#ifndef SHARED_HANDLERS
#include "Sketcher.h"
#endif
```

```
#include "SketcherDoc.h"
#include "PenDialog.h"

#include <propkey.h>

#ifdef _DEBUG
#define new DEBUG_NEW
#endif

// CSketcherDoc


IMPLEMENT_DYNCREATE(CSketcherDoc, CDocument)

// Message map and the rest of the file...
```

This macro defines the base class for CSketcherDoc as CDocument. This is required for the proper dynamic creation of a CSketcherDoc object, including members that are inherited.

The Serialize( ) Function

The class implementation includes the definition of the Serialize() function:

```
void CSketcherDoc::Serialize(CArchive& ar)
{
    if (ar.IsStoring())
    {
        // TODO: add storing code here
    }
    else
    {
        // TODO: add loading code here
    }
}
```

This function serializes the data members of the class. The argument to the function, ar, is a reference to an object of the CArchive class. The IsStoring() member of this class object returns TRUE if the operation is to store data members in a file, and FALSE if the operation is to read back data members from a previously stored document.

Because the Application Wizard has no knowledge of what data your document contains, the process of writing and reading this information is up to you, as indicated by the comments. To understand how you do this, let's look a little more closely at the CArchive class.

The CArchive Class

The CArchive class is the engine that drives the serialization mechanism. It provides an MFC-based equivalent of the stream operations in C++ that you used for reading from the keyboard and writing to the screen in the console program examples. A CArchive object provides a mechanism for streaming your objects to a file, or recovering them as an input stream, automatically reconstituting the objects of your class in the process.

A CArchive object has a CFile object associated with it that provides disk input/output capability for binary files, and provides the connection to the physical file. Within the serialization process, the CFile object takes care of all the specifics of the file input and output operations, and the CArchive object deals with the logic of structuring the object data to be written, or reconstructing the objects from the information read. You need to worry about the details of the associated CFile object only if you are constructing your own CArchive object. With the document in Sketcher, the framework has already taken care of it and passes the CArchive object that it constructs, ar, to the Serialize() function in CSketcherDoc. You'll be able to use the same object in each of the Serialize() functions you add to the element classes when you implement serialization for them.

The CArchive class overloads the extraction and insertion operators (>> and <<) for input and output operations, respectively, on objects of classes derived from CObject, plus a range of basic data types. These overloaded operators work with the object types and primitive types shown in the following table.

TYPE	DEFINITION
bool	Boolean value, true or false
float	Standard single precision floating point
double	Standard double precision floating point
BYTE	8-bit unsigned integer
char	8-bit character
wchar_t	16-bit character
short	16-bit signed integer
int	32-bit signed integer
LONG and long	32-bit signed integer
LONGLONG	64-bit signed integer
ULONGLONG	64-bit unsigned integer
WORD	16-bit unsigned integer
DWORD and unsigned int	32-bit unsigned integer
CString	A CString object defining a string
SIZE and CSize	An object defining a size as a cx, cy pair
POINT and CPoint	An object defining a point as an x, y pair
RECT and CRect	An object defining a rectangle by its upper-left and lower-right corners
CObject*	Pointer to CObject

For basic data types in your objects, you use the insertion and extraction operators to serialize the data. To read or write an object of a serializable class that you have derived from `CObject`, you can either call the `Serialize()` function for the object, or use the extraction or insertion operator. Whichever way you choose must be used consistently for both input and output, so you should not output an object using the insertion operator and then read it back using the `Serialize()` function, or vice versa.

Where you don't know the type of an object when you read it, as in the case of the pointers in the list of elements in our document, for example, you must *only* use the `Serialize()` function. This brings the virtual function mechanism into play, so the appropriate `Serialize()` function for the type of object pointed to is determined at run time.

A `CArchive` object is constructed either for storing objects or for retrieving objects. The `CArchive` function `IsStoring()` returns `TRUE` if the object is for output, and `FALSE` if the object is for input. You saw this used in the `Serialize()` member of `CSketcherDoc`.

There are many other member functions of the `CArchive` class that are concerned with the detailed mechanics of the serialization process, but you don't usually need to know about them to use serialization.

Functionality of CObject-Based Classes

There are three levels of functionality available in your classes when they're derived from the MFC class `CObject`. The level you get in your class is determined by which of three different macros you use in the definition of your class:

MACRO	FUNCTIONALITY
`DECLARE_DYNAMIC()`	Support for runtime class information
`DECLARE_DYNCREATE()`	Support for runtime class information and dynamic object creation
`DECLARE_SERIAL()`	Support for runtime class information, dynamic object creation, and serialization of objects

Each of these macros requires that a complementary macro, named with the prefix `IMPLEMENT_` instead of `DECLARE_`, be placed in the file containing the class implementation. As the table indicates, the macros provide progressively more functionality, so I'll concentrate on the third macro, `DECLARE_SERIAL()`, because it provides everything that the preceding macros do and more. This is the macro you should use to enable serialization in your own classes. It requires that the macro `IMPLEMENT_SERIAL()` be added to the file containing the class implementation.

You may be wondering why the document class uses `DECLARE_DYNCREATE()` and not `DECLARE_SERIAL()`. The `DECLARE_DYNCREATE()` macro provides the capability for dynamic creation of the objects of the class in which it appears. The `DECLARE_SERIAL()` macro provides the capability for serialization of the class, plus the dynamic creation of objects of the class, so it incorporates the effects of `DECLARE_DYNCREATE()`. Your document class doesn't need serialization because the framework only has to synthesize the document object and then restore the values of its data members; however, the data members of a document *do* need to be serializable, because this is the process used to store and retrieve them.

The Macros that Add Serialization to a Class

With the DECLARE_SERIAL() macro in the definition of your CObject-based class, you get access to the serialization support provided by CObject. This includes special new and delete operators that incorporate memory leak detection in debug mode. You don't need to do anything to use this because it works automatically. The macro requires the class name to be specified as an argument, so for serialization of the CElement class, you would add the following line to the class definition:

```
DECLARE_SERIAL(CElement)
```

> **NOTE** There's no semicolon required here because this is a macro, not a C++ statement.

It doesn't matter where you put the macro within the class definition, but if you always put it as the first line, you'll always be able to verify that it's there, even when the class definition involves a lot of lines of code.

The IMPLEMENT_SERIAL() macro that you place in the implementation file for the class requires three arguments. The first argument is the class name, the second is the name of the direct base class, and the third argument is an unsigned 32-bit integer identifying a *schema number*, or version number, for your program. This schema number allows the serialization process to guard against problems that can arise if you write objects with one version of a program and read them with another, in which the classes may be different.

For example, you could add the following line to the source file containing the implementation of the CElement class:

```
IMPLEMENT_SERIAL(CElement, CObject, 1001)
```

If you subsequently modify the class definition, you would change the schema number to something different, such as 1002. If the program attempts to read data that was written with a different schema number from that in the currently active program, an exception is thrown. The best place for this macro is as the first line following the #include directives and any initial comments in the .cpp file.

Where CObject is an indirect base class, as in the case of the CLine class for example, each class in the hierarchy must have the serialization macros added for serialization to work in the top-level class. For serialization in CLine to work, the macros must also be added to CElement.

How Serialization Works

The overall process of serializing a document is illustrated in a simplified form in Figure 17-1.

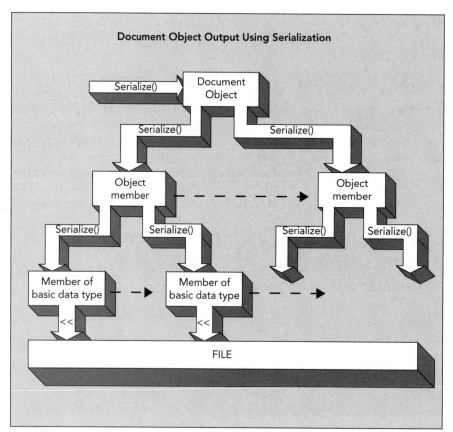

FIGURE 17-1

The Serialize() function in the document object calls the Serialize() function (or uses an overloaded insertion operator) for each of its data members. Where a member is a class object, the Serialize() function for that object serializes each of its data members in turn until eventually, basic data types are written to the file. Because most classes in MFC ultimately derive from CObject, they contain serialization support, so you can almost always serialize MFC class objects.

The data that you'll deal with in the Serialize() member functions of your classes and the application document object are just the data members. The structure of the classes that are involved and any other data necessary to reconstitute your original objects are automatically taken care of by the CArchive object.

Where you derive multiple levels of classes from CObject, the Serialize() function in a class must call the Serialize() member of its direct base class to ensure that the direct base class data members are serialized. Note that serialization doesn't support multiple inheritance, so there can only be one base class for each class defined in a hierarchy.

How to Implement Serialization for a Class

From the previous discussion, I can summarize the steps that you need to take to add serialization to a class:

1. Make sure that the class is derived directly or indirectly from `CObject`.

2. Add the `DECLARE_SERIAL()` macro to the class definition (and to the direct base class if the direct base is not `CObject` or another standard MFC class).

3. Declare the `Serialize()` function as a member function of your class.

4. Add the `IMPLEMENT_SERIAL()` macro to the file containing the class implementation.

5. Implement the `Serialize()` function for your class.

Now let's look at how you can implement serialization for documents in Sketcher.

APPLYING SERIALIZATION

To implement serialization in Sketcher, you must implement the `Serialize()` function in `CSketcherDoc` so that it deals with all of the data members of that class. You need to add serialization to each of the classes that define objects that may be included in a document. Before you start adding serialization to your classes, you should make some small changes to the program to record when a user changes a sketch document. This isn't essential, but it is highly desirable because it enables the program to guard against the document being closed without saving changes.

Recording Document Changes

There's already a mechanism for noting when a document changes. It uses an inherited member of the `CSketcherDoc` class, `SetModifiedFlag()`. By calling this function consistently whenever the document changes, you can record the fact that the document has been altered in a data member of the document class object. This causes a prompt to be automatically displayed when you try to exit the application without saving the modified document. The argument to the `SetModifiedFlag()` function is a value of type `BOOL`, and the default value is `TRUE`. When you have occasion to specify that the document was unchanged, you can call this function with the argument `FALSE`.

At present, there are four occasions when you alter a sketch in the document object:

➤ When you call the `AddElement()` member of `CSketcherDoc` to add a new element.

➤ When you call the `DeleteElement()` member of `CSketcherDoc` to delete an element.

➤ When you call `SendToBack()` for the document object.

➤ When you move an element.

You can handle these situations easily. All you need to do is add a call to `SetModifiedFlag()` to each of the functions involved in these operations. The definition of `AddElement()` appears in the `CSketcherDoc` class definition. You can extend this to:

```
void AddElement(std::shared_ptr<CElement>& pElement) // Add an element to the list
{
  m_Sketch.push_back(pElement);
  UpdateAllViews(nullptr, 0, pElement.get());          // Tell all the views
  SetModifiedFlag();                                   // Set the modified flag
}
```

The definition of `DeleteElement()` is also in the `CSketcherDoc` definition. You should add one line to it, as follows:

```
void DeleteElement(std::shared_ptr<CElement>& pElement)
{
  m_Sketch.remove(pElement);
  UpdateAllViews(nullptr, 0,  pElement.get());         // Tell all the views
  SetModifiedFlag();                                   // Set the modified flag
}
```

The `SendToBack()` function needs to have the same line added:

```
void SendToBack(std::shared_ptr<CElement>& pElement)
{
  if(pElement)
  {
    m_Sketch.remove(pElement);                         // Remove the element from the list
    m_Sketch.push_back(pElement);                      // Put a copy at the end of the list
    SetModifiedFlag();                                 // Set the modified flag
  }
}
```

Moving an element occurs in the `MoveElement()` member of a view object that is called by the handler for the `WM_MOUSEMOVE` message, but you only change the document when the left mouse button is pressed. If there's a right-button click, the element is put back to its original position, so you only need to call the `SetModifiedFlag()` function for the document in the `OnLButtonDown()` function:

```
void CSketcherView::OnLButtonDown(UINT nFlags, CPoint point)
{
  CClientDC aDC{this};                                 // Create a device context
  OnPrepareDC(&aDC);                                   // Get origin adjusted
  aDC.DPtoLP(&point);                                  // convert point to Logical
  CSketcherDoc* pDoc {GetDocument()};                  // Get a document pointer

  if(m_MoveMode)
  { // In moving mode, so drop the element
    m_MoveMode = false;                                // Kill move mode
    auto pElement(m_pSelected);                        // Store selected address
    m_pSelected.reset();                               // De-select the element
    pDoc->UpdateAllViews(nullptr, 0, pElement.get());  // Redraw all the views
    pDoc->SetModifiedFlag();                           // Set the modified flag
  }
  // Rest of the function as before...
}
```

You call the inherited GetDocument() member of the view class to get access to a pointer to the document object and then use this pointer to call the SetModifiedFlag() function.

You now have all the places where you change the sketch. The document object also stores the element type, the element color and the pen width, so you need to track when they change too. Here's how you can update OnColorBlack() for example:

```cpp
void CSketcherDoc::OnColorBlack()
{
    m_Color = ElementColor::BLACK;            // Set the drawing color to black
    SetModifiedFlag();                        // Set the modified flag
}
```

Add the same statement to each of the handlers for the other colors and the element types. The handler for setting the pen width needs to be updated like this:

```cpp
void CSketcherDoc::OnPenWidth()
{
    CPenDialog aDlg;                          // Create a local dialog object
    aDlg.m_PenWidth = m_PenWidth;             // Set pen width as that in the document

    if(aDlg.DoModal() == IDOK)                // Display the dialog as modal
    {
        m_PenWidth = aDlg.m_PenWidth;         // When closed with OK, get the pen width
        SetModifiedFlag();                    // Set the modified flag
    }
}
```

If you build and run Sketcher, and modify a document or add elements to it, you'll now get a prompt to save the document when you exit the program. Of course, the File ⇨ Save menu option doesn't do anything yet except clear the modified flag and save an empty file to disk. You must implement serialization to get the document written to disk, and that's the next step.

Serializing the Document

The first step is to implement the Serialize() function for the CSketcherDoc class. Within this function, you must add code to serialize the data members of CSketcherDoc. The data members that you have declared in the class are as follows:

```cpp
protected:
    ElementType m_Element{ElementType::LINE };    // Current element type
    ElementColor m_Color{ ElementColor::BLACK };  // Current drawing color
    std::list<std::shared_ptr<CElement>> m_Sketch; // A list containing the sketch
    int m_PenWidth{};                             // Current pen width
    CSize m_DocSize { CSize{ 3000, 3000 } };      // Document size
```

These have to be serialized to allow a CSketcherDoc object to be deserialized. You need to insert the statements to store and retrieve these data members in the Serialize() member of the class. However, there is a slight problem. The list< std::shared_ptr<CElement>> object is not serializable because the template is not derived from CObject. In fact, *none* of the STL containers are serializeable, so you always have to take care of serializing STL containers yourself.

All is not lost, however. If you can serialize the objects that the pointers in the container point to, you will be able to reconstruct the container when you read it back.

> **NOTE** The MFC defines container classes such as CList that are serializable. However, if you used these in Sketcher, you would not learn about how you can make a class serializable.

You can implement serialization for the document object with the following code:

```
void CSketcherDoc::Serialize(CArchive& ar)
{
  if (ar.IsStoring())
  {
    ar << static_cast<COLORREF>(m_Color)      // Store the current color
       << static_cast<int>(m_Element)         // the element type as an integer
       << m_PenWidth                          // and the current pen width
       << m_DocSize;                          // and the current document size

    ar << m_Sketch.size();          // Store the number of elements in the list

    // Now store the elements from the list
    for(const auto& pElement : m_Sketch)
      ar << pElement.get();                    // Store the element pointer
  }
  else
  {
    COLORREF color {};
    int elementType {};
    ar >> color                                // Retrieve the current color
       >> elementType                          // the element type as an integer
       >> m_PenWidth                           // and the current pen width
       >> m_DocSize;                           // and the current document size
    m_Color = static_cast<ElementColor>(color);
    m_Element = static_cast<ElementType>(elementType);

    // Now retrieve all the elements and store in the list
    size_t elementCount {};                    // Count of number of elements
    ar >> elementCount;                        // retrieve the element count
    CElement* pElement;
    for(size_t i {} ; i < elementCount ; ++i)
    {
      ar >> pElement;
      m_Sketch.push_back(std::shared_ptr<CElement>(pElement));
    }
  }
}
```

For four of the data members, you just use the extraction and insertion operators that are overloaded in the CArchive class. This won't work for m_Color because the ElementColor type is not serializable. However, you can cast it to type COLORREF, which is serializable because type COLORREF is the same as type long. The m_Element member is of type ElementType, and the serialization process won't handle this directly either. However, you can cast it to an integer for serialization, and then just deserialize it as an integer before casting the value back to ElementType.

For the list of elements, m_Sketch, you first store the count of the number of elements in the list because you will need this to be able to read the elements back. You then write the element pointers that are contained in the shared_ptr objects from the list to the archive in the for loop. Something remarkable happens as a result. The serialization mechanism recognizes that the objects pointed to will be required to reconstruct the document, and will take care of writing those to the archive.

The else clause for the if deals with reading the document object back from the archive. You use the extraction operator to retrieve the first four members from the archive in the same sequence that they were written. The color and element type are read into the local integer variables, color and elementType, and then stored in the m_Color and m_Element members as the correct type.

You read the number of elements recorded in the archive and store it locally in elementCount. Finally, you use elementCount to control the for loop that reads the elements back from the archive and stores them in the list. Note that you don't need to do anything special to take account of the fact that the elements were originally created on the heap. The serialization mechanism takes care of restoring the elements on the heap automatically; all you need to do is pass the pointer for each element to the shared_ptr<CElement> constructor.

In case you are wondering where the list<shared_ptr<CElement>> object comes from when you are deserializing an object, it will be created by the serialization process using the default constructor for the CSketcherDoc class. This is how the basic document object and its uninitialized data members get created. Like magic, isn't it?

That's all you need for serializing the document class data members, but serializing elements from the list causes the Serialize() functions for the element classes to be called to store and retrieve the elements themselves, so you also need to implement serialization for those classes.

Serializing the Element Classes

All the element classes are serializable in principle because their base class, CElement, is derived from CObject. You specified CObject as the base for CElement solely to get support for serialization. Make sure that the default constructor is defined for each of the element classes. The deserialization process requires that this constructor be defined.

You can add support for serialization to each of the element classes by adding the appropriate macros to the class definitions and implementations, and adding the code to the Serialize() member function of each class to serialize its data members. You can start with the base class, CElement, where you need to modify the class definition as follows:

```
class CElement: public CObject
{
DECLARE_SERIAL(CElement)
protected:
  CPoint m_StartPoint;                    // Element position
  int m_PenWidth;                         // Pen width
```

```
        COLORREF m_Color;                              // Color of an element
        CRect m_EnclosingRect;                         // Rectangle enclosing an element

    public:
      virtual ~CElement();
      virtual void Draw(CDC* pDC, std::shared_ptr<CElement> pElement=nullptr) {}
      virtual void Move(const CSize& aSize) {}         // Move an element
      virtual void Serialize(CArchive& ar) override; // Serialize object


      // Get the element enclosing rectangle
      const CRect& GetEnclosingRect() const
      {
        return m_EnclosingRect;
      }

    protected:
      // Constructors protected so they cannot be called outside the class
      CElement();
      CElement(const CPoint& start, COLORREF color, int penWidth = 1);

      // Create a pen
      void CreatePen(CPen& aPen, std::shared_ptr<CElement> pElement)
      {
      if(!aPen.CreatePen(PS_SOLID, m_PenWidth,
                           (this == pElement.get()) ? SELECT_COLOR : m_Color))
        {
          // Pen creation failed
          AfxMessageBox(_T("Pen creation failed."), MB_OK);
          AfxAbort();
        }
      }
    }
};
```

You add the DECLARE_SERIAL() macro and a declaration for the virtual function Serialize(). You already have the default constructor that was created by the Application Wizard. You changed it to protected in the class, although it doesn't matter what its access specification is as long as it appears explicitly in the class definition. It can be public, protected, or private, and serialization still works. If you forget to include a default constructor in a class, though, you'll get an error message when the IMPLEMENT_SERIAL() macro is compiled.

You should add the DECLARE_SERIAL() macro to each of the derived classes CLine, CRectangle, CCircle, CCurve, and CText, with the relevant class name as the argument. You should also add an override declaration for the Serialize() function as a public member of each class.

In the file Element.cpp, you must add the following macro at the beginning:

```
IMPLEMENT_SERIAL(CElement, CObject, VERSION_NUMBER)
```

You can define the static constant VERSION_NUMBER in the Element.h file by adding the definition after the other static constant:

```
static const UINT VERSION_NUMBER {1001};       // Version number for serialization
```

You can then use the same constant when you add the macro to the .cpp file for each of the other element classes. For instance, for the CLine class you should add the line,

```
IMPLEMENT_SERIAL(CLine, CElement, VERSION_NUMBER)
```

and similarly for the other element classes. When you modify any of the classes relating to the document, all you need to do is change the definition of VERSION_NUMBER in the Element.h file, and the new version number applies in all your Serialize() functions.

The Serialize( ) Functions for the Element Classes

You can now implement the Serialize() member function for each of the element classes. Start with the CElement class and add the following definition to Element.cpp:

```
void CElement::Serialize(CArchive& ar)
{
  CObject::Serialize(ar);                 // Call the base class function

  if (ar.IsStoring())
   { // Writing to the file
      ar << m_StartPoint                  // Element position
         << m_PenWidth                    // The pen width
         << m_Color                       // The element color
         << m_EnclosingRect;              // The enclosing rectangle
   }
   else
   {  // Reading from the file
      ar >> m_StartPoint                  // Element position
         >> m_PenWidth                    // The pen width
         >> m_Color                       // The element color
         >> m_EnclosingRect;              // The enclosing rectangle
   }
}
```

This function is of the same form as the one supplied for you in the CSketcherDoc class. All of the data members defined in CElement are supported by the overloaded extraction and insertion operators and so everything is done using those operators. Note that you must call the Serialize() member for the CObject class to ensure that the inherited data members are serialized.

For the CLine class, you can code the function as:

```
void CLine::Serialize(CArchive& ar)
{
  CElement::Serialize(ar);                 // Call the base class function

  if (ar.IsStoring())
  { // Writing to the file
    ar << m_EndPoint;                      // The end point
  }
  else
  { // Reading from the file
    ar >> m_EndPoint;                      // The end point
  }
}
```

The data member is supported by the extraction and insertion operators of the CArchive object ar. You call the Serialize() member of the base class CElement to serialize its data members, and this calls the Serialize() member of CObject. You can see how serialization cascades through the class hierarchy.

The Serialize() member of the CRectangle class is simple:

```
void CRectangle::Serialize(CArchive& ar)
{
  CElement::Serialize(ar);              // Call the base class function
  if (ar.IsStoring())
  { // Writing to the file
    ar << m_BottomRight;                // Bottom-right point for the rectangle
  }
  else
  { // Reading from the file
    ar >> m_BottomRight;
  }
}
```

This calls the direct base class Serialize() function and serializes the bottom-right point for the rectangle.

The function implementation for the CCircle class is identical to that for the CRectangle class:

```
void CCircle::Serialize(CArchive& ar)
{
  CElement::Serialize(ar);              // Call the base class function
  if (ar.IsStoring())
  { // Writing to the file
    ar << m_BottomRight;                // Bottom-right point for the circle
  }
  else
  { // Reading from the file
    ar >> m_BottomRight;
  }
}
```

For the CCurve class, you have rather more work to do. The CCurve class uses a vector<CPoint> container to store the defining points, and because this is not directly serializable, you must take care of it yourself. Having serialized the document, this is not going to be terribly difficult. You can code the Serialize() function as follows:

```
void CCurve::Serialize(CArchive& ar)
{
  CElement::Serialize(ar);              // Call the base class function
  // Serialize the vector of points
  if (ar.IsStoring())
  {
    ar << m_Points.size();             // Store the point count
    // Now store the points
    for)const auto& Point : m_Points)
      ar << point;
  }
```

```
        else
        {
          size_t nPoints {};                  // Stores number of points
          ar >> nPoints;                       // Retrieve the number of points
          // Now retrieve the points
          CPoint point;
          for(size_t i {} i < nPoints; ++i)
          {
            ar >> point;
            m_Points.push_back(point);
          }
        }
      }
    }
```

You first call the base class `Serialize()` function to deal with serializing the inherited members of the class. The technique for storing the contents of the vector is basically the same as you used for serializing the list for the document. You first write the number of elements in the container to the archive, then the elements themselves. The `CPoint` class is serializable, so it takes care of itself. Reading the points back is equally straightforward. You just store each object read from the archive in the vector, `m_Points`, in the `for` loop. The serialization process uses the no-arg constructor for the `CCurve` class to create the basic class object, so the `vector<CPoint>` member is created within this process.

The last class for which you need to add a `Serialize()` implementation is `CText`:

```
      void CText::Serialize(CArchive& ar)
      {
        CElement::Serialize(ar);              // Call the base class function

        if (ar.IsStoring())
        {
            ar << m_String;                    // Store the text string
        }
        else
        {
            ar >> m_String;                    // Retrieve the text string
        }
      }
```

After calling the base class function, you serialize the `m_String` data member using the insertion and extraction operators for `ar`. Although `CString` is not derived from `CObject`, the `CString` class is still fully supported by `CArchive` with these overloaded operators.

EXERCISING SERIALIZATION

That's all you have to do to implement the storing and retrieving of documents in the Sketcher program! The Save and Open menu options in the file menu are now fully operational without adding any more code. If you build and run Sketcher after incorporating the changes I've discussed in this chapter, you'll be able to save and restore files and be automatically prompted to save a modified document when you try to close it or exit from the program without saving, as shown in Figure 17-2.

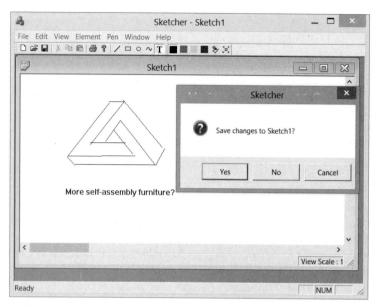

FIGURE 17-2

The prompting works because of the `SetModifiedFlag()` calls that you added everywhere you updated the document. Assuming you have not saved the file previously, if you click the Yes button in the screen shown in Figure 17-2, you'll see the File ⇨ Save As dialog shown in Figure 17-3.

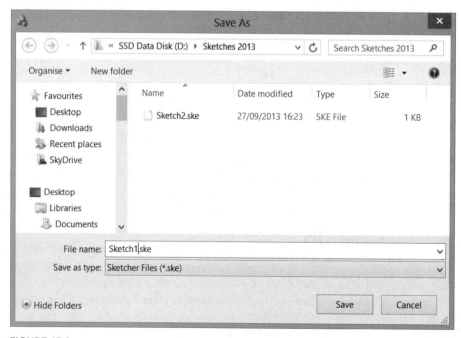

FIGURE 17-3

This is the standard Windows dialog for this menu item. The dialog is fully working, supported by code supplied by the framework. The filename for the document has been generated from that assigned when the document was first opened, and the file extension is automatically defined as `.ske`. The application now has full support for file operations on documents. Easy, wasn't it?

PRINTING A DOCUMENT

It's time to take a look at how you can print a sketch. You already have a basic printing capability implemented in Sketcher, courtesy of the Application Wizard and the framework. The File ➪ Print, File ➪ Print Setup, and File ➪ Print Preview menu items all work. Selecting the File ➪ Print Preview menu item displays a window showing the current Sketcher document on a page, as shown in Figure 17-4.

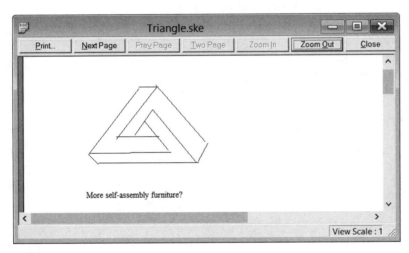

FIGURE 17-4

Whatever is in the current document is placed on a single sheet of paper at the current view scale. If the document's extent is beyond the boundary of the paper, the section of the document off the paper won't be printed. If you select the Print button, this page is sent to your printer.

As a basic capability that you get for free, it's quite impressive, but it's not adequate for our purposes. A typical document in Sketcher may well extend beyond a page, so you would either want to scale the document to fit, or, perhaps more conveniently, print the whole document over as many pages as necessary. You can add your own print processing code to extend the capability of the facilities provided by the framework, but to implement this you first need to understand how printing has been implemented in MFC.

The Printing Process

Printing a document is controlled by the current view. The process is inevitably a bit messy because printing is inherently a messy business, and it potentially involves you in overriding quite a number of inherited functions in your view class. Figure 17-5 shows the logic of the process and the functions involved. It also shows how the sequence of events is controlled by the framework and how printing a document involves calling five inherited members of your view class, which you may need to override. The CDC member functions shown on the left side of the diagram communicate with the printer device driver and are called automatically by the framework.

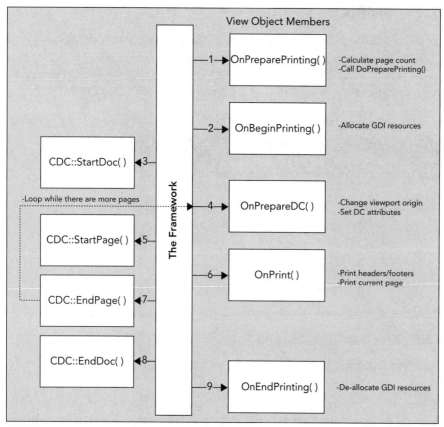

FIGURE 17-5

The typical role of each of the functions in the current view during a print operation is specified in the notes alongside it. The sequence in which they are called is indicated by the numbers on the arrows. In practice, you don't need to implement all of these functions, only those that you want to for your particular printing requirements. Typically, you'll want at least to implement your own versions of OnPreparePrinting(), OnPrepareDC(), and OnPrint(). You'll see an example of how these functions can be implemented in the context of Sketcher a little later in this chapter.

You write data to a printer in the same way as you write data to the display — through a device context. The GDI calls that you use to output text or graphics are device-independent, so they work just as well for a printer as they do for a display. The only difference is the physical output device to which the CDC object applies.

The CDC functions in Figure 17-5 communicate with the device driver for the printer. If the document to be printed requires more than one printed page, the process loops back to call the OnPrepareDC() function for each successive new page, as determined by the EndPage() function. All the functions in your view class that are involved in the printing process are passed a pointer to a CPrintInfo object that provides a link between all the functions that manage the printing process, so let's take a look at the CPrintInfo class in more detail.

The CPrintInfo Class

A CPrintInfo object has a fundamental role in the printing process because it stores information about the print job being executed and details of its status at any time. It also provides functions for accessing and manipulating this data. This object is the means by which information is passed from one view function to another during printing, and between the framework and your view functions.

A CPrintInfo object is created whenever you select the File ⇨ Print or File ⇨ Print Preview menu options. It will be used by each of the functions in the current view that are involved in the printing process, and it is automatically deleted when the print operation ends.

All the data members of CPrintInfo are public. The ones we are interested in for printing sketches are shown in the following table.

MEMBER	USAGE
m_pPD	A pointer to the CPrintDialog object that displays the Print dialog.
m_bDirect	This is set to TRUE by the framework if the print operation is to bypass the Print dialog; otherwise, FALSE.
m_bPreview	A member of type BOOL that has the value TRUE if File ⇨ Print Preview was selected; otherwise, FALSE.
m_bContinuePrinting	A member of type BOOL. If it is TRUE, the framework continues the printing loop shown in the diagram. If it's FALSE, the printing loop ends. You only need to set this variable if you don't pass a page count for the print operation to the CPrintInfo object (using the SetMaxPage() member). In this case, you'll be responsible for signaling when you are finished by setting this variable to FALSE.
m_nCurPage	A value of type UINT that stores the page number of the current page. Pages are usually numbered starting from 1.
m_nNumPreviewPages	A value of type UINT that specifies the number of pages displayed in the Print Preview window. This can be 1 or 2.
m_lpUserData	This is of type LPVOID and stores a pointer to an object that you create. This allows you to create an object to store additional information about the printing operation and associate it with the CPrintInfo object.

continues

(continued)

MEMBER	USAGE
m_rectDraw	A CRect object that defines the usable area of the page in logical coordinates.
m_strPageDesc	A CString object containing a format string used by the framework to display page numbers during print preview.

A CPrintInfo object has the public member functions shown in the following table.

FUNCTION	DESCRIPTION
SetMinPage(UINT nMinPage)	The argument specifies the number of the first page of the document. There is no return value.
SetMaxPage(UINT nMaxPage)	The argument specifies the number of the last page of the document. There is no return value.
GetMinPage() const	Returns the number of the first page of the document as type UINT.
GetMaxPage() const	Returns the number of the last page of the document as type UINT.
GetFromPage() const	Returns the number of the first page of the document to be printed as type UINT. This value is set through the print dialog.
GetToPage() const	Returns the number of the last page of the document to be printed as type UINT. This value is set through the print dialog.

When you're printing a document consisting of several pages, you need to figure out how many printed pages the document will occupy, and store this information in the CPrintInfo object to make it available to the framework. You do this in your version of the OnPreparePrinting() member of the current view.

Page numbers are stored as type UINT. To set the number of the first page in the document, you call the SetMinPage() function for the CPrintInfo object, which accepts the page number as the argument. There's no return value. To set the number of the last page, you call SetMaxPage(). If you later want to retrieve these values, you call the GetMinPage() and GetMaxPage() functions for the CPrintInfo object.

The page numbers that you supply are stored in the CPrintDialog object pointed to by the m_pPD member of the CPrintInfo object and displayed in the dialog that pops up when you select File ⇨ Print... from the menu. The user can then specify the numbers of the first and last pages that are to be printed. You can retrieve the page numbers entered by the user by calling the GetFromPage() and GetToPage() members of the CPrintInfo object. In each case, the value returned is of type UINT. The dialog automatically verifies that the numbers of the first and last pages to be printed are within the range you supplied by specifying the minimum and maximum pages of the document.

You now know what functions you can implement in the view class to manage printing for yourself, with the framework doing most of the work. You also know what information is available through the `CPrintInfo` object that is passed to the functions concerned with printing. You'll get a much clearer understanding of the detailed mechanics of printing by implementing a basic multipage print capability for Sketcher documents.

IMPLEMENTING MULTIPAGE PRINTING

With the mapping mode in Sketcher set to `MM_ANISOTROPIC,` the unit of measure for the elements and the view extent is one hundredth of an inch. With the unit of size being a fixed physical measure, ideally you want to print objects at their actual size.

With the document size specified as 3000 × 3000 units, you can create documents up to 30 inches square, which spreads over quite a few sheets of paper if you fill the whole area. It requires a little more effort to work out the number of pages necessary to print a sketch than with a typical text document because in most instances you'll need a two-dimensional array of pages to print a complete sketch document.

To avoid overcomplicating the problem, we will assume that you're printing on a normal sheet of paper (either A4 size or 8 1/2 × 11 inches) and that you are printing in portrait orientation (which means the long edge is vertical). With either paper size, you'll print the document in a central portion of the paper measuring 7.5 inches × 10 inches. With these assumptions, you don't need to worry about the actual paper size; you just need to chop the document into 750 × 1000−unit chunks, where a unit is 0.01 inches. For a document larger than one page, you'll divide up the document as illustrated in the example in Figure 17-6.

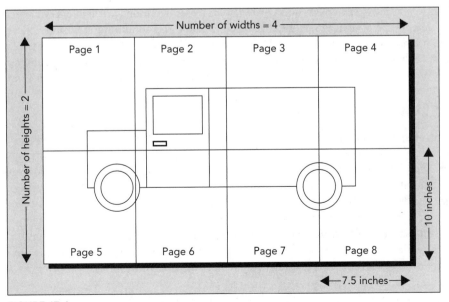

FIGURE 17-6

As you can see, you'll be numbering the pages row-wise, so in this case, pages 1 to 4 are in the first row and pages 5 to 8 are in the second.

Getting the Overall Document Size

To figure out how many pages a particular document occupies, you need to know how big the sketch is, and for this, you want the rectangle that encloses everything in the document. You can do this easily by adding a function GetDocExtent() to the document class, CSketcherDoc. Add the following declaration to the public interface for CSketcherDoc:

```
CRect GetDocExtent() const;    // Get the bounding rectangle for the whole document
```

The implementation is no great problem. The code for it is:

```
// Get the rectangle enclosing the entire document
CRect CSketcherDoc::GetDocExtent() const
{
  if(m_Sketch.empty())                                // Check for empty sketch
    return CRect {0,0,1,1};
  CRect docExtent {m_Sketch.front()->GetEnclosingRect()}; // Initial doc extent
  for(auto& pElement : m_Sketch)
    docExtent.UnionRect(docExtent, pElement->GetEnclosingRect());

  docExtent.NormalizeRect();
  return docExtent;
}
```

You can add this function definition to the SketcherDoc.cpp file.

If the sketch is empty, you return a very small CRect object. The initial size of the document extent is the rectangle enclosing the first element in the list. The process then loops through every element in the document, getting the bounding rectangle for each element and combining it with docExtent. The UnionRect() member of the CRect class calculates the smallest rectangle that contains the two rectangles you pass as arguments, and stores that value in the CRect object for which the function is called. Therefore, docExtent keeps increasing in size until all the elements are contained within it.

Storing Print Data

The OnPreparePrinting() function in the view class is called by the application framework to enable you to initialize the printing process for your document. The basic initialization that's required is to provide information about how many pages are in the document, which is information that the print dialog will display. You should also store information about the pages that your document requires, so you can use it later in the other view functions involved in the printing process. You can create an object of your own class type in the OnPreparePrinting() member of the view class to store this information and store a pointer to the object in the CPrintInfo object that the framework makes available. I adopted this approach primarily to show you how this mechanism works; in many cases you'll find it easier just to store the data in your view object.

You'll need to store the number of pages running the width of the document, m_nWidths, and the number of rows of pages down the length of the document, m_nLengths. You'll also store the upper-left corner of the rectangle enclosing the document data as a CPoint object, m_DocRefPoint, because you'll need this when you work out the position of a page to be printed from its page number. You can store the filename for the document in a CString object, m_DocTitle, so that you can add it as a title to each page. It will also be useful to record the size of the printable area within the page. The definition of the class to accommodate these is:

```
#pragma once

class CPrintData
{
public:
  UINT printWidth {1000};      // Printable page width - units 0.01 inches
  UINT printLength {1000};     // Printable page length - units 0.01 inches
  UINT m_nWidths;              // Page count for the width of the document
  UINT m_nLengths;            // Page count for the length of the document
  CPoint m_DocRefPoint;        // Top-left corner of the document contents
  CString m_DocTitle;          // The name of the document

};
```

The class definition specifies default values for the printable area that corresponds to an A4 page with half-inch margins all round. You can change this to suit your environment, and, of course, you can change the values programmatically in a CPrintData object.

Of course, you could define a constructor for the class and initialize the values of printWidth and printLength there. However, all the data members are public so you can always set their values directly. The CPrintData class is just a vehicle for packaging data items relating to the printing process so there is no necessity for complicating it. Specifying default values for members obviates the need to write constructors and thus simplifies the class definition.

You can add a new header file with the name PrintData.h to the project by right-clicking the Header Files folder in the Solution Explorer pane and then selecting Add ➪ New Item from the pop-up. You can now enter the class definition in the new file. You don't need an implementation file for this class. Because an object of this class is only going to be used transiently, you don't need to use CObject as a base or to consider any other complication.

The printing process starts with a call to OnPreparePrinting() so I'll explore how you should implement that next.

Preparing to Print

The Application Wizard has already added versions of OnPreparePrinting(), OnBeginPrinting(), and OnEndPrinting() to CSketcherView. The base code provided for OnPreparePrinting() calls DoPreparePrinting() in the return statement, as you can see:

```
BOOL CSketcherView::OnPreparePrinting(CPrintInfo* pInfo)
{
  // default preparation
  return DoPreparePrinting(pInfo);
}
```

The DoPreparePrinting() function displays the Print dialog using information about the number of pages to be printed that is defined in the CPrintInfo object. Whenever possible, you should calculate the number of pages to be printed and store it in the CPrintInfo object before this call occurs. Of course, in many circumstances, you may need information from the device context for the printer before you can do this — when you're printing a document where the number of pages is going to be affected by the size of the font to be used for example — in which case it won't be possible to get the page count before you call DoPreparePrinting(). In these circumstances you can compute the number of pages in the OnBeginPrinting() member, which receives a pointer to the device context as an argument. This function is called by the framework after OnPreparePrinting(), so the information entered in the Print dialog is available. This means that you can also take account of the paper size selected by the user in the Print dialog.

Assuming that the page size is large enough to accommodate a 7.5-inch × 10-inch area to draw the document data, you can calculate the number of pages in OnPreparePrinting(). The code to do this is:

```
BOOL CSketcherView::OnPreparePrinting{CPrintInfo* pInfo}
{
  CPrintData* printData {new CPrintData};    // Create a print data object
  CSketcherDoc* pDoc {GetDocument()};        // Get a document pointer
  CRect docExtent {pDoc->GetDocExtent()};    // Get the whole document area

  printData->m_DocRefPoint = docExtent.TopLeft();// Save document reference point
  printData->m_DocTitle = pDoc->GetTitle();      // Save the document filename


  // Calculate how many printed page widths are required
  // to accommodate the width of the document
  printData->m_nWidths = static_cast<UINT>(ceil(
              static_cast<double>(docExtent.Width())/printData->printWidth));

  // Calculate how many printed page lengths are required
  // to accommodate the document length
  printData->m_nLengths = static_cast<UINT>(
          ceil(static_cast<double>(docExtent.Height())/printData->printLength));

  // Set the first page number as 1 and
  // set the last page number as the total number of pages
  pInfo->SetMinPage(1);
  pInfo->SetMaxPage(printData->m_nWidths*printData->m_nLengths);
  pInfo->m_lpUserData = printData;          // Store address of PrintData object
  return DoPreparePrinting(pInfo);
}
```

You first create a CPrintData object on the heap and store its address locally in the pointer. After getting a pointer to the document, you get the rectangle enclosing all of the elements in the document by calling the function GetDocExtent() that you added to the document class earlier in this chapter. You then store the corner of this rectangle in the m_DocRefPoint member of the CPrintData object, and put the name of the file that contains the document in m_DocTitle.

The next two lines of code calculate the number of pages across the width of the document, and the number of pages required to cover the length. The number of pages to cover the width is computed by dividing the document width by the width of the print area on a page and rounding up to the next highest integer using the ceil() function that is declared in the cmath header. For example, ceil(2.1) returns 3.0, ceil(2.9) also returns 3.0, and ceil(-2.1) returns -2.0. A similar calculation to that for the number of pages across the width of a document produces the number to cover the length. The product of these two values is the total number of pages to be printed, and this is the value that you'll supply for the maximum page number. The last step is to store the address of the CPrintData object in the m_lpUserData member of the pInfo object.

Don't forget to add an #include directive for PrintData.h to the SketcherView.cpp file.

Cleaning Up after Printing

Because you created the CPrintData object on the heap, you must ensure that it's deleted when you're done with it. You do this by adding code to the OnEndPrinting() function:

```
void CSketcherView::OnEndPrinting(CDC* /*pDC*/, CPrintInfo* pInfo)
{
    // Delete our print data object
    delete static_cast<CPrintData*>(pInfo->m_lpUserData);
}
```

That's all that's necessary for this function in the Sketcher program, but in some cases, you'll need to do more. Your one-time final cleanup should be done here. Make sure that you remove the comment delimiters (/* */) from the second parameter name; otherwise, your function won't compile. The default implementation comments out the parameter names because you may not need to refer to them in your code. Because you use the pInfo parameter, you must uncomment it; otherwise, the compiler reports it as undefined. You don't need to add anything to the OnBeginPrinting() function in the Sketcher program, but you'd need to add code to allocate any GDI resources, such as pens, if they were required throughout the printing process. You would then delete these as part of the clean-up process in OnEndPrinting().

Preparing the Device Context

At the moment, Sketcher calls OnPrepareDC() for the view object which sets up the mapping mode as MM_ANISOTROPIC to take account of the scaling factor. You must make some additional changes so that the device context is properly prepared in the case of printing:

```
void CSketcherView::OnPrepareDC(CDC* pDC, CPrintInfo* pInfo)
{
  CScrollView::OnPrepareDC(pDC, pInfo);
  CSketcherDoc* pDoc {GetDocument()};
  pDC->SetMapMode(MM_ANISOTROPIC);            // Set the map mode
  CSize DocSize {pDoc->GetDocSize()};         // Get the document size
  pDC->SetWindowExt(DocSize);                 // Now set the window extent

  // Get the number of pixels per inch in x and y
  int xLogPixels {pDC->GetDeviceCaps(LOGPIXELSX)};
  int yLogPixels {pDC->GetDeviceCaps(LOGPIXELSY)};

  // Calculate the viewport extent in x and y
  int scale {pDC->IsPrinting() ? 1 : m_Scale}; // If we are printing, use scale 1
  int xExtent {(DocSize.cx*scale*xLogPixels)/100};
```

```
    int yExtent {(DocSize.cy*scale*yLogPixels)/100};

    pDC->SetViewportExt(xExtent, yExtent);      // Set viewport extent
}
```

This function is called by the framework for output to the printer as well as to the screen. You should make sure that a scale of 1 is used to set the mapping from logical coordinates to device coordinates when you're printing. If you left everything as it was, the output would be at the current view scale, but you'd need to take account of the scale when calculating how many pages were required, and how you set the origin for each page.

You determine whether or not you have a printer device context by calling the IsPrinting() member of the current CDC object, which returns TRUE if you are printing. When you have a printer device context you set the scale to 1. Of course, you must change the statements calculating the viewport extent to use the local variable scale rather than the m_Scale member of the view.

Printing the Document

You write the data to the printer device context in the OnPrint() function. This is called once for each page. You need to add an override for this function to CSketcherView, using the Properties window for the class. Select OnPrint from the list of overrides and then click <Add> OnPrint in the right column.

You can obtain the page number of the page to be printed from the m_nCurPage member of the CPrintInfo object that is passed to the function. You can then use this value to work out the coordinates of the point in the document that corresponds to the upper-left corner of the current page. The way to do this is best understood using an example, so imagine that you are printing page 7 of an 8-page document, as illustrated in Figure 17-7.

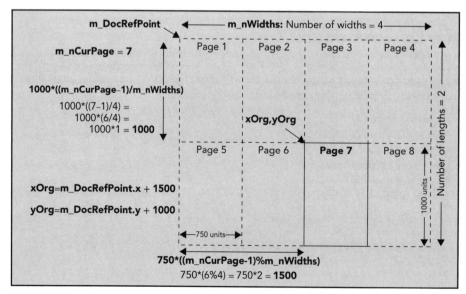

FIGURE 17-7

Remember that these are in logical coordinates and x is positive from left to right and y is increasingly negative from top to bottom. You can get an index to the horizontal position of the page by decrementing the page number by 1 and taking the remainder after dividing by the number of page widths required for the width of the document. Multiplying the result by printWidth produces the x-coordinate of the upper-left corner of the page, relative to the upper-left corner of the rectangle enclosing the elements in the document. Similarly, you can determine the index to the vertical position of the document by dividing the current page number reduced by 1 by the number of page widths required for the horizontal width of the document. By multiplying the result by print-Length, you get the relative y-coordinate of the upper-left corner of the page. You can express this in the following statements:

```
CPrintData* p {static_cast<CPrintData*>(pInfo->m_lpUserData)};
int xOrg {p->m_DocRefPoint.x {static_cast<int>( p->printWidth*
                                ((pInfo->m_nCurPage - 1)%(p->m_nWidths)))}};
int yOrg {p->m_DocRefPoint.y {static_cast<int>( p->printLength*
                                ((pInfo->m_nCurPage - 1)/(p->m_nWidths)))}};
```

It would be nice to print the filename of the document at the top of each page and, perhaps, a page number at the bottom, but you want to be sure you don't print the document data over the filename and page number. You also want to center the printed area on the page. You can do this by moving the origin of the coordinate system in the printer device context *after* you have printed the filename. This is illustrated in Figure 17-8.

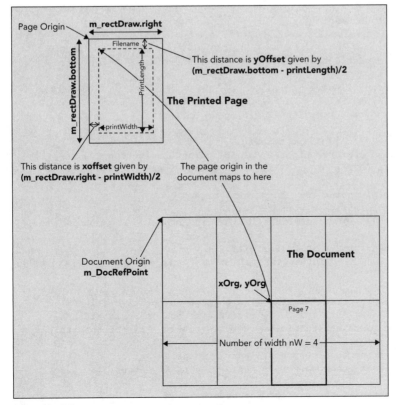

FIGURE 17-8

Figure 17-8 illustrates the correspondence between the printed page area in the device context and the page to be printed in the reference frame of the document data. The diagram shows the expressions for the offsets from the page origin for the printWidth by printLength area where you are going to print the page. You want to print the information from the document in the dashed area shown on the printed page in Figure 17-8, so you need to map the xOrg, yOrg point in the document to the position shown in the printed page, which is displaced from the page origin by the offset values xOffset and yOffset.

By default, the origin in the coordinate system that you use to define elements in the document is mapped to the origin of the device context, but you can change this. The CDC object provides a SetWindowOrg() function for this purpose. This enables you to define a point in the document's logical coordinate system that you want to correspond to the origin in the device context, in this case the point where (0,0) for the printer output will be. It's important to save the old origin that's returned from the SetWindowOrg() function. You must restore the old origin when you've finished drawing the current page; otherwise the m_rectDraw member of the CPrintInfo object is not set up correctly when you print the next page.

The point in the document that you want to map to the origin of the page has the coordinates xOrg-xOffset,yOrg-yOffset. This may not be easy to visualize, but remember that by setting the window origin, you're defining the point that maps to the viewport origin. If you think about it, you should see that the xOrg, yOrg point in the document is where you want it on the page.

The complete code for printing a page of the document is:

```
// Print a page of the document
void CSketcherView::OnPrint(CDC* pDC, CPrintInfo* pInfo)
{
  CPrintData* p{static_cast<CPrintData*>(pInfo->m_lpUserData)};

  // Output the document filename
  pDC->SetTextAlign(TA_CENTER);           // Center the following text
  pDC->TextOut(pInfo->m_rectDraw.right/2, 20, p->m_DocTitle);
  CString str;
  str.Format(_T("Page %u"), pInfo->m_nCurPage);
  pDC->TextOut(pInfo->m_rectDraw.right/2, pInfo->m_rectDraw.bottom-20, str);
  pDC->SetTextAlign(TA_LEFT);             // Left justify text

  // Calculate the origin point for the current page
  int xOrg {static_cast<int>(p->m_DocRefPoint.x +
                    p->printWidth*((pInfo->m_nCurPage - 1)%(p->m_nWidths)))};

  int yOrg {static_cast<int>( p->m_DocRefPoint.y +
                    p->printLength*((pInfo->m_nCurPage - 1)/(p->m_nWidths)))};


  // Calculate offsets to center drawing area on page as positive values
  int xOffset {static_cast<int>((pInfo->m_rectDraw.right - p->printWidth)/2)};
  int yOffset {static_cast<int>((pInfo->m_rectDraw.bottom - p->printLength)/2)};

  // Change window origin to correspond to current page & save old origin
  CPoint OldOrg {pDC->SetWindowOrg(xOrg - xOffset, yOrg - yOffset)};

  // Define a clip rectangle the size of the printed area
  pDC->IntersectClipRect(xOrg, yOrg, xOrg + p->printWidth, yOrg + p->printLength);
```

```
    OnDraw(pDC);                         // Draw the whole document
    pDC->SelectClipRgn(nullptr);         // Remove the clip rectangle
    pDC->SetWindowOrg(OldOrg);           // Restore old window origin
}
```

The first step is to initialize the local pointer, p, with the address of the CPrintData object that is stored in the m_lpUserData member of the object to which pInfo points. You then output the filename that you squirreled away in the CPrintData object. The SetTextAlign() member function of the CDC object allows you to define the alignment of subsequent text output in relation to the reference point you supply for the text string in the TextOut() function. The alignment is determined by the constant passed as an argument to the function. You have three possibilities for specifying the horizontal alignment of the text, as shown in the following table.

CONSTANT	ALIGNMENT
TA_LEFT	The point is at the left of the bounding rectangle for the text, so the text is to the right of the point specified. This is the default alignment.
TA_RIGHT	The point is at the right of the bounding rectangle for the text, so the text is to the left of the point specified.
TA_CENTER	The point is at the center of the bounding rectangle for the text.

You define the x-coordinate of the filename on the page as half the page width, and the y-coordinate as 20 units, which is 0.2 inches, from the top of the page.

After outputting the name of the document file as centered text, you output the page number centered at the bottom of the page. You use the Format() member of the CString class to format the page number stored in the m_nCurPage member of the CPrintInfo object. This is positioned 20 units up from the bottom of the page. You then reset the text alignment to the default setting, TA_LEFT.

The SetTextAlign() function also allows you to change the position of the text vertically by OR-ing a second flag with the justification flag. The second flag can be any of those shown in the following table.

CONSTANT	ALIGNMENT
TA_TOP	Aligns the top of the rectangle bounding the text with the point defining the position of the text. This is the default.
TA_BOTTOM	Aligns the bottom of the rectangle bounding the text with the point defining the position of the text.
TA_BASELINE	Aligns the baseline of the font used for the text with the point defining the position of the text.

The next action in `OnPrint()` uses the method that I discussed for mapping an area of the document to the current page. You get the document drawn on the page by calling the `OnDraw()` function that is used to display the document in the view. This potentially draws the entire document, but you can restrict what appears on the page by defining a *clip rectangle*. A clip rectangle encloses a rectangular area in the device context within which output appears. Output is suppressed outside of the clip rectangle. It's also possible to define irregularly shaped areas for clipping, called *regions*.

The initial default clipping area defined in the print device context is the page boundary. You define a clip rectangle that corresponds to the `printWidth` by `printLength` area centered in the page. This ensures that you draw only in this area and the filename and page number will not be overwritten.

After the current page has been drawn by the `OnDraw()` function call, you call `SelectClipRgn()` with a `nullptr` argument to remove the clip rectangle. If you don't do this, output of the document title is suppressed on all pages after the first, because it lies outside the clip rectangle that would otherwise remain in effect in the print process until the next time `IntersectClipRect()` gets called.

Your final action is to call `SetWindowOrg()` again to restore the window origin to its original location, as discussed earlier in this chapter.

Getting a Printout of the Document

To get your first printed Sketcher document, you just need to build the project and execute the program (once you've fixed any typos). If you try File ⇨ Print Preview and click on the Two Page button, you should get something similar to the window shown in Figure 17-9.

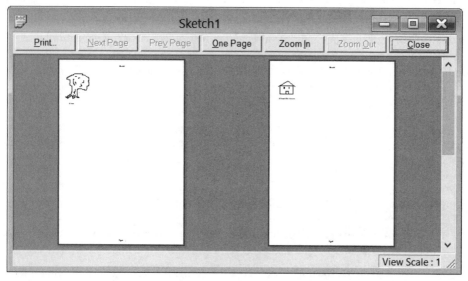

FIGURE 17-9

You get print preview functionality completely for free. The framework uses the code that you've supplied for the normal multipage printing operation to produce page images in the Print Preview window. What you see in the Print Preview window should be exactly the same as appears on the printed page.

SUMMARY

In this chapter, you have implemented the capability to store a document on disk in a form that allows you to read it back and reconstruct its constituent objects using the serialization processes supported by MFC. You have also implemented the capability to print sketches in the Sketcher application. If you are comfortable with how serialization and printing work in Sketcher, you should have little difficulty with implementing serialization and printing in any MFC application.

EXERCISES

1. Update the code in the `OnPrint()` function in Sketcher so that the page number is printed at the bottom of each page of the document in the form "Page *n* of *m*," where *n* is the current page number and *m* is the total number of pages.

2. As a further enhancement to the `CText` class in Sketcher, change the implementation so that scaling works properly with text. (*Hint*: Look up the `CreatePointFont()` function in the online help.)

➤ **WHAT YOU LEARNED IN THIS CHAPTER**

TOPIC	CONCEPT
Serialization	Serialization is the process of transferring objects to a file. Deserialization reconstructs objects from data in a file.
MFC Serialization	To serialize objects in an MFC application, you must identify the class as serializable. To do this you use the `DECLARE_SERIAL()` macro in the class definition and the `IMPLEMENT_SERIAL()` macro in the file containing the class implementation.
Serializable classes in an MFC application	For a class to be serializable in an MFC application, it must have `CObject` as a direct or indirect base class, it must implement a no-arg constructor and implement the `Serialize()` function as a class member.
Printing with the MFC	To provide the ability to print a document in an MFC application, you must implement your versions of the `OnPreparePrinting()`, `OnBeginPrinting()`, `OnPrepareDC()`, `OnPrint()`, and `OnEndPrinting()` functions in the document view class.
The `CPrintInfo` object	A `CPrintInfo` object is created by the MFC framework to store information about the printing process. You can store the address of your own class object that contains print information in a pointer in the `CPrintInfo` object.

18

Programming for Windows 8

WHAT YOU WILL LEARN IN THIS CHAPTER:

➤ How applications written for Windows 8 differ from desktop applications

➤ What XAML is and how you use it

➤ How you create the user interface (UI) for an application targeting Windows 8

➤ The characteristics of the interface to the Windows 8 operating system

➤ How to create a project for Windows 8

➤ How to create the UI for an application graphically

➤ How to modify UI elements in C++ code

➤ How to implement event handling

➤ How you can animate UI elements

WROX.COM CODE DOWNLOADS FOR THIS CHAPTER

You can find the wrox.com code downloads for this chapter on the Download Code tab at www.wrox.com/go/beginningvisualc. The code is in the Chapter 18 download and individually named according to the names throughout the chapter.

WINDOWS STORE APPLICATIONS

Applications written for the Windows 8 UI are called Windows Store apps. There is a great deal of detail involved in a comprehensive explanation of how you program these, certainly more than enough to fill an entire book. Consequently this chapter will just provide you with a start down the path, a toe in the water. After a brief outline of the basics, most of the chapter is devoted to walking you through developing a Windows Store app using C++, so it's learning by doing.

A Windows Store app is very different from a regular Windows desktop application such as Sketcher. The application context is different, the structure of the code is different, and the way the user interacts with the application is different. This is because Windows Store apps are aimed primarily toward tablets with touch screens, and are distributed through the Microsoft application store. Because of the nature of the target platform, apps run in a sandbox that insulates an application from the environment in which it is executing and limits what it can do. Access to files, network connections, and the hardware are all constrained. You interact with a desktop application through the mouse and the keyboard, whereas you interact with a Windows Store app using gestures through the touch-sensitive screen. When you run a Windows Store app on your PC, mouse clicks result in tap events that arise when you tap a touch screen.

> **NOTE** Windows 8 is more user-friendly on a desktop machine if you have two displays. If your graphics card allows it, a second display will make life easier. One display will always show the familiar Windows desktop, and both can show it when you have multiple desktop applications running. It is also very easy to switch between the Windows 8 Start screen and the desktop. The taskbar can be on both displays too.

You must have Visual Studio 2013 installed under Windows 8 to enable its Windows 8 development capabilities. You will also need to obtain a Windows 8 developer license, but this is simple — and free. Windows desktop applications under Windows 8 still use the Win32 API. Windows Store apps use the Windows Runtime (WinRT), which provides the language-independent sandbox.

> **NOTE** Windows Store apps use non-standard extensions to C++. It is possible to write Windows Store apps in standard C++ if you use the WinRT C++ Template Library (WRL). This involves relatively low-level programming with the API and WinRT objects, and is beyond the scope of this book.

The appearance of a Windows Store app and its behavior are defined separately. You define what an app does in C++. You define its UI in the eXtensible Application Markup Language (XAML). You don't need to be an expert in XAML to create the UI for an application although a basic understanding of it helps a lot. UI design capabilities are provided by the Design pane that enables you to create a UI in a similar manner to the way you created a dialog in the Sketcher. Creating the UI graphically generates the required XAML and related C++ code automatically. You also get a lot of help from IntelliSense when you need to modify the XAML. You'll get experience with doing both through the example in this chapter.

The definition of the UI and the operations for a Windows Store app are separate, so in principle the development of the UI in XAML and the coding of the operations in C++ can be separate activities. I say "in principle" because the separation cannot be total. How the C++ code needs to be implemented is very dependent on how the UI is defined in XAML. You can synthesize UI components in code, so in many instances you have a choice as to how a component is created.

DEVELOPING WINDOWS STORE APPS

Visual C++ provides specialized facilities for developing Windows Store apps that differ in many respects from what you have used up to now. To get an understanding of the development environment for them you should now create a project for a Windows Store app. You'll be exploring and working with this project throughout this chapter.

Create a new C++ project by pressing Ctrl+Shift+N. Select the Windows Store option for Visual C++ in the left pane and click on the Blank App (XAML) template. This template creates a project with no UI controls predefined, just a Grid layout element covering the entire page, which is otherwise empty, so you'll create everything else from scratch later in this chapter. You can give the project the name MemoryTest and choose a folder for the solution if you don't like the default. Click OK to start the project creation. You'll need to sign up for a developer license to proceed, if you don't already have one. Follow the dialog prompts for doing this to allow the project to be created.

Display the Solution Explorer pane. The first thing to note is that there are two .xaml files in the list. App.xaml defines the application and MainPage.xaml defines the UI page. A Windows Store app has one or more pages that define the UI, and each is defined by a separate .xaml file. Double-click MainPage.xaml to display it. Loading Designer, which enables you to create and modify the UI, will take a while the first time. You'll eventually see two editing panes. The Design pane where you can extend and modify the UI page graphically is at the top, and below is the XAML for what you see at the top. The XAML defines what is displayed in the Design pane. You can work with either the XAML or the Design pane, and changes you make in one will be automatically reflected in the other. Keep this project open because I'll be referring to it throughout the chapter.

I'll discuss three topics in a little more detail before developing the MemoryTest project further:

➤   The basics of the Windows Runtime

➤   The C++/CX extensions to Standard C++ and how they relate to the WinRT

➤   The nature of XAML and how it defines UI components

WINDOWS RUNTIME CONCEPTS

WinRT is an object-oriented API for Windows Store apps. WinRT is language neutral, so you can use it with JavaScript and C# as well as C++. It provides the sandbox, in which Windows Store apps execute, and limits the extent to which they can access the operating system and hardware resources.

WinRT applications use different terminology from what you have seen so far. A method is an alternative term for a member function in C++ parlance so these terms are interchangeable. You have learned about message handler functions that are called when a Windows message or event occurs in a desktop application. In a Windows Store app, a delegate is a function object that encapsulates a method to be called to handle events of a particular type.

WinRT Namespaces

The classes that define WinRT objects are distributed within a large number of namespaces. To give you an idea of the extent of WinRT, there are well over 100 namespaces, each of which contains several, and in some cases many, class definitions. Classes that represent a particular set of UI components are in the same namespace and generally the namespace name gives you an idea of what it contains. The `Windows::UI::Xaml::Controls` namespace, for example, contains classes that define controls such as buttons, checkboxes, and list boxes. In general, namespaces that relate to the definition or operation of the UI have names that start with `Windows::UI`, and those that start with `Windows::UI::Xaml` relate to XAML types that you use to specify a UI.

You can define your own class types in a Windows Store app. If you define a class for objects that are to be passed to a WinRT component, the class must be within a namespace and must be defined differently from standard C++. I'll explain how shortly.

> **TIP** You will find it useful to have the reference documentation for the WinRT namespaces displayed in your browser while reading this chapter and when you are developing your own Windows Store apps. At the moment, you can find it at `http://msdn.microsoft.com/en-us/library/windows/apps/br211377.aspx`.

WinRT Objects

WinRT is an object-oriented API where the objects are similar to Component Object Model (COM) objects. COM provides a mechanism for defining objects that can be accessed and operated on in different programming languages. A COM object is different from the C++ class objects you have been using up to now. You cannot store a COM object in a variable; you can only store a reference to it. COM objects are reference counted, which means that a record of the number of separate references to an object is maintained. When the reference count for a COM object reaches zero, it will be destroyed and any resources the object owns will be released. This is similar to how `std::shared_ptr` smart pointers work.

If you use naked COM object references, you are responsible to call functions at the appropriate times to keep the reference count correct. However, in WinRT, you are not using naked COM objects; WinRT objects have the management of their reference counts built-in. WinRT objects are created on the heap but you don't have to worry about deleting them because they take care of their own destruction.

Because they are essentially COM objects, WinRT objects can be complicated to work with using standard C++. To work with COM objects you must understand the interfaces involved and stick to the rules for using them. For this reason, Visual C++ includes a set of Microsoft-specific C++ language extensions that hide the complexity of working with WinRT objects, which makes your code much easier to write. These language extensions are referred to as C++/CX, from C++ Component Extensions. When you use C++/CX to work with WinRT objects, you can still use all of the standard C++ language and library facilities, including the STL. Any data passed to or received from the WinRT is always in terms of WinRT objects though, and you must always use C++/CX class types to reference them.

C++ COMPONENT EXTENSIONS (C++/CX)

All data that you pass to, or receive from, the WinRT must be WinRT objects. You cannot pass objects of standard C++ class types to WinRT components. There are two types of WinRT objects — value types that have pass-by-value semantics and `ref class` types that are passed by reference. Data of any of the fundamental C++ types will be converted to a WinRT value type automatically, so you can always use these in your Windows Store apps. `ref class` (or `ref struct`) types are the WinRT equivalents of the standard C++ `class` (or `struct`) types. All variables of `ref class` types store references, not objects. C++/CX provides additional language syntax for defining WinRT types and for working with WinRT objects.

C++/CX Namespaces

There are three C++/CX namespaces that contain things you should know about. These are the default namespaces that contain WinRT type definitions:

➤ The `Platform` namespace includes value types corresponding to C++ fundamental types.

➤ The `Platform::Collections` namespace includes container classes for WinRT types.

➤ The `Windows::Foundation::Collections` namespace provides functions supporting the containers in the `Platform::Collections` namespace.

The `Platform` namespace contains, among others, the following built-in WinRT types:

TYPE	USE
Object	The ultimate base class for all WinRT types. A reference of this type can represent any WinRT type.
String	An immutable Unicode character string. You must use this string type to pass strings to WinRT components.
Boolean	A value that is the equivalent of type `bool`.
SizeT	An unsigned data type that represents the size of an object.
IntPtr	A signed pointer value.
UIntPtr	An unsigned pointer value.
Guid	A 16-byte value that represents a globally unique identifier.

Note that `Boolean`, `Guid`, `SizeT`, `IntPtr`, and `UIntPtr` are value types and `Object` and `String` are ref class types. You are likely to use the `String` class most often, to represent text. The `Platform` namespace also includes the `Array` class that defines a one-dimensional array of object references. You cannot use standard C++ arrays to hold WinRT object references. You cannot define multidimensional arrays with C++/CX.

The containers in the `Platform::Collections` namespace store WinRT object references. It provides `Map` and `Vector` collection class types as well as `MapView` and `VectorView` types that provide read-only collections. You'll be using a `Vector` in the `MemoryTest` example.

The `Windows::Foundation::Collections` namespace defines `begin()` and `end()` functions that return iterators for the collection class reference that you pass as the argument. You can use these iterators to apply the functions in the STL `algorithm` header to a `Vector` container. You will use these in the `MemoryTest` example. The namespace also defines a `back_inserter()` function that returns an iterator you use to insert a value at the end of a collection, and a `to_vector()` function that returns the contents of a `Vector` you pass to the function as an STL `std::vector` object.

Defining WinRT Class Types

You cannot use standard C++ classes to define objects to use with the WinRT. The C++/CX language extensions provide an easy way to create ref class types and work with WinRT class objects. You define a WinRT class type using the `ref class` keyword, which indicates that the class is a WinRT type. The class definition in the `MainPage.xaml.h` file for the `MemoryTest` application looks like this:

```
namespace MemoryTest
{
  /// <summary>
  /// An empty page that can be used on its own or navigated to within a Frame.
  /// </summary>
  public ref class MainPage sealed
  {
  public:
    MainPage();
  };
}
```

`MainPage` is defined as a `ref class` so a reference to a `MainPage` object can be passed to or received from a WinRT method. The `sealed` keyword prevents this class from being used as a base class. The namespace name is the project name. Remember, all WinRT class types must be defined in a namespace.

Here's how you might define your own ref class type:

```
namespace MemoryTest
{
public ref class Card sealed
  {
  public:
    // Public members...

  private:
```

```
        // Private members...

    protected:
      // Protected members...

    internal:
      // Internal members...
    };
  }
```

Members of a ref class can be standard C++ types and ref class types, but members of standard C++ types can only appear in the `internal` or `private` sections of the class.

When a Windows Store app is compiled, information about the ref class types it includes is recorded in a `.winmd` file as metadata. If you compile the `MemoryTest` debug configuration, you'll see the `MemoryTest.winmd` file in the `MemoryTest\Debug\MemoryTest` folder for the project. The `.winmd` file specifies the public and protected interface to the ref class types in the application that can be accessed by other development languages such as C# and JavaScript. Only `public` ref classes defined in a namespace will appear in metadata. You can use non-public ref class types in your application if you don't want the class interface to appear in the metadata. `ref class` members in the `internal` and `private` sections of a class are not published in metadata.

All `public` and `protected` data members of a ref class type must be defined as *properties*. They cannot be ordinary data members. A *property* is a data member that has a privately stored value that you access through public `get()` and `set()` methods. You define a property using the `property` keyword. The names of properties begin with an uppercase letter by convention. Here's the `Card` class with two properties defined:

```
public ref class Card sealed
{
public:
  property Platform::String^ Type;
  property Windows::UI::Xaml::Media::SolidColorBrush^ Color;
};
```

The `Type` and `Color` properties are *trivial properties*, for which the compiler inserts `get()` or `set()` method calls automatically when you retrieve or store a value. Thus you access data members that are trivial properties as though they were ordinary public data members. The compiler supplies default implementations of the `get()` and `set()` methods for a property that simply retrieve or assign the value. You can define the `get()` and `set()` methods for a property explicitly when you need something more than the default behavior. Here's how you could define the `Type` property in the `Card` class with `get()` and `set()` methods:

```
property Platform::String^ Type
{
  Platform::String^ get() { return m_type;  }
  void set(Platform::String^ newType)  { m_type = newType;  }
}

private:
Platform::String^ m_type;
```

I'll explain the notation for specifying ref class variables types in the next section. The get() and set() methods here are the same as the defaults that are created by the compiler but they could be more complicated. You can omit the set() method definition and just define a get() method, in which case the property will be read-only.

The C++/CX syntax for defining a class can include the partial keyword. This is used to specify that a class definition is not complete and there is an additional part of the definition elsewhere. The MainPage class that you have seen in the MemoryTest example is not the whole story. The definition you saw earlier complements a partial definition of the same class. You can see the partial definition if you switch to Class View, extend MainPage and then Partial Definitions in the pane by clicking the arrows at the left, then double-click MainPage. The class definition looks like this:

```
partial ref class MainPage :
            public ::Windows::UI::Xaml::Controls::Page,
            public ::Windows::UI::Xaml::Markup::IComponentConnector
{
public:
    void InitializeComponent();
     virtual void Connect(int connectionId, ::Platform::Object^ target);

private:
    bool _contentLoaded;
};
```

The pane tab showing this code appears in a pane at the extreme right with the tab shaded mauve. The Mauve tab is a "preview" tab (hover the mouse over the tab to see the Preview tooltip). Once you start typing into the document, then the Mauve tab becomes blue and moves to the left. When you change the XAML, the class will be updated. The class here is defined using the partial keyword, and the previous definition that you saw is combined with this to form the complete MainPage class. UI elements that you create using XAML will have corresponding members defined in this class that reference WinRT component objects.

Variables of Ref Class Types

A variable of a ref class type is called a handle because it stores a reference to an object, not the object itself. A handle is like a smart pointer in standard C++. When you assign the value of one ref class variable to another, the handle is copied, not the object. The only way you can get two identical ref class objects is to create them explicitly. You specify a ref class type for a variable using the class type name followed by ^, which is referred to as a hat symbol. Here's an example of defining a ref class variable:

```
SolidColorBrush^ redBrush =
                    ref new SolidColorBrush(Windows::UI::Colors::Red);
```

This defines redBrush as a handle to a SolidColorBrush object, which is an object that defines a brush that fills an area with a particular color. This ref class definition is in the Windows::UI::Xaml::Media namespace. A WinRT object is created using ref new, and is destroyed automatically when no reference to it exists. If you create a ref class object in a function and the only reference is stored in a local variable, the object will be destroyed when the function returns.

The argument to the `SolidColorBrush` constructor is a constant member of the `Colors` class. This class defines a large number of members that represent standard colors.

You can use the `auto` keyword when creating ref class objects:

```
auto redBrush = ref new SolidColorBrush(Windows::UI::Colors::Red);
```

This does the same as the previous statement.

You could create an array that holds handles to ref class objects like this:

```
auto brushes = ref new Platform::Array<SolidColorBrush^>(10);
```

The `brushes` array stores 10 handles to `SolidColorBrush` objects. You specify the element type between the angle brackets following the `Array` class name. Here it is `SolidColorBrush^` — a handle to a `SolidColorBrush` object.

You can create an array of handles with a set of initializers:

```
Platform::Array<SolidColorBrush^>^ colors =
                    {redBrush, greenBrush, blueBrush, yellowBrush};
```

The `colors` array is a handle to an array that will contain four elements initialized with the `SolidColorBrush^` handles that appear between the braces. You can omit the `=` here.

Accessing Members of a Ref Class Object

You use the `->` operator with an object reference to access a member of the object. Here's an example:

```
auto brush = ref new Windows::UI::Xaml::Media::SolidColorBrush();
brush->Color = Windows::UI::Colors::White;
```

This creates the `brush` reference to a `SolidColorBrush` object and sets its `Color` property to `Colors::White`. The notation for calling a method for an object is exactly the same as referencing a property — you just use `->` between the handle and the method name.

Event Handlers

A method that handles events for a UI element is a regular C++ function with a particular signature that will depend on the element type. A typical event handler declaration in a class looks like this:

```
void Button_Tapped_1(Platform::Object^ sender,
                Windows::UI::Xaml::Input::TappedRoutedEventArgs^ e);
```

This declaration for a button event handler was created automatically. It executes when the button is tapped on a tablet or when it is clicked with the mouse. The first parameter is the handle to the UI object that originated the event. You need to cast this to the appropriate type before you use it. The second argument provides additional information about the event. Event handlers for UI elements generally have two parameters with the first parameter of type `Platform::Object^` referencing the object originating the event. The type of the second parameter varies because it is a reference to an object representing the event. Generally, event handlers have a `void` return type. The address of an event handler is recorded in a delegate, which is an object that has similarities to a function pointer in standard C++.

The delegate type for button tapped events is defined as:

```
public delegate void RoutedEventHandler(
Platform::Object^ sender, Windows::UI::Xaml::RoutedEventArgs^ e);
```

Any method that has the signature of this delegate can be added to a delegate of this type. The `TappedRoutedEventArgs` class is derived from `RoutedEventArgs`, so the `Button_Tapped_1()` handler function is consistent with this. You won't need to worry about the intricacies of delegates and event handler functions in this chapter because handler functions for UI component events are defined and registered automatically. All you have to worry about is what the handler function is going to do when it is called.

Casting Ref Class References

In the previous section you learned that you receive a reference to the object causing an event as type `Object^` and you must cast this in order to call methods for the type of object it actually is. You can use `static_cast` with references to WinRT objects, but it is better to use `safe_cast<T>` where `T` is the destination type. `safe_cast<T>` will throw a WinRT compatible exception if the cast fails.

Here's an example:

```
void Button_Tapped_1(Object^ sender, TappedRoutedEventArgs^ e)
{
  Button^ button  = safe_cast<Button^>(sender);
  button->Background = redBrush;
}
```

The `Button` class is in the `Windows::UI::Xaml::Controls` namespace. The first statement in the handler casts `sender` to type `Button^`. The next sets the value of the `Background` property to `redBrush`.

THE EXTENSIBLE APPLICATION MARKUP LANGUAGE (XAML)

XAML is a language that is defined in the eXtensible Markup Language (XML). XML is a meta-language that is used for defining a wide range of application-specific languages. XAML looks a bit like HTML in that it consists of tags and attributes with embedded text, but don't be fooled — XAML is quite different, There are rigid rules for writing XAML correctly; there's none of the flexibility you have when writing HTML. You use XAML to define a set of elements in a hierarchy that specify the UI for a Windows Store app. The UI for an application consists of one or more pages, and each page is defined by a separate XAML file with the extension `.xaml`.

The XAML definition for a page includes the controls and their layout. It also associates C++ functions with events that originate from user interaction with the controls in the UI. The XAML definition of a UI component will have an associated C++ class that encapsulates the component and its characteristics. A UI page defined by a `.xaml` file will have an associated `.h` file that contains the definition of the class, and an associated `.cpp` file that contains the class implementation.

XAML Elements

A XAML file always contains XAML elements arranged in a hierarchy. A XAML element has a type name that is case sensitive. You can define a XAML element by a start tag — `<Grid>`, for example — followed by some optional element content, followed by an end tag — such as `</Grid>`. You can also define an element by a single tag called a start-end tag — for example, `<Grid/>`. A tag is always delimited by a pair of angle brackets, `<>`. All tags contain an element type name that is unique — `Grid` in the preceding examples.

In general, an element can contain other elements between its start and end tags. These are called *child elements* of the enclosing element. The enclosing element is the parent for its child elements. Elements must not overlap so an end tag must always have the same type name as a matching start tag that precedes it, and a child element must be completely enclosed between the start and end tags for its parent. There is always just one root element in a file that encloses all the other elements; specifying more than one root element is not legal XAML.

A XAML element typically has attributes that specify properties for whatever is being defined; the color, dimensions, and orientation of a control, for example.

Here's a XAML element that defines a button control:

```
<Button x:Name="okButton" Background="Blue" Width="150" Click="HandleOK">
OK
</Button>
```

The element type name is `Button`. This defines a button control that is labeled `OK`. The label specification appears between the start tag on the first line, and the end tag, `</Button>`. The items following the type name in the start tag are attributes that define values for properties for the button control; each attribute definition is separated from the next by a space. The `x:Name` property value specifies a name that you can use in C++ code to reference the button object. This name must be different from any other names that you assign in this way in the XAML file. The `Background` property value specifies the background color for the button. `Width` defines its width in pixels. The `Click` property value specifies the name of the function in the C++ class associated with the UI page that will be called when the button is clicked. Property values are always specified by a string in XAML.

> **NOTE** The name for a control that is specified in the XAML for a UI page will not exist in the C++ code in your project until you save the XAML file, so always save the file before you add code that references objects defined in XAML. After a name is defined, IntelliSense will help you choose the function to call for the object in C++.

You could define the previous button with a single tag:

```
<Button x:Name="okButton" Background="Blue" Width="150"
        Click="HandleOK" Content="OK"/>
```

This defines the same button control as the preceding example but using a start-end tag. The forward slash preceding the closing angle bracket indicates the end of the start-end tag. The button label is now defined by the Content property value. The slash preceding the closing angle bracket indicates that this is both a start and an end tag.

Here's an example of an element with child elements:

```
<StackPanel Height="400" Width="900"
            HorizontalAlignment="Left" VerticalAlignment="Top">
    <Button x:Name="okButton" Background="Blue" Width="150"
            Click="HandleOK" Content="OK"/>
    <Button x:Name="cancelButton" Background="Blue" Width="150"
            Click="HandleCancel" Content="Cancel"/>
</StackPanel>
```

The StackPanel element has two child elements that are buttons. Note how the child elements are indented with respect to the parent. Child elements are indented in this way to make the structure of the XAML easier to see.

When necessary, you can add comments in XAML. A XAML comment looks like this:

```
<!-- This is a comment. -->
```

A XAML comment starts with <!-- and ends with -->. You can define a comment spanning several lines:

```
<!--
    This is a comment that is spread
    over two lines.
-->
```

The root element for a page looks like this:

```
<Page
    x:Class="MemoryTest.MainPage"

    xmlns="http://schemas.microsoft.com/winfx/2006/xaml/presentation"
    xmlns:x="http://schemas.microsoft.com/winfx/2006/xaml"
    xmlns:local="using:MemoryTest"
    xmlns:d="http://schemas.microsoft.com/expression/blend/2008"
    xmlns:mc="http://schemas.openxmlformats.org/markup-compatibility/2006"
    mc:Ignorable="d">
</Page>
```

This is the root element for the MainPage in the MemoryTest example. The stuff following Page between the angle brackets in the start tag are properties that identify the page and the set of rules for the XAML in the file. The xmlns property value, for example, identifies the namespace name for the XAML specification. This is just a unique identifier and does not necessarily relate to a real web page. All the elements that define the page must appear between the Page start and end tags.

UI Elements in XAML

The entities that you can add to the Design pane are in the Toolbox pane, shown in Figure 18-1. You have a wide range of elements, including controls, elements that define a layout for several controls, and shapes such as ellipses and rectangles. When you add a control to the Design pane, the XAML that defines the control is added to the .xaml file for the page immediately. You can amend the dimensions and location of the control by interacting with the graphic in the Design pane. This will cause the property values in the XAML for an element to be updated. You can also amend the values of properties in the XAML and the changes will be reflected in the Design pane.

You can change the properties of an element through the Properties pane. You can see this if you click on the `Grid` element in the listing for `MainPage.xaml` in the `MemoryTest` project to display the Properties pane. It will look like Figure 18-2, where I have extended the Layout and Appearance properties. If Properties is not showing, just select the element in the Design pane and press Alt+Enter or select from the View ⇨ Other Windows menu to display the pane.

The Properties pane does not necessarily display all the properties that an element has.

FIGURE 18-1

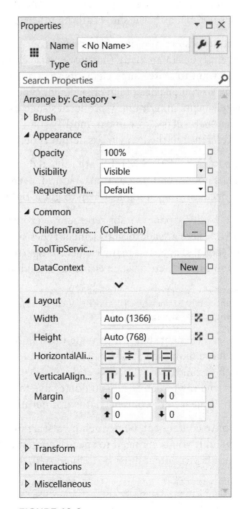

FIGURE 18-2

Every XAML element has a corresponding WinRT class type. A Button element in XAML is defined by the Button class in the WinRT. For each element in the XAML for a page, there will be a WinRT object created in the application. If you define a value for the x:Name property for a XAML element, there will be a member of the page class that has that name. The member is a handle for the WinRT object.

A WinRT object that defines a UI component typically will be of a derived type. For example, the Ellipse class that is defined in the Windows::UI::Xaml::Shapes namespace has the inheritance hierarchy shown in Figure 18-3. The Properties pane will show all the properties that are relevant to the definition of an Ellipse element, and many of these are inherited. This does not mean that it shows all the inherited properties.

Knowing which properties are inherited is important when you store UI object references of different types in an array that stores base class references. For example, you might want to store shape elements such as Rectangle and Ellipse in an array so you declare the array element type as the base class type, Shape^. The elements inherit many properties such as Fill, Height, and Width from the Shape class, so you can modify the values of these without casting a reference in the array to its actual type.

As I said earlier, changes to the XAML file are reflected in the Design pane. Modifying XAML is not as daunting as it may sound, even if you are not an expert in XAML, because you get a lot of help to get it right from IntelliSense.

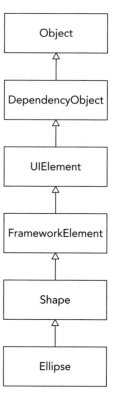

FIGURE 18-3

The controls in the Toolbox pane do not represent everything that you can define in XAML. There are additional element types such as Polygon, which defines a polygonal shape, and many element properties can be defined by other XAML elements. Clearly, you can only create such elements by adding the XAML for them. Here's an example:

```
<Polygon x:Name="triangle" Fill="Red" Points="0,70 70,70 35,0"
         HorizontalAlignment="Center" VerticalAlignment="Center"
         Height="70" Width="70"/>
```

This defines a Polygon element that is a triangle filled in red. The vertices are defined by the Points property values. It has a name specified by the x:Name property value so you reference the object for this UI element with triangle in your C++ code. A Polygon element cannot have content, so you can only use a start-end tag to define it. You don't have to remember this. You will see a warning if you try to insert an element with content that is not permitted.

Elements that can have content can be defined by a start tag and an end tag with the XAML for the content between them. If you don't need to specify content, you can use just a single start-end tag. Elements that cannot have content must be defined with a single start-end tag. Look at this:

```
<Ellipse x:Name="circle" Height="100" Margin="10" Width="100"
         HorizontalAlignment="Center" VerticalAlignment="Center">
  <Ellipse.Fill>
    <SolidColorBrush x:Name="blueBrush" Color="Blue"/>
  </Ellipse.Fill>
</Ellipse>
```

This defines an `Ellipse` element with the name `circle`, so you can use `circle` to reference the shape in C++. The `Margin` property specifies the distance between the `Ellipse` element and the four edges of its parent cell. A single value for the property applies to all four edges so the distance between the ellipse and its parent will be 10 here. You are not limited to a single property value though. When you specify more than one, the values can be separated by spaces or commas. With two values for the `Margin` property value, the first specifies both left and right margins and the second the top and bottom margins. If you specify four values they are the left, top, right, and bottom margins.

The ellipse will display as a circle with a diameter of 100 that is filled in blue. The color fill for the interior of the shape is specified by a nested `Ellipse.Fill` element that defines the `Fill` property value for the `Ellipse` element. An `Ellipse` element cannot have independent content, but it can have elements that define its property values. The color value for the `Fill` property for the `Ellipse` element is specified by a further nested XAML element of type `SolidColorBrush`. The `Color` property value for the `SolidColorBrush` object is `Blue`, which is a standard color. The `SolidColorBrush` element has a name assigned as the value for `x:Name` so you can reference the brush object in code as `blueBrush`. Here's an example:

```
if(circle->Fill == blueBrush)
   circle->Fill = redBrush;
```

This statement compares the `Fill` attribute for the `circle` object to `blueBrush`. If they match, the `Fill` property value is changed to another `SolidColorBrush` object: `redBrush`.

You could try entering the XAML for the ellipse in the `MemoryTest` project. Type the XAML immediately before the `</Grid>` end tag in the `MainPage.xaml` file. You'll see the blue circle displayed in the Design pane. You can delete the XAML afterwards and the circle will disappear from the Design pane.

Attached Properties

When you set property values in XAML, you are setting values for the property members of the WinRT object that defines the element. A XAML element can also have *attached properties*. An *attached property* allows a child element to set a value for a property belonging to a parent element. A child references a property belonging to a parent by qualifying the property name with the type name for the parent. The value for an attached property can be specified as a property in a child or as another child element. Here's an example of using an attached property:

```
<Grid Margin="0,0,10,0">
   <Grid.RowDefinitions>
      <RowDefinition Height="100*"/>
      <RowDefinition Height="100*"/>
   </Grid.RowDefinitions>
   <Grid.ColumnDefinitions>
      <ColumnDefinition Width="75*"/>
      <ColumnDefinition Width="75*"/>
   </Grid.ColumnDefinitions>
   <Rectangle Height="70" Width="70" Grid.Row="0" Grid.Column="0"/>
   <Rectangle Height="70" Width="70" Grid.Row="0" Grid.Column="1"/>
</Grid>
```

The `Grid.Row` and `Grid.Column` specifications in the `Rectangle` elements are attached properties. They specify values for the `Row` and `Column` properties in the parent `Grid` element and define where the `Rectangle` elements are to be located in the grid.

A code snippet in the previous section shows an attached property specified by a child element:

```
<Ellipse Height="100" Margin="10" Width="100"
        HorizontalAlignment="Center" VerticalAlignment="Center">
  <Ellipse.Fill>
    <SolidColorBrush x:Name="blueBrush" Color="Blue"/>
  </Ellipse.Fill>
</Ellipse>
```

The `Ellipse.Fill` child element specifies the `Fill` property for the parent `Ellipse` element.

Parents and Children

A parent element knows its children and a child element knows its parent. Elements that have `Windows::UI::Xaml::FrameworkElement` as a base inherit the `Parent` property, which has a value that is a reference to the parent object. The parent reference is of type `DependencyObject^`, which is a base for the `UIElement` class that is defined in the `Windows::UI::Xaml` namespace. Thus you will need a way to figure out what the actual parent type is when you want to work with it in your code.

Elements that can have children have `Windows::UI::Xaml::Controls::Panel` as a base, from which they inherit the `Children` property. `Children` has a value that defines a collection of child elements. The value is a reference to an object of type `UIElementCollection` that is defined in the `Windows::UI::Xaml::Controls` namespace. The references to the child elements are stored in the collection as type `UIElement`. You can use the `Children` property value to access the child elements in your code without having to specify individual names in XAML. You'll see how you access and use a collection of child elements in the `MemoryTest` example.

Control Elements

There are many control elements, as you will have seen in the Toolbox pane that is shown in Figure 18-1. Most of these are contained in the `Windows::UI::Xaml::Controls` namespace, but types that define shapes are in the `Windows::UI::Xaml::Shapes` namespace. As you might expect, several of these are functionally very similar to controls for a desktop application, and these include `Button`, `CheckBox`, `ComboBox`, `ListBox`, and `TextBox` elements. The `Rectangle` element defines a rectangle that can be optionally filled and it has a similar set of properties to an `Ellipse` element; a `Rectangle` element also has additional properties over an `Ellipse` such as `RadiusX` and `RadiusY` that specify how the corners are to be rounded.

The `FlipView` control is interesting. It can flip sequentially through the items in a collection under the control of your code. The items can be anything; text or images, for example. The collection of items can be a static set, or items can be added programmatically. This control also has built-in animation capability.

Layout Elements

The principle layout elements that control how control elements are arranged on a UI page are `Grid` and `StackPanel` from the `Windows::UI::Xaml::Controls` namespace. They each arrange elements in a different way. A `Grid` provides a rectangular grid of cells in which you can place elements, whereas a `StackPanel` provides a linear stack of elements that can be horizontal or vertical. The `Grid` element is perhaps the most frequently used layout control. You would typically have at least one `Grid` in a UI page covering the entire page area, as in the case of the default blank page in the `MemoryTest` project. This provides a primary arrangement to which you add other elements. A `Grid` element can have one or more rows and columns, and you can reference individual rows or columns by an index, where index values start from zero. You identify a particular `Grid` cell by a row index plus a column index, and you locate a control in a grid cell by specifying a row index and a column index for it. `Grid` cells can contain elements of any type, including `Grid` and `StackPanel` elements, and you can place several elements in a cell so they are superimposed. Child elements in a grid can span several grid cells. You'll be working with grids in the `MemoryTest` example.

A `Canvas` element can contain multiple UI elements as children that are located relative to the left side and top of the `Canvas` element. This means that you have complete freedom as to how the child elements are arranged. Here's an example:

```
<Canvas Background="Azure" Height="200" Width="200">
    <Rectangle Fill="Blue" Canvas.Left="20" Canvas.Top="5"
            Height="70" Width="70"/>
    <Ellipse Fill="Red" Canvas.Left="100" Canvas.Top="100"
            Height="30" Width="70"/>
</Canvas>
```

`Left` and `Top` are attached properties so they are qualified by the parent name in the child elements. The values are in pixels here.

Handling Events for UI Elements

A UI element has properties that identify its event handlers. Each type of event will have a unique property. For example, the `Tapped` property value defines the handler for the event that arises when an element is tapped on a touch screen or clicked in the desktop environment. The majority of event properties for an element are inherited. Most UI elements have the `UIElement` class that is in the `Windows::UI::Xaml` namespace as a base class. `UIElement` has many properties for events, including the following:

➤ `PointerEntered`

➤ `PointerExited`

➤ `PointerMoved`

➤ `PointerPressed`

➤ `Tapped`

➤ `DoubledTapped`

➤ `RightTapped`

This is a subset of the event properties in `UIElement`. All elements derived from this class will inherit all the event properties it defines. The names are self-explanatory. When you want to handle an event, you specify the name of the event handler as the property value. Here's an example:

```
<Rectangle Tapped="Rectangle_Tapped" Fill="Blue" Height="50" Width="100"/>
```

When the rectangle defined by this element is tapped or clicked, the `Rectangle_Tapped()` function will be called. You can specify any name you like for the handler. You can use the Properties pane to define an event handler instead of modifying the XAML directly. This will set the value for the selected property and create the definition for the handler in the class that defines the page containing the UI element. You'll see how this works in the context of the `MemoryTest` example.

When you write the name for a handler as a property value directly in a XAML element, you can right-click the name and select Go To Definition to go to its code. If the event handler doesn't exist, Visual Studio will create it for you and navigate to the code it has created.

Elements have properties that control whether or not particular events are enabled for an element. This allows you to define a handler for a particular event and then control whether or not the events actually occur by setting a property value. The `IsTapEnabled` and `IsDoubleTapEnabled` properties can have values `"true"` or `"false"` that determine whether the `Tapped` or `DoubleTapped` events are enabled.

Whether or not an element is visible is determined by the value of its `Visibility` property. The value can be `"Visible"` or `"Collapsed"`, the latter being invisible. The possible values for the `Visibility` property are defined by the `Visibility` enum class in the `Windows::UI::Xaml` namespace. You need to know this when you are controlling the visibility of an element in code.

You can also control the transparency of an element by setting its `Opacity` property value. The value can be from 0 to 1.0, where 0 is completely transparent and 1.0 is completely opaque.

CREATING A WINDOWS STORE APP

You are now going to develop the `MemoryTest` project into a working program. You will use a diverse range of controls just for the experience rather than for implementing the application in the most elegant way. Of course, this means that the example will not be as consistent in its design as it should be, but it will show you how to work with several of the controls you have available. The approach I'll describe will give you the experience of using the UI Designer pane to create the UI for the example as well as extending and modifying the XAML to expand it. Again, this is not the ideal approach in practice, but it's a good way to try out various possibilities.

The application will implement a memory testing game. It will display a set of 24 cards that are face down initially. The 24 cards consist of 12 matching pairs. The face of each card will be a circle, a square, or a triangle, colored red, green, blue, or yellow, so there are 12 different cards. To play the game you turn up two cards by clicking or tapping them. If the pair match in shape and color they remain turned up. If they don't match you click either card to turn it back over. Ideally you need to memorize what the cards were. You win the game when you have found all matching pairs.

Application Files

If you look at the Solution Explorer pane, you'll see two .xaml files. App.xaml defines the application object and MainPage.xaml defines the main page of the UI. In general, there will be a XAML file for each UI page. The MemoryTest game will need only one page.

If you extend the MainPage.xaml entry by clicking the arrow that appears on the left, you'll see there are two source files, MainPage.xaml.h that contains the MainPage class definition for the main page, and MainPage.xaml.cpp that contains the class implementation. Your modifications to the code can be in either of these files. You will be adding to both files in the example. The MainPage class is a ref class so it defines a WinRT object. The class is specified with the sealed keyword, so you cannot derive another class from it.

The MainPage class definition in MainPage.xaml.h is not complete. None of the details of the UI are defined. There's another file, MainPage.g.h, which defines the rest of the class. This file doesn't appear in the Solution Explorer pane because you must not modify it. The contents are created for you from the XAML for the main page.

The Package.appxmanifest file defines properties that apply when the application is deployed. If you double-click the filename in the Solution Explorer pane you'll see a dialog pane where you can set the path for the logo for the application and specify its orientation as well as other characteristics. The default images for the application are shown in the Assets list in the Solution Explorer pane. You would typically define your own image files for these. You can set permissions for the application on the Capabilities tab that determine what hardware and other resources the application is able to access. I won't be going into details of how you modify any of the settings in this file. The first development task for the application is to design and specify the UI for the game in XAML.

Defining the User Interface

First you must decide the broad layout of the application page — what goes where. You have complete flexibility here, so my choice is arbitrary and undoubtedly not the best. I decided on the arrangement shown in Figure 18-4.

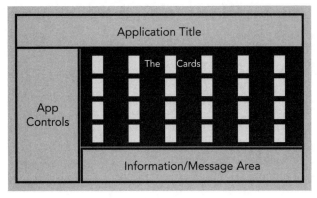

FIGURE 18-4

The application title is the full width of the top of the UI and the 4 × 6 arrangement of cards will be in the rectangular area below the title and to the right. Controls for the game will be in a column at the left, and an information or message area will be at the bottom. You can now add rows and columns to the page grid to provide for this arrangement.

Double-click `MainPage.xaml` to display the XAML and the Design pane. You can select any element to be current by clicking it in the Design pane or clicking its XAML, so select the main page grid. Its properties are displayed in the Properties pane. If you move the cursor just above the upper edge of the grid you will see a vertical orange line appear that divides the grid into two columns. The line follows the cursor as you move it and you select a position by clicking it. You can add horizontal lines that divide the grid into rows with the same procedure with the mouse cursor on the vertical grid boundaries. Add two horizontal dividers and one vertical divider so the grid has the three rows and two columns shown in Figure 18-5.

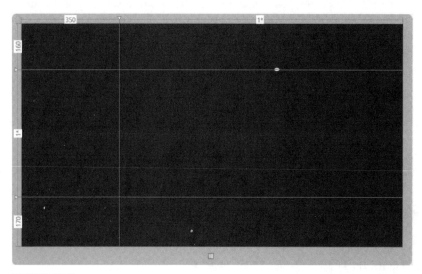

FIGURE 18-5

You can specify how the dimensions of a row or column are measured. If you hover the cursor over any of the column dimensions that are along the top of the grid, you'll see a pop-up appear. When you click the down arrow in the pop-up, you'll see the menu in Figure 18-6.

The top three menu items set the way the dimensions are measured and have the following meanings:

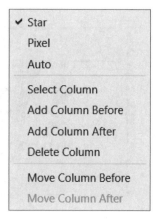

FIGURE 18-6

> **Star:** A * dimension means that measurements are relative. If your grid has two columns with widths specified as "4*" and "6*", the first column will occupy 40% of the overall width and the second column 60%. Three columns with widths, "2*", "3*", and "5*" will occupy 20%, 30%, and 50% of the total grid width. "1*" is implied for a lone "*". With * specification of dimensions for grid rows and columns, the dimensions of the columns and rows will resize proportionately when you resize the grid.

> **Pixel:** This means measurements are absolute in pixels, although such dimensions may be adjusted when the UI is rendered.

> **Auto:** You can use this to make a dimension occupy the available space, whatever it is. For example, with two columns you could specify the first in pixels: "150" for example. If you specify the second column width as "Auto", the second column will occupy the remaining grid width.

You can modify the option for the dimension for each row and column either by selecting from the pop-up menu for each dimension, or you can just use appropriate values for the Height and Width properties for the rows and columns in the XAML, as you'll see. You should not hard-code fixed dimensions for your UI elements. By using Star or Auto specifications, you allow your application to adapt to the screen size on which it is executing.

Grid rows are defined in XAML by a Grid.RowDefinitions element that has a nested RowDefinition element for each row, and the grid columns are defined in a similar way. You can amend the row heights and column widths in the grid by modifying the Height and Width property values for the RowDefinition and ColumnDefinition elements in the XAML. I changed the widths of the columns and the heights of the rows to the values shown in Figure 18-5 so you should try that too. The XAML for my grid now looks like this:

```
<Grid Background="{ThemeResource ApplicationPageBackgroundThemeBrush}">
    <Grid.RowDefinitions>
        <RowDefinition Height="160"/>
        <RowDefinition Height="*"/>
        <RowDefinition Height="170"/>
    </Grid.RowDefinitions>
    <Grid.ColumnDefinitions>
        <ColumnDefinition Width="350"/>
        <ColumnDefinition Width="*"/>
    </Grid.ColumnDefinitions>
</Grid>
```

You can add a UI element to any cell of a grid and that includes another grid. An element can also occupy several cells in a row or column. When you add an element in the Design pane, the element is added as a child of the currently selected element. You must always make sure that the correct element is selected for the parent of a new element. You can select an element by clicking it in the Design pane, or by clicking its type name in the XAML.

You'll add an element to display the title that will occupy the whole of the top row. You can reference grid rows and columns by index values starting from 0 and I'll refer to a particular grid cell in the text as (row_Index, column_Index), so cell (2,1) is the second cell in the third row.

Creating the Title

You can add a child `Grid` element to the existing grid to provide a background for the application title. Click Toolbox on the right of the Visual Studio application window to display it. If it is not shown, you can display it by pressing Ctrl+Alt+X. Click Grid in the list. Click on the boundary between cells in the top row of the current grid to add the new `Grid` element to that row, move it so it lies within the top row of the original grid. You can now edit the XAML for the new grid by deleting all the properties except for `Grid.ColumnSpan="2"`. Place the cursor immediately before the `/>` at the end of the new grid element and enter a space followed by `Background`. IntelliSense will prompt with a list so you can select from the list instead of entering the entire property name. Type B between the double quotes to see the list of colors — I chose `Bisque` because it sounds rather nice. The new property value, `Background="Bisque"`, sets the background color for the element. The XAML for the new grid element should be:

```
<!-- The title for the game -->
<Grid Grid.ColumnSpan="2" Background="Bisque"/>
```

The first line is a comment that I added. The new grid should now fill the top row of the original grid and have a nice background color. The value for the `Grid.ColumnSpan` attached property specifies that the grid covers two columns of the parent. There are no dimensions specified so they are determined by the size of the top row of the parent grid.

To enter a new property value in the XAML for an element, just enter a space in the element where you want to place the property and type the first few letters of the property name. IntelliSense will display a list of property names that you can select from by using the arrow keys, as Figure 18-7 shows this.

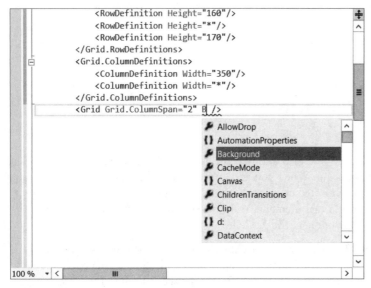

FIGURE 18-7

Pressing Enter with a selection highlighted will create the property. When the value is from a predefined set, IntelliSense will prompt for that too.

You'll use a `RichTextBlock` element to display the title text, just to introduce this element. This is a powerful element for presenting text, but you'll use it in a simple way. It can display several blocks of text each defined by a `Paragraph` child element that can have its own font specification and alignment. Make sure the new grid is selected by clicking its XAML element. Click `RichTextBlock` in the Toolbox pane and then click inside the `Grid` element. The new element will contain a `Paragraph` element as a child; if you need more of these you can add them to the XAML manually. Edit the `RichTextBlock` XAML and its child so that it looks like this:

```
<RichTextBlock FontFamily="Freestyle Script" FontWeight="Bold"
               FontSize="90" TextAlignment="Center" Foreground="Red"
               VerticalAlignment="Center">
    <Paragraph>
      <Run Text="Test Your Memory!"/>
    </Paragraph>
</RichTextBlock>
```

The `FontFamily` property value identifies the font. I chose `"Freestyle Script"` as a fun font for the application tile. I also set the `FontWeight` property value to `"Bold"`. The `FontSize` property value is `"90"` so you have a sizeable title. The `TextAlignment` property value is `"Center"` and the `Foreground` property value is `"Red"` so the text will be centered and in red. The `VerticalAlignment` property value determines how the `RichTextBlock` element is aligned in its parent. The `Run` child element for the `Paragraph` element defines a block of formatted or unformatted text. You could write the `Run` element as:

```
<Run>Test Your Memory!</Run>
```

The complete XAML for the title should now look something like:

```
<!-- The title for the game -->
<Grid Grid.ColumnSpan="2" Background="Bisque">
    <RichTextBlock FontFamily="Freestyle Script" FontWeight="Bold"
                   FontSize="90" TextAlignment="Center" Foreground="Red"
                   VerticalAlignment="Center">
        <Paragraph>
          <Run Text="Test Your Memory!"/>
        </Paragraph>
    </RichTextBlock>
</Grid>
```

I added a comment at the beginning of the block of XAML to identify it. You'll add something to cells (1,0) and (2,0) of the base grid next.

Adding Game Controls

You will add just two game control buttons. There's space for more if you want to develop the game further. One button will be a `Start` button to reset the game with a new random deal of the cards and the other will display instructions on how to play the game. You'll add the functionality for these later.

First select the base grid and add a child `Grid` element from the Toolbox to cell (1,0). Add a horizontal divider so the grid has two equal height rows and a single column. Adjust the properties so the XAML is:

```
<Grid Grid.Row="1" Grid.RowSpan="2" Background="Bisque"
     Margin="0,10,0,0">
  <Grid.RowDefinitions>
      <RowDefinition Height="1*" />
      <RowDefinition Height="1*" />
  </Grid.RowDefinitions>
</Grid>
```

The grid background color is the same as that for the grid holding the title. With the grid row height property values as `"1*"`, the rows will be of equal height and will adjust automatically to fit the space in the parent grid.

Now add a button from the Toolbox in the top cell of the new `Grid` element, with the `Content` value as `"Start"`. Adjust the properties in the XAML for the button so it is:

```
<Button Grid.Row="0" Content="Start" FontSize="32" Foreground="Red"
        Background="Gray" BorderBrush="Black" Height="90" Width="150"
        HorizontalAlignment="Center" VerticalAlignment="Center"/>
```

The background is gray and the border is drawn in black. The button height and width are as you see. The `HorizontalAlignment` and `VerticalAlignment` property values determine how the button is positioned in relation to its container, the top row of the grid.

You are going to implement more UI function with the second button and to allow for this to be added later, you can place the button in a `StackPanel` element that sits in the second row of the grid. After making sure the grid that holds the game controls is selected, click `StackPanel` in the Toolbox pane and click cell (1,0) of the grid. Edit the XAML for the `StackPanel` to:

```
<StackPanel x:Name="ButtonPanel" Grid.Row="1"/>
```

The `x:Name` property value specifies the name by which you can refer to the `StackPanel` object in code.

Add a button in the bottom cell with the `Content` value `"How to Play"`. Make it the same height and width as the Start button. You can make the value of the `Background` property for both buttons `"Gray"`, and the `BorderBrush` property value `"Black"`. The `FontSize` property value for the bottom button can be `"20"`. My XAML for the game controls now looks like this:

```
<!-- Game controls-->
<Grid Grid.Row="1" Grid.RowSpan="2" Background="Bisque" Margin="0,10,0,0">
   <Grid.RowDefinitions>
      <RowDefinition Height="1*" />
      <RowDefinition Height="1*" />
   </Grid.RowDefinitions>
   <Button Grid.Row="0" Content="Start" FontSize="32" Foreground="Red"
           Background="Gray" BorderBrush="Black" Height="90" Width="150"
           HorizontalAlignment="Center" VerticalAlignment="Center"/>
   <StackPanel x:Name="ButtonPanel" Grid.Row="1">
      <Button Content="How to Play" FontSize="20" Foreground="Red"
              Background="Gray" BorderBrush="Black" Height="90" Width="150"
              HorizontalAlignment="Center"/>
   </StackPanel>
</Grid>
```

To the left of the XAML, you'll see a vertical line with a minus sign on the same line as a parent element. Clicking the minus will collapse the XAML into a single line. Clicking the plus sign for a collapsed parent element restores it. This is very helpful when you are working with a lot of XAML, as you'll see later.

You can add another child `Grid` element with the name `"messageArea"` to cover grid cell (2,1) of the top level grid and make the `Background` property value `"Bisque"`. My XAML for this is:

```
<!-- Message area -->
<Grid x:Name="messageArea" Grid.Column="1" Grid.Row="2" Margin="10,0,0,0"
    Background="Bisque"/>
```

You'll place some elements in this grid later. You'll be able to access the grid in code using its handle, `messageArea`. The `Margin` property value here specifies four values so the left margin will be 10 and the other three will be 0.

Creating a Grid to Contain the Cards

You are going to place another grid inside cell (1,1) of the existing grid that will contain the cards. Click `Grid` in the list in the Toolbox pane and then click cell (1,1) of the existing grid. This will display the grid element in the Design pane and add its definition to `MainPage.xaml`. Add five column dividers and three row dividers evenly spaced so the grid has four rows of six cells. You can then edit the XAML for the new grid to the following:

```
<!-- Grid holding the cards -->
<Grid x:Name="cardGrid" Grid.Row="1" Grid.Column="1" Margin="32">
  <Grid.RowDefinitions>
    <RowDefinition Height="4*"/>
    <RowDefinition Height="4*"/>
    <RowDefinition Height="4*"/>
    <RowDefinition Height="4*"/>
  </Grid.RowDefinitions>
  <Grid.ColumnDefinitions>
    <ColumnDefinition Width="6*"/>
    <ColumnDefinition Width="6*"/>
    <ColumnDefinition Width="6*"/>
    <ColumnDefinition Width="6*"/>
    <ColumnDefinition Width="6*"/>
    <ColumnDefinition Width="6*"/>
  </Grid.ColumnDefinitions>
</Grid>
```

Now you have a grid defined to hold the cards; the next step is to decide how a card will be represented.

Defining a Card

A card has two sides. The front will show one of three shapes filled in one of four colors. The back will just show the string `"???"`. There are many ways you could represent a card. For example, you could define the front and back of each card as separate elements, each with a suitable child. This would mean 48 elements for the complete pack of cards. Alternatively, you could define the front of a card as an element containing the three possible shapes, and the back as another with a child to display the string. I decided on yet another approach. I'll explain where we are headed. This will make it easier for you to understand the steps that follow.

Each grid cell will display either the front or the back of a card. As I said, the front of a card can contain a circle, a square, or a triangle in any of four colors: red, green, blue, or yellow. A card back will be the string "???". To make this possible, you can locate instances of all three shape elements — `Ellipse`, `Rectangle`, and `Polygon`, plus a `TextBlock` for the card back, inside a `Grid` element that will determine their sizes. This `Grid` element will be placed in another `Grid` element sitting in a cell of the card grid that will provide the background color for both the front and back of the cards. Thus a single card is a `Grid` element containing a `Grid` element that contains three shape elements and a `TextBlock`. If you place one of these nested `Grid` elements with its children in each cell of `cardGrid`, you can display the front or back of any card by judiciously setting the `Visibility` property for the child elements of the grid element for the card. You can start by creating the elements that define the card for cell (0,0) of `cardGrid`.

Creating a Card

Create the `Grid` element in `cardGrid` cell (0,0) by selecting `cardGrid`, clicking the `Grid` control in the Toolbox pane list, then clicking the `cardGrid` cell (0,0). Edit the XAML to the following:

```
<Grid Grid.Row="0" Grid.Column="0" Background="Azure" Margin="5"/>
```

The value of the `Background` property is "Azure", which will be the color of the background for the front and back of a card. If you want the background to be different between the front and the back, you can set the `Background` property value programmatically, depending on which side of the card was showing. The `Margin` property value will create a boundary of 5 pixels between the edge of each card and the `cardGrid` cell it occupies. This element will be visible at all times because it represents the background for both the front and the back of a card.

Make sure the grid that you just added is selected and place another `Grid` element from the Toolbox in it. This will contain the shapes and the `TextBlock` element and determine the size of them. Edit its properties to the following:

```
<Grid Margin="10" Width="50" Height="50"/>
```

This has margins of 10 pixels all around and has a height and width of 50 which will determine that the child elements will have a height and width of 50 pixels.

Now you can add the shapes that define the front of a card and the `TextBlock` that defines the back to this inner `Grid` element.

Creating a Square

You can define a square with the `Rectangle` XAML element. The corresponding WinRT `Rectangle` class is defined along with other shapes in the `Windows::UI::Xaml::Shapes` namespace. Add a `Rectangle` element from the Toolbox pane to the interior of the `Grid` element that you just added. You'll see that the XAML for the `Grid` element now has a start and end tag and the `Rectangle` element appears between them. Edit the XAML for the `Rectangle` element to the following:

```
<Rectangle Fill="Blue" Stroke="Black" Tapped="Shape_Tapped"/>
```

This will define a square because the parent `Grid` element forces the dimensions of the `Rectangle` element to be 50. The border is black and the fill color is blue. It doesn't matter what color you set here because you will change it programmatically when you decide which card will be placed in each cell of `cardGrid`. The value for the `Tapped` property is the name of the handler function to be called for `Tapped` events on the rectangle. It doesn't exist yet but you'll create it a bit later in this chapter. A `Tapped` event occurs when an element is tapped on a touch screen or clicked with the mouse. The same handler will service `Tapped` events for all elements that appear on the fronts of all the cards.

Creating a Circle

The XAML for a circle will be almost identical to that for a square, so I think you can add the element directly, immediately after the XAML for the rectangle:

```
<Ellipse Fill="Red" Stroke="Black" Tapped="Shape_Tapped"/>
```

The only differences are the element name and the fill color. The `Ellipse` element defines a circle because the size will be determined by the parent `Grid` element to be 50 × 50 pixels. You'll be setting the fill color programmatically, as with the rectangle.

Creating a Triangle

There's no control in the Toolbox that defines a triangle. You have to enter XAML to create a triangle. You'll use a `Polygon` element, which defines a closed polygon by a series of points with as many vertices as you like. A triangle is defined by three points, and you define the coordinates of the points in the value for the `Points` property. The points are defined by a string containing a series of integer coordinates separated by spaces or commas. Obviously there must be an even number of coordinates in the string because each point is defined by an *x,y* pair. The coordinate system has its origin at the top left of the element area with positive *x* running from left to right and positive *y* from top to bottom, just like a window. Add a `Polygon` element to the `Grid` element, following the `Ellipse` element. The XAML should be like this:

```
<Polygon Fill="Green" Points="0,50 50,50 25,0"
         HorizontalAlignment="Center" VerticalAlignment="Center"
         Stroke="Black" Tapped="Shape_Tapped" />
```

The element properties can be in any order, so if yours are in a different sequence it doesn't matter. I have used commas to separate *x* and *y* in a pair and spaces between coordinate pairs for the `Polygon` element. You could use all spaces or all commas as separators if you wish. If you want an inverted triangle you could define the value of the `Points` property as `"0,0 50,0 25,50"`. The `Stroke` property value specifies the color for the outline of the polygon.

Creating the Card Back

The back of a card will be represented by a `TextBlock` element so select that in the Toolbox pane and place it in the `Grid` element that contains the shapes. You can then edit the `TextBlock` XAML element to the following:

```
<TextBlock TextWrapping="Wrap" Text="???" Foreground="Black" FontSize="32"
           FontWeight="Bold"
           VerticalAlignment="Center" HorizontalAlignment="Center"
           Tapped="Cardback_Tapped"/>
```

The text that will be displayed is specified by the Text property value. The Foreground property value determines the color for the text. The font size and weight are defined by the FontSize and FontWeight property values. There are other TextBlock properties that define the font characteristics such as FontStyle and FontFamily, but I'll leave you to explore those possibilities.

The complete XAML for the card in cell (0,0) in cardGrid should be like this:

```
<Grid Grid.Row="0" Grid.Column="0" Background="Azure" Margin="5">
    <Grid Margin="10" Width="50" Height="50">
        <Rectangle Fill="Blue" Stroke="Black" Tapped="Shape_Tapped" />
        <Ellipse Fill="Red" Stroke="Black" Tapped="Shape_Tapped" />
        <Polygon Fill="Green" Points="0,50 50,50 25,0"
                 HorizontalAlignment="Center" VerticalAlignment="Center"
                 Stroke="Black" Tapped="Shape_Tapped" />
        <TextBlock TextWrapping="Wrap" Text="???" Foreground="Black"
                 FontSize="32" FontWeight="Bold"
                 VerticalAlignment="Center" HorizontalAlignment="Center"
                 Tapped="Cardback_Tapped" />
    </Grid>
</Grid>
```

Save the file. It's a good idea to save the project files when you make changes. With the UI for one card created, the rest of the cards will be a piece of cake.

Adding Event Handling

You haven't finished the UI yet so it may seem premature to start talking about event handlers for the cards, but because there are only two, and these will be the same for every card, you might as well add them now. You will want to respond to Tapped events from each of the shape elements and the TextBlock element that represents the card back. You won't respond to events on the Grid elements in the cardGrid cells, so they are essentially inert.

Let's start with the square on a card. In the XAML for the Rectangle element, right-click the value of the Tapped property and select Go To Definition from the context menu. Alternatively, just press F12 with the cursor in the Tapped property value. The MainPage.xaml.cpp file contents will be displayed and you'll see that an implementation for the Shape_Tapped() handler has been added. Return to the XAML and repeat the process for the property value for the Tapped handler in the TextBlock element. You have added all the handlers you need for the cards and you'll add the code for these later. Easy, wasn't it?

It would be nice to highlight the card that is touched or is under the mouse cursor when the game is played. One way to do this is to implement handlers for the PointerEntered and PointerExited events for the Grid element that defines the background color for a card as azure. You'll be able to implement these handlers so the background color changes as the cursor enters and exits the area occupied by the element. You can do this via the Properties pane, just for the experience.

Click the Grid element with the azure color and display the Properties pane for it. Display the event handlers for the element by clicking the rightmost button at the top of the Properties pane (there's a tooltip displayed when you hover the cursor over the button). Enter Card_Entered as the value for the `PointerEntered` property and press Enter. This will create the handler implementation and display it. Return to the XAML and repeat the process for the `PointerExited` event. The value for the `PointerExited` event can be `Card_Exited`. You'll code these handlers to deal with any card.

You can now define the other card positions in the UI.

Creating All the Cards

You have 23 more cards to create in the UI. When you have completed these you'll appreciate the ability to collapse the XAML for parent elements. Repeating the preceding process 23 times would be very tedious indeed, but fortunately there's a shortcut.

The contents of `cardGrid` cell (1,0) will be exactly the same as that for grid cell (0,0), apart from the value of the `Grid.Row` attached property in the `Grid` element that defines the background color, which will be `"1"`. Thus you can create the contents of `cardGrid` cell (1,0) by copying the `Grid` XAML element, including its child elements, and setting the value of `Grid.Row` to `"1"`. The new `Grid` element will be:

```
<Grid Grid.Row="1" Grid.Column="0" Background="Azure" Margin="5"
    PointerEntered="Card_Entered" PointerExited="Card_Exited">
  <Grid Margin="10" Width="50" Height="50">
    <!--
    ... Rectangle, Ellipse, Polygon and TextBlock elements as before...
    -->
  </Grid>
</Grid>
```

The child elements stay exactly the same. The `Shape_Tapped()` handler will be called for the `Tapped` event for all shapes, and `Tapped` events originating from any of the `TextBlock` elements representing card backs will be handled by the `Cardback_Tapped()` function. The `Card_Entered()` and `Card_Exited()` handler functions will process events from both `Grid` elements.

Of course, you can create the XAML for `cardGrid` cells (2,0) and (3,0) in exactly the same way; just change the values of the `Grid.Row` property for these to `"2"` and `"3"`. When you have completed that you'll see the entire first column of the grid is populated with cards in the Design pane.

The XAML for the cards in column two of `cardGrid` will be the same as the XAML for column one, except that the `Grid.Column` attached property value in the `Grid` elements will be `"1"`. Therefore, you can create the XAML for column two by duplicating the four `Grid` elements that define column one cards, and setting the `Grid.Column` attached property value for each `Grid` element in the new set to `"1"`. I'm sure you'll be able to deduce how to fill the remaining columns of `cardGrid`. When you are done, there should be 24 `Grid` elements, each with the same children, and 24 identical cards in the Design pane. You should be able to compile and execute `MemoryTest` now and see how the UI looks. By default, the app will execute directly in your Windows 8 environment. You can execute it in the Simulator, which is much more helpful. Just select Simulator instead of Local Machine in the drop-down on the toolbar. The application window in the simulator will look like Figure 18-8.

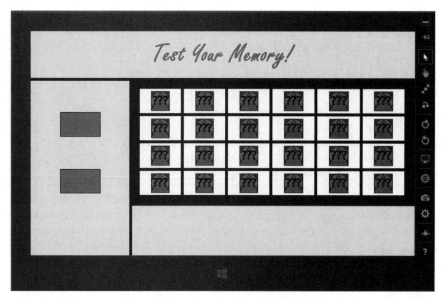

FIGURE 18-8

Hovering the cursor over the buttons on the right of the simulator window will tell you what they do. To terminate the simulator, just right-click the simulator window icon in the Windows taskbar and click Close.

> **NOTE** *Visual Studio has advanced features that allow you to define resources you can use as templates in your XAML. This would allow you to define the nature of a card once in a resource and use the resource to define each card in the UI. This means that if you later needed to change the cards, you would only have to change the resource but a discussion of resource templates is outside the scope of this book.*

Implementing Game Operations

You need to put the framework in place in the MainPage class to make the game work as you want. You will need a few additional data members as well as a number of additional functions. You can do this manually or use the capabilities in Class View you are familiar with. I'll assume in the text that you'll add the code directly to the .h or .cpp file for the MainPage class, but you can use Class View facilities if you prefer.

First you must decide what you want to do and how it's going to work. The elements in each cardGrid cell must be set up so that they represent a particular card. For this you need access to the Grid element in each cell, the Grid element that that contains, and its child shape and TextBlock elements that define the front and back of each card. You'll be referencing the elements that define a card often so you won't want to extract them every time. None of them have names, so you must find and store references to them somehow.

You can access child elements through the value of the Children property for a parent. The Children property value for cardGrid is a collection of its child elements, and these are the Grid elements in the cells that provide the background color for the cards. You can extract references to these objects from the collection recorded as the value of the Children property for cardGrid. You can then extract the child element for each of these in a similar way, which will be a reference to the Grid element containing the shapes and the TextBlock. If you store the references that you extract, you can use them later without repeating the extraction process. Arrays are the best choice to store them because there will be 24 of each type.

You will need the following member functions in the MainPage class:

➤ A SetUpUIState() member function that will set up the arrays that store references to the child elements in cardGrid and set their initial state.

➤ An InitializeCardPack() member function to create a pack of 24 cards. It will be easiest to keep the definition of a pack of cards separate from the XAML elements that represent the cards in the UI. This means you'll also need to define a Card class to represent a card.

➤ An InitializeGame() member function that will set up a new game with cards randomly shuffled.

➤ There are several discrete operations you need in the MainPage class that each will require a member function.

You will probably need some helper methods to accommodate code that is repeated. The MainPage constructor will have to be extended to initialize your own data members. You also have to implement all the event handlers. There's a way to go yet! Before you start extending the MainPage class, let's get the definition of the Card class out of the way.

Defining the Card Class

A card is defined by the type and color of the shape on the front of the card plus the TextBlock object that defines the back. You can define this class as a ref class type for the experience. Add a header file to the MemoryTest project with the name Card.h. You can press Ctrl+Shift+A to open the dialog to do this. You can add the basic definition for the class as:

```
#pragma once
namespace MemoryTest
{
  ref class Card
  {
    // Members to be defined...
  };
}
```

The class must be defined within the project namespace, MemoryTest. You could define it as public to get it into the .winmd file but you don't need to.

You will use Card objects in two ways. First, the specification for a particular card with a given shape type and color will be a Card object. Second, a card in a particular grid cell of cardGrid will also be a Card object. Thus, an array of 24 Card objects can define the shuffled pack of cards and also identify the objects in the UI corresponding to those cards.

A Card object will record the shape, its type, and its color. You can store the shape type as a handle to a String object that is the name of the class type for the shape: "Ellipse", "Rectangle", or "Polygon". You can store the color as a handle to a SolidColorBrush object. This is a good choice because the Background property value for a shape is of type Brush^, and Brush is the base class for SolidColorBrush. The specific shape object for a card will be one of the three types of shapes, so you can store this as a handle to the base class type for shapes, which is type Shape^. The Shape class is defined in the Windows::UI::Xaml::Shapes namespace. The handle to the element that is the back of a card can be a handle to a Windows::UI::Xaml::Controls::TextBlock object. If you make these public properties of the class, they will be easy to access. Here's the complete Card class definition:

```
#pragma once
namespace MemoryTest
{
  public ref class Card sealed
  {
  public:
    Card() {}

    // Copy constructor
    Card(Card^ card)
    {
      Type = card->Type;
      Color = card->Color;
      Shape = card->Shape;
      Back = card->Back;
    }

  public:
    property Platform::String^ Type;                         // Shape type
    property Windows::UI::Xaml::Media::SolidColorBrush^ Color; // Color
    property Windows::UI::Xaml::Shapes::Shape^ Shape;        // Shape handle
    property Windows::UI::Xaml::Controls::TextBlock^ Back;   // Card back
  };
}
```

The class must be specified as sealed because it defines public constructors. If you don't define it as sealed, the code will not compile. You don't need to define any member functions beyond the default constructor and the copy constructor. You will need the copy constructor to create pairs of identical cards.

Adding Data Members to the MainPage Class

You can make all the members you add to the MainPage class private. The first data member to add will store the number of cards:

```
size_t cardCount;                          // The number of cards
```

You'll initialize this in the MainPage constructor. Next you can add arrays to store the handles to the shapes in cardGrid to the MainPage class definition:

```
Platform::Array<Windows::UI::Xaml::Controls::Grid^>^ grids;
Platform::Array<Windows::UI::Xaml::Shapes::Ellipse^>^ circles;
```

```
Platform::Array<Windows::UI::Xaml::Shapes::Rectangle^>^ squares;
Platform::Array<Windows::UI::Xaml::Shapes::Polygon^>^ triangles;
Platform::Array<Windows::UI::Xaml::Controls::TextBlock^>^ cardBacks;
```

These arrays will each have `cardCount` elements.

You will also need an array of `Card` objects:

```
Platform::Array<Card^>^ cardPack;                    // The pack of cards
```

You'll need an `#include` directive for `Card.h` in `MainPage.xaml.h`. You can create the `cardPack` array in the `MainPage` constructor with `cardCount` elements, each storing a handle to a `Card` object. You'll be shuffling the handles in this array for each new game because it is the deck of cards for the game.

You can add members that are handles to `String` objects that will store the type names for the child elements in `cardGrid`:

```
// Type names for card elements
Platform::String^ typeCircle;
Platform::String^ typeSquare;
Platform::String^ typeTriangle;
```

These also must be initialized in the `MainPage` constructor. You will be able to determine the precise type name for an object referenced by a `Shape^` handle by comparing it to these members. You'll need more data members when you implement the event handlers, but that will suffice for now.

Adding Member Functions

You can add the three member functions identified earlier:

```
private:
  // Game functions
  void InitializeCardPack(); // Initialize cardPack to two of each card
  void SetUpUIState();       // Initialize the child elements of cardGrid
  void InitializeGame();     // Set up a game with a shuffled cardPack
```

If you put empty definitions for these functions in `MainPage.xaml.cpp`, the application will be compilable:

```
// Initialize the pack of cards so it contains 12 different pairs
void MainPage::InitializeCardPack()
{
  // Code to be added here...
}

// Set up the initial UI state and stores elements in grid cell order
void MainPage::SetUpUIState()
{
  // Code to be added here...
}

// Shuffle the cards and deal
void MainPage::InitializeGame()
{
  // Code to be added here...
}
```

The basic initialization for the game will be done in the `MainPage` constructor, so let's look at that next.

Initialize the MainPage Object

All the basic initialization for the game will be done in the `MainPage` class constructor. The default implementation includes a call to the `InitializeComponent()` function that sets up the UI components. Be sure to put any code that references UI component objects after this function call. You can amend the constructor definition to the following:

```
MainPage::MainPage()
{
  InitializeComponent();

  // cardCount is number of rows x number of columns in cardGrid
  cardCount =
          cardGrid->ColumnDefinitions->Size*cardGrid->RowDefinitions->Size;

  // Initialize type names for card elements
  typeCircle = Ellipse::typeid->FullName;
  typeSquare = Rectangle::typeid->FullName;
  typeTriangle = Polygon::typeid->FullName;

  // Create arrays to store element handles for the cards
  // Each type is in a separate array and will be stored in card sequence
  circles = ref new Array<Ellipse^>(cardCount);
  triangles = ref new Array<Polygon^>(cardCount);
  squares = ref new Array<Rectangle^>(cardCount);
  cardBacks = ref new Array<TextBlock^>(cardCount);
  grids = ref new Array<Grid^>(cardCount);
  InitializeCardPack();
  SetUpUIState();
  InitializeGame();
}
```

You initialize `cardCount` to the number of cells in `cardGrid`, as the product of the numbers of rows and columns. Next, you initialize the members that store the type names for the shapes. The expression `Ellipse::typeid` results in a handle of type `Platform::Type` that identifies the `Ellipse` type. The `FullName` property value for a `Type` object is a handle to a `String` object containing the type name. Every WinRT object inherits the `GetType()` function from the `Object` base class, which returns a handle to the `Type` object for the object. Thus you obtain the actual type name for a shape object referenced through a `Shape^` handle by calling its inherited `GetType()` member and accessing the `FullName` property value of the object that it returns.

The arrays that hold handles for the `Grid` objects in `cardGrid` and the child elements of the `Grid` objects each have `cardCount` elements. After the basic data initialization in the constructor, you call the three new member functions to initialize the card pack, set up the states of the UI elements, and initialize the game with a shuffled card pack.

To use the shape type names without qualifying them with the namespace name, you need to add the following `using` directive to `MainPage.xaml.cpp`:

```
using namespace Windows::UI::Xaml::Shapes;
```

Initializing the Card Pack

You are going to create `cardCount` `Card` objects and store the handles in the `cardPack` array. There must be 12 pairs of identical `Card` objects. The 12 different cards comprise cards with three different shapes in each of four different colors. You can create these by iterating over the four colors in a loop, and over the three shape types in an inner loop. Here's how that looks:

```
void MainPage::InitializeCardPack()
{
  // Create arrays of the shape types and colors
  Array<String^>^ shapeTypes {typeCircle, typeSquare, typeTriangle};
  Array<SolidColorBrush^>^ colors {
                    ref new SolidColorBrush(Windows::UI::Colors::Red),
                    ref new SolidColorBrush(Windows::UI::Colors::Green),
                    ref new SolidColorBrush(Windows::UI::Colors::Blue),
                    ref new SolidColorBrush(Windows::UI::Colors::Yellow)
                                  };
  // Initialize the card pack
  cardPack = ref new Array<Card^>(cardCount);
  size_t packIndex {};                        // Index to cardPack array
  Card^ card;
  for(auto color : colors)
  {
    for(auto shapeType : shapeTypes)
    {
      card = ref new Card();                  // Create a card...
      card->Type = shapeType;                 // with the current type...
      card->Color = color;                    // ... and color
      card->Shape = nullptr;                  // we will find the shape...
      card->Back = nullptr;                   // ...and back later.
      cardPack[packIndex++] = card;           // Store the card and...
      cardPack[packIndex++] = ref new Card(card); // ...a copy in the pack.
    }
  }
}
```

You first create arrays holding the possible colors and shape types. You initialize the elements in the `cardPack` array with two copies of each `Card` representing a card with a given shape of a particular color. After executing this function, the `cardPack` array will contain the pack of 24 cards arranged in sequence. They will need to be shuffled for a game.

Setting Up the Child Elements of cardGrid

The `SetUpUIState()` method will set the elements in each cell of `cardGrid` so only the back of the card is visible. This implies setting the child shape elements for each cell in `cardGrid` as not visible. Whether or not an element is visible is determined by its `Visibility` property value. This can be `Visible` or `Collapsed`, where these values are defined by the `Visibility` enum class in the `Windows::UI::Xaml` namespace.

The method will store the handles to the `Grid` elements that are children of `cardGrid` in the `grids` array and store the handles to the shapes that are children of each `Grid` child in the array of the appropriate shape type. The child elements that are `TextBlock` handles are stored in the `cardBacks` array. The elements in the arrays that store handles to shapes, card backs, and grids need to be in the same order as their occurrence in `cardGrid`. Here's the code:

```
void MainPage::SetUpUIState()
{
  // Handle to the collection of grids in cardGrid
  auto elements = cardGrid->Children;

  size_t index {};                    // Index to shape arrays
  size_t rowLength(cardGrid->ColumnDefinitions->Size);// Length of a grid row

  // Iterate over the child elements to cardGrid and store
  // the Grid^ handles in the grids array in sequence
  for(UIElement^ element : elements)
  {
    String^ elementType = element->GetType()->FullName; // Get element type
    if(Grid::typeid->FullName == elementType)            // Make sure it's a Grid
    {
      auto grid = safe_cast<Grid^>(element);
      auto row = cardGrid->GetRow(grid);                 // Get the grid row
      auto column = cardGrid->GetColumn(grid);           // and column location.
      index = row*rowLength + column;                    // Index for row/column
      grids[index] = grid;                               // Save the grid
      // A grid in each cell contains another grid as child.
      // We know that's always the case so get the child-grid:
      grid = safe_cast<Grid^>(grid->Children->GetAt(0));
      auto shapes = grid->Children;                      // Get the child shapes
      // Iterate over the child elements to the current Grid and store
      // the shape element handles in the array for their type in sequence
      for(UIElement^ element : shapes)
      {
        elementType = element->GetType()->FullName;      // Get element type

        // Store a circle in circles array & do the same for the other elements
        // Only card backs will be visible - all other shapes collapsed.
        if(typeCircle == elementType)
        {
          circles[index] = safe_cast<Ellipse^>(element);
          element->Visibility = Windows::UI::Xaml::Visibility::Collapsed;
        }
        else if(typeSquare == elementType)
        {
          squares[index] = safe_cast<Rectangle^>(element);
          element->Visibility = Windows::UI::Xaml::Visibility::Collapsed;
        }
        else if(typeTriangle == elementType)
        {
          triangles[index] = safe_cast<Polygon^>(element);
          element->Visibility = Windows::UI::Xaml::Visibility::Collapsed;
        }
        else if(TextBlock::typeid->FullName == elementType)
        {
```

```
        cardBacks[index] = safe_cast<TextBlock^>(element);
        element->Visibility = Windows::UI::Xaml::Visibility::Visible;
      }
    }
  }
 }
}
```

To access the child elements of a parent you obtain a handle to the collection of child elements from the value of its `Children` property. You then iterate over the elements in this collection and cast the `UIElement^` handles to the type of element actually stored. With child elements of `cardGrid` it's easy because the handles are all of type `Grid^` and each of these has a `Grid` child. With child elements of these `Grid` objects, you have to do a little work to determine the type.

The outer range-based `for` loop iterates over the collection of `Grid` child elements in `cardGrid`. The `GetRow()` and `GetColumn()` functions for a `Grid` object return the row and column index respectively, for the child element referenced by the handle you pass as the argument. For each inner `Grid` element, you iterate over the collection of its child elements. By comparing the type name of each child with the shape type names, you are able to determine the type of element referenced by the handle and thus store the handle in the appropriate array. The conversion of child handles is done using `safe_cast`, which throws an exception if the cast is not valid, so you'll know when something goes wrong.

Initializing the Game

The game play involves turning up two cards to see if they match. You will need to record the two cards that are turned up, the count of pairs found, and the handles to the `Card` objects in pairs that have been found. Add the following `private` members to the `MainPage` class:

```
// Game records
Card^   card1Up;                                  // 1st card turned up
Card^   card2Up;                                  // 2nd card turned up
size_t pairCount;                                 // Number of pairs found
Platform::Collections::Vector<Card^>^ pairsFound; // Cards in pairs found
```

`card1Up` and `card2Up` store handles to the cards turned up. `pairCount` records the number of pairs found and when this reaches 12, the game is over. `pairsFound` is a collection that records handles to the `Card` objects in the pairs. You'll use this to manage what cards can cause events.

You can initialize these members in the constructor:

```
MainPage::MainPage() : card1Up {}, card2Up {}, pairCount {}
{
  InitializeComponent();
  // cardCount is number of rows x number of columns in cardGrid
  cardCount =
        cardGrid->ColumnDefinitions->Size*cardGrid->RowDefinitions->Size;
  pairsFound = ref new Platform::Collections::Vector<Card^>(cardCount);

  // Code as before...
}
```

Initializing the game involves shuffling the cards. Add a `private` member function to do this, `ShuffleCards()`, to the `MainPage` class definition:

```
void ShuffleCards();                       // Shuffle the cards
```

You can add an empty definition to `MainPage.xaml.cpp` that you'll complete in the next section:

```
void MainPage::ShuffleCards()
{
  // Code to be added later...
}
```

The `InitializeGame()` function must shuffle the cards in `cardPack`, then set up the elements in `cardGrid` to reflect the order of the cards in `cardPack`. It must also ensure that the UI elements just display the card backs. Here's the code to do that:

```
void MainPage::InitializeGame()
{
  card1Up = card2Up = nullptr;              // No cards up
  pairCount = 0;                            // No pairs found
  pairsFound->Clear();                      // Clear pairs record
  // Null the handles to UI elements
  for(auto card : cardPack)
  {
    card->Shape = nullptr;
    card->Back = nullptr;
  }
  ShuffleCards();                           // Shuffle cardPack

  // Set the shapes in the Grid elements to represent the cards dealt
  for(size_t i {}; i < cardCount; ++i)
  {
    cardPack[i]->Back = cardBacks[i];
    if(cardPack[i]->Type == typeCircle)
    {
      circles[i]->Fill = cardPack[i]->Color;
      cardPack[i]->Shape = circles[i];
    }
    else if(cardPack[i]->Type == typeSquare)
    {
      squares[i]->Fill = cardPack[i]->Color;
      cardPack[i]->Shape = squares[i];
    }
    else if(cardPack[i]->Type == typeTriangle)
    {
      triangles[i]->Fill = cardPack[i]->Color;
      cardPack[i]->Shape = triangles[i];
    }
    cardPack[i]->Shape->IsTapEnabled = true;

    // Set up UI to show card backs & enable events
    cardBacks[i]->Visibility = Windows::UI::Xaml::Visibility::Visible;
    cardBacks[i]->IsTapEnabled = true;
    // Ensure background grids are hit test visible & opaque
    grids[i]->IsHitTestVisible = true;
```

```
        grids[i]->Opacity = 1;
        // Ensure all shapes are invisible & opaque
        circles[i]->Visibility = Windows::UI::Xaml::Visibility::Collapsed;
        squares[i]->Visibility = Windows::UI::Xaml::Visibility::Collapsed;
        triangles[i]->Visibility = Windows::UI::Xaml::Visibility::Collapsed;
        circles[i]->Opacity = 1;
        squares[i]->Opacity = 1;
        triangles[i]->Opacity = 1;
    }
}
```

After the game records have been reset, the first loop nulls the handles to shapes and card backs in the `Card` objects. The second loop sets the `Shape` property value of each `Card` object to a handle to the appropriate shape from one of the arrays storing shapes. It also sets the `Back` property value to a handle for the corresponding card back element. The loop also resets grids, card backs, and shapes to their initial state. An `Opacity` property of 1 is completely opaque. Setting the `IsHitTestVisible` property value for an element to `true` allows hit testing to work in the area of the element. This means that the clicking or tapping of the element can be detected. Setting the value to `false` would inhibit events resulting from clicking or tapping the element or its child elements.

Shuffling the Cards

You can use the `random_shuffle()` function that is defined in the STL algorithm header with elements stored in a Platform::Array object. There are two versions of the function. The simple version takes two arguments that are iterators specifying the first and one-past-the-last items in the sequence to be shuffled. To get the begin and end iterators for the array of cards, you must use the special versions of `begin()` and `end()` from the `Windows::Foundations::Collections` namespace.

By default, `random_shuffle()` uses an internal random number generator seeded with a fixed value so you will always get the same sequence of shuffled card decks. This can be useful for testing, but it's not what we want. However, you can provide a function object that represents a random number generator as the third argument to `random_shuffle()`. The function object you supply must accept a single argument, n, and return a random value from 0 to n-1 inclusive.

I mentioned in Chapter 10 that the `random` header provides a wide range of random number generators, one of which we can use to create a random number generator to use with `random_shuffle()`. You can define an `std::uniform_int_distribution` class object that represents a uniform distribution of random integers within a specified inclusive range. In a uniform distribution each value is equally likely. You can define an object for integers from 1 to n inclusive like this:

```
size_t n {52};
std::uniform_int_distribution<int> distribution(1, n);
```

`distribution` is a functor so to obtain a random value from the distribution that it represents, you call its `operator()()` member function with a random number generator as the argument. Here's an example:

```
std::random_device gen;              // Random number source
size_t value {distribution(gen)};    // Random value from 1 to n
```

You met the `random_device` type back in Chapter 10. An object of this type is a functor that generates random values in the range from 1 to 2^{32}. The gen object that is passed to the `distribution` functor ensures that a random selection from the uniform distribution of integers is returned each time it is called.

We can use a `uniform_int_distribution` object in a lambda expression that we can pass to the `random_shuffle()` function as the random number generator for sorting the cards.

You can implement the `ShuffleCards()` function to produce a shuffled deck like this:

```
void MainPage::ShuffleCards()
{
  std::random_device gen;                    // Random number source
  std::random_shuffle(begin(cardPack), end(cardPack),
    [&gen](size_t n) {
                      std::uniform_int_distribution<int> distribution(1, n);
                      return distribution(gen)-1;  });
}
```

This shuffles the Card object references in the `cardPack` array. It uses the `begin()` and `end()` functions to create iterators for the `cardPack` array that you pass to `random_shuffle()`. The third argument is a lambda expression with a single parameter n that returns a value in the range 0 to n-1 inclusive, which is exactly what the `random_shuffle()` function requires to replace the default random number generator. The random value that the `distribution` functor returns is in the range 1 to n. Subtracting 1 produces a value in the range that we want, from 0 to n-1.

Add the following directives to `MainPage.xaml.cpp`:

```
#include <algorithm>
#include <random>
```

The `algorithm` header is for `random_shuffle()` and the `random` header provides the `random_device` and `uniform_int_distribution` types.

Highlighting the UI Cards

You can highlight a card when the mouse cursor is over it by implementing the `Card_Entered()` and `Card_Exited()` handlers. You can highlight a card simply by changing its color, which means changing the `Background` property value for the `Grid` object that caused the event in the `Card_Entered()` handler:

```
void MemoryTest::MainPage::Card_Entered(Platform::Object^ sender,
              Windows::UI::Xaml::Input::PointerRoutedEventArgs^ e)
{
  safe_cast<Grid^>(sender)->Background = steelBrush;
}
```

You know that `sender` must be a handle to a `Grid` object so you cast it to type `Grid^`. You set the value of the `Background` property to the color provided by a `SolidColorBrush` object that is referenced by `steelBrush`. You can add this handle and a handle to a `SolidColorBrush` of the original color as a class member to avoid creating an object each time the handler is called.

Add the following to the `MainPage` class as `private` members:

```
Windows::UI::Xaml::Media::SolidColorBrush^ steelBrush;  // Card highlighted
Windows::UI::Xaml::Media::SolidColorBrush^ azureBrush;  // Card normal
```

You can initialize these in the `MainPage` constructor:

```
MainPage::MainPage()  : card1Up {}, card2Up {}, pairCount {}
{
  InitializeComponent();
  // Brushes for card colors
  steelBrush = ref new SolidColorBrush(Windows::UI::Colors::SteelBlue);
  azureBrush = ref new SolidColorBrush(Windows::UI::Colors::Azure);

  // Rest of the code as before...
}
```

A card will be returned to its original color by the `Card_Exited()` handler:

```
void MemoryTest::MainPage::Card_Exited(Platform::Object^ sender,
          Windows::UI::Xaml::Input::PointerRoutedEventArgs^ e)
{
  safe_cast<Grid^>(sender)->Background = azureBrush;
}
```

If you recompile and execute the application, you should be able to see card highlighting in action.

Handling Card Back Events

Clicking the back of a card turns over the card. This is handled by the `Cardback_Tapped()` member of `MainPage`. If it is the first card turned over, the card is recorded in `card1Up` and the member function is done. If another card is already turned over, which is signaled by `card1Up` being non-null, then the card originating the current event is the second card. In this case the function must check if the cards are the same. If they are, a pair has been found, so the function will update `pairCount` and disable events for these cards. It will also store the handles to the cards in the `pairsFound` vector. It will also fade the cards a bit to show they are no longer in the game.

If they are not the same, the player must click either upturned card to turn them both back over, before trying for another pair. To ensure this happens, the function will disable events for all the other cards, which will be those showing the backs. When the front of either of the two cards is clicked, the `Shape_Tapped()` handler will be called, which should turn over both cards to show the backs and restore events to all the other cards.

Here's how the code for `Cardback_Tapped()` looks to do that:

```
void MemoryTest::MainPage::Cardback_Tapped(Platform::Object^ sender,
                Windows::UI::Xaml::Input::TappedRoutedEventArgs^ e)
{ // There may be 0 or 1 cards already turned over
  // If there is 1, the card handle will be in card1Up
  TextBlock^ cardBack = safe_cast<TextBlock^>(sender); // Always a card back handle
  cardBack->Visibility = Windows::UI::Xaml::Visibility::Collapsed; // Hide the back
  // Find the card for the back so the shape can be made visible
  Card^ theCard;
  for(auto card : cardPack)
  {
```

```
      if(cardBack == card->Back)
      { // We have found the card so show the front
        card->Shape->Visibility = Windows::UI::Xaml::Visibility::Visible;
        theCard = card;
        break;
      }
    }
    if(!card1Up)
    {
      card1Up = theCard;
    }
    else
    {
      card2Up = theCard;
      if(card1Up->type == card2Up->type && card1Up->Color == card2Up->Color)
      { // We have a pair!
        pairsFound->Append(card1Up);
        pairsFound->Append(card2Up);
        DisableCard(card1Up);
        DisableCard(card2Up);
        card1Up = card2Up = nullptr;
        if(++pairCount == cardCount/2)
          GameOver();
      }
      else
      { // Two cards up but no pair so we now want a Tapped event on either
        // Disable Tapped event for card backs and PointerEntered
        // and PointerExited events for other cards
        for(size_t i {}; i < cardBacks->Length; ++i)
        {
          if(cardBacks[i] == card1Up->Back || cardBacks[i] == card2Up->Back)
            continue;
          cardBacks[i]->IsTapEnabled = false;
          grids[i]->IsHitTestVisible = false;
        }
      }
    }
  }
}
```

Turning a card over involves hiding the back and showing the front. The card back that originated the event is hidden by setting its `Visibility` property to `Collapsed`. The function then searches `cardPack` to find the `Card` object with this back. It shows the front of this card by setting the `Visibility` property value for the shape to `Visible`. It then checks for one or two cards up and proceeds as I described at the beginning of this section. If `pairCount` reaches half the number of cards in the pack, all pairs have been found, so the `GameOver()` function is called to end the game. Add this function as a `private` member of the `MainPage` class:

```
void GameOver();
```

Add a skeleton implementation to the `.cpp` file:

```
void MainPage::GameOver()
{
  // Code to be added later...
}
```

The `Cardback_Tapped()` function calls a helper function, `DisableCardUp()`, so add the following as a `private` member of the `MainPage` class:

```
void DisableCard(Card^ card);
```

The implementation in `MainPage.xaml.cpp` will be:

```cpp
void MainPage::DisableCard(Card^ card)
{
  card->Shape->IsTapEnabled = false;       // Disable Tapped event...
  card->Shape->Opacity = 0.5;

  // Get the parent Grid for shape
  auto grid = safe_cast<Grid^>(card->Shape->Parent);
  grid = safe_cast<Grid^>(grid->Parent);
  grid->IsHitTestVisible = false;          // Disable hit test
  grid->Background = azureBrush;           // Make sure of color
}
```

This disables the `Tapped` event for the `Card` object referenced by the argument and sets its `Opacity` property value to `0.5`, which will make it semi-transparent. It's possible that the background color could be the highlight color so this is set to the normal color to make sure it is that.

Handling Shape Events

When a `Tapped` event for a `Shape` object occurs, there must be at least one card face up because the event could not occur otherwise, and there may be two cards face up. If there's just one, the `Tapped` event handler should just turn the card face down, which allows the player to change his mind about the first selection. If there are two cards face up, they represent a failed pair selection so `Tapped` events from the backs of the other cards will be disabled. Thus for two cards up, the handler must turn the cards over and then enable `Tapped` events for all the backs that are not pairs.

Here's the code for `Shape_Tapped()`:

```cpp
void MemoryTest::MainPage::Shape_Tapped(Platform::Object^ sender,
                    Windows::UI::Xaml::Input::TappedRoutedEventArgs^ e)
{
  // With this event there is always at least one card up but could be two.
  // If only one card is up, the handle is in card1Up
  Shape^ shape = safe_cast<Shape^>(sender);
  if(card1Up && card2Up)
  { // Two cards up so turn over both cards
    card1Up->Shape->Visibility = Windows::UI::Xaml::Visibility::Collapsed;
    card1Up->Back->Visibility = Windows::UI::Xaml::Visibility::Visible;
    card2Up->Shape->Visibility = Windows::UI::Xaml::Visibility::Collapsed;
    card2Up->Back->Visibility = Windows::UI::Xaml::Visibility::Visible;

    // Enable events for all card backs and background grids
    for(size_t i {}; i < cardBacks->Length; ++i)
    {
      if(IsFound(cardBacks[i]))
        continue;
```

```
        cardBacks[i]->IsTapEnabled = true;
        grids[i]->IsHitTestVisible = true;
      }
      card1Up = card2Up = nullptr;  // Reset both handles to cards up
    }
    else
    {  // only one card up and it was clicked so turn over the card
      card1Up->Shape->Visibility = Windows::UI::Xaml::Visibility::Collapsed;
      card1Up->Back->Visibility = Windows::UI::Xaml::Visibility::Visible;
      card1Up = nullptr;
    }
  }
}
```

This calls a helper function, IsFound(), that checks whether a card back belongs to a card in a previously found pair. Add the following to the MainPage class, in a private section as always:

```
bool IsFound(Windows::UI::Xaml::Controls::TextBlock^ back);
```

The implementation of the function is:

```
bool MainPage::IsFound(TextBlock^ back)
{
  for(auto cardFound : pairsFound)
  {
    if(cardFound  && cardFound->Back == back) return true;
  }
  return false;
}
```

This iterates over the cards in the pairsFound vector. When the back property value for a card matches the argument, the function returns true. If no card is found, false is returned. At this point you should be able to try out the game. Nothing happens when you find all the pairs and you can't start a new game yet.

Recognizing a Win

GameOver() is called when all pairs have been found. The success should be acknowledged in some way. You could display a message in the message area that recognizes the win. Return to MainPage.xaml. Add a RichTextBlock control to the messageArea Grid element at the bottom of the game grid. You can specify the text using a Paragraph element, as you did with the game title. The XAML for the messageArea element should now be:

```
<Grid x:Name="messageArea" Grid.Column="1" Grid.Row="2" Margin="10,0,0,0"
        Background="Bisque">
  <RichTextBlock x:Name="winMessage" Opacity="0" FontFamily="Freestyle Script"
        FontWeight="Bold" FontSize="90" TextAlignment="Center" Foreground="Red">
    <Paragraph>
      <Run Text="YOU WIN!!!"/>
    </Paragraph>
  </RichTextBlock>
</Grid>
```

Note that the `Opacity` property value for the `RichTextBlock` element is 0, so the text will not be visible. The `GameOver()` function that is called when all pairs have been found can display the content for the `winMessage` element by setting the value for its `Opacity` property to `1.0`:

```
void MainPage::GameOver()
{
  winMessage->Opacity = 1.0;                    // Show the win message
}
```

There may be other messages in the message area so it would be a good idea to provision for hiding any other messages that appear there. You could do this by adding a `private` helper function to the `MainPage` class, which you could implement like this:

```
void MainPage::HideMessages()
{
  auto messageCollection = messageArea->Children;
  for(UIElement^ element : messageCollection)
  {
    element->Opacity = 0;
  }
}
```

This function obtains the collection of child elements for the `Grid` element, `messageArea`. This is defined in the `FrameworkElement` class that is derived from `UIElement`. It iterates over all the child elements in the collection, setting the `Opacity` property value for each to 0.

You can call this helper function in `GameOver()`:

```
void MainPage::GameOver()
{
  HideMessages();                               // Hide any other messages
  winMessage->Opacity = 1.0;                    // Show the win message
}
```

When you find all the pairs, the win message will magically appear.

Handling Game Control Button Events

The two `Button` elements in the `Grid` element at the left of the card grid are game controls. Add `Tapped` event handlers for these with the names `Start_Tapped` and `Show_How_Tapped` through the Properties pane for each.

Let's implement the Start button handler first. When the Start button event occurs, the game should be reset to its initial state with all messages hidden and a new game started with the cards shuffled. This is not too taxing:

```
void MemoryTest::MainPage::Start_Tapped(Platform::Object^ sender,
Windows::UI::Xaml::Input::TappedRoutedEventArgs^ e)
{
  HideMessages();                               // Clear the message area
  InitializeGame();                             // Reset the game
}
```

You have already done the work necessary. Calling `HideMessages()` clears the message area and `InitializeGame()` sets up the cards and elements in `cardGrid` for a new game.

The Show_How_Tapped() handler just needs to display the instructions in the message area. The first step is to add another RichTextBlock element as a child of the messageArea grid. You can do this in the Design pane. Be sure that you add the RichTextBlock element to the Grid element, and not as a child of the RichTextBlock element for the win message. You can specify the content with Paragraph elements, like this:

```
<RichTextBlock x:Name="playMessage" Opacity="0" Margin="10 0 0 0">
    <Paragraph FontFamily="Verdana" FontSize="30" FontWeight="Bold"
            Foreground="Green">
      <Run Text="How to Play:"/>
    </Paragraph>
    <Paragraph FontFamily="Verdana" FontSize="20" FontWeight="Normal"
            Foreground="Black">
      <Run Text="The idea is to find all the pairs of matching cards "/>
      <Run Text="by turning up two at a time."/>
    </Paragraph>
    <Paragraph FontFamily="Verdana" FontSize="20" FontWeight="Normal"
                                        Foreground="Black">
      <Run Text="If you find a pair, they will fade "/>
      <Run Text="and you can try for another pair."/>
    </Paragraph>
    <Paragraph FontFamily="Verdana" FontSize="20" FontWeight="Normal"
                                        Foreground="Black">
      <Run Text=
        "If two cards don't match, click either to turn them back over."/>
    </Paragraph>
    <Paragraph FontFamily="Verdana" FontSize="20" FontWeight="Normal"
            Foreground="Black">
      <Run Text="Click the Start button for a new game."/>
    </Paragraph>
</RichTextBlock>
```

These elements are placed just before the end tag for the messageArea Grid element. The Margin property value will inset the text in the Paragraph elements from the left edge of the grid. You can see from this that you can set individual text characteristics for each Paragraph element. The first has a FontSize property value of "30" while the other elements display the text in a 20-point font. You can set any of the text properties individually in each Paragraph element, including the text color. Each Paragraph element starts a new line. If the content for a Paragraph element does not fit on a single line within the width of the parent, the content will spill automatically. The Opacity property for the RichTextBlock element is "0", so it will not be visible initially. When the FontFamily property value is the same for all Paragraph child elements as it is here, you could set it as the value for the FontFamily property for the parent RichTextBlock element. You could then omit the property specification from the child Paragraph elements.

> **NOTE** You must not split the string for the value of a Text property in a Run element over two or more lines but you can put the text in several Run elements as in the preceding code.

You need to display the `playMessage` element when the `Show_How_Tapped()` event handler is called:

```
void MemoryTest::MainPage::Show_How_Tapped(Platform::Object^ sender,

Windows::UI::Xaml::Input::TappedRoutedEventArgs^ e)
{
  HideMessages();                        // Clear the message area
  playMessage->Opacity = 1;              // Show the instructions
}
```

You should now have a fully working game. Figure 18-9 shows the game in progress.

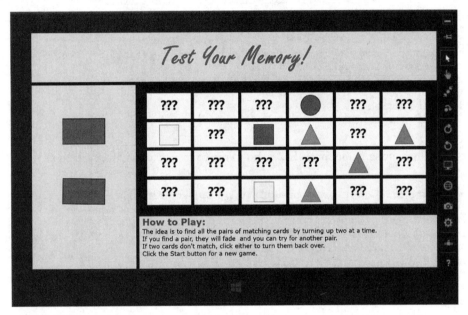

FIGURE 18-9

A `Height` or `Width` property value for an element is not necessarily the value you specify. It may be adjusted during the rendering process and your value is treated as a suggested value that may be modified to suit the context. The `ActualHeight` and `ActualWidth` properties for an element are its rendered height and width. You can see this happening if you adjust the size of the simulator window; you can drag a corner using the mouse. All the elements in the app will adjust in size.

SCALING UI ELEMENTS

The `Loaded` event for the `Page` root element occurs when the complete page has been created and the UI elements have been rendered; it is also called if the application is resized. The outer `Grid` that is the parent of the `Grid` elements for cards will vary its size according to the context. Its `ActualHeight` and `ActualWidth` property values will have been determined when the `Loaded` event handler is called.

Each card is a Grid element of the background color that has a square child Grid element for the contents of the card. The dimensions of the outer Grid element for a card is determined automatically from cardGrid. You could define the height and width of each inner Grid element for a card in terms of the ActualHeight and ActualWidth property values of the outer Grid element. You could therefore calculate the dimensions of the square Grid elements that contain the shapes in a handler for the Loaded event for the Page root element.

Add the Loaded property to the XAML for the Page element with the value as "Page_Loaded", like this:

```
<Page
    xmlns="http://schemas.microsoft.com/winfx/2006/xaml/presentation"
    xmlns:x="http://schemas.microsoft.com/winfx/2006/xaml"
    xmlns:local="using:MemoryTest"
    xmlns:d="http://schemas.microsoft.com/expression/blend/2008"
    xmlns:mc="http://schemas.openxmlformats.org/markup-compatibility/2006"
    x:Class="MemoryTest.MainPage"

    mc:Ignorable="d"
    Loaded="Page_Loaded">
        <!-- All the UI elements -->
</Page>
```

With the cursor in the handler name, press F12 to go to the code. You can implement the handler like this:

```
void MemoryTest::MainPage::Page_Loaded(Platform::Object^ sender,
                                        Windows::UI::Xaml::RoutedEventArgs^ e)
{
  // Scale all card shapes so they squarely fit their grid cells.
  // Iterate over all children of the cardGrid grid.
  for (size_t i {}; i < cardGrid->Children->Size; ++i)
  {
    // Get the small grid in each cell.
    Grid^ grid = safe_cast<Grid^>(cardGrid->Children->GetAt(i));

    // Get the small grid inside the small grid.
    Grid^ childGrid = safe_cast<Grid^>(grid->Children->GetAt(0));

    // Calculate the scaling factor to keep everything square.
    double scale = 1.0;
    if (grid->ActualWidth >= grid->ActualHeight)
    { // Landscape mode
      scale = 0.8*grid->ActualHeight / childGrid->ActualHeight;
    }
    else
    { // Portrait mode
      scale = 0.8*grid->ActualWidth / childGrid->ActualWidth;
    }

    // Apply scaling factor.
    auto scaleTransform = ref new ScaleTransform();
    scaleTransform->ScaleX = scale;
    scaleTransform->ScaleY = scale;
```

```
        childGrid->RenderTransformOrigin = Point(0.5, 0.5);    // Center of object
        childGrid->RenderTransform = scaleTransform;
    }
}
```

This iterates over all the children of `cardGrid` that are the outer `Grid` elements. The scaling for the inner `Grid` element that houses the shapes needs to be different, depending on whether the game is displayed in landscape or portrait orientation. You define the height and width of the inner to be 80% of the ratio of the outer and inner `Grid` heights in landscape, or the ratio of the widths in portrait orientation. Scaling is achieved using a `ScaleTransform` object. The `ScaleTransform` class is defined in the `Windows::UI::Xaml::Media` namespace. The `ScaleX` and `ScaleY` property values specify a scaling factor to be applied in the *x* and *y* directions. You apply the scaling transform by defining the `RenderTransform` property value for `childGrid` to be the `ScaleTransform` object that you created. The `RenderTransform` property value specifies a transformation that is to be applied when `childGrid` is rendered along with its children. The transform is applied relative to the origin that is specified by the `RenderTransformOrigin` property value, where a value of 0,0 is the top-left corner of the element and 1,1 is the bottom-right corner.

The `RenderTransform` property is inherited from `UIElement`, so you can define a transform for any element type that has `UIElement` as a base and the transform will be applied to the element as well as any child elements when it is rendered. The transform can do other things to an element. Setting `ScaleX` to -1 for instance will flip the element about the render transform origin. If you try the game again and rotate to portrait mode it doesn't look good. You can improve this by changing the value of the `Width` property for the left column to 200:

```
<Grid.ColumnDefinitions>
    <ColumnDefinition Width="200"/>
    <ColumnDefinition Width="*"/>
</Grid.ColumnDefinitions>
```

Of course there's huge potential for enhancing the game further. I'll finish by introducing one more thing you can do in a Windows Store app.

TRANSITIONS

Transitions are elements that provide the capability for animation of UI elements. The WinRT types for transition elements are in the `Windows::UI::Xaml::Media::Animation` namespace. I'll just introduce you to a couple of animations in `MemoryTest`.

Application Startup Transitions

The `EntranceThemeTransition` element provides animation for controls when they are first displayed. When you apply it to an element with children such as `cardGrid`, the child elements will appear in sequence, rather than all together. This makes the initial presentation of the game window more pleasing. Here's how you can implement an `EntranceThemeTransition` for `cardGrid` child elements:

```
<Grid x:Name="cardGrid" Grid.Row="1" Grid.Column="1" Margin="32">
    <Grid.RowDefinitions>
```

```
        <!-- Elements defining the rows... -->
    </Grid.RowDefinitions>

    <Grid.ColumnDefinitions>
        <!-- Elements defining the columns... -->
    </Grid.ColumnDefinitions>

    <!-- Animate the display of the cards -->
    <Grid.ChildrenTransitions>
        <TransitionCollection>
            <EntranceThemeTransition/>
        </TransitionCollection>
    </Grid.ChildrenTransitions>

    <!-- Child elements defining the cards... -->
</Grid>
```

`Grid.ChildrenTransitions` is an attached property for a `Grid` element that is inherited from the `Panel` class. It has a property value of type `TransitionCollection` that represents a collection of one or more transitions. Transitions are objects that have `Transition` as a base class. The `Transition` class is in the `Windows::UI::Xaml::Media::Animation` namespace. There is just one element in the `TransitionCollection` for `cardGrid` and that is an `EntranceThemeTransition`. This transition does what you see for elements when they are first displayed. With these additional elements in `cardGrid`, the cards will animate into view in sequence when the application starts. You can apply this to any element or set of elements to get this behavior when the application is first displayed.

Storyboard Animations

I hope the second transition I'll introduce will open the door to you exploring more possibilities. I'll apply this transition to the button that shows how to play the game. This is much more complicated than the `cardGrid` transition because it introduces several elements involved in defining transitions. The transition applies to a transform for the button in the `StackPanel` element in the game controls grid. The `Button` element with the `Content` value `"How to Play"` will have a child element that specifies the transform. The XAML for the button is now this:

```
<Button Content="How to Play" FontSize="20" Foreground="Red"
        Background="Gray" BorderBrush="Black" Height="90" Width="150"
        HorizontalAlignment="Center" Tapped="Show_How_Tapped">

    <!-- This defines a transform that applies to the button -->
    <Button.RenderTransform>
        <RotateTransform x:Name="buttonRotate" />
    </Button.RenderTransform>

</Button>
```

`Button.RenderTransform` is an attached property that has a value of type `RotateTransform` here. The content can be of any type that has `Transform` as a base, which includes `ScaleTransform`, `SkewTransform`, or `TranslateTransform`. A transform element can be subject to an animation that operates on a property of the transform. In the case of the `RotateTransform`, you are going to animate the `Angle` property value, which is the angle through which the element to which the transform applies — the button in this case — is rotated.

The mechanism for animating the `Angle` property value for the `RotateTransform` that is applied to the button will be provided by a `Storyboard` element that controls one or more animations that are specified by its children. You'll define the `StoryBoard` element as a resource for the `StackPanel` parent of the button. It will be a child of a `StackPanel.Resource` element, which is an attached property of the `StackPanel` element.

> **NOTE** The `Resource` element that is an attached property value for the `StackPanel` element is local, but you can also define resources at a global level for your application.

A `StoryBoard` element has child elements that each define an animation. A `StoryBoard` element can control the start time and duration of the animations that are its children through its `Duration` and `BeginTime` property values, and the child elements can also specify these properties independently. You are going to keep it very simple and just apply one animation. This will be a `DoubleAnimation` element that can animate any property value of type `double`. This animation varies the value to which it applies linearly between two limits. You specify the range by the `From` and `To` property values for the `DoubleAnimation` element. You specify the time over which the variation will occur by its `Duration` property value, which is of the form `"hh:mm:ss[.fractional seconds]"` where `hh` is from 0 to 23 hours, `mm` is from 0 to 59 minutes, and `ss` is from 0 to 59 seconds and you can optionally specify fractions of a second. You specify the `BeginTime` value in the same way. The `BeginTime` property value is the delay before the animation starts.

Here's the complete set of XAML for the `Grid` element that contains the buttons, including the animation:

```
<!-- Game controls-->
<Grid Grid.Row="1" Grid.RowSpan="2" Background="Bisque" Margin="0,10,0,0">
  <Grid.RowDefinitions>
     <RowDefinition Height="1*" />
     <RowDefinition Height="1*" />
  </Grid.RowDefinitions>

  <Button Grid.Row="0" Content="Start" FontSize="32" Foreground="Red"
          Background="Gray" BorderBrush="Black" Height="90" Width="150"
          HorizontalAlignment="Center" VerticalAlignment="Center"
          Tapped="Start_Tapped"/>

<StackPanel x:Name="ButtonPanel" Grid.Row="1">

<!-- This Child element contains resources that can be used in the panel
  -->
  <StackPanel.Resources>
    <!-- This defines one or more animations as a resource.
        The value for x:Name is the name you use in C++ to start
        the animation.
     -->

    <Storyboard x:Name="playButtonTurn">
        <!-- This defines an animation that will start 5 seconds after
            the animation is initiated. The animation and its reverse
            will each last 3 seconds.
```

```
                    -->
            <DoubleAnimation From="1" To="90"
                             Duration="00:00:3" BeginTime="00:00:5"
                             Storyboard.TargetName="buttonRotate"
                             Storyboard.TargetProperty="Angle"
                             AutoReverse="True">

        <!-- The easing function determines how the animation operates.
             This particular easing function defines an elastic animation
             by its springiness and the number of oscillations.
         -->
              <DoubleAnimation.EasingFunction>
                <!-- This function specifies how the Angle property value
                     changes.
                 -->
                <ElasticEase Oscillations="5" Springiness="1"
                             EasingMode="EaseOut"/>
              </DoubleAnimation.EasingFunction>

            </DoubleAnimation>
          </Storyboard>
        </StackPanel.Resources>

        <Button Content="How to Play" FontSize="20" Foreground="Red"
                Background="Gray" BorderBrush="Black" Height="90" Width="150"
                HorizontalAlignment="Center" Tapped="Show_How_Tapped">

          <!-- This defines a transform that applies to the button -->
            <Button.RenderTransform>
                <RotateTransform x:Name="buttonRotate" />
            </Button.RenderTransform>

        </Button>
      </StackPanel>
    </Grid>
```

You start the animation in C++ by calling the `Begin()` function for the `StoryBoard` object that you can reference through its handle, `playButtonTurn`. The value of the `StoryBoard.TargetName` attached property in the `DoubleAnimation` element identifies the transform to which the child animation applies. This is the name for the `RotateTransform` for the button. The `From` and `To` property values in the `DoubleAnimation` element specify the range over which the `Angle` property for the `RotateTransform` will be varied. Here it's from 1 to 90 degrees. The `Angle` property is identified by the value of the `StoryBoard.TargetProperty` attached property. Specifying `AutoReverse` as `"True"` for the `DoubleAnimation` element causes the animation to execute first forward, then in reverse. The `Duration` property value applies to both.

The algorithm the `DoubleAnimation` applies to a property is defined by an *easing function*. There are several elements that define easing functions and the corresponding WinRT types are in the `Windows::UI::Xaml::Media::Animation` namespace. My choice is `ElasticEase`. This has a `Springiness` property that determines the springiness of the animation. The larger the value for this, the more elastic the animation is. The `Oscillations` property value is the number of oscillations in the animation. Other easing functions include `BounceEase`, `CubicEase`, `QuarticEase`, `QuinticEase`, and `SineEase`.

You can initiate the animation when the How to Play button is clicked:

```
void MemoryTest::MainPage::Show _ How _ Tapped(Platform::Object^ sender,
                                Windows::UI::Xaml::Input::TappedRoutedEventArgs^ e)
{
  HideMessages();                            // Clear the message area
  playButtonTurn->Begin();                   // Start the animation
  playMessage->Opacity = 1;                  // Show the instructions
}
```

If you have entered the XAML and code correctly, you should see an interesting effect 5 seconds after you click the button.

SUMMARY

As I said at the beginning, this chapter is a very brief introduction to programming Windows Store apps. I have had to omit a lot of detail and pick what I think are the features that you need to understand at the outset. My objective with this chapter has been to show that while developing a Windows Store app is not trivial, it's not that difficult. There's a lot of code involved — inevitably with Windows — but when you break it down it's easy to manage. I hope I have given you enough of an insight to delve deeper into writing Windows Store apps.

➤ WHAT YOU LEARNED IN THIS CHAPTER

TOPIC	CONCEPT
Windows Store apps	A Windows Store app is targeted at tablets or desktop PCs running Windows 8 and executes in a sandbox that limits access to resources in the environment.
Windows Runtime (WinRT)	WinRT is the Windows API for Windows Store apps. It is an object-oriented API that is language neutral, and WinRT objects are COM objects. WinRT objects are reference counted.
C++/CX	C++/CX is a set of Microsoft-specific extensions to standard C++ that make it easier to work with the WinRT. C++/CX includes the ability to define class types that are compatible with WinRT, and to define handle types that store handles to ref class objects.
XAML	XAML is a language for specifying the user interface in a Windows Store app. When an application is compiled, code is generated that creates the UI elements defined by the XAML.
XAML elements	A XAML element is defined by a start tag and an end tag or by a start-end tag. A XAML element can contain other elements called child elements. Start and end tags for XAML elements must not overlap. The start and end tags for a child element must both be between the start and end tags of the parent.
XAML files	A XAML file comprises a set of nested XAML elements with a single root element. Each page in the UI for a Windows Store app is defined by a separate XAML file.

INDEX